Portable Australian Authors

HENRY KINGSLEY

PORTABLE AUSTRALIAN AUTHORS

This series provides carefully selected volumes introducing major
Australian writers and movements. The format is designed for
compactness and for pleasurable reading. Each volume is intended
to meet a need not hitherto met by any single book. Each is edited by
an authority distinguished in his field, who adds an introductory
essay and other helpful material.

General Editor: L.T. Hergenhan

Also in this Series:

Marcus Clarke edited by Michael Wilding
Henry Lawson edited by Brian Kiernan
Five Plays for Stage, Radio, and Television edited by Alrene Sykes
The 1890s: Stories, Verse, and Essays edited by Leon Cantrell
Rolf Boldrewood edited by Alan Brissenden
The Jindyworobaks edited by Brian Elliott
Hal Porter edited by Mary Lord
Barbara Baynton edited by Sally Krimmer and Alan Lawson
Joseph Furphy edited by John Barnes

In Preparation:

New Guinea Images in Australian Literature edited by Nigel Krauth
Science Fiction edited by Van Ikin

Portable
Australian Authors

Henry Kingsley

Edited with an Introduction by

J.S.D. Mellick

University of Queensland Press
St Lucia • London • New York

Typeset by Watson Ferguson & Co, Brisbane
Printed and bound by Warren Printing Co. Ltd, Hong Kong

Distributed in the United Kingdom, Europe, the Middle East, Africa, and the Caribbean by Prentice-Hall International, International Book Distributors Ltd, 66 Wood Lane End, Hemel Hempstead, Herts., England.

National Library of Australia
Cataloguing-in-Publication data

Kingsley, Henry, 1830-1876.
  Henry Kingsley.

  (Portable Australian authors ISSN 0156-6636)
  ISBN 0 7022 1750 6.
  ISBN 0 7022 1760 3 (pbk.).

  I. Mellick, J.S.D. (John Stanton Davis), 1920-.
  II. Title. (Series: Portable Australian authors).

A828'.109

Library of Congress Cataloging in Publication Data

Kingsley, Henry, 1830-1876.
  Henry Kingsley.
  (Portable Australian authors)
  Bibliography: p.
  I. Mellick, J. S. D., 1920-   . II. Title. III. Series.
  PR4845.K5A6 1982   823'.8   81-19990
  ISBN 0-7022-1750-6   AACR2
  ISBN 0-7022-1760-3 (pbk.)

Contents

**PART 4   Australian Reviews and Articles on Explo-
            ration   517**

**PART 5   Extracts from *The Daily Review*
            (Edinburgh)   569**

PART 6   Selected Criticism   585

Acknowledgments

Acknowledgments are due to the libraries and institutions from which material used in this collection was obtained during research for my Ph.D. dissertation on Henry Kingsley at the University of Queensland (1978), and which records fully the names of the many individuals and institutions who assisted; to the Trustees of the Henry W. and Albert A. Berg Collection (The New York Public Library, Astor, Lenox and Tilden Foundation) and the De Coursey Fales Collection for permission to use material in their possession; and to the editor of *Australian Literary Studies* where some of the results of that research first appeared. I am grateful to Mr Cecil Hadgraft and Dr Laurie Hergenhan for useful suggestions; and to Mr and Mrs E.D. Mackinnon, Mr and Mrs Robt Barr-Smith, Mrs E. Richardson, Mr R. Chirnside, Mr J. Crosthwaite, Mr and Mrs J. Gillespie, Mr J. Hunter, Mr Robt Jamieson, Mr and Mrs Jas. Richardson, Mr and Mrs R.J. Scott, and Mr Roger Venables for particular help received. The University of California is deserving of special mention for permission to use the facsimile of one page of *The Hillyars and the Burtons*. Finally, acknowledgment is made of the work of earlier writers on Henry Kingsley.

Acknowledgments

Introduction

Although not so widely known as his elder brother Charles, Henry Kingsley (1830–76) had twenty-four works, apart from uncollected short stories, essays, and articles, published between 1859 and 1877, two of them posthumous publications.[1] Of his novels *The Recollections of Geoffry Hamlyn*, *Ravenshoe*, and *The Hillyars and the Burtons* are still in print today and are those by which he is best known. Written between 1858–65, these three were reasonably successful and represent, with some qualifications, Henry Kingsley's best work. Most critics tend to agree that his writing ability gradually deteriorated after 1865. Distractions arising from his wife's illnesses, and his constant need of money, were among the principal, but not the only, causes. Letters written by Kingsley to Alexander Macmillan, for example, suggest that, in addition to meeting the expectations of Victorian readers, the attitudes of the author's family and his publisher might have had more to do with the nature of his writing than has been realized. Although one may have reservations about the literary quality of the work of both Charles and Henry Kingsley, an early prediction that Henry's novels might outlast those of his older brother[2] still seems relevant, one hundred years after their deaths.[3] The "Australian" novels have a secure and important place in literary history.

Henry Kingsley was educated in the late 1840s at King's College, London, and in the early 1850s at Worcester College, Oxford.[4] His time at Oxford was, to say the least, not characterized by academic distinctions, and he left in 1853 without taking a degree—an obvious act of folly in mid-Victorian England when, to be without qualification, property, or position, was to court economic disaster.

The critical questions raised by Kingsley's novels have been well aired (see bibliography), but aspects of his life have remained elusive. While not neglecting criticism this introduction is designed mainly to relate the works and the life by drawing on new biographical evidence.

Attracted to Australia by the goldrushes of the mid-nineteenth century, Kingsley arrived in Melbourne in December 1853 to begin what Leslie Stephen describes as a period of "desultory employment".[5] After pitching camp on the outskirts of Melbourne, Kingsley, with his friend, Henry Pares Venables—a nephew of the explorer, Charles Sturt—proceeded to Bendigo to look for gold. Of this he later wrote:

> No one who has not done a little of the "exfodiuntur opes" can understand exactly what the gold fever is like. . . . All . . . sports are as nothing to gold hunting; especially where it runs nuggety. To see IT—it itself, Mammon's own bait, which rules the world as at present constituted; the sweet, heavy, delicious lump of yellow metal, which marries your palm so lovingly: to see it itself—the thing for which parliaments legislate first, and men, otherwise good citizens, lie, forge, and cheat widow and orphan: to see this peep with its indescribable golden gleam out of dirty gravel is a thing which maddens men. See the wondrous sight for yourself before you utterly condemn the men who are driven mad by the lust of it.[6]

By June 1854 Kingsley had had enough of the diggings and was working at Willi Mitchell's station, Langi Willi, in Western Victoria—to which property he was to return as a guest in 1857 on an introduction given him by Rolf Boldrewood. Certain details in "*My Landladies—Chapters of a Digger's Life*" show Kingsley's familiarity with the area and events connected with it. He writes of shooting in the nearby Australian Pyrenees; of being at Red Hill at Chewton, near Castlemaine, after most had left; of the Avoca River beginning to flood in the "cold bitter June of the southern hemisphere";[7] and of riding over to Mitchell's, which was some thirty miles away from Avoca.[8]

His stay at Langi Willi was not lengthy. Just as he rejected the routine of King's School, the self-discipline of Oxford, and the life of the diggings, so, too, did Kingsley reject the daily routine of sheep tending and station work at Langi Willi in 1854. Erne Hillyar's sentiments in *The Hillyars and the Burtons* echo Kingsley's own feelings: "I've cut the Bush. I'm sick of it. The place is unbearable since your cousin Samuel has given up coming there; he was the only person worth speaking to. I've read all the books. I'm sick of the smell of sheep; I'm sick of the sight of a saddle; I am, oh! so utterly sick of those long grey plains . . ." (ch.LVIII).

When camped at Expedition Pass, Mt. Alexander, Kingsley had been practically on Hume and Hovell's 1824 route to Port Phillip. This undoubtedly quickened his interest in early Australian exploration and resulted not only in his later articles on the subject, but also in his decision to follow their route northwards to Sydney. In early 1856 he was back in Victoria,[9] after a journey of almost epic proportions.

After leaving Langi Willi, Kingsley went to the Ovens diggings where, on Christmas Eve 1854, in Beechworth,[10] he heard reports of the Omeo disaster from returning survivors. Reports in *The Ovens and Murray Advertiser* between 27 January and 17 March 1855, as well as those in *The Constitution* on 12 July 1856, leave no doubt that the Omeo rush they refer to was that of chapter LXII in *The Hillyars and the Burtons*. Many diggers, hopes buoyed by reports of large finds of gold, trekked to Omeo only to find themselves deluded. The hoax was aggravated by the hardships of the return routes to Mitta Mitta and Beechworth.

Travelling north he felt, as he wrote later in *Ravenshoe*, "as one feels when a stranger in a new land, one rides forth alone into the forest on some distant expedition, and sees the new world" (ch.LI). This world, which was that of the Kiewa valley, he described at greater length in "The New Church at the Mistibithiwong":[11]

Kauna coming for so many centuries from his mountain range . . . had seen but little save now and then a flock of emus, or a tribe of wandering savages; and Neila Neila crawling past spur to spur of the ranges which vexed her, had seen little beyond glorious birds and lofty timber. They were destined to see things very new and strange: "For the first things are passed," as says my Bible for 1582. . . . The first symptoms of the new order on the Mistibithiwong was the appearance, for the first time since creation, of a lean-faced, bold-eyed young Englishman, who splashed wearily through the river on a tired, high-bred horse; and then, having ridden for a time up and down the gullies and flats of the Mistibithiwong, among the wandering Kangaroos, who seeing a mounted man for the first time, thought *he* was a Kangaroo, went back again, and left the parrots, the cockatoos, and lorikeets, to scold one another and not him.

In *The Boy in Grey*, Kingsley makes further reference to the area, this time associating it with loneliness and death:

> "What place is this,' said Philarete, "so solemn, so sad, and yet so beautiful."
> "This is the Creek Mistibethiwong, the Creek of the Lost Footsteps: follow me," [replied the cockatoo].
> So he flew a little way and lighted on a tree, under which there lay a human figure on its side, withered long since by rain and sun, with the cheek pressed in the sand. So lies Leichardt [sic], so lay Wills.[12]

A melancholy awareness of the pathos of man's isolation and his mortality pervades the passage, and reveals Kingsley's response to a land where "first things" still remained and were not yet a dim memory.

After Albury, the Sydney road proceeded in the general direction of Yass, Queanbeyan, and Lake George where, in *Geoffry Hamlyn*, Tom Troubridge unknowingly met George Hawker in a public house (ch.XXXI). Other references to New South Wales exist in his writings but those dealing with Hamlyn's visit to Hawker in Sydney gaol seem best to show Kingsley's sense of history and use of detail: it was "a wild dreary day in the spring: a day of furious wind and cutting rain; a day when . . . ships creaked and groaned at the wharfs [sic], and the harbour was a sheet of wind-driven foam, and the domain was strewn with boughs".[13]

Even a slight knowledge of early Sydney shows Kingsley's deftness in making a scene convey more than the apparent. In the 1840s the expanse known as the Domain was cleared, planted, and provided with carriage drives. Subsequently the band of the 99th Regiment played there, listened to by the "fashionables and unfashionables of Sydney".[14] Thus it is that Kingsley, with a knowledge of Sydney's social customs, was emphasizing the bleakness of the day by stressing the emptiness of the Domain, and making "the wild dreary day" a sombre portent of Hawker's fate.

According to Kingsley, Major Buckley and Geoffry Hamlyn had only to take "a sharp walk" from their hotel near the harbour to arrive at the gaol. This is, as it turns out, based on fact. Darlinghurst gaol (opened in June 1841) was located too far away to be termed a "sharp walk", so Kingsley had another, nearer site, in mind—the first gaol in Sydney—in Essex Street, between Harrington and George Streets, near the harbour. As Kingsley wrote: "[After leaving Hawker in gaol] . . . Neither spoke a word till we came to a corner in George Street, nearest the wharf: and then the Major

turned back upon me suddenly, and I thought he had been unable
to face the terrible gust which came sweeping up from the harbour"
(ch.XLIV). Kingsley, then, has referred not only to the customs of
early Sydney but also to its landmarks to enhance the realism of the
scene. Such detail would have been known to readers familiar with
Sydney of the 1830s—the period usually associated with the
settlement of the Omeo area[15]—and sets the novel in that period.

Kingsley's further impressions of Sydney, and of New South
Wales, are given in *Geoffry Hamlyn* and the excerpt from *Reginald
Hetherege* included in this collection. A report that he served in the
Sydney Mounted Police seems to be more a matter of tradition than
fact as contemporary registers of the police record neither his
enlistment nor his discharge.

Late in 1855 Kingsley left Sydney and travelled southwards to the
headwaters of the Belloury River (the present Tuross River), and
entered the northern part of Gippsland known then as Combermere
County, and regarded at that time as part of the Monaro. His exact
route cannot be identified but it seems most likely that he proceeded
via a cattle route linking the Monaro in New South Wales with
Omeo Plains—via Cottage Creek, Moonbah, Jacob's Ladder,
Snowy River, Pinch River, Cobberas, and Omeo.[16] His presence in
Gippsland is evident from his references in *Geoffry Hamlyn*,[17] *The
Hillyars and the Burtons*,[18] and his paintings which are held in the
Mitchell Library, Sydney,[19] but his subsequent route to Melbourne
is uncertain. Indications are that he travelled overland.[20]

By February 1856 Kingsley was back in Melbourne, having
trekked over sixteen hundred kilometres, a remarkable feat for a
colonial let alone a visitor. He could well claim, as Boldrewood
records in *Babes in the Bush,* that he had acquired "a great deal of
colonial experience",[21] and knew "both sides" of colonial society.[22]
Bruce Sutherland, writing in *The Australian Quarterly*, considered
that Kingsley found in Australia both hardship and hospitality. The
beauty of its landscape he sensed as well as saw, and portrayed it in
his writing.[23] Undoubtedly he knew more of the harsher aspects of
colonial life than has been acknowledged, and more than he
introduced into his fiction. This resulted from Victorian taboos,
perhaps, rather than from personal preference.

Kingsley's mistake may well have been, as Brian Elliott suggests,
not in coming to Australia but in going back to England for
"Australia enlivened and activated his imagination".[24] But return
to England Kingsley did, leaving Australia in February 1858 and
disembarking in England in May 1858. From his Australian years

he appears to have taken back little else but experience, indifferent health, and some portions of a manuscript belonging to his first novel, a romance entitled *The Recollections of Geoffrey Hamlyn*. This was published by Macmillan and Co., London, in 1859, and followed by two further romances, *Ravenshoe* (1862), and *The Hillyars and the Burtons* (1865).

For some years after it appeared, *Geoffry Hamlyn* was widely regarded as the best novel that had been written about Australia. It was later supplanted by the more realistic works, Marcus Clarke's *His Natural Life* (1874) and Joseph Furphy's *Such is Life* (1903), the one with its scenes of convict life and the other of itinerant pastoral workers. *Geoffry Hamlyn* and *The Hillyars and the Burtons* give readers of Australian literature important pictures of life in Australia which were well regarded by Kingsley's contemporaries.[25] The former novel deals primarily with the successes in Australia of well-born but impoverished immigrants who survive the problems of translocation and settlement. In process of doing so they become wealthy squatters who are able to return "home" to England and resume life on their former ancestral holdings. The latter novel treats mainly of two families, one nobly born, the other a blacksmith's family. In Australia a reversal of status takes place and the lowly tradesman finds that his skills, being much in demand, make him an "aristocrat of labour" and a figure of some note in Victoria. His situation is further improved by the fortunate acquisition of new wealth in the form of a copper mine discovered on his property. He has found in the new land a life never possible to him in England. The nobleman, on the other hand, has little or nothing to offer in the way of skills in the colony and is severely handicapped in his efforts to establish himself.

These stories serve to record Kingsley's impressions of Australia in the 1830s and the 1850s, many years after the first convict settlement at Port Jackson in 1788. His writing shows a deep awareness of the "newness" of Australia and exalts it in almost biblical language. In *Geoffry Hamlyn* he praises the immensity of the country: "A new heaven and a new earth! Tier beyond tier, height above height, the great wooded ranges go rolling away westward, till on the lofty skyline they are crowned with a gleam of everlasting snow . . . All creation is new and stirring . . ."[26] The almost paradisal quality of the flora and fauna move him similarly: ". . . Then a green swamp; through the tall reeds the native companion, King of Cranes, waded majestic; the brilliant porphyry water hen, with scarlet bill and legs, flashed like a sapphire among the emerald-green water-sedge . . ."[27] Australia inspired not only a sense of the sublime, but also a sense of strangeness:

> The country through which they walked was one of the richest and most beautiful in the world, but it was not ready for human habitation. It was still in its cruel, pitiless phase. It was only in the state of preparation,—a state which it requires generally a great sacrifice of human life to alter into a state of readiness for what we choose to call a state of civilization. It was exceedingly rich, and it looked wonderfully beautiful. Every morning, great inexorable Mother Nature looked over the eastern hill tops, passing through phases of crimson glory into orange glory, until she had done her day's work, and laid all the magnificent landscape to sleep, under a haze of crystalline blue. And then she would sleep herself; and say, dreamily, "Children! children! here is room for millions of you. Come." And then in the evening she would wake up once more, into new glories of crimson and purple, and once more fall asleep into dark night, sighing sometimes, in dry wandering winds, which rustled through the grass upon the thirsty wolds, "Children! children! you have come too soon, and you must die."[28]

Kingsley began to write *Geoffry Hamlyn* at Langi Willi, near Skipton, Victoria, and finished the major portion of the novel in England. His letters to Macmillan not only answer this longstanding question,[29] but also give some insights as to why Kingsley preferred the romantic mode in which his books are written, to a realistic presentation of life as he must have encountered it in Australia.

After returning from Australia in 1858 he lived with his parents at Eversley, England. From there he wrote to Macmillan (undated letter September 1858) about *Geoffry Hamlyn:* "I am hard at work on the next chapter and am getting on at a good pace and shall be ready to meet the world at Christmas". He was working consistently despite the ill health to which he refers in the same letter: "The coats of the stomach (says Doctor) are in a deuce of a state and won't be right for some time. I wish I had a new stomach".

But it was not only ill health and an approaching publication date that troubled Kingsley. His father was ill and an indication of how it affected him is given in another letter (2 January 1859) to Macmillan: "My father is too failing to attend to the duties of his living, in fact he requires constant care, and so my mother has to go to town and I am left here to take care of him". Shortly after this the father was paralyzed and Kingsley's work was interrupted by nursing duties with the result that the December 1858 deadline was not met. A little later an offer of £50 was received from Boston publishers, Ticknor and Fields, for the prepublication proofs of the book (undated letter March 1859). After taking advice from his brother, Charles, and checking with Alexander Macmillan, Henry accepted the offer.

Charles Kingsley, meanwhile, had been supervising what his younger brother was writing and Henry was reshaping the work in accordance with Charles' criteria. "The faults", wrote Henry to Macmillan (undated letter March 1859), "I have laboriously mended, against my own judgment in some instances". But this was not the only check he was to receive while the work was in hand. Macmillan had views about the content of the book and his wishes had to be respected. It was Macmillan's influence which caused the early part of *Geoffry Hamlyn* to be expanded to almost one third of the finished novel. This resulted in more of the action being set in Dartmoor and Devon, no doubt to meet the tastes of English readers. That it was Macmillan's suggestion can be seen from the letter (undated March 1859) where Henry Kingsley writes: ". . . I shall attend and enlarge the first part and send it for your perusal, attending to the suggestion you made to me the other day".

This was not all. Macmillan might have stated his requirements, and Charles his, but there was yet one more critic to satisfy, sick though he was—Henry's father. "I have taken my father's advice", wrote Kingsley (undated letter March 1859), "in eliminating everything in the book which might prevent it lying on a drawing room table". As Kingsley was finding, experiencing life was one thing, using it in a novel another. His preference for romance rather than realism appears to have derived, at least partly, from the constraints of family and publisher. One can only conjecture what he could have written that would have been potentially offensive to Victorian drawing room society. For instance, in early 1859, Henry recorded that he had received a lecture from Charles "about a certain scene being too coarse" and that he had to rewrite it so that "you may read any part of it out in a drawing room full of young ladies". Henry may have been to Australia but evidently no colonial roughness of scene or expression was to be allowed to taint his work as an author or, for that matter, affect the already established position the Kingsleys had achieved in mid-Victorian England.

If Henry had strong feelings about the effect of these restrictions on his writing he seems not to have protested overmuch. It was the

Australian adventure which had given him the material for his novel and enhanced its potential interest. It was to be English conformity which would stifle his original presentation of life, cause him to turn to romance away from realism, and take into account as part of his audience a "room full of young ladies".

The "Philistines" had to be respected and for the moment "the tie that binds"—in this case his advisers—was to bind subtly and tightly, so much so that the dedication of his second novel, *Ravenshoe*, reads: "To my brother, Charles Kingsley, I dedicate this tale, in token of a love which only grows stronger as we both get older". Victorian "respectability" working through publisher and family was already exacting its price. In receiving "help" from Macmillan, his brother, and his father, Henry *was*, in effect, replacing an imagination enlivened while in Australia with one governed by stifling Victorian values. This, in turn, precluded his depicting much of what he saw in Australia as being essentially different.

In the same letter as that dealing with Charles' strictures, Kingsley makes it clear that chapter **XXX** of *Geoffry Hamlyn* was written in Australia. This chapter was later published separately by Macmillan in 1871 as a book for children, *The Lost Child*. It is a sentimental tale of a child lost in the Australian bush, and is reminiscent of a similarly entitled tale, occurring in Cornish folk lore, with its references to pixies, the child's being attracted by the delights of the forest, and the imaginative response of the child.[30] In the Cornish tale the child survives, Kingsley's child does not.

In another letter to Macmillan (undated September 1858), Henry Kingsley described Macmillan's request to "round off" his novel as "what we painters . . . do when . . . softening the various groups one into another so as to form not a succession of objects but a picture". To a large extent he did this in *Geoffry Hamlyn*. Mary Hawker, who eloped with a ne'er-do-well husband, is the only figure who may be considered of particular interest as a character although the focus of the novel is not really on her. The story is, as Kingsley says through its narrator, Geoffry Hamlyn, "neither more nor less than an account of what befel certain of my acquaintances during a period extending over twenty years . . . yet it has been my object, neither to dwell on the one hand unnecessarily on the more unimportant passages, nor on the other hand to omit anything which may be supposed to bear on the general course of events . . . I must push on too, for there is a long period of dull stupid prosperity . . . which we must get over as quickly as is decent".[31] The structural plan of the novel was "a gloomy beginning leading up to a happy and prosperous conclusion". This, he wrote to Macmillan, he believed "to be within the bounds of art".

When *Geoffry Hamlyn* was finally published in England early in 1859, Macmillan was located in Cambridge and Kingsley was temporarily at St Leonard's. He worked steadily, going up to Cambridge when necessary to see Macmillan, and availed himself of Charles' help with the proof reading. At the same time he was looking ahead to publication arrangements and Australia was in his mind, but not to the extent that might be expected. "Pray write to Irving", he wrote, "I shall be much obliged to you. The 'Argus' a Melbourne newspaper is the principal paper and I doubt not he will manage matters for you as you wish". Along with the copy of the novel he wanted Macmillan to send to Irving (professor of Classics at Melbourne University), another copy was to go to his old friend, H.P. Venables, the Oxford graduate who had accompanied him to Australia in 1853. Other than these no personal copies were sent to Australia by Macmillan. The publisher's list filed among the Kingsley letters[32] is quite detailed regarding the recipients and one may wonder about Kingsley's relationships with known acquaintances in Australia. In this connection three names stand out—T.A. Browne ("Rolf Boldrewood") of Squattleseamere, Chas. Hamilton Macknight of Dunmore, and Willi Mitchell of Langi Willi, all of whom had been his hosts—all were overlooked. Insofar as newspapers were concerned, copies of *Geoffry Hamlyn* were sent not only to *The Argus*, but also to *The Age, The Melbourne Herald,* and the *Sydney Morning Herald.* Although the book received careful attention and was granted a favourable reception in Australia, it was reviewed sparsely. Reviewers in both England and Australia were critical of the novel but the grounds of disparagement "were interestingly different in some respects".[33]

Kingsley received £600 from Macmillan on publication, and when acknowledging receipt stated that he had recommenced work on *Ravenshoe* which he had begun when at Oxford. This, together with reports of his writing in Australia, and his encouragement of Nathanael Walter Swan (1835–84),[34] seems to indicate that even during his undergraduate years Kingsley aspired to be a writer. As early as his first novel, though, he realized there were drawbacks as well as advantages in having a brother prominent both as clergyman and novelist. In an undated letter of June 1859, he complained that he saw no "reason for comparison to be made with Charles" which was, as he saw it, "like comparing Louis Napoleon to his uncle". Despite this, his work was inevitably associated with that of Charles Kingsley.

To some extent the statement in *Geoffry Hamlyn*, that the novel was an account of events involving Hamlyn's acquaintances, needs to be read against a background of contemporary views and attitudes. *Fraser's Magazine* of October 1863 gives a fair indication of some emigrants' attitudes when it records: "Probably most of the settlers who now flock to New Zealand hope to return speedily with fortunes to spend in England; but the statement does not hold equally true of Australia, and most assuredly not of Canada" (p.460). The writer makes this observation because "Canada, and still more Australia and New Zealand, are all lands which have enriched their colonists, some of them with incredible wealth" (p.461). The hope of the characters in *Geoffry Hamlyn* to rebuild personal fortunes in Australia was, for the period in which the novel was set, an acceptable aim. That young Buckley would want to return to Clere to buy back ancestral lands may seem odd to some present day Australians, "offensive" to others (as it was to Furphy), but natural, indeed expected, to those Englishmen of the nineteenth century who aspired to wealth and land ownership. George E. Boxall, writing in *Macmillan's Magazine* in 1899,[35] reviewed the English presence in Australia in terms of "The Evolution of the Australian" and wrote:

> The average Englishman of the first half of the present century was mightily proud of his country and himself. His victories under Wellington and Nelson had induced him to believe that one Englishman was physically a match for three Frenchmen, and he proclaimed that belief as loudly as possible. He was convinced that there was no other country on earth to compare with his island-home; and he was as proud of being able to say "I am an Englishman" as any old Roman of them all was of proclaiming *"Romanus sum"* ... Inferior to the born Englishman ...[young native-born] Australians were also taught that England was the most beautiful country in the world. Even the fogs [in Australia] were an advantage, because they relieved the Englishman from the continuous glare of the blazing sun. Everything English, in fact, was seen through spectacles which hid all defects and magnified all virtues.

By the time Kingsley arrived in Australia, the usage of such terms as "Currency" and "Sterling" to denote locally or English-born Australian residents was unknown to the newcomers of the Roaring

Fifties, but as Boxall states, "the belief it had once represented continued as firm as ever, and native-born Australians were spoken of by English residents in an indulgent manner". It is easy, therefore, to see the relevance of contemporary English attitudes to Kingsley's characters, and discussions in the novel affecting Australia and Britain. *Geoffry Hamlyn* faithfully, if on the whole uncritically, reflects certain influential *attitudes* of Kingsley's time and this is one of its main appeals. To demand of the novel other qualities of realism, or "Australianness", is to ignore what it does offer. G.A. Wilkes, for example, sees in *Geoffry Hamlyn* evidence that while "Kingsley is not a novelist of exceptional powers . . . as a myth-maker his instincts are generally sure, overcoming local failures in the execution . . . critics have been slow to recognise the exact mode [mythic and heroic] with which they are dealing".[36]

A contemporary, Cuthbert Fetherstonhaugh, said of the book: "*Geoffry Hamlyn*, too, although very truthfully portraying life in Australia, all the time bears the impress of the Britisher who wrote it. The author is never heart and soul with the Australian bush or with the Australian bushman. The Britisher is sticking out all the time".[37] Kingsley *was* English and wrote, therefore, from an English stance. To argue against that is to expect the book to be something other than "an account of what befel certain of my acquaintances during a period of twenty years", some two decades before the goldrushes of the fifties. It is a romance, its world the struggle of effort rewarded, and the movement of its narrative faithful to the vision of Improvement to which Macaulay attributed the British rise to power over six generations in his *History of England from the Accession of James II*. *The Hillyars and the Burtons*, by way of contrast, gives a different post-goldrush picture of Australia with characters drawn from the English nobility, tradesmen, goldseekers, and parliamentarians. Pervading the narrative is a sense of Man's mortality and the transience of human life, while Nature is not shown to be benign but rather as "cruel and pitiless". If effort was rewarded in *Geoffry Hamlyn*, the world of *The Hillyars and the Burtons* is "no place of rewards and punishments". Although a romance, Leonie Kramer aptly describes it as being "hardly romantic at all".

The effects of translocation, bushrangers, cattle droving, encounters with Aborigines, the kangaroo hunt, the bushfire, and the lost child are all aspects of station living which the Australian of the day recognized as part of colonial life, and which, from Kingsley onwards, formed part of station romances. In this respect Kingsley proved both observant and seminal. He made use of historical incidents such as the Spanish Galleon near Warrnambool, of which one painting exists as well as many local references: of the attack by Aborigines on Faithfull's station on the Ovens in 1838; of the 1851 bushfire in Victoria, subsequently remembered as Black Thursday for many years; of the child lost at Avoca; of the story of Bogong Jack; and of other details which lie beyond the scope of this introduction.

Scenes of Devon, England, as well as his mention of towns and villages in the early part of the book are factually based. In Australia, although the setting of the book is the Monaro and Gippsland, Kingsley chooses freely from other areas to suit his purposes. The flora, for instance, mentioned on the ride to Cape Chatham (ch.XXXIV), occurs in the vicinity of Cape Conran, Gippsland, but the coastline is more akin to that seen on the Southern Ocean coast of Victoria, the graveyard of many ships which failed to reach Port Phillip after the long voyage out from England. The characters and their social graces are similar, too, to those who settled in the Western District of Victoria in the early days. A reading of Fetherstonhaugh's *After Many Days*, Margaret Kiddle's *Men of Yesterday*, and Rolf Boldrewood's *Old Melbourne Memories*, to mention but three of the many sources available, soon shows this to be so.

Furphy has been mentioned so often for his criticism of Kingsley's "virgin-souled" schoolboys (*Such is Life*, ch.IV), that one connection between them, albeit slight, may be mentioned. In "Wild Sports of the Far South" (omitted from this volume for reasons of space, but see bibliography), Kingsley records that his characters stayed overnight at Costello's, beyond Kangaroo Grounds, Victoria, en route to the Goulburn River valley, via what would have been known then as Insolvency Gap. This station was De Castella's, formerly owned by the Ryrie brothers who overlanded from the Monaro, NSW, to Victoria. Hubert de Castella wrote *Les Squatters Australiens* as a rebuttal of *Les Voleurs d'Or* by Celeste Mogadon (or de Chabrillan), describing its author as being "of great celebrity and small virtue".[38] Ryrie's head gardener was, between 1843 and 1850, Samuel Furphy, father of Joseph (1841–1912) who was born on the property. "Wild Sports of the Far South" concerns itself with fishing on the Goulburn, a kangaroo hunt (the use of which, as a device, Kingsley believed overdone in emigrant stories), an emu hunt, and shooting, before the characters return "Home". It appeared in *Macmillan's Magazine* in May 1859, almost about the time *Geoffry Hamlyn* was published, and contained a comment by Kingsley about stories which dealt with returning migrants who had prospered in Australia:

> I won't bore you much more, my dear reader, with kangaroo hunting. I expect the British public has had nearly enough of it. No cheap periodical can get along for many months without an emigrant story, in which the kangaroos are pretty sure to be prominent, and in which a mechanic [tradesman] and his family, after an unsuccessful career at home (not at all their own fault, you understand), rapidly accumulate a gigantic fortune in Australia, and in the hour of need relieve (let us suppose with tea and damper) the unprincipled swell who caused their ruin.

This is almost, but not quite, *Geoffry Hamlyn*. In many ways, too, Hamlyn the narrator, is almost, but not quite, Henry Kingsley.

In *Geoffry Hamlyn*, Henry Kingsley preserves a record of an Australia which has long since passed away, and which evolved not only from convicts, soldiers, and governors, but also from emigrants prepared to risk resettlement "down under", hoping to improve their estate in life, whether in land, gold, or circumstance, whatever the outcome. If Kingsley has treated the subject in a romantic rather than a realistic manner, I suspect his own sense of adventure and the appeal of the heroic made a contribution. As Michael Sadleir observed in *Things Past*: "He had an intense sympathy for decayed splendour, for buildings and families and individuals whose great days are gone, leaving a once proud structure to neglect or defacement. . . . His worship of the beauty of boyhood and young manhood is fundamentally as much a lament for the evanescence of loveliness as admiration for the loveliness itself . . . he may be fairly termed—the prose laureate of wasted beauty . . ."[39]

That Kingsley should regard explorers in an heroic light is really not surprising even if he writes little of the daily wrestle with the land and little, too, of the melancholy sadness which he brought to it and sensed there during his travels. The Chelsea library of his father's rectory was well stocked with tales of adventure and exploration, and his articles on Eyre and Sturt reveal an ability to recount with feeling and admiration the exploits of both. Sturt well earned, in Kingsley's opinion, the title of Father of Australian Exploration, while Eyre's stoic journey brought not the immortality that Eyre hoped for but recognition of a feat which seemed only of passing interest—few in Melbourne or Sydney remembered the exploit. But, Kingsley wrote, "that dreadful band of country has never been invaded since, and Baxter's bones still lie out on the desolate down, bleaching in the winds". The note of lament is not far absent when he reflects on the past or its exploits.

The remaining fiction and articles give a glimpse of the goldfields ("My Landladies"); of Melbourne and the Western District of Victoria ("Travelling in Victoria"); of Australian country life and bushrangers ("The Two Cadets" and *Reginald Hetherege*); of the melancholy sense of alienation encountered in the depths of the forest-clad Great Dividing Range (*The Boy in Grey*); and an example of mateship as well as a reference to bush-madness (*The Mystery of the Island*). The articles on emigration carry in them a tone which seems to arise from a first-hand encounter with the areas, although, in the case of Queensland, this arises principally from transferred references such as: "In the old times we have known perfectly ignorant gentlemen received on first-class stations like gentlemen, and taught their trade, merely because they could be trusted as men of higher education and responsibility". Undoubtedly, this is a reference to Kingsley's first arrival at Langi Willi in the winter of 1854.

"A Word of Remonstrance with some Novelists" gives a reminder of the moral view of literature, and of the place of morality in literature that Henry Kingsley shared with many other Victorian novelists, good and bad. "I do not protest", he wrote, "against the introduction of wickedness into art, living as we do in a wicked world. I believe 'terror and pity purge the human heart', but let wickedness be painted as William Hogarth painted it, in its loathsome, ghastly, downward career, ending in the gallows, the kennel, the mad-house. Do not let us have liars and cheats, and false wives, transformed by a touch into dying saints and honourable matrons. Do not let crime or its penalty be the crucible which converts our dross into gold."

On the other hand Kingsley was generous and perceptive enough as a critic to admire what he was clearly unable to be to any extent in his own work—the "explorer into the dark recesses of the human soul", as he described Nathaniel Hawthorne. With the exception of Goldsmith and Thackeray he rated Hawthorne as perhaps the greatest master of style in the English language and commended him to "everyone interested in the critical study of English literature and style". His article on the naming of characters shows a ready appreciation of Scott's wit, and leaves no doubt of his admiration for Scott as a writer.

Although Kingsley encountered hardships in Australia the experience was not to be of value to him after his return to England.

Except for a few years, his later life could not be described as successful either professionally or financially. After an unfortunate marriage in 1864—he was ever after beset with money problems—Kingsley moved from Wargrave, where he had been living, to Edinburgh in 1869 in order to become editor of *The Daily Review*. While there he went as the paper's correspondent to the Franco-Prussian War of 1870 but was recalled because his articles were too realistic for his employers. In an excerpt from "The Influence of Travel" he states his views on travel, war, and newspapers, and reveals himself as a thoughtful observer of topical events:

> For my own part, I cannot find words sufficient to overrate my detestation of war, unless some great principle is to be gained by it . . . It will come some day—not yet—when it would be dangerous for any king who depends on his throne for the principle of nationality to let his people see much of other peoples; but this power is passing out of the hands of all princes, presidents and parliaments. . . . Newspapers, with all their enormous value, are sad mischiefmakers sometimes. Nations will never get to know one another through their newspapers: a hundred things prevent any newspaper from giving the public opinion of more than a certain section of the community . . . East, west, south, and north, the travelling nations are civilising; while the untravelling ones, equally able, equally brave, seem to spend the most of their time in cutting one another's throats.[40]

His views, an unusual editorial approach, and the precarious finances of the paper, resulted in his relinquishing the editorship and returning to London in 1871. In mid-1875 he moved to Cuckfield, Sussex, where he died of throat cancer in May 1876. His last years were marked by an estrangement from his brother, Charles, and a declining literary ability. Shortly before he died he was visited by Leslie Stephen and Anne Thackeray Ritchie to whom he said, "They tell me I am going to die. I don't *feel* like a dying man",[41] and went on to talk of books and everyday things. Very soon afterwards they learned of his death. He was buried in Cuckfield churchyard where he lies alone, the grave looking out over the Sussex Downs.

Minor he may have been as a writer but, as John Barnes has noted, "*Geoffry Hamlyn* is one of the foundation novels in Australian literary history . . . [and] . . . marked a beginning of Australian prose fiction".[42] By gaining such recognition Kingsley finally won his long struggle to be known for himself rather than as the younger brother of Charles Kingsley. In doing so he fulfilled the 1896 prediction: "Only in one particular does it seem safe to predict . . . Henry Kingsley is certain of a permanent place in the literature of the young country where he experienced both the best and worst experiences of his life."⁴³ Whether Australia was the scene of his "best and worst experiences" is open to question. Few, though, would disagree with his place in its literature.

Notes

1. Kingsley's first six novels were printed in England by Macmillan and Co., and in USA by Ticknor and Fields, Boston. Nine of his novels were printed for continental sale by Tauchnitz of Leipzig.

2. Clement Shorter, "A Note on Henry Kingsley" in *The Recollections of Geoffry Hamlyn* (London: Ward, Lock & Bowden, 1895), p.vii.

3. Charles Kingsley died 23 January 1875, and Henry on 24 May 1876.

4. A reference to a "strain of homosexuality" in S.M. Ellis, *Henry Kingsley 1830–76 Towards a Vindication* (London: Grant Richards Pronto, 1931), p.37 is not substantiated by either contemporary or later sources, and the episode in "Jackson of Paul's" which gave rise to Ellis' comment is regarded by Michael Sadleir as a David and Jonathan affair. This judgment, considered in the light of Kingsley's classical background, his love of painting, and his eye for beauty, explains his admiration of male beauty. In any case, such admiration falls into perspective when it is recalled that he admired beauty of landscape and animals, and rated love for a woman superior to any which existed between men.

5. Sidney Lee ed., *Dictionary of National Biography* (London: Smith, Elder, 1909), pp.181–82.

6. *Tales of Old Travel*, p.282.

7. "Avoca River—Rises in the Amphitheatre Ranges and proceeds northerly about 110 miles . . . It only runs during the wet season". Frederich Acheson C.E., "Collection and Storage of Water" in *The Victorian Government Prize Essays, 1860* (Melbourne, 1861), p.38.

8. Mitchell is again linked with Avoca in *Stretton* (ch.XLIX).

9. J.S.D. Mellick, Ph.D. thesis, University of Queensland, 1978, ch.IX.

10. "The Last Two Abyssinian Books".

11. The original of "Mistibithiwong", which Kingsley spells variously, is, according to Mr John Crosthwaite of "The Hermitage", Wodonga, undoubtedly Mt Murramurrangbong, on Hume and Hovell's route— the watershed for several creeks in the area. The names "Kauna" and "Neila Neila" are clearly Kiewa and Mitta Mitta respectively.

12. Ch.XIV.

13. Ch.XLIV.

14. Geoffrey Scott, *Sydney's Highways of History* (Melbourne: Georgian House, 1958), p.170.

15. A.M. Pearson, *Echoes from the Mountains* (Omeo Shire Council, 1969), p.21.

16. J.V. Pendergast, *Pioneers of the Omeo District* (n.p., 1968), pp. 12–13.

17. Ch.XLII.

18. Ch.LXII.

19. Rosilyn Baxter, "Henry Kingsley and the Australian Landscape", *Australian Literary Studies* IV, no. 4 (October 1970): 395–98.

20. *Tales of Old Travel*, note, p.336.

21. *Babes in the Bush* (London: Macmillan, 1900), pp.230–31. Boldrewood's characters are identified in papers held by the Latrobe Library, MS5767, Box 145/4(a).

22. Rolf Boldrewood, *A Sydneyside Saxon* (London: Macmillan, 1891), p.9.

23. 17 no. 2 (June 1945): 103.

24. "The Composition of Geoffry Hamlyn: The Legend and the Facts", *Australian Literary Studies* 3 (October 1968): 281.

25. Cuthbert Fetherstonhaugh, *After Many Days*, 2nd ed. (Sydney: John Andrew, 1918), p.42; C.W. Darley, letter 27 August 1919 to Fetherstonhaugh (Mitchell Library, Sydney, No. B1504); Marcus Clarke's Preface, *Long Odds* (1869); and Rolf Boldrewood, *Old Melbourne Memories*, ed. C.E. Sayers (1969), p.149.

26. Ch.XVII.

27. Ch.XXXIV.

28. *The Hillyars and the Burtons*, ch.LXXII.

29. Henry W. and Albert A. Berg Collection, The New York Public Library, Astor, Lenox and Tilden Foundation.

30. Robert Hunt, *Cornish Folk-Lore* (Truro: Top Mark Press, n.d.), pp.8–9.

31. Ch.XXII.

32. Berg Collection.

33. L.T. Hergenhan, "*Geoffry Hamlyn* through Contemporary Eyes", *Australian Literary Studies*, 2 (December 1966): 289–95.

34. N. Walter Swan, *A Couple of Cups Ago and Other Stories* (Melbourne: Cameron, Laing, 1885), p.xii.

35. 80 (June 1899): 125–30.

36. "Kingsley's *Geoffry Hamlyn*: A Study in Literary Survival", *Southerly*, 32 (1972): 243–54.

37. *After Many Days*, p.42.

38. H. de Castella, *John Bull's Vineyard* (Melbourne: Sands and McDougall, 1886), p.23.

39. *Things Past* (London: Constable, 1944), p.14.

40. *Tinsley's Magazine*, 10 (Feb. 1872): 59–67.

41. Clement Shorter, p.xxii.

42. *Henry Kingsley and Colonial Fiction*, Australian Writers and their Work series, (Melbourne: OUP, 1971), p.44.

43. Desmond Byrne, *Australian Writers* (London: Bentley, 1896), p.91.

A Note on the Text

The Chapman and Hall 1877 edition of *The Recollections of Geoffry Hamlyn* has been selected as copy text for facsimile reproduction in this Portable volume because it does not differ substantially from the first edition (the main exceptions are given below), and because it is the earliest one volume edition available. S. M. Ellis states that the first edition was inscribed "To/ My Father and Mother/ This book/ The Fruit of so many weary years separation/ is dedicated/ with the deepest love and affection" (p.269). He writes further that in the second edition, one volume, 1860, the word "reverence" was substituted for "affection". I have not sighted a first edition so inscribed and the two first editions of *The Recollections of Geoffry Hamlyn* (1859) held by The British Library both use the word "reverence".

Major differences occur in the two editions under Contents: chapter XII is entitled "In which a very muscular Christian indeed comes on stage" in the 1859 edition, and "In which a new face is introduced by means of a rat and a terrier" in the 1877 edition; chapter XIII—"The Discovery of the Forgeries" (1859) and "The Discovery" (1877); chapter XX—"Christmas Day in the Bush" (1859) and "A Warm Christmas Day" (1877); and chapter XXI— "Settling Down" (1859) and "Jim Stockbridge begins to take another view of matters" (1877). In the 1859 edition, chapters XX and XXI are headed in the text, as distinct from the Contents, as shown in the 1877 edition where the headings agree in both places.

The sources of the text for the articles and extracts in this volume are given in footnotes. Slight changes in quotation marks and spelling have been made to standardize the text to UQP house style, but Kingsley's idiosyncratic spelling of Australian place names and flora and fauna has been retained.

PART 1

The Recollections of
Geoffry Hamlyn

GEOFFRY HAMLYN.

BY

HENRY KINGSLEY,

AUTHOR OF
"HILLYARS AND BURTONS,"
"AUSTIN ELLIOT,"
"RAVENSHOE,"
ETC.

NEW EDITION.

LONDON:
CHAPMAN AND HALL, 193 PICCADILLY.

TO

MY FATHER AND MOTHER

This Book

THE FRUIT OF SO MANY WEARY YEARS OF SEPARATION

IS DEDICATED

WITH THE DEEPEST LOVE AND REVERENCE.

CONTENTS.

CHAPTER I.

CHAPTER II.

CHAPTER III.

CHAPTER IV.

CHAPTER V

CHAPTER VI.

CHAPTER VII.

CHAPTER VIII.

CONTENTS.

CHAPTER IX.

CONTENTS.

CONTENTS.

CONTENTS.

CHAPTER XLII.

CHAPTER XLIII.

CHAPTER XLIV.

CHAPTER XLV.

CHAPTER XLVI.

CHAPTER XLVII.

CHAPTER XLVIII.

THE RECOLLECTIONS

OF

GEOFFRY HAMLYN.

CHAPTER I.

INTRODUCTORY

NEAR the end of February 1857, I think about the 20th or so, though it don't much matter; I only know it was near the latter end of summer, burning hot, with the bushfires raging like volcanoes on the ranges, and the river reduced to a slender stream of water, almost lost upon the broad white flats of quartz shingle. It was the end of February, I said, when Major Buckley, Captain Brentwood (formerly of the Artillery), and I, Geoffry Hamlyn, sat together over our wine in the veranda at Baroona, gazing sleepily on the grey plains that rolled away east and north-east towards the sea.

We had sat silent for some time, too lazy to speak, almost to think. The beautiful flower-garden which lay before us, sloping towards the river, looked rather brown and sere, after the hot winds, although the orange-trees were still green enough, and vast clusters of purple grapes were ripening rapidly among the yellowing vine-leaves. On the whole, however, the garden was but a poor subject of contemplation for one who remembered it in all its full November beauty, and so my eye travelled away to the left, to a broad paddock of yellow grass which bounded the garden on that side, and there I watched an old horse feeding.

A very old horse indeed, a horse which seemed to have reached the utmost bounds of equine existence. And yet such a beautiful beast. Even as I looked some wild young colts were let out of the stock-yard, and came galloping and whinnying towards him, and then it was eight to see the old fellow as he trotted towards them, with his

B

nose in the air, and his tail arched, throwing his legs out before him with the ease and grace of a four-year-old, and making me regret that he wasn't my property and ten years younger;—altogether, even then, one of the finest horses of his class I had ever seen, and suddenly a thought came over me, and I grew animated.

"Major Buckley," I said, "what horse is that?"

"What horse is that?" repeated the major very slowly. "Why, my good fellow, old Widderin, to be sure."

"Bless me!" I said; "You don't mean to say that that old horse is alive still?"

"He looks like it," said the major. "He'd carry you a mile or two yet."

"I thought he had died while I was in England," I said. "Ah, major, that horse's history would be worth writing."

"If you began," answered the major, "to write the history of the horse, you must write also the history of everybody who was concerned in those circumstances which caused Sam to take a certain famous ride upon him. And you would find that the history of the horse would be reduced into very small compass, and that the rest of your book would assume proportions too vast for the human intellect to grasp."

"How so?" I said.

He entered into certain details, which I will not give.

"You would have," he said, "to begin at the end of the last century, and bring one gradually on to the present time. Good heavens! just consider."

"I think you exaggerate," I said.

"Not at all," he answered. "You must begin the histories of the Buckley and Thornton families in the last generation. The Brentwoods also, must not be omitted,—why there's work for several years. What do you say, Brentwood?"

"The work of a life-time;" said the captain.

"But suppose I were to write a simple narrative of the principal events in the histories of the three families, which no one is more able to do than myself, seeing that nothing important has ever happened without my hearing of it;—how, I say, would you like that?"

"If it amused you to write it, I am sure it would amuse us to read it," said the major.

"But you are rather old to turn author," said Captain Brentwood; "you'll make a failure of it; in fact, you'll never get through with it."

I replied not, but went into my bedroom, and returning with a thick roll of papers threw it on the floor—as on the stage the honest notary throws down the long-lost will,—and there I stood for a moment with my arms folded, eyeing Brentwood triumphantly.

"It is already done, captain," I said. "There it lies."

The captain lit a cigar, and said nothing; but the major said, "Good gracious me! and when was this done?"

"Partly here, and partly in England. I propose to read it aloud to you, if it will not bore you."

"A really excellent idea," said the major. "My dear!"—this last was addressed to a figure which was now seen approaching us up a long vista of trellised vines. A tall figure dressed in grey. The figure, one could see as she came nearer, of a most beautiful old woman.

Dressed I said in grey, with a white handkerchief pinned over her grey hair, and a light Indian shawl hanging from her shoulders. As upright as a dart, she came towards us through the burning heat, as calmly and majestically as if the temperature had been delightfully moderate. A hoary old magpie accompanied her, evidently of great age, and from time to time barked like an old bulldog, in a wheezy whisper.

"My dear," said the major; "Hamlyn is going to read aloud some manuscript to us."

"That will be very delightful, this hot weather," said Mrs. Buckley. "May I ask the subject, old friend?"

"I would rather you did not, my dear madam; you will soon discover, in spite of a change of names, and perhaps somewhat of localities."

"Well, go on," said the major; and so on I went with the next chapter, which is the first of the story.

The reader will probably ask:

"Now, who on earth is Major Buckley? and who is Captain Brentwood? and last, not least, who the Dickens are you?" If you will have patience, my dear sir, you will find it all out in a very short time—Read on.

CHAPTER II.

THE COURTSHIP AND MARRIAGE OF JOHN THORNTON, CLERK, AND THE BIRTH OF SOME ONE WHO TAKES RATHER A CONSPICUOUS PART IN OUR STORY.

SOMETIME between the years 1780 and 1790, young John Thornton, then a Servitor at Christ Church, fell in love with pretty Jane Hickman, whose father was a well-to-do farmer, living not far down the river from Oxford; and shortly before he took his degree, he called formally upon old Hickman, and asked his daughter's hand. Hickman was secretly well pleased that his daughter should marry a scholar and a gentleman like John Thornton, and a man too who could knock over his bird, or kill his trout in the lasher with any one. So after some decent hesitation he told him, that as soon as he got a living, good enough to support Jane as she had been accustomed to live, he might take her home with a father's blessing, and a hundred pounds to buy furniture. And you may take my word for it, that there was not much difficulty with the young lady, for in fact the thing had long ago been arranged between them, and she was anxiously waiting in the passage to hear her father's decision, all the time that John was closeted with him.

John came forth from the room well pleased and happy. And that evening when they two were walking together in the twilight by the quiet river, gathering cowslips and fritillaries, he told her of his good prospects, and how a young lord, who made much of him, and treated him as a friend and an equal, though he was but a Servitor—and was used to sit in his room talking with him long after the quadrangle was quiet, and the fast men had reeled off to their drunken slumbers—had only three days before promised him a living of 300*l.* a-year, as soon as he should take his priest's orders. And when they parted that night, at the old stile in the meadow, and he saw her go gliding home like a white phantom under the dark elms, he thought joyfully, that in two short years they would be happily settled, never more to part in this world, in his peaceful vicarage in Dorsetshire.

Two short years, he thought. Alas! and alas! Before two years were gone, poor Lord Sandston was lying one foggy November morning on Hampstead Heath, with a bullet through his heart. Shot down at the commencement of a noble and useful career by a brainless gambler—a man who did all things ill, save billiards and pistol-shooting; his beauty and his strength hurried to corruption, and his wealth to the senseless *debauchée* who hounded on his murderer to insult him. But I have heard old Thornton tell, with proud tears, how my lord, though outraged and insulted, with no course open to him but to give the villain the power of taking his life, still fired in the air, and went down to the vault of his forefathers without the guilt of blood upon his soul.

So died Lord Sandston, and with him all John's hopes of advancement. A curate now on 50*l.* a-year; what hope had he of marrying? And now the tearful couple, walking once more by the river in desolate autumn, among the flying yellow leaves, swore constancy, and agreed to wait till better times should come.

So they waited. John in his parish among his poor people and his school-children, busy always during the day, and sometimes perhaps happy. But in the long winter evenings, when the snow lay piled against the door, and the wind howled in the chimney; or worse, when the wind was still, and the rain was pattering from the eaves, he would sit lonely and miserable by his desolate hearth, and think with a sigh of what might have been had his patron lived. And five-and-twenty years rolled on until James Brown, who was born during the first year of his curateship, came home a broken man, with one arm gone, from the battle of St. Vincent. And the great world roared on, and empires rose and fell, and dull echoes of the great throes without were heard in the peaceful English village, like distant thunder on a summer's afternoon, but still no change for him.

But poor Jane bides her time in the old farm-house, sitting constant and patient behind the long low latticed window, among the geraniums and roses, watching the old willows by the river. Five-and-twenty times she sees those willows grow green, and the meadow brighten up with flowers, and as often she sees their yellow leaves driven before the strong south wind, and the meadow grow dark and hoar before the breath of autumn. Her father was long since dead, and she was bringing up her brother's children. Her raven hair was streaked with grey, and her step was not so light, nor her laugh so loud, yet still she waited and hoped, long after all hope seemed dead.

But at length a brighter day seemed to dawn for them ; for the bishop, who had watched for years John Thornton's patient industry and blameless conversation, gave him, to his great joy and astonishment, the living of Drumston, worth 350*l.* a-year. And now, at last, he might marry if he would. True, the morning of his life was gone long since, and its hot noon spent in thankless labour ; but the evening, the sober, quiet evening, yet remained, and he and Jane might still render pleasant for one another the downward road toward the churchyard, and hand-in-hand walk more tranquilly forward to meet that dark tyrant Death, who seemed so terrible to the solitary watcher.

A month or less after John was installed, one soft grey day in March, this patient couple walked slowly arm-in-arm up the hill, under the lychgate, past the dark yew that shadowed the peaceful graves, and so through the damp church porch, up to the old stone altar, and there were quietly married, and then walked home again. No feasting or rejoicing was there at that wedding ; the very realization of their long deferred hopes was a disappointment. In March they were married, and before the lanes grew bright with the primroses of another spring, poor Jane was lying in a new-made grave, in the shadow of the old grey tower.

But, though dead, she yet lived to him in the person of a bright-eyed baby, a little girl, born but three months before her mother's death. Who can tell how John watched and prayed over that infant, or how he felt that there was something left for him in this world yet, and thought that if his child would live, he should not go down to the grave a lonely desolate man. Poor John!—who can say whether it would not have been better if the mother's coffin had been made a little larger, and the baby had been carried up the hill, to sleep quietly with its mother, safe from all the evil of this world.

But the child lived and grew, and, at seventeen, I remember her well, a beautiful girl, merry, impetuous, and thoughtless, with black waving hair and dark blue eyes, and all the village loved her and took pride in her. For they said—" She is the handsomest and the best in the parish."

————

CHAPTER III.

THE HISTORY OF (A CERTAIN FAMILY LIVING IN) EUROPE, FROM THE BATTLE OF TRAFALGAR TO THE PEACE OF 1818, CONTAINING FACTS HITHERTO UNPUBLISHED.

AMONG all the great old commoner families of the south of England, who have held the lands of their forefathers through every change of dynasty and religion, the Buckleys of Clere stand deservedly high among the brightest and the oldest. All down the stormy page of this great island's history one sees, once in about a hundred years, that name in some place of second-rate honour at least, whether as admiral, general, or statesman ; and yet, at the beginning of this present century, the representative of the good old family was living at Clere House, a palace built in the golden times of Elizabeth, on 900l. a-year, while all the county knew that it took 300l. to keep Clere in proper repair.

The two Stuart revolutions had brought them down from county princes to simple wealthy squires, and the frantic efforts made by Godfrey Buckley, in the " South Sea " scheme to retrieve the family fortunes, had well nigh broke them. Year by year they saw acre after acre of the broad lands depart, and yet Marmaduke Buckley lived in the home of his ancestors, and the avenue was untouched by axe or saw.

He was a widower, with two sons, John and James. John had been to sea from his earliest youth, and James had joined his regiment a year or more. John had been doing the state good service under his beloved Collingwood; and on the 19th October, 1805, when Nelson and Collingwood made tryst to meet at the gates of hell, John Buckley was one of the immortals on the deck of the " Royal Sovereign." And when the war fog rolled away to leeward, and Trafalgar was won, and all seas were free, he lay dead in the cockpit, having lived just long enough to comprehend the magnitude of the victory.

Brave old Marmaduke was walking up and down the terrace at Clere uneasy and impatient. Beside him was the good old curate who had educated both the boys, and wearily and oft they turned to watch down the long vista of the ancient avenue for the groom, who had been despatched to Portsmouth to gain some tidings of the lieutenant. They had heard of the victory, and, in their simple way, had praised God for it, drinking a bottle of the rarest old wine to his Majesty's health and the confusion of his enemies, before they knew whether they themselves were among the number of the mourners. And now, as they paced the terrace, every moment they grew more anxious and uneasy for the long delayed intelligence.

Some trifle took them into the flower-garden, and, when they came back, their hearts leapt up, for the messenger was there dismounted, opening the gate. The curate ran down the steps, and taking a black-edged letter from the sorrowful groom, gave it into the trembling hands of the old man with a choking sob. He opened it and glanced over it, and then, throwing it towards his friend, walked steadily up the steps, and disappeared within the dark porch.

It was just three hasty lines from the great Collingwood himself. That brave heart, in the midst of the din of victory, had found time to scrawl a word to his old schoolmate, and tell him that his boy had died like a hero, and that he regretted him like a son.

The old man sat that evening in the western gallery, tearless and alone, brooding over his grief. Three times the curate had peeped in, and as often had retreated, fearful of disturbing the old man's solemn sorrow. The autumn sun had gone down in wild and lurid clouds, and the gallery was growing dark and gloomy, when the white figure of a beautiful girl entering silently at the lower door came gliding up the darkening vista, past the light of the windows and the shadow of the piers, to where the old man sat under the high north window, and knelt at his feet, weeping bitterly.

It was Agnes Talbot, the daughter of his nearest neighbour and best friend, whom the curate had slyly sent for, thinking in his honest heart that she would make a better comforter than he, and rightly; for the old man, bending over her, lifted up his voice and wept, speaking for the first time since he heard of his bereavement, and saying, "Oh, my boy, my boy!"

"He is gone, sir," said Agnes, through her tears; "and gone the way a man should go. But there is another left you yet; remember him."

"Aye, James," said he; "alas, poor James! I wonder if he knows it. I wish he were here."

"James is here," said she. "He heard of it before you, and came posting over as fast as he could, and is waiting outside to know if you can see him."

The door at the lower end of the gallery opened, and a tall and noble-looking young man strode up and took his father's hand.

He was above the ordinary height of man, with a grand broad forehead and bold blue eyes. Old Marmaduke's heart warmed up as he parted his curling hair, and he said,

"Thank God, I've got one left still! The old house will not perish yet, while such a one as you remains to uphold it."

After a time they left him, at his own request, and walked out together through the dark rooms towards the old hall.

"Agnes, my beloved, my darling!" said James, drawing his arm round her waist; "I knew I should find you with him like a ministering angel. Say something to comfort me, my love. You never could love John as I did; yet I know you felt for him as your brother, as he soon would have been, if he had lived."

"What can I say to you, my own?" she replied, "save to tell you that he fell as your brother should fall, amongst the foremost, fighting for his country's existence. And, James, if you must go before me, and leave me a widow before I am a bride, it would render more tolerable the short time that would be left me before I followed you, to think that you had fallen like him."

"There will be a chance of it, Agnes," said James, "for Stuart, they say, is going to Italy, and I go with him. There will be a long and bloody war, and who knows how it will end? Stay you here quiet with the old man, my love, and pray for me; the end will come some day. I am only eighteen and an ensign; in ten years I may be a colonel."

They parted that night with tears and kisses, and a few days afterwards James went from among them to join his regiment.

From that time Agnes almost lived with old Marmaduke. Her father's castle could be seen over the trees from the windows of Clere, and every morning, wet or dry, the old man posted himself in the great north window of the gallery to watch her coming. All day she would pervade the gloomy old mansion like a ray of sunlight, now reading to him, now leading him into the flower-garden in fine weather, till he grew quite fond of flowers for her sake, and began even to learn the names of some of them. But oftenest of all she would sit working by his side, while he told her stories of times gone by, stories which would have been dull to any but her, but which she could listen to and applaud. Best of all she liked to hear him talk of James, and his exploits by flood and field from his youth up; and so it was that this quiet couple never tired one another, for their hearts were set upon the same object.

Sometimes her two sisters, noble and beautiful girls, would come to see him; but they, indeed, were rather intruders, kind and good as they were. And sometimes old Talbot looked round to see his old friend, and talked of bygone fishing and hunting, which roused the old man up and made him look glad for half a day after. Still, however, Agnes and the old curate were company enough for him, for they were the only two who loved his absent son as well as he. The love which had been divided between the two, seemed now to be concentrated upon the one, and yet this true old Briton never hinted at James' selling out and coming home, for he said that the country had need of every one then, more particularly such a one as James.

Time went on, and he came back to them from Corunna, and spending little more than a month at home, he started away once more; and next they heard of him at Busaco, wounded and promoted. Then they followed him in their hearts along the path of glory, from Talavera by Albuera and Vittoria, across the Pyrenees. And while they were yet reading a long-delayed letter, written from Toulouse at midnight—after having been to the theatre with Lord Wellington, wearing a white cockade—he broke in on them again, to tell them the war was well-nigh over, and that he would soon come and live with them in peace.

Then what delightful reunions were there in the old gallery window, going over all the weary campaigns once more; pleasant rambles, too, down by the river-side in the sweet May evenings, old Marmaduke and the curate discreetly walking in front, and James and Agnes loitering far behind. And in the succeeding winter after they were married, what pleasant rides had they to meet the hounds, and merry evenings before the bright wood-fire in the hall. Never were four people more happy than they. The war was done, the disturber was confined, and peace had settled down upon the earth.

Peace, yes. But not for long. Spring came on, and with it strange disquieting rumours, growing more certain day by day, till the terrible news broke on them that the faithless tyrant had broke loose again, and that all Europe was to be bathed in blood once more by his insane ambition.

James had sold out of the army, so that when Agnes first heard the intelligence she thanked God that her husband at least would be safe at home during the storm. But she was soon to be undeceived. When the news first came, James had galloped off to Portsmouth, and late in the evening they saw him come riding slowly and sadly up the avenue. She was down at the gate before he could dismount, and to her eager inquiries if the news were true, he replied,

"All too true, my love; and I must leave you this day week."

"My God!" said she; "leave me again, and not six months married? Surely the king has had you long enough; may not your wife have you for a few short months?"

"Listen to me, dear wife," he replied. "All the Peninsular men are volunteering, and I must not be among the last, for ever, man is wanted now. Buonaparte is joined by the whole army, and the craven king has fled. If England and Prussia can combine to strike a blow before he gets head, thousands and hundreds of thousands of lives will be spared. But let him once get firmly seated, and then, hey! for ten years' more war. Beside the thing is done; my name went in this morning."

She said, "God's will be done;" and he left his young bride and his old father once again. The nightingale grew melodious in the midnight woods, the swallows nestled again in the chimneys, and day by day the shadows under the old avenue grew darker and darker till merry June was half gone; and then one Saturday came the rumour of a great defeat.

All the long weary summer Sabbath that followed, Agnes and Marmaduke silently paced the terrace, till the curate—having got through his own services somehow, and broken down in the "prayer during war and tumults,"—came hurrying back to them to give what comfort he could.

Alas! that was but little. He could only speculate whether or not the duke would give up Brussels, and retire for reinforcements. If the the two armies could effect a union, they would be near about the strength of the French, but then the Prussians were cut to pieces; so the curate broke down, and became the worst of the three.

Cheer up, good souls! for he you love shall not die yet for many long years. While you are standing there before the porch, dreading the long anxious night, Waterloo has been won, and he—having stood the appointed time in the serried square, watching the angry waves of French cavalry dash in vain against the glittering wall of bayonets—is now leaning against a gun in the French position, alive and well, though fearfully tired, listening to the thunder of the Prussian artillery to the north, and watching the red sun go down across the wild confusion of the battle-field.

But home at Clere none slept that night, but met again next morning weary and harassed. All the long three days none of them spoke much, but wandered about the house uneasily. About ten o'clock on the Wednesday night they went to bed, and the old man slept from sheer weariness.

It was twelve o'clock when there came a clang at the gate, and a sound of horses' feet on the gravel. Agnes was at the window in a moment.

"Who goes there?" she cried.

"An orderly from Colonel Mountford at Portsmouth," said a voice below. "A letter for Mr. Buckley."

She sent a servant to undo the door; and going to the window again, she inquired, trembling,—

"Do you know what the news is, orderly?"

" A great victory, my dear," said the man, mistaking her for one of the servants. " Your master is all right. There's a letter from him inside this one."

" And I daresay," Mrs. Buckley used to add, when she would tell this old Waterloo story, as we called it, " that the orderly thought me a most heartless domestic, for when I heard what he said, I burst out laughing so loud, that old Mr. Buckley woke up to see what was the matter, and when heard, he laughed as loud as I did."

So he came back to them again with fresh laurels, but Agnes never felt safe, till she heard that the powers had determined to chain up her *bête noir*, Buonaparte, on a lonely rock in the Atlantic, that he might disturb the world no more. Then at last she began to believe that peace might be a reality, and a few months after Waterloo, to their delight and exultation, she bore a noble boy.

And as we shall see more of this boy, probably, than of any one else in these following pages, we will, if you please, appoint him hero, with all the honours and emoluments thereunto pertaining. Perhaps when I have finished, you will think him not so much of a hero after all. But at all events you shall see how he is an honest upright gentleman, and in these times, perhaps such a character is preferable to a hero.

Old Marmaduke had been long failing, and two years after this he had taken to his bed, never to leave it again alive. And one day when the son and heir was rolling and crowing on his grandfather's bed, and Agnes was sewing at the window, and James was tying a fly by the bedside, under the old man's directions; he drew the child towards him, and beckoning Agnes from the window spoke thus :—

" My children, I shan't be long with you, and I must be the last of the Buckleys that die at Clere. Nay, I mean it, James ; listen carefully to me : when I go, the house and park must go with me. We are very poor as you well know, and you will be doing injustice to this boy if you hang on here in this useless tumble-down old palace, without money enough to keep up your position in the county. You are still young, and it would be hard for you to break up old associations. It got too hard for me lately, though at one time I meant to do it. The land and the house are the worst investment you can have for your money, and if you sell, a man like you may make money in many ways. Gordon the brewer is dying to have the place, and he has more right to it than we have, for he has ten acres round to our one. Let him have the estate and found a new family ; the people will miss us at first, God bless 'em, but they'll soon get used to Gordon, for he's a kindly man, and a just, and I am glad that we shall have so good a successor. Remember your family and your ancestors, and for that reason don't hang on here, as I said

before, in the false position of an old county family without money,
like the Singletons of Hurst, living in a ruined hall, with a miserable
overcropped farm, a corner of the old deer park, under their drawing-
room window. No, my boy, I would sooner see you take a farm
from my lord, than that. And now I am tired with talking, and so
leave me, but after I am gone, remember what I have said."

A few days after this the old man passed peacefully from the
world without a sigh.

They buried him in the family vault under the chancel windows. And he was the last of the Buckleys that slept in the grave
of his forefathers. And the old arch beneath the east window
is built up for ever.

Soon after he was gone, the Major, as I shall call him in future,
sold the house and park, and the few farms that were left, and
found himself with twelve thousand pounds, ready to begin the world
again. He funded his money and made up his mind to wait a few
years and see what to do ; determining that if no other course should
open, he would emigrate to Canada—the paradise of half-pay
officers. But in the meantime he moved into Devonshire, and took
a pretty little cottage which was to let, not a quarter of a mile from
Drumston Vicarage.

Such an addition to John Thornton's little circle of acquaintances
was very welcome. The Major and he very soon became fast friends,
and noble Mrs. Buckley was seldom a day without spending an hour
at least, with the beautiful, wilful Mary Thornton.

CHAPTER IV.

SOME NEW FACES.

THE twilight of a winter's evening, succeeding a short and stormy
day, was fast fading into night, and old John Thornton sat dozing in
his chair before the fire, waiting for candles to resume his reading.
He was now but little over sixty, yet his hair was snowy white, and his
face looked worn and aged. Any one who watched his countenance
now in the light of the blazing wood, might see by the down-drawn
brows and uneasy expression that the old man was unhappy and
disquieted.

The book that lay in his lap was a volume of Shakespeare, open at
the " Merchant of Venice." Something he had come across in
that play had set him thinking. The book had fallen on his knees,
and he sat pondering till he had fallen asleep. Yet even in his

slumber the uneasy expression stayed upon his face, and now and then he moved uneasily in his chair.

What could there be to vex him? Not poverty at all events, for not a year ago a relation, whom he had seldom seen, and of late years entirely lost sight of, had left him 5,000*l.* and a like sum to his daughter Mary. And his sister, Miss Thornton, a quiet good old maid, who had been a governess all her life, had come to live with him, so that he was now comfortably off, with the only two relations he cared about in the world staying with him to make his old age comfortable. Yet notwithstanding all this, John was unhappy.

His daughter Mary sat sewing in the window, ostensibly for the purpose of using the last of the daylight. But the piece of white muslin in her hand claimed but a small part of her attention. Sometimes she gave a stitch or two; but then followed a long gaze out of the window, across the damp gravel and plushy lawn, towards the white gate under the leafless larches. Again with an impatient sigh she would address herself to her sewing, but once more her attention would wander to the darkening garden; so at length she rose, and leaning against the window, began to watch the white gate once more.

But now she starts, and her face brightens up, as the gate swings on its hinges, and a tall man comes with rapid eager step up the walk. John moves uneasily in his sleep, but unnoticed by her, for she stands back in the shadow of the curtain, and eagerly watches the new comer in his approach. Her father sits up in his chair, and after looking sadly at her for a moment, then sinks back with a sigh, as though he would wish to go to sleep again and wake no more.

The maid, bringing in candles, met the new comer at the door, and, carrying in the lights before him, announced—

" Mr. George Hawker."

I remember his face indistinctly as it was then. I remember it far better as it was twenty years after. Yet I must try to recall it for you as well as I can, for we shall have much to do with this man before the end. As the light from the candles fell upon his figure while he stood in the doorway, any man or woman who saw it would have exclaimed immediately, " What a handsome fellow!" and with justice; for if perfectly regular features, splendid red and brown complexion, faultless white teeth, and the finest head of curling black hair I ever saw, could make him handsome, handsome he was without doubt. And yet the more you looked at him the less you liked him, and the more inclined you felt to pick a quarrel with him. The thin lips, the everlasting smile, the quick suspicious glance, so rapidly shot out from under the overhanging eyebrows, and as quickly withdrawn, were fearfully repulsive, as well as a trick he had of always clearing his throat before he spoke, as if to gain time to frame a lie. But, perhaps, the strangest thing about him was the shape of his head, which, I believe, a child would have observed: The young fellows in those times knew little enough about phrenology. I doubt, indeed, if I had ever heard the word, and yet among the village lads that man went by the name of " flat-headed George." The forehead was both low and narrow, sloping a great way back, while the larger part of the skull lay low down behind the ears. All this was made the more visible by the short curling hair which covered his head.

He was the only son of a small farmer, in one of the distant outlying hamlets of Drumston, called Woodlands. His mother· had died when he was very young, and he had had but little education, but had lived shut up with his father in the lonely old farm-house. And strange stories were in circulation among the villages about that house, not much to the credit of either father or son, which stories John Thornton must in his position as clergyman have heard somewhat of, so that one need hardly wonder at his uneasiness when he saw him enter.

For Mary adored him; the rest of the village disliked and distrusted him; but she, with a strange perversity, loved him as it seldom falls to the lot of man to be loved—with her whole heart and soul.

" I have brought you some snipes, Mr. Thornton," said he, in his most musical tones. " The white frost last night has sent them down off the moor as thick as bees, and this warm rain will soon send them all back again. I only went round through Fernworthy and Combe, and I have killed five couple."

" Thank you, Mr. George, thank you," said John, " they are not so plentiful as they were in old times, and I don't shoot so well either as I used to do. My sight's going, and I can't walk far. It is nearly time for me to go, I think."

" Not yet, sir, I hope; not yet for a long time," said George Hawker, in an offhand sort of way. But Mary slipped round, kissed his forehead, and took his hand quietly in hers.

John looked from her to George, and dropped her hand with a sigh, and soon the lovers were whispering together again in the darkness of the window.

But now there is a fresh footfall on the garden walk, a quick, rapid, decided one. Somebody bursts open the hall-door, and, without shutting it, dashes into the parlour, accompanied by a tornado of damp air, and announces in a loud, though not unpleasant voice, with a foreign accent—

" I have got the new Scolopax."

He was a broad, massive built man, about the middle height, with a square determined set of features, brightened up by a pair of merry blue eyes. His forehead was, I think, the finest I ever saw; so high, so broad, and so upright; and, altogether, he was the sort of man that in a city one would turn round and look after, wondering who he was.

He stood in the doorway, dripping, and without "Good-even," or salutation of any sort, exclaimed—

" I have got the new Scolopax !"

" No !" cried old John, starting up all alive, " Have you though ? How did you get him ? Are you sure it is not a young Jack ? Come in and tell us all about it. Only think."

" The obstinacy and incredulity of you English," replied the new comer, totally disregarding John's exclamations, and remaining dripping in the doorway, " far exceeds anything I could have conceived, if I had not witnessed it. If I told you once, I told you twenty times, that I had seen the bird on three distinct occasions in the meadow below Reel's mill ; and you each time threw your jacksnipe theory in my face. To-day I marked him down in the bare ground outside Haveldon wood, than ran at full speed up to the jager, and offered him five shillings if he would come down and shoot the bird I showed him. He came, killed the bird in a style that I would give a year's tobacco to be master of, and remarked as I paid him his money, that he would like to get five shillings for every one of those birds he could shoot in summer time. The jolter-head thought it was a sandpiper, but he wasn't much farther out than you with your jacksnipes. Bah !"

" My dear Doctor Mulhaus," said John mildly, " I confess myself to have been foolishly incredulous, as to our little place being honoured by such a distinguished stranger as the new snipe. But come in to the fire, and smoke your pipe, while you show me your treasure. Mary, you know, likes tobacco, and Mr. George, I am sure," he added, in a slightly altered tone, " will excuse it."

Mr. George would be charmed. But the Doctor, standing staring at him open-eyed for a moment, demanded in an audible whisper—

" Who the deuce is that ?"

" Mr. George Hawker, Doctor, from the Woodlands. I should have thought you had met him before."

" Never," replied the Doctor. " And I don't—and I mean I have had the honour of hearing of him from Stockbridge. Excuse me, sir, a moment. I am going to take a liberty. I am a phrenologist." He advanced across the room to where George sat, laid his hand on his forehead, and drawing it lightly and slowly back through his black curls, till he reached the nape of his neck, ejaculated a " Hah !" which might mean anything, and retired to the fire.

He then began filling his pipe, but before it was filled set it suddenly on the table, and drawing from his coat-pocket a cardboard box, exhibited to the delighted eyes of the vicar that beautiful little brown-mottled snipe, which now bears the name of Colonel Sabine, and having lit his pipe, set to work with a tiny penknife, and a pot of arsenical soap, all of which were disinterred from the vast coat-pocket before mentioned, to reduce the plump little bird to a loose mass of skin and feathers, fit to begin again his new life in death in a glass-case in some collector's museum.

George Hawker had sat very uneasy since the Doctor's phrenological examination, and every now and then cast fierce angry glances at him from under his lowered eyebrows, talking but little to Mary. But now he grows more uneasy still, for the gate goes again, and still another footfall is heard approaching through the darkness.

That is James Stockbridge. I should know that step among a thousand. Whether brushing through the long grass of an English meadow in May time, or quietly pacing up and down the orange alley in the New World, between the crimson snow and the blazing west; or treading lightly across the wet ground at black midnight, when the cattle are restless, or the blacks are abroad; or even, I should think, staggering on the slippery deck, when the big grey seas are booming past, and the good ship seems plunging down to destruction.

He had loved Mary dearly since she was almost a child; but she, poor pretty fool, used to turn him to ridicule, and make him fetch and carry for her like a dog. He was handsomer, cleverer, stronger, and better tempered than George Hawker, and yet she had no eyes for him, or his good qualities. She liked him in a sort of way; nay, it might even be said that she was fond of him. But what she liked better than him was to gratify her vanity, by showing her power over the finest young fellow in the village, and to use him as a foil to aggravate George Hawker. My aunt Betsy (spinster) used to say, that if she were a man, sooner than stand that hussy's airs (meaning Mary's) in the way young Stockbridge did, she'd cut and run to America, which, in the old lady's estimation, was the last resource left to an unfortunate human creature, before suicide.

As he entered the parlour, John's face grew bright, and he held out his hand to him. The Doctor, too, shoving his spectacles on his forehead, greeted him with a royal salute, of about twenty-one short words; but he got rather a cool reception from the lovers in the window. Mary gave him a quiet good evening, and George hoped with a sneer that he was quite well, but directly the pair were whispering together once more in the shadow of the curtain.

So he sat down between the Doctor and the Vicar. James, like all the rest of us, had a profound respect for the Doctor's learning, and old John and he were as father and son; so a better matched trio could hardly be found in the parish, as they sat there before the cheerful blaze, smoking their pipes.

"A good rain, Jim; a good, warm, kindly rain after the frost," began the Vicar.

"A very good rain, sir," replied Jim.

"Some idiots," said the Doctor, "take the wing bones out first. Now, my method of beginning at the legs and working forward, is infinitely superior. Yet that ass at Crediton, after I had condescended to show him, persisted his own way was the best." All this time he was busy skinning his bird.

"How are your Southdowns looking, Jim?" says the Vicar. "Foot-rot, eh?"

"Well, yes, sir," says James, "they always will, you know, in these wet clays. But I prefer 'em to the Leicesters, for all that."

"How is scapegrace Hamlyn?" asked the Vicar.

"He is very well, sir. He and I have been out with the harriers to-day."

"Ah! taking you out with the harriers instead of minding his business; just like him. He'll be leading you astray, James, my boy. Young men like you and he, who have come to be their own masters so young, ought to be more careful than others. Besides, you see, both you and Hamlyn, being 'squires, have got an example to set to the poorer folks."

"We are neither of us so rich as some of the farmers, sir."

"No; but you are both gentlemen born, you see, and, therefore, ought to be in some way models for those who are not."

"Bosh," said the Doctor. "All this about Hamlyn's going out hare-hunting."

"I don't mind it once a week," said the Vicar, ignoring the Doctor's interruption; "but *four times* is rather too much. And Hamlyn has been out four days this week. Twice with Wrefords, and twice with Holes. He can't deny it."

Jim couldn't, so he laughed. "You must catch him, sir," he said, "and give him a real good wigging. He'll mind you. But catch him soon, sir, or you won't get the chance. Doctor, do you know anything about New South Wales?"

"Botany Bay," said the Vicar abstractedly, "convict settlement in South Seas. Jerry Shaw begged the Judge to hang him instead of sending him there. Judge wouldn't do it though; Jerry was too bad for that."

"Hamlyn and I are thinking of selling up and going there," said Jim. "Do you know anything about it, Doctor?"

"What!" said the Doctor; "the mysterious hidden land of the great South Sea. Tasman's land, Nuyt's land, Leuwin's land, De Witt's land, any fool's land who could sail round, and never have the sense to land and make use of it—the new country of Australasia. The land with millions of acres of fertile soil, under a splendid climate, calling aloud for some one to come and cultivate them.

C

The land of the Eucalypti and the Marsupials, the land of deep forests and boundless pastures, which go rolling away westward, plain beyond plain, to none knows where. Yes; I know something about it."

The Vicar was "knocked all of a heap" at James's announcement, and now, slightly recovering himself, said—

"You hear him. He is going to Botany Bay. He is going to sell his estate, 250 acres of the best land in Devon, and go and live among the convicts. And who is going with him? Why, Hamlyn the wise. Oh dear me. And what is he going for?"

That was a question apparently hard to answer. If there was a reason, Jim was either unwilling or unable to give it. Yet I think that the real cause was standing there in the window, with a look of unbounded astonishment on her pretty face.

"Going to leave us, James!" she cried, coming quickly towards him. "Why, whatever shall I do without you?"

"Yes, Miss Mary," said James somewhat huskily; "I think may say that we have settled to go. Hamlyn has got a letter from a cousin of his who went from down Plymouth way, and who is making a fortune; and besides, I have got tired of the old place somehow, lately. I have nothing to keep me here now, and there will be a change, and a new life there. In short," said he, in despair of giving a rational reason, "I have made up my mind."

"Oh!" said Mary, while her eyes filled with tears, "I shall be so sorry to lose you."

"I too," said James, "shall be sorry to start away beyond seas and leave all the friends I care about save one behind me. But times are hard for the poor folks here now, and if I, as 'squire, set the example of going, I know many will follow. The old country, Mr. Thornton," he continued, "is getting too crowded for men to live in without a hard push, and depend on it, when poor men are afraid to marry for fear of having children which they can't support, it is time to move somewhere. The hive is too hot, and the bees must swarm, so that those that go will both better themselves, and better those they leave behind them, by giving them more room to work and succeed. It's hard to part with the old farm and the old faces now, but perhaps in a few years, one will get to like that country just as one does this, from being used to it, and the old country will seem only like a pleasant dream after one has awoke."

"Think twice about it, James, my boy," said the Vicar.

"Don't be such an ass as to hesitate," said the Doctor impatiently. "It is the genius of your restless discontented nation to go blundering about the world like buffaloes in search of fresh pasture. You have founded already two or three grand new empires, and you are now going to form another; and men like you ought to have their fingers in the pie."

" Well, God speed you, and Hamlyn too, wherever you go. Are you going home, Mr. Hawker ? "

George, who hated James from the very bottom of his heart, was not ill-pleased to hear there would be a chance of soon getting rid of him. He had been always half jealous of him, though without the slightest cause, and to-night he was more so than ever, for Mary, since she had heard of James' intended departure, had grown very grave and silent. He stood, hat in hand, ready to depart, and as usual, when he meant mischief, spoke in his sweetest tones.

" I am afraid I must be saying good evening, Mr. Thornton. Why, James," he added, " this is something quite new. So you are going to Botany without waiting to be sent there. Ha ! ha ! Well, I wish you every sort of good luck. My dear friend, Hamlyn, too. What a loss he'll be to our little society, so sociable and affable as he always is to us poor farmers' sons. You'll find it lonely there though. You should get a wife to take with you. Oh, yes, I should certainly get married before I went. Good night."

All this was meant to be as irritating as possible ; but as he went out at the door he had the satisfaction to hear James' clear honest laugh mingling with the Vicar's, for, as George had closed the door, the Doctor had said, looking after him—

" Gott in Himmel, that young man has got a skull like a tom-cat."

This complimentary observation was lost on Mary, who had left the room with George. The Vicar looked round for her, and sighed when he missed her.

" Ah ! " said he ; " I wish he was going instead of you."

" So does the new colony, I'll be bound," added the Doctor.

Soon after this the party separated. When James and the Doctor stood outside the door, the latter demanded, " Where are you going ? "

" To Sydney, I believe, Doctor."

" Goose. I mean now."

" Home."

" No, you ain't," said the Doctor ; " you are going to walk up to Hamlyn's with me, and hear me discourse." Accordingly, about eleven o'clock, these two arrived at my house, and sat before the fire till half-past three in the morning ; and in that time the doctor had given us more information about New South Wales than we had been able to gather from ordinary sources in a month.

CHAPTER V.

IN WHICH THE READER IS MADE ACCOMPLICE TO A MISPRISION OF FELONY.

THOSE who only know the river Taw as he goes sweeping, clear and full, past orchards and farmhouses, by woods and parks, and through long green meadows, after he has left Dartmoor, have little idea of the magnificent scene which rewards the perseverance of any one who has the curiosity to follow him up to his granite cradle between the two loftiest eminences in the West of England.

On the left, Great Cawsand heaves up, down beyond down, a vast sheet of purple heath and golden whin, while on the right the lofty serrated ridge of Yestor starts boldly up, black against the western sky, throwing a long shadow over the wild waste of barren stone at his feet.

Some Scotchmen, perhaps, may smile at my applying the word " magnificent " to heights of only 2,100 feet. Yet I have been among mountains which double Ben Nevis in height, and with the exception of the Murray Gates in Australia, and a glen in Madeira, whose name I have forgotten, I have never seen among them the equal of some of the northern passes of Dartmoor for gloomy magnificence. For I consider that scenery depends not so much on height as on abruptness.

It is an evil, depressing place. Far as the eye can reach up the glen and to the right, it is one horrid waste of grey granite; here and there a streak of yellow grass or a patch of black bog; not a tree nor a shrub within the sky-line. On a hot summer's day it is wearisome enough for the lonely angler to listen to the river crawling lazily through the rocks that choke his bed, mingled with the clocking of some water-moved boulder, and the chick-chick of the stone-chat, or the scream of the golden plover over head. But on a wild winter's evening, when day is fast giving place to night, and the mist shrouds the hill, and the wild wind is rushing hoarse through tor and crag, it becomes awful and terrible in the extreme.

On just such a night as that, at that time when it becomes evident that the little light we have had all day is about to leave us, a lonely watcher was standing by the angry swelling river in the most desolate part of the pass, at a place where a vast confusion of formless rocks crosses the stream, torturing it into a hundred boiling pools and hissing cascades.

He stood on the summit of a cairn close to the river, and every now and then, shading his eyes with his hand, he looked eastward through the driving rain, as though expecting some one who came not. But at length, grown tired of watching, he with an oath descended to a sheltered corner among the boulders, where a smouldering peat-fire was giving out more smoke than heat, and, crouching over it, began to fan the embers with his hat.

He was a somewhat short, though powerful man, in age about forty, very dark in complexion, with black whiskers growing half over his chin. His nose was hooked, his eyes were black and piercing, and his lips thin. His face was battered like an old sailor's, and every careless, unstudied motion of his body was as wild and reckless as could be. There was something about his *toute ensemble*, in short, that would have made an Australian police-man swear to him as a convict without the least hesitation.

There were redeeming points in the man's face, too. There was plenty of determination, for instance, in that lower jaw; and as he bent now over the fire, and his thoughts wandered away to other times and places, the whole appearance of the man seemed to change and become milder and kindlier; yet when some slight noise makes him lift his head and look round, there is the old expression back again, and he looks as reckless and desperate as ever; what he is is more apparent, and the ghost of what he might have been has not wholly departed.

I can picture to myself that man scowling behind the bayonet line at Maida, or rapidly and coolly serving his gun at Trafalgar, helping to win the dominion of all seas, or taking his trick at the helm through arctic iceblocks with Parry, or toiling on with stead-fast Sturt, knee-deep in the sand of the middle desert, patiently yet hopelessly scanning the low quivering line of the north-west horizon.

In fifty situations where energy and courage are required, I can conceive that man a useful citizen. Yet here he is on the lone moor, on the winter's night, a reckless, cursing, thrice convicted man. His very virtues,—his impatient energy and undeniable courage,—his greatest stumbling-blocks, leading him into crimes which a lazy man or a coward would have shrunk from. Deserted apparently by God and man, he crouched there over the low fire, among his native rocks, and meditated fresh villanies.

He had been transported at eighteen for something, I know not what, which earned transportation in those days, and since then his naturally violent temper, aggravated instead of being broken by penal discipline, had earned him three fresh convictions in the colony. From the last of these sentences he had escaped, with a cunning and address which had baffled the vigilance of the Sydney police, good as they were, and had arrived home, two years before this time, after twenty-one years' absence, at his native village in the moor.

None there knew him, or even guessed who he was. His brother, a small farmer, who would have taken him to his heart had he recog-nised him, always regarded him as a suspicious stranger; and what cut him deeper still, his mother, his old, half-blind, palsied mother, whose memory he had in some sort cherished through the horrors of the hulk, the convict-ship, the chain-gang, and the bush, knew him not. Only once, when he was speaking in her presence, she said abruptly,—

"The voice of him is like the voice of my boy that was took away. But he was smooth-faced, like a girl, and ye're a dark, wrinkled man. 'Sides, he died years agone, over the water."

But the old lady grew thoughtful and silent from that day, and three weeks after she was carried up to her grave,—

> "By the little grey church on the windy hill."

At the funeral, William Lee, the man whom I have been describing, pushed quietly through the little crowd, and as they threw the first earth on the coffin, stood looking over the shoulder of his brother, who was unconscious of his existence.

Like many men who have been much in great solitudes, and have gone days and weeks sometimes without meeting a fellow-creature, he had acquired the habit of thinking aloud, and if any one had been listening they would have heard much such a soliloquy as the following, expletives omitted, or rather softened :—

" A brutal cold country this, for a man to camp out in. Never a buck-log to his fire, no, nor a stick thicker than your finger for seven mile round; and if there was, you'd get a month for cutting it. If the young 'un milks free this time, I'll be off to the bay again, I know. But will he? By George, he shall though. The young snob, I know he daren't but come, and yet it's my belief he's late just to keep me soaking out in the rain. Whew! it's cold enough to freeze the tail off a tin possum; and this infernal rubbish won't burn, at least not to warm a man. If it wasn't for the whisky I should be dead. There's a rush of wind; I am glad for one thing there is no dead timber overhead. He'll be drinking at all the places coming along to get his courage up to bounce me, but there ain't a public-house on the road six miles from this, so the drink will have pretty much died out of him by the time he gets to me, and if I can get him to sit in this rain, and smoke 'backer for five minutes, he won't be particular owdacious. I'll hide the grog, too, between the stones. He'll be asking for a drink the minute he comes. I hope Dick is ready; he is pretty sure to be. He's a good little chap, that Dick; he has stuck to me well these **five** years. I wouldn't like to trust him with another man's horse, though. But this other one is no good; he's got all the inclination to go the whole hog, and none of the pluck necessary. If he ever is lagged, he will be a worse one than ever I was, or Dick either. There he is, for a hundred pounds."

A faint " halloo !" sounded above the war of the weather; and Lee, putting his hand to his mouth, replied with that strange cry, so well known to all Australians—" Coeé."

A man was now heard approaching through the darkness, now splashing deep into some treacherous moss hole with a loud curse, now blundering among loose-lying blocks of stone. Lee waited till he was quite close, and then seizing a bunch of gorse lighted it at his fire and held it aloft; the bright blaze fell full upon the face and features of George Hawker.

"A cursed place and a cursed time," he began, "for an appointment. If you had wanted to murder me, I could have understood it. But I am pretty safe, I think; your interest don't lie that way."

"Well, well, you see," returned Lee, "I don't want any meetings on the cross up at my place in the village. The whole house ain't mine, and we don't know who may be listening. I am suspected enough already, and it wouldn't look well for you to be seen at my place. Folks would have begun axing what for."

"Don't see it," said George. "Besides, if you did not want to see me at home, why the devil do you bring me out here in the middle of the moor? We might have met on the hill underneath the village, and when we had done business gone up to the public-house. D——d if I understand it."

He acquiesced sulkily in the arrangement, however, because he saw it was no use talking about it, but he was far from comfortable. He would have been still less so had he known that Lee's shout had brought up a confederate, who was now peering over the rocks, almost touching his shoulder.

"Well," said Lee, "here we are, so we had better be as comfortable as we can this devil's night."

"Got anything to drink?"

"Deuce a swipe of grog have I. But I have got some real Barret's twist, that never paid duty as I know'd on, so just smoke a pipe before we begin talking, and show you aint vexed."

"I'd sooner have had a drop of grog, such a night as this."

"We must do as the Spaniards do, when they can't get anything," said Lee; "go without."

They both lit their pipes, and smoked in silence for a few minutes, till Lee resumed:—

"If the witches weren't all dead, there would be some of them abroad to-night; hear that?"

"Only a whimbrel, isn't it?" said George.

"That's something worse than a whimbrel, I'm thinking," said the other. "There's some folks don't believe in witches and the like," he continued; "but a man that's seen a naked old hag of a gin ride away on a myall-bough, knows better."

"Lord!" said George. "I shouldn't have thought you'd have believed in the like of that—but I do—that old devil's dam, dame Parker, that lives alone up in Hatherleigh Wood, got gibbering some infernal nonsense at me the other day, for shooting her black cat. I made the cross in the road though, so I suppose it won't come to anything."

" Perhaps not," said Lee; " but I'd sooner kill a man than a black cat."

Another pause. The tobacco, so much stronger than any George had been accustomed to, combined with the cold, made him feel nervous and miserable.

" When I was a boy," resumed Lee, " there were two young brothers made it up to rob the squire's house, down at Gidleigh. They separated in the garden after they cracked the crib, agreeing to meet here in this very place, and share the swag, for they had got nigh seventy pound. They met and quarrelled over the sharing up; and the elder one drew out a pistol, and shot the younger dead. The poor boy was sitting much where you are sitting now, and that long tuft of grass grew up from his blood."

" I believe that's all a lie," said George; " you want to drive me into the horrors with your humbugging tales."

Lee, seeing that he had gone far enough, if not too far, proposed, somewhat sulkily, that they should begin to talk about what brought them there, and not sit crouching in the wet all night.

" Well," said George, " it's you to begin. What made you send for me to this infernal place ? "

" I want money," said Lee.

" Then you'd better axe about and get some," said George; " you'll get none from me. I am surprised that a man with your knowledge of the world should have sent me such a letter as you did yesterday, I am indeed—What the devil's that ? "

He started on his feet. A blaze of sudden light filled the nook where they were sitting, and made it as bright as day, and a voice shouted out,

" Ha, ha, ha ! my secret coves, what's going on here ? something quiet and sly, eh ? something worth a fifty-pound note, eh ? Don't you want an arbitrator, eh ? Here's one, ready made."

" You're playing a dangerous game, my flashman, who ever you are," said Lee, rising savagely. " I've shot a man down for less than that. So you've been stagging this gentleman and me, and listening, have you ? For just half a halfpenny," he added, striding towards him, and drawing out a pistol, " you shouldn't go home this night."

" Don't you be a fool, Bill Lee ; " said the new comer. " I saw the light and made towards it, and as I come up I heard some mention made of money. Now then, if my company is disagreeable, why I'll go, and no harm done."

" What ! it's you, is it ? " said Lee ; " well, now you've come, you may stop and hear what it's all about. I don't care, you are not very squeamish, or at least needn't to be."

George saw that the arrival of this man was preconcerted, and cursed Lee bitterly in his heart, but he sat still, and thought how he could out-manœuvre them.

"Now," said Lee, "I ain't altogether sorry that you have come, for I want to tell you a bit of a yarn, and ask your advice about my behaviour. This is about the state of the case. A young gentleman, a great friend of mine, was not very many years ago, pretty much given up to fast living, cock-fighting, horse-racing, and many other little matters which all young fellows worth anything are pretty sure to indulge in, and which are very agreeable for the time, but which cost money, and are apt to bring a man into low society. When I tell you that he and I first met in Exeter, as principals in crossing a fight, you may be sure that these pursuits *had* brought the young gentleman into *very* low company indeed. In fact, he was over head and ears in debt, raising money in every way he could, hook or crook, square or cross, to satisfy certain creditors, who were becoming nasty impatient and vexatious. I thought something might be made of this young gentleman, so finding there was no pride about him, I cultivated his acquaintance, examined his affairs, and put him up to the neatest little fakement in the world, just showed him how to raise two hundred pounds, and clear himself with everybody, just by signing his father's name, thereby saving the old gent the trouble of writing it (he is very infirm, is dad), and anticipating by a few years what must be his own at last. Not to mention paying off a lot of poor publicans and horse-dealers, who could not afford to wait for their money. Blowed if I don't think it the most honest action he ever did in his life. Well, he committed the—wrote the name I mean,—and stood two ten-pound notes for the information, quite handsome. But now this same young gent is going to marry a young lady with five thousand pounds in her own right, and she nearly of age. Her father, I understand, is worth another five thousand, and very old; so that what he'll get ultimately if he marries into that family, counting his own expectations, won't be much less I should say than twenty thousand pounds. Now I mean to say, under these circumstances, I should be neglecting my own interests most culpably, if I didn't demand from him the trifling sum of three hundred pounds for holding my tongue."

"Why, curse you," broke in Hawker, "you said two hundred yesterday."

"Exactly so," said Lee, "but that *was* yesterday. To-morrow, if the job ain't settled, it'll be four, and the day after five. It's no use, George Hawker," he continued; "you are treed, and you can't help yourself. If I give information you swing, and you know it; but I'd rather have the money than see the man hanged. But mind," said he, with a snarl, "if I catch you playing false, by the Lord, I'll hang you for love."

For an instant the wretched George cast a hurried glance around, as if considering what wild chance there was of mastering his two enemies, but that glance showed him that it was hopeless, for they both stood close together, each holding in his hand a cocked pistol, so in despair he dropped his eyes on the fire once more, while Lee chuckled inwardly at his wise foresight in bringing an accomplice.

"By Jove," he said to himself, "it's lucky Dick's here. If I had been alone, he'd have been at me then like a tiger. It would have been only man to man, but he would have been as good as me; he'd have fought like a rat in a corner."

George sat looking into the embers for a full half minute, while the others waited for his answer, determined that he should speak first. At length he raised his head, and said hoarsely, looking at neither of them,—

"And where am I to get three hundred pounds?"

"A simple question very easily answered," said Lee. "Do what you did before, with half the difficulty. You manage nearly everything now your father is getting blind, so you need hardly take the trouble of altering the figures in the banker's book, and some slight hint about taking a new farm would naturally account for the old man's drawing out four or five hundred. The thing's easier than ever."

"Take my advice, young man," said Dick, "and take the shortest cut out of the wood. You see my friend here, William, has got tired of these parts, as being, you see, hardly free and easy enough for him, and he wants to get back to a part of the world he was rather anxious to leave a few years ago. If he likes to take me back with him, why he can. I rather fancy the notion myself. Give him the money, and in three months we'll both be fourteen thousand odd miles off. Meanwhile, you marry the young lady, and die in your bed, an honest gentleman, at eighty-four, instead of being walked out some cold morning to a gallows at twenty-two."

"Needs must where the devil drives," replied George. "You shall have the money this day week. And now let me go, for I am nearly froze dead."

"That's the talk," said Lee; "I knew you would be reasonable. If it hadn't been for my necessities, I am sure I never would have bothered you. Well, good night."

George rose and departed eastward, towards the rising moon, while Lee and his companion struck due west across the moor. The rain had ceased, and the sky was clear, so that there was not much difficulty in picking their way through the stones and moss-hags. Suddenly Lee stopped, and said to his comrade, with an oath,—

"Dick, my boy, I didn't half like the way that dog left us."

"Nor I either," replied the other. "He has got some new move in his head, you may depend on it. He'll give you the slip if he can."

"Let him try it," said Lee; "oh, only just let him try it."

And then the pair of worthies walked home.

— · —

CHAPTER VI.

GEORGE HAWKER GOES TO THE FAIR—WRESTLES, BUT GETS THROWN ON HIS BACK—SHOOTS AT A MARK, BUT MISSES IT.

LEE had guessed rightly. When George found himself so thoroughly entrapped, and heard all his most secret relations with Lee so openly discussed before a third man, he was in utter despair, and saw no hope of extrication from his difficulties. But this lasted for a very short time. Even while Lee and Dick were still speaking, he was reflecting how to turn the tables on them, and already began to see a sparkle of hope glimmering afar.

Lee was a returned convict, George had very little doubt of that. A thousand queer expressions he had let fall in conversation had shown him that it was so. And now, if he could but prove it, and get Lee sent back out of the way. And yet that would hardly do after all. It would be difficult to identify him. His name gave no clue to who he was. There were a thousand or two of Lees hereabouts, and a hundred William Lees at least. Still it was evident that he was originally from this part of the country; it was odd no one had recognised him.

So George gave up this plan as hopeless. "Still," said he, "there is a week left; surely I can contrive to bowl him out somehow." And then he walked on in deep thought.

He was crossing the highest watershed in the county by an open, low-sided valley on the southern shoulder of Cawsand. To the left lay the mountain, and to the right tors of weathered granite, dim in the changing moonlight. Before him was a small moor-pool, in summer a mere reedy marsh, but now a bleak tarn, standing among dangerous mosses, sending ghostly echoes across the solitude, as the water washed wearily against the black peat shores, or rustled among the sere skeleton reeds in the shallow bays.

Suddenly he stopped with a jar in his brain and a chill at his heart. His breath came short, and raising one hand, he stood beating the ground for half a minute with his foot. He gave a stealthy glance around, and then murmured hoarsely to himself,—

"Aye, that would do; that would do well. And I could do it, too, when I was half-drunk."

Was that the devil, chuckling joyous to himself across the bog?

No, only an innocent little snipe, getting merry over the change of weather, bleating to his companions as though breeding time were come round again.

Crowd close, little snipes, among the cup-moss and wolf's foot, for he who stalks past you over the midnight moor, meditates a foul and treacherous murder in his heart.

Yes, it had come to that, and so quickly. He would get this man Lee, who held his life in his hand, and was driving him on from crime to crime, to meet him alone on the moor if he could, and shoot him. What surety had he that Lee would leave him in peace after this next extortion? none but his word,—the word of a villain like that. He knew what his own word was worth; what wonder if he set a small value on Lee's? He might be hung as it was; he would be hung for something. Taw Steps was a wild place, and none were likely to miss either Lee or his friend. It would be supposed they had tramped off as they came. There could be no proof against him, none whatever. No one had ever seen them together. They must both go. Well, two men were no worse than one. Hatherleigh had killed four men with his own hand at Waterloo, and they gave him a medal for it. They were likely honest fellows enough, not such scoundrels as these two.

So arguing confusedly with himself, only one thing certain in his mind, that he was committed to the perpetration of this crime, and that the time for drawing back was passed long ago, he walked rapidly onwards towards the little village where he had left his horse in an outhouse, fearing to trust him among the dangerous bogs which he had himself to cross to gain the rendezvous at Taw Steps.

He rapidly cleared the moor, and soon gained the little grey street, lying calm and peaceful beneath the bright winter moon, which was only now and then obscured for a moment by the last flying clouds of the late storm hurrying after their fellows. The rill which ran brawling loud through the village, swollen by the late rains, at length forced on his perception that he was fearfully thirsty, and that his throat was parched and dry.

"This is the way men feel in hell, I think," said he. "Lord! let me get a drink while I can. The rich man old Jack reads about couldn't get one for all his money."

He walked up to a stone horse-trough, a little off the road. He stooped to drink, and started back with an oath. What pale, wild, ghastly face was that, looking at him out of the cool calm water? Not his own, surely? He closed his eyes, and, having drunk deep, walked on refreshed. He reached the outhouse where his horse was tied, and, as he was leading the impatient animal forth, one of the children within the cottage adjoining woke up and began to cry. He waited still a moment, and heard the mother arise and soothe it; then a window overhead opened, and a woman said—

" Is that you, Mr. Hawker ? "

" Aye," said he, " it's me. Come for the horse."

He was startled at the sound of his own voice. It was like another man's. But like the voice of some one he seemed to know, too. A new acquaintance.

" It will be morn soon," resumed the woman. " The child is much worse to-night, and I think he'll go before daybreak. Well, well—much sorrow saved, maybe. I'll go to bed no more to-night, lest my boy should be off while I'm sleeping. Good night, sir. God bless you. May you never know the sorrow of losing a first-born."

Years after he remembered those random words. But now he only thought that if the brat should die, there would be only one pauper less in Bickerton. And so thinking, mounted and rode on his way.

He rode fast, and was soon at home. He had put his horse in the stable, and, shoeless, was creeping up to bed, when, as he passed his father's door, it opened, and the old man came out, light in hand.

He was a very infirm old man, much bent, though evidently at one time he had been of great stature. His retreating forehead, heavy grey eyebrows, and loose sensual mouth, rendered him no pleasing object at any time, and, as he stood in the doorway now, with a half drunken satyr-like leer on his face, he looked perfectly hideous.

" Where's my pretty boy been ? " he piped out. " How pale he looks. Are you drunk, my lad ? "

" No ! wish I was," replied George. " Give me the keys, dad, and let me get a drink of brandy. I've been vexed, and had nought to drink all night. I shall be getting the horrors if I don't have something before I go to bed."

The old man got him half a tumbler of brandy from his room, where there was always some to be had, and following him into his room, sat down on the bed.

" Who's been vexing my handsome son ? " said he ; " my son that I've been waiting up for all night. Death and gallows to them, whoever they are. Is it that pale-faced little parson's daughter ? Or is it her tight-laced hypocrite of a father, that comes whining here with his good advice to me who know the world so well ? Never mind, my boy. Keep a smooth face, and play the humbug till you've got her, and her money, and then break her impudent little heart if you will. Go to sleep, my boy, and dream you are avenged on them all."

" I mean to be, father, on some of them, I tell you," replied George.

" That's right, my man. Good night."

" Good night, old dad," said George. As he watched him out of

the room, a kinder, softer expression came on his face. His father
was the only being he cared for in the world.

He slept a heavy and dreamless sleep that night, and when he
woke for the first time, the bright winter's sun was shining into his
room, and morning was far advanced.

He rose, strengthened and refreshed by his sleep, with a light
heart. He began whistling as he dressed himself, but suddenly
stopped, as the recollection of the night before came upon him.
Was it a reality, or only a dream? No: it was true enough. He
has no need to whistle this morning. He is entangled in a web of
crime and guilt from which there is no escape.

He dressed himself, and went forth into the fresh morning air for
a turn, walking up and down on the broad gravel walk before the
dark old porch.

A glorious winter's morning. The dismal old stone-house, many-
gabled, held aloft its tall red chimneys towards the clear blue sky,
and looked bright and pleasant in the sunshine. The deep fir and
holly woods which hemmed it in on all sides, save in front, were
cheerful with sloping gleams of sunlight, falling on many a patch of
green moss, red fern, and bright brown last year's leaves. In front,
far below him, rolled away miles of unbroken woodland, and in the
far distance rose the moor, a dim cloud of pearly grey.

A robin sat and sung loud beside him, sole songster left in the
wintry woods, but which said, as plain as bird could say, could he
have understood it, "See, the birds are not all dead in this dreary
winter time. I am still here, a pledge from my brothers. When yon
dim grey woods grow green, and the brown hollows are yellow with
kingcups and primroses, the old melody you know so well shall begin
again, and the thrush from the oak top shall answer to the golden-
toned blackbird in the copse, saying—'Our mother is not dead,
but has been sleeping. She is awake again—let all the land
rejoice.'"

Little part had that poor darkened mind in such thoughts as
these. If any softening influence were upon him this morning, he
gave no place to it. The robin ceased, and he only heard the croak
of a raven, an old inhabitant of these wild woods, coming from the
darkest and tallest of the fir-trees. Then he saw his father approaching along the garden walk.

One more chance for thee, unhappy man. Go up to him now,
and tell him all. He has been a kind father to you, with all his
faults. Get him on your side, and you may laugh Lee to scorn.
Have you not the courage to tell him?

For a moment he hesitated, but the dread of his father's burst of
anger kept him silent. He hardened his heart, and, whistling,
waited for the old man to come up.

"How is he this morning?" said his father. "What has he

got his old clothes on for, and such fine ones as he has in his drawer ?"

" Why should I put on my best clothes this day, father ?"

" Aint'ee going down to revels ?"

" True," said George. " I had forgotten all about it. Yes; I shall go down, of course."

" Are you going to play (wrestle) ?" asked the father.

" Maybe I may. But come in to breakfast. Where's Madge ?"

" In-doors," said the father, " waiting breakfast—mortal cross."

" Curse her crossness," said George. " If I were ye, dad, I'd kick her out in the lane next time she got on one of her tan-rams."

A tall woman about forty stepped out of the house as he uttered these words. " Ye hear what he says, William Hawker," she said. " Ye hear what ye're own lawful son says. He'd kick me out in the lane. And ye'd stand there and let him, ye old dog ; I don't doubt."

" Hush, George," said the old man. " You don't know what you're saying, boy. Go in, Madge, and don't be a fool ; you bring it on yourself."

The woman turned in a contemptuous way and walked in. She was a very remarkable looking person. Tall and upright, at least six feet high, with swarthy complexion, black eyes, and coal-black hair, looped up loosely in a knot behind. She must have been very beautiful as a young girl, but was now too fierce and hawkish look-ing, though you would still call her handsome. She was a full-blooded gipsy, of one of the best families, which, however, she totally denied. When I say that she bore the worst of characters morally, and had the reputation besides of being a witch of the highest acquirements,—a sort of double first at Satan's university,—I have said all I need to say about her at present.

These three sat down to breakfas not before each of them, how-ever, had refreshed themselves with a dram. All the meal through, the old man and Madge were quarrelling with one another, till at length the contest grew so fierce that George noticed it, a thing he very seldom took the trouble to d .

" I tell thee," said the old ma , " ye'll get no more money this week. What have 'ee done with the last five pounds ?"

George knew well enough, she had given it to him. Many a time did she contrive to let him have a pound or two, and blind the old man as to where it was gone. The day before he had applied to her for some money and she had refused, and in revenge, George had recommended his father to turn her out, knowing that she could hear every word, and little meaning it in reality.

" Ye *stingy old beast*," she replied, very slowly and distinctly, " I wish ye were dead and out of the way. I'll be doing it myself some of these odd times." And looking at him fixedly and pointing her finger, she began the Hebrew alphabet—Aleph, Beth, &c. from the 119th Psalm.

" I won't have it," screamed the old man. " Stop, or I'll kill you, I will ——! George, you won't see your father took before your eyes. Stop her !"

" Come, quiet, old girl; none of that ;" said George, taking her round the waist and putting his hand before her mouth. " Be reasonable now." She continued to look at the old man with a smile of triumph for a short time, and then said, with a queer laugh :

" It's lucky you stopped me. Oh, very lucky indeed. Now, are you going to give the money, you old Jew ?"

She had carried the day, and the old man sulkily acquiesced. George went up stairs, and having dressed himself to his taste, got on horseback and rode down to the village, which was about three miles.

This was the day of the Revels, which corresponds pretty well with what is called in other parts of England a pleasure fair ; that is to say, although some business might be done, yet it was only a secondary object to amusement.

The main village of Drumston was about a mile from the church which I have before noticed, and consisted of a narrow street of cob-houses, whitewashed and thatched, crossing at right angles, by a little stone bridge, over a pretty, clear trout-stream. All around the village, immediately behind the backs of the houses, rose the abrupt red hills, divided into fields by broad oak hedges, thickly set with elms. The water of the stream, intercepted at some point higher up, was carried round the crown of the hills for the purposes of irrigation, which, even at this dead season, showed its advantages by the brilliant emerald green of the tender young grass on the hill-sides. Drumston, in short, was an excellent specimen of a close, dull, dirty, and, I fear, not very healthy Devonshire village in the red country.

On this day the main street, usually in a state of ancle-deep mud six months in the year, was churned and pounded into an almost knee-deep state, by four or five hundred hobnail shoes in search of amusement. The amusements were various. Drinking (very popular), swearing (ditto), quarrelling, eating pastry ginger-bread and nuts (female pastime), and looking at a filthy Italian, leading a still more filthy monkey, who rode on a dog (the only honest one of the three). This all day, till night dropped down on a scene of drunkenness and vice, which we had better not seek to look at further. Surely, if ever man was right, old Joey Bender, the methodist shoemaker, was right, when he preached against the revels for four Sundays running, and said roundly that he would sooner see all his congregation leave him and go up to the steeple-house top all in a body, than that they should attend such a crying abomination.

The wrestling, the only honest sensible amusement to be had, was not in much favour at Drumston. Such wrestling as there was was carried on in a little croft behind the principal of the public-houses, for some trifling prize, given by the publicans. Into this place, James Stockbridge and myself had wandered on the afternoon of the day in question, having come down to the revel to see if we could find some one we wanted.

There was a small ring of men watching the performances, and talking, each and all of them, not to his neighbour, or to himself, but to the ambient air, in the most unintelligible Devonshire jargon, rendered somewhat more barbarous than usual by intoxication. Frequently one of them would address one of the players in language more forcible than choice, as he applauded some piece of *finesse*, or condemned some clumsiness on the part of the two youths who were struggling about in the centre, under the impression they were wrestling. There were but two moderate wrestlers in the parish, and those two were George Hawker and James Stockbridge. And James and myself had hardly arrived on the ground two minutes, before George, coming up, greeted us.

After a few common-place civilities, he challenged James to play. "Let us show these muffs what play is," said he; "it's a disgrace to the county to see such work."

James had no objection; so, having put on the jackets, they set to work to the great admiration of the bystanders, one of whom, a drunken tinker, expressed his applause in such remarkable language that I mildly asked him to desist, which of course made him worse.

The two wrestlers made very pretty play of it for some time, till James, feinting at some outlandish manœuvre, put George on his back by a simple trip, akin to scholar's-mate at chess.

George fell heavily, for they were both heavy men. He rose from the ground and walked to where his coat was, sulkily. James thinking he might have been hurt, went up to speak to him; but the other, greeting him with an oath, turned and walked away through the crowd.

He was in a furious passion, and he went on to the little bridge that crossed the stream. We saw him standing looking into the water below, when a short light-looking man came up to him, and having spoken to him for a few minutes, walked off in the direction of Exeter, at a steady, rapid pace.

That man was Dick, the companion of Lee (I knew all this afterwards). George was standing as I have described on the bridge, when he came up to him, and touching him, said:

"I want to speak to you a moment, Mr. Hawker."

D

George turned round, and when he saw who it was, asked, angrily, "What the —— do you want?"

"No offence, sir. You see, I'm in trouble, there's a warrant out against me, and I must fly. I am as hard-up as a poor cove could be; can you give me a trifle to help me along the road?"

Here was a slice of good luck; to get rid of this one so easily. George gave him money, and having wished him farewell, watched him striding steadily up the long hill towards Exeter with great satisfaction; then he went back to the public-house, and sat drinking an hour or more. At last he got out his horse to ride homeward.

The crowd about the public-house door was as thick as ever, and the disturbance greater. Some of the women were trying to get their drunken husbands home, one man had fallen down dead-drunk beside the door in the mud, and his wife was sitting patiently beside him. Several girls were standing wearily about the door, dressed in their best, each with a carefully-folded white-pocket-handkerchief in her hand for show, and not for use, waiting for their sweethearts to come forth when it should suit them; while inside the tap all was a wild confusion of talk, quarrelling, oaths, and smoke enough to sicken a scavenger.

These things are changed now, or are chan ng, year by year. Now we have our rural policeman keeping some ort of order, and some show of decency. And indeed these little fairs, the curse of the country, are gradually becoming extinct by the exertions of a more energetic class of county magistrates; and though there is probably the same amount of vice, public propriety is at all events more respected. I think I may say that I have seen as bad, or even worse, scenes of drunkenness and disorder at an English fair, as ever I have in any Australian mining town.

George Hawker was so hemmed in by the crowd that he was unable to proceed above a foot's-pace. He was slowly picking his way through the people, when he felt some one touching him on the leg, and, looking round, saw Lee standing beside him.

"What, Lee, my boy, you here?" said he; "I have just seen your amiable comrade—he seems to be in trouble."

"Dick's always in trouble, Mr. Hawker," replied he. "He has no care or reason; he isn't a bad fellow, but I'm always glad when he is out of my way; I don't like being seen with him. This is likely to be his last time, though. He is in a serious scrape, and, by way of getting out of it, he is walking into Exeter, along the high road, as if nothing was the matter. There's a couple of traps in Belston after him now, and I came down here to keep secure. By-the-bye, have you thought of that little matter we were talking about the other night? To tell you the truth, I don't care how soon I am out of this part of the country."

"Oh! ah!" replied George, "I've thought of it, and it's all right. Can you be at the old place the day after to-morrow?"

"That can I," said Lee, "with much pleasure."

"You'll come alone this time, I suppose," said George. I suppose you don't want to share our little matter with the whole country?"

"No fear, Mr. George; I will be there at eight punctual, and alone."

"Well, bye-bye," said George, and rode off.

It was getting late in the evening when he started, and ere he reached home it was nearly dark. For the last mile his road lay through forest-land: noble oaks, with a plentiful under-growth of holly, over-shadowed a floor of brown leaves and red fern; and at the end of the wood nearest home, where the oaks joined his own fir plantations, one mighty gnarled tree, broader and older than all the rest, held aloft its withered boughs against the frosty sky.

This oak was one of the bogie haunts of the neighbourhood. All sorts of stories were told about it, all of which George, of course, believed; so that when his horse started and refused to move forward, and when he saw a dark figure sitting on the twisted roots of the tree, he grew suddenly cold, and believed he had seen a ghost.

The figure rose, and stalked towards him through the gathering gloom; he saw that it held a baby in its arms, and that it was tall and noble-looking. Then a new fear took possession of him, not supernatural; and he said in a low voice—"Ellen!"

"That was my name once, George Hawker," replied she, standing beside him, and laying her hand upon his horse's shoulder. "I don't know what my name is now, I'm sure; it surely can't remain the same, and me so altered."

"What on earth brings you back just at this time, in God's name?" asked George.

"Hunger, cold, misery, drunkenness, disease. Those are the merry companions that lead me back to my old sweetheart. Look here, George, should you know him again?"

She held up a noble child about a year old, for him to look at. The child, disturbed from her warm bosom, began to wail.

"What! cry to see your father, child?" she exclaimed. "See what a bonnie gentleman he is, and what a pretty horse he rides, while we tread along through the mire."

"What have you come to me for, Ellen?" asked George. "Do you know that if you are seen about here just now you may do me a great injury?"

"I don't want to hurt you, George," she replied; "but I must have money. I cannot work, and I dare not show my face here. Can't you take me in to-night, George, only just to-night, and let me lie by the fire? I'll go in the morning; but I know it's going to freeze, and I do dread the long cold hours so. I have lain out two nights, now, and I had naught to eat all day. Do'ee take me in, George; for old love's sake, do!"

She was his own cousin, an orphan, brought up in the same house with him by his father. Never very strong in her mind, though exceedingly pretty, she had been early brought to ruin by George. On the birth of a boy, about a year before, the old man's eyes were opened to what was going on, and in a furious rage he turned her out of doors, and refused ever to see her again. George, to do him justice, would have married her, but his father told him, if he did so, he should leave the house with her. So the poor thing had gone away and tried to get needlework in Exeter, but her health failing, and George having ceased to answer all applications from her, she had walked over, and lurked about in the woods to gain an interview with him.

She laid her hand on his, and he felt it was deadly cold. "Put my coat over your shoulders, Nelly, and wait an instant while I go and speak to Madge. I had better let her know you are coming; then we shan't have any trouble."

He rode quickly through the plantation, and gave his horse to a boy who waited in front of the door. In the kitchen he found Madge brooding over the fire, with her elbows on her knees, and without raising her head or turning round, she said:

"Home early, and sober! what new mischief are you up to?"

"None, Madge, none! but here's the devil to pay. Ellen's come back. She's been lying out these three nights, and is awful hard up. It's not my fault, I have sent her money enough, in all conscience."

"Where is she?" inquired Madge, curtly.

"Outside, in the plantation."

"Why don't you bring her in, you treacherous young wolf?" replied she. "What did you bring her to shame for, if you are going to starve her?"

"I was going to fetch her in," said George, indignantly; "only I wanted to find out what your temper was like, you vicious old cow. How did I know but what you would begin some of your tantrums, and miscall her?"

"No fear o' that! no fear of pots and kettles with me! lead her in, lad, before she's frozen!"

George went back for her, and finding her still in the same place, brought her in. Madge was standing erect before the fire, and, walking up to the unfortunate Ellen, took her baby from her, and made her sit before the fire.

"Better not face the old man," said she; "he's away to the revels, and he'll come home drunk. Make yourself happy for to-night, at all events."

The poor thing began to cry, which brought on such a terrible fit of coughing that Madge feared she would rupture a blood-vessel. She went to get her a glass of wine, and returned with a candle, and then, for the first time, they saw what a fearful object she was.

"Oh!" she said to George, "you see what I am now. I ain't long for this world. Only keep me from worse, George, while I am alive, and do something for the boy afterwards, and I am content. You're going to get married, I know, and I wish you well. But don't forget this poor little thing when it's motherless. If you do, and let him fall into vice, you'll never be lucky, George."

"Oh, you ain't going to die, old Nelly," said George; "not for many years yet. You're pulled down, and thin, but you'll pick up again with the spring. Now, old girl, get some supper out before he comes home."

They gave her supper, and put her to bed. In the morning, very early, George heard the sound of wheels below his bedroom window; and looking out, saw that Madge was driving out of the yard in a light cart, and, watching her closely, saw her pick up Ellen and the child just outside the gate. Then he went to bed again, and, when he awoke, he heard Madge's voice below, and knew she was come back.

He went down, and spoke to her. "Is she gone?" he asked.

"In course she is," replied Madge. "Do you think I was going to let her stay till the old man was about?"

"How much money did you give her, besides what she had from me?"

"I made it five pounds in all; that will keep her for some time, and then you must send her some more. If you let that wench starve, you ought to be burnt alive. A *man* would have married her in spite of his father."

"A likely story," said George, "that I was to disinherit myself for her. However, she shan't want at present, or we shall have her back again. And that won't do, you know."

"George," said Madge, "you promise to be as great a rascal as your father."

The old man had, as Madge prophesied, come home very drunk the night before, and had lain in bed later than usual, so that, when he came to breakfast, he found George, gun in hand, ready to go out.

"Going shooting, my lad?" said the father. "Where be going?"

"Down through the hollies for a woodcock. I'll get one this morning, it's near full moon."

All the morning they heard him firing in the bottom below the house, and at one o'clock he came home, empty-handed.

"Why, George!" said his father, "what hast thee been shooting at? I thought 'ee was getting good sport."

" I've been shooting at a mark," he replied.

" Who be going to shoot now, eh, George?" asked the old man.

" No one as I know of," he replied.

" Going over to Eggesford, eh, Georgey? This nice full moon is about the right thing for thee. They Fellowes be good fellows to keep a fat haunch for their neighbours."

George laughed, as he admitted the soft impeachment of deer-stealing, but soon after grew sullen, and all the afternoon sat over the fire brooding and drinking. He went to bed early, and had just got off his boots, when the door opened, and Madge came in."

" What's up to now, old girl?" said George.

" What are you going to be up to, eh?" she asked, " with your gun?"

" Only going to get an outlying deer," said he.

" That's folly enough, but there's a worse folly than that. It's worse folly to wipe out money-scores in blood. It's a worse folly if you are in a difficulty to put yourself in a harder one to get out of the first. It's a worse ——"

" Why, you're mad," broke in George. " Do you think I am fool enough to make away with one of the keepers?"

" I don't know what you are fool enough to do. Only mind my words before it's too late."

She went out, and left him sitting moodily on the bed. " What a clever woman she is," he mused. " How she hits a thing off. She's been a good friend to me. I've a good mind to ask her advice. I'll think about it to-morrow morning."

But on the morrow they quarrelled about something or another, and her advice was never asked. George was moody and captious all day; and at evening, having drunk hard, he slipped off, and, gun in hand, rode away through the darkening woods towards the moor.

It was dark before he had got clear of the labyrinth of lanes through which he took his way. His horse he turned out in a small croft close to where the heather began; and, having hid the saddle and bridle in a hedge, strode away over the moor with his gun on his shoulder.

He would not think; he would sooner whistle; distance seemed like nothing to him; and he was surprised and frightened to find himself already looking over the deep black gulf through which the river ran before he thought he was half-way there.

He paused to look before he began to descend. A faint light still lingered in the frosty sky to the south-west, and majestic Yestor rose bold and black against it. Down far, far beneath his feet was the river, dimly heard, but not seen; and, as he looked to where it should be, he saw a little flickering star, which arrested his attention. That must be Lee's fire—there he began to descend.

Boldly at first, but afterwards more stealthily, and now more silently still, for the fire is close by, and it were well to give him no notice. It is in the old place, and he can see it now, not ten yards before him, between two rocks.

Nearer yet a little, with cat-like tread. There is Lee, close to the fire, sitting on the ground, dimly visible, yet clearly enough for his purpose. He rests the gun on a rock, and takes his aim.

He is pinioned from behind by a vigorous hand, and a voice he knows cries in his ear—"Help, Bill, or you'll be shot!"

The gun goes off in the scuffle, but hurts nobody, and Lee running up, George finds the tables completely turned, and himself lying, after a few desperate struggles, helplessly pinioned on the ground.

Dick had merely blinded him by appearing to go to Exeter. They both thought it likely that he would attack Lee, but neither supposed he would have stolen on him so treacherously. Dick had just noticed him in time, and sprung upon him, or Lee's troubles would have been over for ever.

"You treacherous young sweep, you shall hang for this," were Lee's first words. " Ten thousand pounds would not save you now. Dick, you're a jewel. If I had listened to you, I shouldn't have trusted my life to the murdering vagabond. I'll remember to-night, my boy, as long as I live."

Although it appeared at first that ten thousand pounds would not prevent Lee handing George over to justice, yet, after a long and stormy argument, it appeared that the lesser sum of five hundred would be amply sufficient to stay any ulterior proceedings, provided the money was forthcoming in a week. So that ultimately George found himself at liberty again, and, to his great astonishment, in higher spirits than he could have expected.

"At all events," said he to himself, as he limped back, lame and bruised, "I have not got *that* on my mind. Even if this other thing was found out, there is a chance of getting off. Surely my own father wouldn't prosecute—though I wouldn't like to trust to it, unless I got Madge on my side."

His father, I think I have mentioned, was too blind to read, and George used to keep all his accounts; so that nothing would seem at first to look more easy than to imitate his father's signature, and obtain what money he wished. But George knew well that the old man was often in the habit of looking through his banker's book, with the assistance of Madge, so that he was quite unsafe without her. His former embezzlement he had kept secret, by altering some figure in the banker's book; but this next one, of such a much larger amount, he felt somewhat anxious about. He, however, knew his woman well, and took his measures accordingly.

On the day mentioned, he met Lee, and gave him the money agreed on; and having received his assurances that he valued his life too much to trouble him any more, saw him depart, fully expecting that he should have another application at an early date; under which circumstances, he thought he would take certain precautions which should be conclusive.

But he saw Lee no more. No more for many, many years, But how and when they met again, and who came off best in the end, this tale will truly and sufficiently set forth hereafter.

CHAPTER VII.

MAJOR BUCKLEY GIVES HIS OPINION ON TROUT-FISHING, ON EMIGRATION, AND ON GEORGE HAWKER.

SPRING had come again, after a long wet winter, and every orchard-hollow blushed once more with apple-blossoms. In warm sheltered southern valleys hedges were already green, and even the tall hedgerow-elms began, day after day, to grow more shady and dense.

It was a bright April morning, about ten o'clock, when Mary Thornton, throwing up her father's study-window from the outside, challenged him to come out and take a walk; and John, getting his hat and stick, immediately joined her in front of the house.

" Where is your aunt, my love ? " said John.

" She is upstairs," said Mary. " I will call her."

She began throwing gravel at one of the upper windows, and crying out, " Auntie ! Auntie ! "

The sash was immediately thrown (no, that is too violent a word —say lifted) up, and a beautiful old lady's face appeared at the window.

" My love," it said, in a small, soft voice, " pray be careful of the windows. Did you want anything, my dear ? "

" I want you out for a walk, Auntie; so come along."

" Certainly, my love. Brother, have you got your thick kerchief in your pocket ? "

" No," said the Vicar, " I have not, and I don't mean to have."

Commencement of a sore-throat lecture from the window, cut short by the Vicar, who says,—

" My dear, I shall be late if you don't come." (Jesuitically on his part, for he was going nowhere.)

So she comes accordingly, as sweet-looking an old maid as ever you saw in your life. People have no right to use up such beautiful women as governesses. It's a sheer waste of material. Miss Thornton had been a governess all her life; and now, at the age of five-and-forty, had come to keep her brother's house for him, add her savings to his, and put the finishing touch on Mary's somewhat rough education.

"My love," said she, "I have brought you your gloves."

"Oh, indeed, Auntie, I won't wear them," said Mary. "I couldn't be plagued with gloves. Nobody wears them here."

"Mrs. Buckley wears them, and it would relieve my mind if you were to put them on, my dear. I fear my lady's end was accelerated by, unfortunately, in her last illness, catching sight of Lady Kate's hands after she had been assisting her brother to pick green walnuts."

Mary was always on the eve of laughing at these aristocratic recollections of her aunt; and to her credit be it said, she always restrained herself, though with great difficulty. She, so wildly brought up, without rule or guidance in feminine matters, could not be brought to comprehend that prim line-and-rule life, of which her aunt was the very impersonation. Nevertheless, she heard what Miss Thornton had to say with respect; and if ever she committed an extreme *gaucherie*, calculated to set her aunt's teeth on edge, she always discovered what was the matter, and mended it as far as she was able.

They stood on the lawn while the glove controversy was going on, and a glorious prospect there was that bright spring morning. In one direction the eye was carried down a long, broad, and rich vale, intersected by a gleaming river, and all the way down set thick with hamlet, farm, and church. In the dim soft distance rose the two massive towers of a cathedral, now filling all the country side with the gentle melody of their golden-toned bells, while beyond them, in the misty south, there was a gleam in the horizon, showing where the sky

"Dipped down to sea and sands."

"It's as soft and quiet as a Sunday," said the Vicar; "and what a fishing day! I have half a mind—Hallo! look here."

The exclamation was caused by the appearance on the walk of a very tall and noble-looking man, about thirty, leading a grey pony, on which sat a beautiful woman with a child in her arms. Our party immediately moved forward to meet them, and a most friendly greeting took place on both sides, Mary at once taking possession of the child.

This was Major Buckley and his wife Agnes. I mentioned before that, after Clere was sold, the Major had taken a cottage in Drumston, and was a constant visitor on the Vicar; generally calling for the old gentleman to come fishing or shooting, and leaving his wife and his little son Samuel in the company of Mary and Miss Thornton.

"I have come, Vicar, to take you out fishing," said he. "Get your rod and come. A capital day. Why, here's the Doctor."

So there was, standing among them before any one had noticed him.

" I announce," said he, " that I shall accept the most agreeable invitation that any one will give me. What are you going to do, Major ? "

" Going fishing."

" Ah ! and you, madam ? " turning to Miss Thornton.

" I am going to see Mrs. Lee, who has a low fever, poor thing."

" Which Mrs. Lee, madam ? "

" Mrs. Lee of Eyford."

" And which Mrs. Lee of Eyford, madam ? "

" Mrs. James Lee."

" Junior or senior ? " persevered the Doctor.

" Junior," replied Miss Thornton, laughing.

" Ah ! " said the Doctor, " now we have it. I would suggest that all the Mrs. Lees in the parish should have a ticket with a number on it, like the *voituriers*. Buckley, lay it before the quarter-sessions. If you say the idea came from a foreigner, they will adopt it immediately. Miss Thornton, I will do myself the honour of accompanying you, and examine the case."

So the ladies went off with the Doctor, while the Vicar and Major Buckley turned to go fishing.

" I shall watch you, Major, instead of fishing myself," said the Vicar. " Where do you propose going ? "

" To the red water," said the Major. Accordingly they turn down a long, deep lane, which looks certainly as if it would lead one to a red brook, for the road and banks are of a brick-colour. And so it does, for presently before them they discern a red mill, and a broad, pleasant ford, where a crystal brook dimples and sparkles over a bed of reddish-purple pebbles.

" It is very clear," says the Major. " What's the fly to be, Vicar? "

" That's a very hard question to answer," says the Vicar. " Your Scotchman, eh ? or a small blue dun ? "

" We'll try both," says the Major ; and in a very short time it becomes apparent that the small dun is the man, for the trout seem to think that it is the very thing they have been looking for all day, and rise at it two at a time.

They fish downwards ; and after killing half-a-dozen half-pound fish, come to a place where another stream joins the first, making it double its original size, and here there is a great oak-root jutting into a large deep pool.

The Vicar stands back, intensely excited. This is a sure place for a big fish. The Major, eager but cool, stoops down and puts his flies in just above the root at once ; not as a greenhorn would, taking a few wide casts over the pool first, thereby standing a chance of hooking a little fish, and ruining his chance for a big one ; and at the second trial a deep-bodied brown fellow, about two pounds, dashes at the treacherous little blue, and gulps him down.

Then what a to-do is there. The Vicar jumping about on the grass, giving all sorts of contradictory advice. The Major, utterly despairing of ever getting his fish ashore, fighting a losing battle with infinite courage, determined that the trout shall remember him, at all events, if he does get away. And the trout, furious and indignant, but not in the least frightened, trying vainly to get back to the old root. Was there ever such a fish?

But the Major is the best man, for after ten minutes troutie is towed up on his side to a convenient shallow, and the Vicar puts on his spectacles to see him brought ashore. He scientifically pokes him in the flank, and spans him across the back, and pronounces *ex cathedrâ*—

" You'll find, sir, there won't be a finer fish, take him all in all, killed in the parish this season."

" Ah, it's a noble sport," says the Major. " I shan't get much more of it, I'm afraid."

" Why shouldn't you ? "

" Well, I'll tell you," says the Major. " Do you know how much property I have got ? "

" No, indeed."

" I have only ten thousand pounds ; and how am I to bring up a family on the interest of that ? "

" I should fancy it was quite enough for you," said the Vicar ; " you have only one son."

" How many more am I likely to have, eh ? And how should I look to find myself at sixty with five boys grown up, and only 300*l*. a-year ? "

" That is rather an extreme case," said the Vicar ; " you would be poor then, certainly."

" Just what I don't want to be. Besides wanting to make some money, I am leading an idle life here, and am getting very tired of it. And so—" he hesitated.

" And so ? " said the Vicar.

" I am thinking of emigrating. To New South Wales. To go into the sheep-farming line. There."

" There indeed," said the Vicar. " And what has put you up to it?"

" Why, my wife and I have been thinking of going to Canada for some time, and so the idea is not altogether new. The other day Hamlyn (you know him) showed me a letter from a cousin of his who is making a good deal of money there. Having seen that letter, I was much struck with it, and having made a great many other inquiries, I laid the whole information before my wife, and begged her to give me her opinion."

" And she recommended you to stay at home in peace and comfort," interposed the Vicar.

" On the contrary, she said she thought we ought by all means to go," returned the Major.

" Wonderful, indeed. And when shall you go ? "

" Not for some time, I think. Not for a year."

" I hope not. What a lonely old man I shall be when you are all gone."

" Nay, Vicar, I hope not," said the Major. " You will stay behind to see your daughter happily married, and your grandchildren about your knees."

The Vicar sighed heavily, and the Major continued.

" By-the-bye, Miss Thornton seems to have made a conquest already. Young Hawker seems desperately smitten ; did it ever strike you ? "

" Yes, it has struck me ; very deep indeed," said the Vicar ; " but what can I do ? "

" You surely would not allow her to marry him ? "

" How can I prevent it ? She is her own mistress, and I never could control her yet. How can I control her when her whole heart and soul is set on him ? "

" Good God ! " said the Major, " do you really think she cares for him ? "

" Oh, she loves him with her whole heart. I have seen it a long while."

" My dear friend, you should take her away for a short time, and see if she will forget him. Anything sooner than let her marry him."

" Why should she not marry him ? " said the Vicar. " She is only a farmer's grand-daughter. We are nobody, you know."

" But he is not of good character."

" Oh, there is nothing more against him than there is against most young fellows. He will reform and be steady. Do you know anything special against him ? " asked the Vicar.

" Not actually against him ; but just conceive, my dear friend, what a family to marry into ! His father—I speak the plain truth— is a most disreputable, drunken old man, living in open sin with a gipsy woman of the worst character, by whom George Hawker has been brought up. What an atmosphere of vice ! The young fellow himself is universally disliked, and distrusted too, all over the village. Can you forgive me for speaking so plain ? "

" There is no forgiveness necessary, my good friend ; " said the Vicar. " I know how kind your intentions are. But I cannot bring myself to have a useless quarrel with my daughter merely because I happen to dislike the object of her choice. It would be quite a useless quarrel. She has always had her own way, and always will."

" What does Miss Thornton say ? " asked the Major.

" Nothing, she never does say anything. She regards Hawker as Mary's accepted suitor ; and though she may think him vulgar, she would sooner die than commit herself so far as to say so. She has been so long under others, and without an opinion save theirs, that she cannot form an opinion at all."

They had turned and were walking home, when the Vicar, sticking his walking-cane upright in the grass, began again.

" It is the most miserable and lamentable thing that ever took place in this world. Look at my sister again : what a delicate old maid she is ! used to move and be respected, more than most governesses are, in the highest society in the land. There'll be a home for her when I die ! Think of her living in the house with any of the Hawkers ; and yet, sir, that woman's sense of duty is such that she'd die sooner than leave her niece. Sooner be burnt at the stake than go one inch out of the line of conduct she has marked out for herself."

The Vicar judged his sister most rightly : we shall see that hereafter.

" A man of determination and strength of character could have prevented it at the beginning, you would say. I dare say he might have ; but I am not a man of determination and strength of character. I never was, and I never shall be."

" Do you consider it in the light of a settled question, then," said the Major, " that your daughter should marry young Hawker ? "

" God knows. She will please herself. I spoke to her at first about encouraging him, and she began by laughing at me, and ended by making a scene whenever I spoke against him. I was at one time in hopes that she would have taken a fancy to young Stockbridge ; but I fear I must have set her against him by praising him too much. It wants a woman, you know, to manage those sort of things."

" It does, indeed."

" You see, as I said before, I have no actual reason to urge against Hawker, and he will be very rich. I shall raise my voice against her living in the house with that woman Madge—in fact, I won't have it ; but take it all in all, I fear I shall have to make the best of it."

Major Buckley said no more, and soon after they got home. There was Mrs. Buckley, queenly and beautiful, waiting for her husband ; and there was Mary, pretty, and full of fun ; there also was the Doctor, smoking and contemplating a new fern ; and Miss Thornton, with her gloved-hands folded, calculating uneasily what amount of detriment Mary's complexion would sustain in consequence of walking about without her bonnet in an April sun.

One and all cried out to know what sport ; and little Sam tottered forward demanding a fish for himself, which, having got, he at once put into his mouth head foremost. The Doctor, taking off his spectacles, examined the contents of the fish-basket, and then demanded :

" Now, my good friend, why do you give yourself the trouble to catch trout in that round-about way, requiring so much skill and

patience ? In Germany we catch them with a net—a far superior way, I assure you. Get any one of the idle young fellows about the village to go down to the stream with a net, and they will get more trout in a day than you would in a week."

"What!" said the Major, indignantly; "put a net in my rented water?—If I caught any audacious scoundrel carrying a net within half a mile of it, I'd break his neck. You can't appreciate the delights of fly-fishing, doctor—you are no sportsman."

"No, I ain't," said the Doctor; "you never said anything truer than that, James Buckley. I am nothing of the sort. When I was a young man, I had a sort of brute instinct, which made me take the same sort of pleasure in killing a boar that a cat does in killing a mouse; but I have outlived such barbarism."

"Ha, ha !" said the Vicar; "and yet he gave ten shillings for a snipe. And he's hand-and-glove with every poacher in the parish."

"The snipe was a new species, sir," said the Doctor, indignantly; "and if I do employ the hunters to collect for me, I see no inconsistency in that. But I consider this fly-fishing mania just of a piece with your *idiotic,* I repeat it, *idiotic* institution of fox-hunting. Why, if you laid baits poisoned with *nux vomica* about the haunts of those animals, you would get rid of them in two years."

The Doctor used to delight in aggravating the Major by attacking English sports; but he had a great admiration for them nevertheless.

The Major got out his wife's pony; and setting her on it, and handing up the son and heir, departed home to dinner. They were hardly inside the gate when Mrs. Buckley began:

"My dear husband, did you bring him to speak of the subject we were talking about ? "

"He went into it himself, wife, tooth and nail."

"Well ? "

"Well! indeed, my dear Agnes, do you know that, although I love the old man dearly, I must say I think he is rather weak."

"So I fear," said Mrs. Buckley; "but he is surely not so weak as to allow that young fellow to haunt the house, after he has had a hint that he is making love to Mary ? "

"My dear, he accepts him as her suitor. He says he has been aware of it for some time, and that he has spoken to Mary about it, and made no impression; so that now he considers it a settled thing."

"What culpable weakness ! So Mary encourages him, then ? "

"She adores him, and won't hear a word against him."

"Unfortunate girl!" said Mrs. Buckley, "and with such a noble young fellow as Stockbridge ready to cut off his head for her ! It is perfectly inconceivable."

"Young Hawker is very handsome, my dear, you must remember."

"Is he?" said Mrs. Buckley. "*I* call him one of the most evil-looking men I ever saw."

"My dear Agnes, I think if you were to speak boldly to her, you might do some good. You might begin to undermine this unlucky infatuation of her's; and I am sure, if her eyes were once opened, that the more she saw him, the less she would like him."

"I think, James," said Mrs. Buckley, "that it becomes the duty of us, who have been so happy in our marriage, to prevent our good old vicar's last days from being rendered miserable by such a mésalliance as this. I am very fond of Mary; but the old Vicar, my dear, has taken the place of your father to me."

"He is like a second father to me too," said the Major; "but he wants a good many qualities that my own father had. He hasn't his energy or determination. Why, if my father had been in his place, and such an ill-looking young dog as that came hanging about the premises, my father would have laid his stick about his back. And it would be a good thing if somebody would do it now."

Such was Major Buckley's opinion.

CHAPTER VIII.

THE VICAR HEARS SOMETHING TO HIS ADVANTAGE.

"My dear," said old Miss Thornton, that evening, "I have consulted Mrs. Buckley on the sleeves, and she is of opinion that they should be pointed."

"Do you think," said Mary, "that she thought much about the matter?"

"She promised to give the matter her earnest attention," said Miss Thornton; "so I suppose she did. Mrs. Buckley would never speak at random, if she once promised to give her real opinion."

"No, I don't think she would, Auntie, but she is not very particular in her own dress."

"She always looks like a thorough lady, my dear: Mrs. Buckley is a woman whom I could set before you as a model for imitation far sooner than myself."

"She is a duck, at all events," said Mary; "and her husband is a darling."

Miss Thornton was too much shocked to say anything. To hear a young lady speak of a handsome military man as a "darling," went quite beyond her experience. She was considering how much bread and water and backboard she would have felt it her duty to give Lady Kate, or Lady Fanny, in old times, for such an expression, when the Vicar, who had been dozing, woke up and said:—

"Bless us, what a night! The equinoctial gales come back again. This rain will make up for the dry March with a vengeance; I am glad I am safely housed before a good fire."

Unlucky words! he drew nearer to the fire, and began rubbing his knees; he had given them about three rubs, when the door opened and the maid's voice was heard ominous of evil.

"Thomas Jewel is worse, sir, and if you please his missis don't expect he'll last the night; and could you just step up?"

"Just stepping up," was a pretty little euphemism for walking three long miles dead in the teeth of a gale of wind, with a fierce rushing tropical rain. One of the numerous tenders of the ship Jewel (74), had just arrived before the wind under bare poles, an attempt to set a rag of umbrella having ended in its being blown out of the bolt-ropes, and the aforesaid tender Jewel was now in the vicarage harbour of refuge, reflecting what an awful job it would have in beating back against the monsoon.

"Who has come with this message?" said the Vicar, entering the kitchen followed by Miss Thornton and Mary.

"Me, sir," says a voice from the doorway.

"Oh, come in, will you," said the Vicar; "it's a terrible night, is it not?"

"Oh Loord!" said the voice in reply—intending that ejaculation for a very strong affirmative. And advancing towards the light, displayed a figure in a long brown great-coat, reaching to the ancles, and topped by some sort of head-dress, resembling very closely a small black carpet bag, tied on with a red cotton handkerchief. This was all that was visible, and the good Vicar stood doubting whether it was male or female, till catching sight of an immense pair of hob-nail boots peeping from the lower extremity of the coat, he made up his mind at once, and began:—

"My good boy—"

There was a cackling laugh from under the carpet-bag, and a harsh grating voice replied:

"I be a gurl."

"Dear me," said the Vicar, "then what do you dress yourself in that style for?—So old Jewel is worse."

"Us don't think a'll live the night."

"Is the doctor with him?" said the Vicar.

"The 'Talian's with un."

By which he understood her to mean Dr. Mulhaus, all foreigners being considered to be Italians in Drumston. An idea they got, I take it, from the wandering organ men being of that nation.

"Well," said the Vicar, "I will start at once, and come. It's a terrible night."

The owner of the great-coat assented with a fiendish cackle, and departed. The Vicar, having been well wrapped up by his sister and daughter, departed also, with a last injunction from Miss Thornton to take care of himself.

Easier said than done, such a night as this. A regular south-westerly gale, accompanied by a stinging, cutting rain, which made it almost impossible to look to windward. Earth and sky seemed mixed together, and each twig and bough sent a separate plaint upon the gale, indignant at seeing their fresh-acquired honours torn from them and scattered before the blast.

The Vicar put his head down and sturdily walked against it. It was well for him that he knew every inch of the road, for his know-ledge was needed now. There was no turn in the road after he had passed the church, but it took straight away over the high ground up to Hawker's farm on the woodlands.

Old Jewel, whom he was going to see, had been a hind of Hawker's for many years; but about a twelvemonth before the present time he had left his service, partly on account of increasing infirmity, and partly in consequence of a violent quarrel with Madge. He was a man of indifferent character. He had been married once in his life, but his wife only lived a year, and left him with one son, who had likewise married and given to the world seven as barbarous, neglected, young savages as any in the parish. The old man, who was now lying on his deathbed, had been a sort of confidential man to old Hawker, retained in that capacity on account, the old man said once in his drink, of not having any wife to worm family affairs out of him. So it was generally believed by the village folks, that old Jewel was in possession of some fearful secrets (such as a murder or two, for instance, or a brace of forgeries), and that the Hawkers daren't turn him out of the cottage where he lived for their lives.

Perhaps some of these idle rumours may have floated through the Vicar's brain as he fought forwards against the storm; but if any did, they were soon dismissed again, and the good man's thoughts carried into a fresh channel. And he was thinking what a fearful night this would be at sea, and how any ship could live against such a storm, when he came to a white gate, which led into the deep woods surrounding Hawker's house, and in a recess of which lived old Jewel and his family.

Now began the most difficult part of his journey. The broader road that led from the gate up to the Hawkers' house was plainly perceptible, but the little path which turned up to the cottage was not so easily found, and when found, not easily kept on such a black wild night as this. But, at length, having hit it, he began to follow it with some difficulty, and soon beginning to descend rapidly, he caught sight of a light, and, at the same moment, heard the rushing of water.

"Oh," said he to himself, "the water is come down, and I shall have a nice job to get across it. Any people but the Jewels would

E

have made some sort of a bridge by now; but they have been content with a fallen tree ever since the old bridge was carried away."

He scrambled down the steep hill side with great difficulty, and
not without one or two nasty slips, which, to a man of his age, was
no trifle, but at length stood trembling with exertion before a flooded
brook, across which lay a fallen tree, dimly seen in the dark against
the gleam of the rushing water.

"I must stand and steady my nerves a bit after that tumble," he
said, "before I venture over there. That's the 'Brig of Dread'
with a vengeance. However, I never came to harm yet when I was
after duty, so I'll chance it."

The cottage stood just across the brook, and he hallooed aloud for
some one to come. After a short time the door opened, and a man
appeared with a lantern.

"Who is there?" demanded Dr. Mulhaus' well-known voice.
"Is it you, Vicar?"

"Aye," rejoined the other, "it's me at present; but it won't be
me long if I slip coming over that log. Here goes," he said, as he
steadied himself and crossed rapidly, while the Doctor held the light.
"Ah," he added, when he was safe across, "I knew I should get
over all right."

"You did not seem very certain about it just now," said the
Doctor. "However, I am sincerely glad you are come. I knew
no weather would stop you."

"Thank you, old friend," said the Vicar; "and how is the
patient?"

"Going fast. More in your line than mine. The man believes
himself bewitched."

"Not uncommon," said the Vicar, "in these parts; they are
always bothering me with some of that sort of nonsense."

They went in. Only an ordinary scene of poverty, dirt, and vice,
such as exists to some extent, in every parish, in every country on the
globe. Nothing more than that, and yet a sickening sight enough.

A squalid, damp, close room, with the earthen floor sunk in
many places and holding pools of water. The mother smoking in
the chimney corner, the eldest daughter nursing an illegitimate
child, and quarrelling with her mother in a coarse, angry tone. The
children, ragged and hungry, fighting for the fireside. The father
away, at some unlawful occupation probably, or sitting drinking
his wages in an alehouse. That was what they saw, and what
any man may see to-day for himself in his own village, whether in
England or Australia, that working man's paradise. Drink, dirt,
and sloth, my friends of the working orders, will produce the same
effects all over the world.

As they came in the woman of the house rose and curtseyed to
the Vicar, but the eldest girl sat still and turned away her head. The

Vicar, after saluting her mother, went gently up to her, and patting the baby's cheek, asked her kindly how she did. The girl tried to answer him, but could only sob. She bent down her head again over the child, and began rocking it to and fro.

"You must bring it to be christened," said the Vicar kindly. "Can you come on Wednesday?"

"Yes, I'll come," she said with a sort of choke. And now the woman having lit a fresh candle, ushered them into the sick man's room.

"Typhus and scarlatina!" said the Doctor. "How this place smells after being in the air. He is sensible again, I think."

"Quite sensible," the sick man answered aloud. "So you've come, Mr. Thornton; I'm glad of it; I've got a sad story to tell you; but I'll have vengeance if you do your duty. You see the state I am in!"

"Ague!" said the Vicar.

"And who gave it me?"

"Why, God sent it to you," said the Vicar. "All people living in a narrow wet valley among woodlands like this, must expect ague."

"I tell you she gave it to me. I tell you she has overlooked me; and all this doctor's stuff is no use, unless you can say a charm as will undo her devil's work."

"My good friend," said the Vicar, "you should banish such fancies from your mind, for you are in a serious position, and ought not to die in enmity with any one."

"Not die in enmity with her? I'd never forgive her till she took off the spell."

"Whom do you mean?" asked the Vicar.

"Why, that infernal witch, Madge, that lives with old Hawker," said the man excitedly. "That's who I mean!"

"Why, what injury has she done you?"

"Bewitched me, I tell you! Given me these shaking fits. She told me she would, when I left; and so she has, to prevent my speaking. I might a spoke out anytime this year, only the old man kept me quiet with money; but now it's nigh too late!"

"What might you have spoken about?" asked the Vicar.

"Well, I'll just relate the matter to you," said the man, speaking fast and thick, "and I'll speak the truth. A twelvemonth agone, this Madge and me had a fierce quarrel, and I miscalled her awful, and told her of some things she wasn't aware I knew of; and then she said, 'If ever a word of that escapes your lips, I'll put such a spell on ye that your bones shall shake apart.' Then I says, If you do, your bastard son shall swing."

"Who do you mean by her bastard son?"

"Young George Hawker. He is not the son of old Mrs. Hawker!"

Madge was brought to bed of him a fortnight before her mistress; and when she bore a still-born child, old Hawker and I buried it in the wood, and we gave Madge's child to Mrs. Hawker, who never knew the difference before she died."

" On the word of a dying man, is that true?" demanded the Vicar.

" On the word of a dying man that's true, and this also. I says to Madge, ' Your boy shall swing, for I know enough to hang him.' And she said, ' Where are your proofs?' and I—O Lord! O Lord! she's at me again."

He sank down again in a paroxysm of shivering, and they got no more from him. Enough there was, however, to make the Vicar a very silent and thoughtful man, as he sat watching the sick man in the close stifling room.

" You had better go home, Vicar," said the Doctor; " you will make yourself ill staying here. I do not expect another lucid interval."

" No," said the Vicar, " I feel it my duty to stay longer. For my own sake too. What he has let out bears fearfully on my happiness, Doctor."

" Yes, I can understand that, my friend, from what I have heard of the relations that exist between your daughter and that young man. You have been saved from a terrible misfortune, though at the cost, perhaps, of a few tears, and a little temporary uneasiness."

" I hope it may be as you say," said the Vicar. " Strange, only to-day Major Buckley was urging me to stop that acquaintance."

" I should have ventured to do so too, Vicar, had I been as old a friend of yours as Major Buckley."

" He is not such a very old friend," said the Vicar; " only of two years' standing, yet I seem to have known him ten."

At daybreak the man died, and made no sign. So as soon as they had satisfied themselves of the fact, they departed, and came out together into the clear morning air. The rain-clouds had broken, though when they had scrambled up out of the narrow little valley where the cottage stood, they found that the wind was still high and fierce, and that the sun was rising dimly through a yellow haze of driving scud.

They stepped out briskly, revived by the freshness of all around, and had made about half the distance home, when they descried a horseman coming slowly towards them. It seemed an early time for any one to be abroad, and their surprise was increased at seeing that it was George Hawker returning home.

" Where can he have been so early?" said the Doctor.

" So late, you mean," said the Vicar; " he has not been home all night. Now I shall brace up my nerves and speak to him."

" My good wishes go with you, Vicar," said the Doctor, and walked on, while the other stopped to speak with George Hawker.

" Good morning, Mr. Thornton. You are early a-foot, sir."

"Yes, I have been sitting up all night with old Jewel. He is dead."

"Is he indeed, sir?" said Hawker. "He won't be much loss, sir, to the parish. A sort of happy release, one may say, for every one but himself."

"Can I have the pleasure of a few words with you, Mr. Hawker?"

"Surely, sir," said he, dismounting. "Allow me to walk a little on the way back with you?"

"What I have to say, Mr. Hawker," said the Vicar, "is very short, and, I fear, also very disagreeable to all parties. I am going to request you to discontinue your visits to my house altogether, and, in fact, drop our acquaintance."

"This is very sudden, sir," said Hawker. "Am I to understand, sir, that you cannot be induced by any conduct of mine to reconsider this decision?"

"You are to understand that such is the case, sir."

"And this is final, Mr. Thornton?"

"Quite final, I assure you," said the Vicar; "nothing on earth should make me flinch from my decision."

"This is very unfortunate, sir," said George. "For I had reason to believe that you rather encouraged my visits than otherwise."

"I never encouraged them. It is true I permitted them. But since then circumstances have come to my ears which render it imperative that you should drop all communication with the members of my family, more especially, to speak plainly, with my daughter."

"At least, sir," said George, "let me know what charge you bring against me."

"I make no charges of any sort," replied the Vicar. "All I say is, that I wish the intercourse between you and my daughter to cease; and I consider, sir, that when I say that, it ought to be sufficient. I conceive that I have the right to say so much without question."

"I think you are unjust, sir; I do, indeed," said George.

"I may have been unjust, and I may have been weak, in allowing an intimacy (which I do not deny, mind you) to spring up between my daughter and yourself. But I am not unjust now, when I require that it should cease. I begin to be just."

"Do you forbid me your house, sir?"

"I forbid you my house, sir. Most distinctly. And I wish you good-day."

There was no more to be said on either side. George stood beside his horse, after the Vicar had left him, till he was fairly out of ear-shot. And then, with a fierce oath, he said,—

"You puritanical old humbug, I'll do you yet. You've heard about Nell and her cursed brat. But the daughter ain't always the same way of thinking with the father, old man,"

The Vicar walked on, glad enough to have got the interview over, till he overtook the Doctor, who was walking slowly till he came up. He felt as though the battle was gained already, though he still rather dreaded a scene with Mary.

"How have you sped, friend?" asked the Doctor. "Have you given the young gentleman his *congée*?"

"I have," he replied. "Doctor, now half the work is done, I feel what a culpable coward I have been not to do it before. I have been deeply to blame. I never should have allowed him to come near us. Surely, the girl will not be such a fool as to regret the loss of such a man. I shall tell her all I know about him, and after that I can do no more. No more? I never had her confidence. She has always had a life apart from mine. The people in the village, all so far below us in every way, have been to me acquaintances, and only that; but they have been her world, and she has seen no other. She is a kind, affectionate daughter, but she would be as good a daughter to any of the farmers round as she is to me. She is not a lady. That is the truth. God help the man who brings up a daughter without a wife."

"You do her injustice, my friend," said the Doctor. "I understand what you mean, but you do her injustice. All the female society she has ever seen, before Mrs. Buckley and your sister came here, was of a rank inferior to herself, and she has taken her impressions from that society to a great extent. But still she is a lady; compare her to any of the other girls in the parish, and you will see the difference."

"Yes, yes, that is true," said the Vicar. "You must think me a strange man to speak so plainly about my own daughter, Doctor, and to you, too, whom I have known so short a time. But one must confide in somebody, and I have seen your discretion manifested so often that I trust you."

They had arrived opposite the Vicar's gate, but the Doctor, resisting all the Vicar's offers of breakfast, declined to go in. He walked homeward toward his cottage-lodgings, and as he went he mused to himself somewhat in this style,—

"What a good old man that is. And yet how weak. I used to say to myself when I first knew him, what a pity that a man with such a noble intellect should be buried in a country village, a pastor to a lot of ignorant hinds. And yet he is fit for nothing else, with all his intelligence, and all his learning. He has no go in him,— no back to his head. Contrast him with Buckley, and see the difference. Now Buckley, without being a particularly clever man, sees the right thing, and goes at it through fire and water. But our old Vicar sees the right, and leaves it to take care of itself. He can't manage his own family even. That girl is a fine girl, a very fine girl. A good deal of character about her. But her animal passions are so strong that she would be a Tartar for any one to manage. She will be too much for the Vicar. She will marry that man in the end. And if he don't use her properly, she'll hate him as much as she loves him now. She is more like an Italian than an English girl. Hi! there's a noble Rhamnea!"

The Vicar went into his house, and found no one up but the maids, who were keeping that saturnalia among the household gods, which, I am given to understand, goes on in every well-regulated household before the lords of the creation rise from their downy beds. I have never seen this process myself, but I am informed, by the friend of my heart, who looked on it once for five minutes, and then fled, horror struck, that the first act consists in turning all the furniture upside down, and beating it with brooms. Further than this, I have no information. If any male eye has penetrated these awful secrets beyond that, let the owner of that eye preserve a decent silence. There are some things that it is better not to know. Only let us hope, brother, that you and I may always find ourselves in a position to lie in bed till it is all over. In Australia, it may be worth while to remark, this custom, with many other religious observances, has fallen into entire desuetude.

The Vicar was very cross this morning. He had been sitting up all night, which was bad, and he had been thinking these last few minutes that he had made a fool of himself, by talking so freely to the Doctor about his private affairs, which was worse. Nothing irritated the Vicar's temper more than the feeling of having been too free and communicative with people who did not care about him, a thing he was very apt to do. And, on this occasion, he could not disguise from himself that he had been led into talking about his daughter to the Doctor, in a way which he characterised in his own mind as being " indecent."

As I said, he was cross. And anything in the way of clearing up or disturbance always irritated him, though he generally concealed it. But there was a point at which his vexation always took the form of a protest, more or less violent. And that point was determined by any one meddling with his manuscript sermons.

So, on this unlucky morning, in spite of fresh-lit fires smoking in his face, and fenders in dark passages throwing him headlong into lurking coalscuttles, he kept his temper like a man, until coming into his study, he found his favourite discourse on the sixth seal lying on the floor by the window, his lectures on the 119th Psalm on the hearthrug, and the maid fanning the fire with his *chef d'œuvre*, the Waterloo thanksgiving.

Then, I am sorry to say, he lost his temper. Instead of calling the girl by her proper name, he addressed her as a distinguished Jewish lady, a near relation of King Ahab, and, snatching the sermon from her hand, told her to go and call Miss Mary, or he'd lay his stick about her back.

The girl was frightened—she had never seen her master in this state of mind before. So she ran out of the room, and, having fetched Mary, ensconced herself outside the door to hear what was the matter.

Mary tripped into the room looking pretty and fresh. " Why, father," she said, " you have been up all night. I have ordered you a cup of coffee. How is old Jewel ?"

" Dead," said the Vicar. " Never mind him. Mary, I want to speak to you, seriously, about something that concerns the happiness of your whole life."

" Father," she said, " you frighten me. Let me get you your coffee before you begin, at all events."

" Stay where you are, I order you," said the father. " I will have no temporizing until the matter grows cold. I will speak now ; do you hear. Now, listen."

She was subdued, and knew what was coming. She sat down, and waited. Had he looked in her face, instead of in the fire, he would have seen an expression there which he would little have liked —a smile of obstinacy and self-will.

"I am not going to mince matters, and beat about the bush, Mary," he began. " What I say I mean, and will have it attended to. You are very intimate with young Hawker, and that intimacy is very displeasing to me."

" Well ? " she said.

" Well," he answered. " I say it is not well. I will not have him here."

" You are rather late, father," she said. " He has had the run of this house these six months. You should have spoken before."

" I speak now, miss," said the Vicar, succeeding in working himself into a passion, " and that is enough. I forbid him the house, now ! "

" You had better tell him so, father. I won't."

" I daresay you won't," said the Vicar. " But I have told him so already this morning."

" You have ! " she cried. " Father, you had no right to do that. You encouraged him here. And now my love is given, you turn round and try to break my heart."

" I never encouraged him. You all throw that in my face. You have no natural affection, girl. I always hated the man. And now I have heard things about him sufficient to bar him from any honest man's house."

" Unjust ! " she said. " I will never believe it."

" I daresay you won't," said the Vicar. " Because you don't want to. You are determined to make my life miserable. There was Jim Stockbridge. Such a noble, handsome, gentlemanly young fellow, and nothing would please you but to drive him wild, till he left the country. Now, go away, and mind what I have said. You mean to break my heart, I see."

She turned as she was going out. "Father," she said, "is James Stockbridge gone?"

"Yes; gone. Sailed a fortnight ago. And all your doing. Poor boy, I wonder where he is now."

Where is he now? Under the cliffs of Madeira. Standing on the deck of a brave ship, beneath a rustling cloud of canvas, watching awe-struck that noble island, like an aërial temple, brown in the lights, blue in the shadows, floating between a sapphire sea and an azure sky. Far aloft in the air is Ruivo, five thousand feet overhead, father of the great ridges and sierras that run down jagged and abrupt, till they end in wild surf-washed promontories. He is watching a mighty glen that pierces the mountain, dark with misty shadows. He is watching the waterfalls that stream from among the vineyards into the sea below, and one long white monastery, perched up among the crags above the highway of the world.

Borne upon the full north wind, the manhood and intelligence of Europe goes past, day by day, in white winged ships. And above all, unheeding, century after century, the old monks have vegetated there, saying their masses, and ringing their chapel bells, high on the windy cliff.

CHAPTER IX.

WHEN THE KYE CAME HAME.

AND when Mary had left the room, the Vicar sat musing before the fire in his study. "Well," said he to himself, "she took it quieter than I thought she would. Now, I can't blame myself. I think I have shown her that I am determined, and she seems inclined to be dutiful. Poor dear girl, I am sorry for her. There is no doubt she has taken a fancy to this handsome young scamp. But she must get over it. It can't be so very serious as yet. At all events I have done my duty, though I can't help saying that I wish I had spoken before things went so far."

The maid looked in timidly, and told him that breakfast was ready. He went into the front parlour, and there he found his sister making tea. She looked rather disturbed, and, as the Vicar kissed her, he asked her "where was Mary?"

"She is not well, brother," she answered. "She is going to stay up-stairs, I fear something has gone wrong with her."

" She and I had some words this morning," answered he, and that happens so seldom, that she is a little upset, that is all."

" I hope there is nothing serious, brother," said Miss Thornton.

" No ; I have only been telling her that she must give up receiving George Hawker here. And she seems to have taken a sort of fancy to his society, which might have grown to something more serious. So I am glad I spoke in time."

" My dear brother, do you think you have spoken in time ? I have always imagined that you had determined, for some reason which I was not master of, that she should look on Mr. Hawker as her future husband. I am afraid you will have trouble. Mary is self-willed."

Mary was very self-willed. She refused to come down-stairs all day, and, when he was sitting down to dinner, he sent up for her. She sent him for an answer, that she did not want any dinner, and that she was going to stay where she was.

The Vicar ate his dinner notwithstanding. He was vexed, but, on the whole, felt satisfied with himself. This sort of thing, he said to himself, was to be expected. She would get over it in time. He hoped that the poor girl would not neglect her meals, and get thin. He might have made himself comfortable if he had seen her at the cold chicken in the back kitchen.

She could not quite make the matter out. She rather fancied that her father and Hawker had had some quarrel, the effects of which would wear off, and that all would come back to its old course. She thought it strange too that her father should be so different from his usual self, and this made her uneasy. One thing she was determined on, not to give up her lover, come what would. So far in life she had always had her own way, and she would have it now. All things considered, she thought that sulks would be her game. So sulks it was. To be carried on until the Vicar relented.

She sat up in her room till it was evening. Twice during the day her aunt had come up, and the first time she had got rid of her under pretence of headache, but the second time she was forced in decency to admit her, and listen entirely unmodified to a long discourse, proving, beyond power of contradiction, that it was the duty of every young Englishwoman to be guided entirely by her parents in the choice of a partner for life. And how that Lady Kate, as a fearful judgment on her for marrying a captain of artillery against the wishes of her noble relatives, was now expiating her crimes on 400*l.* a-year, and when she might have married a duke.

Lady Kate was Miss Thornton's " awful example," her " naughty girl." She served to point many a moral of the old lady's. But Lady Fanny, her sister, was always represented as the pattern of all Christian virtues—who had crowned the hopes of her family and well-wishers by marrying a gouty marquis of sixty-three, with fifty

thousand a-year. On this occasion, Mary struck the old lady dumb—"knocked her cold," our American cousins would say—by announcing that she considered Lady Fanny to be a fool, but that Lady Kate seemed to be a girl of some spirit. So Miss Thornton left her to her own evil thoughts, and, as evening began to fall, Mary put on her bonnet, and went out for a walk.

Out by the back door, and round through the shrubbery, so that she gained the front gate unperceived from the windows; but ere she reached it she heard the latch go, and found herself face to face with a man.

He was an immensely tall man, six foot at least. His long heavy limbs loosely hung together, and his immense broad shoulders slightly rounded. In features he was hardly handsome, but a kindly pleasant looking face made ample atonement for want of beauty. He was dressed in knee breeches, and a great blue coat, with brass buttons, too large even for him, was topped by a broad-brimmed beaver hat, with fur on it half an inch long. In age, this man was about five-and-twenty, and well known he was to all the young fellows round there for skill in all sporting matters, as well as for his kind-heartedness and generosity.

When he saw Mary pop out of the little side walk right upon him, he leaned back against the gate and burst out laughing. No, hardly "burst out." His laughter seemed to begin internally and silently, till, after one or two rounds, it shook the vast fabric of his chest beyond endurance, and broke out into so loud and joyous a peal that the blackbird fled, screeching indignantly, from the ivy-tree behind him.

"What! Thomas Troubridge," said Mary. "My dear cousin, how are you? Now, don't stand laughing there like a great gaby, but come and shake hands. What on earth do you see to laugh at in me?"

"Nothing, my cousin Poll, nothing," he replied. "You know that is my way of expressing approval. And you look so pretty standing there in the shade, that I would break any man's neck who didn't applaud. Shake hands, says you, I'll shake hands with a vengeance." So saying, he caught her in his arms, and covered her with kisses.

"You audacious," she exclaimed, when she writhed herself free. "I'll never come within arm's-length of you again. How dare you?"

"Only cousinly affection, I assure you, Poll. Rather more violent than usual at finding myself back in Drumston. But entirely cousinly."

"Where have you been, then, Tom?" she asked.

"Why, to London, to be sure. Give us ano——"

"You keep off, sir, or you'll catch it. What took you there?"

"Went to see Stockbridge and Hamlyn off."

"Then, they are gone?" she asked.

"Gone, sure enough. I was the last friend they'll see for many a long year."

"How did Stockbridge look? was he pretty brave?"

"Pretty well. Braver than I was. Mary, my girl, why didn't ye marry him?"

"What—you are at me with the rest, are you?" she answered.

"Why, because he was a gaby, and you're another; and I wouldn't marry either of you to save your lives—now then!"

"Do you mean to say you would not have me, if I asked you? Pooh! pooh! I know better than that, you know." And again the shrubbery rang with his laughter.

"Now, go in, Tom, and let me get out," said Mary. "I say Tom, dear, don't say you saw me. I am going out for a turn, and I don't want them to know it."

Tom twisted up his great face into a mixture of mystery, admiration, wonder, and acquiescence, and, having opened the gate for her, went in.

But Mary walked quickly down a deep narrow lane, overarched with oak, and melodious with the full rich notes of the thrush, till she saw down the long vista, growing now momentarily darker, the gleaming of a ford where the road crossed a brook.

Not the brook where the Vicar and the Major went fishing. Quite a different sort of stream, although they were scarcely half a mile apart, and joined just below. Here all the soil was yellow clay, and, being less fertile, was far more densely wooded than any of the red country. The hills were very abrupt, and the fields but sparely scattered among the forest land. The stream itself, where it crossed the road, flowed murmuring over a bed of loose blue slate pebbles, but both above and below this place forced its way, almost invisible, through a dense oak wood, deeply tangled with under-growth.

A stone foot-bridge spanned the stream, and having reached this, it seemed as if she had come to her journey's end. For leaning on the rail she began looking into the water below, though starting and looking round at every sound.

She was waiting for some one. A pleasant place this to wait in. So dark, so hemmed in with trees, and the road so little used; spring was early here, and the boughs were getting quite dense already. How pleasant to see the broad red moon go up behind the feathery branches, and listen to the evensong of the thrush, just departing to roost, and leaving the field clear for the woodlark all night. There were a few sounds from the village, a lowing of cows, and the noise of the boys at play; but they were so tempered down by the distance, that they only added to the evening harmony.

There is another sound now. Horses' feet approaching rapidly from the side opposite to that by which she has come; and soon a horseman comes in sight, coming quickly down the hill. When he sees her he breaks into a gallop, and only pulls up when he is at the side of the brook below her.

This is the man she was expecting—George Hawker. Ah, Vicar! how useless is your authority when lovers have such intelligence as this. It were better they should meet in your parlour, under your own eye, than here, in the budding spring-time, in this quiet spot under the darkening oaks.

Hawker spoke first. " I guessed," he said, " that it was just possible you might come out to-night. Come down off the bridge, my love, and let us talk together while I hang up the horse."

So as he tied the horse to a gate, she came down off the bridge. He took her in his arms and kissed her. " Now, my Poll," said he, " I know what you are going to begin talking about."

" I daresay you do, George," she answered. " You and my father have quarrelled."

" The quarrel has been all on one side, my love," he said; " he has got some nonsense into his head, and he told me when I met him this morning, that he would never see me in his house again."

" What has he heard, George? it must be something very shocking to change him like that. Do you know what it is?"

" Perhaps I do," he said; " but he has no right to visit my father's sins on me. He hates me, and he always did; and he has been racking his brains to find out something against me. That rascally German doctor has found him an excuse, and so he throws in my teeth, as fresh discovered, what he must have known years ago."

" I don't think that, George. I don't think he would be so deceitful."

" Not naturally he wouldn't, I know; but he is under the thumb of that doctor; and you know how *he* hates me—If you don't I do."

" I don't know why Dr. Mulhaus should hate you, George."

" I do though; that sleeky dog Stockbridge, who is such a favourite with him, has poisoned his mind, and all because he wanted you and your money, and because you took up with me instead of him."

" Well now," said Mary; " don't go on about him—he is gone, at all events; but you must tell me what this is that my father has got against you."

" I don't like to. I tell you it is against my father, not me."

" Well!" she answered; " if it was any one but me, perhaps, you ought not to tell it; but you ought to have no secrets from me, George—I have kept none from you."

" Well, my darling, I will tell you then: you know Madge, at our place?"

" Yes; I have seen her."

" Well, it's about her. She and my father live together like man and wife, though they ain't married; and the Vicar must have known that these years, and yet now he makes it an excuse for getting rid of me."

" I always thought she was a bad woman," said Mary; " but you are wrong about my father. He never knew it till now I am certain; and of course, you know, he naturally won't have me go and live in the house with a bad woman."

" Does he think then, or do you think," replied George, with virtuous indignation, " that I would have thought of taking you there? No, I'd sooner have taken you to America!"

" Well, so I believe, George."

" This won't make any difference in you, Mary? No, I needn't ask it, you wouldn't have come here to meet me to-night if that had been the case."

" It ought to make a difference, George," she replied; " I am afraid I oughtn't to come out here and see you, when my father don't approve of it."

" But you will come, my little darling, for all that;" he said. " Not here though—the devil only knows who may be loitering round here. Half a dozen pair of lovers a night perhaps—no, meet me up in the croft of a night. I am often in at Gosford's of an evening, and I can see your window from there, you put a candle in the right-hand corner when you want to see me, and I'll be down in a very few minutes. I shall come every evening and watch."

" Indeed," she said, " I won't do anything of the sort'; at least, unless I have something very particular to say. Then, indeed, I might do such a thing. Now I must go home or they will be missing me."

" Stay a minute, Mary," said he; " you just listen to me. They will, some of them, be trying to take my character away. You won't throw me off without hearing my defence, dear Mary, I know you won't. Let me hear what lies they tell of me, and don't you condemn me unheard because I come from a bad house. Tell me that you'll give me a chance of clearing myself with you, my girl, and I'll go home in peace and wait."

What girl could resist the man she loved so truly, when he pleaded so well? With his arm about her waist, and his handsome face bent over her, lit up with what she took to be love. Not she, at all events. She drew the handsome face down towards her, and as she kissed him fervently, said:

" I will never believe what they say of you, love. I should die if I lost you. I will stay by you through evil report and good report. What is all the world to me without you?"

And she felt what she said, and meant it. What though the words in which she spoke were borrowed from the trashy novels she was always reading—they were true enough for all that. George saw that they were true, and saw also that now was the time to speak about what he had been pondering over all day.

"And suppose, my own love," he said ; " that your father should stay in his present mind, and not come round ? "

" Well ! " she said.

"What are we to do ?" he asked ; " are we to be always content with meeting here and there, when we dare ? Is there nothing further ? "

"What do you mean ?" she said in a whisper. "What shall we do ? "

" Can't you answer that ? " he said softly. " Try."

" No, I can't answer. You tell me what."

" Fly ! " he said in her ear. " Fly, and get married, that's what I mean."

" Oh ! that's what you mean," she replied. " Oh, George, I should not have courage for that."

" I think you will, my darling, when the time comes. Go home and think about it."

He kissed her once more, and then she ran away homeward through the dark. But she did not run far before she began to walk slower and think.

" Fly with him," she thought. " Run away and get married. What a delightfully wild idea. Not to be entertained for a moment, of course, but still what a pleasant notion. She meant to marry George in the end ; why not that way as well as any other ? She thought about it again and again, and the idea grew more familiar. At all events, if her father should continue obstinate, here was a way out of the difficulty. He would be angry at first, but when he found he could not help himself he would come round, and then they would all be happy. She would shut her ears to anything they said against George. She could not believe it. She would not. He should be her husband, come what might. She would dissemble, and keep her father's suspicions quiet. More, she would speak lightly of George, and make them believe she did not care for him. But most of all, she would worm from her father everything she could about him. Her curiosity was aroused, and she fancied, perhaps, George had not told her all the truth. Perhaps he might be entangled with some other woman. She would find it all out if she could."

So confusedly thinking she reached home, and approaching the door, heard the noise of many voices in the parlour. There was evidently company, and in her present excited state nothing would

suit her better ; so sliding up to her room, and changing her dress
a little, she came down and entered the parlour.

" Behold," cried the Doctor, as she entered the room, " the
evening-star has arisen at last. My dear young lady, we have been
loudly lamenting your absence and indisposition."

" I have been listening to your lamentations, Doctor," she replied.
" They were certainly loud, and from the frequent bursts of laughter, I judged they were getting hysterical, so I came down."

There was quite a party assembled. The Vicar and Major
Buckley were talking earnestly together. Troubridge and the
Doctor were side by side, while next the fire was Mrs. Buckley,
with young Sam asleep on her lap, and Miss Thornton sitting quietly
beside her.

Having saluted them all, Mary sat down by Mrs. Buckley, and
began talking to her. Then the conversation flowed back into the
channel it had been following before her arrival.

" I mean to say, Vicar," said the Major, " that it would be better to
throw the four packs into two. Then you would have less squab-
bling and bickering about the different boundaries, and you would
kill the same number of hares with half the dogs."

" And you would throw a dozen men out of work, sir," replied
the Vicar, " in this parish and the next, and that is to be considered ; and about half the quantity of meat and horseflesh would
be consumed, which is another consideration. I tell you I believe
things are better as they are."

" I hear they got a large stern-cabin ; did they, Mr. Troubridge ?"
said the Doctor. " I hope they'll be comfortable. They should
have got more amidships if they could. They will be sick the longer
in their position."

" Poor boys ! " said Troubridge ; " they'll be more heart-sick than
stomach-sick, I expect. They'd half-repented before they sailed."

Mary sat down by Mrs. Buckley, and had half an hour's agreeable
conversation with her, till they all rose to go. Mrs. Buckley was
surprised at her sprightliness and good spirits, for she had expected
to find her in tears. The Doctor had met the Major in the morning, and told him what had passed the night before, so Mrs. Buckley
had come in to cheer Mary up for the loss of her lover, and to her
surprise found her rather more merry than usual. This made the
good lady suspect at once that Mary did not treat the matter very
seriously, or else was determined to defy her father, which, as Mrs.
Buckley reflected, she was perfectly able to do, being rich in her
own right, and of age. So when she was putting on her shawl to
go home, she kissed Mary, and said kindly,—

" My love, I hope you will always honour and obey your father,
and I am sure you will always, under all circumstances, remember
that I am your true friend. Good night."

And having bidden her good night, Mary went in. The Doctor was gone with the Major, but Tom Troubridge sat still before the fire, and as she came in was just finishing off one of his thundering fits of laughter at something that the Vicar had said.

"My love," said the Vicar, "I am so sorry you have been poorly, though you look better to-night. Your dear aunt has been to Tom's room, so there is nothing to do, but to sit down and talk to us."

"Why, cousin Tom," she said, laughing, "I had quite forgc' you; at least, quite forgot you were going to stay here. Why, what a time it is since I saw you."

"Isn't it?" he replied; "such a very long time. If I remember right, we met last out at the gate. Let's see. How long was that ago?"

"You ought to remember," she replied; "you're big enough. Well, good night. I'm going to bed."

She went to her room, but not to bed. She sat in the window, looking at the stars, pale in the full moonlight, wondering. Wondering what George was doing. Wondering whether she would listen to his audacious proposal. And wondering, lastly, what on earth her father would say if she did.

CHAPTER X.

IN WHICH WE SEE A GOOD DEAL OF MISCHIEF BREWING.

A MONTH went on, and May was well advanced. The lanes had grown dark and shadowy with their summer bravery; the banks were a rich mass of verdure once more, starred with wild-rose and eglantine; and on the lesser woodland stream, the king fern was again concealing the channel with brilliant golden fronds; while brown bare thorn-thickets, through which the wind had whistled savagely all winter, were now changed into pleasant bowers, where birds might build and sing.

A busy month this had been for the Major. Fishing every day, and pretty near all day, determined, as he said, to make the most of it, for fear it should be his last year. There was a beaten path worn through the growing grass all down the side of the stream by his sole exertions; and now the May-fly was coming, and there would be no more fishing in another week, so he worked harder than ever. Mrs. Buckley used to bring down her son and heir, and sit under an oak by the river-side, sewing. Pleasant, long days they were when dinner would be brought down to the old tree, and she would spend the day there, among the long meadow-grass, purple and yellow with flowers, bending under the soft west wind. Pleasant to hear the corncrake by the hedge-side, or the moorhen in the water. But pleasantest of all was the time when her husband, tired of fishing, would come and sit beside her, and the boy, throwing his lately-petted flowers to the wind, would run crowing to the spotted beauties which his father had laid out for him on the grass.

The Vicar was busy in his garden, and the Doctor was often helping him, although the most of his time was spent in natural history, to which he seemed entirely devoted. One evening they had been employed rather later than usual, and the Doctor was just gone, when the Vicar turned round and saw that his sister was come out, with her basket and scissors, to gather a fresh bouquet for the drawing-room.

So he went to join her, and as he approached her he admired her with an affectionate admiration. Such a neat, trim figure, with the snow-white handkerchief over her head, and her white garden gloves; what a contrast to Mary, he thought; "Both good of their sort, though," he added.

"Good evening, brother," began Miss Thornton. "Was not that Dr. Mulhaus went from you just now?"

"Yes, my dear."

"You had letters of introduction to Dr. Mulhaus, when he came to reside in this village?" asked Miss Thornton.

"Yes; Lord C——, whom I knew at Oxford, recommended me to him."

"His real name, I daresay, is not Mulhaus. Do you know what his real name is, brother?"

How very awkward plain plump questions of this kind are. The Vicar would have liked to answer "No," but he could not tell a lie. He was also a very bad hand at prevaricating; so with a stammer, he said "Yes!"

"So do I!" said Miss Thornton.

"Good Lord, my dear, how did you find it out?"

"I recognised him the first instant I saw him, and was struck dumb. I was very discreet, and have never said a word even to you till now; and, lately, I have been thinking that you might know, and so I thought I would sound you."

"I suppose you saw him when you were with her ladyship in Paris, in '14?"

"Yes; often," said Miss Thornton. "He came to the house several times. How well I remember the last. The dear girls and I were in the conservatory in the morning, and all of a sudden we heard the door thrown open, and two men coming towards us talking from the breakfast-room. We could not see them for the plants but when we heard the voice of one of them, the girls got into a terrible flutter, and I was very much frightened myself. However, there was no escape, so we came round the corner on them as bold as we could, and there was this Dr. Mulhaus, as we call him, walking with him."

" With him ?—with who ? "

" The Emperor Alexander, my dear, whose voice we had recognised ; I thought you would have known whom I meant."

" My dear love," said the Vicar, " I hope you reflect how sacred that is, and what a good friend I should lose if the slightest hint as to who he was, were to get among the gentry round. You don't think he has recognised you ? "

" How is it likely, brother, that he would remember an English governess, whom he never saw but three times, and never looked at once ? I have often wondered whether the Major recognised him."

" No ; Buckley is a Peninsular man, and although at Waterloo, never went to Paris. Lans—Mulhaus, I mean, was not present at Waterloo. So they never could have met. My dear discreet old sister, what tact you have ! I have often said to myself, when I have seen you and he together, ' If she only knew who he was ;'— and to think of your knowing all the time. Ha ! ha ! ha ! That's very good."

" I have lived long where tact is required, my dear brother. See, there goes young Mr. Hawker ! "

" I'd sooner see him going home than coming here. Now, I'd go out for a turn in the lanes, but I know I should meet half a dozen couples courting, as they call it. Bah ! So I'll stay in the garden."

The Vicar was right about the lanes being full of lovers. Never a vista that you looked down but what you saw a ghostly pair, walking along side by side. Not arm in arm, you know. The man has his hands in his pockets, and walks a few feet off the woman. They never speak to one another—I think I don't go too far in saying that. I have met them and overtaken them, and come sharp round corners on to them, but I never heard them speak to one another. I have asked the young men themselves whether they ever said anything to their sweethearts, and those young men have answered, " No ; that they didn't know as they did." So that I am inclined to believe that they are contented with that silent utterance of the heart which is so superior to the silly whisperings one hears on dark ottomans in drawing-rooms.

But the Vicar had a strong dislike to lovers' walks. He was a practical man, and had studied parish statistics for some years, so that his opinion is entitled to respect. He used to ask, why an honest girl should not receive her lover at her father's house, or in broad daylight, and many other impertinent questions which we won't go into, but which many a west-country parson has asked before, and never got an answer to.

Of all pleasant places in the parish, surely one of the pleasantest for a meeting of this kind was the old oak at the end of Hawker's plantation, where George met Nelly a night we know of. So quiet and lonely, and such pleasant glimpses down long oaken glades, with a bright carpet of springing fern. Surely there will be a couple here this sweet May evening.

So there is! Walking this way too! George Hawker is one of them; but we can't see who the other is. Who should it be but Mary, though, with whom he should walk, with his arm round her waist talking so affectionately. But see, she raises her head. Why! that is not Mary. That is old Jewel's dowdy, handsome, brazen-faced grandaughter.

"Now I'm going home to supper, Miss Jenny," he says. "So you pack off, or you'll have your amiable mother asking after you. By-the-bye, your sister's going to be married, ain't she?"

He referred to her elder sister—the one that the Vicar and the Doctor saw nursing a baby the night that old Jewel died.

"Yes," replied the girl. "Her man's going to have her at last; that's his baby she's got, you know; and it seems he'll sooner make her work for keeping it, than pay for it hisself. So they're going to be married; better late than never."

George left her and went in; into the gloomy old kitchen, now darkening rapidly. There sat Madge before the fire, in her favourite attitude, with her chin on her hand and her elbow on her knee.

"Well, old woman," said he, "where's the old man?"

"Away to Colyton fair," she answered.

"I hope he'll have the sense to stay there to-night, then," said George. "He'll fall off his horse in a fit coming home drunk some of these nights, and be found dead in a ditch!"

"Good thing for you if he was!"

"May be," said George; "but I'd be sorry for him, too!"

"You would," she said laughing. "Why, you young fool, you'd be better off in fifty ways!"

"Why, you unnatural old vixen," said he indignantly, "do you miscall a man for caring for his own father? Aye, and not such a bad 'un either; and that's a thing I'm best judge of!"

"He's been a good father to you, George, and I like you the better, lad, for speaking up for him. He's an awful old rascal, my boy, but you'll be a worse if you live!"

"Now, stop that talk of yours, Madge, and don't go on like a mad woman, or else we shall quarrel; and that I don't want, for I've got something to tell you. I want your help, old girl!"

"Aye, and you'll get it, my pretty boy; though you never tell me aught till you are forced."

" Well, I'm going to tell you something now ; so keep your ears open. Madge, where is the girl ? "

" Up-stairs."

" Where's the man ? "

" Outside, in the stable, doing down your horse. Bend over the fire, and whisper in my ear, lad ! "

" Madge, old girl," he whispered, as they bent their heads together,—" I've wrote the old man's name where I oughtn't to have done."

" What ! again ! " she answered. " Three times ! For God's sake, mind what you are at, George."

" Why," said he, astonished, " did you know I'd done it before ? "

" Twice I know of," she said. " Once last year, and once last month. How do you think he'd have been so long without finding it out if it hadn't been for me ? And what a fool you were not to tell me before. Why, you must be mad. I as near let the cat out of the bag coming over that last business in the book without being ready for it, as anything could be. However, it's all right at present. But what's this last ? "

" Why, the five hundred. I only did it twice."

" You mustn't do it again, George. You were a fool ever to do it without me. We are hardly safe now, if he should get talking to the bank people. However, he never goes there, and you must take care he don't."

" I say, Madge," said George, " what would he do if he found it out ? "

" I couldn't answer for him," said she. " He likes you best of anything next his money ; and sometimes I am afraid he wouldn't spare even you if he knew he had been robbed. You might make yourself safe for any storm, if you liked."

" How ? "

" Marry that little doll Thornton, and get her money. Then, if it came to a row, you could square it up."

" Well," said George, " I am pushing that on. The old man won't come round, and I want her to go off with me, but she can't get her courage up yet."

" Well, at all events," said Madge, " you should look sharp. There's a regular tight-laced mob about her, and they all hate you. There's that Mrs. Buckley. Her conversation will be very different from yours, and she'll see the difference, and get too proud for the like of you. That woman's a real lady, and that's very dangerous, for she treats her like an equal. Just let that girl get over her first fancy for you, and she'll care no more about you than nothing. Get hold of her before she's got tired of you."

" And there's another thing," said George. " That Tom Troubridge is staying there again."

" That's very bad," said Madge. " She is very likely to take a fancy to him. He's a fine young fellow. You get her to go off with you. I'll find the money, somehow. Here comes the old man."

Old Hawker came in half-drunk and sulky.

" Why, George," he said ; " you at home. I thought you'd have been down, hanging about the parson's. You don't get on very fast with that girl, lad. I thought you'd have had her by now. You're a fool, boy."

He reeled up to bed, and left the other two in the kitchen.

" George," said Madge, " tell us what you did with that last money."

" I ain't going to tell you," he answered.

" Ha, ha ! " she said ; " you hadn't need to hide anything from me now."

" Well, I like to tell you this least of all," he said. " That last money went to hush up the first matter."

" Did any one know of the first matter, then ? " said Madge aghast.

" Yes ; the man who put me up to it."

" Who was that ? "

" No one you know. William Lee of Belston."

" No one I know," she answered sarcastically. " Not know my old sweetheart, Bill Lee of Belston. And I the only one that knew him when he came back. Well, I've kept that to myself, because no good was to be got by peaching on him, and a secret's always worth money. Why, lad, I could have sent that man abroad again quicker than he come, if I had a-wanted. Why hadn't you trusted me at first ? You'd a-saved five hundred pound. You'll have him back as soon as that's gone."

" He'd better mind himself, then," said George vindictively.

" None o' that now," said Madge ; " that's what you were after the other night with your gun. But nothing came of it ; I saw that in your face when you came home. Now get off to bed ; and if Bill Lee gives you any more trouble, send him to me."

He went to bed, but instead of sleeping lay thinking.

" It would be a fine thing," he thought, " to get her and her money. I am very fond of her for her own sake, but then the money would be the making of me. I ought to strike while the iron is hot. Who knows but what Nell might come gandering back in one of her tantrums, and spoil everything. Or some of the other girls might get talking. And this cursed cheque, too ; that ought to be provided against. What a fool I was not to tell Madge about it before. I wonder whether she is game to come, though I think she is ; she has been very tender lately. It don't look as if she was getting tired of me, though she might take a fancy into her head about Troubridge. I daresay her father is putting him up to it ; though, indeed, that would be sure to set her against him. If he hadn't done that with Stockbridge, she'd have married him, I believe. Well, I'll see her to-morrow night, and carry on like mad. Terribly awkward it will be, though, if she won't. However, we'll see. There's a way to make her;" and so he fell asleep.

As Somebody would have it, the very next day the Vicar and Mary had a serious quarrel. Whether his digestion was out of order; whether the sight of so many love-couples passing his gate the night before had ruffled him and made him bilious; or whether some one was behindhand with his tithe, we shall never know. Only we know, that shortly after dinner they disagreed about some trifle, and Mary remained sulky all the afternoon; and that at tea-time, driven on by pitiless fate, little thinking what was hanging over him, he made some harsh remark, which brought down a flood of tears. Whereat, getting into a passion, he told Mary, somewhat unjustly, that she was always sulking, and was making his life miserable. That it was time that she was married. That Tom Troubridge was an excellent young fellow, and that he considered it was her duty to turn her attention immediately to gaining his affections.

Mary said, with tearful indignation, that it was notorious that he was making love to Miss Burrit of Paiskow. And that if he wasn't, she'd never, never, think of him, for that he was a great, lumbering, stupid, stupid fool. There now.

Then the Vicar got into an unholy frame of mind, and maddened by Mary's tears, and the sight of his sister wiping her frightened face with her handkerchief, said, with something like an asseveration, that she was always at it. That she was moping about, and colloguing with that infamous young scoundrel, Hawker. That he would not have it. That if he found him lurking about his premises, he'd either break his neck himself, or find some one who could; and a great deal more frantic nonsense, such as weak men generally indulge in when they get in a passion; much better left unsaid at any time, but which on this occasion, as the reader knows, was calculated to be ruinous.

Mary left the room, and went to her own. She was in a furious passion against her father, against all the world. She sat on the bed for a time, and cried herself quiet. It grew dark, and she lit a candle, and put it in the right corner of the window, and soon after, wrapping a shawl around her, she slipped down the back-stairs, and went into the croft.

Not long before she heard a low whistle, to which she replied, and in a very few minutes felt George's arm round her waist, and his cheek against hers.

" I knew you would not disappoint me to-night, my love," he began. " I have got something particular to say to you. You seem out of sorts to-night, my dear. It's not my fault, is it ? "

"Not yours, George. Oh no," she said. "My father has been very cruel and unjust to me, and I have been in a great passion and very miserable. I am so glad you came to-night, that I might tell you how very unhappy I was."

"Tell me everything, my love. Don't keep back any secrets from me."

"I won't indeed, George. I'll tell you everything. Though some of it will make you very angry. My father broke out about you at tea-time, and said that you were hanging about the place, and that he wouldn't have it. And then he said that I ought to marry Tom Troubridge, and that I said I'd never do. And then he went on worse again. He's quite changed lately, George. I ain't at all happy with him."

"The cure is in your own hands, Mary. Come off with me. I can get a licence, and we could be married in a week or so, or two. Then, what follows? Why, your father is very angry. He is that at present. But he'll of course make believe he is in a terrible way. Well, in a few weeks he'd see it was no use carrying on. That his daughter had married a young man of property, who was very fond of her, and as she was very fond of. And that matters might be a deal worse. That a bird in hand is worth two in the bush. And so he'll write a kind affectionate letter to his only child, and say that he forgives her husband for her sake. That's how the matter will end, depend upon it."

"Oh, George, George! if I could only think so."

"Can you doubt it? Use your reason, my dear, and ask yourself what he would gain by holding out. You say he's so fond of you."

"Oh, I know he is."

"Well, my darling, he wouldn't show it much if he was angry very long. You don't know what a change it will make when the thing's once done. When I am his son-in-law he'll be as anxious to find out that I'm a saint as he is now to make me out a sinner. Say yes, my girl."

"I am afraid, George."

"Of nothing. Come, you are going to say yes, now."

"But when, George? Not yet?"

"To-morrow night."

"Impossible! Sunday evening?"

"The better the day the better the deed. Come, no refusal now, it is too late, my darling. At ten o'clock I shall be here, under your window. One kiss more, my own, and good night."

CHAPTER XI.

IN WHICH THE VICAR PREACHES A FAREWELL SERMON.

WHO has not seen the misery and despair often caused in a family by the senseless selfishness of one of its members? Who has not felt enraged at such times, to think that a man or woman should presume on the affection and kindheartedness of their relatives, and yet act as if they were wholly without those affections themselves? And, lastly, who of us all is guiltless of doing this? Let him that is without sin among us cast the first stone.

The Spring sun rose on the Sabbath morning, as if no trouble were in store for any mortal that day. The Vicar rose with the sun, for he had certain arrears of the day's sermons to get through, and he was in the habit of saying that his best and clearest passages were written with his window open, in the brisk morning air.

But although the air was brisk and pleasant this morning, and all nature was in full glory, the inspiration did not come to the Vicar quite so readily as usual. In fact, he could not write at all, and at one time was thinking of pleading ill health, and not preaching, but afterwards changed his mind, and patched the sermons up somehow, making both morning and afternoon five minutes shorter than usual.

He felt queer and dull in the head this morning. And, after breakfast, he walked to church with his sister and daughter, not speaking a word. Miss Thornton was rather alarmed, he looked so dull and stupid. But Mary set it all down to his displeasure at her.

She was so busy with far other thoughts at church that she did not notice the strange halting way in which her father read the service—sometimes lisping, sometimes trying twice before he could pronounce a word at all. But, after church, Miss Thornton noticed it to her; and she also noticed, as they stood waiting for him under the lychgate, that he passed through the crowd of neighbours, who stood as usual round the porch to receive him, without a word, merely raising his hat in salutation. Conduct so strange that Miss Thornton began to cry, and said she was sure her brother was very ill. But Mary said it was because he was still angry with her that he spoke to no one, and that when he had forgotten his cause of offence he would be the same again.

At lunch, the Vicar drank several glasses of wine, which seemed to do him good; and by the time he had, to Miss Thornton's great astonishment, drunk half a bottle, he was quite himself again. Mary was all this time in her room, and the Vicar asked for her. But Miss Thornton said she was not very well.

"Oh, I remember," said the Vicar, "I quarrelled with her last night. I was quite in the wrong, but, my dear sister, all yesterday and to-day I have been so nervous, I have not known what I said or did. I shall keep myself up to the afternoon service with wine, and to-morrow we will see the Doctor. Don't tell Mary I'm ill. She will think she is the cause, poor girl."

Afternoon service went off well enough. When Mary heard his old familiar voice strong, clear, and harmonious, filling the aisles and chapels of the beautiful old church, she was quite reassured. He seemed stronger than usual even, and never did the congregation listen to a nobler or better sermon from his lips, than the one they heard that spring afternoon ; the last, alas, they ever had from their kind old Vicar.

Mary could not listen to it. The old innocent interest she used to have in her father's success in preaching was gone. As of old, sitting beneath the carved oak screen, she heard the sweet simple harmony of the evening hymn roll up, and die in pleasant echoes among the lofty arches overhead. As of old, she could see through the rich traceried windows the moor sloping far away, calm and peaceful, bathed in a misty halo of afternoon sunshine. All these familiar sights and sounds were the same, but she herself was different. She was about to break rudely through from the old world of simple routine and homely pleasure, and to cast herself unthinking into a new world of passion and chance, and take the consequences of such a step, let them be what they might. She felt as if she was the possessor of some guilty secret, and felt sometimes as if some one would rise in church and denounce her. How would all these quiet folks talk of her to-morrow morning? That was not to be thought of. She must harden her heart and think of nothing. Only that to-morrow she would be far away with her lover.

Poor Mary ! many a woman, and many a man, who sat so quiet and calm in the old church that afternoon, had far guiltier secrets than any you ever had, to trouble them, and yet they all drank, slept, and died, as quietly as many honest and good men. Poor girl ! let us judge as kindly of her as we can, for she paid a fearful penalty for her self-will. She did but break through the prejudices of her education, we may say ; and if she was undutiful, what girls are not, under the influence of passion? If such poor excuses as these will cause us to think more kindly of her, let us make them, and leave the rest to God. Perhaps, brother, you and I may stand in a position to have excuses made for us, one day ; therefore, we will be charitable.

My lord was at church that afternoon, a very rare circumstance, for he was mostly at his great property in the north, and had lately been much abroad for his health. So when Miss Thornton and Mary joined the Vicar in the main aisle, and the three went forth into the churchyard, they found the villagers drawn respectfully back upon the graves, and his lordship waiting in close confabulation with farmer Wreford, to receive the Vicar as he came out.

A tall, courtly, grizzled-looking man he was, with clear grey eyes, and a modulated harmonious voice. Well did their lordships of the upper-house know that voice, when after a long sleepy debate it aroused them from ambrosial slumbers, with biting sarcasm, and most disagreeably told truths. And most heartily did a certain proportion of their lordships curse the owner of that voice, for a talented, eloquent, meddlesome innovator. But on all his great estates he was adored by the labourers and town's-folk, though hated by the farmers and country 'squires; for he was the earliest and fiercest of the reform and free-trade warriors.

He came up to the Vicar with a pleasant smile. "I have to thank you, Mr. Thornton, for a most charming sermon, though having the fault common to all good things, of being too short. Miss Thornton, I hope you are quite well; I saw Lady D—— the other day, and she begged that when I came down here, I would convey her kindest love to you. I think she mentioned that she was about to write to you."

"I received a letter from her ladyship last week," said Miss Thornton; "informing me that dear Lady Fanny had got a son and heir."

"Happy boy," said my Lord; "fifty thousand a year, and nothing to do for it, unless he likes. Besides a minority of at least ten years; for L—— is getting very shaky, Miss Thornton, and is still devotely given to stewed mushrooms. Nay, my dear lady, don't look distressed, she will make a noble young dowager. This must be your daughter, Mr. Thornton—pray introduce me."

Mary was introduced, and his Lordship addressed a few kindly commonplaces to her, to which she replied with graceful modesty. Then he demanded of the Vicar, "where is Dr. Mulhaus, has he been at church this afternoon?"

At that moment the Doctor, attended by the old clerk, was head and shoulders into the old oak chest that contained the parish registers, looking for the book of burials for sixteen hundred and something. Not being able to get to the bottom, he got bodily in, as into a bath, and after several dives succeeded in fishing it up from the bottom, and standing there absorbed for a few minutes, up to his middle in dusty parchments and angry moths, he got his finger on a particular date, and dashed out of church, book in hand, and hatless, crying, "Vicar, Vicar!" just as the villagers had cleared off, and my lord was moving away with the Vicar to the parsonage, to take dinner.

When his Lordship saw the wild dusty figure come running out of the church porch with the parish register in his hand, and no hat on his head, he understood the position immediately. He sat down on a tombstone, and laughed till he could laugh no longer.

"No need to tell me," he said through his laughter, "that he is unchanged; just as mad and energetic as ever, at whatever he takes in hand, whether getting together impossible ministries, or searching the parish-register of an English village. How do you do, my dear old friend?"

"And how do you do, old democrat?" answered the Doctor. "Politics seem to agree with you; I believe you would die without vexation—just excuse me a moment. Look you here, you infidel," to the Vicar, showing him the register; "there's his name plain— 'Burrows, Curate of this parish, 1698.'—Now what do you say?"

The Vicar acquiesced with a sleepy laugh, and proposed moving homewards. Miss Thornton hoped that the Doctor would join them at dinner as usual. The Doctor said of course, and went back to fetch his hat, my Lord following him into the church. When the others had gone down the hill, and were waiting for the nobleman and the Doctor at the gate, Miss Thornton watched the two coming down the hill. My Lord stopped the Doctor, and eagerly demonstrated something to him with his forefinger on the palm of his hand; but the Doctor only shook his head, and then the pair moved on.

My Lord made himself thoroughly agreeable at dinner, as did also the Doctor. Mary was surprised too at the calm highbred bearing of her aunt, the way she understood and spoke of every subject of conversation, and the deference with which they listened to her. It was a side of her aunt's character she had never seen before, and she felt it hard to believe that that intellectual dignified lady, referred to on all subjects, was the old maid she had been used to laugh at, and began to feel that she was in an atmosphere far above what she was accustomed to.

"All this is above me," she said to herself; "let them live in this sphere who are accustomed to it, I have chosen wiser, out of the rank in which I have been brought up. I would sooner be George Hawker's wife than sit there, crushed and bored by their highflown talk."

Soon after dinner she retired with her aunt; they did not talk much when they were alone, so Mary soon retired to her room, and having made a few very slight preparations, sat down at the window. The time was soon to come, but it was very cold; the maids were out, as they always were on Sunday evening, and there was a fire in the kitchen,—she would go and sit there—so down she went.

She wished to be alone, so when she saw a candle burning in the kitchen she was disappointed, but went in nevertheless. My Lord's groom, who had been sitting before the fire, rose up and saluted her. A handsome young man, rather square and prominent about the jaws, but nevertheless foolish and amiable looking. The sort of man one would suppose, who, if his lord were to tell him to jump into the pit Tophet, would pursue one of two courses, either jump in himself, without further to do, or throw his own brother in with profuse apologies. From the top of his sleek round head to the sole of his perfect top-boot, the model and living exponent of what a servant should be—fit to be put into a case and ticketed as such.

He saluted her as she came in, and drawing a letter from his hat, put it into her astonished hands. "My orders were, Miss, that I was not to give it to you unless I saw you personally."

She thanked him and withdrew to read it. It was a scrawl from George Hawker, the first letter she had ever received from him, and ran as follows:—

" My Heart's Darling,

" I shall be in the croft to-night, according to promise, ready to make you the happiest woman in England, so I know you won't fail. My Lord is coming to church this afternoon, and will be sure to dine with you. So I send this present by his groom, Sam; a good young chap, which I have known since he was so high, and like well, only that he is soft, which is not to his disadvantage.

G. H."

She was standing under the lamp reading this when she heard the dining-room door open, and the men coming out from their wine. She slipped into the room opposite, and stood listening in the dark. She could see them as they came out. There was my Lord and the Doctor first, and behind came Major Buckley, who had dropped in, as his custom was, on Sunday evening, and who must have arrived while she was upstairs. As they passed the door, inside which she stood, his Lordship turned round and said:—

" I tell you what, my dear Major, if that old Hawker was a tenant of mine, I'd take away his lease, and, if I could, force him to leave the parish. One man of that kind does incalculable harm in a village, by lowering the tone of the morality of the place. That's the use of a great landlord if he does his duty. He can punish evildoers whom the law does not reach."

" Don't say anything more about him," said the Doctor in a low voice. " It's a tender subject in this house."

" It is, eh !" said my Lord; " thanks for the hint, good—bah ! —Mulhaus. Let us go up and have half an hour with Miss Thornton before I go !"

They went up, and then her father followed. He seemed flushed, and she thought he must have been drinking too much wine. After they were in the drawing-room, she crept upstairs and listened. They were all talking except her father. It was half-past nine, and she wished they would go. So she went into her bedroom and waited. The maids had come home, and she heard them talking to the groom in the kitchen. At ten o'clock the bell was rung, and my Lord's horse ordered. Soon he went, and not long afterwards the Major and the Doctor followed. Then she saw Miss Thornton go to her room, and her father walk slowly to his; and all was still throughout the house.

She took her hat and shawl and slipped down stairs shoeless into her father's study. She laid a note on his chimney-piece, which she had written in the morning, and opening the back-door fled swiftly forth, not daring to look behind her. Quickly, under the blinking stars, under the blooming apple-trees, out to the croft-gate, and there was George waiting impatiently for her, according to promise.

"I began to fear you were not coming, my dear. Quick, jump!"

She scrambled over the gate, and jumped into his arms; he hurried her down the lane about a hundred yards, and then became aware of a dark object in the middle of the road.

"That's my gig, my dear. Once in that, and we are soon in Exeter. All right, Bob?"

"All right!" replied a strange voice in the dark, and she was lifted into the gig quickly; in another moment George was beside her, and they were flying through the dark steep lanes at a dangerous speed.

The horse was a noble beast—the finest in the country side— and, like his driver, knew every stock and stone on the road; so that ere poor Mary had recovered her first flurry, they had crossed the red ford, and were four miles on the road towards the capital, and began to feel a little more cheerful, for she had been crying bitterly.

"Don't give way, Polly," said George.

"No fear of my giving way now, George. If I had been going to do that, I'd have done it before. Now tell us what you are going to do? I have left everything to you."

"I think we had better go straight on to London, my dear," he replied, "and get married by licence. We could never stop in Exeter; and if you feel up to it, I should like to get off by early coach to-morrow morning. What do you say?"

"By all means! Shall we be there in time?"

"Yes; two hours before the coach starts."

"Have you money enough, George?" she asked.

"Plenty!" he replied.

"If you go short, you must come to me, you know," she said.

They rattled through the broad streets of a small country town just as the moon rose. The noble minster, which had for many years been used as the parish church, slept quietly among the yews and gravestones; all the town was still; only they two were awake, flying, she thought, from the fellowship of all quiet men. Was her father asleep now? she wondered. What would Miss Thornton say in the morning? and many other things she was asking herself, when she was interrupted by George saying, "Only eight miles to Exeter; we shall be in by daybreak."

So they left Crediton Minster behind them, and rolled away along the broad road by the river, beneath the whispering poplars.

* * * * * *

As Miss Thornton was dressing herself next morning she heard the Vicar go down into his study as usual. She congratulated herself that he was better, from being up thus early, but determined, nevertheless, that he should see a doctor that day, who might meet and consult with Dr. Mulhaus.

Then she wondered why Mary had not been in. She generally came into her aunt's room to hook-and-eye her, as she called it; but not having come this morning, Miss Thornton determined to go to her, and accordingly went and rapped at her door.

No answer. "Could the girl have been fool enough?" thought Miss Thornton. "Nonsense! no! She must be asleep!"

She opened the door and went in. Everything tidy. The bed had not been slept in. Miss Thornton had been in at an elopement and a famous one, before; so she knew the symptoms in a moment. Well she remembered the dreadful morning when Lady Kate went off with Captain Brentwood, of the Artillery. Well she remembered the Countess going into hysterics. But this was worse than that; this touched her nearer home.

"Oh you naughty girl! Oh you wicked, ungrateful girl; to go and do such a thing at a time like this, when I've been watching the paralysis creeping over him day by day! How shall I tell him? How shall I ever tell him? He will have a stroke as sure as fate. He was going to have one without this. I dare not tell him till breakfast, and yet I ought to tell him at once. I was brought into the world to be driven mad by girls. Oh dear, I wish they were all boys, and we might send them to Eton and wash our hands of them. Well, I must leave crying, and prepare for telling him."

She went into his study, and at first could not see him; but he was there—a heap of black clothes lay on the hearthrug, and Miss Thornton running up, saw that it was her brother, speechless, senseless, clasping a letter in his hand.

She saw that the worst was come, and nerved herself for work, like a valiant soul as she was. She got him carried to his bed by the two sturdy maids, and sent an express for Dr. Mulhaus, and another for the professional surgeon. Then she took from her pocket the letter which she had found in the poor Vicar's hand, and, going to the window, read as follows:

"When you get this, father, I shall be many miles away. I have started to London with George Hawker, and God only knows whether you will see me again. Try to forgive me, father, and if not, forget that you ever had a daughter who was only born to give you trouble. —Your erring but affectionate Mary."

It will be seen by the reader that this unlucky letter, written in agitation and hurry, contained no allusion whatever to marriage, but rather left one to infer that she was gone with Hawker as his mistress. So the Vicar read it again and again, each time more mistily, till sense and feeling departed, and he lay before his hearth a hopeless paralytic.

At that moment Mary, beside George, was rolling through the fresh morning air, up the beautiful Exe valley. Her fears were gone with daylight and sunshine, and as he put his arm about her waist, she said,

" I am glad we came outside."

" Are you quite happy now ? " he asked.

" Quite happy ! "——

CHAPTER XII.

IN WHICH A NEW FACE IS INTRODUCED, BY MEANS OF A RAT AND A TERRIER.

FOR the first four weeks that the Vicar lay paralyzed, the neighbouring clergymen had done his duty ; but now arose a new difficulty at Drumston. Who was to do the duty while the poor Vicar lay there on his back speechless ?

" How," asked Miss Thornton of Tom Troubridge, " are we to make head against the dissenters now ? Let the duty lapse but one single week, my dear friend, and you will see the chapels overflowing once more. My brother has always had a hard fight to keep them to church, for they have a natural tendency to dissent here. And a great number don't care what the denominations are, so long as there is noise enough."

" If that is the case," answered Tom, " old Mark Hook's place of worship should pay best. I'd back them against Bedlam any day."

" They certainly make the loudest noise at a Revival," said Miss Thornton. " But what are we to do ? "

" That I am sure I don't know, my dearest auntie," said Troubridge, " but I am here, and my horse too, ready to go any amount of errands."

" I see no way," said Miss Thornton, " but to write to the Bishop."

" And I see no way else," said Tom, " unless you like to dress me up as a parson, and see if I would do."

Miss Thornton wrote to the Bishop, with whom she had some

acquaintance, and told him how her brother had been struck down with paralysis, and that the parish was unprovided for: that if he would send any gentleman he approved of, she would gladly receive him at Drumston.

Armed with this letter, Tom found himself, for the first time in his life, in an episcopal palace. A sleek servant in black opened the door with cat-like tread, and admitted him into a dark, warm hall; and on Tom's saying, in a hoarse whisper, as if he was in church, that he had brought a note of importance, and would wait for an answer, the man glided away, and disappeared through a spring-door, which swung to behind him. Tom thought it would have banged, but it didn't. Bishops' doors never bang.

Tom had a great awe for your peers spiritual. He could get on well enough with a peer temporal, particularly if that proud aristocrat happened to be in want of a horse; but a bishop was quite another matter.

So he sat rather uncomfortable in the dark, warm hall, listening to such dull sounds as could be heard in the gloomy mansion. A broad oak staircase led up from the hall into lighter regions, and there stood, on a landing above, a lean, wheezy old clock, all over brass knobs, which, as he looked on it, choked, and sneezed four.

But now there was a new sound in the house. An indecent, secular sound. A door near the top of the house was burst violently open, and there was a scuffle. A loud voice shouted twice unmistakeably and distinctly, "So-o, good bitch!" And then the astounded Tom heard the worrying of a terrier, and the squeak of a dying rat. There was no mistake about it; he heard the bones crack. Then he made out that a dog was induced to go into a room on false pretences, and deftly shut up there, and then he heard a heavy step descending the stairs towards him.

But, before there was time for the perpetrator of these sacrileges to come in sight, a side door opened, and the Bishop himself came forth with a letter in his hand (a mild, clever, gentlemanly-looking man he was too, Tom remarked) and said,—

"Pray is there not a messenger from Drumston here?"

Tom replied that he had brought a letter from his cousin the Vicar. He had rather expected to hear it demanded, "Where is the audacious man who has dared to penetrate these sacred shades?" and was agreeably relieved to find that the Bishop wasn't angry with him.

"Dear me," said the Bishop; "I beg a thousand pardons for keeping you in the hall; pray walk into my study."

So in he went and sat down. The Bishop resumed,—

"You are Mr. Thornton's cousin, sir?"

Tom bowed. "I am about the nearest relation he has besides his sister, my lord."

G

"Indeed," said the Bishop. "I have written to Miss Thornton to say that there is a gentleman, a relation of my own, now living in the house with me, who will undertake Mr. Thornton's duties, and I dare say, also, without remuneration. He has nothing to do at present.—Oh, here is the gentleman I spoke of!"

Here was the gentleman he spoke of, holding a dead rat by the tail, and crying out,—

"Look here, uncle; what did I tell you? I might have been devoured alive, had it not been for my faithful Fly, your enemy."

He was about six feet or nearly so in height, with a highly intellectual though not a handsome face. His brown hair, carelessly brushed, fell over a forehead both broad and lofty, beneath which shone a pair of bold, clear grey eyes. The moment Troubridge saw him he set him down in his own mind as a "goer," by which he meant a man who had go, or energy, in him. A man, he thought, who was thrown away as a parson.

The Bishop, ringing the bell, began again, "This is my nephew, Mr. Frank Maberly."

The sleek servant entered.

"My dear Frank, pray give that rat to Sanders, and let him take it away. I don't like such things in the study."

"I only brought it to convince you, uncle," said the other. "Here you are, Sanders!"

But Sanders would have as soon shaken hands with the Pope. He rather thought the rat was alive; and taking the tongs, he received the beast at a safe distance, while Tom saw a smile of contempt pass over the young curate's features.

"You'd make a good missionary, Sanders," said he; and turning to Troubridge, continued, "Pray excuse this interlude, sir. You don't look as if you would refuse to shake me by my ratty hand."

Tom thought he would sooner shake hands with him than fight him, and was so won by Maberly's manner, that he was just going to say so, when he recollected the presence he was in, and blushed scarlet.

"My dear Frank," resumed his uncle, "Mr. Thornton of Drumston is taken suddenly ill, and I want you to go over and do his duties for him till he is better."

"Most certainly, my dear lord; and when shall I go?"

"Say to-morrow; will that suit your household, sir?" said the Bishop.

Tom replied, "Yes, certainly," and took his leave. Then the Bishop, turning to Frank, said,—

"The living of Drumston, nephew, is in my gift; and if Mr. Thornton does not recover, as is very possible, I shall give it to you. I wish you, therefore, to go to Drumston, and become acquainted with your future parishioners. You will find Miss Thornton a most charming old lady."

Frank Maberly was the second son of a country gentleman of good property, and was a very remarkable character. His uncle had always said of him, that whatever he chose to take up he would be first in ; and his uncle was right. At Eton he was not only the best cricketer and runner, but decidedly the best scholar of his time. At Cambridge, for the first year, he was probably the noisiest man in his college, though he never lived what is called " hard ; " but in the second year he took up his books once more, and came forth third wrangler and first class, and the second day after the class-list came out, made a very long score in the match with Oxford. Few men were more popular, though the fast men used to call him crotchety ; and on some subjects, indeed, he was very impatient of contradiction. And most of his friends were a little disappointed when they heard of his intention of going into the Church. His father went so far as to say,—

" My dear Frank, I always thought you would have been a lawyer."

" I'd sooner be a———well, never mind what."

" But you might have gone into the army, Frank," said his father.

" I am going into the army, sir," he said ; " into the army of Christ."

Old Mr. Maberly was at first shocked by this last expression from a son who rarely or never talked on religious matters, and told his wife so that night.

" But," he added, " since I've been thinking of it, I'm sure Frank meant neither *blague* nor irreverence. He is in earnest. I never knew him tell a lie ; and since he was six years old he has known how to call a spade a spade."

" He'll make a good parson," said the mother.

" He'll be first in that, as he is in everything else," said the father.

" But he'll never be a bishop," said Mrs. Maberly.

" Why not ? " said the husband, indignantly.

" Because, as you say yourself, husband, he will call a spade a spade."

" Bah ! you are a radical," said the father.   " Go to sleep."

At the time of John Thornton's illness, he had been ordained about a year and a half. He had got a title for orders, as a curate, in a remote part of Devon, but had left it in consequence of a violent disagreement with his rector, in which he had been most fully borne out by his uncle, who, by the bye, was not the sort of man who would have supported his own brother, had he been in the wrong. Since then Frank Maberly had been staying with his uncle, and, as he expressed it, " working the slums " at Exeter.

Miss Thornton sat in the drawing-room at Drumston the day after Tom's visit to the Bishop, waiting dinner for the new Curate.

Tom and she had been wondering how he would come. Miss Thornton said, probably in the Bishop's carriage; but Tom was inclined to think he would ride over. The dinner time was past some ten minutes, when they saw a man in black put his hand on the garden-gate, vault over, and run breathless up to the hall-door. Tom had recognised him and dashed out to receive him, but ere he had time to say "good day" even, the new comer pulled out his watch, and having looked at it, said in a tone of vexation:—

"Twenty-one minutes, as near as possible; nay, a little over. By Jove! how pursy a fellow gets mewed up in town! How far do you call it, now, from the Buller Arms?"

"It is close upon four miles," said Tom, highly amused.

"So they told me," replied Frank Maberly. "I left my port-manteau there, and the landlord-fellow had the audacity to say in conversation that I couldn't run the four miles in twenty minutes. It's lucky a parson can't bet, or I should have lost my money. But the last mile is very much up-hill, as you must allow."

"I'll tell you what, sir," said Tom; "there isn't a man in this parish would go that four mile under twenty minutes. If any man could, I ought to know of it."

Miss Thornton had listened to this conversation with wonder not unmixed with amusement. At first she had concluded that the Bishop's carriage was upset, and that Frank was the breathless messenger sent forward to chronicle the mishap. But her tact soon showed the sort of person she had to deal with, for she was not unacquainted with the performances of public schoolboys. She laughed when she called to mind the *bouleversement* that used to take place when Lord Charles and Lord Frederick came home from Harrow, and invaded her quiet school-room. So she advanced into the passage to meet the new-comer with one of her pleasantest smiles.

"I must claim an old woman's privilege of introducing myself, Mr. Maberly," she said. "Your uncle was tutor to the B——s, when I was governess to the D——s; so we are old acquaintances."

"Can you forgive me, Miss Thornton?" he said, "for running up to the house in this lunatic sort of way? I am still half a school-boy, you know. What an old jewel she is!" he added to himself.

Tom said: "May I show you your room, Mr. Maberly?"

"If you please, do," said Frank; and added, "Get out, Fly; what are you doing here?"

But Miss Thornton interceded for the dog, a beautiful little black and tan terrier, whose points Tom was examining with profound admiration.

"That's a brave little thing, Mr. Maberly," said he, as he showed him to his room. "I should like to put in my name for a pup."

They stood face to face in the bed-room as he said this, and Frank, not answering him, said abruptly :—

" By Jove ! what a splendid man you are ! What do you weigh, now ? "

" Close upon eighteen stone, just now, I should think ; " said Tom.

" Ah, but you are carrying a little flesh," said Frank.

" Why, yes ; " said Tom. " I've been to London for a fortnight."

" That accounts for it," said Frank. " Many dissenters in this parish ? "

" A sight of all sorts," said Tom. " They want attracting to church here ; they don't go naturally, as they do in some parts."

" I see," said Frank ; " I suppose they'll come next Sunday though, to see the new parson ; my best plan will be to give them a stinger, so that they'll come again."

" Why, you see," said Tom, " it's got about that there'll be no service next Sunday, so they'll make an excuse for going to Meeting. Our best plan will be, for you and I to go about and let them know that there's a new minister. Then you'll get them together, and after that I leave it to you to keep them. Shall we go down to dinner ? "

They came together going out of the door, and Frank turned and said :—

" Will you shake hands with me ? I think we shall suit one another."

" Aye ! that we shall," said Tom heartily ; " you're a man's parson ; that's about what you are. But," he added, seriously ; " you wouldn't do among the old women, you know."

At dinner, Miss Thornton said, " I hope, Mr. Maberly, you are none the worse after your run ? Are you not afraid of such violent exercise bringing on palpitation of the heart ? "

" Not I, my dear madam," he said. " Let me make my defence for what, otherwise, you might consider mere boyish folly. I am passionately fond of athletic sports of all kinds, and indulge in them as a pleasure. No real man is without some sort of pleasure, more or less harmless. Nay, even your fanatic is a man who makes a pleasure and an excitement of religion. My pleasures are very harmless ; what can be more harmless than keeping this shell of ours in the highest state of capacity for noble deeds ? I know," he said, turning to Tom, " what the great temptation is that such men as you or I have to contend against. It is ' the pride of life ; ' but if we know that and fight against it, how can it prevail against us ? It is easier conquered than the lust of the flesh, or the lust of the eye, though some will tell you that I can't construe my Greek Testament, and that the ' pride of life ' means something very different. I hold my opinion, however, in spite of them. Then, again, although

I have taken a good degree (not so good as I might, though), I consider that I have only just begun to study. Consequently, I read hard still, and shall continue to do so the next twenty years, please God. I find my head the clearer, and my intellect more powerful in consequence of the good digestion produced by exercise; so I mean to use it till I get too fat, which will be a long while first." .

"Ain't you afraid," said Tom, laughing. " of offending some of your weaker brothers' consciences, by running four miles, because a publican said you couldn't?"

"Disputing with a publican might be an error of judgment," said Frank. "Bah! *might* be—it *was;* but with regard to running four miles—no. It is natural and right that a man at five-and-twenty should be both able and willing to run four miles, a parson above all others, as a protest against effeminacy. With regard to consciences, those very tender-conscienced men oughtn't to want a parson at all."

Miss Thornton had barely left the room, to go up to the Vicar, leaving Tom and Frank Maberly over their wine, when the hall-door was thrown open, and the well-known voice of the Doctor was heard exclaiming in angry tones :—

"If! sir, if! always at if's. ' If Blucher had destroyed the bridge,' say you, as if he ever meant to be such a Vandal. And if he had meant to do it, do you think that fifty Wellesleys in one would have stayed him? No, sir; and if he had destroyed every bridge on the Seine, sir, he would have done better than to be overruled by the counsels of Wellington (glory go with him, however! He was a good man). And why, forsooth?—because the English bore the brunt at Waterloo, in consequence of the Prussians being delayed by muddy roads."

"And Ligny," said the laughing voice of Major Buckley. "Oh, Doctor, dear! I like to make you angry, because then your logic is so very outrageous. You are like the man who pleaded not guilty of murder : first, because he hadn't done it; secondly, that he was drunk when he did it; and thirdly, that it was a case of mistaken identity."

"Ha, ha!" laughed the Doctor, merrily, recovering his good humour in a moment. "That's an Irish story for a thousand pounds. There's nothing English about that. Ha! ha!".

They were presented to Frank as the new Curate. The Doctor, after a courteous salutation, put on his spectacles, and examined him carefully. Frank looked at him all the time with a quiet smile, and in the end the Doctor said—

"Allow me the privilege of shaking hands with you, sir. Shall I be considered rude if I say that I seldom or never saw a finer head than yours on a man's shoulders? And judging by the face, it is well lined."

" Like a buck-basket," said Frank, " full of dirty linen. Plenty of it, and of some quality, but not in a state fit for use yet. I will have it washed up, and wear such of it as is worth soon."

The Doctor saw he had found a man after his own heart, and it was not long before Frank and he were in the seventh heaven of discussion. Meanwhile, the Major had drawn up alongside of Tom, and said—

" Any news of the poor little dove that has left the nest, old friend ?"

" Yes," said Tom, eagerly ; " we have got a letter. Good news, too."

" Thank God for that," said the Major. " And where are they?"

" They are now at Brighton."

" What's that ? " said the Doctor, turning round. " Any news?"

They told him, and then it became necessary to tell Frank Maberly what he had not known before, that the Vicar had a daughter who had " gone off."

" One of the prettiest, sweetest creatures, Mr. Maberly," said the Major, " that you ever saw in your life. None of us, I believe, knew how well we loved her till she was gone."

" And a very remarkable character, besides," said the Doctor. " Such a force of will as you see in few women of her age. Obscured by passion and girlish folly, it seemed more like obstinacy to us. But she has a noble heart, and, when she has outlived her youthful fancies, I should not be surprised if she turned out a very remarkable woman."

CHAPTER XIII.

THE DISCOVERY.

ONE morning the man who went once a-week from old Hawker's, at the Woodlands, down to the post, brought back a letter, which he delivered to Madge at the door. She turned it over and examined it more carefully than she generally did the old man's letters, for it was directed in a clerk-like hand, and was sealed with a big and important-looking seal, and when she came to examine this seal, she saw that it bore the words " B. and F. Bank." " So, they are at it again, are they ? " she said. " The deuce take 'em, I say : though for that matter I can't exactly blame the folks for looking after their own. Well, there's no mistake about one thing, he must see this letter, else some of 'em will be coming over and blowing the whole thing. He will ask me to read it for him, and

I'll do so, right an end. Lord, what a breeze there'll be ! I hope I shall be able to pull my lad through, though it very much depends on the old 'un's temper. However, I shall soon know."

Old Hawker was nearly blind, and although an avaricious, suspicious old man, as a general rule, trusted implicitly on ordinary occasions to George and Madge in the management of his accounts, reflecting, with some reason, that it could not be their interest to cheat him. Of late, however, he had been uneasy in his mind. Madge, there was no denying, had got through a great deal more money than usual, and he was not satisfied with her account of where it had gone. She, we know, was in the habit of supplying George's extravagances in a way which tried all her ingenuity to hide from him, and he, mistrusting her statements, had determined as far as he could to watch her.

On this occasion she laid the letter on the breakfast table, and waited his coming down, hoping that he might be in a good humour, so that there might be some chance of averting the storm from George. Madge was much terrified for the consequences, but was quite calm and firm.

Not long before she heard his heavy step coming down the stairs, and soon he came into the room, evidently in no favourable state of mind.

" If you don't kill or poison that black tom-cat," was his first speech, " by the Lord I will. I suppose you keep him for some of your witchwork. But if he's the devil himself, as I believe he is, I'll shoot him. I won't be kept out of my natural sleep by such a devil's brat as that. He's been keeping up such a growling and a scrowling on the hen-house roof all night, that I thought it was Old Scratch come for you, and getting impatient. If you must keep an imp of Satan in the house, get a mole, or a rat, or some quiet beast of that sort, and not such a vicious toad as him."

" Shoot him after breakfast if you like," she said. " He's no friend of mine. Get your breakfast, and don't be a fool. There's a letter for you; take and read it."

" Yah ! Read it, she says, and knows I'm blind," said Hawker. " You artful minx, you want to read it yourself."

He took the letter up, and turned it over and over. He knew the seal, and shot a suspicious glance at her. Then, looking at her fixedly, he put it in his breast-pocket, and buttoned up his coat.

" There !" he said. " I'll read it. Oh yes, believe me, I'll read it. You Jezebel ! "

" You'd better eat your meat like a Christian man," she answered, " and not make such faces as them."

" Where's the man ?" he asked.

" Outside, I suppose."

" Tell him I want the gig. I'm going out for a drive. A pleasure drive, you know. All down the lane, and back again. Cut along and tell him, before I do you a mischief."

She saw he was in one of his evil humours, when nothing was to be done with him, and felt very uneasy. She went and ordered the gig, and when he had finished breakfast, he came out to the door.

"You'd best take your big coat," she said, "else you'll be getting cold, and be in a worse temper than you are,—and that's bad enough, Lord knows, for a poor woman to put up with."

"How careful she is!" said Hawker. "What care she takes of the old man! I've left you ten thousand pounds in my will, ducky. Good-bye."

He drove off, and left her standing in the porch. What a wild, tall figure she was, standing so stern and steadfast there in the morning sun!—a woman one would rather have for a friend than an enemy.

Hawker was full of other thoughts than these. Coupling his other suspicions of Madge with the receipt of this letter from the bank, he was growing very apprehensive of something being wrong. He wanted this letter read to him, but whom could he trust? Who better than his old companion Burrows, who lived in the valley below the Vicarage? So, whipping up his horse, he drove there, but found he was out. He turned back again, puzzled, going slowly, and as he came to the bottom of the hill, below the Vicarage, he saw a tall man leaning against the gate, and smoking.

"He'll do for want of a better," he said to himself. "He's an honest-going fellow, and we've always been good friends, and done good business together, though he is one of that cursed Vicarage lot."

So he drew up when he came to the gate. "I beg your pardon, Mr. Troubridge," he said, with a very different tone and manner to what we have been accustomed to hear him use, "but could you do a kindness for a blind old man? I have no one about me that I can trust since my son is gone away. I have reason to believe that this letter is of importance; could you be so good as to read it to me?"

"I shall be happy to oblige you, Mr. Hawker," said Tom. "I am sorry to hear that your sight is so bad."

"Yes; I'm breaking fast," said Hawker. "However, I shan't be much missed. I don't inquire how the Vicar is, because I know already, and because I don't think he would care much for my inquiries, after the injury my son has done him. I will break the seal. Now may I trouble you?"

Tom Troubridge read aloud:—

"B. and F. Bank. [Such a date.]

"SIR,—May I request that you will favour me personally with a call, at the earliest possible opportunity, at my private office, 166, Broad Street? I have reason to fear that two forged cheques, bearing your signature, have been inadvertently cashed by us. The amount, I am sorry to inform you, is considerable. I need not further urge your immediate attention. This is the third communication we have made to you on the subject, and are much surprised at receiving no answer. I hope that you will be so good as to call at once.

"Yours, sir, &c., P. ROLLOX, Manager."

"I thank you, Mr. Troubridge," said the old man, quietly and politely. "You see I was not wrong when I thought that this letter was of importance. May I beg as a favour that you would not mention this to any one?"

"Certainly, Mr. Hawker. I will respect your wish. I hope your loss may not be heavy."

"The loss will not be mine though, will it?" said old Hawker. "I anticipate that it will fall on the bank. It is surely at their risk to cash cheques. Why, a man might sign for all the money I have in their hands, and surely they would be answerable for it?"

"I am not aware how the law stands, Mr. Hawker," said Troubridge. "Fortunately, no one has ever thought it worth while to forge my name."

"Well, I wish you a good day, sir, with many thanks," said Hawker. "Can I do anything for you in Exeter?"

Old Hawker drove away rapidly in the direction of Exeter; his horse, a fine black, clearing the ground in splendid style. Although a cunning man, he was not quick in following a train of reasoning, and he was half-way to Exeter before he had thoroughly comprehended his situation. And then, all he saw was that somebody had forged his name, and he believed that Madge knew something about it.

"I wish my boy George was at home," he said. "He'd save me getting a lawyer now. I am altogether in the hands of those Bank folks if they like to cheat me, though it's not likely they'd do that. At all events I will take Dickson with me."

Dickson was an attorney of good enough repute. A very clever quiet man, and a good deal employed by old Hawker, when his business was not too disreputable. Some years before, Hawker had brought some such excessively dirty work to his office, that the lawyer politely declined having anything to do with it, but recommended him to an attorney who he thought would undertake it. And from that time the old fellow treated him with marked respect, and spoke everywhere of him as a man to be trusted: such an effect had the fact of a lawyer refusing business had on him!

He reached Exeter by two o'clock, so rapidly had he driven. He went at once to Dickson's, and found him at home, busy swinging the poker, in deep thought, before the fireplace in his inner office. He was a small man, with an impenetrable expressionless face, who never was known to unbend himself to a human being. Only two facts were known about him. One was, that he was the best swimmer in Exeter, and had saved several lives from drowning; and the other was, that he gave away (for him) large sums in private charity.

Such was the man who now received old Hawker, with quiet politeness; and having sent his horse round to the inn stable by a clerk, sat down once more by the fire, and began swinging the poker, and waiting for the other to begin the conversation.

"If you are not engaged, Mr. Dickson," said Hawker, "I would be much obliged to you if you could step round to the B. and F. Bank with me. I want you to witness what passes, and to read any letters or papers for me that I shall require."

The attorney put down the poker, got his hat, and stood waiting, all without a word.

"You won't find it necessary to remark on anything that occurs, Mr. Dickson, unless I ask your opinion."

The attorney nodded, and whistled a tune. And then they started together through the crowded street.

The bank was not far, and Hawker pushed his way in among the crowd of customers. It was some time before he could get hold of a clerk, there was so much business going on. When, at last, he did so, he said—"I want to see Mr. Rollox; he told me to call on him at once."

"He is engaged at present," said the clerk. "It is quite impossible you can see him."

"You don't know what you are talking about, man," said Hawker. "Send in and tell him Mr. Hawker, of Drumston, is here."

"Oh, I beg your pardon, Mr. Hawker. I have only just come here, and did not know you. Porter, show Mr. Hawker in."

They went into the formal bank parlour. There was the leather writing table, the sheet almanac, the iron safe, and all the weapons by which bankers war against mankind, as in all other sanctuaries of the kind. Moreover, there was the commander-in-chief himself, sitting at the table. A bald, clever, gentlemanly-looking man, who bowed when they came in. "Good day, Mr. Hawker. I am obliged to you for calling at last. We thought something was wrong. Mr. Dickson, I hope you are well. Are you attending with Mr. Hawker, or are you come on private business?"

The attorney said—"I'm come at his request," and relapsed into silence.

"Ah!" said the manager. "I am, on the whole, glad that Mr. Hawker has brought a professional adviser with him. Though," he added, laughing, "it is putting me rather at a disadvantage, you know. Two to one,—eh?"

"Now, gentlemen, if you will be so good as to close the door carefully, and be seated, I will proceed to business, hoping that you

will give me your best attention. About six or eight months ago,—
'et me be particular, though," said he, referring to some papers,—
" that is rather a loose way of beginning. Here it is. The fourth
of September last year—yes. On that day, Mr. Hawker, a cheque
was presented at this bank, drawn ' in favour of bearer,' and signed
in your name, for two hundred pounds, and cashed, the person who
presented it being well known here."

" Who ? " interrupted Hawker.

" Excuse me, sir," said the manager ; " allow me to come to that
hereafter. You were about to say, I anticipate, that you never
drew a cheque 'on bearer' in your life. Quite true. That ought
to have excited attention, but it did not till a very few weeks ago,
our head-clerk, casting his eyes down your account, remarked on the
peculiarity, and, on examining the cheque, was inclined to believe
that it was not in your usual handwriting. He intended communi-
cating with me, but was prevented for some days by my absence ;
and, in the meantime, another cheque, similar, but better imitated,
was presented by the same person, and cashed, without the knowledge
of the head-clerk. On the cheque coming into his hands, he repri-
manded the cashier, and he and I, having more closely examined
them, came to the conclusion that they were both forgeries. We
immediately communicated with you, and, to our great surprise,
received no answer either to our first or second application. We,
however, were not idle. We ascertained that we could lay our
hands on the utterer of the cheques at any moment, and tried a third
letter to you, which has been successful."

" The two letters you speak of have never reached me, Mr. Rollox," said Hawker. " I started off on the receipt of yours this
morning—the first I saw. I am sorry, sir, that the bank should lose
money through me ; but, by your own showing, sir, the fault lay with
your own clerks."

" I have never attempted to deny it, Mr. Hawker," said the
manager. " But there are other matters to be considered. Before
I go on, I wish to give you an opportunity of sending away your
professional adviser, and continuing this conversation with me
alone."

They both turned and looked at the lawyer. He was sitting with
his hands in his pockets, and one would have thought he was whistling, only no sound came. His face showed no signs of intelligence
in any feature save his eyes, and they were expressive of the wildest
and most unbounded astonishment.

" I have nothing to do in this matter, sir," said Hawker, " that
I should not wish Mr. Dickson to hear. He is an honourable man,
and I confide in him thoroughly."

" So be it, then, Mr. Hawker," said the manager. " I have as
high an opinion of my friend Mr. Dickson as you have ; but I warn

you, that some part of what will follow will touch you very unpleasantly."

" I don't see how," said Hawker; " go on, if you please."

" Will you be good enough to examine these two cheques, and say whether they are genuine or not ? "

" I have only to look at the amount of this large one, to pronounce it an impudent forgery," said Hawker. " I have not signed so large a cheque for many years. There was one last January twelvemonth of £400, for the land at Highcot, and that is the largest, I believe, I ever gave in my life."

" There can be no doubt they are forgeries. Your sight, I believe, is too bad to swear easily to your own signature ; but that is quite enough. Now, I have laid this case before our governor, Lord C——, and he went so far as to say that, under the painful circumstances of the case, if you were to refund the money, the bank might let the matter drop ; but that, otherwise, it would be their most painful duty to prosecute."

" *I* refund the money !" laughed Hawker ; " you are playing with me, sir. Prosecute the dog ; I will come and see him hung ! Ha ! ha !"

" It will be a terrible thing if we prosecute the utterer of these cheques," said the manager.

" Why ? " said Hawker. " By-the-bye, you know who he is, don't you ? Tell me who it is ? "

" Your own son, Mr. Hawker," said the manager, almost in a whisper.

Hawker rose and glared at them with such a look of deadly rage that they shrank from him appalled. Then, he tottered to the mantelpiece and leant against it, trying to untie his neckcloth with feeble, trembling fingers.

" Open your confounded window there, Rollox," cried the lawyer, starting up. " Where's the wine ? Look sharp, man ! "

Hawker waved to him impatiently to sit down, and then said, at first gasping for breath, but afterwards more quietly :

" Are you sure it was he that brought those cheques ? "

" Certainly, sir," said the manager. " You may be sure it was he. Had it been any one else, they would not have been cashed without more examination ; and on the last occasion he accounted rather elaborately for your drawing such a large sum."

Hawker recovered himself and sat down.

" Don't be frightened, gentlemen," he said. " Not this time. I've something to do before that comes. It won't be long, the doctor says, but I must transact some business first. O Lord ! I see it all now. That cursed, cursed woman and her boy have been hoodwinking me and playing with me all this time, have they ? Oh, but I'll have my vengeance on 'em—one to the stocks, and another to the gallows.

I, unfortunately, can't give you any information where that man is that has the audacity to bear my name, sir," said he to the manager. " His mother at one time persuaded me that he was a child of mine; but such infernal gipsy drabs as that can't be depended on, you know. I have the honour to wish you a very good afternoon, sir, thanking you for your information, and hoping your counsel will secure a speedy conviction. I shall probably trouble you to meet me at a magistrate's to-morrow morning, where I will take my oath in his presence that those cheques are forgeries. You will find alterations in my banker's book, too, I expect. We'll look into it all to-morrow. Come along, Dickson, my sly little weasel; I've a gay night's work for you; I'm going to leave all my property to my cousin Nick, my bitterest enemy, and a lawsuit with it that'll break his heart. There's fun for the lawyers,—eh, my boy!"

So talking, the old man strode firmly forth, with a bitter, malignant scowl on his flushed face. The lawyer followed him, and, when they were in the street, Hawker again asked him to come to the inn and make his will for him.

" I'll stay by you, Hawker, and see that you don't make a fool of yourself. I wish you would not be so vindictive. It's indecent; you'll be ashamed of it to-morrow; but, in the meantime, it's indecent."

" Ha, ha!" laughed Hawker; " how quietly he talks! One can see that he hasn't had a bastard child fathered on him by a gipsy hag. Come along, old fellow; there's fifty pounds' worth of work for you this week, if I only live through it!"

He took the lawyer to the inn, and they got dinner. Hawker ate but little, for him, but drank a good deal. Dickson thought he was getting drunk; but when dinner was over, and Hawker had ordered in spirits-and-water, he seemed sober enough again.

" Now, Mr. Dickson," said he, " I am going to make a fresh will to-morrow morning, and I shall want you to draw it up for me. After that I want you to come home with me and transact business. You will do a good day's work, I promise you. You seem to me now to be the only man in the world I can trust. I pray you don't desert me."

" As I said before," replied the lawyer, " I won't desert you; but listen to me. I don't half like the sudden way you have turned against your own son. Why don't you pay this money, and save the disgrace of that unhappy young man? I don't say anything about your disinheriting him—that's no business of mine—but don't be witness against him. The bank, or rather my Lord C——, has been very kind about it. Take advantage of their kindness and hush the matter up."

" I know you ain't in the pay of the bank," said Hawker, " so I won't charge you with it. I know you better than to think you'd

!end yourself to anything so mean; but your conduct looks suspicious. If you hadn't done me a few disinterested kindnesses lately, I should say that they'd paid you to persuade me to stop this, so as they might get their money back, and save the cost of a prosecution. But I ain't so far gone as to believe that; and so I tell you, as one man to another, that if you'd come suddenly on such a mine of treason and conspiracy as I have this afternoon, and found a lad that you have treated as, and tried to believe was, your own son, you'd be as bad as me. Every moment I think of it, it comes out clearer. That woman that lives with me has palmed that brat of hers on me as my child; and he and she have been plundering me these years past. The money that woman has made away with would build a ship, sir. What she's done with it, her master, the devil, only knows; and I've said nought about it, because she's a witch, and I was afraid of her. But now I've found her out. She has stopped the letters that they wrote to me about this boy's forgery, and that shows she was in it. She shall pack. I won't prosecute her; no. I've reasons against that; but I'll turn her out in the world without a sixpence. You see I'm quiet enough now!"

"You're quiet enough," said the lawyer, "and you've stated your case very well. But are you sure this lad is not your son?"

"If I was sure that he was," said Hawker, "it wouldn't make any difference, as I know on. Ah, man, you don't know what a rage I'm in. If I chose, I could put myself into such an infernal passion at this moment as would bring on a 'plectic fit, and lay me dead on the floor. But I won't do it, not yet. I'll have another drop of brandy, and sing you a song. Shall I give 'ee 'Roger a-Maying,' or what'll ye have?"

"I'll have you go to bed, and not take any more brandy," said the lawyer. "If you sing, get in one of the waiters, and sing to him; he'd enjoy it. I'm going home, but I shall come to breakfast to-morrow morning, and find you in a different humour."

"Good night, old mole," said Hawker; "good night, old bat, old parchment skin, old sixty per cent. Ha, ha! If a wench brings a brat to thee, old lad, chuck it out o' window, and her after it. Thou can only get hung for it, man. They can only hang thee once, and that is better than to keep it and foster it, and have it turn against thee when it grows up. Good night."

Dickson came to him in the morning, and found him in the same mind. They settled down to business, and Hawker made a new will. He left all his property to his cousin (a man he had had a bitter quarrel with for years), except £100 to his groom, and £200 to Tom Troubridge, "for an act of civility" (so the words ran), "in reading a letter for a man who ought to have been his enemy." And when the will (a very short one) was finished, and the lawyer proposed getting two of his clerks as witnesses, Hawker told him to fold it up and keep it ; that he would get it witnessed by-and-by.

" You're coming home with me," he said, " and we'll get it witnessed there. You'll see why, when its done."

Then they went to the manager of the bank, and got him to go before a magistrate with him, whilst he deposed on oath that the two cheques, before mentioned, were forgeries, alleging that his life was so uncertain that the criminal might escape justice by his sudden death. Then he and Dickson went back to the inn, and after dinner started together to drive to Drumston.

They had been so engaged with business that they had taken no notice of the weather. But when they were clear of the northern suburbs of the town, and were flying rapidly along the noble turnpike-road that turning eastward skirts the broad Exe for a couple of miles before turning north again, they remarked that a dense black cloud hung before them, and that everything foreboded a violent thunder-storm.

" We shall get a drowning before we reach your place, Hawker," said the lawyer. " I'm glad I brought my coat."

" Lawyers never get drowned," said Hawker, " though I believe you have tried it often enough."

When they crossed the bridge, and turned to the north, along the pretty banks of the Creedy, they began to hope that they would leave it on the right ; but ere they reached Newton St. Cyres they saw that it was creeping up overhead, and, stopping a few minutes in that village, perceived that the folks were all out at their doors talking to one another, as people do for company's sake when a storm is coming on.

Before they got to Crediton they could distinguish, above the sound of the wheels, the thunder groaning and muttering perpetually, and as they rattled quickly past the grand old minster a few drops of rain began to fall.

The boys were coming out of the Grammar School in shoals, laughing, running, whooping, as the manner of boys is. Hawker drove slowly as he passed through the crowd, and the lawyer took that opportunity to put on his great-coat.

" We've been lucky so far," he said, " and now we are going to pay for our good luck. Before it is too late, Hawker, pull up and stay here. If we have to stop all night, I'll pay expenses ; I will indeed. It will be dark before we are home. Do stop."

" Not for a thousand pound," said Hawker. " I wouldn't baulk myself now for a thousand pound. Hey ! fancy turning her out such a night as this without sixpence in her pocket. Why, a man like you, that all the county knows, a man who has got two gold medals for bravery, ain't surely afraid of a thunderstorm ? "

" I ain't afraid of the thunderstorm, but I am of the rheumatism," said the other. " As for a thunderstorm, you're as safe out of doors as in ; some say safer. But you're mistaken if you suppose I don't fear death, Hawker. I fear it as much as any man."

" It didn't look like it that time you soused in over the weir after the groom lad," said Hawker.

" Bah ! man," said the lawyer ; " I'm the best swimmer in Devon. That was proved by my living in that weir in flood time. So I have less to fear than any one else. Why, if that boy hadn't been as quiet and plucky as he was, I knew I could kick him off any minute, and get ashore. Hallo; that's nearer."

The storm burst on them in full fury, and soon after it grew dark. The good horse, however, stepped out gallantly, though they made but little way; for, having left the high road and taken to the narrow lanes, their course was always either up hill or down, and every bottom they passed grew more angry with the flooding waters as they proceeded. Still, through darkness, rain, and storm, they held their way till they saw the lights of Drumston below them.

" How far is it to your house, Hawker?" said the lawyer. " This storm seems to hang about still. It is as bad as ever. You must be very wet."

" It's three miles to my place, but a level road, at least all up-hill, gently rising. Cheer up ! We won't be long."

They passed through the village rapidly, lighted by the lightning. The last three miles were done as quickly as any part of the journey, and the lawyer rejoiced to find himself before the white gate that led up to Hawker's house.

It was not long before they drew up to the door. The storm seemed worse than ever. There was a light in the kitchen, and when Hawker had halloed once or twice, a young man ran out to take the horse.

" Is that you, my boy?" said Hawker. " Rub the horse down, and come in to get something. This ain't a night fit for a dog to be out in ; is it ?"

" No, indeed, sir," said the man. " I hope none's out in it but what likes to be."

They went in. Madge looked up from arranging the table for supper, and stared at Hawker keenly. He laughed aloud, and said,—

" So you didn't expect me to-night, deary, eh ?"

" You've chose a bad night to come home in, old man," she answered.

" A terrible night, ain't it ? Wouldn't she have been anxious if she'd a' known I'd been out ?"

" Don't know as I should," she said. " That gentleman had better get dried, and have his supper."

" I've got a bit of business first, deary. Where's the girl ?"

" In the other kitchen."

" Call her.—Lord! listen to that."

A crash of thunder shook the house, heard loud above the rain, which beat furiously against the windows. Madge immediately returned with the servant girl, a modest, quiet-looking creature, evidently in terror at the storm.

" Get out that paper, Dickson, and we'll get it signed."

The lawyer produced the will, and Madge and the servant girl were made to witness it. Dickson, having dried the signatures, took charge of it again ; and then Hawker turned round fiercely to Madge.

" That's my new will," he said ; " my new will, old woman. Oh, you cat! I've found you out."

Madge saw a storm was coming, worse than the one which raged and rattled outside, and she braced her nerves to meet it.

" What have you found out, old man?" she said quietly.

" I've found out that you and that young scoundrel have been robbing and cheating me in a way that would bring me to the workhouse in another year. I have found out that he has forged my name for nearly a thousand pounds, and that you've helped him. I find that you yourself have robbed me of hundreds of pounds, and that I have been blinded, and cozened, and hoodwinked by two that I kept from the workhouse, and treated as well as I treated myself. That's what I have found out, gipsy."

" Well?" was all Madge said, standing before him with her arms folded.

" So I say," said Hawker ; " it is very well. The mother to the streets, and the boy to the gallows."

" You wouldn't prosecute him, William ; your own son?"

" No, I shan't," he replied ;—" but the Bank will."

" And couldn't you stop it?"

" I could. But if holding up my little finger would save him, I wouldn't do it."

" Oh, William," she cried, throwing herself on her knees ; " don't look like that. I confess everything ; visit it on me, but spare that boy."

" You confess, do you?" he said. " Get up. Get out of my house ; you shan't stay here."

But she would not go, but hanging round him, kept saying, " Spare the boy, William, spare the boy!" over and again, till he struck her in his fury, and pulled her towards the door.

" Get out and herd with the gipsies you belong to," he said. " You witch, you can't cry now."

" But," she moaned, " oh, not such a night as this, William ; not to-night. I am frightened of the storm. Let me stay to-night. I am frightened of the lightning. Oh, I wouldn't turn out your door such a night as this."

" Out, out, you devil ! "

" Oh, William, only one—"

" Out, you Jezebel, before I do you a mischief."

He had got the heavy door open, and she passed out, moaning low to herself. Out into the fierce rain and the black darkness; and the old man held open the door for a minute, to see if she were gone.

No. A broad, flickering riband of light ineffable wavered for an instant of time before his eyes, lighting up the country far and wide ; but plainly visible between him and the blaze was a tall, dark, bare-headed woman, wildly raising her hands above her head, as if imploring vengeance upon him, and, ere the terrible explosion which followed had ceased to shake the old house to its foundations, he shut the door, and went muttering alone up to his solitary chamber.

The next morning the groom came into the lawyer's room, and informed him that when he went to call his master in the morning, he had found the bed untouched, and Hawker sitting half undressed in his arm-chair, dead and cold.

CHAPTER XIV.

THE MAJOR'S VISIT TO THE " NAG'S-HEAD."

MAJOR BUCKLEY and his wife stood together in the verandah of their cottage, watching the storm. All the afternoon they had seen it creeping higher and higher, blacker and more threatening up the eastern heavens, until it grew painful to wait any longer for its approach. But now that it had burst on them, and night had come on dark as pitch, they felt the pleasant change in the atmosphere, and, in spite of the continuous gleam of the lightning, and the eternal roll and crackle of the thunder, they had come out to see the beauty and majesty of the tempest.

They stood with their arms entwined for some time, in silence ; but after a crash louder than any of those which had preceded it, Major Buckley said :—

" My dearest Agnes, you are very courageous in a thunderstorm."

" Why not, James ? " she said ; " you cannot avoid the lightning, and the thunder won't harm you. Most women fear the sound of the thunder more than anything, but I suspect that Ciudad Rodrigo made more noise than this, husband ? "

" It did indeed, my dear. More noise than I ever heard in any storm yet. It is coming nearer."

"I am afraid it will shake the poor Vicar very much," said Mrs. Buckley. "Ah, there is Sam crying."

They both went into the sitting-room; little Sam had petitioned to go to bed on the sofa till the storm was over, and now, awakened by the thunder, was sitting up in his bed, crying out for his mother.

The Major went in and lay down by the child on the sofa, to quiet him. "What!" said he, "Sammy, you're not afraid of thunder, are you?"

"Yes! I am," said the child; "very much indeed. I am glad you are come, father."

"Lightning never strikes good boys, Sam," said the Major.

"Are you sure of that, father?" said the little one.

That was a poser; so the Major thought it best to counterfeit sleep; but he overdid it, and snored so loud, that the boy began to laugh, and his father had to practise his deception with less noise. And by degrees, the little hand that held his moustache dropped feebly on the bedclothes, and the Major, ascertaining by the child's regular breathing that his son was asleep, gently raised his vast length, and proposed to his wife to come into the verandah again.

"The storm is breaking, my love," said he; "and the air is deliciously cool out there. Put your shawl on and come out."

They went out again; the lightning was still vivid, but the thunder less loud. Straight down the garden from them stretched a broad gravel walk, which now, cut up by the rain into a hundred water channels, showed at each flash like rivers of glittering silver. Looking down this path toward the black wood during one of the longest continued illuminations of the lightning, they saw for an instant a dark, tall figure, apparently advancing towards them. Then all the prospect was wrapped again in tenfold gloom.

Mrs. Buckley uttered an exclamation, and held tighter to her husband's arm. Every time the garden was lit up, they saw the figure nearer and nearer, till they knew that it was standing before them in the darkness; the Major was about to speak, when a hoarse voice, heard indistinctly above the rushing of the rain, demanded:

"Is that Major Buckley?"

At the same minute the storm-light blazed up once more, and fell upon an object so fearful and startling that they both fell back amazed. A woman was standing before them, tall, upright, and bareheaded; her long black hair falling over a face as white and ghastly as a three days' corpse; her wild countenance rendered more terrible by the blue glare of the lightning shining on the rain that streamed from every lock of her hair and every shred of her garments. She looked like some wild daughter of the storm, who had lost her way, and came wandering to them for shelter.

"I am Major Buckley," was the answer. "What do you want? But in God's name come in out of the rain."

" Come in and get your things dried, my good woman," said Mrs. Buckley. " What do you want with my husband such a night as this?"

" Before I dry my things, or come in, I will state my business," said the woman, coming under the verandah. " After that I will accept your hospitality. This is a night when polecats and rabbits would shelter together in peace ; and yet such a night as this, a man turns out of his house the woman who has lain beside him twenty years."

" Who are you, my good soul?" said the Major.

" They call me Madge the Witch," she said ; " I lived with old Hawker, at the Woodlands, till to-night, and he has turned me out. I want to put you in possession of some intelligence that may save much misery to some that you love."

" I can readily believe that you can do it," said the Major, " but pray don't stand there ; come in with my wife, and get your things dried."

" Wait till you hear what I have to say : George Hawker, my son—"

" Your son—good God!"

" I thought you would have known that. The Vicar does. Well, this son of mine has run off with the Vicar's daughter."

" Well ?"

" Well, he has committed forgery. It'll be known all over the country to-morrow, and even now I fear the runners are after him. If he is taken before he marries that girl, things will be only worse than they are. But never mind whether he does or not, perhaps you differ with me ; perhaps you think that, if you could find the girl now, you could stop her and bring her home ; but you don't know where she is. I do, and if you will give me your solemn word of honour as a gentleman to give him warning that his forgery for five hundred pounds is discovered, I will give you his direction."

The Major hesitated for a moment, thinking.

" If you reflect a moment, you must see how straightforward my story is. What possible cause can I have to mislead you? I know which way you will decide, so I wait patiently."

" I think I ought to say yes, my love," said the Major to his wife ; " if it turned out afterwards that I neglected any opportunity of saving this poor girl (particularly if this tale of the forgery be true), I should never forgive myself."

" I agree with you, my dear," said Mrs. Buckley. " Give your promise, and go to seek her."

" Well, then," said the Major ; " I give you my word of honour that I will give Hawker due warning of his forgery being discovered, if you will give me his direction. I anticipate that they are in London, and I shall start to-night, to be in time for the morning coach. Now, will you give me the address?"

"Yes!" said Madge. "They are at the Nag's Head, Buckingham Street, Strand, London; can you remember that?"

"I know where the street is," said the Major; "now will you go into the kitchen, and make yourself comfortable? My dear, you will see my valise packed? Ellen, get this person's clothes dried, and get her some hot wine. By-the-bye," said he, following her into the kitchen, "you must have had a terrible quarrel with Hawker, for him to send you out such a night as this?"

"It was about this matter," she said: "the boy forged on his father, and I knew it, and tried to screen him. My own son, you know."

"It was natural enough," said the Major. "You are not deceiving me, are you? I don't see why you should, though."

"Before God, I am not. I only want the boy to get warning."

"You must sleep here to-night," said the Major; "and to-morrow you can go on your way, though, if you cannot conveniently get away in the morning, don't hurry, you know. My house is never shut against unfortunate people. I have heard a great deal of you, but I never saw you before; you must be aware, however, that the character you have held in the place is not such as warrants me in asking you to stay here for any time."

The Major left the kitchen, and crossed the yard. In a bedroom above the stable slept his groom, a man who had been through his campaigns with him from first to last. It was to waken him that the Major took his way up the narrow stairs towards the loft.

"Jim," he said, "I want my horse in an hour."

The man was out of bed in a moment, and while he was dressing, the Major continued:—

"You know Buckingham Street, Strand, Jim, don't you? When you were recruiting you used to hang out at a public-house there, unless I am mistaken."

"Exactly so, sir! We did; and a many good chaps we picked up there, gents and all sorts. Why, it was in that werry place, Major, as we 'listed Lundon; him as was afterwards made sergeant for being the first man into Sebastian, and arterwards married Skettles: her as fell out of eighteen stories at Brussels looking after the Duke, and she swore at them as came to pick her up, she did; and walked in at the front door as bold as brass."

"There, my good lad," said the Major; "what's the good of telling such stories as that? Nobody believes them, you know. Do you know the Nag's Head there? It's a terribly low place, is it not?"

"It's a much changed if it ain't, sir," said Jim, putting on his breeches. "I was in there not eighteen months since. It's a fighting-house; and there used to be a dog show there, and a reunion of vocal talent, and all sorts of villanies."

"Well, see to the horse, Jim, and I'll sing out when I'm ready," said the Major, and went back into the house.

He came back through the kitchen, and saw that Madge was being treated by the maids with that respect that a reputed witch never fails to command; then, having sat for some time talking to his wife, and finding that the storm was cleared off, he kissed his sleeping child and its mother, and mounting his horse in the stable-yard, rode off towards Exeter.

In the morning, when Mrs. Buckley came down stairs, she inquired for Madge. They told her she had been up some time, and, having got some breakfast, was walking up and down in front of the house. Going there, Mrs. Buckley found her. Her dress was re-arranged with picturesque neatness, and a red handkerchief pinned over her rich dark hair, that last night had streamed wild and wet in the tempest. Altogether, she looked an utterly different being from the strange, storm-beaten creature who had craved their hospitality the night before. Mrs. Buckley admired the bold, upright, handsome figure before her, and gave her a cheery "good morning."

"I only stayed," said Madge, "to wish you good-bye, and thank you for your kindness. When they who should have had some pity on me turned me out, you took me in!"

"You are heartily welcome," said Mrs. Buckley. "Cannot I do more for you? Do you want money? I fear you must!"

"None, I thank you kindly," she replied; "that would break the spell. Good-bye!"

"Good-bye!" said Mrs. Buckley.

Madge stood in front of the door and raised her hand.

"The blessing of God," she said, "shall be upon the house of the Buckleys, and more especially upon you and your husband, and the boy that is sleeping inside. He shall be a brave and a good man, and his wife shall be the fairest and best in the country side. Your kine shall cover the plains until no man can number them, and your sheep shall be like the sands of the sea. When misfortune and death and murder fall upon your neighbours, you shall stand between the dead and the living, and the troubles that pass over your heads shall be like the shadow of the light clouds that fly across the moor on a sunny day. And when in your ripe and honoured old age you shall sit with your husband, in a garden of your own planting, in the lands far away, and see your grand-children playing around you, you shall think of the words of the wild, lost gipsy woman, who gave you her best blessing before she went away and was seen no more."

Mrs. Buckley tried to say "Amen," but found herself crying. Something there was in that poor creature, homeless, penniless, friendless, that made her heart like wax. She watched her as she strode down the path, and afterwards looked for her re-appearing on a high exposed part of the road, a quarter of a mile off, thinking she would take that way. But she waited long, and never again saw that stern, tall figure, save in her dreams.

She turned at last, and one of the maids stood beside her.

"Oh, missis," she said, "you're a lucky woman to-day. There's some in this parish would have paid a hundred pounds for such a fortune as that from her. It'll come true,—you will see!"

"I hope it may, you silly girl," said Mrs. Buckley; and then she went in and knelt beside her sleeping boy, and prayed that the blessing of the gipsy woman might be fulfilled.

*　　　*　　　*　　　*　　　*

It was quite late on the evening of his second day's journey that the Major, occupying the box-seat of the "Exterminator," dashed with comet-like speed through so much of the pomps and vanities of this wicked world as showed itself in Piccadilly at half-past seven on a spring afternoon.

"Hah!" he soliloquised, passing Hyde-park Corner, "these should be the folks going out to dinner. They dine later and later every year. At this rate they'll dine at half-past one in twenty years' time. That's the Duke's new house; eh, coachman? By George, there's his Grace himself, on his brown cob; God bless him! There are a pair of good-stepping horses, and old Lady E—— behind 'em, by Jove!—in her war-paint and feathers— pinker than ever. She hasn't got tired of it yet. She'd dance at her own funeral if she could. And there's Charley Bridgenorth in the club balcony—I wonder what he finds to do in peace time?— and old B—— talking to him. What does Charley mean by letting himself be seen in the same balcony with that disreputable old fellow? I hope he won't get his morals corrupted! Ah! So here we are! eh?"

He dismounted at the White Horse Cellar, and took a hasty dinner. His great object was speed; and so he hardly allowed himself ten minutes to finish his pint of port before he started into the street, to pursue the errand on which he had come.

It was nearly nine o'clock, and he thought he would be able to reach his destination in ten minutes. But it was otherwise ordered. His evil genius took him down St. James's Street. He tried to persuade himself that it was the shortest way, though he knew all the time that it wasn't. And so he was punished in this way: he had got no further than Crockford's, when, in the glare of light opposite the door of that establishment, he saw three men standing, one of whom was talking and laughing in a tone perhaps a little louder than it is customary to use in the streets nowadays. Buckley knew that voice well (better, perhaps, among the crackle of musketry than in the streets of London), and, as the broad-shouldered owner of it turned his jolly, handsome face towards him, he could not suppress a low laugh of satisfaction. At the same moment the before-mentioned man recognised him, and shouted out his name.

"Busaco Buckley, by the Lord," he said, "revisiting once more the glimpses of the gas lamps! My dear old fellow, how are you, and where do you come from?"

The Major found himself quickly placed under a lamp for inspection, and surrounded by three old and well-beloved fellow-campaigners. What could a man do under the circumstances? Nothing, if human and infallible, I should say, but what the Major did—stay there, laughing and joking, and talking of old times, and freshen up his honest heart, and shake his honest sides with many an old half-forgotten tale of fun and mischief.

"Now," he said at last, "you must let me go. You Barton (to the first man he recognised), you are a married man; what are you doing at Crockford's?"

"The same as you are," said the other,—"standing outside the door. The pavement's free, I suppose. I haven't been in such a place these five years. Where are you staying, old boy?"

The Major told them, and they agreed to meet at breakfast next morning. Then, after many farewells, and callings back, he pursued his way towards the Strand, finding to his disgust that it was nearly ten o'clock.

He, nevertheless, held on his way undiscouraged, and turning by degrees into narrower and narrower streets, came at last on one quieter than the others, which ended abruptly at the river.

It was a quiet street, save at one point, and that was where a blaze of gas (then recently introduced, and a great object of curiosity to the Major) was thrown across the street, from the broad ornamented windows of a flash public-house. Here there was noise enough. Two men fighting, and three or four more encouraging, while a half-drunken woman tried to separate them. From the inside, too, came a noise of singing, quarrelling, and swearing, such as made the Major cross the road, and take his way on the darker side of the street.

But when he got opposite the aforesaid public-house, he saw that it was called the "Nag's Head," and that it was kept by one J. Trotter. "What an awful place to take that girl to!" said the Major. "But there may be some private entrance, and a quiet part of the house set by for a hotel." Nevertheless, having looked well about him, he could see nothing of the sort, and perceived that he must storm the bar.

But he stood irresolute for a moment. It looked such a very low place, clean and handsome enough, but still the company about the door looked so very disreputable. "J. Trotter!" he reflected. "Why, that must be Trotter the fighting-man. I hope it may be; he will remember me."

So he crossed. When he came within the sphere of the gas lamps, those who were assisting at the fight grew silent, and gazed upon him with open eyes. As he reached the door one of them remarked, with a little flourish of oaths as a margin or garland round his remark, that "of all the swells he'd ever seen, that 'un was the biggest, at all events."

Similarly, when they in the bar saw that giant form, the blue coat and brass buttons, and, above all, the moustache (sure sign of a military man in those days), conversation ceased, and the Major then and there became the event of the evening. He looked round as he came in, and, through a door leading inwards, he saw George Hawker himself, standing talking to a man with a dog under each arm.

The Major was not deceived as to the identity of J. Trotter. J. Trotter, the hero of a hundred fights, stood himself behind his own bar, a spectacle for the gods. A chest like a bull, a red neck, straight up and down with the back of his head, and a fist like a seal's flipper, proclaimed him the prize-fighter; and his bright grey eye, and ugly laughing face, proclaimed him the merry, good-humoured varlet that he was.

What a wild state of amazement he was in when he realized the fact that Major Buckley of the —th was actually towering aloft under the chandelier, and looking round for some one to address! With what elephantine politeness and respect did he show the Major into a private parlour, sweeping off at one round nearly a dozen pint-pots that covered the table, and then, shutting the door, stand bowing and smiling before his old pupil!

"And so you are gone into business, John, are you?" said the Major. "I'm glad to see it. I hope you are doing as well as you deserve."

"Much better than that," said the prize-fighter. "Much better than *that*, sir, I assure you."

"Well, I'm going to get you to do something for me," said the Major. "Do you know, John, that you are terribly fat?"

"The business allus does make flesh, sir. More especially to coves as has trained much."

"Yes, yes, John, I am going from the point. There is a young man of the name of Hawker here?"

The prize-fighter remained silent, but a grin gathered on his face. "I never contradicts a gentleman," he said. "And if you say he's here, why, in course, he is here. But I don't say he's here; you mind that, sir."

"My good fellow, I saw him as I came in," said the Major.

"Oh, indeed," said the other; "then that absolves me from any responsibility. He told me to deny him to anybody but one, and you ain't she. He spends a deal of money with me, sir; so, in course, I don't want to offend him. By-the-bye, sir, excuse me a moment."

The Major saw that he had got hold of the right man, and waited willingly. The fighting-man went to the door, and called out, " My dear." A tall, good-looking woman came to the bar, who made a low curtsey on being presented to the Major. " My dear," repeated Trotter, " the south side." " The particular, I suppose," she said. " In course," said he. So she soon appeared with a bottle of Madeira, which was of such quality that the Major, having tasted it, winked at the prize-fighter, and the latter laughed, and rubbed his hands.

" Now," said the Major, " do you mind telling me whether this Hawker is here alone ?"

" He don't live here. He only comes here of a day, and sometimes stays till late. This evening a pretty young lady —yes, a *lady*—come and inquired for him in my bar, and I was struck all of a heap to see such a creature in such a place, all frightened out of her wits. So I showed her through in a minute, and up stairs to where my wife sits, and she waited there till he come in. And she hadn't been gone ten minutes when you come."

The Major swore aloud, without equivocation or disguise. " Ah," he said, " If I had not met Barton ! Pray, Trotter, have you any idea where Hawker lives ?"

" Not the least in the world, further than it's somewhere Hampstead way. That's a thing he evidently don't want known."

" Do you think it likely that he and that young lady live in the same house ? I need not disguise from you that I am come after her, to endeavour to get her back to her family."

" I know they don't live in the same house," said Trotter, " because I heard her say to-night, before she went away, ' Do look round, George,' she says, ' at my house for ten minutes, before you go home.'"

" You have done me a great kindness," said the Major, " in what you have told me. I don't know how to thank you."

" It's only one," said the prize-fighter, " in return for a many you done me ; and you are welcome to it, sir. Now, I expect you'd like to see this young gent ; so follow me if you please."

Through many passages, past many doors, he followed him, until they left the noise of the revelry behind, and at last, at the end of a long dark passage, the prize-fighter suddenly threw open a door, and announced—" Major Buckley !"

There were four men playing at cards, and the one opposite to him was George Hawker. The Major saw at a glance, almost before any one had time to speak, that George was losing money, and that the other three were confederates.

The prize-fighter went up to the table and seized the cards; then, after a momentary examination, threw both packs in the fire.

"When gents play cards in my house, I expect them to use the cards I provides at the bar, and not private packs, whether marked or not. Mr. Hawker, I warned you before about this; you'll lose every sixpence you're worth, and then you will say it was done at my house, quite forgetting to mention that I warned you of it repeatedly."

But George took no notice of him. "Really, Major Buckley," he began, "this is rather—"

"Rather an intrusion, you would say—eh, Mr. Hawker?" said the Major; "so it is, but the urgency of my business must be my apology. Can you give me a few words alone?"

George rose and came out with them. The prize-fighter showed them into another room, and the Major asked him to stand in the passage, and see that no one was listening; "you see, John," he added, "we are very anxious not to be overheard."

"I am not at all particular myself," said George Hawker. "I have nothing to conceal."

"You will alter your mind before I have done, sir," said the Major.

George didn't like the look of affairs.—How came it that the Major and the prize-fighter knew one another so well? What did the former mean by all this secrecy? He determined to put a bold face on the matter.

"Miss Thornton is living with you, sir, I believe?" began the Major.

"Not at all, sir; Miss Thornton is in lodgings of her own. I have the privilege of seeing her for a few hours every day. In fact, I may go as far as to say that I am engaged to be married to her, and that that auspicious event is to come off on Thursday week."

"May I ask you to favour me with her direction?" said the Major.

"I am sorry to disoblige you, Major Buckley, but I must really decline;" answered George. "I am not unaware how disinclined her family are to the connexion; and, as I cannot but believe that you come on their behalf, I cannot think that an interview would be any thing but prejudicial to my interest. I must remind you, too, that Miss Thornton is of age, and her own mistress in every way."

While George had been speaking, it passed through the Major's mind: "What a checkmate it would be, if I were to withhold the information I have, and set the runners on him, here! I might save the girl, and further the ends of justice; but my hands are tied by the promise I gave that woman,—how unfortunate!"

"Then, Mr. Hawker," he said aloud, "I am to understand that you refuse me this address?"

" I am necessitated to refuse it most positively, sir."

" I am sorry for it. I leave it to your conscience. Now, I have got a piece of intelligence to give you, which I fear will be somewhat unpalatable—I got your address at this place from a woman of the name of Madge—"

" You did !" exclaimed George.

" Who was turned out of doors by your father, the night before last, in consequence, I understood, of some misdeeds of hers having come to light. She came immediately to my house, and offered to give me your direction, on condition of my passing my word of honour to deliver you this message : ' that the forgery (£500 was the sum mentioned, I think) was discovered, and that the Bank was going to prosecute.' I of course form no judgment as to the truth or falsehood of this : I leave you to take your own measures about it —only I once again ask you whether you will give me an interview with Miss Thornton ? "

George had courage enough left to say hoarsely and firmly, " No !"

" Then," replied the Major, " I must call you to witness that I have performed my errand to you faithfully. I beg, also, that you will carry all our kindest remembrances to Miss Thornton, and tell her that her poor father was struck with paralysis when he missed her, and that he is not expected to live many weeks. And I wish you good night."

He passed out, and down the stairs ; as he passed the public parlour-door, he heard a man bawling out a song, two or three lines of which he heard, and which made him blush to the tips of his ears, old soldier as he was.

As he walked up the street, he soliloquised : " A pretty mess I've made of it—done him all the service I could, and not helped her a bit—I see there is no chance of seeing her, though I shall try. I will go round Hampstead to-morrow, though that is a poor chance. In Paris, now, or Vienna, one could find her directly. What a pity we have no police ! "

CHAPTER XV.

THE BRIGHTON RACES, AND WHAT HAPPENED THEREAT.

GEORGE HAWKER just waited till he heard the retiring footsteps of the Major, and then, leaving the house, held his way rapidly towards Mary's lodgings, which were in Hampstead ; but finding he would be too late to gain admittance, altered his course when he was close to the house, and went to his own house, which was not more than a few hundred yards distant. In the morning he went to her, and she ran down the garden to meet him before the servant had time to open the door, looking so pretty and bright. " Ah, George ! " said she, " you never came last night, after all your promises. I shall be glad when it's all over, George, and we are together for good."

"It won't be long, first, my dear," he answered ; "we must manage to get through that time as well as we can, and then we'll begin to sound the old folks. You see I am come to breakfast."

" I expected you," she said ; " come in and we will have such a pleasant chat, and after that you must take me down the town, George, and we will see the carriages."

" Now, my love," said George ; " I've got to tell you something that will vex you ; but you must not be down-hearted about it, you know. The fact is, that your friends, as they call themselves, moving heaven and earth to get you back, by getting me out of the way, have hit on the expedient of spreading false reports about me, and issuing scandals against me. They found out my address at the Nag's Head, and came there after me not half an hour after you were gone, and I only got out of their way by good luck. You ought to give me credit for not giving any living soul the secret of our whereabouts, so that all I have got to do is to keep quiet here until our little business is settled, and then I shall be able to face them boldly again, and set everything straight."

" How cruel ! " she said ; " how unjust ! I will never believe anything against you, George."

" I am sure of that, my darling ;" he said, kissing her. " But now, there is another matter I must speak about, though I don't like to,—I am getting short of money, love."

" I have got nearly a hundred pounds, George," she said ; "and, as I told you, I have five thousand pounds in the funds, which I can sell out at any time I like."

" We shall do well, then, my Polly. Now let us go for a walk."

All that week George stayed with her quietly, till the time of residence necessary before they could be married was expired. He knew that he was treading on a mine, which at any time might burst and blow his clumsy schemes to the wind. But circumstances were in his favour, and the time came to an end at last. He drank hard all the time without letting Mary suspect it, but afterwards, when it was all over, wondered at his nerve and self-possession through all those trying days, when he was forced eternally to have a smile or a laugh ready, and could not hear a step behind him without thinking of an officer, or look over his head without thinking he saw a gallows in the air.

It was during this time that he nursed in his heart a feeling of desperate hatred and revenge against William Lee, which almost became the leading passion of his life. He saw, or thought he saw, that this man was the author of all the troubles that were gathering so thick around his head, and vowed, if chance threw the man in his way again, that he would take ample and fearful vengeance, let it cost what it might. And though this feeling may have sometimes grown cold, yet he never, (as we shall see), to the last day forgot or forgave the injuries this man had done him.

Mary was as innocent of business as a child, and George found little difficulty in persuading her, that the best thing she could do under present circumstances, was to sell out the money she had in the funds, and place it in a bank, to be drawn on as occasion should require; saying that they should be so long perhaps, before they had any other fund to depend on, that they might find it necessary to undertake some business for a living, in which case, it would be as well to have their money under command at a moment's notice.

There was, not far from the bank, an old Stock-broker, who had known her father and herself for many years, and was well acquainted with all their affairs, though they had but little intercourse by letter. To him she repaired, and, merely informing him that she was going to marry without her father's consent, begged him to manage the business for her; which he, complimenting her upon her good fortune in choosing a time when the funds were so high, immediately undertook; at the same time recommended her to a banker, where she might open an account.

On the same day that this business was concluded, a licence was procured, and their wedding fixed for the next day. "Now," thought George, as he leapt into bed on that night, " let only to-morrow get over safely, and I can begin to see my way out of the wood again."

And in the morning they were married in Hampstead church. Parson, clerk, pew-opener, and beadle, all remarked what a handsome young couple they were, and how happy they ought to be; and the parson departed, and the beadle shut up the church, and the mice came out again, and ate the Bibles, and the happy pair walked away down the road, bound together by a strong chain, which nothing could loose but death. They went to Brighton. Mary had said she would so like to see the sea; and the morning after they arrived there—the morning after their wedding—Mary wrote an affectionate penitential letter to her father, telling him that she was married, and praying his forgiveness.

They were quite gay at Brighton, and she recovered her spirits wonderfully at first. George soon made acquaintances, who soon got very familiar, after the manner of their kind,— greasy, tawdry, bedizened bucks,—never asleep, always proposing a game of cards, always carrying off her husband. Mary hated them, while she was at times proud to see her husband in such fine company.

Such were the eagles that gathered round the carcass of George

Hawker; and at last these eagles began to bring the hen-birds with them, who frightened our poor little dove with the amplitude and splendour of their feathers, and their harsh, strange notes. George knew the character of those women well enough; but already he cared little enough about his wife, even before they had been a month married, going on the principle that the sooner she learned to take care of herself, the better for her; and after they had been married little more than a month, Mary thought she began to see a change in her husband's behaviour to her.

He grew sullen and morose, even to her. Every day almost he would come to her with a scowl upon his face; and when she asked if he was angry with her, would say, " No, that he wasn't angry with her; but that things were going wrong—altogether wrong; and if they didn't mend, he couldn't see his way out of it at all."

But one night he came home cheerful and hilarious, though rather the worse for liquor. He showed her a roll of notes which he had won at roulette—over a hundred pounds—and added, " That shall be the game for me in future, Polly; all square and above board there."

" My dear George, I wish you'd give up gambling."

" So I will, some of these fine days, my dear. I only do it to pass the time. It's cursed dull having nothing to do."

" To-morrow is the great day at the races, George. I wish you would take me; I never saw a horse-race."

" Ay, to be sure," said he; " we'll go, and, what's more, we'll go alone. I won't have you seen in public with those dowdy drabs."

So they went alone. Such a glorious day as it was—the last happy day she spent for very long ! How delightful it was, all this rush and crush, and shouting and hubbub around, while you were seated in a phaeton, secure above the turmoil ! What delight to see all the beautiful women in the carriages, and, grandest sight of all, which struck awe and admiration into Mary's heart, was the great Prince himself, that noble gentleman, in a gutter-sided hat, and a wig so fearfully natural that Mary secretly longed to pull his hair.

But princes and duchesses were alike forgotten when the course was cleared for the great event of the day, and, one by one, the sleek beauties came floating along, above the crowd, towards the starting-post. Then George, leaving Mary in the phaeton to the care of their landlady, pushed his way among the crowd, and, by dint of hard squeezing, got against the rail. He had never seen such horses as these; he had never known what first-class horse-racing was. Here was a new passion for him, which, like all his others, should only by its perversion end in his ruin.

He had got some money on one of the horses, though he, of course, had never seen it. There was a cheer all along the line, and a dark bay fled past towards the starting-post, seeming rather to belong to the air than the ground. By George," he said, aloud, as the blood mounted to his face, and tingled in his ears, " I never saw such a sight as that before."

He was ashamed of having spoken aloud in his excitement, but a groom who stood by said, for his consolation,—

" I don't suppose you ever did sir, nor no man else. That's young Velocipede, and that's Chiffney a-ridin' him. You'll see that horse walk over for everything next year."

But now the horses come down, five of them abreast, at a walk, amid a dead silence from the crowd, three of them steady old stagers, but two jumping and pulling. " Back, Velocipede; back, Lara!" says the starter; down goes the flag, they dart away, and then there is a low hum of conversation, until a murmur is heard down the course, which swells into a roar as you notice it. The horses are coming. One of the royal huntsmen gallops by, and then, as the noise comes up towards you, you can hear the maddening rush of the horses' feet upon the turf, and, at the same time, a bay and a chestnut rush past in the last fierce struggle, and no man knows yet who has won.

Then the crowd poured once more over the turf, and surged and cheered round the winning horses. Soon it came out that Velocipede had won, and George, turning round delighted, stood face to face with a gipsy woman.

She had her hood low on her head, so that he could not see her face, but she said, in a low voice, " Let me tell your fortune."

" It is told already, mother," said George. " Velocipede has won; you won't tell me any better news than that this day, I know."

" No, George Hawker, I shan't," replied the gipsy, and, raising her hood for an instant, she discovered to his utter amazement the familiar countenance of Madge.

" Will you let me tell your fortune now, my boy ? " she said.

" What, Madge, old girl ! By Jove, you shall. Well, who'd a' thought of seeing you here ? "

" I've been following you, and looking for you ever so long," she said. " They at the Nag's Head didn't know where you were gone, and if I hadn't been a gipsy, and o' good family, I'd never have found you."

" You're a good old woman," he said. " I suppose you've some news for me ? "

" I have," she answered; " come away after me."

He followed her into a booth, and they sat down. She began the conversation.

" Are you married ? " she asked.

" Ay · a month since."

ɪ

" And you've got her money ? "

" Yes," he said ; " but I've been walking into it."

" Make the most of it," said Madge. " Your father's dead."

" Dead ! "

" Ay, dead. And what's worse, lad, he lived long enough to alter his will."

" Oh, Lord ! What do you mean ? "

" I mean," she said, " that he has left all his money to your cousin. He found out everything, all in a minute, as it were ; and he brought a new will home from Exeter, and I witnessed it. And he turned me out of doors, and, next morning, after I was gone, he was found dead in his bed. I got to London, and found no trace of you there, till, by an accident, I heard that you had been seen down here, so I came on. I've got my living by casting fortins, and begging, and cadging, and such like. Sometime I've slept in a barn, and sometime in a hedge, but I've fought my way to you, true and faithful, through it all, you see."

" So he's gone," said George, between his teeth, " and his money with him. That's awful. What an unnatural old villain ! "

" He got it into his head at last, George, that you weren't his son at all."

" The lunatic !—and what put that into his head ? "

" He knew you weren't his wife's son, you see, and he had heard some stories about me before I came to live with him, and so, at the last, he took to saying he'd nought to do with you."

" Then you mean to say——"

" That you are my boy," she said, " my own boy. Why, lad, who but thy own mother would a' done for thee what I have ? And thou never thinking of it all these years ! Blind lad ! "

" Good God ! " said George. " And if I had only known that before, how differently I'd have gone on. How I'd have sneaked and truckled, and fetched and carried for him ! Bah, it's enough to drive one mad. All this hide-and-seek work don't pay, old woman. You and I are bowled out with it. How easy for you to have given me a hint of this years ago, to make me careful ! But you delight in mystery and conglomeration, and you always will. There—I ain't ungrateful, but when I think of what we've lost, no wonder I get wild. And what the devil am I to do now ? "

" You've got the girl's money to go on with," she said.

" Not so very much of it," he replied. " I tell you I've been playing like—never mind what, this last month, and I've lost every night. Then I've got another woman in tow, that costs—oh curse her, what don't she cost, what with money and bother ?—In short, if I don't get something from somewhere, in a few months I shall be in Queer Street. What chance is there of the parson's dying ? "

" It don't matter much to you when he dies, I expect," said she,

" for you may depend that those that's got hold of him won't let his money come into your hands. He's altered his will, you may depend on it."

" Do you really think so?"

" I should think it more probable than not. You see that old matter with the Bank is known all over the country, although they don't seem inclined to push it against you, for some reason. Yet it's hardly likely that the Vicar would let his money go to a man who couldn't be seen for fear of a rope."

" You're a raven, old woman," he said. " What am I to do?"

" Give up play, to begin with."

" Well?"

" Start some business with what's left."

" Ha, ha! Well, I'll think of it. You must want some money, old girl! Here's a fipunnote."

" I don't want money, my boy; I'm all right," she said.

" Oh, nonsense; take it."

" I won't," she answered. " Give me a kiss, George."

He kissed her forehead, and bent down his head reflecting. When he looked up she was gone.

He ran out of the booth and looked right and left, but saw her nowhere. Then he went sulkily back to his wife. He hardly noticed her, but said it was time to go home. All the way back, and after they had reached their lodgings, he kept the same moody silence, and she, frightened at some unheard-of calamity, forbore to question him. But when she was going to bed she could withhold her anxiety no longer, and said to him,—

" Oh, George, you have got some bad news; let me share it with you. If it is anything about my father, I implore you to tell me. How is it I have got no answer to the letter I wrote a month ago?"

He answered her savagely, " I don't know anything about your father, and I don't care. I've got bad news, d—d bad news, if that will make you sleep the sounder. And, once for all, you'll find it best, when you see me sulky, not to give me any of your tantrums in addition. Mind that."

He had never spoken to her like that before. She went to her bed crushed and miserable, and spent the night in crying, while he went forth and spent the night with some of his new companions, playing wildly and losing recklessly, till the summer morning sun streamed through the shutters, and shone upon him desperate and nigh penniless, ripe for a fall lower than any he had had as yet.

CHAPTER XVI.

THE END OF MARY'S EXPEDITION.

LET us hurry over what is to follow. I who knew her so well can have no pleasure in dwelling over her misery and degradation. And he who reads these pages will, I hope, have little sympathy with the minor details of the life of such a man as George Hawker.

Some may think that she has been punished enough already, for leaving her quiet happy home to go away with such a man. "She must have learnt already," such would say, "that he cares nothing for her. Let her leave her money behind, and go back to her father to make such amends as she may for the misery she has caused him." Alas, my dear madam, who would rejoice in such a termination of her troubles more than myself? But it is not for me to mete out degrees of punishment. I am trying with the best of my poor abilities to write a true history of certain people whom I knew. And I, no more than any other human creature, can see the consequences that will follow on any one act of folly or selfishness, such as this poor foolish girl has committed. We must wait and watch, judging with all charity. Let you and me go on with her even to the very end.

Good men draw together very slowly. Yet it is one of the greatest happinesses one is capable of, to introduce two such to one another, and see how soon they become friends. But bad men congregate like crows or jackals, and when a new one appears, he is received into the pack without question, as soon as he has given proof sufficient of being a rascal.

This was the case with George Hawker. His facility for making acquaintance with rogues and blacklegs was perfectly marvellous. Any gentleman of this class seemed to recognise him instinctively, and became familiar immediately. So that soon he had round him such a circle of friends as would have gone hard to send to the dogs the most honourable and virtuous young man in the three kingdoms.

When a new boy goes to school, his way is smoothed very much at first by the cakes and pocket-money he brings with him. Till these are gone he must be a weak boy indeed who cannot (at a small school) find some one to fight his battles and fetch and carry for him. Thackeray has thought of this (what does he not think of?) in his little book, "Dr. Birch," where a young sycophant is represented saying to his friend, who has just received a hamper, "Hurrah, old fellow, *I'll lend you my knife.*" This was considered so true to nature, on board a ship in which I once made a long voyage, that it passed into a proverb with us, and if any one was seen indulging in a luxury out of the way at dinner,—say an extra bottle of wine out of his private store,—half-a-dozen would cry out at once, "Hurrah, old fellow, I'll lend you my knife:" a modest way of requesting to be asked to take a glass of wine better than that supplied by the steward.

In the same way, George Hawker was treated by the men he had got round him as a man who had a little property that he had not got rid of, and as one who was to be used with some civility, until his money was gone, and he sank down to the level of the rest of them—to the level of living by his wits, if they were sharp enough to make a card or billiard sharper; or otherwise to find his level among the proscribed of society, let that be what it might.

And George's wits were not of the first order, or the second ; and his manners and education were certainly not those of a gentleman, or likely to be useful in attracting such unwary persons as these Arabs of the metropolis preyed upon. So it happened that when all his money was played away, which came to pass in a month or two, the higher and cleverer class of rascals began to look uncommonly cold upon him.

At first poor crushed Mary used to entertain of an evening some of the *élite* among the card-sharpers of London—men who actually could have spoken to a gentleman in a public place, and not have got kicked. These men were polite, and rather agreeable, and one of them, a Captain Saxon, was so deferential to her, and seemed so entirely to understand her position, that she grew very fond of him, and was always pleased to see him at her house.

Though, indeed, she saw but little of any men who came there, soon after any of them arrived, she used to receive a signal from George, which she dared not disobey, to go to bed. And when she lay there, lonely and sleepless, she could detect, from the absence of conversation, save now and then a low, fierce oath, that they were playing desperately, and at such times she would lie trembling and crying. Once or twice, during the time she remembered these meetings, they were rudely broken upon by oaths and blows, and on one particular occasion, she heard one of the gamesters, when infuriated, call her husband "a d—d swindling dog of a forger."

In these times, which lasted but a few months, she began to reflect what a fool she had been, and how to gratify her fancy she had thrown from her everything solid and worth keeping in the world. She had brought herself to confess, in bitterness and anguish, that he did not love her, and never had, and that she was a miserable unhappy dupe. But, notwithstanding, she loved him still, though she dreaded the sight of him, for she got little from him now but oaths and taunts.

It was soon after their return from Brighton that he broke out, first on some trivial occasion, and cursed her aloud. He said he hated the sight of her pale face, for it always reminded him of ruin and misery; that he had the greatest satisfaction in telling her that he was utterly ruined; that his father was dead, and had left his money elsewhere, and that her father was little better; that she would soon be in the workhouse; and, in fine, said everything that his fierce, wild, brutal temper could suggest.

She never tempted another outbreak of the kind; that one was too horrible for her, and crushed her spirit at once. She only tried by mildness and submission to deprecate his rage. But every day he came home looking fiercer and wilder; as time went on her heart sunk within her, and she dreaded something more fearful than she had experienced yet.

As I said, after a month or two, his first companions began to drop off, or only came, bullying and swearing, to demand money. And now another class of men began to take their place, the sight of whom made her blood cold—worse dressed than the others, and worse mannered, with strange, foul oaths on their lips. And then, after a time, two ruffians, worse looking than any of the others, began to come there, of whom the one she dreaded most was called Maitland.

He was always very civil to her; but there was something about him, his lowering, evil face, and wild looks, which made him a living nightmare to her. She knew he was flying from justice, by the way he came and went, and by the precaution always taken when he was there. But when he came to live in the room over theirs, and when, by listening at odd times, she found that he and her husband were engaged in some great villany, the nature of which she could not understand, then she saw that there was nothing to do, but in sheer desperation to sit down and wait the catastrophe.

About this time she made another discovery, that she was penniless, and had been so some time. George had given her money from time to time to carry on household expenses, and she contrived to make these sums answer well enough. But one day, determined to know the worst, she asked him, at the risk of another explosion, how their account stood at the bank? He replied in the best of his humours, apparently, "that the five thousand they had had there had been overdrawn some six weeks, and that, if it hadn't been for his exertions in various ways, she'd have been starved out before now."

" All gone !" she said ; " and where to ?"

" To the devil," he answered. " And you may go after it."

" And what are we to do now, George ?"

" The best we can."

" But the baby, George ? I shall lie-in in three months."

" You 'must take your chance, and the baby too. As long as there's any money going you'll get some of it. If you wrote to your father you might get some."

" I'll never do that," she said.

" Won't you?" said he ; " I'll starve you into it when money gets scarce."

Things remained like this till it came to be nearly ten months from their marriage. Mary had never written home but once, from Brighton, and then, as we know, the answer had miscarried ; so she, conceiving she was cast off by her father, had never attempted to communicate with him again. The time drew nigh that she should be confined, and she got very sick and ill, and still the man Maitland lived in the house, and he and George spent much of their time away together at night.

Yet poor Mary had a friend who stayed by her through it all— Captain Saxon, the great billiard sharper. Many a weary hour, when she was watching up anxious and ill, for her husband, this man would come and sit with her, talking agreeably and well about many things ; but chiefly about the life he used to lead before he fell so low as he was then.

He used to say, " Mrs. Hawker, you cannot tell what a relief and pleasure it is to me to have a *lady* to talk to again. You must conceive how a man brought up like myself misses it."

" Surely, Captain Saxon," she would say, " you have some relations left. Why not go back to them ? "

" They wouldn't own me," he said. " I smashed everything, a fine fortune amongst other things, by my goings on ; and they very properly cast me off. I never got beyond the law, though. Many well-known men speak to me now, but they won't play with me, though ; I am too good. And so you see I play dark to win from young fellows, and I am mixed up with a lot of scoundrels. A man brought an action against me the other day to recover two hundred pounds I won of him, but he couldn't do anything. And the judge said, that though the law couldn't touch me, yet I was mixed up notoriously with a gang of sharpers. That was a pleasant thing to hear in court, wasn't it ?—but true."

" It has often surprised me to see how temperate you are, Captain Saxon," she said.

" I am forced to be," he said ; " I must keep my hand steady. See there ; it's as firm as a rock. No ; the consolation of drink is denied me ; I have something to live for still. I'll tell you a secret. I've insured my life very high in favour of my little sister whom I ruined, and who is out as a governess. If I don't pay up to the last, you see, or if I commit suicide, she'll lose the money. I pay very high, I assure you. On one occasion not a year ago, I played for the money to pay the premium only two nights before it would have been too late. There was touch and go for you ! But my hand was as steady as a rock, and after the last game was over I fainted."

" Good Lord," she said, " what a terrible life ! But suppose you fall into sickness and poverty. Then you may fall into arrear, and she will lose everything after all."

He laughed aloud. A strange wild laugh. "No," said he; "I am safe there, if physicians are to be believed. Sometimes, when I am falling asleep, my heart begins to flutter and whirl, and I sit up in bed, breathless and perspiring till it grows still again. Then I laugh to myself, and say, 'Not this time then, but it can't be long now.' Those palpitations, Mrs. Hawker, are growing worse and worse each month. I have got a desperate incurable heart complaint, that will carry me off, sudden and sure, without warning, I hope to a better sort of world than this."

"I am sorry for you, Captain Saxon," she said, sobbing, "so very, very sorry for you!"

"I thank you kindly, my good friend," he replied. "It's long since I had so good a friend as you. Now change the subject. I want to talk to you about yourself. You are going to be confined."

"In a few days, I fear," she said.

"Have you money?"

"My husband seems to have money enough at present, but we have none to fall back upon."

"What friends have you?"

"None that I can apply to."

"H'm," he said. "Well, you must make use of me, and as far as I can manage it, of my purse too, in case of an emergency. I mean, you know, Mrs. Hawker," he added, looking full at her, "to make this offer to you as I would to my own sister. Don't in God's name refuse my protection, such as it is, from any mistaken motives of jealousy. Now tell me, as honestly as you dare, how do you believe your husband gets his living?"

"I have not the least idea, but I fear the worst."

"You do right," he said. "Forewarned is forearmed, and, at the risk of frightening you, I must bid you prepare for the worst. Although I know nothing about what he is engaged in, yet I know that the man Maitland, who lives above, and who you say is your husband's constant companion, is a desperate man. If anything happens, apply to me straightway, and I will do all I can. My principal hope is in putting you in communication with your friends. Could you not trust me with your story, that we might take advice together?"

She told him all from beginning to the end, and at the last she said, "If the worst should come, whatever that may be, I would write for help to Major Buckley, for the sake of the child that is to come."

"Major Buckley!"—he asked eagerly,—"do you mean James Buckley of the —th?"

"The same man," she replied, "my kindest friend."

" Oh, Lord ! " he said, growing pale, " I've got one of these spasms coming on. A glass of water, my dear lady, in God's name ! "

He held both hands on his heart, and lay back in his chair a little, with livid lips, gasping for breath. By degrees his white hands dropped upon his lap, and he said with a sigh, " Nearer still, old friend, nearer than ever. Not far off now."

But he soon recovered and said, " Mrs. Hawker, if you ever see ·hat man Buckley again, tell him that you saw Charley Biddulph, who was once his friend, fallen to be the consort of rogues and thieves, cast off by every one, and dying of a heart complaint; but tell him he could not die without sending a tender love to his good old comrade, and that he remembered him and loved him to the very end."

" And I shall say too," said Mary, " when all neglected me, and forgot me, this Charles Biddulph helped and cheered me; and when I was fallen to the lowest, that he was still to me a courteous gentleman, and a faithful adviser; and that but for him and his goodness I should have sunk into desperation long ago. Be sure that I will say this too."

The door opened, and George Hawker came in.

" Good evening, Captain Saxon," said he. " My wife seems to make herself more agreeable to you than she does to me. I hope you are pleased with her. However, you are welcome to be. I thank God I ain't jealous. Where's Maitland ? "

" He has not been here to-night, George," she said, timidly.

" Curse him, then. Give me a candle ; I'm going up-stairs. Don't go on my account, Captain Saxon. Well, if you will, good night."

Saxon bade him good night, and went. George went up into Maitland's room, where Mary was never admitted ; and soon she heard him hammer, hammering at metal, overhead. She was too used to that sound to take notice of it ; so she went to bed, but lay long awake, thinking of poor Captain Saxon.

Less than a week after that she was confined. She had a boy, and that gave her new life. Poorly provided for as that child was, he could not have been more tenderly nursed or more prized and loved, if he had been born in the palace, with his Majesty's right honourable ministers in the ante-room, drinking dry Sillery in honour of the event.

Now she could endure what was to come better. And less than a month after, just as she was getting well again, all her strength and courage were needed. The end came.

She was sitting before the fire, about ten o'clock at night, nursing her baby, when she heard the street-door opened by a key ; and the next moment her husband and Maitland were in the room.

" Sit quiet, now, or I'll knock your brains out with the poker," said George; and, seizing a china ornament from the chimney-piece, he thrust it into the fire, and heaped the coals over it.

" We're caught like rats, you fool, if they have tracked us," said Maitland; " and nothing but your consummate folly to thank for it. I deserve hanging for mixing myself up with such a man in a thing like this. Now, are you coming; or do you want half-an-hour to wish your wife good-bye?"

George never answered that question. There was a noise of breaking glass down-stairs, and a moment after a sound of several feet on the stair.

" Make a fight for it," said Maitland, "if you can do nothing else. Make for the back-door."

But George stood aghast, while Mary trembled in every limb. The door was burst open, and a tall man coming in said, "In the King's name, I arrest you, George Hawker and William Maitland, for coining."

Maitland threw himself upon the man, and they fell crashing over the table. George dashed at the door, but was met by two others. For a minute there was a wild scene of confusion and struggling, while Mary crouched against the wall with the child, shut her eyes, and tried to pray. When she looked round again she saw her husband and Maitland securely handcuffed, and the tall man, who first came in, wiping the blood from a deep cut in his forehead, said,

" There is nothing against this woman, is there, Sanders?"

" Nothing, sir, except that she is the prisoner Hawker's wife."

" Poor woman!" said the tall man. " She has been lately confined, too. I don't think it will be necessary to take her into custody. Take away the prisoners; I shall stay here and search."

He began his search by taking the tongs and pulling the fire to pieces. Soon he came to the remnants of the china ornament which George had thrown in; and, after a little more raking, two or three round pieces of metal fell out of the grate.

" A very green trick," he remarked. " Well, they must stay there to cool before I can touch them; " and turning to Mary said, " Could you oblige me with some sticking-plaster? Your husband's confederate has given me an ugly blow."

She got some, and put it on for him. " Oh, sir!" she said, " Can you tell me what this is all about?"

" Easy, ma'am," said he. " Maitland is one of the most notorious coiners in England, and your husband is his confederate and assistant. We've been watching, just to get a case that there would be no trouble about, and we've got it."

" And if it is proved?" she asked, trembling.

He looked very serious. " Mrs. Hawker, I know your history,

as well as your husband's, the same as if you told it to me. So I am sorry to give a lady who is in misfortune more pain than I can help; but you know coining is a hanging matter."

She rocked herself wildly to and fro, and the chair where she sat, squeezing the child against her bosom till he cried. She soothed him again without a word, and then said to the officer, who was searching every nook and cranny in the room:

"Shall you be obliged to turn me out of here, or may I stay a few nights?"

"You can stay as long as you please, madam," he said; "that's a matter with your landlady, not me. But if I was you I'd communicate with my friends, and get some money to have my husband defended."

"They'd sooner pay for the rope to hang him," she said. "You seem a kind and pitiful sort of man; tell me honestly, is there any chance for him?"

"Honestly, none. There may be some chance of his life; but there is evidence enough on this one charge, leave alone others, mind you, to convict twenty men. Why, we've evidence of two forgeries committed on his father before ever he married you; so that, if he is acquitted on this charge, he'll be arrested for another outside the court."

All night long she sat up nursing the child before the fire, which from time to time she replenished. The officers in possession slept on sofas, and dozed in chairs; but when the day broke she was still there, pale and thoughtful, sitting much in the same place and attitude as she did before all this happened, the night before, which seemed to her like a year ago, so great was the change since then. "So," thought she, "he was nothing but a villain after all. He had merely gained her heart for money's sake, and cast her off when it was gone. What a miserable fool she had been, and how rightly served now, to be left penniless in the world!"

Penniless, but not friendless. She remembered Captain Saxon, and determined to go to him and ask his advice. So when the strange weird morning had crept on, to such time as the accustomed crowd began to surge through the street, she put on her bonnet, and went away for the first time to seek him at his lodgings, in a small street, leading off Piccadilly.

An old woman answered the door. "The Captain was gone," she said, "to Boulogne, and wouldn't be back yet for a fortnight. Would she leave any name?"

She hardly thought it worth while. All the world seemed to have deserted her now; but she said, more in absence of mind than for any other reason, "Tell him that Mrs. Hawker called, if you please."

"Mrs. Hawker!" the old woman said; "there's a letter for you, ma'am, I believe; and something particular too, 'cause he told me to keep it in my desk till you called. Just step in, if you please."

Mary followed her in, and she produced a letter directed to Mrs. Hawker. When Mary opened it, which she did in the street, after the door was shut, the first thing she saw was a bank-note for five pounds, and behind it was the following note :—

" I am forced to go to Boulogne, at a moment's notice, with a man whom I must not lose sight of. Should you have occasion to apply to me during my absence (which is fearfully probable), I have left this, begging your acceptance of it, in the same spirit as that in which it was offered ; and I pray you to accept this piece of advice at the same time :—

" Apply instantly to your friends, and go back to them at once. Don't stop about London on any excuse. You have never known what it is to be without money yet ; take care you never do. When a man or a woman is poor and hungry, there is a troop of devils who always follow such, whispering all sorts of things to them. They are all, or nearly all, known to me : take care you do not make their acquaintance.

" Yours most affectionately,
                " CHARLES BIDDULPH."

What a strange letter, she thought. He must be mad. Yet there was method in his madness, too. Devils such as he spoke of had leant over her chair and whispered to her before now, plain to be heard. But that was in the old times, when she sat brooding alone over the fire at night. She was no longer alone now, and they had fled—fled, scared at the face of a baby.

She went home and spoke to the landlady. But little was owing, and that she had money enough to pay without the five pounds that the kind gambler had given her. However, when she asked the landlady whether she could stay there a week or two longer, the woman prayed her with tears to begone ; that she and her husband had brought trouble enough on them already.

But there was still a week left of their old tenancy, so she held possession in spite of the landlady ; and from the police-officers, who were still about the place, she heard that the two prisoners had been committed for trial, and that that trial would take place early in the week at the Old Bailey.

Three days before the trial she had to leave the lodgings, with but little more than two pounds in the world. For those three days she got lodging as she could in coffee-houses and such places, always meeting, however, with that sort of kindness and sympathy from the women belonging to them which could not be bought for money. She was in such a dull state of despair, that she was happily insensible to all smaller discomforts, and on the day of the trial she endeavoured to push into the court with her child in her arms.

The crowd was too dense, and the heat was too great for her, so she came outside and sat on some steps on one side of a passage. Once she had to move as a great personage came up, and then one of the officers said,—

"Come, my good woman, you mustn't sit there, you know. That's the judge's private door."

"I beg pardon," she said, "and I will move, if you wish me. But they are trying my husband for coining, and the court is too hot for the child. If you will let me sit there, I will be sure to get out of the way when my lord comes past."

The man looked at her as if it was a case somewhat out of his experience, and went away. Soon, however, he came back again, and after staring at her a short time, said,—

"Do you want anything, missis? Anything I can get?"

"I am much obliged to you, nothing," she said; "but if you can tell me how the trial is going on, I shall be obliged to you."

He shook his head and went away, and when he returned, telling her that the judge was summing up, he bade her follow him, and found her a place in a quiet part of the court. She could see her husband and Maitland standing in the dock, quite close to her, and before them the judge was calmly, slowly, and distinctly giving the jury the history of the case from beginning to end. She was too much bewildered and desperate to listen to it, but she was attracted by the buzz of conversation which arose when the jury retired. They seemed gone a bare minute to her, when she heard and understood that the prisoners were found guilty. Then she heard Maitland sentenced to death, and George Hawker condemned to be transported beyond the seas for the term of his natural life, in consideration of his youth; so she brought herself to understand that the game was played out, and turned to go.

The officer who had been kind to her stopped her, and asked her "where she was going?" She answered, "To Devonshire," and passed on, but almost immediately pushed back to him through the crowd, which was pouring out of the doors, and thanked him for his kindness to her. Then she went out with the crowd into the street, and almost instinctively struck westward.

Through the western streets, roaring with carriages, crowded with foot passengers, like one in a dream; past the theatres, and the arches, and all the great, rich world, busy seeking its afternoon pleasure: through the long suburbs, getting more scattered as she went on, and so out on to the dusty broad western highway: a lonely wanderer, with only one thought in her throbbing head, to reach such home as was left her before she died.

At the first quiet spot she came to she sat down and forced herself to think. Two hundred miles to go, and fifteen shillings to keep her. Never mind, she could beg; she had heard that some made a trade of begging, and did well; hard if she should die on the road. So she pushed on through the evening toward the sinking sun, till the milestones passed slower and slower, and then she found shelter in a tramps' lodging-house, and got what rest she could. In a week she was at Taunton. Then the weather, which had hitherto been fair and pleasant, broke up, and still she held on (with the rain beating from the westward in her face, as though to stay her from her refuge), dizzy and confused, but determined still, along the miry high-road.

She had learnt from a gipsy woman, with whom she had walked in company for some hours, how to carry her child across her back, slung in her shawl. So, with her breast bare to the storm, she fought her way over the high bleak downs, glad and happy when the boy ceased his wailing, and lay warm and sheltered behind her, swathed in every poor rag she could spare from her numbed and dripping body.

Late on a wild rainy night she reached Exeter, utterly penniless, and wet to the skin. She had had nothing to eat since noon, and her breast was failing for want of nourishment and over-exertion. Still it was only twenty miles further. Surely, she thought, God had not saved her through two hundred such miles, to perish at last. The child was dry and warm, and fast asleep, and if she could get some rest in one of the doorways in the lower part of the town, till she was stronger, she could fight her way on to Drumston; so she held on to St. Thomas's, and finding an archway drier than the others, sat down, and took the child upon her lap.

Rest!—rest was a fiction; she was better walking—such aches, and cramps, and pains in every joint! She would get up and push on, and yet minute after minute went by, and she could not summon courage.

She was sitting with her beautiful face in the light of a lamp. A woman well and handsomely dressed was passing rapidly through the rain, but on seeing her stopped and said :—

" My poor girl, why do you sit there in the damp entry such a a night as this ?"

" I am cold, hungry, ruined; that's why I sit under the arch," replied Mary, rising up.

" Come home with me," said the woman : "I will take care of you."

" I am going to my friends," replied she.

" Are you sure they will be glad to see you, my dear," said the woman, " with that pretty little pledge at your bosom ?"

" I care not," said Mary, " I told you I was desperate."

" Desperate, my pretty love," said the woman ; " a girl with beauty like yours should never be desperate ; come with me."

Mary stepped forward and struck her, so full and true that the woman reeled backwards, and stood whimpering and astonished.

"Out! you false jade," said Mary; "you are one of those devils that Saxon told me of, who come whispering, and peering, and crowding behind those who are penniless and deserted; but I have faced you, and struck you, and I tell you to go back to your master, and say that I am not for him."

The woman went crying and frightened down the street, thinking that she had been plying her infamous trade on a lunatic; but Mary sat down again and nursed the child.

But the wind changed a little, and the rain began to beat in on her shelter; she arose, and went down the street to seek a new one.

She found a deep arch, well sheltered, and, what was better, a lamp inside, so that she could sit on the stone step, and see her baby's face. Dainty quarters, truly! She went to take possession, and started back with a scream.

What delusion was this? There, under the lamp, on the step, sat a woman, her own image, nursing a baby so like her own that she looked down at her bosom to see if it was safe. It must be a fancy of her own disordered brain; but no—for when she gathered up her courage, and walked towards it, a woman she knew well started up, and, laughing wildly, cried out,

"Ha! ha! Mary Thornton."

"Ellen Lee?" said Mary, aghast.

"That's me, dear," replied the other; "you're welcome, my love, welcome to the cold stones, and wet streets, and to hunger and drunkenness, and evil words, and the abomination of desolation. That's what we all come to, my dear. Is that his child?"

"Whose?" said Mary. "This is George Hawker's child."

"Hush, my dear!" said the other; "we never mention his name in our society, you know. This is his too—a far finer one than yours. Cis Jewell had one of his too, a poor little rat of a thing that died, and now the minx is flaunting about the High-street every night, in her silks and her feathers as bold as brass. I hope you'll have nothing to say to her; you and I will keep house together. They are looking after me to put me in the madhouse. You'll come too, of course."

"God have mercy on you, poor Nelly!" said Mary.

"Exactly so, my dear," the poor lunatic replied. "Of course He will. But about him you know. You heard the terms of his bargain?"

"What do you mean?" asked Mary.

"Why, about him you know, G—— H——, Madge the witch's son. He sold himself to the deuce, my dear, on condition of ruining a poor girl every year. And he has kept his contract hitherto. If he don't, you know —— come here, I want to whisper to you."

The poor girl whispered rapidly in her ear; but Mary broke away from her and fled rapidly down the street, poor Ellen shouting after her, "Ha, ha! the parson's daughter, too,—ha, ha!"

"Let me get out of this town, O Lord!" she prayed most earnestly, "if I die in the fields." And so she sped on, and paused not till she was full two miles out of the town towards home, leaning on the parapet of the noble bridge that even then crossed the river Exe.

The night had cleared up, and a soft and gentle westerly breeze was ruffling the broad waters of the river, where they slept deep, dark, and full above the weir. Just below where they broke over the low rocky barrier, the rising moon showed a hundred silver spangles among the broken eddies.

The cool breeze and the calm scene quieted and soothed her, and, for the first time for many days, she began to think.

She was going back, but to what? To a desolated home, to a heart-broken father, to the jeers and taunts of her neighbours. The wife of a convicted felon, what hope was left for her in this world? None. And that child that was sleeping so quietly on her bosom, what a mark was set on him from this time forward!—the son of Hawker the coiner! Would it not be better if they both were lying below there in the cold still water, at rest?

But she laughed aloud. "This is the last of the devils he talked of," said she. "I have fought the others and beat them. I won't yield to this one."

She paused abashed, for a man on horseback was standing before her as she turned. Had she not been so deeply engaged in her own thoughts she might have heard him merrily whistling as he approached from the town, but she heard him not, and was first aware of his presence when he stood silently regarding her, not two yards off.

"My girl," he said, "I fear you're in a bad way. I don't like to see a young woman, pretty as I can see you are even now, standing on a bridge, with a baby, talking to herself."

"You mistake me," she said, "I was not going to do that; I was resting and thinking."

"Where are you going?" he asked.

"To Crediton," she replied. "Once there, I should almost fancy myself safe."

"See here," he said; "my waggon is coming up behind. I can give you a lift as far as there. Are you hungry?"

"Ah," she said, "if you knew. If you only knew!"

They waited for the waggon's coming up, for they could hear the horses' bells chiming cheerily across the valley. "I had an only daughter went away once," he said. "But, glory to God! I got her back again, though she brought a child with her. And I've grown to be fonder of that poor little base-born one than anything in this world. So cheer up."

"I am married," she said; "this is my lawful boy, though it were better, perhaps, he had never been born."

"Don't say that, my girl," said the old farmer, for such she took him to be, "but thank God you haven't been deceived like so many are."

The waggon came up and was stopped. He made her take such refreshment as was to be got, and then get in and lie quiet among the straw till in the grey morning they reached Crediton. The weather had grown bad again, and long before sunrise, after thanking and blessing her benefactor, poor Mary struck off once more, with what strength she had left, along the deep red lanes, through the driving rain.

CHAPTER XVII.

EXODUS.

BUT let us turn and see what has been going forward in the old parsonage this long weary year. Not much that is noteworthy, I fear. The chronicle of a year's sickness and unhappiness, would be rather uninteresting, so I must get on as quick as I can.

The Vicar only slowly revived from the fit in which he fell on the morning of Mary's departure to find himself hopelessly paralytic, unable to walk without support, and barely able to articulate distinctly. It was when he was in this state, being led up and down the garden by the Doctor and Frank Maberly, the former of whom was trying to attract his attention to some of their old favourites, the flowers, that Miss Thornton came to him with the letter which Mary had written from Brighton, immediately after their marriage.

It was, on the whole, a great relief for the Vicar. He had dreaded to hear worse than this. They had kept from him all knowledge of Hawker's forgery on his father, which had been communicated to them by Major Buckley. So that he began to prepare his mind for the reception of George Hawker as a son-in-law, and to force himself to like him. So with shaking palsied hand he wrote :—

"Dear Girl,—In sickness or sorrow, remember that I am still your father. I hope you will not stop long in London, but come back and stay near me. We must forget all that has passed, and make the best of it.—JOHN THORNTON."

Miss Thornton wrote :—

"My dearest foolish Mary,—How could you leave us like that, my love! Oh, if you had only let us know what was going on, I could have told you such things, my dear. But now you will never know them, I hope. I hope Mr. Hawker will use you kindly. Your father hopes that you and he may come down and live near him, but

K

we know that 1. .mpossible. If your father were to know of your husband's fearful delinquencies, it would kill him at once. But when trouble comes on you, my love, as it must in the end, remember that there is still a happy home left you here."

These letters she never received. George burnt them without giving them to her, so that for a year she remained under the impression that they had cast her off. So only at the last did she, as the sole hope of warding off poverty and misery from her child, determine to cast herself upon their mercy.

The year had nearly passed, when the Vicar had another stroke, a stroke that rendered him childish and helpless, and precluded all possibility of his leaving his bed again. Miss Thornton found that it was necessary to have a man servant in the house now, to move him, and so on. So one evening, when Major and Mrs. Buckley and the Doctor had come down to sit with her, she asked, " did they know a man who could undertake the business ? "

" I do," said the Doctor. " I know a man who would suit you exactly. A strong knave enough. An old soldier."

" I don't think we should like a soldier in the house, Doctor," said Miss Thornton. " They use such very odd language sometimes, you know."

" This man never swears," said the Doctor.

" But soldiers are apt to drink sometimes, you know, Doctor," said Miss Thornton. " And that wouldn't do in this case."

" I've known the man all my life," said the Doctor with animation. " And I never saw him drunk."

" He seems faultless, Doctor," said the Major, smiling.

" No, he is not faultless, but he has his qualifications for the office, nevertheless. He can read passably, and might amuse our poor old friend in that way. He is not evil tempered, though hasty, and I think he would be tender and kindly to the old man. He had a father once himself, this man, and he nursed him to his latest day, as well as he was able, after his mother had left them and gone on the road to destruction. And my man has picked up some knowledge of medicine too, and might be a useful ally to the physician."

" A paragon ! " said Mrs. Buckley, laughing. " Now let us hear his faults, dear Doctor."

" They are many," he replied, " I don't deny. But not such as to make him an ineligible person in this matter. To begin with, he is a fool—a dreaming fool, who once mixed himself up with politics, and went on the assumption that truth would prevail against humbug. And when he found his mistake, this fellow, instead of staying at his post, as a man should, he got disgusted, and beat a cowardly retreat, leaving his duty unfulfilled. When I look at one side of this man's life, I wonder why such useless fellows as he were born into the world. But I opine that every man is of some use, and that my friend may still have manhood enough left in him to move an old paralytic man in his bed."

" And his name, Doctor? You must tell us that," said Mrs. Buckley, looking sadly at him.

" I am that man," said the Doctor, rising. " Dear Miss Thornton, you will allow me to come down and stay with you. I shall be so glad to be of any use to my old friend, and I am so utterly useless now."

What could she say, but " yes," with a thousand thanks, far more than she could express? So he took up his quarters at the Vicarage, and helped her in the labour of love.

The Sunday morning after he came to stay there, he was going down stairs, shortly after daybreak, to take a walk in the fresh morning air, when on the staircase he met Miss Thornton, and she, putting sixpence into his hand, said,

" My dear Doctor, I looked out of window just now, and saw a tramper woman sitting on the door-step. She has black hair and a baby, like a gipsy. And I am so nervous about gipsies, you know. Would you give her that and tell her to go away?"

The Doctor stepped down with the sixpence in his hand to do as he was bid. Miss Thornton followed him. He opened the front door, and there sure enough sat a woman, her hair, wet with the last night's rain, knotted loosely up behind her hatless head. She sat upon the door-step rocking herself to and fro, partly it would seem from disquietude, and partly to soothe the baby which was lying on her lap crying. Her back was towards him, and the Doctor only had time to notice that she was young, when he began,—

" My good soul, you mustn't sit there, you know. It's Sunday morning, and ——"

No more. He had time to say no more. Mary rose from the step and looked at him.

" You are right, sir, I have no business here. But if you will tell him that I only came back for the child's sake, he will hear me. I couldn't leave it in the workhouse, you know."

Miss Thornton ran forward, laughing wildly, and hugged her to her honest heart. " My darling!" she said, " My own darling! I knew she would find her home at last. In trouble and in sorrow I told her where she was to come. Oh happy trouble, that has brought our darling back to us!"

" Aunt! aunt!" said Mary, " don't kill me. Scold me a little, aunt dear, only a little."

" Scold you, my darling! Never, never! Scold you on this happy Sabbath morn! Oh! never, my love."

And the foolishness of these two women was so great that the Doctor had to go for a walk. Right down the garden, round the cow-yard, and in by the back way to the kitchen, where he met

Frank, and told him what had happened. And there they were at it again. Miss Thornton kneeling, wiping poor Mary's blistered feet before the fire; while the maid, foolishly giggling, had got possession of the baby, and was talking more affectionate nonsense to it than ever baby heard in this world before.

Mary held out her hand to him, and when he gave her his vast brown paw, what does she do, but put it to her lips and kiss it?— as if there was not enough without that. And, to make matters worse, she quoted Scripture, and said, " Forasmuch as ye have done it unto the least of these, ye have done it unto me." So our good Doctor had nothing left but to break through that cloak of cynicism which he delighted to wear, (Lord knows why!) and to kiss her on the cheek, and to tell her how happy she had made them by coming back, let circumstances be what they might.

Then she told them, with bursts of wild weeping, what those circumstances were. And at last, when they were all quieted, Miss Thornton boldly volunteered to go up and tell the Vicar that his darling was returned.

So she went up, and Mary and the Doctor waited at the bed-room door and listened. The poor old man was far gone beyond feeling joy or grief to any great extent. When Miss Thornton raised him in his bed, and told him that he must brace up his nerves to hear some good news, he smiled a weary smile, and Mary looking in saw that he was so altered that she hardly knew him.

" I know," he said, lisping and hesitating painfully, " what you are going to tell me, sister. She is come home. I knew she would come at last. Please tell her to come to me at once; but I can't see him yet. I must get stronger first." So Mary went in to him, and Miss Thornton came out and closed the door. And when Mary came down stairs soon afterwards she could not talk to them, but remained a long time silent, crying bitterly.

The good news soon got up to Major Buckley's, and so after church they saw him striding up the path, leading the pony carrying his wife and baby. And while they were still busy welcoming her back, came a ring at the door, and a loud voice, asking if the owner of it might come in.

Who but Tom Troubridge! Who else was there to raise her four good feet off the ground, and kiss her on both cheeks, and call her his darling little sister! Who else was there who could have changed their tears into laughter so quick that their merriment was wafted up to the Vicar's room, and made him ring his bell, and tell them to send Tom up to him! And who but Tom could have lit the old man's face up with a smile, with the history of a new colt, that my lord's mare Thetis had dropped last week!

That was her welcome home. To the home she had dreaded coming to, expecting to be received with scorn and reproaches. To the home she had meant to come to only as a penitent, to leave her child there and go forth into the world to die. And here she found herself the honoured guest—treated as one who had been away on a journey, whom they had been waiting and praying for all the time, and who came back to them sooner than expected. None hold the force of domestic affection so cheap as those who violate it most rudely. How many proud unhappy souls are there at this moment, voluntarily absenting themselves from all that love them in the world, because they dread sneers and cold looks at home! And how many of these, going back, would find only tears of joy to welcome them, and hear that ever since their absence they had been spoken of with kindness and tenderness, and loved, perhaps, above all the others!

After dinner, when the women were alone together, Mrs. Buckley began,—

" Now, my dear Mary, you must hear all the news. My husband has had a letter from Stockbridge."

" Ah, dear old Jim!" said Mary; " and how is he?"

" He and Hamlyn are quite well," said Mrs. Buckley, " and settled. He has written such an account of that country to Major Buckley, that he, half persuaded before, is now wholly determined to go there himself."

" I heard of this before," said Mary. " Am I to lose you, then, at once?"

" We shall see," said Mrs. Buckley; " I have my ideas. Now, who do you think is going beside?"

" Half Devonshire, I should think," said Mary; " at least, all whom I care about."

" It would seem so, indeed, my poor girl," said Mrs. Buckley; " for your cousin Troubridge has made up his mind to come."

" There was a time when I could have stopped him," she thought; " but that is gone by now." And she answered Mrs. Buckley:—

" Aunt and I will stay here, and think of you all. Shall we ever hear from you? It is the other side of the world, is it not?"

" It is a long way; but we must wait, and see how things turn out. We may not have to separate after all. See, my dear; are you fully aware of your father's state? I fear you have only come home to see the last of him. He probably will be gone before this month is out. You see the state he is in. And when he is gone, have you reflected what to do?"

Mary, weeping bitterly, said, " No; only that she could never live in Drumston, or anywhere where she was known."

" That is wise, my love," said Mrs. Buckley, " under the circumstances. Have you made up your mind where to go, Miss Thornton, when you have to leave the Vicarage for a new incumbent?"

" I have made up my mind," answered Miss Thornton, " to go wherever Mary goes, if it be to the other end of the earth. We will be Ruth and Naomi, my dear. You would never get on without me."

"That is what I say," said Mrs. Buckley. "Never leave her. Why not come away out of all unhappy associations, and from the scorn and pity of your neighbours, to live safe and happy with all the best friends you have in the world?"

"What do you mean?" said Mary, "Ah, if we could only do so!"

"Come away with us," said Mrs. Buckley, with animation; "come away with us, and begin a new life. There is Troubridge looking high and low for a partner with five thousand pounds. Why should not Miss Thornton and yourself be his partners?"

"Ah me!" said Miss Thornton. "And think of the voyage! But I shall not decide on anything; Mary shall decide."

*   *   *   *   *   *

Scarcely more than a week elapsed from the day that Mary came home, when there came a third messenger for old John Thornton, and one so peremptory that he arose and followed it in the dead of night. So, when they came to his bedside in the morning, they found his body there, laid as it was when he wished them good night, but cold and dead. He himself was gone, and nothing remained but to bury his body decently beside his wife's, in the old churchyard, and to shed some tears, at the thought that never, by the fireside, or in the solemn old church, they should hear that kindly voice again.

And then came the disturbance of household gods, and the rupture of life-old associations. And although they were begged by the new comer not to hurry or incommode themselves, yet they too wished to be gone from the house whence everything they loved had departed.

Their kind true friend Frank was presented with the living, and they accepted Mrs. Buckley's invitation to stay at their house till they should have decided what to do. It was two months yet before the Major intended to sail, and long before those two months were past, Mary and Miss Thornton had determined that they would not rend asunder the last ties they had this side of the grave, but would cast in their lot with the others, and cross the weary sea with them towards a more hopeful land.

One more scene, and we have done with the Old World for many a year. Some of these our friends will never see it more, and those who do will come back with new thoughts and associations, as strangers to a strange land. Only those who have done so know how much effort it takes to say, "I will go away to a land where none know me or care for me, and leave for ever all that I know and love." And few know the feeling which comes upon all men after it is done,—the feeling of isolation, almost of terror, at having gone so far out of the bounds of ordinary life; the feeling of self-distrust and cowardice at being alone and friendless in the world, like a child in the dark.

*   *   *   *   *   *

A golden summer's evening is fading into a soft cloudless summer's night, and Doctor Mulhaus stands upon Mount Edgecombe, looking across the trees, across the glassy harbour, over the tall men-of-war, out beyond the silver line of surf on the breakwater, to where a tall ship is rapidly spreading her white wings, and speeding away each moment more rapidly before a fair wind, towards the south-west. He watches it growing more dim, minute by minute, in distance and in darkness, till he can see no longer; then brushing a tear from his eye he says aloud:—

"There goes my English microcosm. All my new English friends with whom I was going to pass the rest of my life, peaceful and contented, as a village surgeon. Pretty dream, two years long! Truly man hath no sure abiding place here. I will go back to Prussia, and see if they are all dead, or only sleeping."

So he turned down the steep path under the darkening trees, towards where he could see the town lights along the quays, among the crowded masts.

CHAPTER XVIII.

THE FIRST PUFF OF THE SOUTH WIND.

A NEW heaven and a new earth! Tier beyond tier, height above height, the great wooded ranges go rolling away westward, till on the lofty sky-line they are crowned with a gleam of everlasting snow. To the eastward they sink down, breaking into isolated forest-fringed peaks, and rock-crowned eminences, till with rapidly straightening lines they fade into the broad grey plains, beyond which the Southern Ocean is visible by the white sea-haze upon the sky.

All creation is new and strange. The trees, surpassing in size the largest English oaks, are of a species we have never seen before. The graceful shrubs, the bright-coloured flowers, ay, the very grass itself, are of species unknown in Europe; while flaming lories and brilliant parroquets fly whistling, not unmusically, through the gloomy forest, and over head in the higher fields of air, still lit up by the last rays of the sun, countless cockatoos wheel and scream in noisy joy, as we may see the gulls do about an English headland. To the northward a great glen, sinking suddenly from the saddle on which we stand, stretches away in long vista, until it joins a broader valley, through which we can dimly see a full-fed river winding along in gleaming reaches, through level meadow land, interspersed with clumps of timber.

We are in Australia. Three hundred and fifty miles south of Sydney, on the great watershed which divides the Belloury from the Maryburnong, since better known as the Snowy-river of Gipps-land.

As the sun was going down on the scene I have been describing, James Stockbridge and I, Geoffry Hamlyn, reined up our horses on the ridge above-mentioned, and gazed down the long gully which lay stretched at our feet. Only the tallest trees stood with their higher boughs glowing with the gold of the departing day, and we stood undetermined which route to pursue, and half inclined to camp at the next waterhole we should see. We had lost some cattle, and among others a valuable imported bull, which we were very anxious to recover. For five days we had been passing on from run to run, making inquiries without success, and were now fifty long miles from home in a southerly direction. We were beyond the bounds of all settlement; the last station we had been at was twenty miles to the north of us, and the occupiers of it, as they had told us the night before, had only taken up their country about ten weeks, and were as yet the furthest pioneers to the southward.

At this time Stockbridge and I had been settled in our new home about two years, and were beginning to get comfortable and con-tented. We had had but little trouble with the blacks, and having taken possession of a fine piece of country, were flourishing and well to do.

We had never heard from home but once, and that was from Tom Troubridge, soon after our departure, telling us that if we succeeded he should follow, for that the old place seemed changed now we were gone. We had neither of us left any near relations behind us, and already we began to think that we were cut off for ever from old acquaintances and associations, and were beginning to be resigned to it.

Let us return to where he and I were standing alone in the forest. I dismounted to set right some strap or another, and, instead of getting on my horse again at once, stood leaning against him, looking at the prospect, glad to ease my legs for a time, for they were cramped with many hours' riding.

Stockbridge sat in his saddle immoveable and silent as a statue, and when I looked in his face I saw that his heart had travelled further than his eye could reach, and that he was looking far beyond the horizon that bounded his earthly vision, away to the pleasant old home which was home to us no longer.

"Jim," said I, "I wonder what is going on at Drumston now?"

"I wonder," he said softly.

A pause.

Below us, in the valley, a mob of jackasses * were shouting and laughing uproariously, and a magpie was chanting his noble vesper hymn from a lofty tree.

"Jim," I began again, "do you ever think of poor little Mary now?"

"Yes, old boy, I do," he replied; "I can't help it; I was thinking of her then—I am always thinking of her, and, what's more, I always shall be. Don't think me a fool, old friend, but I love that girl as well now as ever I did. I wonder if she has married that fellow Hawker?"

"I fear there is but little doubt of it," I said; "try to forget her, James. Get in a rage with her, and be proud about it; you'll make all your life unhappy if you don't."

He laughed. "That's all very well, Jeff, but it's easier said than done.—Do you hear that? There are cattle down the gully."

There was some noise in the air, beside the evening rustle of the south wind among the tree-tops. Now it sounded like a far-off hubbub of waters, now swelled up harmonious, like the booming of cathedral bells across some rich old English valley on a still summer's afternoon.

"There are cattle down there, certainly," I said, "and a very large number of them; they are not ours, depend upon it: there are men with them, too, or they would not make so much noise. Can it be the blacks driving them off from the strangers we stayed with last night, do you think? If so, we had best look out for ourselves."

"Blacks could hardly manage such a large mob as there are there," said James. "I'll tell you what I think it is, old Jeff; it's some new chums going to cross the watershed, and look for new country to the south. If so, let us go down and meet them: they will camp down by the river yonder."

James was right. All doubt about what the new comers were was solved before we reached the river, for we could hear the rapid detonation of the stock-whips loud above the lowing of the cattle; so we sat and watched them debouche from the forest into the broad river meadows in the gathering gloom: saw the scene so venerable and ancient, so seldom seen in the Old World—the patriarchs moving into the desert with all their wealth, to find a new pasture-ground. A simple primitive action, the first and simplest act of colonization, yet producing such great results on the history of the world, as did the parting of Lot and Abraham in times gone by.

First came the cattle lowing loudly, some trying to stop and

* Dacelo Gigantea.

graze on the rich pasture after their long day's travel, some heading noisily towards the river, now beginning to steam with the rising evening mist. Now a lordly bull, followed closely by two favourite heifers, tries to take matters into his own hands, and cut out a route for himself, but is soon driven ignominiously back in a lumbering gallop by a quick-eyed stockman. Now a silly calf takes it into his head to go for a small excursion up the range, followed, of course, by his doting mother, and has to be headed in again, not without muttered wrath and lowerings of the head from madame. Behind the cattle come horsemen, some six or seven in number, and last, four drays, bearing the household goods, come crawling up the pass.

We had time to notice that there were women on the foremost dray, when it became evident that the party intended camping in a turn of the river just below. One man kicked his feet out of the stirrups, and sitting loosely in his saddle, prepared to watch the cattle for the first few hours till he was relieved. Another lit a fire against a fallen tree, and while the bullock-drivers were busy unyoking their beasts, and the women were clambering from the dray, two of the horsemen separated from the others, and came forward to meet us.

Both of them I saw were men of vast stature. One rode upright, with a military seat, while his companion had his feet out of his stirrups, and rode loosely, as if tired with his journey. Further than this, I could distinguish nothing in the darkening twilight; but, looking at James, I saw that he was eagerly scanning the strangers, with elevated eyebrow and opened lips. Ere I could speak to him, he had dashed forward with a shout, and when I came up with him, wondering, I found myself shaking hands, talking and laughing, everything in fact short of crying, with Major Buckley and Thomas Troubridge.

"Range up alongside here, Jeff, you rascal," said Tom, "and let me get a fair hug at you. What do you think of this for a lark; eh ?—to meet you out here, all promiscuous, in the forest, like Prince Arthur ! We could not go out of our way to see you, though we knew where you were located, for we must hurry on and get a piece of country we have been told of on the next river. We are going to settle down close by you, you see. We'll make a new Drumston in the wilderness."

"This is a happy meeting, indeed, old Tom," I said, as we rode towards the drays, after the Major and James. "We shall have happy times, now we have got some of our old friends round us. Who is come with you ? How is Mrs. Buckley ?"

"Mrs. Buckley is as well as ever, and as handsome. My pretty little cousin, Mary Hawker, and old Miss Thornton are with us; the poor old Vicar is dead."

"Mary Hawker with you ?" I said. "And her husband, Tom ?

"Hardly, old friend. We travel in better company," said he. "George Hawker is transported for life."

"Alas, poor Mary!" I answered. "And what for?"

"Coining," he answered. "I'll tell you the story another time. To-night let us rejoice."

I could not but watch James, who was riding before us, to see how he would take this news. The Major, I saw, was telling him all about it, but James seemed to take it quite quietly, only nodding his head as the other went on. I knew how he would feel for his old love, and I turned and said to Troubridge,—

"Jim will be very sorry to hear of this. I wish she had married him."

"That's what we all say," said Tom. "I am sorry for poor Jim. He is about the best man I know, take him all in all. If that fellow were to die, she might have him yet, Hamlyn."

We reached the drays. There sat Mrs. Buckley on a log, a noble, happy matron, laughing at her son as he toddled about, busy gathering sticks for the fire. Beside her was Mary, paler and older-looking than when we had seen her last, with her child upon her lap, looking sad and worn. But a sadder sight for me was old Miss Thornton, silent and frightened, glancing uneasily round, as though expecting some new horror. No child for her to cling to and strive for. No husband to watch for and anticipate every wish. A poor, timid, nervous old maid, thrown adrift in her old age upon a strange sea of anomalous wonders. Every old favourite prejudice torn up by the roots. All old formulas of life scattered to the winds!

She told me in confidence that evening that she had been in sad trouble all day. At dinner-time some naked blacks had come up to the dray, and had frightened and shocked her. Then the dray had been nearly upset, and her hat crushed among the trees. A favourite and precious bag, which never left her, had been dropped in the water; and her Prayer-book, a parting gift from Lady Kate, had been utterly spoiled. A hundred petty annoyances and griefs, which Mary barely remarked, and which brave Mrs. Buckley, in her strong determination of following her lord to the ends of the earth, and of being as much help and as little incumbrance to him as she could, had laughed at, were to her great misfortunes. Why, the very fact, as she told me, of sitting on the top of a swinging jolting dray was enough to keep her in a continual state of agony and terror, so that when she alit at night, and sat down, she could not help weeping silently, dreading lest any one should see her.

Suddenly, Mary was by her side, kneeling down.

"Aunt," she said, "dearest aunt, don't break down. It is all my wicked fault. You will break my heart, auntie dear, if you cry like that. Why did ever I bring you on this hideous journey?"

"How could I leave you in your trouble, my love?" said Miss

Thornton. You did right to come, my love. We are among old friends. We have come too far for trouble to reach us. We shall soon have a happy home again now, and all will be well."

So she, who needed so much comforting herself, courageously dried her tears and comforted Mary. And when we reached the drays, she was sitting with her hands folded before her in serene misery.

" Mary," said the Major, " here are two old friends."

He had no time to say more, for she, recognising Jim, sprang up, and, running to him, burst into hysterical weeping.

" Oh, my good old friend !" she cried ; " oh, my dear old friend ! Oh, to meet you here in this lonely wilderness ! Oh, James, my kind old brother ! "

I saw how his big heart yearned to comfort his old sweetheart in her distress. Not a selfish thought found place with him. He could only see his old love injured and abandoned, and nought more.

" Mary," he said, " what happiness to see you among all your old friends come to live among us again ! It is almost too good to believe in. Believe me, you will get to like this country as well as old Devon soon, though it looks so strange just now. And what a noble boy, too ! We will make him the best bushman in the country when he is old enough."

So he took the child of his rival to his bosom, and when the innocent little face looked into his, he would see no likeness to George Hawker there. He only saw the mother's countenance as he knew her as a child in years gone by.

" Is nobody going to notice me or my boy, I wonder ?" said Mrs. Buckley. " Come here immediately, Mr. Stockbridge, before we quarrel."

In a very short time all our party were restored to their equanimity, and were laying down plans for pleasant meetings hereafter. And long after the women had gone to bed in the drays, and the moon was riding high in the heavens, James and myself, Troubridge and the Major, sat before the fire ; and we heard, for the first time, of all that had gone on since we left England, and of all poor Mary's troubles. Then each man rolled himself in his blanket, and slept soundly under the rustling forest-boughs.

In the bright cool morning, ere the sun was up, and the belated opossum had run back to his home in the hollow log, James and I were a-foot looking after our horses. We walked silently side by side for a few minutes, until he turned and said :—

" Jeff, old fellow, of course you will go on with them, and stay until they are settled ?"

" Jim, old fellow," I replied, " of course you will go on with them, and stay till they are settled ?"

He pondered a few moments, and then said, " Well, why not ?

I suppose she can be still to me what she always was? Yes, I will go with them."

When we returned to the dray we found them all astir, preparing for a start. Mrs. Buckley, with her gown tucked up, was preparing breakfast, as if she had been used to the thing all her life. She had an imperial sort of way of manœuvring a frying-pan, which did one good to see. It is my belief, that if that woman had been called upon to groom a horse, she'd have done it in a ladylike way.

While James went among the party to announce his intention of going on with them, I had an opportunity of looking at the son and heir of all the Buckleys. He was a sturdy, handsome child about five years old, and was now standing apart from the others, watching a bullock-driver yoking-up his beast. I am very fond of children, and take great interest in studying their characters; so I stood, not unamused, behind this youngster, as he stood looking with awe and astonishment at the man, as he managed the great, formidable beasts, and brought each one into his place; not, however, without more oaths than one would care to repeat. Suddenly the child, turning and seeing me behind him, came back, and took my hand.

"Why is he so angry with them?" the child asked at once. "Why does he talk to them like that?"

"He is swearing at them," I said, "to make them stand in their places."

"But they don't understand him," said the boy. "That black and white one would have gone where he wanted it in a minute; but it couldn't understand, you know; so he hit it over the nose. Why don't he find out how they talk to one another? Then he'd manage them much better. He is very cruel."

"He does not know any better," I said. "Come with me and get some flowers."

"Will you take me up?" he said. "I mustn't run about, for fear of snakes."

I took him up, and we went to gather flowers.

"Your name is Samuel Buckley, I think," said I.

"How did you know that?"

"I remember you when you were a baby," I said. "I hope you may grow to be as good a man as your father, my lad. See, there is mamma calling for us."

"And how far south are you going, Major?" I asked at breakfast.

"No further than we can help," said the Major. "I stayed a night with my old friend Captain Brentwood, by the way; and there I found a man who knew of some unoccupied country down here, which he had seen in some bush expedition. We found the ground he mentioned taken up; but he says there is equally good on the next river. I have bought him and his information."

" We saw good country away to the south yesterday," I said.
" But are you wise to trust this man ? Do you know anything about
him ?"

" Brentwood has known him these ten years, and trusts him
entirely ; though, I believe, he has been a convict. If you are
determined to come with us, Stockbridge, I will call him up, and
examine him about the route. William Lee, just step here a
moment."

A swarthy and very powerfully built man came up. No other
than the man I have spoken of under that name before. He was
quite unknown either to James or myself, although, as he told us
afterwards, he had recognised us at once, but kept out of our sight
as much as possible, till by the Major's summons he was forced to
come forward.

" What route to-day, William ?" asked the Major.

" South and by east across the range. We ought to get down to
the river by night, if we're lucky."

So, while the drays were getting under way, the Major, Tom,
James, and myself rode up to the saddle where we had stood the
night before, and gazed south-east across the broad prospect, in the
direction that the wanderers were to go.

" That," said the Major, " to the right there, must be the great
glen out of which the river comes ; and there, please God, we will
rest our weary bodies and build our house. Odd, isn't it, that I
should have been saved from shot and shell when so many better
men were put away in the trench, to come and end my days in a
place like this ? Well, I think we shall have a pleasant life of it,
watching the cattle spread further across the plains year after year,
and seeing the boy grow up to be a good man. At all events, for
weal or woe, I have said good-bye to old England, for ever and
a day."

The cattle were past, and the drays had arrived at where we
stood. With many a hearty farewell, having given a promise to
come over and spend Christmas-day with them, I turned my horse's
head homewards and went on my solitary way.

CHAPTER XIX.

I HIRE A NEW HORSEBREAKER.

I MUST leave them to go their way towards their new home, and
follow my own fortunes a little, for that afternoon I met with an
adventure quite trifling indeed, but which is not altogether without
interest in this story.

I rode on till high noon, till having crossed the valley of the Belloury, and followed up one of its tributary creeks, I had come on to the water system of another main river, and the rapid widening of the gully whose course I was pursuing assured me that I could not be far from the main stream itself. At length I entered a broad flat intersected by a deep and tortuous creek, and here I determined to camp till the noon-day heat was past, before I continued my journey, calculating that I could easily reach home the next day.

Having watered my horse, I turned him loose for a graze, and, making such a dinner as was possible under the circumstances, I lit a pipe and lay down on the long grass, under the flowering wattle-trees, smoking, and watching the manœuvres of a little tortoise, who was disporting himself in the waterhole before me. Getting tired of that I lay back on the grass, and watched the green leaves waving and shivering against the clear blue sky, given up entirely to the greatest of human enjoyments—the after-dinner pipe, the pipe of peace.

Which is the pleasantest pipe in the day? We used to say at home that a man should smoke but four pipes a-day: the matutinal, another I don't specify, the post-prandial, and the symposial or convivial, which last may be infinitely subdivided, according to the quantity of drink taken. But in Australia this division won't obtain, particularly when you are on the tramp. Just when you wake from a dreamless sleep beneath the forest boughs, as the east begins to blaze, and the magpie gets musical, you dash to the embers of last night's fire, and after blowing many fire-sticks find one which is alight, and proceed to send abroad on the morning breeze the scene of last night's dottle. Then, when breakfast is over and the horses are caught up and saddled, and you are jogging across the plain, with the friend of your heart beside you, the burnt incense once more goes up, and conversation is unnecessary. At ten o'clock when you cross the creek (you always cross a creek about ten if you are in a good country), you halt and smoke. So after dinner in the lazy noon-tide, one or perhaps two pipes are necessary, with, perhaps, another about four in the afternoon, and last, and perhaps best of all, are the three or four you smoke before the fire at night, when the day is dying and the opossums are beginning to chatter in the twilight. So that you find that a fig of Barret's twist, seventeen to the pound, is gone in the mere hours of day-light, without counting such a casualty as waking up cold in the night, and going at it again.

So I lay on my back dreaming, wondering why a locust who was in full screech close by, took the trouble to make that terrible row when it was so hot, and hoping that his sides might be sore with the exertion, when to my great astonishment I heard the sound of feet brushing through the grass towards me. "Black fellow," I said to myself; but no, those were shodden feet that swept along so wearily.

I raised myself on my elbow, with my hand on my pistol, and reconnoitred.

There approached me from down the creek a man, hardly reaching the middle size, lean and active-looking, narrow in the flanks, thin in the jaws, his knees well apart; with a keen bright eye in his head. His clothes looked as if they had belonged to ten different men; and his gait was heavy, and his face red, as if from a long hurried walk; but I said at once, " Here comes a riding man, at all events, be it for peace or war."

" Good day, lad," said I.

" Good day, sir."

" You're rather off the tracks for a foot-man," said I. " Are you looking for your horse?"

" Deuce a horse have I got to my name, sir,—have you got a feed of anything? I'm nigh starved."

" Ay, surely: the tea's cold; put it on the embers and warm it a bit; here's beef, and damper too, plenty."

I lit another pipe and watched his meal. I like feeding a real hungry man; it's almost as good as eating oneself — sometimes better.

When the edge of his appetite was taken off he began to talk; he said first—

" Got a station anywheres about here, sir?"

" No, I'm Hamlyn of the Durnongs, away by Maneroo."

" Oh! ay; I know you, sir; which way have you come this morning?"

" Southward; I crossed the Belloury about seven o'clock."

" That, indeed! You haven't seen anything of three bullock drays and a mob of cattle going south?"

" Yes! I camped with such a lot last night!"

" Not Major Buckley's lot?"

" The same."

" And how far were they on?"

" They crossed the range at daylight this morning;—they're thirty miles away by now."

He threw his hat on the ground with an oath: " I shall never catch them up. I daren't cross that range on foot into the new country, and those black devils lurking round. He shouldn't have left me like that;—all my own fault, though, for staying behind! No, no, he's true enough—all my own fault. But I wouldn't have left him so, neither; but, perhaps, he don't think I'm so far behind."

I saw that the man was in earnest, for his eyes were swimming; —he was too dry for tears; but though he looked a desperate scamp, I couldn't help pitying him and saying,—

" You seem vexed you couldn't catch them up; were you going along with the Major, then?"

" No, sir; I wasn't hired with him; but an old mate of mine, Bill Lee, is gone along with him to show him some country, and I was going to stick to him and see if the Major would take me; we haven't been parted for many years, not Bill and I haven't; and the worst of it is, that he'll think I've slipped away from him, instead of following him fifty mile on foot to catch him. Well! it can't be helped now; I must look round and get a job somewhere till I get a chance to join him. Were you travelling with them, sir?"

" No, I'm after some cattle I've lost; a fine imported bull, too, —worse luck! We'll never see him again, I'm afraid, and if I do find them, how I am to get them home single-handed I don't know."

" Do you mean a short-horned Durham bull with a key brand? Why, if that's him, I can lay you on to him at once; he's up at Jamieson's, here to the west. I was staying at Watson's last night, and one of Jamieson's men stayed in the hut—a young hand; and, talking about beasts, he said that there was a fine short-horned bull come on to their run with a mob of heifers and cows, and they couldn't make out who they belonged to; they were all different brands."

" That's our lot for a thousand," says I; " a lot of store cattle we bought this year from the Hunter, and haven't branded yet,—more shame to us."

" If you could get a horse and saddle from Jamieson's, sir," said he, " I could give you a hand home with them: I'd like to get a job somehow, and I am well used to cattle."

" Done with you," said I;"Jamieson's isn't ten miles from here, and we can do that to-night if we look sharp. Come along, my lad."

So I caught up the horse, and away we went. Starting at right angles with the sun, which was nearly overhead, and keeping to the left of him—holding such a course, as he got lower, that an hour and half, or thereabouts, before setting he should be in my face, and at sundown a little to the left; which is the best direction I can give you for going about due west in November, without a compass— which, by the way, you always ought to have.

My companion was foot-sore, so I went slowly; he, however, shambled along bravely when his feet got warm. He was a talk- ative, lively man, and chattered continually.

" You've got a nice place up at the Durnongs, sir," said he; " I stayed in your huts one night. It's the comfortablest bachelor station on this side. You've got a smart few sheep, I expect?"

" Twenty-five thousand. Do you know these parts well?"

" I knew that country of yours long before any of it was took up."

" You've been a long while in the country, then?"

" I was sent out when I was eighteen; spared, as the old judge said, on account of my youth: that's eleven years ago."

" Spared, eh? It was something serious, then."

" Trifling enough : only for having a rope in my hand."

" They wouldn't lag a man for that," said I.

" Ay, but," he replied, " there was a horse at the end of the rope.
I was brought up in a training stable, and somehow there's something
in the smell of a stable is sure to send a man wrong if he don't take
care. I got betting and drinking, too, as young chaps will, and lost
my place, and got from bad to worse till I shook a nag, and got
bowled out and lagged. That's about my history, sir ; will you give
me a job now ? " And he looked up, laughing.

" Ay, why not ? " said I. " Because you tried hard to go to the
devil when you were young and foolish, it don't follow that you
should pursue that line of conduct all your life. You've been in a
training stable, eh ? If you can break horses, I may find you something to do."

" I'll break horses against any man in this country—though that's
not saying much, for I ain't seen not what I call a breaker since I've
been here ; as for riding, I'd ridden seven great winners before I was
eighteen ; and that's what ne'er a man alive can say. Ah, those
were the rosy times ! Ah for old Newmarket ! "

" Are you a Cambridgeshire man, then ? "

" Me ? Oh, no ; I'm a Devonshire man.   I come near from where
Major Buckley lived some years. Did you notice a pale, pretty-
looking woman, was with him—Mrs. Hawker ? "

I grew all attention.   " Yes," I said, " I noticed her."

" I knew her husband well," he said, " and an awful rascal he
was : he was lagged for coining, though he might have been for half-
a-dozen things besides."

" Indeed ! " said I ; " and is he in the colony ? "

" No ; he's over the water, I expect."

" In Van Diemen's Land, you mean ? "

" Just so," he said ; " he had better not show Bill Lee much of
his face, or there'll be mischief."

" Lee owes him a grudge, then ? "

" Not exactly that," said my communicative friend, " but I don't
think that Hawker will show much where Lee is."

" I am very glad to hear it," I thought to myself.   " I hope
Mary may not have some trouble with her husband still."

" What is the name of the place Major Buckley comes from ? " I
inquired.

" Drumston."

" And you belong there too ? "   I knew very well, however, that
he did not, or I must have known him."

" No," he answered ; " Okehampton is my native place. But you
talk a little Devon yourself, sir."

The conversation came to a close, for we heard the barking of dogs, and saw the station where we were to spend the night. In the morning I went home, and my new acquaintance, who called himself Dick, along with me. Finding that he was a first-rate rider, and gentle and handy among horses, I took him into my service permanently, and soon got to like him very well.

CHAPTER XX.

A WARM CHRISTMAS DAY.

ALL through November and part of December, I and our Scotch overseer, Georgy Kyle, were busy as bees among the sheep. Shearers were very scarce, and the poor sheep got fearfully " tomahawked" by the new hands, who had been a very short time from the barracks. Dick, however, my new acquaintance, turned out a valuable ally, getting through more sheep and taking off his fleece better than any man in the shed. The prisoners, of course, would not work effectually without extra wages, and thus gave a deal of trouble; knowing that there was no fear of my sending them to the magistrate (fifty miles off) during such a busy time. However, all evils must come to an end some time or another, and so did shearing, though it was nearly Christmas before our wool was pressed and ready for the drays.

Then came a breathing time. So I determined, having heard nothing of James, to go over and spend my Christmas with the Buckleys, and see how they were getting on at their new station; and about noon on the day before Boxing-day, having followed the track made by their drays from the place I had last parted with them, I reined up on the cliffs above a noble river, and could see their new huts, scarce a quarter of a mile off, on the other side of the stream.

They say that Christmas-day is the hottest day in the year in those countries, but some days in January are, I think, generally hotter. To-day, however, was as hot as a salamander could wish. All the vast extent of yellow plain to the eastward quivered beneath a fiery sky, and every little eminence stood like an island in a lake of mirage. Used as I had got to this phenomenon, I was often tempted that morning to turn a few hundred yards from my route, and give my horse a drink at one of the broad glassy pools that seemed to lie right and left. Once the faint track I was following headed straight towards one of these apparent sheets of water, and I was even meditating a bathe, but, lo! when I was a hundred yards or so off, it began to dwindle and disappear, and I found nothing but the same endless stretch of grass, burnt up by the midsummer sun.

For many miles I had distinguished the new huts, placed at the apex of a great cape of the continent of timber which ran down from the mountains into the plains. I thought they had chosen a strange place for their habitation, as there appeared no signs of a water-course near it. It was not till I pulled up within a quarter of a mile of my destination that I heard a hoarse roar as if from the bowels of the earth, and found that I was standing on the edge of a glen about four hundred feet deep, through which a magnificent snow-fed river poured ceaselessly, here flashing bright among bars of rock, there lying in dark, deep reaches, under tall, white-stemmed trees.

The scene was so beautiful and novel that I paused and gazed at it. Across the glen, behind the houses, rose up a dark mass of timbered ranges, getting higher and steeper as far as the eye could reach, while to the north-east the river's course might be traced through the plains by the timber that fringed the water's edge, and sometimes feathered some tributary gully almost to the level of the flat lofty table-land. On either side of it, down behind down folded one over the other, and, bordered by great forests, led the eye towards the river's source, till the course of the deep valley could no longer be distinguished, lost among the distant ranges; but above where it had disappeared, rose a tall blue peak with streaks of snow.

I rode down a steep pathway, and crossed a broad gravelly ford. As my horse stopped to drink I looked delighted up the vista which opened on my sight. The river, partly overshadowed by tall trees, was hurrying and spouting through upright columns of basalt, which stood in groups everywhere like the pillars of a ruined city; in some places solitary, in others, clustered together like fantastic buildings; while a hundred yards above was an island, dividing the stream, on which, towering above the variety of low green shrubs which covered it, three noble fern trees held their plumes aloft, shaking with the concussion of the falling water.

I crossed the river. A gully, deep at first, but getting rapidly shallower, led up by a steep ascent to the table-land above, and as I reached the summit I found myself at Major Buckley's front door. They had, with good taste, left such trees as stood near the house—a few deep-shadowed light-woods and black wattles, which formed pretty groups in what I could see was marked out for a garden. Behind, the land began to rise, at first, in park-like timbered forest glades, and further back, closing into dense deep woodlands.

"What a lovely place they will make of this in time!" I said to myself; but I had not much time for cogitation. A loud, cheerful voice shouted: "Hamlyn, you are welcome to Baroona!" and close to me I saw the Major, carrying his son and heir in his arms, advancing to meet me from the house-door.

"You are welcome to Baroona!" echoed the boy; "and a merry Christmas and a happy New-year to you!"

I went into the house and was delighted to find what a change a few weeks of busy, quiet, and *home* had made in the somewhat draggle-tailed and disconsolate troop that I had parted with on their road. Miss Thornton, with her black mittens, white apron, and spectacles, had found herself a cool corner by the empty fire-place, and was stitching away happily at baby linen. Mrs. Buckley, in the character of a duchess, was picking raisins, and Mary was helping her; and, as I entered, laughing loudly, they greeted me kindly with all the old sacred good wishes of the season.

" I very much pity you, Mr. Hamlyn," said Mrs. Buckley, " at having outlived the novelty of being scorched to death on Christmas-day. My dear husband, please refresh me with reading the thermometer ! "

" One hundred and nine in the shade," replied the Major, with a chuckle.

" Ah, dear ! " said Mrs. Buckley. " If the dear old rheumatic creatures from the alms-house at Clere could only spend to-morrow with us, how it would warm their old bones ! Fancy how they are crouching before their little pinched grate just now ! "

" Hardly that, Mrs. Buckley," I said laughing ; "they are all snug in bed now. It is three o'clock in the morning, or thereabouts, at home, you must remember. Miss Thornton, I hope you have got over your journey."

" Yes, and I can laugh at all my mishaps now," she replied ; " I have just got homely and comfortable here, but we must make one more move, and that will be the last for me. Mary and Mr. Troubridge have taken up their country to the south-west, and as soon as he has got our house built, we are going to live there."

" It is not far, I hope," said I.

" A trifle : not more than ten miles," said Miss Thornton ; " they call the place Toonarbin. Mary's run joins the Major's on two sides, and beyond again, we already have neighbours, the Mayfords. They are on the river again ; but we are on a small creek towards the ranges. I should like to have been on the river, but they say we are very lucky."

" I am so glad to see you," said Mary ; " James Stockbridge said you would be sure to come ; otherwise, we should have sent over for you. What do you think of my boy ? "

She produced him from an inner room. He was certainly a beautiful child, though very small, and with a certain painful likeness to his father, which even I could see, and I could not help comparing him unfavourably, in my own mind, with that noble six-year-old Sam Buckley, who had come to my knee where I sat, and was looking in my face as if to make a request.

" What is it, my prince ? " I asked.

He blushed, and turned his handsome gray eyes to a silver-handled riding-whip that I held in my hand. " I'll take such care of it," he whispered, and, having got it, was soon astride of a stick, full gallop for Banbury Cross.

James and Troubridge came in. To the former I had much to tell that was highly satisfactory about our shearing ; and from the latter I had much to hear about the state of both the new stations, and the adventures of a journey he had had back towards Sydney to fetch up his sheep. But these particulars will be but little interesting to an English reader, and perhaps still less so to an Australian. I am writing a history of the people themselves, not of their property. I will only say, once for all, that the Major's run contained very little short of 60.000 acres of splendidly grassed plain-land, which he took up originally with merely a few cattle, and about 3,000 sheep ; but which, in a few years, carried 28,000 sheep comfortably. Mrs. Hawker and Troubridge had quite as large a run ; but a great deal of it was rather worthless forest, badly grassed ; which Tom, in his wisdom, like a great many other new chums, had thought superior to the bleak plains on account of the shelter. Yet, notwithstanding this disadvantage, they were never, after a year or two, with less than 15,000 sheep, and a tolerable head of cattle. In short, in a very few years, both the Major and Troubridge, by mere power of accumulation, became very wealthy people.

Christmas morn rose bright ; but ere the sun had time to wreak his fury upon us, every soul in the household was abroad, under the shade of the lightwood trees, to hear the Major read the Litany.

A strange group we were. The Major stood with his back against a tree-stem, and all his congregation were ranged around him. To his right stood Miss Thornton, her arms folded placidly before her ; and with her, Mary and Mrs. Buckley, in front of whom sat the two boys : Sam, the elder, trying to keep Charles, the younger, quiet. Next, going round the circle, stood the old housekeeper, servant of the Buckleys for thirty years ; who now looked askance off her Prayer-book to see that the two convict-women under her charge were behaving with decorum. Next, and exactly opposite the Major, were two free servants : one a broad, brawny, athletic-looking man, with, I thought, not a bad countenance ; and the other a tall, handsome, foolish-looking Devonshire lad. The round was completed by five convict man-servants, standing vacantly looking about them ; and Tom, James, and myself, who were next the Major.

The service, which he read in a clear manly voice, was soon over, and we returned to the house in groups. I threw myself in the way of the two free servants, and asked,—

" Pray, which of you is William Lee ?"—for I had forgotten him.

The short thickset man I had noticed before touched his hat and said that he was. That touching of the hat is a very rare piece of courtesy from working men in Australia. The convicts are forced to do it, and so the free men make it a point of honour not to do so.

"Oh!" said I, "I have got a groom who calls himself Dick. I found him sorefooted in the bush the day I met the Major. He was trying to pick you up. He asked me to tell you that he was afraid to cross the range alone on account of the blacks, or he would have come up with you. He seemed anxious lest you should think it was his fault."

"Poor chap!" said Lee. "What a faithful little fellow it is! Would it be asking a liberty if you would take back a letter for me, sir?"

I said, "No; certainly not."

"I am much obliged to you, sir," he said. "I am glad Dick has got with *a gentleman.*"

That letter was of some importance to me, though I did not know it till after, but I may as well say why now. Lee had been a favourite servant of my father's, and when he got into trouble my father had paid a counsel to defend him. Lee never forgot this, and this letter to Dick was shortly to the effect that I was one of the *right sort*, and was to be taken care of, which injunction Dick obeyed to the very letter, doing me services for pure good will, which could not have been bought for a thousand a-year.

After breakfast arose the question, "What is to be done?" Which Troubridge replied to by saying: "What could any sensible man do such weather as this, but get into the water and stop there?"

"Shall it be, 'All hands to bathe,' then?" said the Major.

"You won't be without company," said Mrs. Buckley, "for the black fellows are camped in the bend, and they spend most of their time in the water such a day as this."

So James and Troubridge started for the river with their towels, the Major and I promising to follow them immediately, for I wanted to look at my horse, and the Major had also something to do in the paddock. So we walked together.

"Major," said I, when we had gone a little way, "do you never feel anxious about Mary Hawker's husband appearing and giving trouble?"

"Oh, no!" said he. "The man is safe in Van Diemen's Land. Besides, what could he gain? I, for one, without consulting her, should find means to pack him off again. There is no fear."

"By the bye, Major," I said, "have you heard from our friend Doctor Mulhaus since your arrival? I suppose he is at Drumston still?"

"Oh dear, no!" said he. "He is gone back to Germany. He is going to settle there again. He was so sickened of England when all his friends left, that he determined to go home. I understood that he had some sort of patrimony there, on which he will end his days. Wherever he goes, God go with him, for he is a noble fellow!"

"Amen," I answered. And soon after, having got towels, we proceeded to the river; making for a long reach a little below where I had crossed the night before.

"Look there!" said the Major. "There's a bit for one of your painters! I wish Wilkie or Martin were here."

I agreed with him. Had Etty been on the spot he would have got a hint for one of his finest pictures; and though I can give but little idea of it in writing, let me try. Before us was a long reach of deep, still water, unbroken by a ripple, so hemmed in on all sides by walls of deep green black wattle, tea-tree, and delicate silver acacia, that the water seemed to flow in a deep shoreless rift of the forest, above which the taller forest trees towered up two hundred feet, hiding the lofty cliffs, which had here receded a little back from the river.

The picture had a centre, and a strange one. A little ledge of rock ran out into deep water, and upon it, rising from a heap of light-coloured clothing, like a white pillar, in the midst of the sombre green foliage, rose the naked carcass of Thomas Troubridge, Esq., preparing for a header, while at his feet were grouped three or four black fellows, one of whom as we watched slid off the rock like an otter. The reach was covered with black heads belonging to the savages, who were swimming in all directions, while groups of all ages and both sexes stood about on the bank in Mother Nature's full dress.

We had a glorious bathe, and then sat on the rock, smoking, talking, and watching the various manœuvres of the blacks. An old lady, apparently about eighty, with a head as white as snow, topping her black body (a flourbag cobbler, as her tribe would call her), was punting a canoe along in the shallow water on the opposite side of the river. She was entirely without clothes, and in spite of her decrepitude stood upright in the cockleshell, handling it with great dexterity. When she was a little above us, she made way on her barque, and shot into the deep water in the middle of the stream, evidently with the intention of speaking us. As, however, she was just half-way across, floating helplessly, unable to reach the bottom with the spear she had used as a puntpole in the shallower water, a mischievous black imp canted her over, and souse she went into the river. It was amazing to see how boldly and well the old woman struck out for the shore, keeping her white head well out of the water; and having reached dry land once more, sat down on her haunches, and began scolding with a volubility and power which would soon have silenced the loudest tongue in old Billingsgate.

Her anger, so far from wearing out, grew on what fed it; so that her long-drawn yells, which seemed like parentheses in her jabbering discourse, were getting each minute more and more acute, and we were just thinking about moving homewards, when a voice behind us sang out,—

"Hallo, Major! Having a little music, eh? What a sweet song that old girl is singing! I must write it down from dictation, and translate it, as Walter Scott used to do with the old wives' ballads in Scotland."

"I have no doubt it would be quite Ossianic—equal to any of the abusive scenes in Homer. But, my dear Harding, how are you? You are come to eat your Christmas dinner with us, I hope?"

"That same thing, Major," answered the new comer. "Troubridge and Stockbridge, how are you? This, I presume, is your partner, Hamlyn?"

We went back to the house. Harding, I found, was half-owner of a station to the north-east, an Oxford man, a great hand at skylarking, and an inveterate writer of songs. He was good-looking too, and gentlemanlike, in fact, a very pleasant companion in every way.

Dinner was to be at six o'clock, in imitation of home hours; but we did not find the day hang heavy on our hands, there was so much to be spoken of by all of us. And when that important meal was over we gathered in the open air in front of the house, bent upon making Christmas cheer.

"What is your last new song, eh, Harding?" said the Major; "now is the time to ventilate it."

"I've been too busy shearing for song-writing, Major."

Soon after this we went in, and there we sat till nearly ten o'clock, laughing, joking, singing, and drinking punch. Mary sat between James Stockbridge and Tom, and they three spoke together so exclusively and so low, that the rest of us were quite forgotten. Mary was smiling and laughing, first at one and then at the other, in her old way, and now and then as I glanced at her I could hardly help sighing. But I soon remembered certain resolutions I had made, and tried not to notice the trio, but to make myself agreeable to the others. Still my eyes wandered towards them again intuitively. I thought Mary had never looked so beautiful before. Her complexion was very full, as though she were blushing at something one of them had said to her, and while I watched I saw James rise and go to a jug of flowers, and bring back a wreath of scarlet Kennedia, saying:—

"Do us a favour on Christmas night, Mary; twine this in your hair."

She blushed deeper than before, but she did it, and Tom helped her. There was no harm in that, you say, for was he not her cousin? But still I could not help saying to myself, "Oh Mary, Mary, if you were a widow, how long would you stay so?"

"What a gathering it is, to be sure!" said Mrs. Buckley!—
"all the old Drumstonians who are alive collected under one roof."

"Except the Doctor," said the Major.

"Ah, yes, dear Doctor Mulhaus. I am so sad sometimes to
think that we shall never see him again."

"I miss him more than any one," said the Major. "I have no
one to contradict me now."

"I shall have to take that duty upon me, then," said his wife.

"Hark! there is Lee come back from the sheep station. Yes,
that must be his horse. Call him in and give him a glass of grog.
I was sorry to send him out to-day."

"He is coming to make his report," said Mrs. Buckley; "there
is his heavy tramp outside the door."

The door was opened, and the new comer advanced to where the
glare of the candles fell upon his face.

Had the Gentleman in Black himself advanced out of the darkness at that moment, with his blue bag on his arm and his bundle
of documents in his hand, we should not have leapt to our feet and
cried out more suddenly than we did then. For Doctor Mulhaus
stood in the middle of the room, looking around him with a bland
smile.

CHAPTER XXI.

HE stood in the candle-light, smiling blandly, while we all
stayed for an instant, after our first exclamation speechless with
astonishment.

The Major was the first who showed signs of consciousness, for I
verily believe that one half of the company at least believed him to
be a ghost. "You are the man," said the Major, "who in the flesh
called himself Maximilian Mulhaus! Why are you come to trouble
us, O spirit?—not that we shouldn't be glad to see you if you were
alive, you know, but—my dear old friend, how are you?"

Then we crowded round him, all speaking at once and trying to
shake hands with him. Still he remained silent, and smiled. I,
looking into his eyes, saw that they were swimming, and divined
why he would not trust himself to speak. No one hated a show of
emotion more than the Doctor, and yet his brave warm heart would
often flood his eyes in spite of himself.

He walked round to the fire-place, and, leaning against the board
that answered for a chimney-piece, stood looking at us with beam-
ing eyes, while we anxiously waited for him to speak.

" Ah ! " he said at length, with a deep sigh, " this does me good
I have not made my journey in vain. A man who tries to live in
this world without love must, if he is not a fool, commit suicide in a
year. I went to my own home, and my own dogs barked at me.
Those I had raised out of the gutter, and set on horseback, splashed
mud on me as I walked. I will go back, I said, to the little English
family who loved and respected me for my own sake, though they be
at the ends of the earth. So I left those who should have loved me
with an ill-concealed smile on their faces, and when I come here I
am welcomed with tears of joy from those I have not known five
years. Bah ! Here is my home, Buckley : let me live and die with
you."

" Live ! " said the Major—" ay, while there's a place to live in ;
don't talk about dying yet, though,—we'll think of that presently.
I can't find words enough to give him welcome. Wife, can you ? "

" Not I, indeed," she said ; " and what need ? He can see a
warmer welcome in our faces than an hour's clumsy talk could give
him. I say, Doctor, you are welcome, now and for ever. Will that
serve you, husband ? "

I could not help looking at Miss Thornton. She sat silently staring
at him through it all, with her hands clasped together, beating them
upon her knee. Now, when all was quiet, and Mrs. Buckley and
Mary had run off to the kitchen to order the Doctor some supper, he
seemed to see her for the first time, and bowed profoundly. She
rose, and, looking at him intently, sat down again.

The Doctor had eaten his supper, and Mrs. Buckley had made him
something to drink with her own hands ; the Doctor had lit his pipe,
and we had gathered round the empty fire-place, when the Major
said,—

" Now, Doctor, do tell us your adventures, and how you have
managed to drop upon us from the skies on Christmas-day."

" Soon told, my friend," he answered. " See here. I went back
to Germany because all ties in England were broken. I went to
Lord C——— : I said, ' I will go back and see the palingenesis of my
country ; I will see what they are doing, now the French are in the
dust.' He said, ' Go, and God speed you ! ' I went. What did I
find ? Beggars on horseback everywhere, riding post-haste to the
devil—not as good horsemen, either, but as tailors of Brentford, and
crowding one another into the mud to see who would be there first.
' Let me get out of this before they ride over me,' said I. So I
came forth to England, took ship, and here I am."

" A most lucid and entirely satisfactory explanation of what you
have been about, I must say," answered the Major ; " however, I
must be content."

At this moment, little Sam, who had made his escape in the
confusion, came running in, breathless. " Papa ! Papa ! " said he,

" Lee has come home with a snake seven feet long." Lee was at the door with the reptile in his hand—a black snake, with a deep salmon-coloured belly, deadly venomous, as I knew. All the party went out to look at it, except the Doctor and Miss Thornton, who stayed at the fire-place.

" Mind your hands, Lee!" I heard James say; " though the brute is dead, you might prick your fingers with him."

I was behind all the others, waiting to look at the snake, which was somewhat of a large one, and worth seeing, so I could not help overhearing the conversation of Miss Thornton and the Doctor, and having heard the first of it my ears grew so unnaturally quickened, that I could not for the life of me avoid hearing the whole, though I was ashamed of playing eavesdropper.

" My God, sir!" I heard her say, " what new madness is this? Why do you persist in separating yourself from your family in this manner?"

" No madness at all, my dear madam," he answered; " you would have done the same under the circumstances. My brother was civil, but I saw he would rather have me away and continue his steward-ship. And so I let him."

Miss Thornton put another question which I did not catch, and the sense of which I could not supply, but I heard his answer plainly: it was,—

" Of course I did, my dear lady, and, just as you may suppose, when I walked up the Ritter Saal, there was a buzz and a giggle, and not one held out his hand save noble Von H——; long life to him!"

" But ——?" said Miss Thornton, mentioning somebody, whose name I could not catch.

" I saw him bend over to M—— as I came up to the Presence, and they both laughed. I saw a slight was intended, made my devoirs, and backed off. The next day he sent for me, but I was off and away. I heard of it before I left England."

" And will you never go back?" she said.

" When I can with honour, not before; and that will never be till he is dead, I fear; and his life is as good as mine. So, hey for natural history, and quiet domestic life, and happiness ·with my English friends! Now, am I wise or not?"

" I fear not," she said.

The Doctor laughed, and taking her hand, kissed it gallantly; by this time we had all turned round, and were coming in.

" Now, Doctor," said the Major, " If you have done flirting with Miss Thornton, look at this snake."

" A noble beast, indeed," said the Doctor. " Friend," he added to Lee, " if you don't want him, I will take him off your hands for a sum of money. He shall be pickled, as I live."

" He is very venomous, sir," said Lee. " The blacks eat 'em, it's true, but they always cut the head off first. I'd take the head off, sir, before I ventured to taste him."

We all laughed at Lee's supposing that the Doctor meant to make a meal of the deadly serpent, and Lee laughed as loudly as anybody.

" You see, sir," he said, " I've always heard that you French gents ate frogs, so I didn't know as snakes would come amiss."

" Pray don't take me for a Frenchman, my good lad," said the Doctor; " and as for frogs, they are as good as chickens."

" Well, I've eaten guaners myself," said Lee, " though I can't say much for them. They're uglier than snakes any way."

Lee was made to sit down and take a glass of grog. So, very shortly, the conversation flowed on into its old channel, and, after spending a long and pleasant evening, we all went to bed.

James and I slept in the same room; and, when we were going to bed, I said,—

" James, if that fellow were to die, there would be a chance for you yet."

" With regard to what?" he asked.

" You know well enough, you old humbug," I said; " with regard to Mary Hawker,—née Thornton!"

" I doubt it, my lad," he said. " I very much doubt it indeed; and, perhaps, you have heard that there must be two parties to a bargain, so that even if she were willing to take me, I very much doubt if I would ask her."

" No one could blame you for that," I said, " after what has happened. There are but few men who would like to marry the widow of a coiner."

" You mistake me, Jeff. You mistake me altogether," he answered, walking up and down the room with one boot off. " That would make but little difference to me. I've no relations to sing out about a mésalliance, you know. No, my dear old fellow, not that; but—Jeff, Jeff! you are the dearest friend I have in the world."

" Jim, my boy," I answered, " I love you like a brother. What is it?"

" I have no secrets from you, Jeff," he said; " so I don't mind telling you." Another hesitation! I grew rather anxious. " What the deuce is coming?" I thought. " What can she have been up to? Go on, old fellow," I added aloud; " let's hear all about it."

He stood at the end of the room, looking rather sheepish. " Why, the fact is, old fellow, that I begin to suspect that I have outlived any little attachment I had in that quarter. I've been staying in the house two months with her, you see: and, 'n fact!—in fact!" —here he brought up short again.

"James Stockbridge," I said, sitting up in bed, " you atrocious humbug ; two months ago you informed me, with a sigh like a groggy pair of bellows, that her image could only be effaced from your heart by death. You have seduced me, whose only fault was loving you too well to part with you, into coming sixteen thousand miles to a barbarous land, far from kindred and country, on the plea that your blighted affections made England less endurable than— France, I'll say for argument ;—and now, having had two months' opportunity of studying the character of the beloved one, you coolly inform me that the whole thing was a mistake. I repeat that you are a humbug."

" If you don't hold your tongue, and that quick," he replied, " I'll send this boot at your ugly head. Now, then ! "

I ducked, fully expecting it was coming, and laughed silently under the bed-clothes. I was very happy to hear this—I was very happy to hear that a man, whom I really liked so well, had got the better of a passion for a woman who I knew was utterly incapable of being to him what his romantic high-flown notions required a wife to be. " If this happy result," I said to myself, " can be rendered the more sure by ridicule, that shall not be wanting. Meanwhile, I will sue for peace, and see how it came about."

I rose again and saw he had got his other boot half off, and was watching for me. " Jim," said I, " you ain't angry because I laughed at you, are you ? "

" Angry ! " he answered. " I am never angry with you, and you know it. I've been a fool, and I ought to be laughed at."

" Pooh ! " said I, " no more a fool than other men have been before you, from father Adam downwards."

" And he was a most con—"

" There," I interrupted : " don't abuse your ancestors. Tell me why you have changed your mind so quick ? "

" That's a precious hard thing to do, mind you ; " he answered. " A thousand trifling circumstances, which taken apart are as worthless straws, when they are bound up together become a respectable truss, which is marketable, and ponderable. So it is with little traits in Mary's character, which I have only noticed lately, nothing separately ; yet, when taken together, are, to say the least, different to what I had imagined while my eyes were blinded. To take one instance among fifty ; there's her cousin Tom, one of the finest fellows that ever stepped ; but still I don't like to see her, a married woman, allowing him to pull her hair about, and twist flowers in it."

This was very true, but I thought that if James instead of Tom had been allowed the privilege of decorating her hair, he might have looked on it with different eyes. James, I saw, cared too little about her to be very jealous, and so I saw that there was no fear of any coolness between him and Troubridge, which was a thing to be rejoiced at, as a quarrel would have been a terrible blow on our little society.

"Jim," said I, "I have got something to tell you. Do you know, I believe there is some mystery about Doctor Mulhaus."

"He is a walking mystery," said Jim: "but he is a noble good fellow, though unhappily a frog-eater."

"Ah! but I believe Miss Thornton knows it."

"Very like," said Jim, yawning.

I told him all the conversation I overheard that evening.

"Are you sure she said 'the king'?" he asked.

"Quite sure," I said; "now, what do you make of it?"

"I make this of it," he said: "that it is no earthly business of ours, or we should have been informed of it; and if I were you, I wouldn't breathe a word of it to any mortal soul, or let the Doctor suspect that you overheard anything. Secrets where kings are concerned are precious sacred things, old Jeff. Good night!"

CHAPTER XXII.

SAM BUCKLEY'S EDUCATION.

This narrative which I am now writing is neither more nor less than an account of what befel certain of my acquaintances during a period extending over nearly, or quite, twenty years, interspersed, and let us hope embellished, with descriptions of the country in which these circumstances took place, and illustrated by conversations well known to me by frequent repetition, selected as throwing light upon the characters of the persons concerned. Episodes there are, too, which I have thought it worth while to introduce, as being more or less interesting, as bearing on the manners of a country but little known, out of which materials it is difficult to select those most proper to make my tale coherent; yet it has been my object, neither to dwell on the one hand unnecessarily on the more unimportant passages, nor on the other hand to omit anything which may be supposed to bear on the general course of events.

Now, during all the time above mentioned, I, Geoffry Hamlyn, have happened to lead a most uninteresting, and with few exceptions prosperous existence. I was but little concerned, save as a hearer, in the catalogue of exciting accidents and offences which I chronicle. I have looked on with the deepest interest at the love-making, and ended a bachelor; I have witnessed the fighting afar off, only joining the battle when I could not help it, yet I am a steady old fogey, with a mortal horror of a disturbance of any sort. I have sat drinking with the wine-bibbers, and yet at sixty my hand is as steady as a rock. Money has come to me by mere accumulation; I have taken more pains to spend it than to make it; in short, all through my life's dream, I have been a spectator and not an actor, and so in this story I shall keep myself as much as possible in the background, only appearing personally when I cannot help it.

Acting on this resolve I must now make my *congé*, and bid you farewell for a few years, and go back to those few sheep which James Stockbridge and I own in the wilderness, and continue the history of those who are more important than myself. I must push on too, for there is a long period of dull stupid prosperity coming to our friends at Baroona and Toonarbin, which we must get over as quickly as is decent. Little Sam Buckley also, though at present a most delightful child, will soon be a mere uninteresting boy. We must teach him to read and write, and ride, and what not, as soon as possible, and see if we can't find a young lady—well, I won't anticipate, but go on. Go on, did I say?—jump on, rather—two whole years at once.

See Baroona now. Would you know it? I think not. That hut where we spent the pleasant Christmas-day you know of is degraded into the kitchen, and seems moved backward, although it stands in the same place, for a new house is built nearer the river, quite overwhelming the old slab hut in its grandeur—a long low wooden house, with deep cool verandahs all round, already festooned with passion flowers, and young grape-vines, and fronted by a flower garden, all a-blaze with petunias and geraniums.

It was a summer evening, and all the French windows reaching to the ground were open to admit the cool south wind, which had just come up, deliciously icily cold after a scorching day. In the verandah sat the Major and the Doctor over their claret (for the Major had taken to dining late again now, to his great comfort), and in the garden were Mrs. Buckley and Sam watering the flowers, attended by a man who drew water from a new-made reservoir near the house.

" I think, Doctor," said the Major, " that the habit of dining in the middle of the day is a gross abuse of the gifts of Providence, and I'll prove it to you. What does a man dine for?—answer me that."

" To satisfy his hunger, *I* should say," answered the Doctor.

" Pooh! pooh! stuff and nonsense, my good friend," said the Major; " you are speaking at random. I suppose you will say, then, that a black fellow is capable of dining?"

" Highly capable, as far as I can judge from what I have seen," replied the Doctor. " A full-grown fighting black would be ashamed if he couldn't eat a leg of mutton at a sitting."

" And you call that *dining?* " said the Major. " I call it gorging. Why, those fellows are more uncomfortable after food than before. I have seen them sitting close before the fire and rubbing their stomachs with mutton fat to reduce the swelling. Ha! ha! ha! —dining, eh? Oh, Lord!"

"Then if you don't dine to satisfy your hunger, what the deuce do you eat dinners for at all?" asked the Doctor.

"Why," said the Major, spreading his legs out before him with a benign smile, and leaning back in his chair, "I eat my dinner, not so much for the sake of the dinner itself, as for the after-dinnerish feeling which follows: a feeling that you have nothing to do, and that if you had you'd be shot if you'd do it. That, to return to where I started from, is why I won't dine in the middle of the day."

"If that is the way you feel after dinner, I certainly wouldn't."

"All the most amiable feelings in the human breast," continued the Major, "are brought out in their full perfection by dinner. If a fellow were to come to me now and ask me to lend him ten pounds, I'd do it, provided, you know, that he would fetch out the cheque-book and pen and ink."

"Laziness is nothing," said the Doctor, "unless well carried out. I only contradicted you, however, to draw you out; I agree entirely. Do you know, my friend, I am getting marvellously fond of this climate."

"So am I. But then you know, Doctor, that we are sheltered from the north wind here by the snow-ranges. The summer in Sydney, now, is perfectly infernal. The dust is so thick you can't see your hand before you."

"So I believe," said the Doctor. "By the bye, I got a new butterfly to-day: rather an event, mind you, here, where there are so few."

"What is he?"

"An Hipparchia," said the Doctor, "Sam saw him first and gave chase."

"You seem to be making quite a naturalist of my boy, Doctor. I am sincerely obliged to you. If we can make him take to that sort of thing it may keep him out of much mischief."

"He will never get into much," said the Doctor, "unless I am mistaken; he is the most docile child I ever came across. It is a pleasure to be with him. What are you going to do with him?"

"He must go to school, I am afraid," said the Major with a sigh; "I can't bring my heart to part with him; but his mother has taught him all she knows, so I suppose he must go to school and fight, and get flogged, and come home with a pipe in his mouth, and an oath on his lips, with his education completed. I don't fancy his staying here among these convict servants, when he is old enough to learn mischief."

"He'll learn as much mischief at a colonial school, I expect," said the Doctor, "and more too. All the evil he hears from these fellows will be like the water on a duck's back ; whereas, if you send him to school in a town, he'll learn a dozen vices he'll never hear of here. Get him a tutor."

" That is easier said than done, Doctor. It is very hard to get a respectable tutor in the colony."

" Here is one at your hand," said the Doctor.   " Take me."

" My dear friend," said the Major, jumping up, " I would not have dared to ask such a thing. If you would undertake him for a short time ?"

" I will undertake the boy's education altogether. Potztausend, and why not ! It will be a labour of love, and therefore the more thoroughly done. What shall he learn, now ? "

" That I must leave to you."

" A weighty responsibility," said the Doctor.   " No Latin or Greek, I suppose ? They will be no use to him here."

" Well—no ; I suppose not. But I should like him to learn his Latin grammar. You may depend upon it there's something in the Latin grammar."

" What use has it been to you, Major ? "

" Why, the least advantage it has been to me is to give me an insight into the construction of languages, which is some use. But while I was learning the Latin grammar, I learnt other things besides, of more use than the construction of any languages, living or dead. First, I learnt that there were certain things in this world that *must* be done. Next, that there were people in this world, of whom the Masters of Eton were a sample, whose orders must be obeyed without question. Third, I found that it was pleasanter in all ways to do one's duty than to leave it undone. And last, I found out how to bear a moderate amount of birching without any indecent outcry."

" All very useful things," said the Doctor.   " Teach a boy one thing well, and you show him how to learn others. History, I suppose ?"

" As much as you like, Doctor. His mother has taught him his catechism, and all that sort of thing, and she is the fit person, you know. With the exception of that and the Latin grammar, I trust everything to your discretion."

" There is one thing I leave to you, Major, if you please, and that is corporal chastisement. I am not at all sure that I could bring myself to flog Sam, and, if I did, it would be very inefficiently done."

" Oh, I'll undertake it," said the Major, " though I believe I shall have an easy task. He won't want much flogging."

At this moment Mrs. Buckley approached with a basketful of fresh-gathered flowers. " The roses don't flower well, here, Doctor," she said, " but the geraniums run mad. Here is a salmon-coloured one for your button-hole."

" He has earned it well, Agnes," said her husband. " He has decided the discussion we had last night by offering to undertake Sam's education himself."

" And God's blessing on him for it!" said Mrs. Buckley, warmly. " You have taken a great load off my mind, Doctor. I should never have been happy if that boy had gone to school. Come here, Sam."

Sam came bounding into the verandah, and clambered up on his father, as if he had been a tree. He was now eleven years old, and very tall and well-formed for his age. He was a good-looking boy, with regular features, and curly chestnut hair. He had, too, the large grey-blue eye of his father, an eye that never lost for a moment its staring expression of kindly honesty, and the lad's whole countenance was one which, without being particularly handsome, or even very intelligent, won an honest man's regard at first sight.

" My dear Sam," said his mother, " leave off playing with your father's hair, and listen to me, for I have something serious to say to you. Last night your father and I were debating about sending you to school, but Doctor Mulhaus has himself offered to be your tutor, thereby giving you advantages, for love, which you never could have secured for money. Now, the least we can expect of you, my dear boy, is that you will be docile and attentive to him."

" I will try, Doctor dear," said Sam. " But I am very stupid sometimes, you know."

So the good Doctor, whose head was stored with nearly as much of human knowledge as mortal head could hold, took simple, guileless little Sam by the hand, and led him into the garden of knowledge. Unless I am mistaken, these two will pick more flowers than they will dig potatoes in the aforesaid garden, but I don't think that two such honest souls will gather much unwholesome fruit. The danger is that they will waste their time, which is no danger at all, but a certainty.

I believe that such an education as our Sam got from the Doctor would have made a slattern and a *fainéant* out of half the boys in England. If Sam had been a clever boy, or a conceited boy, he would have ended with a superficial knowledge of things in general, imagining he knew everything when he knew nothing, and would have been left in the end, without a faith either religious or political, a useless, careless man.

This danger the Doctor foresaw in the first month, and going to the Major abruptly, as he walked up and down the garden, took his arm, and said,—

" See here, Buckley. I have undertaken to educate that boy of yours, and every day I like the task better, and yet every day I see that I have undertaken something beyond me. His appetite for knowledge is insatiable, but he is not an intellectual boy; he makes no deductions of his own, but takes mine for granted. He has no commentary on what he learns, but that of a dissatisfied idealist like me, a man who has been thrown among circumstances sufficiently favourable to make a prime minister out of some men, and yet who has ended by doing nothing. Another thing: this is my first attempt at education, and I have not the schoolmaster's art to keep him to details. Every day I make new resolutions, and every day I break them. The boy turns his great eyes upon me in the middle of some humdrum work, and asks me a question. In answering, I get off the turnpike road, and away we go from lane to lane, from one subject to another, until lesson-time is over, and nothing done. And, if it were merely time wasted, it could be made up, but he remembers every word I say, and believes in it like gospel, when I myself couldn't remember half of it to save my life. Now, my dear fellow, I consider your boy to be a very sacred trust to me, and so I have mentioned all this to you, to give you an opportunity of removing him to where he might be under a stricter discipline, if you thought fit. If he was like some boys, now, I should resign my post at once; but, as it is, I shall wait till you turn me out, for two reasons. The first is, that I take such delight in my task, that I do not care to relinquish it; and the other is, that the lad is naturally so orderly and gentle, that he does not need discipline, like most boys."

"My dear Doctor," replied Major Buckley, "listen to me. If we were in England, and Sam could go to Eton, which, I take it you know, is the best school in the world, I would still earnestly ask you to continue your work. He will probably inherit a great deal of money, and will not have to push his way in the world by his brains; so that close scholarship will be rather unnecessary. I should like him to know history well and thoroughly; for he may mix in the political life of this little colony by and by. Latin grammar, you know," he said, laughing, "is indispensable. Doctor, I trust my boy with you because I know that you will make him a gentleman, as his mother, with God's blessing, will make him a Christian."

So, the Doctor buckled to his task again, with renewed energy; to Euclid, Latin grammar, and fractions. Sam's good memory enabled him to make light of the grammar, and the fractions too were no great difficulty, but the Euclid was an awful trial. He couldn't make out what it was all about. He got on very well until he came nearly to the end of the first book, and then getting among the parallelogram "props," as we used to call them, (may their fathers' graves be defiled!) he stuck dead. For a whole evening did he pore patiently over one of them till A B, setting to C D, crossed hands, poussetted, and whirled round "in Sahara waltz" through his throbbing head. Bed-time, but no rest! Whether he slept or not he could not tell. Who could sleep with that long-bodied, ill-tempered-looking parallelogram A H standing on the bed-clothes, and crying out in tones loud enough to waken the house, that it never had been, nor ever would be equal to the fat jolly square C K? So, in the morning, Sam woke to the consciousness that he was farther off from the solution than ever, but, having had a good cry, went into the study and tackled to it again.

No good! Breakfast time, and matters much worse! That long peaked-nose vixen of a triangle A H C, which yesterday Sam had made out was equal to half the parallelogram and half the square, now had the audacity to declare that she had nothing to do with either of them; so what was to be done now?

After breakfast Sam took his book and went out to his father, who was sitting smoking in the verandah. He clambered up on to his knee, and then began :—

"Father, dear, see here; can you understand this? You've got to prove, you know,—oh, dear! I've forgot that now."

"Let's see," said the Major; "I'm afraid this is a little above me. There's Brentwood, now, could do it; he was in the Artillery, you know, and learnt fortification, and that sort of thing. I don't think I can make much hand of it, Sam."

But Sam had put his head upon his father's shoulder, and was crying bitterly.

"Come, come, my old man," said the Major, "don't give way, you know; don't be beat."

"I can't make it out at all," said Sam, sobbing. "I've got such a buzzing in my head with it! and if I can't do it I must stop; because I can't go on to the next till I understand this. Oh, dear me!"

"Lay your head there a little, my boy, till it gets clearer: then perhaps you will be able to make it out. You may depend on it that you ought to learn it, or the good Doctor wouldn't have set it to you; never let a thing beat you, my son."

So Sam cried on his father's shoulder a little, and then went in with his book; and not long after, the Doctor looked in unperceived, and saw the boy with his elbows on the table and the book before him. Even while he looked a big tear fell plump into the middle of A H; so the Doctor came quietly in and said,—

"Can't you manage it, Sam?"

Sam shook his head.

"Just give me hold of the book; will you, Sam?"

Sam complied without word or comment; the Doctor sent it flying through the open window, half-way down the garden. "There!" said he, nodding his head, "that's the fit place for him this day: you've had enough of him at present; go and tell one of the blacks to dig some worms, and we'll make holiday and go a fishing."

Sam looked at the Doctor, and then through the window at his old enemy lying in the middle of the flower-bed. He did not like to see the poor book, so lately his master, crumpled and helpless, fallen from its high estate so suddenly. He would have gone to its assistance, and picked it up and smoothed it, the more so as he felt that he had been beaten.

The Doctor seemed to see everything. "Let it lie here, my child," he said; "you are not in a position to assist a fallen enemy; you are still the vanquished party. Go and get the worms."

He went, and when he came back he found the Doctor sitting beside his father in the verandah, with a penknife in one hand and the ace of spades in the other. He cut the card into squares, triangles, and parallelograms, while Sam looked on, and, demonstrating as he went, fitted them one into the other, till the boy saw his bugbear of a proposition made as clear as day before his eyes.

"Why," said Sam, "that's as clear as need be. I understand it. Now may I pick the book up, Doctor?"

History was the pleasantest part of all Sam's tasks, for they would sit in the little room given up for a study, with the French windows open looking on the flower-garden, Sam reading aloud and the Doctor making discursive commentaries. At last, one day the Doctor said,—

"My boy, we are making too much of a pleasure of this: you must really learn your dates. Now tell me the date of the accession of Edward the Sixth."

No returns.

"Ah! I thought so: we must not be so discursive. We'll learn the dates of the Grecian History, as being an effort of memory, you not having read it yet."

But this plan was rather worse than the other; for one morning, Sam having innocently asked, at half-past eleven, what the battle of Thermopylæ was, Mrs. Buckley coming in, at one, to call them to lunch, found the Doctor, who had begun the account of that glorious fight in English, and then gone on to German, walking up and down the room in a state of excitement, reciting to Sam, who did not know δ from ψ, the soul-moving account of it from Herodotus in good sonorous Greek. She asked, laughing, "What language are you talking now, my dear Doctor?"

"Greek, madam, Greek! and the very best of Greek!"

"And what does Sam think of it? I should like you to learn Greek, my boy, if you can."

"I thought he was singing, mother," said Sam; but after that the lad used to sit delighted, by the river side, when they were fishing, while the Doctor, with his musical voice, repeated some melodious ode of Pindar's.

And so the intellectual education proceeded, with more or less energy; and meanwhile the physical and moral part was not forgotten, though the two latter, like the former, were not very closely attended to, and left a good deal to Providence. (And, having done your best for a boy, in what better hands can you leave him?) But the Major, as an old soldier, had gained a certain faith in the usefulness of physical training; so, when Sam was about twelve, you might have seen him any afternoon on the lawn, with his father, the Major, patiently teaching him singlestick, and Sam as patiently learning, until the boy came to be so marvellously active on his legs, and to show such rapidity of eye and hand, that the Major, on one occasion, having received a more than usually agonizing cut on the forearm, remarked that he thought he was not quite so active on his pins as formerly, and that he must hand the boy over to the Doctor.

"Doctor," said he that day, "I have taught my boy ordinary sword play till, by Jove, sir, he is getting quicker than I am. I wish you would take him in hand and give him a little fencing."

"Who told you I could fence?" said the Doctor.

"Why, I don't know; no one, I think. I have judged, I fancy, more by seeing you flourish your walking-stick than anything else. You are a fencer, are you not?"

The Doctor laughed. He was in fact a consummate *maître d'armes;* and Captain Brentwood, before spoken of, no mean fencer, coming to Baroona on a visit, found that our friend could do exactly as he liked with him, to the Captain's great astonishment. And Sam soon improved under his tuition, not indeed to the extent of being a master of the weapon; he was too large and loosely built for that; but, at all events, so far as to gain an upright and elastic carriage, and to learn the use of his limbs.

The Major issued an edict, giving the most positive orders against its infringement, that Sam should never mount a horse without his special leave and licence. He taught him to ride, indeed, but would not give him much opportunity for practising it. Once or twice a-week he would take him out, but seldom oftener. Sam, who never dreamt of questioning the wisdom and excellence of any of his father's decisions, rather wondered at this; pondering in his own mind how it was that, while all the lads he knew around, now getting pretty numerous, lived, as it were, on horseback, never walking a quarter of a mile on any occasion, he alone should be discouraged from it. "Perhaps," he said to himself one day, "he doesn't want me to make many acquaintances. It is true, Charley Delisle smokes and swears, which is very ungentlemanly; but Cecil Mayford, Dad says, is a perfect little gentleman, and I ought to see as much of him as possible, and yet he wouldn't give me a horse to go to their muster. Well, I suppose he has some reason for it."

One holiday the Doctor and the Major were sitting in the verandah after breakfast, when Sam entered to them, and, clambering on to his father as his wont was, said,—

"See here, father! Harry is getting in some young beasts at the stock-yard hut, and Cecil Mayford is coming over to see if any of theirs are among them; may I go out and meet him?"

"To be sure, my boy; why not?"

"May I have Bronsewing, father? He is in the stable."

"It is a nice cool day, and only four miles; why not walk out, my boy?"

Sam looked disappointed, but said nothing.

"I know all about it, my child," said the Major; "Cecil will be there on Blackboy, and you would like to shew him that Bronsewing is the superior pony of the two. That's all very natural; but still I say, get your hat, Sam, and trot through the forest on your own two legs, and bring Cecil home to dinner."

Sam still looked disappointed, though he tried not to show it. He went and got his hat, and, meeting the dogs, got such a wild welcome from them that he forgot all about Bronsewing Soon his father saw him merrily crossing the paddock with the whole kennel of the establishment, Kangaroo dogs, cattle dogs, and colleys, barking joyously around him.

"There's a good lesson manfully learnt, Doctor," said the Major; "he has learnt to sacrifice his will to mine without argument, because he knows I have always a reason for things. I want that boy to ride as little as possible, but he has earned an exception in his favour to-day.—Jerry!" (After a few calls the stableman appeared.) "Put Mr. Samuel's saddle on Bronsewing, and mine on Ricochette, and bring them round."

So Sam, walking cheerily forward singing, under the light and shadow of the old forest, surrounded by his dogs, hears horses' feet behind him, and looking back sees his father riding and leading Bronsewing saddled.

"Jump up, my boy," said the Major; "Cecil shall see what Bronsewing is like, and how well you can sit him. The reason I altered my mind was that I might reward you for acting like a man, and not arguing. Now, I don't want you to ride much yet for a few years. I don't want my lad to grow up with a pair of bow legs like a groom, and probably something worse, from living on horseback before his bones are set. You see I have good reason for what I do."

But I think that the lessons Sam liked best of all were the swimming lessons, and at a very early age he could swim and dive like a black, and once when disporting himself in the water, when not more than thirteen, poor Sam nearly had a stop put to his bathing for ever, and that in a very frightful manner

His father and he had gone down to bathe one hot noon; the Major had swum out and was standing on the rock wiping himself, while Sam was still disporting in the mid-river; as he watched the boy he saw what seemed a stick upon the water, and then, as he perceived the ripple around it, the horrible truth burst on the affrighted father: it was a large black snake crossing the river, and poor little Sam was swimming straight towards it, all unconscious of his danger.

The Major cried out and wav d his hand; the boy seeing something was wrong, turned and made for the shore, and the next moment his father, bending his body back, hurled himself through the air and alighted in the water alongside of him, clutching him round the body, and heading down the river with furious strokes.

"Don't cling, Sam, or get frightened; make for the shore."

The lad, although terribly frig tened at he knew not what, with infinite courage seconded his father's efforts although he felt sinking. In a few minutes they were safe on the bank, in time for them to see the reptile land, and crawling up the bank disappear among the rocks.

"God has been very good to us, my son. You have been saved from a terrible death. Mind you don't breathe a word to your mother about this."

That night Sam dreamt that he was in the coils of a snake, but waking up found that his father was laid beside him in his clothes with one arm round his neck, so he went to sleep again and thought no more of the snake.

"My son, if sinners entice thee, consent thou not"—a saying which it is just possible you have heard before. I can tell you where it comes from: it is one of the apothegms of the king of a little eastern nation who at one time were settled in Syria, and whose writings are not much read now-a-days, in consequence of the vast mass of literature of a superior kind which this happy century has produced. I can recommend the book, however, as containing some original remarks, and being generally worth reading. The meaning of the above quotation (and the man who said it, mind you, had at one time a reputation for shrewdness), is, as I take it, that a man's morals are v y much influenced by the society he is thrown among; and although in these parliamentary times we know that kings must of necessi be fools, yet in this instance I think that the man shows some glimmerings of reason, for his remark tallies singularly with my own personal observation; so, acting on this, while I am giving you the history of this little wild boy of the bush, I cannot do better than give some account of the companions with whom he chiefly assorted out of school-hours.

With broad intelligent forehead, with large loving hazel eyes, with a frill like Queen Elizabeth, with a brush like a fox; deep in the brisket, perfect in markings of black, white, and tan; in sagacity a Pitt, in courage an Anglesey, Rover stands first on my list, and claims to be king of Colley-dogs. In politics I should say Conservative of the high Protectionist sort. Let us have no strange dogs about the place to grub up sacred bones, or we will shake out our frills and tumble them in the dust. Domestic cats may mioul in the garden at night to a certain extent, but a line must be drawn; after that they must be chased up trees and barked at, if necessary, all night. Opossums and native cats are unfit to cumber the earth, and must be hunted into holes, wherever possible. Cows and other horned animals must not come into the yard, or even look over the garden fence, under penalties. Black fellows must be barked at, and their dogs chased to the uttermost limits of the habitable globe. Such were the chief points of the creed subscribed to by Sam's dog Rover.

All the love that may be between dog and man, and man and dog, existed between Sam and Rover. Never a fresh cheery morning when the boy arose with the consciousness of another happy day before him, but that the dog was waiting for him as he stepped from his window into clear morning air. Never a walk in the forest, but that Rover was his merry companion. And what would lessons have been without Rover looking in now and then with his head on one side, and his ears cocked, to know when he would be finished and come out to play?

Oh, memorable day, when Sam got separated from his father in Yass, and, looking back, saw a cloud of dust in the road, and dimly descried Rover, fighting valiantly against fearful odds, with all the dogs in the township upon him! He rode back, and prayed for assistance from the men lounging in front of the public-house; who, pitying his distress, pulled off all the dogs till there were only left Rover and a great white bulldog to do battle. The fight seemed going against Sam's dog; for the bulldog had him by the neck, and held him firm, so that he could do nothing. Nevertheless, mind yourself, master bulldog; you've only got a mouthful of long hair there; and when you do let go, I think, there is danger for you in those fierce gleaming eyes, and terrible grinning fangs.

Sam was crying; and the men round were saying, "Oh! take the bulldog off; the colley's no good to him,"—when a man suddenly appeared at Sam's side, and called out,

"I'll back the colley for five pounds, and here's my money!"

Half-a dozen five pound notes were ready for him at once; and he had barely got the stakes posted before the event proved he was right. In an evil moment for him the bulldog loosed his hold, and, ere he had time to turn round, Rover had seized him below the eye, and was dragging him about the road, worrying him as he would an opossum: so the discomfited owner had to remove his bulldog to save his life. Rover, after showing his teeth and shaking himself, came to Sam as fresh as a daisy; and the new comer pocketed his five pounds.

" I am so much obliged to you," said Sam, turning to him, " for taking my dog's part! They were all against me."

" I'm much obliged to your dog, sir, for winning me five pounds so easy. But there ain't a many bad dogs or bad men either, about Major Buckley's house."

" Then you know us?" said Sam.

" Ought to it, sir. An old Devonshire man. Mr. Hamlyn's stud-groom, sir—Dick."

Well, as I am going to write Rover's life, in three volumes post octavo, I won't any further entrench on my subject matter, save to say that, while on the subject of Sam's education, I could not well omit a notice of the aforesaid Rover. For I think all a man can learn from a dog, Sam learnt from him; and that is something. Now let us go on to the next of his notable acquaintances.

Who is this glorious, blue-eyed, curly-headed boy, who bursts into the house like a whirlwind, making it ring again with merry laughter? This is Jim Brentwood, of whom we shall see much anon.

At Waterloo, when the French cavalry were coming up the hill, and our artillerymen were running for the squares, deftly trundling their gun-wheels before them, it happened that there came running towards the square where Major Buckley stood like a tower of strength (the tallest man in the regiment), an artillery officer, begrimed with mud and gunpowder, and dragging a youth by the collar, or rather, what seemed to be the body of a youth. Some cried out to him to let go; but he looked back, seeming to measure the distance between the cavalry and the square, and then, never loosing his hold, held on against hope. Every one thought he would be too late; when some one ran out of the square (men said it was Buckley), and, throwing the wounded lad over his shoulder, ran with him into safety; and a cheer ran along the line from those who saw him do it. Small time for cheering then; for neither could recover his breath before there came a volley of musketry, and all around them, outside the bayonets, was a wild sea of fierce men's faces, horses' heads, gleaming steel, and French blasphemy. A strange scene for the commencement of an acquaintance! And yet it throve; for that same evening, Buckley, talking to his Colonel, saw the artillery officer coming towards them, and asked who he might be?

" That," said the Colonel, " is Brentwood of the Artillery, who ran away with Lady Kate Bingley, and they haven't a rap to bless themselves with, sir. It was her brother that you and he fetched into the square to-day."

And so began a friendship which lasted the lives of both men; and, I doubt not, will last their sons' lives too. For Brentwood lived within thirty miles of the Major, and their sons spent much of their time together, having such a friendship for one another as only boys can have.

Captain Brentwood's son Jim was a very different boy to Sam, though a very fine fellow too. Mischief and laughter were the apparent objects of his life; and when the Doctor saw him approaching the house, he used to put away Sam's lesson-books with a sigh and wait for better times. The Captain had himself undertaken his son's education, and, being a somewhat dreamy man, excessively attached to mathematics, Jim had got, altogether, a very remarkable education indeed; which, however, is hardly to our purpose just now. Brentwood, I must say, was a widower, and a kind-hearted, easy-going man; he had, besides, a daughter, who was away at school. Enough of them at present.

The next of Sam's companions who takes an important part in this history is Cecil Mayford—a delicate, clever little dandy, and courageous withal; with more brains in his head, I should say, than Sam and Jim could muster between them. His mother was a widow, who owned the station next down the river from the Buckleys', distant about five miles, and which, since the death of her husband, Doctor Mayford, she had managed with the assistance of an overseer. She had, besides Cecil, a little daughter of great beauty.

Also, I must here mention that the next station below Mrs. Mayford's, on the river, distant by the windings of the valley fifteen miles, and yet, in consequence of a bend, scarcely ten from Major Buckley's at Baroona, was owned and inhabited by Yahoos (by name Donovan), with whom we had nothing to do. But this aforesaid station, which is called Garoopna, will shortly fall into other hands, when you will see that many events of deep importance will take place there, and many pleasant hours spent there by all our friends, more particularly one—by name Sam.

There is one other left of whom I must say something here, and more immediately. The poor, puling little babe, born in misery and disaster, Mary Hawker's boy Charles!

Toonarbin was but a short ten miles from Baroona, and, of course, the two families were as one. There was always a hostage from the one house staying as a visitor in the other; and, under such circumstances, of course, Charles and Sam were much together, and, as time went on, got to be firm friends.

Charles was two years younger than Sam; the smallest of all the lads, and perhaps the most unhappy. For the truth must be told: he was morose and uncertain in his temper; and although all the other boys bore with him most generously, as one of whom they had heard that he was born under some great misfortune, yet he was hardly a favourite amongst them; and the poor boy, sometimes perceiving this, would withdraw from his play, and sulk alone, resisting all the sober, kind inducements of Sam, and the merry, impetuous persuasions of Jim, to return.

But he was a kind, good-hearted boy, nevertheless. His temper was not under control; but, after one of his fierce, volcanic bursts of ill-humour, he would be acutely miserable and angry with himself for days, particularly if the object of it had been Jim or Sam, his two especial favourites. On one occasion, after a causeless fit of anger with Jim, while the three were at Major Buckley's together, he got his pony and rode away home secretly, speaking to no one. The other two lamented all the afternoon that he had taken the matter so seriously, and were debating even next morning going after him to propitiate him, when Charles reappeared, having apparently quite recovered his temper, but evidently bent upon something.

He had a bird, a white corrella, which could talk and whistle surprisingly, probably, in fact, the most precious thing he owned. This prodigy he had now brought back in his basket as a peace-offering, and refused to be comforted, unless Jim accepted it as a present.

" But see, Charley," said Jim, " I was as much in the wrong as you were" (which was not fact, for Jim was perfectly innocent). " I wouldn't take your bird for the world."

But Charles said that his mother approved of it, and if Jim didn't take it he'd let it fly.

" Well, if you will, old fellow," said Jim, " I'll tell you what I would rather have. Give me Fly's dun pup instead, and take the bird home."

So this was negotiated after a time, and the corrella was taken back to Toonarbin, wildly excited by the journey, and calling for strong liquor all the way home.

Those who knew the sad circumstances of poor Charles's birth (the Major, the Doctor, and Mrs. Buckley) treated him with such kindness and consideration that they won his confidence and love. In any of his Berserk fits, if his mother were not at hand, he would go to Mrs. Buckley and open his griefs ; and her motherly tact and kindness seldom failed to still the wild beatings of that poor, sensitive, silly little heart, so that in time he grew to love her as only second to his mother.

Such is my brief and imperfect, and I fear tedious account of Sam's education, and of the companions with whom he lived, until the boy had grown into a young man, and his sixteenth birthday came round, on which day, as had been arranged, he was considered to have finished his education, and stand up, young as he was, as a man.

Happy morning, and memorable for one thing at least—that his father, coming into his bedroom and kissing his forehead, led him

out to the front door, where was a groom holding a horse handsomer
than any Sam had seen before, which pawed the gravel impatient to
be ridden, and ere Sam had exhausted half his expressions of wonder
and admiration—that his father told him the horse was his, a birth-
day-present from his mother.

CHAPTER XXIII.

TOONARBIN.

" But," I think I hear you say, " what has become of Mary Hawker
all this time ?   You raised our interest about her somewhat, at first,
as a young and beautiful woman, villain-beguiled, who seemed, too,
to have a temper of her own, and promised, under circumstances, to
turn out a bit of a b—mst—ne.   What is she doing all this time ?
Has she got fat, or had the small-pox, that you neglect her like this ?
We had rather more than we wanted of her and her villanous husband
in the first part of this volume ; and now nothing.   Let us, at all
events, hear if she is dead or alive.   And her husband, too,—
although we hope, under Providence, that he has left this wicked
world, yet we should be glad to hear of it for certain.   Make inquiries,
and let us know the result.   Likewise, be so good as inform us,
how is Miss Thornton ?"

To all this I answer humbly, that I will do my best.   If you will
bring a dull chapter on you, duller even than all the rest, at least
read it, and exonerate me.   The fact is, my dear sir, that women
like Mary Hawker are not particularly interesting in the piping
times of peace.   In volcanic and explosive times they, with their
wild animal passions, become tragical and remarkable, like baronesses
of old.   But in tranquil times, as I said, they fall into the background, and show us the value and excellence of such placid, noble
helpmates, as the serene, high-bred Mrs. Buckley.

A creek joined the river about a mile below the Buckleys' station,
falling into the main stream with rather a pretty cascade, which
even at the end of the hottest summer poured a tiny silver thread
across the black rocks.   Above the cascade the creek cut deep into
the table land, making a charming glen, with precipitous bluestone
walls, some eighty or ninety feet in height, fringed with black wattle
and lightwood, and here and there, among the fallen rocks nearest
the water, a fern tree or so, which last I may say are no longer there,
Dr. Mulhaus having cut the hearts out of them and eaten them for
cabbage.   Should you wander up this little gully on a hot summer's
day, you would be charmed with the beauty of the scenery, and the
shady coolness of the spot ; till coming upon a black snake coiled

away among the rocks, like a rope on the deck of a man of war, you would probably withdraw, not without a strong inclination to "shy" at every black stick you saw for the rest of the day. For this lower part of the Moira creek was, I am sorry to say, the most troubled locality for snakes, diamond, black, carpet, and other, which I ever happened to see.

But following this creek you would find that the banks got rapidly less precipitous, and at length it swept in long curves through open forest glades, spreading, too, into deep dark water-holes, only connected by gravelly fords, with a slender stream of clear water running across the yellow pebbles. These water-holes were the haunts of the platypus and the tortoise. Here, too, were flocks of black duck and teal, and as you rode past, the merry little snipe would rise from the water's edge, and whisk away like lightning through the trees. Altogether, a pleasant woodland creek, alongside of which, under the mighty box-trees, ran a sandy road, bordered with deep beds of bracken fern, which led from Baroona of the Buckleys to Toonarbin of the Hawkers.

A pleasant road, indeed, winding through the old forest straight towards the mountains, shifting its course so often that every minute some new vista opened upon you, till at length you came suddenly upon a clear space, beyond which rose a picturesque little granite cap, at the foot of which you saw a charming house, covered with green creepers, and backed by huts, sheepyards, a woolshed, and the usual concomitants of a flourishing Australian sheep station. Behind all again towered lofty, dark hanging woods, closing the prospect.

This is Toonarbin, where Mary Hawker, with her leal and trusty cousin Tom Troubridge for partner, has pitched her tent, after all her spasmodic, tragical troubles, and here she is leading as happy, and by consequence as uninteresting, an existence as ever fell to the lot of a handsome woman yet.

Mary and Miss Thornton had stayed with the Buckleys until good cousin Tom had got a house ready to receive them, and then they moved up and took possession. Mary and Tom were from the first co-partners, and, latterly, Miss Thornton had invested her money, about £2,000, in the station. Matters were very prosperous, and, after a few years, Tom began to get weighty and didactic in his speech, and to think of turning his attention to politics.

To Mary the past seemed like a dream—as an old dream, wellnigh forgotten. The scene was so changed that at times she could hardly believe that all those dark old days were real. Could she, now so busy and happy, be the same woman who sat worn and frightened over the dying fire with poor Captain Saxon? Is she the same woman whose husband was hurried off one wild night, and transported for coining? Or is all that a hideous imagination?

No. Here is the pledge and proof that it is all too terribly real. This boy, whom she loves so wildly and fiercely, is that man's son, and his father, for aught she knows, is alive, and only a few poor hundred miles off. Never mind; let it be forgotten as though it never was. So she forgot it, and was happy.

But not always. Sometimes she could not but remember what she was, in spite of the many kind friends who surrounded her, and the new and busy life she led. Then would come a fit of despondency, almost of despair, but the natural elasticity of her temper soon dispersed these clouds, and she was her old self again.

Her very old self, indeed. That delicate-minded, intellectual old maid, Miss Thornton, used to remark with silent horror on what she called Mary's levity of behaviour with men, but more especially with honest Tom Troubridge. Many a time, when the old lady was sitting darning (she was always darning; she used to begin darning the things before they were a week out of the draper's shop), would her tears fall upon her work, as she saw Mary sitting with her child in her lap, smiling, while the audacious Tom twisted a flower in her hair, in the way that pleased him best. To see anything wrong, and to say nothing, was a thing impossible. She knew that speaking to Mary would only raise a storm, and so, knowing the man she had to deal with, she determined to speak to Tom.

She was not long without her opportunity. Duly darning one evening, while Mary was away putting her boy to bed, Tom entered from his wine. Him, with a combination of valour and judgment, she immediately attacked, acting upon a rule once laid down to Mary—"My dear, if you want to manage a man, speak to him after dinner."

"Mr. Troubridge," said Miss Thornton. "May I speak a few words to you on private affairs?"

"Madam," said Tom, drawing up a chair, "I am at your service night or day."

"A younger woman," said Miss Thornton, "might feel some delicacy in saying what I am going to say. But old age has its privileges, and so I hope to be forgiven."

"Dear Miss Thornton," said Tom, "You must be going to say something very extraordinary if it requires forgiveness from me."

"Nay, my dear kinsman," said Miss Thornton; "if we begin exchanging compliments, we shall talk all night, and never get to the gist of the matter after all. Here is what I want to say. It seems to me that your attentions to our poor Mary are somewhat more than cousinly, and it behoves me to remind you that she is still a married woman. Is that too blunt? Have I offended you?"

"Nay—no," said Tom; "you could never offend me. I think you are right too. It shall be amended, madam."

And after this Mary missed many delicate little attentions that Tom had been used to pay her. She thought he was sulky on some account at first, but soon her good sense showed her that, if they two were to live together, she must be more circumspect, or mischief would come.

For, after all, Tom had but small place in her heart. Heart filled almost exclusively with this poor sulky little lad of hers, who seemed born to trouble, as the sparks went upward. In teething even, aggravating beyond experience, and afterwards suffering from the whole list of juvenile evils in such a way as boy never did before; coming out of these troubles too, with a captious, disagreeable temper, jealous in the extreme,—not a member who, on the whole, adds much to the pleasure of the little household,—yet with the blindest love towards some folks. Instance his mother, Thomas Troubridge, and Sam Buckley.

For these three the lad had a wild hysterical affection, and yet none of them had much power over him. Once by one unconsidered word arouse the boy's obstinacy, and all chance of controlling him was gone. Then, your only chance was to call in Miss Thornton, who had a way of managing the boy, more potent than Mary's hysterics, and Tom's indignant remonstrances, or Sam's quiet persuasions.

For instance,—once, when he was about ten years old, his mother set him to learn some lesson or another, when he had been petitioning to go off somewhere with the men. He was furiously naughty, and threw the book to the other end of the room, all the threats and scoldings of his mother proving insufficient to make him pick it up again. So that at last she went out, leaving him alone, triumphant, with Miss Thornton, who said not a word, but only raised her eyes off her work, from time to time, to look reproachfully on the rebellious boy. He could stand his mother's anger, but he could not stand those steady wondering looks that came from under the old lady's spectacles. So that, when Mary came in again, she found the book picked up, and the lesson learned. Moreover, it was a fortnight before the lad misbehaved himself again.

In sickness and in health, in summer and in winter, for ten long years after they settled at Toonarbin, did this noble old lady stand beside Mary as a rock of refuge in all troubles, great or small. Always serene, patient, and sensible, even to the last; for the time came when this true and faithful servant was removed from among them to receive her reward.

One morning she confessed herself unable to leave her bed; that was the first notice they had. Doctor Mayford, sent for secretly, visited her. "Break up of the constitution," said he,—"no organic disease,"—but shook his head. "She will go," he added, "with the first frost. I can do nothing." And Dr. Mulhaus, being con-

N

sulted, said he was but an amateur doctor, but concurred with **Dr.** Mayford. So there was nothing to do but to wait for the end as patiently as might be.

During the summer she got out of bed, and sat in a chair, which Tom used to lift dexterously into the verandah. There she would sit very quietly; sometimes getting Mrs. Buckley, who came and lived at Toonarbin that summer, to read a hymn for her; and, during this time, she told them where she would like to be buried.

On a little knoll, she said, which lay to the right of the house, barely two hundred yards from the window. Here the grass grew shorter and closer than elsewhere, and here freshened more rapidly beneath the autumn rains. Here, on winter's evenings, the slanting sunbeams lingered longest, and here, at such times, she had been accustomed to saunter, listening to the sighing of the wind, in the dark funeral sheoaks and cypresses, like the far-off sea upon a sandy shore. Here, too, came oftener than elsewhere a flock of lories, making the dark low trees gay with flying living blossoms. And here she would lie with her feet towards the east, her sightless eyes towards that dreary ocean which she would never cross again.

One fresh spring morning she sat up and talked serenely to Mrs. Buckley, about matters far higher and more sacred than one likes to deal with in a tale of this kind, and, after a time, expressed a wish for a blossom of a great amaryllis which grew just in front of her window.

Mrs. Buckley got the flower for her; and so, holding the crimson-striped lily in her delicate, wasted fingers, the good old lady passed from this world without a struggle, as decently and as quietly as she had always lived in it.

* * * * *

This happened when Charles was about ten years old, and, for some time, the lad was subdued and sad. He used to look out of the window at night towards the grave, and wonder why they had put her they all loved so well, to lie out there under the wild-sweeping winter rain. But, by degrees, he got used to the little square white railing on the sheoak knoll, and, ere half a year was gone, the memory of his aunt had become very dim and indistinct.

Poor Mary, too, though a long while prepared for it, was very deeply and sincerely grieved at Miss Thornton's death; but she soon recovered from it. It came in the course of nature, and, although the house looked blank and dull for a time, yet there was too much life all around her, too much youthful happy life, to make it possible to dwell very long on the death of one who had left them full of years and honour. But Lord Frederick (before spoken of incidentally in this narrative), playing billiards at Gibraltar, about a year after this, had put into his hand a letter, from which, when opened, there fell a lock of silver grey hair on the green cloth, which he carefully picked up, and, leaving his game, went home to his quarters. His comrades thought it was his father who was dead, and when they heard it was only his sister's old governess, they wondered exceedingly; "for Fred," said they, "is not given to be sentimental."

And now, in a year or two, it began to be very difficult to keep Master Charley in order. When he was about thirteen, there was a regular guerilla-war between him and his mother, on the subject of learning, which ended, ultimately, in the boy flatly refusing to learn anything. His natural capacities were but small, and, under any circumstances, knowledge would only have been acquired by him with infinite pains. But, as it was, with his selfishness fostered so excessively by his mother's indulgence, and Tom's good-humoured carelessness, it became totally impossible to teach him anything. In vain his mother scolded and wept, in vain Tom represented to him the beauties and excellences of learning—learn the boy would not; so that at fourteen he was given up in despair by his mother, having learnt nearly enough of reading, writing, and ciphering, to carry on the most ordinary business of life,—a most lamentable state of things for a lad who, in after life, would be a rich man, and who, in a young and rapidly-rising country, might become, by the help of education, politically influential.

I think that when Samuel Buckley and James Brentwood were grown to be young men of eighteen or nineteen, and he was about seventeen or so, a stranger would have seen a great deal of difference between the two former and the latter, and would, probably, have remarked that James and Sam spoke and behaved like two gentlemen, but that Charles did not, but seemed as though he had come from a lower grade in society,—with some truth too, for there was a circumstance in his bringing up which brought him more harm than all his neglect of learning, and all his mother's foolish indulgences.

Both Major Buckley and Captain Brentwood made it a law of the Medes and Persians, that neither of their sons should hold any conversation with the convict servants, save in the presence of competent authorities; and, indeed, they both, as soon as increased emigration enabled them, removed their old household servants, and replaced them by free men, newly arrived: a lazy independent class, certainly, with exaggerated notions of their own importance in this new phase of their life, but without the worse vices of the convicts. This rule, even in such well-regulated households, was a very hard one to get observed, even under flogging penalties; and, indeed, formed the staple affliction of poor thoughtless Jim's early life, as this little anecdote will show:—

One day going to see Captain Brentwood, when Jim was about ten years old, I met that young gentleman (looking, I thought, a little out of sorts) about two hundred yards from the house. He turned with me to go back, and, after the first salutations, I said,—

"Well, Jim, my boy, I hope you've been good since I saw you last?"

"Oh dear, no," was the answer, with a shake of the head that meant volumes.

"I'm sorry to hear that; what is the matter?"

"I've been *catching* it," said Jim, in a whisper, coming close alongside of me. "A tea-stick as thick as my forefinger all over." —Here he entered into particulars, which, however harmless in themselves, were not of a sort usually written in books.

"That's a bad job," I said; "what was it for?"

"Why, I slipped off with Jerry to look after some colts on the black swamp, and was gone all the afternoon; and so Dad missed me; and when I got home didn't I *catch it!* Oh Lord, I'm all over blue wales; but that ain't the worst."

'What's the next misfortune?" I inquired.

"Why, when he got hold of me he said, 'Is this the first time you have been away with Jerry, sir?' and I said 'Yes' (which was the awfullest lie ever you heard, for I went over to Barker's with him two days before); then he said, 'Well, I must believe you if you say so. I shall not disgrace you by making inquiries among the men;' and then he gave it me for going that time, and since then I've felt like Cain and Abel for telling him such a lie. What would you do, —eh?"

"I should tell him all about it," I said.

"Ah, but then I shall catch it again, don't you see! Hadn't I better wait till these wales are gone down?"

"I wouldn't, if I were you," I answered; "I'd tell him at once."

"I wonder why he is so particular," said Jim; "the Delisles and the Donovans spend as much of their time in the huts as they do in the house."

"And fine young blackguards they'll turn out," I said; in which I was right in those two instances. And although I have seen young fellows brought up among convicts who have turned out respectable in the end, yet it is not a promising school for good citizens.

But at Toonarbin no such precautions as these were taken with regard to Charles. Tom was too careless, and Mary too indulgent. It was hard enough to restrain the boy during the lesson hours, falsely so called. After that he was allowed to go where he liked, and even his mother sometimes felt relieved by his absence; so that he was continually in the men's huts, listening to their yarns— sometimes harmless bush adventures, sometimes, perhaps, ribald stories which he could not understand; but one day Tom Troubridge coming by the hut looked in quietly, and saw master Charles smoking a black pipe, (he was not more than fourteen,) and heard such a conversation going on that he advanced suddenly upon them, and ordered the boy home in a sterner tone than he had ever used to him before, and looked out of the door till he had disappeared. Then he turned round to the men.

There were three of them, all convicts, one of whom, the one he had heard talking when he came in, was a large, desperate-looking fellow. When these men mean to deprecate your anger, I have remarked they always look you blankly in the face; but if they mean to defy you and be impudent, they never look at you, but always begin fumbling and fidgetting with something. So when Tom saw that the big man before mentioned (Daniel Harvey by name) was stooping down before the fire, he knew he was going to have a row, and waited.

"So boss," began the ruffian, not looking at him, "we ain't fit company for the likes of that kinchin,—eh?"

"You're not fit company for any man except the hangman," said Tom, looking more like six-foot-six than six-foot-three.

"Oh my —— colonial oath!" said the other; "oh my —— 'cabbage tree!' So there's going to be a coil about that scrubby little myrnonger; eh? Don't you fret your bingy,* boss; he'll be as good a man as his father yet."

For an instant a dark shadow passed over Tom's face.

"So," he thought, "these fellows know all about George Hawker, eh? Well, never mind; what odds if they do?" And then he said aloud, turning round on Harvey, "Look you here, you dog; if I ever hear of your talking in that style before that boy, or any other boy, by George I'll twist your head off!"

He advanced towards him, as if to perform that feat on the spot; in a moment the convict had snatched his knife from his belt and rushed upon him.

Very suddenly indeed; but not quite quick enough to take the champion of Devon by surprise. Ere he was well within reach Tom had seized the hand that held the knife, and with a backward kick of his left foot sent the embryo assassin sprawling on his back on the top of the fire, whence Tom dragged him by his heels, far more astonished than burnt. The other two men had, meanwhile, sat taking no notice, or seeming to take none, of the disturbance. Now however, one of them spoke, and said,—

"I'm sure, sir, you didn't hear me say nothing wrong to the young gent," and so on, in a whining tone, till Tom cut him short by saying that, "if he had any more nonsense among them, he would send 'em all three over to Captain Desborough, to the tune of fifty (lashes) a-piece."

After this little émeute Charles did not dare to go into the huts, and soon after these three men were exchanged. But there remained

* As a specimen of colonial slang, the above is not in the least exaggerated.

one man whose conversation and teaching, though not, perhaps, so openly outrageously villanous as that of the worthy Harvey, still had a very unfortunate effect on his character.

This was a rather small, wiry, active man, by name Jackson, a native, colonially convicted,* very clever among horses, a capital light-weight boxer, and in running superb, a pupil and *protégé* of the immortal "flying pieman," † (May his shadow never be less !) a capital cricketer, and a supreme humbug. This man, by his various accomplishments and great tact, had won a high place in Tom Troubridge's estimation, and was put in a place of trust among the horses; consequently having continual access to Charles, to whom he made himself highly agreeable, as being heir to the property; giving him such insights into the worst side of sporting life, and such truthful accounts of low life in Sydney, as would have gone far to corrupt a lad of far stronger moral principle than he.

And so, between this teaching of evil and neglect of good, Mary Hawker's boy did not grow up all that might be desired. And at seventeen, I am sorry to say, he got into a most disreputable connexion with a Highland girl, at one of the Donovans' out-station huts; which caused his kindly guardian, Tom Troubridge, a great deal of vexation, and his mother the deepest grief, which was much increased at the same time by something I will relate in the next chapter.

So sixteen years rolled peacefully away, chequered by such trifling lights and shadows as I have spoken of. The new generation, the children of those whom we knew at first, are now ready to take their places, and bear themselves with more or less credit in what may be going on. And now comes a period which in the memory of all those whom I have introduced to you ranks as the most important of their lives. To me, looking back upon nearly sixty years of memory, the events which are coming stand out from the rest of my quiet life, well defined and remarkable, above all others. As looking on our western moors, one sees the long straight sky-line, broken only once in many miles by some fantastic Tor.

CHAPTER XXIV.

IN WHICH MARY HAWKER LOSES ONE OF HER OLDEST SWEETHEARTS.

SIXTEEN years of peace and plenty had rolled over the heads of James Stockbridge and myself, and we had grown to be rich. Our

* A man born in the colony, of European parents, convicted of some crime committed in the colony.

† A great Australian pedestrian; now, I believe, gathered to his fathers.

agent used to rub his hands, and bow, whenever our high mightinesses visited town. There was money in the bank, there was claret in the cellar, there were race-horses in the paddock; in short, we were wealthy prosperous men—James a magistrate.

November set in burning hot, and by the tenth the grass was as dry as stubble; still we hoped for a thunder-storm and a few days' rain, but none came. December wore wearily on, and by Christmas the smaller creeks, except those which were snow-fed, were reduced to a few muddy pools, and vast quantities of cattle were congregated within easy reach of the river, from other people's runs, miles away.

Of course, feed began to get very scarce, yet we were hardly so bad off yet as our neighbours, for we had just parted with every beast we could spare, at high prices, to Port Phillip, and were only waiting for the first rains to start after store cattle, which were somewhat hard to get near the new colony.

No rain yet, and we were in the end of January; the fountains of heaven were dried up, but now all round the northern horizon the bush fires burnt continually, a pillar of smoke by day, and a pillar of fire by night.

Nearer, by night, like an enemy creeping up to a beleaguered town. The weather had been very still for some time, and we took precaution to burn great strips of grass all round the paddocks to the north, but, in spite of all our precautions, I knew that, should a strong wind come on from that quarter, nothing short of a miracle would save us.

But as yet the weather was very still, not very bright, but rather cloudy, and a dense haze of smoke was over everything, making the distances look ten times as far as they really were, and rendering the whole landscape as grey and melancholy as you can conceive. There was nothing much to be done, but to sit in the verandah, drinking claret-and-water, and watching and hoping for a thunder-storm.

On the third of February the heat was worse than ever, but there was no wind; and as the sun went down among the lurid smoke, red as blood, I thought I made out a few white brush-shaped clouds rising in the north.

Jim and I sat there late, not talking much. We knew that if we were to be burnt out our loss would be very heavy; but we thanked God that even were we to lose everything it would not be irreparable, and that we should still be wealthy. Our brood mares and racing stock were our greatest anxiety. We had a good stack of hay, by which we might keep them alive for another month, supposing all the grass was burnt; but if we lost that, our horses would probably die. I said at last,—

" Jim, we may make up our minds to have the run swept. The fire is burning up now."

" Yes, it is brightening," said he, " but it must be twenty miles off still, and if it comes down with a gentle wind we shall save the paddocks and hay. There is a good deal of grass in the lower paddock. I am glad we had the forethought not to feed it down. Well, fire or no fire, I shall go to bed."

We went to bed, and, in spite of anxiety, mosquitoes, and heat, I fell asleep. In the grey morning I was awakened, nearly suffocated, by a dull continuous roar. It was the wind in the chimney. The north wind, so long imprisoned, had broke loose, and the boughs were crashing, and the trees were falling, before the majesty of his wrath.

I ran out, and met James in the verandah. " It's all up," I said. " Get the women and children into the river, and let the men go up to windward with the sheep-skins.* I'll get on horseback, and go out and see how the Morgans get on. That obstinate fellow will wish he had come in now."

Morgan was a stockman of ours, who lived, with a wife and two children, about eight miles to the northward. We always thought it would have been better for him to move in, but he had put it off, and now the fire had taken us by surprise.

I rode away, dead-up wind. Our station had a few large trees about it, and then all was clear plain and short grass for two miles; after that came scrubby ranges, in an open glade of which the Morgans' hut stood. I feared, from the density of the smoke, that the fire had reached them already, but I thought it my duty to go and see, for I might meet them fleeing, and help them with the children.

I had seen many bush-fires, but never such a one as this. The wind was blowing a hurricane, and, when I had ridden about two miles into scrub, high enough to brush my horse's belly, I began to get frightened. Still I persevered, against hope; the heat grew more fearful every moment; but I reflected that I had often ridden up close to a bush-fire, turned when I began to see the flame through the smoke, and cantered away from it easily.

Then it struck me that I had never yet seen a bush-fire in such a hurricane as this. Then I remembered stories of men riding for their lives, and others of burnt horses and men found in the bush. And, now, I saw a sight which made me turn in good earnest.

I was in lofty timber, and, as I paused, I heard the mighty crackling of fire coming through the wood. At the same instant the blinding smoke burst into a million tongues of flickering flame, and I saw the fire—not where I had ever seen it before—not creeping along among the scrub—but up aloft, a hundred and fifty feet over-

---

* Sheep-skins, on sticks, used for beating out the fire when in short grass.

head. It had caught the dry bituminous tops of the higher boughs, and was flying along from tree-top to tree-top like lightning. Below, the wind was comparatively moderate, but, up there, it was travelling twenty miles an hour. I saw one tree ignite like gun-cotton, and then my heart grew small, and I turned and fled.

I rode as I never rode before. There were three miles to go ere I cleared the forest, and got among the short grass, where I could save myself—three miles! Ten minutes nearly of intolerable heat, blinding smoke, and mortal terror. Any death but this! Drowning were pleasant, glorious to sink down into the cool sparkling water. But, to be burnt alive! Fool that I was to venture so far! I would give all my money now to be naked and penniless, rolling about in a cool pleasant river.

The maddened, terrified horse went like the wind, but not like the hurricane—that was too swift for us. The fire had outstripped us over-head, and I could see it dimly through the infernal choking reek, leaping and blazing a hundred yards before us, among the feathery foliage, devouring it, as the south wind devours the thunder clouds. Then I could see nothing. Was I clear of the forest? Thank the Lord, yes—I was riding over grass.

I managed to pull up the horse, and as I did so, a mob of kangaroos blundered by, blinded, almost against me, noticing me no more in their terror than if I had been a stump or a stone. Soon the fire came hissing along through the grass scarcely six inches high, and I walked my horse through it; then I tumbled off on the blackened ground, and felt as if I should die.

I lay there on the hot black ground. My head felt like a block of stone, and my neck was stiff so that I could not move my head. My throat was swelled and dry as a sand-hill, and there was a roaring in my ears like a cataract. I thought of the cool waterfalls among the rocks far away in Devon. I thought of everything that was cold and pleasant, and then came into my head about Dives praying for a drop of water. I tried to get up, but could not, so lay down again with my head upon my arm.

It grew cooler, and the atmosphere was clearer. I got up, and, mounting my horse, turned homeward. Now I began to think about the station. Could it have escaped? Impossible! The fire would fly a hundred yards or more such a day as this even in low plain. No, it must be gone! There was a great roll in the plain between me and home, so that I could see nothing of our place—all around the country was black, without a trace of vegetation. Behind me were the smoking ruins of the forest I had escaped from, where now the burnt-out trees began to thunder down rapidly, and before, to the south, I could see the fire raging miles away.

So the station is burnt, then? No! For as I top the ridge, there it is before me, standing as of old—a bright oasis in the desert of burnt country round. Ay! the very hay-stack is safe! And the paddocks?—all right!—glory be to God!

I got home, and James came running to meet me.

"I was getting terribly frightened, old man," said he. "I thought you were caught. Lord save us, you look ten years older than you did this morning!"

I tried to answer, but could not speak for drought. He ran and got me a great tumbler of claret-and-water; and, in the evening, having drunk about an imperial gallon of water, and taken afterwards some claret, I felt pretty well revived.

Men were sent out at once to see after the Morgans, and found them perfectly safe, but very much frightened; they had, however, saved their hut, for the fire had passed before the wind had got to its full strength.

So we were delivered from the fire; but still no rain. All day, for the next month, the hot north wind would blow till five o'clock, and then a cool southerly breeze would come up and revive us; but still the heavens were dry, and our cattle died by hundreds.

On the eighteenth of March, we sat in the verandah looking still over the blackened unlovely prospect, but now cheerfully and with hope; for the eastern sky was piled up range beyond range with the scarlet and purple splendour of cloud-land, and, as darkness gathered, we saw the lightning, not twinkling and glimmering harmlessly about the horizon, as it had been all the summer, but falling sheer in violet-coloured rivers behind the dark curtain of rain that hung from the black edge of a teeming thunder-cloud.

We had asked our overseer in that night, being Saturday, to drink with us; he sat very still, and talked but little, as was his wont. I slapped him on the back, and said:—

"Do you remember, Geordie, that muff in Thalaba who chose the wrong cloud? He should have got you or me to choose for him; we wouldn't have made a mistake, I know. We would have chosen such a one as yon glorious big-bellied fellow. See how grandly he comes growling up!"

"It's just come," said he, "without the praying for. When the fire came owre the hill the other day, I just put up a bit prayer to the Lord, that He'd spare the haystack, and He spared it. (I didna stop working, ye ken; I worked the harder; if ye dinna mean to work, ye should na pray.) But I never prayed for rain,— I didna, ye see, like to ask the Lord to upset all his gran' laws of electricity and evaporation, just because it would suit us. I thocht He'd likely ken better than mysel. Hech, sirs, but that chiel's riding hard!"

A horseman appeared making for the station at full speed; when he was quite close, Jim called out, "By Jove, it is Doctor Mulhaus!" and we ran out into the yard to meet him.

Before any one had time to speak, he shouted out: " My dear boys, I'm so glad I am in time : we are going to see one of the grandest electrical disturbances it has ever been my lot to witness. I reined up just now to look, and I calculated that the southern point of explosion alone is discharging nine times in the minute. How is your barometer ? "

" Haven't looked, Doctor."

" Careless fellow," he replied, " you don't deserve to have one."

" Never mind, sir, we have got you safe and snug out of the thunder-storm. It is going to be very heavy I think. I only hope we will have plenty of rain."

" Not much doubt of it," said he. " Now, come into the verandah and let us watch the storm."

We went and sat there; the highest peaks of the great cloud alps, lately brilliant red, were now cold silver grey, harshly defined against a faint crimson background, and we began to hear the thunder rolling and muttering. All else was deadly still and heavy.

" Mark the lightning ! " said the Doctor ; " that which is before the rain-wall is white, and that behind violet-coloured. Here comes the thundergust."

A fierce blast of wind came hurrying on, carrying a cloud of dust and leaves before it. It shook the four corners of the house and passed away. And now it was a fearful sight to see the rain-spouts pouring from the black edge of the lower cloud as from a pitcher, nearly overhead, and lit up by a continuous blaze of lightning. Another blast of wind, now a few drops, and in ten minutes you could barely distinguish the thunder above the rattle of the rain on the shingles.

It warred and banged around us for an hour, so that we could hardly hear one another speak. At length the Doctor bawled,—

" We shall have a crack closer than any yet, you'll see ; we always have one particular one ;—our atmosphere is not restored to its balance yet,—there ! "

The curtains were drawn, and yet, for an instant, the room was as bright as day. Simultaneously there came a crack and an explosion, so loud and terrifying, that, used as I was to such an event, I involuntarily jumped up from my seat.

" Are you all right here ?" said the Doctor ; and, running out into the kitchen, shouted, " Any one hurt ? "

The kitchen girl said that the lightning had run all down her back like cold water, and the housekeeper averred that she thought the thunder had taken the roof of the house off. So we soon perceived that nothing was the matter, and sat down again to our discourse, and our supper. " Well," began I, " here's the rain come at last. In a fortnight there will be good grass again. We ought to start and get some store cattle."

"But where?" replied James, "We shall have to go a long way for them; every one will be wanting the same thing now. We must push a long way north, and make a depôt somewhere westward. Then we can pick them up by sixes and sevens at a time. When shall we go?"

"The sooner the better."

"I think I will come with you," said the Doctor. "I have not been a journey for some time."

"Your conversation, sir," I said, "will shorten the journey by one-half"—which was sincerely said.

Away we went northward, with the mountains on our left, leaving snow-streaked Kosciusko nearly behind us, till a great pass, through the granite walls, opened up to the westward, up which we turned, Mount Murray towering up the south. Soon we were on the Murrumbidgee, sweeping from side to side of his mountain valley in broad curves, sometimes rushing hoarse, swollen by the late rains, under beds of high timber, and sometimes dividing broad meadows of rich grass, growing green once more under the invigorating hand of autumn. All nature had awakened from her deep summer sleep, the air was brisk and nimble, and seldom did three happier men ride on their way than James, the Doctor, and I.

Good Doctor! How he beguiled the way with his learning—in ecstasies all the time, enjoying everything, animate or inanimate, as you or I would enjoy a new play or a new opera. How I envied him! He was like a man always reading a new and pleasant book. At first the stockmen rode behind, talking about beasts, and horses, and what not—often talking about nothing at all, but riding along utterly without thought, if such a thing could be. But soon I noticed they would draw up closer, and regard the Doctor with some sort of attention, till toward the evening of the second day, one of them, our old acquaintance Dick, asked the Doctor a question, as to why, if I remember right, certain trees should grow in certain localities, and there only. The Doctor reined up alongside him directly, and in plain forcible language explained the matter: how that some plants required more of one sort of substance than another, and how they get it out of particular soils; and how, in the lapse of years, they had come to thrive best on the soil that suited them, and had got stunted and died out in other parts. "See," said he, "how the turkey holds to the plains, and the pheasant (lyre-bird) to the scrub, because each one finds its food there. Trees cannot move; but by time, and by positively refusing to grow on unkindly soils, they arrange themselves in the localities which suit them best."

So after this they rode with the Doctor always, both hearing him and asking him questions, and at last, won by his blunt kindliness, they grew to like and respect him in their way, even as we did.

So we fared on through bad weather and rough country, enjoying a journey which, but for him, would have been a mere trial of patience. Northward ever, through forest and plain, over mountain and swamp, across sandstone, limestone, granite, and rich volcanic land, each marked distinctly by a varying vegetation. Sometimes we would camp out, but oftener managed to reach a station at night. We got well across the dry country between the Murrumbidgee and the Lachlan, now abounding with pools of water ; and, having crossed the latter river, held on our course towards Croker's Range, which we skirted ; and, after having been about a fortnight out, arrived at the lowest station on the Macquarrie late in the afternoon.

This was our present destination. The owner was a friend of ours, who gave us a hearty welcome, and, on our inquiries as to store cattle, thought that we might pick up a good mob of them from one station or another. " We might," said he, " make a depôt for them, as we collected them, on some unoccupied land down the river. It was poor country, but there was grass enough to keep them alive. He would show us a good place. in a fork, where it was impossible to cross on two sides, and where they would be easily kept together ; that was, if we liked to risk it."

" Risk what ?" he asked.

" Blacks," said he. " They are mortal troublesome just now down the river. I thought we had quieted them, but they have been up to their old games lately, spearing cattle, and so on. I don't like, in fact, to go too far down there alone. I don't think they are Macquarrie blacks ; I fancy they must have come up from the Darling, through the marshes."

We thought we should have no reason to be afraid with such a strong party as ours ; and Owen, our host, having some spare cattle, we were employed for the next three days in getting them in. We got nearly a hundred head from him.

The first morning we got there the Doctor had vanished ; but the third evening, as we were sitting down to supper, in he came, dead beat, with a great bag full of stones. When we had drawn round the fire, I said :

" Have you got any new fossils for us to see ?"

" Not one," said he ; " only some minerals."

" Do not you think, sir," said Owen, our host, " that there are some ores of metals round this country ? The reason I ask you is, we so often pick up curious-coloured stones, like those we get from the miners at home, in Wales, where I come from."

" I think you will find some rich mines near here soon. Stay ; it can do you no harm. I will tell you something : three days ago I followed up the river, and about twenty miles above this spot I became attracted by the conformation of the country, and remarked it as being very similar to some very famous spots in South America. ' Here,' I said to myself, ' Maximilian, you have your volcanic disturbance, your granite, your clay, slate, and sandstone upheaved, and seamed with quartz;—why should you not discover here, what is certainly here, more or less?'—I looked patiently for two days, and I will show you what I found."

He went to his bag and fetched an angular stone about as big as one's fist. It was white, stained on one side with rust-colour, but in the heart veined with a bright yellow metallic substance, in some places running in delicate veins into the stone, in others breaking out in large shining lumps.

" That's iron-pyrites." said I, as pat as you please.

" Goose !" said the Doctor ; " look again."

I looked again, it was certainly different to iron-pyrites ; it was brighter, it ran in veins into the stone ; it was lumpy, solid, and clean. I said, " It is very beautiful ; tell us what it is ?"

" Gold !" said he, triumphantly, " getting up and walking about the room in an excited way; " that little stone is worth a pound ; there is a quarter of an ounce in it. Give me ten tons, only ten cartloads such stone as that, and I would buy a principality."

Every one crowded round the stone open-mouthed, and James said :

" Are you sure it is gold, Doctor ?"

" He asks me if I know gold, when I see it,—me, you understand, who have scientifically examined all the best mines in Peru, not to mention the Minas Geraés in the Brazils ! My dear fellow, to a man who has once seen it, native gold is unmistakeable, utterly so ; there is nothing at all like it."

" But this is a remarkable discovery, sir," said Owen. " What are you going to do ?"

" I shall go to the Government," said he, " and make the best bargain I can."

I had better mention here that he afterwards did go to the Government, and announce his discovery. Rather to the Doctor's disgust, however, though he acknowledged the wisdom of the thing, the courteous and able gentleman who then represented His Majesty, informed him that he was perfectly aware of the existence of gold, but that he for one should assert the prerogative of the Crown, and prevent any one mining on Crown-lands ; as he considered that, were the gold abundant, the effects on the convict population would be eminently disastrous. To which obvious piece of good sense the Doctor bowed his head, and the whole thing passed into oblivion— so much so, that when I heard of Hargreave's discovery in 1851, I had nearly forgotten the Doctor's gold adventure ; and I may here state my belief that the knowledge of its existence was confined to very few, and those well-educated men, who never guessed (how could they without considerable workings ?) how abundant it was. As for the stories of shepherds finding gold and selling it to the Jews in Sydney, they are very mythical, and I for one entirely disbelieve them.

In time we had collected about 250 head of cattle from various points into the fork of the river, which lay further down, some seven miles, than his house. As yet we had not been troubled by the blackfellows. Those we had seen seemed pretty civil, and we had not allowed them to get familiar; but this pleasant state of things was not to last. James and the Doctor, with one man, were away for the very last mob, and I was sitting before the fire at the camp, when Dick, who was left behind with me, asked for my gun to go and shoot a duck. I lent it him, and away he went, while I mounted my horse and rode slowly about, heading back such of the cattle as appeared to be wandering too far.

I heard a shot, and almost immediately another; then I heard a queer sort of scream, which puzzled me extremely. I grew frightened and rode towards the quarter where the shots came from, and almost immediately heard a loud co'oe. I replied, and then I saw Dick limping along through the bushes, peering about him and holding his gun as one does when expecting a bird to rise. Suddenly he raised his gun and fired. Out dashed a black fellow from his hiding place, running across the open, and with his second barrel Dick rolled him over. Then I saw half-a-dozen others rise, shaking their spears; but seeing me riding up, and supposing I was armed, they made off.

"How did this come about, Dick, my lad?" said I. "This is a bad job."

"Well," he said, "I just fired at a duck, and the moment my gun was gone off, up jumped half-a-dozen of them, and sent a shower of spears at me, and one has gone into my leg. They must a' thought that I had a single-barrel gun and waited till I'd fired it; but they found their mistake, the devils; for I gave one of them a charge of shot in his stomach at twenty yards, and dropped him; they threw a couple more spears, but both missed, and I hobbled out as well as I could, loading as I went with a couple of tallow cartridges. I saw this other beast skulking, and missed him first time, but he has got something to remember me by now."

"Do you think you can ride to the station and get some help?" said I. "I wish the others were back."

"Yes," he replied, "I will manage it, but I don't like to leave you alone."

"One must stay," I said, "and better the sound man than the wounded one. Come, start off, and let me get to the camp, or they will be plundering that next."

I started him off and ran back to the camp. Everything was safe as yet, and the ground round being clear, and having a double-barrel gun and two pistols, I was not so very much frightened. It is no use to say I was perfectly comfortable, because I wasn't. A French-man writing this, would represent himself as smoking a cigar, and singing with the greatest nonchalance. I did neither. Being an Englishman, I may be allowed to confess that I did not like it.

I had fully made up my mind to fire on the first black who showed himself, but I did not get the opportunity. In about two hours I heard a noise of men shouting and whips cracking, and the Doctor and James rode up with a fresh lot of cattle.

I told them what had happened, and we agreed to wait and watch till news should come from the station, and then to start. There was, as we thought, but little danger while there were four or five together; but the worst of it was, that we were but poorly armed. However, at nightfall, Owen and one of his men came down, report-ing that Dick, who had been speared, was getting all right, and bringing also three swords, and a brace of pistols.

James and I took a couple of swords, and began fencing, in play.

" I see," said the Doctor, " that you know the use of a sword, you two."

" Lord bless you !" I said, " we were in the Yeomanry (Landwehr you call it); weren't we, Jim ? I was a corporal."

" I wish," said Owen, " that, now we are together, five of us, you would come and give these fellows a lesson ; they want it badly."

" Indeed," I said, " I think they have had lesson enough for the present. Dick has put down two of them. Beside, we could not leave the cattle."

" I am sorry," said James, " that any of our party has had this collision with them. I cannot bear shooting the poor brutes. Let us move out of this, homeward, to-morrow morning."

Just before dark, who should come riding down from the station but Dick !—evidently in pain, but making believe that he was quite comfortable.

" Why, Dick, my boy," I said, " I thought you were in bed ; you ought to be, at any rate."

" Oh, there's nothing much the matter with me, Mr. Hamlyn," he said. " You will have some trouble with these fellows, unless I am mistaken. *I was told to look after you once*, and I mean to do it."

(He referred to the letter that Lee had sent him years before.)

That night Owen stayed with us at the camp. We set a watch, and he took the morning spell. Everything passed off quietly ; but when we came to examine our cattle in the morning, the lot that James had brought in the night before were gone.

The river, flooded when we first came, had now lowered con-siderably, so that the cattle could cross if they really tried. These last, being wild and restless, had gone over, and we soon found the marks of them across the river.

The Doctor, James, Dick, and I started off after them, having armed ourselves for security. We took a sword a-piece, and each had a pistol. The ground was moist, and the beasts easily tracked; so we thought an easy job was before us, but we soon changed our minds.

Following on the trail of the cattle, we very soon came on the footsteps of a black fellow, evidently more recent than the hoof-marks; then another footstep joined in, and another, and at last we made out that above a dozen blacks were tracking our cattle, and were between us and them.

Still we followed the trail as fast as we could. I was uneasy, for we were insufficiently armed, but I found time to point out to the Doctor, what he had never remarked before, the wonderful difference between the naked foot-print of a white man and a savage. The white man leaves the impression of his whole sole, every toe being distinctly marked, while your black fellow leaves scarce any toe-marks, but seems merely to spurn the ground with the ball of his foot.

I felt very ill at ease. The morning was raw, and a dense fog was over everything. One always feels wretched on such a morning, but on that one I felt miserable. There was an indefinable horror over me, and I talked more than any one, glad to hear the sound of my own voice.

Once the Doctor turned round and looked at me fixedly from under his dark eyebrows. "Hamlyn," he said, "I don't think you are well; you talk fast, and are evidently nervous. We are in no danger, I think, but you seem as if you were frightened."

"So I am, Doctor, but I don't know what at."

Jim was riding first, and he turned and said, "I have lost the black fellows' track entirely: here are the hoof-marks, safe enough, but no foot-prints, and the ground seems to be rising."

The fog was very thick, so that we could see nothing above a hundred yards from us. We had come through forest all the way, and were wet with pushing through low shrubs. As we paused came a puff of air, and in five minutes the fog had rolled away, and a clear blue sky and a bright sun were overhead.

Now we could see where we were. We were in the lower end of a precipitous mountain-gulley, narrow where we were, and growing rapidly narrower as we advanced. In the fog we had followed the cattle-track right into it, passing, unobserved, two great heaps of tumbled rocks which walled the glen; they were thickly fringed with scrub, and, it immediately struck me that they stood just in the place where we had lost the tracks of the black fellows.

I should have mentioned this, but, at this moment, James caught sight of the lost cattle, and galloped off after them; we followed, and very quickly we had headed them down the glen, and were posting homeward as hard as we could go.

I remember well there was a young bull among them that took **the** lead. As he came nearly opposite the two piles of rock which I have mentioned, I saw a black fellow leap on a boulder, and send a spear into him.

He headed back, and the other beasts came against him. Before we could pull up we were against the cattle, and then all was confusion and disaster. Two hundred black fellows were on us at once, shouting like devils, and sending down their spears upon us like rain. I heard the Doctor's voice, above all the infernal din, crying "Viva! Swords, my boys; take your swords!" I heard two pistol shots, and then, with deadly wrath in my heart, I charged at a crowd of them, who were huddled together, throwing their spears wildly, and laid about me with my cutlass like a madman.

I saw them scrambling up over the rocks in wild confusion; then I heard the Doctor calling me to come on. He had reined up, and a few of the discomfited savages were throwing spears at him from a long distance. When he saw me turn to come, he turned also, and rode after James, who was two hundred yards ahead, reeling in his saddle like a drunken man, grinding his teeth, and making fierce clutches at a spear which was buried deep in his side, and which at last he succeeded in tearing out. He went a few yards further, and then fell off his horse on the ground.

We were both off in a moment, but when I got his head on my lap, I saw he was dying. The Doctor looked at the wound, and shook his head. I took his right hand in mine, and the other I held upon his true and faithful heart, until I felt it flutter, and stop for **ever.**

Then I broke down altogether. "Oh! good old friend! Oh! dear old friend, could you not wait for me? Shall I never see you again?"

Yes! I think that I shall see **him** again. When I have crossed the dark river which we must all cross, I think he will be one of those who come down to meet me from the gates of the Everlasting City.

*   *   *   *   *   *

"A man," said the Doctor to me, two days after, when we were sitting together in the station parlour, "who approached as nearly the model which our Great Master has left us as any man I know. I studied and admired him for many years, and now I cannot tell you not to mourn. I can give you no comfort for the loss of such a man, save it be to say that you and I may hope to meet him again, and learn new lessons from him, in a better place than this."

CHAPTER XXV.

IN WHICH THE NEW DEAN OF B—— MAKES HIS APPEARANCE, AND ASTONISHES THE MAJOR OUT OF HIS PROPRIETY.

ONE evening towards the end of that winter Mrs. Buckley and Sam sat alone before the fire, in the quickly-gathering darkness. The candles were yet unlighted, but the cheerful flickering light produced by the combustion of three or four logs of sheoak, topped by one of dead gum, shone most pleasantly on the well-ordered dining-room, on the close-drawn curtains, on the nicely-polished furniture, on the dinner-table, laid with fair array of white linen, silver, and glass, but, above all, on the honest, quiet face of Sam, who sat before his mother in an easy chair, with his head back, fast asleep.

While she is alternately casting glances of pride and affection towards her sleeping son, and keen looks on the gum log, in search of centipedes, let us take a look at her ourselves, and see how sixteen years have behaved to that handsome face. There is change here, but no deterioration. It is a little rounder perhaps, and also a little fuller in colour, but there are no lines there yet. "Happiness and cease-less good temper don't make many wrinkles, even in a warmer climate than old England," says the Major, and says also, confidentially, to Brentwood, "Put a red camelia in her hair, and send her to the opera even now, and see what a sensation she would make, though she is nearer fifty than forty,"—which was strictly true, although said by her husband, for the raven hair is as black as it was when decorated with the moss-roses of Clere, and the eye is as brilliant as when it flashed with the news of Trafalgar.

Now, the beautiful profile is turned again towards the sleeper as he moves. "Poor boy!" she said. "He is quite knocked up. He must have been twenty-four hours in the saddle. However, he had better be after cattle than in a billiard-room. I wonder if his father will be home to-night."

Suddenly Sam awoke. "Heigho!" said he. "I'm nice company, mother. Have I been asleep?"

"Only for an hour or so, my boy," said she. "See; I've been defending you while you slumbered. I have killed three centipedes, which came out of that old gum log. I cut this big one in half with the fire-shovel, and the head part walked away as if nothing had happened. I must tell the man not to give us rotten wood, or some of us will be getting a nip. It's a long fifty miles from Captain Brentwood's," said Mrs. Buckley after a time. "And that's a very good day's work for little Bronsewing, carrying your father."

"And what has been the news since I have been away,—eh, mother?"

"Why, the greatest news is that the Donovans have sold their station, and are off to Port Phillip."

"All the world is moving there," said Sam. "Who has he sold it to?"

"That I can't find out.—There's your father, my love."

There was the noise of horses' feet and merry voices in the little gravelled yard behind the house, heard above a joyous barking of dogs. Sam ran out to hold his father's horse, and soon came into the room again, accompanied by his father and Captain Brentwood.

After the first greetings were over, candles were lighted, and the three men stood on the hearth-rug together—a very remarkable group, as you would have said, had you seen them. You might go a long while in any country without seeing three such men in company.

Captain Brentwood, of Artillery renown, was a square, powerfully built man, say five-foot-ten in height. His face, at first sight, appeared rather a stupid one beside the Major's, expressing rather determination than intelligence; but once engage him in a conversation which interested him, and you would be surprised to see how animated it would become. Then the man, usually so silent, would open up the store-house of his mind, speaking with an eloquence and a force which would surprise one who did not know him, and which made the Doctor often take the losing side of an argument for the purpose of making him speak. Add to this that he was a thoroughly amiable man, and, as Jim would tell you (in spite of a certain severe whipping you wot of), a most indulgent and excellent father.

Major Buckley's shadow had grown no less,—nay, rather greater, since first we knew him. In other respects, there was very little alteration, except that his curling brown hair had grown thinner about the temples, and was receding a little from his forehead. But what cared he for that! He was not the last of the Buckleys.

One remarks now, as the two stand together, that Sam, though but nineteen, is very nearly as tall as his father, and promises to be as broad across the shoulders, some day, being an exception to colonially-bred men in general, who are long and narrow. He is standing and talking to his father.

"Well, Sam," said the Major, "so you're back safe,—eh, my boy! A rough time, I don't doubt. Strange store-cattle are queer to drive at any time, particularly such weather as you have had."

"And such a lot, too!" said Sam. "Tell you what, father, it's lucky you've got them cheap, for the half of them are off the ranges."

"Scrubbers, eh?" said the Major; "well, we must take what we can catch, with this Port Phillip rush. Let's sit down to dinner; I've got some news that will please you. Fish, eh? See there, Brentwood! What do you think of that for a black-fish? What was his weight, my dear?"

"Seven pounds and a half, as the black fellows brought him in," said Mrs. Buckley.

"A very pretty fish," said the Major. "My dear, what is the news?"

"Why, the Donovans have sold their station."

"Ha! ha!" laughed the Major. "Why, we have come from there to-day. Why, we were there last night at a grand party. All the Irishmen in the country side. Such a turmoil I haven't seen since I was quartered at Cove. So that's your news,—eh?"

"And so you stepped on there without calling at home, did you?" said Mrs. Buckley. "And perhaps you know who the purchaser is?"

"Don't you know, my love?"

"No, indeed!" said Mrs. Buckley. "I have been trying to find out these two days. It would be very pleasant to have a good neighbour there,—not that I wish to speak evil of the Donovans: but really they did go on in such terrible style, you know, that one could not go there. Now, tell me who has bought Garoopna."

"One Brentwood, captain of Artillery."

"Nonsense!" said Mrs. Buckley. "Is he not joking now, Captain Brentwood? That is far too good news to be true."

"It is true, nevertheless, madam," said Captain Brentwood. "I thought it would meet with your approval, and I can see by Sam's face that it meets with his. You see, my dear, Buckley has got to be rather necessary to me. I miss him when he is absent, and I want to be more with him. Again, I am very fond of my son Jim, and my son Jim is very fond of your son Sam, and is always coming here after him when he ought to be at home. So I think I shall see more of him when we are ten miles apart than when we are fifty. And, once more, my daughter Alice, now completing her education in Sydney, comes home to keep house for me in a few months, and I wish her to have the advantage of the society of the lady whom I honour and respect above all others. So I have bought Garoopna."

"If that courtly bow is intended for me, my dear Captain," said Mrs. Buckley, "as I cannot but think it is, believe me that your daughter shall be as my daughter."

"Teach her to be in some slight degree like yourself, Mrs. Buckley," said the Captain, "and you will put me under obligations which I can never repay."

"Altogether, wife," said the Major, "it is the most glorious arrangement that ever was come to. Let us take a glass of sherry all round on it. Sam, my lad, your hand! Brentwood, we have none of us ever seen your daughter. She should be handsome."

"You remember her mother?" said the Captain.

"Who could ever forget Lady Kate who had once seen her?" said the Major.

"Well, Alice is more beautiful than her mother ever was."

There went across the table a bright electric spark out of Mrs. Buckley's eye into her husband's, as rapid as those which move the quivering telegraph needles, and yet not unobserved, I think, by Captain Brentwood, for there grew upon his face a pleasant smile, which, rapidly broadening, ended in a low laugh, by no means disagreeable to hear, though Sam wondered what the joke could be until the Captain said,—

"An altogether comical party that last night at the Donovans', Buckley! the most comical I ever was at."

Nevertheless, I don't believe that it was that which made him laugh at all.

"A capital party!" said the Major, laughing. "Do you know, Brentwood, I always liked those Donovans, under the rose, and last night I liked them better than ever. They were not such very bad neighbours, although old Donovan wanted to fight a duel with me once. At all events, the welcome I got last night will make me remember them kindly in future."

"I must go down and call there before they go," said Mrs. Buckley. "People who have been our neighbours so many years must not go away without a kind farewell. Was Desborough there?"

"Indeed, he was. Don't you know he is related to the Donovans?"

"Impossible!"

"Fact my dear I assure you, according to Mrs. Donovan, who told me that the De Novans and the Desboroughs were cognate Norman families, who settled in Ireland together, and have since frequently intermarried."

"I suppose," said Mrs. Buckley, laughing, "that Desborough did not deny it."

"Not at all, my dear: as he said to me privately, 'Buckley, never deny a relationship with a man worth forty thousand pounds, the least penny, though your ancestors' bones should move in their graves.'"

"I suppose," said Mrs. Buckley, "that he made himself as agreeable as usual."

"As usual, my dear. He made even Brentwood laugh; he danced all the evening with that giddy girl Lesbia Burke, who let slip that she remembered me at Naples, in 1805, when she was there with that sad old set, and who consequently must be nearly as old as myself."

"I hope you danced with her," said Mrs. Buckley.

"Indeed I did, my dear. And she wore a wreath of yellow chrysanthemum, no other flowers being obtainable. I assure you we 'kept the flure' in splendid style."

They were all laughing at the idea of the Major dancing, when Sam exclaimed, "Good Lord!"

"What's the matter, my boy?" said the Major.

"I must cry peccavi," said Sam. "Father, you will never forgive me! I forgot till this moment a most important message. I was rather knocked up, you see, and went to sleep, and that sent it out of my head."

"You are forgiven, my boy, be it what it may. I hope it is nothing very serious."

"Well, it is very serious," said Sam. "As I was coming by Hanging Rock, I rode up to the door a minute, to see if Cecil was at home,—and Mrs. Mayford came out and wanted me to get off and come in, but I hadn't time; and she said, 'The Dean is coming here to-night, and he'll be with you to-morrow night, I expect. So don't forget to tell your mother.'"

"To-morrow night!" said Mrs. Buckley, aghast. "Why, my dear boy, that is to-night! What shall I do?"

"Nothing at all, my love," said the Major, "but make them get some supper ready. He can't have expected us to wait dinner till this time."

"I thought," said Captain Brentwood, "that the Dean was gone back to England."

"So he is," said the Major. "But this is a new one. The good old Dean has resigned."

"What is the new one's name?" said the Captain.

"I don't know," said the Major. "Desborough said it was a Doctor Maypole, and that he was very like one in appearance. But you can't trust Desborough, you know; he never remembers names. I hope he may be as good a man as his predecessor."

"I hope he may be no worse," said Captain Brentwood; "but I hope, in addition, that he may be better able to travel, and look after his outlying clergy a little more."

"It looks like it," said the Major, "to be down as far as this, before he has been three months installed."

Mrs. Buckley went out to the kitchen to give orders; and after that they sat for an hour or more over their wine, till at length the Major said,—

"We must give him up in another hour."

Then, as if they had heard him, the dogs began to bark. Rover, who had, against rules, sneaked into the house, and lain *perdu* under the sofa, discovered his retreat by low growling, as though determined to do his duty, let the consequences be what they might. Every now and then, too, when his feelings overpowered him, he would discharge a ' Woof,' like a minute gun at sea.

"That must be him, father," said Sam. "You'll catch it, Mr. Rover!"

He ran out; a tall black figure was sitting on horseback before the door, and a pleasant cheery voice said, " Pray, is this Major Buckley's?"

"Yes, sir," said Sam; " we have been expecting you."

He called for the groom, and held the stranger's horse while he dismounted. Then he assisted him to unstrap his valise, and carried it in after him.

The Major, Mrs. Buckley, and the Captain had risen, and were standing ready to greet the Church dignitary as he came in, in the most respectful manner. But when the Major had looked for a moment on the tall figure in black which advanced towards the fire; instead of saying, " Sir, I am highly honoured by your visit," or " Sir, I bid you most heartily welcome," he dashed forward in the most undignified fashion, upsetting a chair, and seizing the reverend Dean by both hands, exclaimed, " God bless my heart and soul! Frank Maberly!"

It was he: the mad curate, now grown into a colonial dean,— sobered, apparently, but unchanged in any material point: still elastic and upright, looking as if for twopence he would take off the black cut-away coat and the broad-brimmed hat, and row seven in the University eight, at a moment's notice. There seemed something the matter with him though, as he held the Major's two hands in his, and looked on his broad handsome face. Something like a shortness of breath prevented his speech, and, strange, the Major seemed troubled with the same complaint; but Frank got over it first, and said,—

" My dear old friend, I am so glad to see you!"

And Mrs. Buckley said, laying her hand upon his arm, " It seems as if all things were arranged to make my husband and myself the happiest couple in the world. If we had been asked to-night, whom of all people in the world we should have been most glad to see as the new Dean, we should have answered at once, Frank Maberly; and here he is!"

" Then, you did not know whom to expect?" said Frank.

" Not we, indeed," said the Major. " Desborough said the new Dean was a Doctor Maypole; and I pictured to myself an old school-master with a birch rod in his coat tail-pocket. And we have been in such a stew all the evening about giving the great man a proper reception. Ha! ha! ha!"

" And will you introduce me to this gentleman?" said the Dean, moving towards Sam, who stood behind his mother.

" This," said the Major, with a radiant smile, " is my son Samuel, whom, I believe, you have seen before."

" So, the pretty boy that I knew at Drumston," said the Dean, laying his hands on Sam's shoulders, " has grown into this noble gentleman ! It makes me feel old, but I am glad to feel old under such circumstances. Let me turn your face to the light and see if I can recognise the little lad whom I used to carry pickaback across Hatherleigh Water."

Sam looked in his face—such a kindly good placid face, that it seemed beautiful, though by some rules it was irregular and ugly enough. The Dean laid his hand on Sam's curly head, and said, " God bless you, Samuel Buckley," and won Sam's heart for ever.

All this time Captain Brentwood had stood with his back against the chimney-piece, perfectly silent, having banished all expression from his countenance ; now, however, Major Buckley brought up the Dean and introduced him :—

" My dear Brentwood, the Dean of B——; not Dean to us though, so much as our dear old friend Frank Maberly."

" Involved grammar," said the Captain to himself, but, added aloud : " A Churchman of your position, sir, will do me an honour by using my house ; but the Mr. Maberly of whom I have so often heard from my friend Buckley, will do me a still higher honour if he will allow me to enrol him among the number of my friends."

Frank the Dean thought that Captain Brentwood's speech would have made a good piece to turn into Greek prose, in the style of Demosthenes ; but he didn't say so. He looked at the Captain's stolid face for a moment, and said, as Sam thought, a little abruptly :

" I think, sir, that you and I shall get on very well together when we understand one another."

The Captain made no reply in articulate speech, but laughed internally, till his sides shook, and held out his hand. The Dean laughed too, as he took it, and said :

" I met a young lady at the Bishop's the other day, a Miss Brentwood."

" My daughter, sir," said the Captain.

" So I guessed—partly from the name, and partly from a certain look about the eyes, rather unmistakeable. Allow me to say, sir, that I never remember to have seen such remarkable beauty in my life."

They sat Frank down to supper, and when he had done, the conversation was resumed.

" By-the-bye, Major Buckley," said he, " I miss an old friend, who I heard was living with you ; a very dear old friend,—where is Doctor Mulhaus ?"

" Dear Doctor," said Mrs. Buckley, " this is his home indeed, but he is away at present on an expedition with two old Devon friends, Hamlyn and Stockbridge."

" Oh !" said Frank, " I have heard of those men ; they came out here the year before the Vicar died. I never knew either of them, but I well remember how kindly Stockbridge used to be spoken of by every one in Drumston. I must make his acquaintance."

" You will make the acquaintance of one of the finest fellows in the world, Dean," said the Major ; " I know no worthier man than Stockbridge. I wish Mary Thornton had married him."

" And I hear," said Frank, " that the pretty Mary is your next door neighbour, in partnership with that excellent giant Troubridge. I must go and see them to-morrow. I will produce one of those great roaring laughs of his, by reminding him of our first introduction at the Palace, through a rat."

" I am sorry to say," said the Major, " that Tom is away at Port Phillip, with cattle."

" Port Phillip again," said Frank ; " I have heard of nothing else throughout my journey. I am getting bored with it. Will you tell me what you know about it for certain ?"

" Well," said the Major, " it lies about 250 miles south of this, though we cannot get at it without crossing the mountains, in consequence of some terribly dense scrub on some low ranges close to it, which they call, I believe, the Dandenong. It appears, however, when you are there, that there is a great harbour, about forty miles long, surrounded with splendid pastures, which stretch west further than any man has been yet. Take it all in all, I should say it was the best watered and most available piece of country yet discovered in New Holland."

" Any good rivers ?" asked the Dean.

" Plenty of small ones, only one of any size, apparently, which seems to rise somewhere in this direction, and goes in at the head of the bay. They tried years ago to form a settlement on this bay, but Collins, the man entrusted with it, could find no fresh water, which seems strange, as there is, according to all accounts, a fine full-flowing river running by the town."

" They have formed a town there, then ?" said the Dean.

" There are a few wooden houses gone up by the river side. I believe they are going to make a town there, and call it Melbourne ; we may live to see it a thriving place."

The Major has lived to see his words fulfilled—fulfilled in such marvellous sort, that bald bare statistics read like the wildest romance. At the time he spoke, twenty-two years ago from this present year 1858, the Yarra rolled its clear waters to the sea through the unbroken solitude of a primeval forest, as yet unseen by the eye of a white man. Now there stands there a noble city, with crowded wharves, containing with its suburbs not less than 120,000 inhabitants. 1,000 vessels have lain at one time side by side, off the mouth of that little river; and through the low sandy heads that close the great port towards the sea, *thirteen millions sterling* of exports is carried away each year by the finest ships in the world. Here, too, are waterworks constructed at fabulous expense, a service of steam-ships, between this and the other great cities of Australia, vieing in speed and accommodation with the coasting steamers of Great Britain; noble churches, handsome theatres. In short, a great city, which, in its amazing rapidity of growth, utterly surpasses all human experience.

I never stood in Venice contemplating the decay of the grand palaces of her old merchant princes, whose time has gone by for ever. I never watched the slow downfall of a great commercial city; but I have seen what to him who thinks aright is an equally grand subject of contemplation—the rapid rise of one. I have seen what but a small moiety of the world, even in these days, has seen, and what, save in this generation, has never been seen before, and will, I think, never be seen again. I have seen Melbourne. Five years in succession did I visit that city, and watch each year how it spread and grew until it was beyond recognition. Every year the press became denser, and the roar of the congregated thousands grew louder, till at last the scream of the flying engine rose above the hubbub of the streets, and two thousand miles of electric wire began to move the clicking needles with ceaseless intelligence.

Unromantic enough, but beyond all conception wonderful. I stood at the east end of Bourke Street, not a year ago, looking at the black swarming masses, which thronged the broad thoroughfare below. All the town lay at my feet, and the sun was going down beyond the distant mountains; I had just crossed from the front of the new Houses of Legislature, and had nearly been run over by a great omnibus. Partly to recover my breath, and partly, being not used to large cities, to enjoy the really fine scene before me, I stood at the corner of the street in contemplative mood. I felt a hand on my shoulder, and looked round,—it was Major Buckley.

" This is a wonderful sight, Hamlyn," said he.

" When you think of it," I said, " really think of it, you know, how wonderful it is ! "

" Brentwood," said the Major, " has calculated by his mathematics that the progress of the species is forty-seven, decimal eight, more rapid than it was thirty-five years ago."

" So I should be prepared to believe," I said; " where will it all end ? Will it be a grand universal republic, think you, in which war is unknown, and universal prosperity has banished crime ? I may be too sanguine, but such a state of things is possible. This is a sight which makes a man look far into the future."

" Prosperity," said the Major, " has not done much towards

abolishing crime in this town, at all events; and it would not take much to send all this back into its primeval state."

"How so, Major?" said I; "I see here the cradle of a new and mighty empire."

"Two rattling good thumps of an earthquake," said the Major, "would pitch Melbourne into the middle of Port Phillip, and bury all the gold far beyond the reach even of the Ballarat deep-sinkers. The world is very, very, young, my dear Hamlyn. Come down and dine with me at the club."

CHAPTER XXVI.

WHITE HEATHENS.

CAPTAIN BRENTWOOD went back to Garoopna next morning; but Frank Maberly kept to his resolution of going over to see Mary; and, soon after breakfast, they were all equipped ready to accompany him, standing in front of the door, waiting for the horses. Frank was remarking how handsome Mrs. Buckley looked in her hat and habit, when she turned and said to him,—

"My dear Dean, I suppose you never jump over five-barred gates now-a-days? Do you remember how you used to come over the white gate at the Vicarage? I suppose you are getting too dignified for any such thing?"

There was a three-railed fence dividing the lower end of the yard from the paddock. He rammed his hat on tight, and took it flying, with his black coat-tails fluttering like wings; and, coming back laughing, said,—

"There's a bit of the old Adam for you, Mrs. Buckley! Be careful how you defy me again."

The sun was bright overhead, and the land in its full winter verdure, as they rode along the banks of the creek that led to Toonarbin. Frank Maberly was as humorous as ever, and many a merry laugh went ringing through the woodland solitudes, sending the watchman cockatoo screaming aloft to alarm the flock, or startling the brilliant thick-clustered lories (richest coloured of all parrots in the world), as they hung chattering on some silver-leaved acacia, bending with their weight the fragile boughs down towards the clear still water, lighting up the dark pool with strange, bright reflections of crimson and blue; startling, too, the feeding doe-kangaroo, who skipped slowly away, followed by her young one—so slowly that the watching travellers expected her to stop each moment, and could scarcely believe she was in full flight till she topped a low ridge and disappeared.

"That is a strange sight to a European, Mrs. Buckley," said Frank; "a real wild animal. It seems so strange to me, now, to think that I could go and shoot that beast, and account to no man for it. That is, you know, supposing I had a gun, and powder and shot, and, also, that the kangaroo would be fool enough to wait till I was near enough; which, you see, is pre-supposing a great deal. Are they easily approached?"

"Easily enough, on horseback," said Sam, "but very difficult to come near on foot, which is also the case with all wild animals and birds worth shooting in this country. A footman,* you see, they all mistake for their hereditary enemy, the blackfellow; but, as yet, they have not come to distinguish a man on horseback from a four-footed beast. And, this seems to show that animals have their traditions like men."

"Pray, Sam, are not these pretty beasts, these kangaroos, becoming extinct?"

"On sheep-runs, very nearly so. Sheep drive them off directly: but on cattle-runs, so far from becoming extinct, they are becoming so numerous as to be a nuisance; consuming a most valuable quantity of grass."

"How can you account for that?"

"Very easily," said Sam; "their enemies are all removed. The settlers have poisoned, in well-settled districts, the native dogs and eagle-hawks, which formerly kept down their numbers. The blacks prefer the beef of the settlers to bad and hard-earned kangaroo venison; and, lastly, the settlers never go after them, but leave them to their own inventions. So that the kangaroo has better times of it than ever."

"That is rather contrary to what one has heard, though," said Frank.

"But Sam is right, Dean," said the Major. "People judge from seeing none of them on the plains, from which they have been driven by the sheep; but there are as many in the forest as ever."

"The Emu, now," said Frank, "are they getting scarce?"

"They will soon be among the things of the past," said the Major; "and I am sorry for it, for they are a beautiful and harmless bird."

"Major," said Frank, "how many outlying huts have you?"

"Five," said the Major. "Four shepherds' huts, and one store-keeper's in the range, which we call the heifer station."

"You have no church here, I know," said Frank; "but do these men get any sort of religious instruction?"

"None whatever," said the Major. "I have service in my house

---

* Let not Charles or Jeames suppose that they or their brethren of the plush are here spoken of. Could they be mistaken for *blackfellows?* No; the word footman merely means one who goes afoot instead of riding.

on Sunday, but I cannot ask them to come to it, though sometimes the stockmen do come. The shepherds, you know, are employed on Sunday as on any other day. Sheep must eat!"

"Are any of these men convicts?"

"All the shepherds," said the Major. "The stockman and his assistant are free men, but their hut-keeper is bond."

"Are any of them married?"

"Two of the shepherds; the rest single; but I must tell you that on our run we keep up a regular circulation of books among the huts, and my wife sticks them full of religious tracts, which is really about all that we can do without a clergyman."

"Do you find they read your tracts, Mrs. Buckley?" asked Frank.

"No," said Mrs. Buckley, "with the exception, perhaps, of 'Black Giles the Poacher,' which always comes home very dirty. Narrative tracts they will read when there is nothing more lively at hand; but such treatises as 'Are You Ready?' and 'The Sinner's Friend,' fall dead. One copy lasts for years."

"One copy of either of them," said Frank, "would last me some time. Then these fellows, Major, are entirely godless, I suppose?"

"Well, I'll tell you, Dean," said the Major, stopping short, "it's about as bad as bad can be! it can't be worse, sir. If by any means you could make it worse, it would be by sending such men round here as the one who was sent here last. He served as a standing joke to the hands for a year or more; and I believe he was sincere enough, too."

"I must invade some of these huts, and see what is to be done," said Frank. "I have had a hard spell of work in London since old times; but I have seen enough already to tell me that that work was not so hopeless as this will be. I think, however, that there is more chance here than among the little farmers in the settled districts. Here, at all events, I shan't have the rum-bottle eternally standing between me and my man. What a glorious, independent, happy set of men are those said small freeholders, Major! What a happy exchange an English peasant makes when he leaves an old, well-ordered society, the ordinances of religion, the various give-and-take relations between rank and rank, which make up the sum of English life, for independence, godlessness, and rum! He gains, say you! Yes, he gains meat for his dinner every day, and *voilà tout!* Contrast an English workhouse schoolboy—I take the lowest class for example, a class which should not exist—with a small farmer's son in one of the settled districts. Which will make the most useful citizen? Give me the workhouse lad!"

"Oh, but you are over-stating the case, you know, Dean," said the Major. "You must have a class of small farmers! Wherever the land is fit for cultivation it must be sold to agriculturists; or, otherwise, in case of a war, we shall be dependent on Europe and America for the bread we eat. I know some excellent and exemplary men who are farmers, I assure you."

"Of course! of course!" said Frank. "I did not mean quite all I said; but I am angry and disappointed. I pictured to myself the labourer, English, Scotch, or Irish—a man whom I know, and have lived with and worked for some years, emigrating, and, after a few years of honest toil, which, compared to his old hard drudgery, was child's-play, saving money enough to buy a farm. I pictured to myself this man accumulating wealth, happy, honest, godly, bringing up a family of brave boys and good girls, in a country where, theoretically, the temptations to crime are all but removed: this is what I imagined. I come out here, and what do I find? My friend the labourer has got his farm, and is prospering, after a sort. He has turned to be a drunken, godless, impudent fellow, and his wife little better than himself; his daughters dowdy hussies; his sons lanky, lean, pasty-faced, blaspheming blackguards, drinking rum before breakfast, and living by cheating one another out of horses. Can you deny this picture?"

"Yes," said the Major, "I can disprove it by many happy instances, and yet, to say the truth, it is fearfully true in as many more. There is no social influence in the settled districts; there are too many men without masters. Let us wait and hope."

"This is not to the purpose at present, though," said Mrs. Buckley. "See what you can do for us in the bush, my dear Dean. You have a very hopeless task before you, I fear."

"The more hopeless, the greater glory, madam," said Frank, taking off his hat and waving it. Called, Chosen, and Faithful. "There is a beautiful house!"

"That is Toonarbin," said the Major; "and there's Mary Hawker in the verandah."

"Let us see," said Mrs. Buckley, "if she will know him. If she does not recognise him, let no one speak before me."

When they had ridden up and dismounted, Mrs. Buckley presented Frank. "My dear," said she, "the Dean is honouring us by staying at Baroona for a week, and proposes to visit round at the various stations. To-morrow we go to the Mayfords, and next day to Garoopna."

Mary bowed respectfully to Frank, and said, "that she felt highly honoured," and so forth. "My partner is gone on a journey, and my son is away on the run, or they would have joined with me in bidding you welcome, sir."

Frank would have been highly honoured at making their acquaintance.

Mary started, and looked at him again. "Mr. Maberly! Mr.

Maberly!" she said, "your face is changed, but your voice is unchangeable. You are discovered, sir!"

"And are you glad to see me?"

"No!" said Mary, plainly.

"Now," said Mrs. Buckley to herself, "she is going to give us one of her tantrums. I wish she would behave like a reasonable being. She is always bent on making a scene;" but she kept this to herself, and only said aloud: "Mary, my dear! Mary!"

"I am sorry to hear you say so, Mrs. Hawker," said Frank: "but it is just and natural."

"Natural," said Mary, "and just. You are connected in my mind with the most unhappy and most degraded period of my life. Can you expect that I should be glad to see you? You were kind to me then, as is your nature to be, kind and good above all men whom I know. I thought of you always with love and admiration, as one whom I deeply honoured, but would not care to look upon again. As the one of all whom I would have forget me in my disgrace. And now, to-day of all days, just when I have found the father's vices confirmed in the son, you come before me, as if from the bowels of the earth, to remind me of what I was."

Mrs. Buckley was very much shocked and provoked by this, but held her tongue magnanimously. And what do you think, my dear reader, was the cause of all this hysteric tragic nonsense on the part of Mary? Simply this. The poor soul had been put out of temper. Her son Charles, as I mentioned before, had had a scandalous *liaison* with one Meg Macdonald, daughter of one of the Donovans' (now Brentwood's) shepherds. That morning, this brazen hussy, as Mary very properly called her, had come coolly up to the station and asked for Charles. And on Mary's shaking her fist at her, and bidding her be gone, she had then and there rated poor Mary in the best of Gaelic for a quarter of an hour; and Mary, instead of venting her anger on the proper people, had taken her old plan of making herself disagreeable to those who had nothing to do with it, which naturally made Mrs. Buckley very angry, and even ruffled the placid Major a little, so that he was not sorry when he saw in his wife's face, from the expression he knew so well, that Mary was going to "catch it."

"I wish, Mary Hawker," said Mrs. Buckley, "that you would remember that the Dean is our guest, and that on our account alone there is due to him some better welcome than what you have given him."

"Now, you are angry with me for speaking truth too abruptly," said Mary, crying.

"Well, I am angry with you," said Mrs. Buckley. "If that was the truth, you should not have spoken it now. You have no right to receive an old friend like this."

"You are very unkind to me," said Mary. "Just when after

so many years' peace and quietness my troubles are beginning again, you are all turning against me." And so she laid down her head and wept.

"Dear Mrs. Hawker," said Frank, coming up and taking her hand, "if you are in trouble, I know well that my visit is well timed. Where trouble and sorrow are, there is my place, there lies my work. In prosperity my friends sometimes forget me, but my hope and prayer is, that when affliction and disaster come, I may be with them. You do not want me now; but when you do, God grant I may be with you! Remember my words."

She remembered them well.

Frank made an excuse to go out, and Mary, crying bitterly, went into her bedroom. When she was gone, the Major, who had been standing by the window, said,—

"My dear wife, that boy of hers is aggravating her. Don't be too hard upon her."

"My dear husband," said Mrs. Buckley, "I have no patience with her, to welcome an old friend, whom she has not seen for nearly twenty years, in that manner! It is too provoking."

"You see, my love," said the Major, "that her nerves have been very much shaken by misfortune, and at times she is really not herself."

"And I tell you what, mother dear," said Sam, "Charles Hawker is going on very badly. I tell you, in the strictest confidence, mind, that he has not behaved in a very gentlemanlike way in one particular, and if he was any one else but who he is, I should have very little to say to him."

"Well, my dear husband and son," said Mrs. Buckley, "I will go in and make the *amende* to her. Sam, go and see after the Dean."

Sam went out, and saw Frank across the yard playing with the dogs. He was going towards him, when a man entering the yard suddenly came up and spoke to him.

It was William Lee—grown older, and less wild-looking, since we saw him first at midnight·on Dartmoor, but a striking person still. His hair had become grizzled, but that was the only sign of age he showed. There was still the same vigour of motion, the same expression of enormous strength about him as formerly; the principal change was in his face. Eighteen years of honest work, among people who in time, finding his real value, had got to treat him more as a friend than a servant, had softened the old expression of reckless ferocity into one of good-humoured independence. And Tom Troubridge, no careless observer of men, had said once to Major Buckley, that he thought his face grew each year more like what it must have been when a boy. A bold flight of fancy for Tom, but, like all else he said, true.

P

Such was William Lee, as he stopped Sam in the yard, and, with a bold, honest look of admiration, said—

"It makes me feel young to look at you, Mr. Buckley. You are a great stranger here lately. Some young lady to run after, I suppose? Well, never mind; I hope it ain't Miss Blake."

"A man may not marry his grandmother, Lee," said Sam, laughing.

"True for you, sir," said Lee. "That was wrote up in Drumston church, I mind, and some other things alongside of it, which I could say by heart once on a time—all on black boards, with yellow letters. And also, I remember a spick and span new board, about how Anthony Hamlyn (that's Mr. Geoffry Hamlyn's father) ' repaired and beautified this church;' which meant that he built a handsome new pew for himself in the chancel. Lord, I think I see him asleep in it now. But never mind that—I've kept a pup of Fly's for you, sir, and got it through the distemper. Fly's pup, by Rollicker, you know."

"Oh, thank you," said Sam. "I am really much obliged to you. But you must let me know the price, you know, Lee. The dog should be a good one."

"Well, Mr. Buckley," said Lee, "I have been cosseting this little beast up in the hopes you'd accept it as a present. And then, says I to myself, when he takes a new chum out to see some sport, and the dog pulls down a flying doe, and the dust goes up like smoke, and the dead sticks come flying about his ears, he will say to his friends, 'That's the dog Lee gave me. Where's his equal?' So don't be too proud to take a present from an old friend."

"Not I, indeed, Lee," said Sam. "I thank you most heartily."

"Who is this long gent in black, sir?" said Lee, looking towards Frank, who was standing and talking with the Major. "A parson, I reckon."

"The Dean of B——," answered Sam.

"Ah! so,"—said Lee,—"come to give us some good advice? Well, we want it bad enough, I hope some on us may foller it. Seems a man, too, and not a monkey."

"My father says," said Sam, "that he was formerly one of the best boxers he ever saw."

Any further discussion of Frank's physical powers was cut short by his coming up to Sam and saying,—

"I was thinking of riding out to one of the outlying huts, to have a little conversation with the men. Will you come with me?"

"If you will allow me, I shall be delighted beyond all measure."

"I beg your pardon, sir," said Lee, "but I understood you to say that you were going to one of our huts to give the men a discourse. Would you let me take you out to one of them? I'd like well to hear what you'd got to say myself, sir, and I promise you the lads I'll show you want good advice as well as any."

"You will do me infinite service," said Frank. "Sam, if you will excuse me, let me ask you to stay behind. I have a fancy for going up alone. Let me take these men in the rough, and see what I can do unassisted."

"You will be apt to find them uncivil, sir," said Sam. "I am known, and my presence would ensure you outward respect at all events."

"Just what I thought," said Frank. "But I want to see what I can do alone and unassisted. No; stay, and let me storm the place single-handed."

So Lee and he started toward the ranges, riding side by side.

"You will find, sir," said Lee, "that these men, in this here hut, are a rougher lot than you think for. Very like they'll be cheeky. I would almost have wished you'd a' let Mr. Buckley come. He's a favourite round here, you see, and you'd have gone in as his friend."

"You see," said Frank, turning confidentially to Lee, "I am not an ordinary parson. I am above the others. And what I want is not so much to see what I can do myself, but what sort of a reception any parson coming hap-hazard among these men will get. That is why I left Mr. Buckley behind. Do you understand me?"

"I understand you, sir," said Lee. "But I'm afeard."

"What are you afraid of?" said Frank, laughing.

"Why, if you'll excuse me, sir, that you'll only get laughed at."

"That all!" said Frank. "Laughter breaks no bones. What are these men that we are going to see?"

"Why, one," said Lee, "is a young Jimmy (I beg your pardon, sir, an emigrant), the other two are old prisoners. Now see here. These prisoners hate the sight of a parson above all mortal men. And, for why? Because, when they're in prison, all their indulgences, and half their hopes of liberty depend on how far they can manage to humbug the chaplain with false piety.* And so, when they are free again, they hate him worse than any man. I am an an old prisoner myself, and I know it."

"Have you been a prisoner, then?" said Frank, surprised.

"I was transported, sir, for poaching."

"That all!" said Frank. "Then you were the victim of a villanous old law. Do you know," he added, laughing, "that I rather believe I have earned transportation myself? I have a horrible schoolboy recollection of a hare who would squeak in my pocket, and of a keeper passing within ten yards of where I lay hidden. If that is all, give me your hand."

* It must be remembered that Lee's prison experiences went so far back as about 1811.—H. K.

Lee shook his head. " That is what I was sent out for," said he, " but since then there are precious few villanies I have not committed. You hadn't ought to shake hands with me, sir."

Frank laid his hand kindly on his shoulder. " I am not a judge," he said. " I am a priest. We must talk together again. Now, we have no time, for, if I mistake not, there is our destination."

They had been riding through splendid open forest, growing denser as they approached the ranges. They had followed a creek all the way, or nearly so, and now came somewhat suddenly on a large reedy waterhole, walled on all sides by dense stringy-bark timber, thickly undergrown with scrub.* Behind them opened a long vista formed by the gully, through which they had been approaching, down which the black burnt stems of the stringy-bark were agreeably relieved by the white stems of the red and blue gum, growing in the moister and more open space near the creek.† In front of them was a slab hut of rich mahogany colour, by no means an unpleasing object among the dull unbroken green of the forest. In front of it was a trodden space littered with the chips of firewood. A pile of the last article lay a few yards in front of the door. And against the walls of the tenement was a long bench, on which stood a calabash, with a lump of soap and a coarse towel ; a camp oven, and a pair of black-top boots, and underneath which lay a noble cattle dog, who, as soon as he saw them, burst out into furious barking, and prepared to give battle.

" Will you take my horse for me," said Frank to Lee, " while I go inside ?"

" Certainly, sir," said Lee. " But mind the dog."

Frank laughed and jumped off. The dog was unprepared for this. It was irregular. The proper and usual mode of proceeding would have been for the stranger to have stayed on horseback, and for him (the dog) to have barked himself hoarse, till some one came out of the hut and pacified him by throwing billets of wood at him ; no conversation possible till his barking was turned into mourning. He was not up to the emergency. He had never seen a man clothed in black from head to foot before. He probably thought it was the D——l. His sense of duty not being strong enough to outweigh considerations of personal safety, he fled round the house, and being undecided whether to bark or to howl, did both, while Frank opened the door and went in.

The hut was like most other bush huts, consisting of one undivided apartment, formed of split logs, called slabs, set upright in the

* *Scrub.*—I have used, and shall use, this word so often, that some explanation is due to the English reader. I can give no better definition of it than by saying that it means "shrubbery."

† *Creek.*—The English reader must understand that a creek means a succession of waterholes, unconnected for nine months in the year.

ground. The roof was of bark, and the whole interior was stained by the smoke into a rich dark brown, such as Teniers or our own beloved Cattermole would delight in. You entered by a door in one of the long sides, and saw that the whole of the end on your right was taken up by a large fireplace, on which blazed a pile of timber. Round the walls were four bed places, like the bunks on board ship, each filled with a heap of frouzy blankets, and in the centre stood a rough table, surrounded by logs of wood, sawed square off, which served for seats.

The living occupants of the hut were scarcely less rude than the hut itself. One of the bed places was occupied by a sleepy, black-haired, not bad-looking young fellow, clad in greasy red shirt, greasy breeches and boots, and whose shabby plated spurs were tangled in the dirty blankets. He was lying on his back, playing with a beautiful little parrot. Opposite him, sitting up in his bunk, was another young fellow, with a singularly coarse, repulsive countenance, long yellow hair, half-way down his back, clothed like the other in greasy breeches. This last one was puffing at a short black pipe, in an affected way, making far more noise than was necessary in that operation, and seemed to be thinking of something insolent to say to the last speaker, whoever he may have been.

Another man was sitting on the end of the bench before the fire, with his legs stretched out before it. At the first glance Frank saw that this was a superior person to the others. He was dressed like the others in black-top boots, but, unlike the others, he was clean and neat. In fact the whole man was clean and neat, and had a clean-shaved face, and looked respectable, so far as outward appearances were concerned. The fourth man was the hut-keeper, a wicked-looking old villain, who was baking bread.

Frank looked at the sleepy young man with the parrot, and said to himself, " There's a bad case." He looked at the flash, yellow-haired young snob who was smoking, and said, " There's a worse." He looked at the villanous grey-headed old hut-keeper, and said, " There's a hopeless case altogether." But when he looked at the neatly dressed man, who sat in front of the fire, he said, " That seems a more likely person. There is some sense of order in him, at all events. See what I can do with him."

He stood with his towering tall black figure in the doorway. The sleepy young man with the black hair sat up and looked at him in wonder, while his parrot whistled and chattered loudly. The yellow-haired young man looked round to see if he could get the others to join him in a laugh. The hut-keeper said, " Oh, h—!" and attended once more to the cooking; but the neat-looking man rose up, and gave Frank courteously " Good day."

" I am a clergyman," said Frank, " come to pay you a visit, if you will allow me."

Black-hair looks as if astonishment were a new sensation to him, and he was determined to have the most of it. Meanwhile, little parrot taking advantage of his absence of mind, clambers up his breast and nips off a shirt-button, which he holds in his claw, pretending it is immensely good to eat. Hut-keeper clatters pots and pans, while Yellow-hair lies down whistling insolently. These last two seemed inclined to constitute themselves his Majesty's Opposition in the present matter, while Black-hair and the neat man are evidently inclined towards Frank. There lay a boot in front of the fire, which the neat man, without warning, seized and hurled at Yellow-hair, with such skill and precision that the young fellow started upright in bed and demanded, with many verbs and adjectives, what he meant by that?

" I'll teach you to whistle when a gentleman comes into the hut —you Possumguts ! Lie down now, will you ?"

Yellow-hair lay down, and there was no more trouble with him. Hut-keeper, too, seeing how matters were going, left off clattering his pots, and Frank was master of the field.

" Very glad to see you, sir," says the neat man ; " very seldom we get a visit from a gentleman in a black coat, I assure you."

Frank shook hands with him and thanked him, and then, turning suddenly upon Black-hair, who was sitting with his bird on his knee, one leg out of his bunk, and his great black vacant eyes fixed on Frank, said,—

" What an exceedingly beautiful bird you have got there ! Pray, what do you call it ?"

Now it so happened that Black-hair had been vacantly wondering to himself whether Frank's black coat would meet across his stomach, or whether the lower buttons and buttonholes were " dummies." So that when Frank turned suddenly upon him he was, as it were, caught in the fact, and could only reply in a guilty whisper, " Mountain blue."

" Will he talk ? " asked Frank.

" Whistle," says Black-hair, still in a whisper, and then, clearing his throat continued, in his natural tone, " Whistle beautiful. Black fellows gets 'em young out of the dead trees. I'll give you this one if you've a mind."

Frank couldn't think of it ; but could Black-hair get him a young cockatoo, and leave it with Mr. Sam Buckley for transmission ?— would be exceedingly obliged.

Yes, Black-hair could. Thinks, too, what a pleasant sort of chap this parson was. " Will get him a cockatoo certainly."

Then Frank asks, may he read them a bit out of the Bible, and neat man says they will be highly honoured. And Black-hair gets out of his bunk and sits listening in a decently respectful way. Opposition are by no means won over. The old hut-keeper sits sulkily smoking, and the yellow-haired man lies in his bunk with his back towards them. Lee had meanwhile come in, and, after recognitions from those inside, sat quietly down close to the door. Frank took for a text, " Servants, obey your masters," and preached them a sermon about the relations of master and servant, homely, plain, sensible and interesting, and had succeeded in awakening the whole attention and interest of the three who were listening, when the door was opened and a man looked in.

Lee was next the door, and cast his eyes upon the new comer. No sooner had their eyes met than he uttered a loud oath, and, going out with the stranger, shut the door after him.

" What can be the matter with our friend, I wonder ?" asked Frank. " He seems much disturbed."

The neat man went to the door and opened it. Lee and the man who had opened the door were standing with their backs towards them, talking earnestly. Lee soon came back without a word, and, having caught and saddled his horse, rode away with the stranger, who was on foot. He was a large, shabbily-dressed man, with black curly hair; this was all they could see of him, for his back was always towards them.

" Never saw Bill take on like that before," said the neat man. " That's one of his old pals, I reckon. He ain't very fond of meeting any of 'em, you see, since he has been on the square. The best friends in prison, sir, are the worst friends out."

" Were you ever in prison, then ?" said Frank.

" Lord bless you !" said the other, laughing, " I was lagged for forgery."

" I will make you another visit if I can," said Frank. " I am much obliged to you for the patience with which you heard me."

The other ran out to get his horse for him, and had it saddled in no time. " If you will send a parson round," he said, when Frank was mounted, " I will ensure him a hearing, and good bye, sir."

" And God speed you," says Frank. But, lo ! as he turned to ride away, Black-hair the sleepy-headed comes to the hut-door, looking important, and says, " Hi !" Frank is glad of this, for he likes the stupid-looking young fellow better than he fancied he would have done at first, and says to himself, " There's the making of a man in that fellow, unless I am mistaken." So he turns politely to meet him, and, as he comes towards him, remarks what a fine, good-humoured young fellow he is. Black-hair ranges along-side, and, putting his hand on the horse's neck, says, mysteriously—

" Would you like a native companion ?" *

" Too big to carry, isn't it ?" says Frank.

" I'll tie his wings together, and send him down on the ration

---

* A great crane, common in Australia. A capital pet, though dangerous among children; having that strange propensity common to all the cranes and herons, of attacking the eye.

dray," says Black-hair. " You'll come round and see us again, will you ? "

So Frank fares back to Toonarbin, wondering where Lee has gone. But Black-hair goes back into the hut, and taking his parrot from the bed-place, puts it on his shoulder, and sits rubbing his knees before the fire. Yellow-hair and the hut-keeper are now in loud conversation, and the former is asking, in a loud authoritative tone (the neat man being outside), " whether a chap is to be hunted and badgered out of his bed by a parcel of —— parsons ? " To which Hut-keeper says, " No, by ——! A man might as well be in barracks again." Yellow-hair, morally comforted and sustained by this opinion, is proceeding to say, that, for his part, a parson is a useless sort of animal in general, who gets his living by frightening old women, but that this particular parson is an unusually offensive specimen, and that there is nothing in this world that he (Yellow-hair) would like better than to have him out in front of the house for five minutes, and see who was best man,—when Black-hair, usually a taciturn, peaceable fellow, astonishes the pair by turning his black eyes on the other, and saying, with lowering eyebrows,—

" You d——d humbug ! Talk about fighting him ! Always talk about fighting a chap when he's out of the way, when you know you've no more fight in you than a bronsewing. Why, he'd kill you, if you only waited for him to hit you ! And see here : if you don't stop your jaw about him, you'll have to fight me, and that's a little more than you're game for, I'm thinking."

This last was told me by the man distinguished above as " the neat man," who was standing outside, and heard the whole.

When Frank arrived in due time at Toonarbin, and found all there much as he had left it, save that Mary Hawker had recovered her serenity, and was standing expecting him, with Charles by her side. Sam asked him, " Where was Lee ? " and Frank, thinking more of other things, said he had left him at the hut, not thinking it worth while to mention the circumstance of his having been called out— a circumstance which became of great significance hereafter ; for, though we never found out for certain who the man was, we came in the end to have strong suspicions.

However, as I said, all clouds had cleared from the Toonarbin atmosphere, and, after a pleasant meal. Frank, Major and Mrs. Buckley, Sam, and Charles Hawker, rode home to Baroona under the forest arches, and reached the house in the gathering twilight.

The boys were staying behind at the stable as the three elders entered the darkened drawing-room. A figure was in one of the easy chairs by the fire—a figure which seemed familiar there, though the Major could not make out who it was until a well-known voice said,—.

" Is that you, Buckley ? "

It was the Doctor. They both welcomed him warmly home, and waited in the gloom for him to speak, but only saw that he had bent down his head over the fire.

"Are you ill, Doctor?" said Mrs. Buckley.

"Sound in wind and limb, my dear madam, but rather sad at heart. We have had some very severe black fighting, and we have lost a kind old friend—James Stockbridge."

"Is he wounded, then?" said Mrs. Buckley.

"Dead."

"Dead!"

"Speared in the side. Rolled off his horse, and was gone in five minutes."

"Oh, poor James!" cried Mrs. Buckley. "He, of all men! The man who was their champion. To think that he, of all men, should end in that way!"

*   *   *   *   *   *

Charles Hawker rode home that night, and went into the room where his mother was. She was sitting sewing by the fire, and looked up to welcome him home.

"Mother," said he, "there is bad news to tell. We have lost a good friend. James Stockbridge is killed by the blacks on the Macquarrie."

She answered not a word, but buried her face in her hands, and very shortly rose and left the room. When she was alone, she began moaning to herself, and saying,—

"Some more fruit of the old cursed tree! If he had never seen me, he would have died at home, among his old friends, in a ripe, honoured old age."

CHAPTER XXVII.

THE GOLDEN VINEYARD.

On a summer's morning, almost before the dew had left the grass on the north side of the forest, or the belated opossum had gone to his nest, in fact just as the East was blazing with its brightest fire, Sam started off for a pleasant canter through the forest, to visit one of their out-station huts, which lay away among the ranges, and which was called, from some old arrangement, now fallen into disuse, "the heifer station."

There was the hut, seen suddenly down a beautiful green vista in the forest, the chimney smoking cheerily. "What a pretty contrast of colours!" says Sam, in a humour for enjoying everything. "Dark brown hut among the green shrubs, and blue smoke rising above all ; prettily, too, that smoke hangs about the foliage this still morning, quite in festoons. There's Matt at the door !"

A lean, long-legged, clever-looking fellow, rather wide at the knees, with a brown complexion, and not unpleasant expression of face, stood before the door plaiting a cracker for his stockwhip. He looked pleased when he saw Sam, and indeed it must be a surly fellow indeed, who did not greet Sam's honest face with a smile. Never a dog but wagged his tail when he caught Sam's eye.

" You're abroad early this morning, sir," said the man ; " nothing the matter, is there, sir ? "

" Nothing," said Sam, " save that one of Captain Brentwood's bulls is missing, and I came out to tell you to have an extra look round."

" I'll attend to it, sir."

" Hi ! Matt," said Sam, " you look uncommonly smart."

Matt bent down his head, and laughed, in a rather sheepish sort of way.

" Well, you see, sir, I was coming in to the home station to see if the Major could spare me for a few days."

" What, going a courting, eh ?   Well, I'll make that all right for you. Who is the lady,—eh ? "

" Why, its Elsy Macdonald, I believe."

" Elsy Macdonald ! " said Sam.

" Ay, yes, sir. I know what you mean, but she ain't like her sister ; and that was more Mr. Charles Hawker's fault than her own. No ; Elsy is good enough for me, and I'm not very badly off, and begin to fancy I would like some better sort of welcome in the evening than what a cranky old brute of a hut-keeper can give me. So I think I shall bring her home."

" I wish you well, Matt," said Sam ; " I hope you are not going to leave us, though."

" No fear, sir ; Major Buckley is too good a master for that ! "

" Well, I'll get the hut coopered up a bit for you, and you shall be as comfortable as circumstances will permit. Good morning."

" Good morning, sir ; I hope I may see you happily married yourself some of these days."

Sam laughed ; " that would be a fine joke," he thought, " but why shouldn't it be, eh ? I suppose it must come some time or another. I shall begin to look out ; I don't expect I shall be very easily suited. Heigh ho ! "

I expect, however, Mr. Sam, that you are just in the state of mind to fall headlong in love with the first girl you meet with a nose on her face ; let us hope, therefore, that she may be eligible.

But here is home again, and here is the father standing majestic and broad in the verandah, and the mother with her arm round his neck, both waiting to give him a hearty morning's welcome.

And there is Doctor Mulhaus kneeling in spectacles before his new Grevillea Victoriæ, the first bud of which is bursting into life; and the dogs catch sight of him and dash forward, barking joyfully; and as the ready groom takes his horse, and the fat housekeeper looks out all smiles, and retreats to send in breakfast, Sam thinks to himself, that he could not leave his home and people, not for the best wife in broad Australia; but then, you see, he knew no better.

"What makes my boy look so happy this morning?" asked his mother. "Has the bay mare foaled, or have you negotiated James Brentwood's young dog? Tell us, that we may participate."

"None of these things have happened, mother; but I feel in rather a holiday humour, and I'm thinking of going down to Garoopna this morning, and spending a day or two with Jim."

"I will throw a shoe after you for luck," said his mother. "See, the Doctor is calling you."

Sam went to the Doctor, who was intent on his flower. "Look here, my boy; here is something new: the handsomest of the Grevilleas, as I live. It has opened since I was here."

"Ah!" said Sam, "this is the one that came from the Quartz Ranges, last year, is it not? It has not flowered with you before."

"If Linnæus wept and prayed over the first piece of English furze which he saw," said the Doctor, "what everlasting smelling-bottle hysterics he would have gone into in this country! I don't sympathise with his tears much, though, myself; though a new flower is a source of the greatest pleasure to me."

"And so you are going to Garoopna, Sam?" said his father, at breakfast. "Have you heard, my dear, when the young lady is to come home?"

"Next month, I understand, my dear," said Mrs. Buckley. "When she does come I shall go over and make her a visit."

"What is her name, by the bye?" asked the Doctor.

"Alice."

So, behold Sam starting for his visit. The very Brummel of bush-dandies. Hunt might have made his well-fitting cord breeches, Hoby might have made those black-top boots, and Chifney might have worn them before royalty, and not been ashamed. It is too hot for coat or waistcoat; so he wears his snow-white shirt, topped by a blue "bird's-eye-handkerchief," and keeps his coat in his valise, to be used as occasion shall require. His costume is completed with a cabbage-tree hat, neither too new nor too old; light, shady, well ventilated, and three pounds ten, the production, after months of labour, of a private in her Majesty's Fortieth Regiment of Foot: not with long streaming ribands down his back, like a Pitt Street bully, but with short and modest ones as becomes a gentleman,—altogether as fine a looking young fellow, as well dressed, and as well mounted too, as you will find on the country side.

Let me say a word about his horse, too; horse Widderin. None ever knew what that horse had cost Sam. The Major even had a delicacy about asking. I can only discover by inquiry that, at one time, about a year before this, there came to the Major's a travel-ler, an Irishman by nation, who bored them all by talking about a certain " Arcturus " colt, which had been dropped to a happy pro-prietor by his mare " Larkspur," among the Shoalhaven gullies; described by him as a colt the like of which was never seen before; as indeed he should be, for his sire Arcturus, as all the world knows, was bought up by a great Hunter-river horse-breeder from the Duke of C——; while his dam, Larkspur, had for grandsire the great Bombshell himself. What more would you have than that, unless you would like to drive Veno in our dog-cart? However, it so happened that, soon after the Irishman's visit, Sam went away on a journey, and came back riding a new horse; which when the Major saw, he whistled, but discreetly said nothing. A very large colt he was, with a neck like a rainbow, set into a splendid shoulder, and a marvellous way of throwing his legs out;—very dark chestnut in colour, almost black, with longish ears, and an eye so full, honest, and impudent, that it made you laugh in his face. Widderin, Sam said was his name, price and history being suppressed; called after Mount Widderin, to the northward there, whose loftiest sublime summit bends over like a horse's neck, with two peaked crags for ears. And the Major comes somehow to connect this horse with the Arcturus colt mentioned by our Irish friend, and observes that Sam takes to wearing his old clothes for a twelvemonth, and never seems to have any ready money. We shall see some day whether or no this horse will carry Sam ten miles, if required, on such direful emergency too as falls to the lot of few men. However, this is all to come. Now in holiday clothes and in holiday mind, the two noble animals cross the paddock, and so down by the fence towards the river; towards the old gravel ford you may remember years ago. Here is the old flood, spouting and streaming as of yore, through the basalt pillars. There stand the three fern trees, too, above the dark scrub on the island. Now up the rock bank, and away across the breezy plains due North.

Brushing through the long grass tussocks, he goes his way singing, his dog Rover careering joyously before him. The horse is clearly for a gallop, but it is too hot to-day. The tall, flat-topped volcanic hill which hung before him like a grey faint cloud when he started, now rears its fluted columns overhead, and now is getting dim again behind him. But ere noon is high he once more hears the brawling river beneath his feet, and Garoopna is before him on the opposite bank.

The river, as it left Major Buckley's at Baroona, made a sudden bend to the west, a great arc, including with its minor windings nearly twenty-five miles, over the chord of which arc Sam had now been riding, making, from point to point, ten miles or thereabouts. The Mayfords' station, also, lay to the left of him, being on the curved side of the arc, about five miles from Baroona. The reader may, if he please, remember this.

Garoopna is an exceedingly pretty station; in fact, one of the most beautiful I have ever seen. It stands at a point where the vast forests, which surround the mountains in a belt, from ten to twenty miles broad, run down into the plains and touch the river. As at Baroona, the stream runs in through a deep cleft in the table land, which here, though precipitous on the eastern bank, on the western breaks away into a small natural amphitheatre bordered by fine hanging woods, just in advance of which, about two hundred yards from the river, stands the house, a long, low building densely covered with creepers of all sorts, and fronted by a beautiful garden. Right and left of it are the woolsheds, sheepyards, stockyards, men's huts &c.; giving it almost the appearance of a little village; and behind the wooded ranges begin to rise, in some places broken beautifully by sheer scarps of grey rock. The forest crosses the river a little way; so that Sam, gradually descending from the plains to cross, went the last quarter of a mile through a shady sandy forest tract, fringed with bracken, which led down to a broad crossing place, where the river sparkled under tall over-arching red gums and box-trees; and then following the garden fence, found himself before a deep cool-looking porch, in a broad neatly-kept courtyard behind the house.

A groom* came out and took his horse. Rover has enough to do; for there are three or four sheep dogs in the yard, who walk round him on tiptoe, slowly, with their frills out and their tails arched, growling. Rover, also, walks about on tiptoe, arches his tail, and growls with the best of them. He knows that the slightest mistake would be disastrous, and so manœuvres till he gets to the porch, where, a deal of gravel having been kicked backwards, in the same way as the ancients poured out their wine when they drank a toast, or else (as I think is more probable) as a symbol that animosities were to be buried, Rover is admitted as a guest, and Sam feels it safe to enter the house.

A cool, shady hall, hung round with coats, hats, stockwhips; a gun in the corner, and on a slab, the most beautiful nosegay you can imagine. Remarkable that for a bachelor's establishment;—but there is no time to think about it, for a tall, comfortable-looking

---

* Do not let Bob or Tom, when they read this book in the sixteenth edition, before the harness-room stove, suppose that an Australian groom resembles in any way the very neat young man who follows the young ladies in their canters. The dirtiest helper at a university stable would come nearer the mark.

housekeeper, whom Sam has never seen before, comes in from the kitchen and curtseys.

"Captain Brentwood not at home, is he?" said Sam.

"No, sir! Away on the run with Mr. James."

"Oh! very well," says Sam; "I am going to stay a few days."

"Very well, sir; will you take anything before lunch?"

"Nothing, thank you."

"Miss Alice is somewhere about, sir. I expect her in every minute."

"Miss Alice!" says Sam, astonished. "Is she come home?"

"Came home last week, sir. Will you walk in and sit down?"

Sam got his coat out of his valise, and went in. He wished that he had put on his plain blue necktie instead of the blue one with white spots. He would have liked to have worn his new yellow riding-trousers, instead of breeches and boots. He hoped his hair was in order, and tried to arrange his handsome brown curls without a glass, but, in the end, concluded that things could not be mended now, so he looked round the room.

What a charming room it was! A couple of good pictures, and several fine prints on the walls. Over the chimneypiece, a sword, and an old gold-laced cap, on which Sam looked with reverence. Three French windows opened on to a dark cool verandah, beyond which was a beautiful flower-garden. The floor of the room, uncarpeted, shone dark and smooth, and the air was perfumed by vases of magnificent flowers, a hundred pounds worth of them, I should say, if you could have taken them to Covent-garden that December morning. But what took Sam's attention more than anything was an open piano, in a shady recess, and on the keys a little fairy white glove.

"White kid gloves, eh, my lady?" says Sam; "that don't look well." So he looked through the book-shelves, and, having lighted on "Boswell's Johnson," proceeded into the verandah. A colley she-dog was lying at one end, who banged her tail against the floor in welcome, but was too utterly prostrated by the heat and by the persecution of her puppy to get up and make friends. The pup, however, a ball of curly black wool, with a brown-striped face, who was sitting on the top of her with his head on one side, seemed to conclude that a game of play was to be got out of Sam, and came blundering towards him; but Sam was, by this time, deep in a luxurious rocking-chair, so the puppy stopped half way, and did battle with a great black tarantula spider who happened to be abroad on business.

Sam went to the club with his immortal namesake, bullied Bennet Langton, argued with Beauclerk, put down Goldsmith, and extinguished Boswell. But it was too hot to read; so he let the book fall on his lap, and lay a dreaming.

What a delicious verandah is this to dream in! Through the tangled passion-flowers, jessamines and magnolias, what a soft gleam of bright hazy distance, over the plains and far away! The deep river-glen cleaves the table-land, which, here and there, swells into breezy downs. Beyond, miles away to the North, is a great forest-barrier, above which there is a blaze of late snow, sending strange light aloft into the burning haze. All this is seen through an arch in the dark mass of verdure which clothes the trellis-work, only broken through in this one place, as though to make a frame for the picture. He leans back, and gives himself up to watching trifles.

See here. A magpie comes furtively out of the house with a key in his mouth, and, seeing Sam, stops to consider if he is likely to betray him. On the whole, he thinks not; so he hides the key in a crevice, and whistles a tune.

Now enters a cockatoo, waddling along comfortably and talking to himself. He tries to enter into conversation with the magpie, who, however, cuts him dead, and walks off to look at the prospect.

Flop! flop! A great foolish-looking kangaroo comes through the house and peers round him. The cockatoo addresses a few remarks to him, which he takes no notice of, but goes blundering out into the garden, right over the contemplative magpie, who gives him two or three indignant pecks on his clumsy feet, and sends him flying down the gravel walk.

Two bright-eyed little kangaroo rats come out of their box peering and blinking. The cockatoo finds an audience in them, for they sit listening to him, now and then catching a flea, or rubbing the backs of their heads with their fore-paws. But a buck 'possum, who stealthily descends by a pillar from unknown realms of mischief on the top of the house, evidently discredits cockey's stories, and departs down the garden to see if he can find something to eat.

An old cat comes up the garden walk, accompanied by a wicked kitten, who ambushes round the corner of the flowerbed, and pounces out on her mother, knocking her down and severely maltreating her. But the old lady picks herself up without a murmur, and comes into the verandah followed by her unnatural offspring, ready for any mischief. The kangaroo rats retire into their box, and the cockatoo, rather nervous, lays himself out to be agreeable.

But the puppy, born under an unlucky star, who has been watching all these things from behind his mother, thinks at last, "Here is some one to play with," so he comes staggering forth and challenges the kitten to a lark.

She receives him with every sympton of disgust and abhorrence; but he, regardless of all spitting, and tail swelling, rolls her over, spurring and swearing, and makes believe he will worry her to death. Her scratching and biting tell but little on his woolly hide, and he seems to have the best of it out and out, till a new ally appears unexpectedly, and quite turns the tables. The magpie hops up, ranges alongside of the combatants, and catches the puppy such a dig over the tail as sends him howling to his mother with a flea in his ear.

Sam lay sleepily amused by this little drama; then he looked at the bright green arch which separated the dark verandah from the bright hot garden. The arch was darkened, and looking he saw something which made his heart move strangely, something that he has not forgotten yet, and never will.

Under the arch between the sunlight and the shade, bareheaded, dressed in white, stood a girl, so amazingly beautiful, that Sam wondered for a few moments whether he was asleep or awake. Her hat, which she had just taken off, hung on her left arm, and with her delicate right hand she arranged a vagrant tendril of the passion-flower, which in its luxuriant growth had broken bounds and fallen from its place above.—A girl so beautiful that I in all my life never saw her superior. They showed me the other day, in a carriage in the park, one they said was the most beautiful girl in England, a descendant of I know not how many noblemen. But, looking back to the times I am speaking of now, I said at once and decidedly, "Alice Brentwood twenty years ago was more beautiful than she."

A Norman style of beauty, I believe you would call it. Light hair, deep brilliant blue eyes, and a very fair complexion. Beauty and high-bred grace in every limb and every motion. She stood there an instant on tiptoe, with the sunlight full upon her, while Sam, buried in gloom, had time for a delighted look, before she stepped into the verandah and saw him.

She floated towards him through the deep shadow. "I think," she said in the sweetest, most musical little voice, "that you are Mr. Buckley. If so, you are a very old friend of mine by report." So she held out her little hand, and with one bold kind look from the happy eyes, finished Sam for life.

Father and mother, retire into the chimney corner and watch. Your day is done. Doctor Mulhaus, put your good advice into your pocket and smoke your pipe. Here is one who can exert a greater power for good or evil than all of you put together. It was written of old,—"A man shall leave his father and mother and cleave unto his——" Hallo! I am getting on rather fast, I am afraid.

He had risen to meet her. "And you, Miss Brentwood," he said, "are tolerably well known to me. Do you know now that I believe by an exertion of memory I could tell you the year and the month when you began to learn the harp? My dear old friend Jim has kept me quite *au fait* with all your accomplishments."

"I hope you are not disappointed in me," said Alice, laughing.

"No," said Sam. "I think rather the contrary. Are you?"

"I have not had time to tell yet," she said. "I will see how you behave at lunch, which we shall have in half an hour *tête-à-tête*. You have been often here before, I believe? Do you see much change?"

" Not much. I noticed a new piano, and a little glove that I had never seen before. Jim's menagerie of wild beasts is as numerous as ever, I see. He would have liked to be in Noah's Ark."

" And so would you and I, Mr. Buckley," she answered, laughing, " if we had been caught in the flood."

Good gracious! Think of being in Noah's Ark with her!

" You find them a little troublesome, don't you, Miss Brentwood?"

" Well, it requires a good deal of administrative faculty to keep the kitten and the puppy from open collision, and to prevent the magpie from pecking out the cockatoo's eye and hiding it in the flower bed. Last Sunday morning he (the magpie) got into my father's room, and stole thirty-one shillings and sixpence. We got it all back but half a sovereign, and that we shall never see."

The bird thus alluded to broke into a gush of melody, so rich, full, and metallic, that they both turned to look at him. Having attracted attention, he began dancing, crooning a little song to himself, as though he would say, " I know where it is." And lastly he puffed out his breast, put back his bill, and swore two or three oaths that would have disgraced a London scavenger, with such remarkable distinctness too, that there was no misunderstanding him ; so Sam's affectation of not having caught what the bird said, was a dead failure.

" Mr. Buckley," said she, " if you will excuse me I will go and see about lunch. Can you amuse yourself there for half an hour?" Well, he would try. So he retired again to the rocking-chair, about ten years older than when he rose from it. For he had grown from a boy into a man.

He had fallen over head and ears in love, and all in five minutes. Fallen deeply, seriously, in love, to the exclusion of all other sublunary matters, before he had well had time to notice whether she spoke with an Irish brogue or a Scotch (happily she did neither). Sudden, you say: well, yes ; but, in lat. 34°, and lower, whether in the southern or northern atmosphere, these sort of affairs come on with a rapidity and violence only equalled by the thunder-storms of those regions, and utterly surprising to you who perhaps read this book in 52° north, or perhaps higher. I once went to a ball with as free-and-easy, heart-whole a young fellow as any I know, and agreed with him to stay half an hour, and then come away and play pool. In twenty-five minutes by my watch, which keeps time like a ship's chronometer, that man was in the tragic or cut-throat stage of the passion with a pretty little thing of forty, a cattle-dealer's widow, who stopped *his* pool-playing for a time, until she married the great ironmonger in George Street. Romeo and Juliet's little matter was just as sudden, and very Australian in many points. Only mind, that Romeo, had he lived in Australia, instead of taking poison, would probably have

> " Took to drinking ratafia, and thought of poor Miss Baily,'

for full twenty-four hours after the catastrophe.

At least such would have been the case in many instances, but not in all. With some men these suddenly-conceived passions last their lives, and, I should be inclined to say longer, were there not strong authority against it.

But Sam? He saw the last twinkle of her white gown disappear, and then leant back and tried to think. He could only say to himself, "By Jove, I wonder if I can ever bring her to like me. I wish I had known she was here; I'd have dressed myself better. She is a precious superior girl. She might come to like me in time. Heigh ho!"

The idea of his having a rival, or of any third person stepping in between him and the young lady to whom he had thrown his handkerchief, never entered into his Sultanship's head. Also, when he came to think about it, he really saw no reason why she should not be brought to think well of him. "As well me as another," said he to himself; "that's where it is. She must marry somebody, you know!"

Why is she gone so long? He begins to doubt whether he has not after all been asleep and dreaming. There she comes again, however, for the arch under the creepers is darkened again, and he looks up with a pleasant smile upon his face to greet her.

God save us! What imp's trick is this? There, in the porch, in the bright sun, where she stood not an hour ago in all her beauty and grace, stands a hideous, old savage, black as Tophet, grinning; showing the sharp gap-teeth in her apish jaws, her lean legs shaking with old age and rheumatism.

The colley shakes out her frill, and, raising the hair all down her back, stands grinning and snarling, while her puppy barks pot-valiantly between her legs. The little kangaroo rats ensconce themselves once more in their box, and gaze out amazed from their bright little eyes. The cockatoo hooks and clambers up to a safe place in the trellis, and Sam, after standing thunder-struck for a moment, asks, what she wants?

" Make a light," * says the old girl, in a pathetic squeak. Further answer she makes none, but squats down outside, and begins a petulant whine: sure sign that she has a tale of woe to unfold, and is going to ask for something.

" Can that creature," thinks Sam, " be of the same species as the

---

* " Make a light," in blackfellow's gibberish, means simply " See." Here it means, " I'm only come to see how you are getting on," or something of that sort.

beautiful Alice Brentwood? Surely not! There seems as much difference between them as between an angel and an ordinary good woman." Hard to believe, truly, Sam; but perhaps, in some of the great European cities, or even nearer home, in some of the prison barracks, you may chance to find a white woman or two fallen as low as that poor, starved, ill-treated, filthy old savage!

Alice comes out once more, and brings sunshine with her. She goes up to the old lubra with a look of divine compassion on her beautiful face; the old woman's whine grows louder as she rocks herself to and fro. "Yah marah, Yah boorah, Oh boora Yah! Yah Ma!"

"What! old Sally!" says the beautiful girl. "What is the matter? Have you been getting waddy again?"

"Baal!" says she, with a petulant burst of grief.

"What is it, then?" says Alice. "Where is the gown I gave you?"

Alice had evidently vibrated the right chord. The "Yarah Moorah" coronach was begun again; and then suddenly, as if her indignation had burst bounds, she started off with a shrillness and rapidity astonishing to one not accustomed to blackfellows, into something like the following: "Oh Yah (very loud), oh Mah! Barkmaburrawurrah, Barkmamurrahwurrah Oh Ya Barkmanurrawah Yee (in a scream. Then a pause). Oh Mooroo (pause). Oh hinaray (pause). Oh Barknamurrwurrah Yee!"

Alice looked as if she understood every word of it, and waited till the poor old soul had "blown off the steam," and then asked again:

"And what has become of the gown, Sally?"

"Oh dear! Young lubra, Betty (big thief that one) tear it up and stick it along a fire. Oh, plenty cold this old woman. Oh, plenty hungry this old woman. Oh, Yarah Moorah," &c.

"There! go round to the kitchen," said Alice, "and get something to eat. Is it not abominable, Mr. Buckley? I cannot give anything to this old woman but the young lubras take it from her. However, I will 'put the screw on them.' They shall have nothing from me till they treat her better. It goes to my heart to see a woman of that age, with nothing to look forward to but kicks and blows. I have tried hard to make her understand something of the next world: but I can't get it out of her head that when she dies she will go across the water and come back a young white woman with plenty of money. Mr. Sandford, the missionary, says he has never found one who could be made to comprehend the existence of God. However, I came to call you to lunch; will you give me your arm?"

Such a self-possessed, intrepid little maiden, not a bit afraid of him, but seeming to understand and trust him so thoroughly. Not all the mock-modesty and blushing in the world would have won him half so surely, as did her bold, quiet, honest look. Although a very young man, and an inexperienced, Sam could see what a candid, honest, gentle soul looked at him from those kind blue eyes; and she, too, saw something in Sam's broad noble face which attracted her marvellously, and in all innocence she told him so, plump and plain, as they were going into the house.

"I fancy I shall like you very much, Mr. Buckley. We ought to be good friends, you know: your father saved the lives of my father and uncle."

"I never heard of that before," said Sam.

"I dare say not," said Alice. "Your father is not the man to speak of his own noble deeds; yet he ran out of his square and pulled my father and uncle almost from under the hoofs of the French cavalry at Waterloo. It makes my cheeks tingle to tell of it now."

Indeed it did. Sam thought that if it brought such a beautiful flush to her face, and such a flash from her eyes, whenever she told it, that he would get her to tell it again more than once.

But lunch! Don't let us starve our new pair of turtle-doves, in the outset. Sam is but a growing lad, and needs carbon for his muscles, lime for his bones, and all that sort of thing; a glass of wine won't do him any harm either, and let us hope that his new passion is not of such lamentable sort as to prevent his using a knife and fork with credit and satisfaction to himself.

Here, in the dark, cool parlour, stands a banquet for the gods, white damask, pretty bright china, and clean silver. In the corner of the table is a frosted claret-jug, standing, with freezing politeness, upright, his hand on his hip, waiting to be poured out. In the centre, the grandfather of watermelons, half-hidden by peaches and pomegranates, the whole heaped over by a confusion of ruby cherries (oh, for Lance to paint it!). Are you hungry, though? If so, here is a mould of potted-head and a cold wild duck, while, on the sideboard, I see a bottle of pale ale. My brother, let us breakfast in Scotland, lunch in Australia, and dine in France, till our lives' end.

And the banquet being over, she said, as pleasantly as possible, "Now, I know you want to smoke in the verandah. For my part, I should like to bring my work there and sit with you, but, if you had rather not have me, you have only to say that 'you could not think,' &c. &c., and I will obediently take myself off."

But Sam didn't say that. He said that he couldn't conceive anything more delightful, if she was quite sure she did not mind.

Not she, indeed! So she brought her work out, and they sat together. A cool wind came up, bending the flowers, swinging the creepers to and fro, and raising a rushing sound, like the sea, from the distant forest. The magpie having been down the garden when the wind came on, and having been blown over, soon joined them in a very captious frame of mind; and, when Alice dropped a ball of red worsted, he seized it as lawful prize, and away in the house with a hop and a flutter. So both Sam and Alice had to go after him, and hunt him under the sofa, and the bird, finding that he must yield, dropped the ball suddenly, and gave Sam two vicious digs on the fingers to remember him by. But when Alice just touched his hand in taking it from him, he wished it had been a whipsnake instead of a magpie.

So the ball of worsted was recovered, and they sat down again. He watched her nimble fingers on the delicate embroidery; he glanced at her quiet face and down-turned eyelids, wondering who she was thinking of. Suddenly she raised her eyes and caught him in the fact. You could not swear she blushed; it might only be a trifling reflection from one of the red China roses that hung between her and the sun; yet, when she spoke, it was not quite with her usual self-possession; a little hurriedly perhaps.

"Are you going to be a soldier, as your father was?"

Sam had thought for an instant of saying "yes," and then to prove his words true of going to Sydney, and enlisting in the "Half Hundred." * Truth, however, prompting him to say "no," he compromised the matter by saying he had not thought of it.

"I am rather glad of that, do you know," she said. "Unless in India, now, a man had better be anything than a soldier. I am afraid my brother Jim will be begging for a commission some day. I wish he would stay quietly at home."

That was comforting. He gave up all thoughts of enlisting at once. But now the afternoon shadows were beginning to slant longer and longer, and it was nearly time that the Captain and Jim should make their appearance. So Alice proposed to walk out to meet them, and as Sam did not say no, they went forth together.

Down the garden, faint with the afternoon scents of the flowers before the western sun, among petunias and roses, oleander and magnolia; here a towering Indian lily, there a thicket of scarlet geranium and fuchsia. By shady young orange trees, covered with fruit and blossom, between rows of trellissed vines, bearing rich promise of a purple vintage. Among fig trees and pomegranates, and so leaving the garden, along the dry slippery grass, towards the hoarse rushing river, both silent till they reached it. There is a silence that is golden.

They stood gazing on the foaming tide an instant, and then Alice said,—

"My father and Jim will come home by the track across there. Shall we cross and meet them? We can get over just below."

A little lower down, all the river was collected into one headlong race; and a giant tree, undermined by winter floods, had fallen from

---

* The fiftieth, buffs.

one bank to the other, offering a giddy footway across the foaming water.

"Now," said Alice, "if you will go over, I will follow you."

So he ran across, and then looked back to see the beautiful figure tripping fearlessly over, with outstretched arms, and held out his great brown hand to take her tiny fingers as she stepped down from the upturned roots, on to the soft white sand. He would like to have taken them again, to help her up the bank, but she sprang up like a deer, and would not give him the opportunity. Then they had a merry laugh at the magpie, who had fluttered down all this way before them, to see if they were on a foraging expedition, and if there were any plunder going, and now could not summon courage to cross the river, but stood crooning and cursing by the brink. Then they sauntered away through the forest, side by side, along the sandy track, among the knolls of bracken, with the sunlit boughs overhead whispering knowingly to one another in the evening breeze, as they passed beneath.—An evening walk long remembered by both of them.

> "Oh see ye not that pleasant road,
>   That winds along the ferny brae?
> Oh that's the road to fairy land,
>   Where thou and I this e'en must gae."

"And so you cannot remember England, Mr. Buckley?" says Alice.

"Oh dear, no. Stay though, I am speaking too fast. I can remember some few places. I remember a steep, red road, that led up to the church, and have some dim recollection of a vast grey building, with a dark porch, which must have been the church itself. I can see, too, at this moment, a broad green flat, beside a creek, which was covered with yellow and purple flowers, which mother and I made into nosegays. That must be the place my father speaks of as the Hatherleigh Meadows, where he used to go fishing, and, although I must have been there often, yet I can only remember it on one occasion, when he emptied out a basket of fish on the grass for me to look at. My impression of England is, that everything was of a brighter colour than here; and they tell me I am right."

"A glorious country," said Alice; "what would I give to see it?—so ancient and venerable, and yet so amazingly young and vigorous. It seems like a waste of existence for a man to stay here tending sheep, when his birthright is that of an Englishman: the right to move among his peers, and find his fit place in the greatest empire in the world. Never had any woman such a noble destiny before her as this young lady who has just ascended the throne."

But the conversation changed here, and her Majesty escaped criticism for the time. They came to an open space in the forest, thickly grown with thickets of bracken fern, prickly acacia, and here and there a solitary dark-foliaged lightwood. In the centre rose a few blackened posts, the supports of what had once been a hut, and as you looked, you were surprised to see an English rose or two, flowering among the dull-coloured prickly shrubs, which were growing around. A place, as any casual traveller would have guessed, which had a history, and Sam, seeing Alice pause, asked her, "what old hut was this?"

"This," she said, " is the Donovans' old station, where they were burnt out by the blacks."

Sam knew the story well enough, but he would like to hear her tell it; so he made believe to have heard some faint reports of the occurrence, and what could she do, but give him the particulars?

"They had not been here a year," she said; "and Mrs. Donovan had been confined only three days; there was not a soul on the station but herself, her son Murtagh, and Miss Burke. All day the blackfellows were prowling about, and getting more and more insolent, and at night, just as Murtagh shut the door, they raised their yell, and rushed against it. Murtagh Donovan and Miss Burke had guessed what was coming all day, but had kept it from the sick woman, and now, when the time came, they were cool and prepared. They had two double-barrelled guns loaded with slugs, and with these they did such fearful execution from two loop-holes they had made in the slabs, that the savages quickly retired; but poor Miss Burke, incautiously looking out to get a shot, received a spear wound in her shoulder, which she bears the mark of to this day. But the worst was to come. The blackfellows mounted on the roof, tried to take off the bark, and throw their spears into the hut, but here they were foiled again. Wherever a sheet of bark was seen to move they watched, and on the first appearance of an enemy, a charge of shot at a few yards' distance told with deadly effect. Mrs. Donovan, who lay in bed and saw the whole, told my father that Lesbia Burke loaded and fired with greater rapidity and precision than did her cousin. A noble woman, I say."

"Good old Lesbia!" said Sam; "and how did it end?"

"Why, the foolish blacks fired the woolshed, and brought the Delisles upon them; they tried to fire the roof of the hut, but it was raining too hard: otherwise it would have gone hard with poor Miss Burke. See, here is a peach-tree they planted, covered with fruit; let us gather some; it is pretty good, for the Donovans have kept it pruned in memory of their escape."

"But the hut was not burnt," said Sam, " where did it stand?"

"That pile of earth there, is the remains of the old turf chimney. They moved across the river after it happened."

But peaches, when they grow on a high tree, must be climbed for, particularly if a young and pretty girl expresses a wish for them.

And so it fell out, that Sam was soon astride of one of the lower boughs, throwing the fruit down to Alice, who put them one by one into the neatest conceivable little basket that hung on her arm.

And so they were employed, busy and merry, when they heard a loud cheery voice, which made both of them start.

"Quite a scene from 'Paradise Lost,' I declare; only Eve ought to be up the tree handing down the apples to Adam, and not *vice versâ.* I miss a carpet snake, too, who would represent the Deuce, and make the thing complete.—Sam Buckley, how are you?"

It was Captain Brentwood who had come on them so inaudibly along the sandy track, on horseback, and beside him was son Jim, looking rather mischievously at Sam, who did not show to the best of advantage up in the peach-tree; but, having descended, and greetings being exchanged, father and son rode on to dress for dinner, the hour for which was now approaching, leaving Sam and Alice to follow at leisure, which they did; for Captain Brentwood and Jim had time to dress and meet in the verandah, before they saw the pair come sauntering up the garden.

"Father," said Jim, taking the Captain's hand, "how would that do?"

"Marvellous well, I should say;" replied the Captain.

"And so I think, too," said Jim. "Hallo! you two; dinner is ready, so look sharp."

After dinner the Captain retired silently to the chimney-corner, and read his book, leaving the three young people to amuse themselves as they would. Nothing the Captain liked so much as quiet, while he read some abstruse work on Gunnery, or some scientific voyage; but I am sorry to say he had got very little quiet of an evening since Alice came home, and Jim had got some one to chatter to. This evening, however, seemed to promise well, for Alice brought out a great book of coloured prints, and the three sat down to turn them over, Jim, of course, you know, being in the middle.

The book was "Wild Sports of the East," a great volume of coloured lithographs, worth some five-and-twenty guineas. One never sees such books as that now-a-days, somehow; people, I fancy, would not pay that price for them. What modern travels have such plates as the old editions of "Cook's Voyages"? The number of illustrated books is increased tenfold, but they are hardly improved in quality.

But Sam, I think, would have considered any book beautiful in such company. "This," said Alice, "is what we call the 'Tiger Book'—why, you will see directly.—You turn over, Jim, and don't crease the pages."

So Jim turned over, and kept them laughing by his simple remarks, more often affected than real, I suspect. Now they went through the tangled jungle, and seemed to hear the last mad howl of the dying tiger, as the elephant knelt and pinned him to the ground with his tusks. Now they chased a lordly buffalo from his damp lair in the swamp; now they saw the English officers flying along on their Arabs through the high grass with well-poised spears after the snorting hog. They have come unexpectedly on a terrible old tiger; one of the horses swerves, and a handsome young man, losing his seat, seems just falling into the monster's jaws, while the pariah dogs scud away terrified through the grass.

"That chap will be eaten immediately," says Jim.

"He has been in that position ever since I can remember," says Alice; "so I think he is pretty safe."

Now they are with the British army on the march. A scarlet bar stretches across the plain, of which the further end is lost in the white mirage—all in order; walking irresistibly on to the conquest of an empire greater than Haroun Al Raschid's. So naturally done too, that as you look, you think you see the columns swing as they advance, and hear the heavy, weary tramp of the troops above the din and shouting of the crowd of camp-followers, on camels and elephants, which surrounds them. Beyond the plain the faint blue hills pierce the grey air, barred with a few long white clouds, and far away a gleaming river winds through a golden country spanned with long bridges, and fringed with many a fantastic minaret.

"How I should like to see that!" said Alice.

"Would you like to be a countess," said Jim, "and ride on an elephant in a howitzer?"

"Howdah, you goose!" said Alice. "Besides, that is not a countess; that is one of the soldiers' wives. Countesses don't go to India: they stay at home to mind the Queen's clothes."

"What a pleasant job for them," said Jim, "when her Most Gracious Majesty has got the toothache! I wonder whether she wears her crown under her bonnet or over it?"

Captain Brentwood looked up. "My dear boy," he said, "does it not strike you that you are talking nonsense?"

"Did you ever see the old King, father?" said Jim.

"I saw King George the Third many times."

"Ah, but I mean to speak to him."

"Once only, and then he was mad. He was sitting up with her Majesty, waiting for intelligence which I brought. His Royal Highness took the despatches from me, but the King insisted on seeing me."

"And what did he say, father? Do tell us," said Alice eagerly.

"Little enough, my love," said the Captain, leaning back. "He asked, 'Is this the officer who brought the despatches, York?' And his Royal Highness said 'Yes.' Then the King said, 'You bring good news, sir: I was going to ask you some questions, but they are all gone out of my head. Go and get your supper; get your supper, sir.' Poor old gentleman. He was a kindly old man, and I had a great respect for him. Alice, sing us a song, my love."

She sang them "The Burial of Sir John Moore" with such perfect taste and pathos that Sam felt as if the candle had gone out when she finished. Then she turned round and said to him, "You ought to like that song; your father was one of the actors in it."

"He has often told me the story," said Sam, "but I never knew what a beautiful one it was till I heard you sing it."

All pleasant evenings must end, and at last she rose to go to bed. But Sam, before he went off to the land of happy dreams, saw that the little white glove which he had noticed in the morning was lying neglected on the floor; so he quietly secured and kept it. And, last year, opening his family Bible to refer to certain entries, now pretty numerous, in the beginning, I found a little white glove pinned to the fly-leaf, which I believe to be the same glove here spoken of.

CHAPTER XXVIII.

A GENTLEMAN FROM THE WARS.

I NEED hardly say that Sam was sorry when the two days which he had allowed himself for his visit were over. But that evening, when he mentioned the fact that he was going away in the morning, the Captain, Alice, and Jim, all pressed him so eagerly to stay another week, that he consented; the more as there was no earthly reason he knew of why he should go home.

And the second morning from that on which he should have been at home, going out to the stable before breakfast, he saw his father come riding over the plain, and, going to meet him, found that he, too, meditated a visit to the Captain.

"I thought you were come after me, father," said Sam. "By the bye, do you know that the Captain's daughter, Miss Alice, is come home?"

"Indeed!" said the Major; "and what sort of a body is she?"

"Oh, she is well enough. Something like Jim. Plays very well on the piano, and all that sort of thing, you know. Sings too."

"Is she pretty?" asked the Major.

"Oh, well, I suppose she is," said Sam. "Yes; I should say that a great many people would consider her pretty."

They had arrived at the door, and the groom had taken the Major's horse, when Alice suddenly stepped out and confronted them.

The Major had been prepared to see a pretty girl, but he was by no means prepared for such a radiant, lovely, blushing, creature as stepped out of the darkness into the fresh morning to greet him, clothed in white, bareheaded, with

"A single rose in her hair."

As he told his wife, a few days after, he was struck "all of a heap;" and Sam heard him whisper to himself, "By Jove!" before he went up to Alice and spoke.

"My dear young lady, you and I ought not to be strangers, for I recognise you from my recollections of your mother. Can you guess who I am?"

"I recognise you from my recollections of your son, sir," said Alice, with a sly look at Sam; "I should say that you were Major Buckley."

The Major laughed, and, taking her hand, carried it to his lips; a piece of old-fashioned courtesy she had never experienced before, and which won her heart amazingly.

"Come, come, Buckley!" said the quiet voice of Captain Brentwood from the dark passage; "what are you at there with my daughter? I shall have to call out and fight some of you young fellows yet, I see."

Alice went in past her father, stopping to give him a kiss, and disappeared into the breakfast-room. The Captain came out, and shook hands warmly with the Major, and said,

"What do you think of her,—eh?"

"I never saw such beauty before," answered the Major; "never, by Jove! I tell you what, Brentwood, I wish she could come out this season in London. Why, she might marry a duke."

"Let us get her a rouge-pot and a French governess, and send her home by the next ship; eh, Buckley?" said the Captain, with his most sardonic smile. "She would be the better for a little polishing; wouldn't she, eh? Too hoydenish and forward, I am afraid; too fond of speaking the truth. Let's have her taught to amble, and mince, and——Bah, come to breakfast!"

The Major laughed heartily at this tirade of the Captain's. He was fond of teasing him, and I believe the Captain liked to be teased by him.

"And what are you three going to do with yourselves to-day, eh?" asked the Captain at breakfast. "It is a matter of total indifference to me, so long as you take yourselves off somewhere, and leave me in peace."

Alice was spokesman:—"We are going up to the Limestone Gates; Mr. Samuel Buckley has expressed a desire to see them, and so Jim and I thought of taking him there."

This was rather a jesuitical speech. The expedition to the Limestone Gates involved a long ride through very pretty scenery, which she herself had proposed. As for Sam, bless you! he didn't care whether they rode east, west, north, or south, so long as he rode beside her; however, having got his cue, he expressed a strong wish to examine, geologically, the great band of limestone which alternated with the slate towards the mountains, the more particularly as he knew that the Captain and the Major intended to ride out in another direction, to examine some new netting for sheep-yards which the Captain had imported.

If Major Buckley thought Alice beautiful as he had seen her in the morning, he did not think her less so when she was seated on a beautiful little horse, which she rode gracefully and courageously, in a blue riding-habit, and a sweet little grey hat with a plume of companion's feathers hanging down on one side. The cockatoo was on the door-step to see her start, and talked so incessantly in his excitement, that even when the magpie, (who wanted, you know, to see the thing quietly and form his opinion, not to have everybody talking at once,) assaulted him and pulled a feather out of his tail, he could not be quiet. Sam's horse Widderin capered with delight, and Sam's dog Rover coursed far and wide before them, with joyful bark. So they three went off through the summer's day as happy as though all life were one great summer's holiday, and there were no storms below the horizon to rise and overwhelm them; through the grassy flat, where the quail whirred before them, and dropped again as if shot; across the low rolling forest land, where a million parrots fled whistling to and fro, like jewels in the sun; past the old stock-yard, past the sheep-wash hut, and then through forest which grew each moment more dense and lofty, along the faint and narrow track which led into one of the most abrupt and romantic gullies which pierce the Australian Alps.

All this became classic ground to them afterwards, and the causes which made it so were now gathering to their fulfilment, even now, while these three were making happy holiday together, little dreaming of what was to come. Afterwards, years after, they three came and looked on this valley again; not as now, with laughter and jokes, but silently, speaking in whispers, as though they feared to wake the dead.

The road they followed, suddenly rising from the forest, took over the shoulder of a rocky hill, and then, plunging down again, followed a little running creek, up to where a great ridge of slate, crossing the valley, hemmed them in on either side, leaving only room for the creek and the road. Following it further, the glen opened out, sweeping away right and left in broad curves, while straight before them, a quarter of a mile distant, there rose out of the low scrub and fern a mighty wall of limestone, utterly barring all further progress save in a single spot to the left, where the vast grey wall was split, giving a glimpse of another glen beyond. This great natural cleft was the limestone gate which they had come to see, and which was rendered the more wonderful by a tall pinnacle of rock, which stood in the centre of the gap about 300 feet in height, not unlike one of the same kind in Dovedale.

" I don't think I ever saw anything so beautiful," said Alice. " How fine that spire of rock is, shooting up from the feathered shrubs at the base! I will come here some day and try to draw it."

" Wait a minute," said Jim; " you have not seen half yet."

He led them through the narrow pass, among the great boulders which lined the creek. The instant they came beyond, a wind, icy cold, struck upon their cheeks, and Alice, dropping her reins, uttered a cry of awe and wonder, and Sam too exclaimed aloud; for before them, partly seen through crowded tree stems, and partly towering above the forest, lay a vast level wall of snow, flecked here and there by the purple shadow of some flying summer cloud.

A sight so vast and magnificent held them silent for a little; then suddenly, Jim, looking at Alice, saw that she was shivering.

" What is the matter, Alice, my dear?" he said; " let us come away: the snow-wind is too much for you."

" Oh! it is not that!" she said. " Somebody is walking over my grave."

" Oh, that's all!" said Jim; " they are always at it with me, in cold weather. Let 'em. It won't hurt, that I know of."

But they turned homeward, nevertheless; and coming through the rock walls again, Jim said,

" Sam, what was that battle the Doctor and you were reading about one day, and you told me all about it afterwards, you know?"

" Malplacquet?"

" No; something like that, though. Where they got bailed up among the rocks, you know, and fought till they were all killed."

" Thermopylæ?"

" Ah! This must be just such another place, I should think."

" Thermopylæ was by the sea-shore," said Alice.

" Now, I should imagine," said Sam, pointing to the natural glacis formed by the decay of the great wall which they had seen fronting them as they came up, " that a few determined men with rifles, posted among those fern-trees, could make a stand against almost any force."

" But, Sam," said Jim, " they might be cut up by cavalry. Horses could travel right up the face of the slope there. Now, suppose a gang of bushrangers in that fern-scrub; do you think an equal number of police could not turn them out of it? Why, I have seen the place where Moppy's gang turned and fought Desborough on the Macquarrie. It was stronger than this, and yet—you know what he did with them, only kept one small one for hanging, as he elegantly expressed it."

" But I ain't talking of bushrangers," said Sam. " I mean such fellows as the Americans in the War of Independence. See what a dance they led our troops with their bushfighting."

" I wonder if ever there will be a War of Independence here," said Alice.

" I know which side I should be on, if there was," said Sam.

" Which would that be ? " asked Jim.

" My dear friend," said Sam, testily, " how can you, an officer's son, ask me, an officer's son, such a question ? The King's (I beg pardon, the Queen's) side, of course."

" And so would I," said Jim, " if it came to that, you know."

" You would never have the honour of speaking to your sweet sister again, if you were not," said Alice.

" But I don't think those Americans were in the wrong ; do you, Miss Brentwood ? " said Sam.

" Why no ; I don't suppose that such a man as General Washington, for instance, would have had much to do with them if they had been."

" However," said Sam, " we are talking of what will never occur here. To begin with, we could never stand alone against a great naval power. They would shut us up here to starve. We have everything to lose, and nothing to gain by a separation. I would hardly like, myself, for the sake of a few extra pounds taxes, to sell my birthright as an Englishman."

" Conceive," said Alice, " being in some great European city, and being asked if you were British, having to say, No ! "

They were coming through the lower pass, and turned to look back on the beautiful rock-walled amphitheatre, sleeping peaceful and still under the afternoon sun. The next time (so it happened) that Sam and Jim looked at that scene together, was under very different circumstances. Now the fronds of the fern-trees were scarce moved in the summer's breeze, and all was silent as the grave. They saw it again ;—when every fern tuft blazed with musketry, and the ancient cliffs echoed with the shouts of fighting, and the screams of dying men and horses.

" It is very early," said Alice. " Let us ride to the left, and see the great waterfall you speak of, Jim."

It was agreed. Instead of going home they turned through the forest, and debouched on the plains about two miles above Garoopna, and, holding their course to the river, came to it at a place where a great trap dike, crossing, formed a waterfall, over which the river, now full with melting snow, fell in magnificent confusion. They stood watching the grand scene with delight for a short time, and then, crossing the river by a broad, shallow ford, held their way homeward, along the eastern and more level bank, sometimes reining up their horses to gaze into the tremendous glen below them, and

watch the river crawling on through many impediments, and beginning to show a golden light in its larger pools beneath the sloping,
westering sun.

Just as they sighted home, on the opposite side of the river, they
perceived two horsemen before them, evidently on the track between
Major Buckley's and Garoopna. They pushed on to " overhaul
them," and found that it was Doctor Mulhaus, whom they received
with boisterous welcome, and a tall, handsome young gentleman,
a stranger.

" A young gentleman, Sam," said the Doctor, " Mr. Halbert by
name, who arrived during your father's absence with letters of introduction. I begged him to follow your father over here, and, as his
own horse was knocked up, I mounted him at his own request on
Jezebel, he preferring her to all the horses in the paddock on account
of her beauty, after having been duly warned of her wickedness.
But Mr. Halbert seems of the Centaur species, and rather to enjoy
an extra chance of getting his neck broke."

Politeness to strangers was one of the first articles of faith in the
Buckley and Brentwood families : so the young folks were soon on
the best of terms.

" Are you from Sydney way, Mr. Halbert ?" said Sam.

" Indeed," said the young man, " I have only landed in the
country six weeks. I have got three years' leave of absence from
my regiment in India, and, if I can see a chance, I shall cut the
army and settle here."

" Oh ! " said Alice, " are you a soldier, Mr. Halbert ?"

" I have that honour, Miss Brentwood. I am a lieutenant in the
Bengal Horse Artillery."

" That is delightful. I am a soldier's daughter, and Mr. Buckley
here also, as you know, I suppose."

" A soldier's daughter, is he ? " said impudent Jim. " A very
fine girl, too ! "

Sam, and Jim too, had some disrespectful ideas about soldier's
riding qualities ; Sam could not help saying,—

" I hope you will be careful with that mare, Mr. Halbert; I
should not like a guest of ours to be damaged. She's a desperate
brute,—I'm afraid of her myself."

" I think I know the length of her ladyship's foot," said Halbert,
laughing good-naturedly.

As they were speaking, they were passing through a narrow way
in a wattle scrub. Suddenly a blundering kangaroo, with Rover in
full chase, dashed right under the mare's nose and set her plunging
furiously. She tried to wheel round, but, finding herself checked,
reared up three or four times, and at last seemed to stand on her
hind legs, almost overbalancing herself.

Halbert sat like a statue till he saw there was a real chance of her falling back on him; then he slipped his right foot quickly out of the stirrup, and stood with his left toe in the iron, balancing himself till she was quieter; then he once more threw his leg across the saddle, and regained his seat, laughing.

Jim clapped his hands; "By Jove, Sam, we must get some of these army men to teach us to ride, after all!"

"We must do so," said Sam. "If that had been you or I, Jim, with our rough clumsy hands, we should have had the mare back atop of us."

"Indeed," said Alice, "you are a splendid rider, Mr. Halbert: but don't suppose, from Mr. Buckley's account of himself, that he can't ride well; I assure you we are all very proud of him. He can sit some bucking horses which very few men will attempt to mount."

"And that same bucking, Miss Brentwood," said Halbert, "is just what puzzles me utterly. I got on a bucking horse in Sydney the other day, and had an ignominious tumble in the sale-yard, to everybody's great amusement."

"We must give one another lessons, then, Mr. Halbert," said Sam;—"but I can see already, that you have a much finer hand than I."

Soon after they got home, where the rest of the party were watching for them, wondering at their late absence. Halbert was introduced to the Major by the Doctor, who said, "I deliver over to you a guest, a young conqueror from the Himalayas, and son of an old brother warrior. If he now breaks his neck horse-riding, his death will not be at my door; I can now eat my dinner in peace."

After dinner the three young ones, Sam, Alice, and Jim, gathered round the fire, leaving Halbert with the Major and the Captain talking military, and the Doctor looking over an abstruse mathematical calculation, with which Captain Brentwood was not altogether satisfied. Alice and Sam sat in chairs side by side, like Christians, but Jim lay on the floor, between the two, like a blackfellow; they talked in a low voice about the stranger.

"I say," said Jim, "ain't he a handsome chap, and can't he ride? I dare say he's a devil to fight, too,—hear him tell how they pounded away at those Indians in that battle. I expect they'd have made a general of him before now, only he's too young. Dad says he's a very distinguished young officer. Alice, my dear, you should see the wound he's got, a great seam all down his side. I saw it when he was changing his shirt in my room before dinner."

"Poor fellow!" said Alice; "I like him very much. Don't you, Mr. Buckley?"

"I like him exceedingly;—I hope he'll stop with us," continued Jim.

"And I also," said Sam, "but what shall we do to-morrow?"

" Let's have a hunt," said Jim. " Halbert, have you ever been kangaroo hunting ? "

" Never !—I want to go ! "

" Well, we can have a capital hunt to-morrow : Sam has got his dog Fly here, and I'll take one of my best dogs, and we'll have a good run, I dare say."

" I shall come, too," said Alice : " that is," added she, looking shyly at Sam, " if you would be kind enough to take care of me, and let Mr. Halbert and Jim do the riding. But I'm afraid I shall be sadly in your way."

" If you don't go," said Sam, " I shall stay at home : now then ! "

At this minute, the housekeeper came in bearing jugs and glasses. " Eleanor," said Jim, " Is Jerry round ? "

" Yes, sir ; he's coiled somewhere in the woodhouse," said she.

" Just rouse him out and send him in."

" Who is this Jerry who coils in woodhouses ? " said Halbert.

" A tame black belonging to us. He is great at all sorts of hunting ; I want to see if he can find us a flying doe for to-morrow."

Jerry entered, and advanced with perfect self-possession towards the fire. He was a tall savage, with a big black beard, and wavy hair like a Cornishman. He was dressed in an old pair of dandy riding breeches of Jim's, which reached a short way below the knees, fitting closely, and a blue check shirt rolled up above the elbow showing his lean wiry forearm, seamed and scarred with spear wounds and bruises. He addressed nobody, but kept his eyes wandering all over the room ; at length he said, looking at the ceiling,—

" Cobbon thirsty this fellow : you got a drop of brandy ? "

" Jerry," said Jim, having produced the brandy, " you make a light kangaroo."

" All about plenty kangaroo," said Jerry.

" Yowi ; * but mine want it big one flying doe."

" Ah-h-h ! Mine make a light flying doe along a stockyard this morning ; close by, along a fent, you see ! "

" That'll do," says Jim. " We'll be up round the old stockyard after breakfast to-morrow. You, Jerry, come with us."

It was a fresh breezy autumn morning in April, when the four sallied forth, about nine o'clock, for their hunt. The old stockyard stood in the bush, a hundred yards from the corner of the big paddock fence, and among low rolling ranges and gullies, thickly timbered with gum, cherry, and sheoak : a thousand parrots flew swiftly in flocks, whistling and screaming from tree to tree, while wattled-birds and numerous other honey-eaters clustered on the flowering basksias. The spur-winged plover and the curlew ran swiftly among the grass,

* Yowi means yes. But Mr. Hamlyn is a little incorrect in using it here. It is more of a Moreton Bay word.—H. K.

R

and on a tall dead tree white cockatoos and blue cranes watched the intruders curiously.

Alice and Sam rode together soberly, and before them were Halbert and Jim, girt up, ready for the chase. Before them, again, was the active blackfellow, holding the dogs in a leash,—two tall hounds, bred of foxhound and greyhound, with a dash of colley.

A mob of kangaroos crosses their path, but they are all small; so the dogs, though struggling fiercely, are still held tight by Jerry: now he crosses a little ridge before them and looks down into the gully beyond, holding up his hand.

The two young men gather up their reins and settle themselves in their seats. "Now, Halbert," says Jim, "sit fast and mind the trees."

They ride up to the blackfellow; through the low wattles, they can see what is in the gully before them, though the dogs cannot.

"Baal, flying doe this one," says Jerry in a whisper. "Old man this fellow, cobbon matong,* mine think it."

A great six-foot kangaroo was standing about two hundred yards from them, staring stupidly about him.

"Let go, Jerry," said Jim. The dogs released, sprang forward, and, in an instant, saw their quarry, which, with a loud puff of alarm, bounded away up the opposite slope at full speed, taking twenty feet at each spring.

Halbert and Jim dashed off after the dogs, who had got a good start of them, and were laying themselves out to their work right gallantly; Sam's dog, Fly, slightly leading. Both dogs were close on the game, and Halbert said,—

"We are going to have a short run, I'm afraid."

"Talk about that twenty minutes hence," said Jim, settling to his work.

Over range after range they hold their headlong course. Now a bandicoot scuttles away from under their feet to hide in his hollow log; now a mob of terrified cattle huddle together as they sweep by; now they are flying past a shepherd's hut, and the mother runs out to snatch up a child, and bear him out of harm's way, after they are safe past. A puppy, three weeks old, joins the chase with heart and soul, but "caves in" at about fifty yards, and sits him down to bark. Now they are rushing on through a broad flat, with another great range before them. Still always the grey bounding figure holds on, through sunlight and shadow, with the dogs grim and steadfast close in his wake.

The work begins to tell on the horses. Fat Jezebel, who could hardly be held at first, now is none the worse for a little spur; and Jim's lean, long-legged horse, seems to consider that the entertain-

* "Very strong."

ment ought to conclude shortly. "Well done, Fly!" he shouts; "bravely tried, my girl!" She had drawn herself ahead, and made a bold strike at the kangaroo, but missed him. Now the other dog, Bolt, tries it, but without luck; and now they have both dropped a little back, and seem in for another mile or so.

Well done, lass!—there she goes again! With a furious effort she pushes ahead, and seizes the flying beast by the hock—this time with some luck, for down he goes in a cloud of dust and broken sticks, and both the dogs are on him at once. Now he is up again and running, but feebly. And see, what is the matter with the young dog? He runs on, but keeps turning, snapping fiercely at his side, and his footsteps are marked with blood. Poor lad! he has got a bad wound in that last tumble,—the kangaroo has ripped up his flank with a kick from his hind foot. But now the chase is over,—the hunted beast has turned, and is at bay against a tree, Fly standing before him, waiting for assistance, snarling fiercely.

They pulled up. Jim took out a pistol and presented it to Halbert.

"Thank you," said he. "Hair trigger?"

"Yes."

He balanced it for a second, and in another the kangaroo was lying quivering on the ground, shot through the heart.

"Well done!" said Jim. "Now I must look to this dog."

All his flank along the ribs was laid open, and Jim, producing a needle and thread, proceeded to sew it up.

"Will you let me do that for you?" said Halbert.

"I wish you would. I'm fond of the poor thing, and my hand shakes. You've seen the surgeons at work, I expect."

"Yes, indeed." And he tenderly and carefully stitched up the dog's side, while Jim held him.

"What do we do with the game?" said he.

"Oh, Jerry will be along on our tracks presently," said Jim "He brings me the tail, and does what he likes with the rest. I wonder where Sam and Alice are?"

"Oh, they are right enough," said Halbert, laughing. "I dare say they are not very anxious about the kangaroo, or anything else. That's 'a case,' I suppose?"

"Well, I hope it is," said Jim; "but you see I don't know. Girls are so odd."

"Perhaps he has never asked her."

"No; I don't think he has. I wish he would. You are not married, are you?"

"My God — no!" said Halbert, "nor ever shall be."

"Never?"

"Never, Jim. Let me tell you a story as we ride home. You and I shall be good friends, I know. I like you already, though we have only known one another two days. I can see well what you are made of. They say it eases a man's mind to tell his grief. I wish it would mine. Well; before I left England I had secretly engaged myself to marry a beautiful girl, very much like your sister, a governess in my brother-in-law's family. I went off to join my regiment, and left her there with my sister and her husband, Lord Carstone, who treated her as if she was already one of the family—God bless them! Two years ago my father died, and I came into twenty thousand pounds; not much, but enough to get married on in India, particularly as I was getting on in my profession. So I wrote to her to come out to me. She sailed in the Assam, for Calcutta, but the ship never arrived. She was spoken off the Mauritius, but never seen after. The underwriters have paid up her insurance, and everyone knows now that the Assam went down in a typhoon, with all hands."

"God bless you!" said Jim, "I am very sorry for that."

"Thank you. I have come here for change of scene more than anything, but I think I shall go back soon."

"I shall come with you," said Jim. "I have determined to be a soldier, and I know the governor has interest enough to get me into some regiment in India." (I don't believe he had ever thought of it before that morning.)

"If you are determined, he might. His services in India were too splendid to have been forgotten yet."

"I wonder," said Jim, "if he will let me go? I'd like to see Alice married first."

They jogged on in silence for a little, and slowly, on account of the wounded dogs. Then Jim said,—

"Well, and how did you like your sport?"

"Very much indeed; but I thought bush-riding was harder work. We have only had one or two leaps over fallen logs altogether."

"There ain't much leaping, that's a fact. I suppose you have been fox-hunting?"

"My father was a master of hounds," replied Halbert. "On the first day of the season, when the hounds met at home, there would be two hundred horsemen on our terrace, fifty of them, at least, in pink. It was a regular holiday for all the country round. Such horses, too. My father's horse, the Elk, was worth £300, and there were better horses than him to be seen in the field, I promise you."

"And all after a poor little fox!"

"You don't know Charley, I can see," said Halbert. "Poor little fox, indeed! Why, it's as fair a match between the best-tried pack of hounds in England, and an old dog-fox, as one would wish to see. And as hard work as it is to ride up to them, even without a stiff fence at every two hundred yards, to roll you over on your head, if your horse is blown or clumsy. Just consider how many are run, and how few are killed. I consider a fox to be the noblest quarry in the world. His speed, courage, and cunning are wonderful. I have seen a fox run fifteen miles as the crow flies, and only three of us in at the death. That's what I call sport."

"So do I, by Jove!" said Jim. "You have some good sport in India, too?"

"Yes. Pig-sticking is pretty—very pretty, I may say, if you have two or three of the right sort with you. All the Griffins ought to hunt together, though. There was a young fellow, a King's-officer, and a nobleman, too, came out with us the other day, and rode well forward, but as the pig turned he contrived to spear my horse through the pastern. He was full of apologies, and I was outwardly highly polite and indifferent, but internally cursing him up hill and down dale. I went home and had the horse shot; but when I got up next morning, there was a Syce leading up and down a magnificent Australian, a far finer beast than the one which I had lost, which my Lord had sent up to replace my unfortunate nag. I went down to his quarters and refused to accept it; but he forced me in the end, and it gave me a good lesson about keeping my temper over an unavoidable accident, which I don't mean to forget. Don't you think it was prettily done?"

"Yes, I do," said Jim; "but you see these noblemen are so rich that they can afford to do that sort of thing, where you or I couldn't. But I expect they are very good fellows on the whole."

"There are just as large a proportion of good noblemen as there are of any other class—more than that you have no right to expect. I'm a liberal, as my father was before me, and a pretty strong one too; but I think that a man with sixty thousand acres, and a seat in the House of Lords, is entitled to a certain sort of respect. A Grand Seigneur is a very capital institution if he will only stay on his estates some part of the year."

"Ay!" said Jim; who was a shrewd fellow in his way. "They know that here, well enough; look at our Macarthurs and Went-worths,—but then they must be men, and not snobs, as the governor says."

When they got home, they found Sam and Alice sitting in the verandah as comfortable as you please.

"Well," said Jim, "you are a nice lot! This is what you call kangaroo-hunting!"

"Oh, you went too fast for us. Have you killed?"

"Yes! out by the big swamp."

"You have taken your time to get home then."

"Poor Bolt is cut up, and we couldn't go out of a walk. Now give us something to eat, will you, Alice?"

"Well, ring the bell and we will have lunch."

But just as Jim rang the bell, there was a loud voice outside, and the three young men went out to see who it was, and found two horsemen in front of the door.

One, who was still sitting on his horse, was a dark-haired slight young man, Charles Hawker in fact, whom we know already, but the other, who had dismounted, and was leaning against his horse, was a highbred, delicate little fellow, to whom we have yet to be introduced.

He was a slight lad, perhaps not more than eighteen, with one of the pleasantest, handsomest faces of his own that you could wish to see, and also a very intellectual look about him, which impressed you at once with the idea that if he lived he would have made some sort of figure in life. He was one of the greatest dandies, also, in those parts, and after the longest ride used to look as if he had been turned out of a bandbox. On the present occasion he had on two articles of dress which attracted Jim's attention amazingly. The first was a new white hat, which was a sufficiently remarkable thing in those parts at that time; and the second, a pair of yellow leather riding-trousers.

"Why, Cecil Mayford!" said Sam, "how do you do? Charley, how are you? Just in time for lunch. Come in."

Jim was walking round and round Cecil without speaking a word. At last the latter said, "How do *you* do, James Brentwood?"

"How do your breeches do, Cecil?" answered Jim; "that is a much more important question. By the bye, let me introduce you to Mr. Halbert. Also, allow me to have the honour to inform you that my sister Alice is come home from school."

"I am aware of that, and am come over to pay my respects. Sam, leave me alone. If I were to disarrange my dress before I was presented to Miss Brentwood, I would put a period to my existence. Jim, my dear soul, come in and present me. Don't all you fellows come mobbing in, you know."

So Jim took Cecil in, and the other young fellows lounged about the door in the sun. "Where have you come from, Charley?" asked Sam.

"I have been staying at the Mayfords'; and this morning, hearing that you and your father were here, we thought we would come over and stay a bit."

"By the bye," said Sam, "Ellen Mayford was to have come home from Sydney the same time as Alice Brentwood, or thereabouts. Pray, is she come?"

"Oh, yes!" said Charles; "she is come this fortnight, or more."

"What sort of a girl has she grown to be?"

"Well, *I* call her an uncommonly pretty girl. A very nice girl indeed, I should say. Have you heard the news from the north?"

"No!"

"Bushrangers! Nine or ten devils, loose on the upper Macquarrie, caught the publican at Marryong alone in the bush; he had been an overlooker, or some such thing, in old times, so they stripped him, tied him up, gave him four dozen, and left him to the tender mercies of the blowflies, in consequence of which he was found dead next day, with the cords at his wrists cutting down to the bone with the struggles he made in his agony."

"Whew!" said Sam. "We are going to have some of the old-fashioned work over again. Let us hope Desborough will get hold of them before they come this way."

"Some of our fellow-countrymen," said Halbert, "are, it seems to me, more detestably ferocious than savages, when they once get loose."

"Much of a muchness—no better, and perhaps no worse," said Sam. "All men who act entirely without any law in their actions arrive at much the same degree, whether white or black."

"And will this Captain Desborough, whom you speak of, have much chance of catching these fellows?" asked Halbert.

"They will most likely disperse on his approach if he takes any force against them," said Sam. "I heard him say, myself, that the best way was to tempt them to stay and show fight, by taking a small force against them, as our admirals used to do to the French, in the war. By the bye, how is Tom Troubridge? He is quite a stranger to me. I have only seen him twice since he was back from Port Phillip."

"He is off again now, after some rams, up to the north."

"I hope he won't fall in with the bushrangers. Anybody with him?"

"William Lee," answered Charles.

"A good escort. There is lunch going in,—come along."

CHAPTER XXIX.

SAM MEETS WITH A RIVAL, AND HOW HE TREATED HIM.

THAT week one of those runs upon the Captain's hospitality took place which are common enough in the bush, and, although causing a temporary inconvenience, are generally as much enjoyed by the entertainer as entertained. Everybody during this next week came to see them, and nobody went back again. So by the end of the week there were a dozen or fourteen guests assembled, all uninvited, and apparently bent on making a good long stay of it.

Alice, who had expected to be rather put out, conducted everything with such tact and dignity that Mrs. Buckley remarked to Mrs.

Mayford, when they were alone together, "that she had never seen such beauty and such charming domestic grace combined, and that he would be a lucky young fellow who got her for a wife."

"Well, yes, I should be inclined to say so too," answered Mrs. Mayford. "Rather much of the boarding-school as yet, but that will wear off, I dare say. I don't think the young lady will go very long without an offer. Pray, have you remarked anything, my dear madam?"

Yes, Mrs. Buckley had remarked something on her arrival the day before yesterday. She had remarked Sam and Alice come riding over the paddock, and Sam, by way of giving a riding-lesson, holding the little white hand in his, teaching it (the dog!) to hold the reins properly. And on seeing Alice she had said to herself, "That will do." But all this was not what Mrs. Mayford meant, —in fact, these two good ladies were at cross-purposes.

"Well, I thought I did," replied Mrs. Buckley, referring to Sam. "But one must not be premature. They are both very young, and may not know their own minds."

"They seem as if they did," said Mrs. Mayford. "Look there!" Outside the window they saw something which gave Mrs. Buckley a sort of pang, and made Mrs. Mayford laugh.

There was no one in the garden visible but Cecil Mayford and Alice, and she was at that moment busily engaged in pinning a rose into his buttonhole. "The audacious girl!" thought Mrs. Buckley; "I am afraid she will be a daughter of debate among us. I wish she had not come home." While Mrs. Mayford continued,—

"I am far from saying, mind you, my dear Mrs. Buckley, that I don't consider Cecil might do far better for himself. The girl is pretty, very pretty, and will have money. But she is too decided, my dear. Fancy a girl of her age expressing opinions! Why, if I had ventured to express opinions at her age, I——I don't know what my father would have said."

"Depend very much on what sort of opinions they were; wouldn't it?" said Mrs. Buckley.

"No; I mean any opinions. Girls ought to have no opinions at all. There, last night when the young men were talking all together, she must needs get red in the face and bridle up, and say, 'She thought an Englishman who wasn't proud of Oliver Cromwell was unworthy of the name of an Englishman.' Her very words, I assure you. Why, if my daughter Ellen had dared to express herself in that way about a murderous Papist, I'd have slapped her face."

"I don't think Cromwell was a Papist; was he?" said Mrs. Buckley.

"A Dissenter, then, or something of that sort," said Mrs. Mayford. "But that don't alter the matter. What I don't like to see is a young girl thrusting her oar in in that way. However, I shall make no opposition, I can assure you. Cecil is old enough to choose for himself, and a mother's place is to submit. Oh, no, I assure you, whatever my opinions may be, I shall offer no opposition."

"I shouldn't think you would," said Mrs. Buckley, as the other left the room : "rather a piece of luck for your boy to marry the handsomest and richest girl in the country. However, madam, if you think I am going to play a game of chess with you for that girl, or any other girl, why, you are mistaken."

And yet it was very provoking. Ever since she had begun to hear from various sources how handsome and clever Alice was, she had made up her mind that Sam should marry her, and now to be put out like this by people whom they had actually introduced into the house ! It would be a great blow to Sam too. She wished he had never seen her. She would sooner have lost a limb than caused his honest heart one single pang. But, after all, it might be only a little flirtation between her and Cecil. Girls would flirt; but then there would be Mrs. Mayford manœuvring and scheming her heart out, while she, Agnes Buckley, was constrained by her principles only to look on and let things take their natural course.

Now, there arose a coolness between Agnes Buckley and the Mayfords, mother and son, which was never made up—never, oh, never ! Not very many months after this she would have given ten thousand pounds to have been reconciled to the kind-hearted old busy-body ; but then it was too late.

But now, going out into the garden, she found the Doctor busy planting some weeds he had found in the bush, in a quiet corner, with an air of stealth, intending to privately ask the gardener to see after them till he could fetch them away. The magpie, having seen from the window a process of digging and burying going on, had attended in his official capacity, standing behind the Doctor, and encouraging him every now and then with a dance, or a few flute-like notes of music. I need hardly mention that the moment the Doctor's back was turned the bird rooted up every one of the plants, and buried them in some secret spot of his own, where they lie, I believe, till this day.

To the Doctor she told the whole matter, omitting nothing, and then asked his advice. "I suppose," she said, "you will only echo my own determination of doing nothing at all ? "

"Quite so, my dear madam. If she loves Sam, she will marry him ; if she don't, he is better without her."

"That is true," said Mrs. Buckley. "I hope she will have good taste enough to choose my boy."

"I hope so too, I am sure," said the Doctor. "But we must not be very furious if she don't. Little Cecil Mayford is both handsomer and cleverer **than** Sam. We must not forget that, you know."

That evening was the first thoroughly unhappy evening, I think, that Sam ever passed in his life. I am inclined to imagine that his digestion was out of order. If any of my readers ever find themselves in the same state of mind that he was in that night, let them be comforted by considering that there is always a remedy at hand, before which evil thoughts and evil tempers of all kinds fly like mist before the morning sun. How many serious family quarrels, marriages out of spite, alterations of wills, and secessions to the Church of Rome, might have been prevented by a gentle dose of blue pill! What awful instances of chronic dyspepsia are presented to our view by the immortal bard in the characters of Hamlet and Othello! I look with awe on the digestion of such a man as the present King of Naples. Banish dyspepsia and spirituous liquors from society, and you would have no crime, or at least so little that you would not consider it worth mentioning.

However, to return to Sam. He, Halbert, Charles Hawker, and Jim had been away riding down an emu, and had stayed out all day. But Cecil Mayford, having made excuse to stay at home, had been making himself in many ways agreeable to Alice, and at last had attended her on a ride, and on his return had been rewarded with a rose, as we saw. The first thing Sam caught sight of when he came home was Alice and Cecil walking up and down the garden very comfortably together, talking and laughing. He did not like to see this. He dreaded Cecil's powers of entertainment too much, and it made him angry to hear how he was making Alice laugh. Then, when the four came into the house, this offending couple took no notice of them at all, but continued walking up and down in the garden, till Jim, who, not being in love, didn't care twopence whether his sister came in or not, went out to the verandah, and called out "Hi!"

"What now?" said Alice, turning round.

"Why, we're come home," said Jim, "and I want you."

"Then you won't get me, impudence," said Alice, and began walking up and down again. But not long after, having to come in, she just said, "How do, Mr. Halbert?" and passed on, never speaking to Sam. Now there was no reason why she should have spoken to him, but "Good evening, Mr. Buckley," would not have hurt anybody. And now in came Cecil, with that unlucky rose, and Jim immediately began,—

"Hallo, Cis, where did you get your flower?"

"Ah, that's a secret," said Cecil, with an affected look.

"No secret at all," said Alice, coming back. "I gave it to him. He had the civility to stay and take me out for a ride, instead of going to run down those poor pretty emus. And that is his reward. I pinned it into his coat for him." And out she went again.

Sam was very sulky, but he couldn't exactly say with whom. With himself more than anybody, I believe.

"Like Cecil's consummate impudence!" was his first thought; but after he had gone to his room to dress, his better nature came to him, and before dinner came on he was his old self again, unhappy still, but not sulky, and determined to be just.

"What right have I to be angry, even suppose she does come to care more for him than for me? What can be more likely? he is more courtly, amusing, better-looking, they say, and certainly cleverer; oh, decidedly cleverer. He might as well make me his enemy as I make him mine. No; dash it all! He has been like a brother to me ever since he was so high, and I'll be d——d if there shan't be fair play between us two, though I should go into the army through it. But I'll watch, and see how things go."

So he watched at dinner and afterwards, but saw little to comfort him. Saw one thing, nay, two things, most clearly. One was, that Cecil Mayford was madly in love with Alice; and the other was, that poor Cecil was madly jealous of Sam. He treated him differently to what he had ever done before, as though on that evening he had first found his rival. Nay, he became almost rude, so that once Jim looked suddenly up, casting his shrewd blue eyes first on one and then on the other, as though to ask what the matter was. But Sam only said to himself, "Let him go on. Let him say what he will. He is beside himself now, and some day he will be sorry. He shall have fair play, come what will."

But it was hard for our lad to keep his temper sometimes. It was hard to see another man sitting alongside of her all the evening, paying her all those nameless little attentions which somehow, however unreasonably, he had brought himself to think were his right, and no one else's, to pay. Hard to wonder and wonder whether or no he had angered her, and if so, how? Halbert, good heart, saw it all, and sitting all the evening by Sam, made himself so agreeable, that for a time even Alice herself was forgotten. But then, when he looked up, and saw Cecil still beside her, and her laughing and talking so pleasantly, while he was miserable and unhappy, the old chill came on his heart again, and he thought—was the last happy week only a deceitful gleam of sunshine, and should he ever take his old place beside her again?

Once or twice more during the evening Cecil was almost insolent to him, but still his resolution was strong.

"If he is a fool, why should I be a fool? I will wait and see if he can win her. If he does, why there is India for me. If he does not, I will try again. Only I will not quarrel with Cecil, because he is blinded. Little Cecil, who used to bathe with me, and ride pickaback round the garden! No; he shall have fair play. By Jove, he shall have fair play, if I die for it."

And he had some little comfort in the evening. When they had all risen to go to bed, and were standing about in confusion lighting candles, he suddenly found Alice by his side, who said in a sweet, low, musical tone,—

" Can you forgive me ?"

" What have I to forgive, my dear young lady ? " he said softly. " I was thinking of asking your forgiveness for some unknown fault."

" I have behaved so ill to you to-day," she said, " the first of my new friends ! I was angry at your going out after our poor emus, and I was cross to you when you came home. Do let us be friends again."

There was a chance for a reconciliation ! But here was Cecil Mayford thrusting between them with a lit candle just at the wrong moment ; and she gave him such a sweet smile, and such kind thanks, that Sam felt nearly as miserable as ever.

And next morning everything went wrong again. Whether it was merely coquetry, or whether she was angry at their hunting the emus, or whether she for a time preferred Cecil's company, I know not ; but she, during the next week, neglected Sam altogether, and refused to sit beside him, making a most tiresome show of being unable to get on without Cecil Mayford, who squired her here, there, and everywhere, in the most provoking fashion.

But it so happened that the Doctor and the Major sat up later than the others that night, taking a glass of punch together before the fire, and the Major said, abruptly,—

" There will be mischief among the young fellows about that girl. It is a long while since I saw one man look at another as young Mayford did at our Sam to-night. I wish she were out of the way. Sam and Mayford are both desperately in love with her, and one must go to the wall. I wish that boy of mine was keener ; he stayed aloof from her all to-night."

" Don't you see his intention ? " said the Doctor. " I am very much mistaken if I do not. He is determined to leave the field clear for all comers, unless she herself makes some sort of advances to him. ' If she prefers Mayford,' says Sam to himself, ' in the way she appears to, why, she is welcome to him, and I can go home as soon as I am assured of it.' And go home he would, too, and never say one word of complaint to any living soul."

" What a clear, brave, honest soul that lad has ! " said the Major.

" Truly," said the Doctor, " I only know one man who is his equal."

" And who is he ? "

" His father. Good night : good dreams ! "

   *   *   *   *   *

So Sam kept to his resolution of finding out whether or no Alice was likely to prefer Cecil to him. And, for all his watching and puzzling, he couldn't. He had never confided one word of all this to his mother, and yet she knew it all as well as he.

Meanwhile, Cecil was quite changed. He almost hated Sam, and seldom spoke to him, and at the same time hated himself for it. He grew pale, too, and never could be persuaded to join any ; port whatever; while Sam, being content to receive only a few words in the day from My Lady, worked harder than ever, both in the yards and riding. All day he and Jim would be working like horses, with Halbert for their constant companion, and, half an hour before dinner, would run whooping down to the river for their bathe, and then come in clean, happy, hungry—so full of life and youth, that in these sad days of deficient grinders, indigestion, and liver, I can hardly realize that once I myself was as full of blood and as active and hearty as any of them.

There was much to do the week that Alice and Sam had their little tiff. The Captain was getting in the "scrubbers," cattle which had been left, under the not very careful rule of the Donovans, to run wild in the mountains. These beasts had now to be got in, and put through such processes as cattle are born to undergo. The Captain and the Major were both fully stiff for working in the yards, but their places were well supplied by Sam and Jim. The two fathers, with the assistance of the stockman, and sometimes of the sons, used to get them into the yards, and then the two young men would go to work in a style I have never seen surpassed by any two of the same age. Halbert would sometimes go into the yard and assist, or rather hinder; but he had to give up just when he was beginning to be of some use, as the exertion was too violent for an old wound he had.

Meanwhile Cecil despised all these things, and, though a capital hand among cattle, was now grown completely effeminate, hanging about the house all day, making, in fact, " rather a fool of himself about that girl," as Halbert thought, and thought, besides, " What a confounded fool she will make of herself if she takes that little dandy !—not that he isn't a very gentlemanlike little fellow, but that Sam is worth five hundred of him."

One day, it so happened that every one was out but Cecil and Alice ; and Alice, who had been listening to the noises at the stock-yard a long while, suddenly proposed to go there.

" I have never been," she said ; " I should so like to go ! I know I am not allowed, but you need not betray me, and I am sure the others won't. I should so like to see what they are about !"

" I assure you, Miss Brentwood, that it is not a fit place for a lady."

" Why not ?"

Cecil blushed scarlet. If women only knew what awkward questions they ask sometimes! In this instance he made an ass of himself, for he hesitated and stammered.

"Come along!" said she; "you are going to say that it is dangerous—(nothing was further from his thoughts); I must learn to face a little danger, you know. Come along."

"I am afraid," said Cecil, "that Jim will be very angry with me;" which was undoubtedly very likely.

"Never mind Jim," she said; "come along."

So they went, and in the rush and confusion of the beasts' feet got to the yard unnoticed. Sam and Jim were inside, and Halbert was perched upon the rails; she came close behind him and peeped through.

She was frightened. Close before her was Sam, hatless, in shirt and breeches only, almost unrecognisable, grimed with sweat, dust, and filth beyond description. He had been nearly horned that morning, and his shirt was torn from his armpit downwards, showing rather more of a lean muscular flank than would have been desirable in a drawing-room. He stood there with his legs wide apart, and a stick about eight feet long and as thick as one's wrist in his hand; while before him, crowded into a corner of the yard, were a mob of infuriated, terrified cattle. As she watched, one tried to push past him and get out of the yard; he stepped aside and let it go. The next instant a lordly young bull tried the same game, but he was "wanted;" so, just as he came nearly abreast of Sam, he received a frightful blow on the nose from the stick, which turned him.

But only for a moment. The maddened beast shaking his head with a roar rushed upon Sam like a thunderbolt, driving him towards the side of the yard. He stepped on one side rapidly, and then tumbled himself bodily through the rails, and fell with his fine brown curls in the dust, right at the feet of poor Alice, who would have screamed, but could not find the voice.

Jim and Halbert roared with laughter, and Sam, picking himself up, was beginning to join as loud as anybody, when he saw Alice, looking very white and pale, and went towards her.

"I hope you haven't been frightened by that evil-disposed bull, Miss Brentwood," he said pleasantly; "you must get used to that sort of work."

"Hallo, sister!" shouted Jim; "what the deuce brings you here? I thought you were at home at your worsted work. You should have seen what we were at, Cecil, before you brought her up. Now, miss, just mount that rail alongside of Halbert, and keep quiet."

"Oh, do let me go home, Jim dear; I am so frightened!"

"Then you must learn not to be frightened," he said. "Jump up now!"

But meanwhile the bull had the best of it, and had got out of the yard. A long lithe lad, stationed outside on horseback, was in full chase, and Jim, leaping on one of the horses tied to the rails, started off to his assistance. The two chased the unhappy bull as a pair of greyhounds chase a hare, with their whips cracking as rapidly and as loudly as you would fire a revolver. After an excursion of about a mile into the forest, the beast was turned and brought towards the yard. Twice he turned and charged the lad, with the same success. The cunning old stockhorse wheeled round or sprang aside, and the bull went blundering into empty space with two fourteen-foot stock-whips playing on his unlucky hide like rain. At length he was brought in again, and one by one those entitled to freedom were passed out by Sam, and others reserved unto a day of wrath—all but one cow with her calf.

All this time Alice had sat by Halbert. Cecil had given no assistance, for Jim would have done anything rather than press a guest into the service. Halbert asked her, what she thought of the sport?

"Oh, it is horrible," she said. "I should like to go home. I hope it is all over."

"Nearly," said Halbert; "that cow and calf have got to go out. Don't get frightened now; watch your brother and Buckley."

It was a sight worth watching; Sam and Jim advanced towards the maddened beasts to try and get the cow to bolt. The cattle were huddled up at the other end of the yard, and having been so long in hand, were getting dangerous. Once or twice young beasts had tried to pass, but had been driven back by the young men, with a courage and dexterity which the boldest matador in Spain could not have surpassed. Cecil Mayford saw, with his well-accustomed eye, that matters were getting perilous, and placed himself at the rails, holding one ready to slip if the beasts should break. In a moment, how or why none could tell, they made a sudden rush: Jim was borne back, dealing blows about him like a Paladin, and Sam was down, rolled over and over in the dust, just at Alice's feet.

Half-a-dozen passed right over him as he lay. Jim had made good his retreat from the yard, and Cecil had quietly done just the right thing: put up the rail he held, and saved the day's work. The cattle were still safe, but Sam lay there in the dust, motionless.

Before any of them had appreciated what had happened, Alice was down, and, seizing Sam by the shoulders, had dragged him to the fence. Halbert, horrified to see her actually in the presence of the cattle, leaped after her, put Sam through the rails, and lifted her up to her old post on the top. In another instant the beasts swept furiously round the yard, just over the place where they had been standing.

They gathered round Sam, and for an instant thought he was

dead; but just as Jim hurriedly knelt down, and raising his head began to untie his handkerchief, Sam uprose, and, shaking himself and dusting his clothes, said,—

" If it had been any other beast which knocked me down but that poley heifer, I should have been hurt; " and then said that " it was bathing-time, and they must look sharp to be in time for dinner: " three undeniable facts, showing that, although he was a little unsteady on his legs, his intellect had in nowise suffered.

And Halbert, glancing at Alice, saw something in her face that made him laugh; and dressing for dinner in Jim's room, he said to that young gentleman,—

" Unless there are family reasons against it, Jim, which of course I can't speak about, you know, I should say you would have Sam for your brother-in-law in a very short time."

" Do you really think so, now? " said Jim; " I rather fancied she had taken up with Cecil. I like Sam's fist, mind you, better than Cecil's whole body, though he is a good little fellow, too."

" She has been doing that, I think, rather to put Sam on his mettle; for I think he was taking things too easy with her at first; but now, if Cecil has any false hopes, he may give them up; the sooner the better. No woman who was fancy free could stand seeing that noble head of Sam's come rolling down in the dust at her feet; and what courage and skill he exhibited, too! Talk of bull-fights! I have seen one. Bah! it is like this nail-brush to a gold watch, to what I saw to-day. Sam, sir, has won a wife by cattle-drafting."

" If that is the case," said Jim, pensively brushing his hair, " I am very glad that Cecil's care for his fine clothes prevented his coming into the yard; for he is one of the bravest, coolest hands among cattle, I know; he beats me."

" Then he beats a precious good fellow, Jim. A man who could make such play as you did to-day, with a stick, ought to have nothing but a big three-foot of blue steel in his hand, and her Majesty's commission to use it against her enemies."

" That will come," said Jim, " the day after Sam has got the right to look after Alice; not before; the governor is too fond of his logarithms."

When Sam came to dress for dinner he found that he was bruised all over, and had to go to the Captain for " shin plaster," as he called it.

Captain Brentwood had lately been trying homœopathy, which in his case, there being nothing the matter with him, was a decided success. He doctored Sam with Arnica externally, and gave him the five-hundredth of a grain of something to swallow; but what made Sam forget his bruises quicker than these dangerous and violent remedies, was the delightful change in Alice's behaviour.

She was so agreeable that evening, that he was in the seventh heaven; the only drawback to his happiness being poor Cecil Mayford's utter distraction and misery. Next morning, too, after a swim in the river, he handled such a singularly good knife and fork, that Halbert told Jim privately, that if he, Sam, continued to sport such a confoundedly good appetite, he would have to be carried half-a mile on a heifer's horns and left for dead, to keep up the romant'c effect of his tumble the day before.

They were sitting at breakfast, when the door opened, and there appeared before the assembled company the lithe lad I spoke of yesterday, who said,—

" Beg your pardon, sir; child lost, sir."

They all started up. " Whose child?" asked the Captain.

" James Grewer's child, sir, at the wattle hut."

" Oh!" said Alice, turning to Sam, " it is that pretty little boy up the river that we were admiring so last week."

" When was he lost?" asked Major Buckley.

" Two days now, sir," said the lad.

" But the hut is on the plain side of the river," said the Major; " he can't be lost on the plains."

" The river is very low, sir," said the lad; " hardly ancle-deep just there. He may have crossed."

" The black fellows may have found him," suggested Mrs. Buckley.

" They would have been here before now to tell us, if they had, I am afraid," said Captain Brentwood. " Let us hope they may have got him; however, we had better start at once. Two of us may search the river between this and the hut, and two may follow it towards the Mayfords'. Sam, you have the best horse; go down to the hut, and see if you can find any trace across the river, on this side, and follow it up to the ranges. Take some one with you, and, by-the-bye, take your dog Rover."

They were all quickly on the alert. Sam was going to ask Jim to come with him; but as he was putting the saddle on Widderin he felt a hand on his arm, and, turning, saw Cecil Mayford.

" Sam Buckley," said Cecil, " let me ride with you; will you?"

" Who sooner, old friend?" answered Sam heartily: " let us come together by all means, and if we are to go to the ranges, we had better take a blanket a-piece, and a wedge of damper. So if you will get them from the house, I will saddle your horse."

CHAPTER XXX.

HOW THE CHILD WAS LOST, AND HOW HE GOT FOUND AGAIN—WHAT CECIL
SAID TO SAM WHEN THEY FOUND HIM—AND HOW IN CASTING LOTS,
ALTHOUGH CECIL WON THE LOT, HE LOST THE PRIZE.

FOUR or five miles up the river from Garoopna stood a solitary hut,
snug—sheltered by a lofty bare knoll, round which the great river
chafed among the boulders. Across the stream was the forest
sloping down in pleasant glades from the mountain ; and behind the
hut rose the plain four or five hundred feet over head, seeming to
be held aloft by the blue-stone columns which rose from the river
side.

In this cottage resided a shepherd, his wife, and one little boy,
their son, about eight years old. A strange, wild little bush child,
able to speak articulately, but utterly without knowledge or experience of human creatures, save of his father and mother ; unable to
read a line ; without religion of any sort or kind ; as entire a little
savage, in fact, as you could find in the worst den in your city,
morally speaking, and yet beautiful to look on ; as active as a roe,
and, with regard to natural objects, as fearless as a lion.

As yet unfit to begin labour. All the long summer he would
wander about the river bank, up and down the beautiful rock-walled
paradise where he was confined, sometimes looking eagerly across
the water at the waving forest boughs, and fancying he could see
other children far up the vistas beckoning to him to cross and play
in that merry land of shifting lights and shadows.

It grew quite into a passion with the poor little man to get across
and play there ; and one day when his mother was shifting the
hurdles, and he was handing her the strips of green hide which
bound them together, he said to her,—

" Mother, what country is that across the river ? "

" The forest, child."

" There's plenty of quantongs over there, eh, mother, and raspberries ? Why mayn't I get across and play there ? "

" The river is too deep, child, and the Bunyip lives in the water
under the stones."

" Who are the children that play across there ? "

" Black children, likely."

" No white children ? "

" Pixies ; don't go near 'em, child ; they'll lure you on, Lord
knows where. Don't get trying to cross the river, now, or you'll
be drowned."

But next day the passion was stronger on him than ever. Quite early on the glorious cloudless midsummer day he was down by the river side, sitting on a rock, with his shoes and stockings off, paddling his feet in the clear tepid water, and watching the million fish in the shallows—black fish and grayling—leaping and flashing in the sun.

There is no pleasure that I have ever experienced like a child's midsummer holiday. The time, I mean, when two or three of us used to go away up the brook, and take our dinners with us, and come home at night tired, dirty, happy, scratched beyond recognition, with a great nosegay, three little trout, and one shoe, the other one having been used for a boat till it had gone down with all hands out of soundings. How poor our Derby days, our Greenwich dinners, our evening parties, where there are plenty of nice girls, are after that! Depend on it, a man never experiences such pleasure or grief after fourteen as he does before: unless in some cases in his first love-making, when the sensation is new to him.

But, meanwhile, there sat our child, barelegged, watching the forbidden ground beyond the river. A fresh breeze was moving the trees, and making the whole a dazzling mass of shifting light and shadow. He sat so still that a glorious violet and red king-fisher perched quite close, and, dashing into the water, came forth with a fish, and fled like a ray of light along the winding of the river. A colony of little shell parrots, too, crowded on a bough, and twittered and ran to and fro quite busily, as though they said to him, "We don't mind you, my dear; you are quite one of us."

Never was the river so low. He stepped in; it scarcely reached his ancle. Now surely he might get across. He stripped himself, and, carrying his clothes, waded through, the water never reaching his middle all across the long, yellow, gravelly shallow. And there he stood naked and free in the forbidden ground.

He quickly dressed himself, and began examining his new kingdom, rich beyond his utmost hopes. Such quantongs, such raspberries, surpassing imagination; and when tired of them, such fern boughs, six or eight feet long! He would penetrate this region, and see how far it extended.

What tales he would have for his father to-night. He would bring him here, and show him all the wonders, and perhaps he would build a new hut over here, and come and live in it? Perhaps the pretty young lady, with the feathers in her hat, lived somewhere here, too?

There! There is one of those children he has seen before across the river. Ah! ah! it is not a child at all, but a pretty grey beast, with big ears. A kangaroo, my lad; he won't play with you, but skips away slowly, and leaves you alone.

There is something like the gleam of water on that rock. A snake! Now a sounding rush through the wood, and a passing shadow. **An eagle!** He brushes so close to the child, that he strikes at the bird with a stick, and then watches him as he shoots up like a rocket, and, measuring the fields of air in ever-widening circles, hangs like a motionless speck upon the sky; though, measure his wings across, and you will find he is nearer fifteen feet than fourteen.

Here is a prize, though! A wee little native bear, barely eight inches long,—a little grey beast, comical beyond expression, with broad flapped ears, sits on a tree within reach. He makes no resistance, but cuddles into the child's bosom, and eats a leaf as they go along; while his mother sits aloft, and grunts indignant at the abstraction of her offspring, but, on the whole, takes it pretty comfortably, and goes on with her dinner of peppermint leaves.

What a short day it has been! Here is the sun getting low, and the magpies and jackasses beginning to tune up before roosting.

He would turn and go back to the river. Alas! which way?

He was lost in the bush. He turned back and went, as he thought, the way he had come, but soon arrived at a tall, precipitous cliff, which, by some infernal magic, seemed to have got between him and the river. Then he broke down, and that strange madness came on him which comes even on strong men when lost in the forest: a despair, a confusion of intellect, which has cost many a man his life. Think what it must be with a child!

He was fully persuaded that the cliff was between him and home, and that he must climb it. Alas! every step he took aloft carried him further from the river and the hope of safety; and when he came to the top, just at dark, he saw nothing but cliff after cliff, range after range, all around him. He had been wandering through steep gullies all day unconsciously, and had penetrated far into the mountains. Night was coming down, still and crystal-clear, and the poor little lad was far away from help or hope, going his last long journey alone.

Partly perhaps walking, and partly sitting down and weeping, he got through the night; and when the solemn morning came up again he was still tottering along the leading range, bewildered; crying, from time to time, "Mother, mother!" still nursing his little bear, his only companion, to his bosom, and holding still in his hand a few poor flowers he had gathered the day before. Up and on all day, and at evening, passing out of the great zone of timber, he came on the bald, thunder-smitten summit ridge, where one ruined tree held up its skeleton arms against the sunset, and the wind came keen and frosty. So, with failing, feeble legs, upward still, towards the region of the granite and the snow; towards the eyrie of the kite and the eagle.

    *   *   *   *   *   *

Brisk as they all were at Garoopna, none were so brisk as Cecil and Sam. Charles Hawker wanted to come with them, but Sam asked him to go with Jim ; and, long before the others were ready, our two had strapped their blankets to their saddles, and, followed by Sam's dog Rover, now getting a little grey about the nose, cantered off up the river.

Neither spoke at first. They knew what a solemn task they had before them ; and, while acting as though everything depended on speed, guessed well that their search was only for a little corpse, which, if they had luck, they would find stiff and cold under some tree or crag.

Cecil began : " Sam, depend on it that child has crossed the river to this side. If he had been on the plains he would have been seen from a distance in a few hours."

" I quite agree," said Sam. " Let us go down this side till we are opposite the hut, and search for marks by the river side."

So they agreed ; and in half an hour were opposite the hut, and, riding across to it to ask a few questions, found the poor mother sitting on the door-step, with her apron over her head, rocking herself to and fro.

" We have come to help you, mistress," said Sam. " How do you think he is gone ? "

She said, with frequent bursts of grief, that " some days before he had mentioned having seen white children across the water, who beckoned him to cross and play ; that she, knowing well that they were fairies, or perhaps worse, had warned him solemnly not to mind them ; but that she had very little doubt that they had helped him over and carried him away to the forest ; and that her husband would not believe in his having crossed the river."

" Why, it is not knee-deep across the shallow," said Cecil.

" Let us cross again," said Sam : " he *may* be drowned, but I don't think it."

In a quarter of an hour from starting they found, slightly up the stream, one of the child's socks, which in his hurry to dress he had forgotten. Here brave Rover took up the trail like a bloodhound, and before evening stopped at the foot of a lofty cliff.

" Can he have gone up here ? " said Sam, as they were brought up by the rock.

" Most likely," said Cecil. " Lost children always climb from height to height. I have heard it often remarked by old bush hands. Why they do so, God, who leads them, only knows ; but the fact is beyond denial.* Ask Rover what he thinks ? "

* The Author of this book knew a child who, being lost by his father out shooting on one of the flats bordering the Eastern Pyrenees, in Port Phillip, on a Sunday afternoon, was found on the Wednesday following. dead, at an elevation above the Avoca township of between two and three thousand feet.

The brave old dog was half-way up, looking back for them. It took them nearly till dark to get their horses up ; and, as there was no moon, and the way was getting perilous, they determined to camp, and start again in the morning.

They spread their blankets and lay down side by side. Sam had thought, from Cecil's proposing to come with him in preference to the others, that he would speak of a subject nearly concerning them both , but Cecil went off to sleep and made no sign ; and Sam, ere he dozed, said to himself, " By Jove, if he don't speak this journey, I will. It is unbearable that we should not come to some understanding. Poor Cecil ! "

At early dawn they caught up their horses, which had been hobbled with the stirrup leathers, and started afresh. Both were more silent than ever, and the dog, with his nose to the ground, led them slowly along the rocky rib of the mountain, ever going higher and higher.

" It is inconceivable," said Sam, " that the poor child can have come up here. There is Tuckerimbid close to our right, five thousand feet above the river. Don't you think we must be mistaken ? "

" The dog disagrees with you," said Cecil. " He has something before him not very far off. Watch him."

The trees had become dwarfed and scattered ; they were getting out of the region of trees ; the real forest zone was now below them, and they saw they were emerging towards a bald elevated down, and that a few hundred yards before them was a dead tree, on the highest branch of which sat an eagle.

" The dog has stopped," said Cecil ; " the end is near."

" See," said Sam, " there is a handkerchief under the tree."

" That is the boy himself," said Cecil.

They were up to him and off in a moment. There he lay, dead and stiff, one hand still grasping the flowers he had gathered on his last happy play-day, and the other laid as a pillow, between the soft cold cheek and the rough cold stone. His midsummer holiday was over, his long journey was ended. He had found out at last what lay beyond the shining river he had watched so long.

Both the young men knelt beside him for a moment in silence. They had found only what they had expected to find, and yet, now that they had found it, they were far more touched and softened than they could have thought possible. They stayed in silence a few moments, and then Cecil, lifting up his head, said suddenly,—

" Sam Buckley ! there can be no debate between us two, with this lying here between us. Let us speak now."

" There has never been any debate, Cecil," said he, "and there never would be, though this little corpse was buried fathoms deep. It takes two to make a quarrel, Cecil, and I will not be one."

" Sam," said Cecil, " I love Alice Brentwood better than all the world besides."

" I know it."

" And you love her too, as well, were it possible, as I do."

" I know that too."

" Why," resumed Cecil hurriedly, " has this come to pass ? Why has it been my unlucky destiny, that the man I love and honour above all others should become my rival ? Are there no other women in the world ?   Tell me, Sam, why is it forced on me to choose between my best friend and the woman I love dearer than life ?   Why has this terrible emergency come between us ? "

" I will tell you why," said Sam, speaking very quietly, as though fearing to awaken the dead: " to teach us to behave like men of honour and gentlemen, though our hearts break.   That is why, Cecil."

" What shall we do ? " said Cecil.

" Easily answered," said Sam.   " Let her decide for herself.   It may be, mind you, that she will have neither of us.   There has been one living in the house with her lately, far superior in every point to you or I.   How if she thought fit to prefer him ? "

" Halbert ! "

" Yes, Halbert !   What more likely ?   Let you and I find out the truth, Cecil, like men, and abide by it.   Let each one ask her in his turn what chance he has."

" Who first ? "

" See here," said Sam ; "draw one of these pieces of grass out of my hand.   If you draw the longest piece ask her at once.   Will you abide by this ? "

He said " Yes," and drew—the longest piece.

" That is well," said Sam.   " And now no more of this at present. I will sling this poor little fellow in my blanket and carry him home to his mother.   See, Cecil, what is Rover at ? "

Rover was on his hind legs against the tree, smelling at something. When they came to look, there was a wee little grey bear perched in the hollow of the tree.

" What a very strange place for a young bear !" said Cecil.

" Depend on it," said Sam, " that the child had caught it from its dam, and brought it up here.   Take it home with you, Cecil, and give it to Alice."

Cecil took the little thing home, and in time it grew to be between three and four feet high, a grandfather of bears.   The magpie protested against his introduction to the establishment, and used to pluck billfulls of hair from his stomach under pretence of lining a nest, which was never made.   But in spite of this, the good gentle beast lived nigh as long as the magpie—long enough to be caressed by the waxen fingers of little children, who would afterwards gather round their father, and hear how the bear had been carried to the mountains in the bosom of the little boy who lost his way on the granite ranges, and went to heaven, in the year that the bushrangers came down.

Sam carried the little corpse back in his blanket, and that evening helped the father to bury it by the river side. Under some fern trees they buried him, on a knoll which looked across the river, into the treacherous beautiful forest which had lured him to his destruction.

Alice was very sad for a day or two, and thought and talked much about this sad accident, but soon she recovered her spirits again. And it fell out that a bare week after this, the party being all out in one direction or another, that Cecil saw Alice alone in the garden, tending her flowers, and knew that the time was come for him to keep his bargain with Sam and speak to her. He felt like a man who was being led to execution; but screwed his courage to the highest point, and went down to where she was tying up a rose-tree.

"Miss Brentwood," he said, "I am come to petition for a flower."

"You shall have a dozen, if you will," she answered. "Help yourself; will you have a peony or a sun-flower? If you have not made up your mind, let me recommend a good large yellow sun-flower."

Here was a pretty beginning!

"Miss Brentwood, don't laugh at me, but listen to me a moment. I love you above all earthly things besides. I worship the ground you walk on. I loved you from the first moment I saw you. I shall love you as well, ay, better, if that could be, on the day my heart is still, and my hand is cold for ever: can you tell me to hope? Don't drive me, by one hasty half-considered word, to despair and misery for the rest of my life. Say only one syllable of encouragement, and I will bide your time for years and years."

Alice was shocked and stunned. She saw he was in earnest by his looks, and by his hurried, confused way of speaking. She feared she might have been to blame, and have encouraged him, in her thoughtlessness, more than she ought. "I will make him angry with me," she said to herself. "I will treat him to ridicule. It is the only chance, poor fellow!"

"Mr. Mayford," she said, "if I thought you were in jest, I should feel it necessary to tell my father and brother that you had been impertinent. I can only believe that you are in earnest, and I deeply regret that your personal vanity should have urged you to take such an unwarrantable liberty with a girl you have not yet known for ten days."

He turned and left her without a word, and she remained standing where she was, half inclined to cry, and wondering if she had acted right on the spur of the moment—sometimes half inclined to believe that she had been unladylike and rude. When a thing of this kind takes place, both parties generally put themselves in immediate correspondence with a confidant. Miss Smith totters into the apartments of her dearest friend, and falls weeping on the sofa, while Jones rushes madly into Brown's rooms in the Temple, and shying his best hat into the coalscuttle, announces that there is nothing now left for him but to drown the past in debauchery. Whereupon Brown, if he is a good fellow, as all the Browns are, produces the whisky and hears all about it.

So in the present instance two people were informed of what had taken place before they went to bed that night; and those two were Jim and Doctor Mulhaus. Alice had stood where Cecil had left her, thinking, could she confide it to Mrs. Buckley, and ask for advice? But Mrs. Buckley had been a little cross to her that week for some reason, and so she was afraid: and, not knowing anybody else well enough, began to cry.

There was a noise of horses' feet just beyond the fence, and a voice calling to her to come. It was Jim, and, drying her eyes, she went out, and he, dismounting, put his arm round her waist and kissed her.

"Why, my beauty," he said, "who has been making you cry?"

She put her head on his shoulder and began sobbing louder than ever. "Cecil Mayford," she said in a whisper.

"Well, and what the d——l has he been at?" said Jim, in a rather startling tone.

"Wants to marry me," she answered, in a whisper, and hid her face in his coat.

"The deuce doubt he does," said Jim; "who does not? What did you tell him?"

"I told him that I wondered at his audacity."

"Sent him off with a flea in his ear, in fact," said Jim. "Well, quite right. I suppose you would do the same for any man?"

"Certainly I should," she said, looking up.

"If Doctor Mulhaus, now,—eh?"

"I'd box his ears, Jim," she said, laughing: "I would, indeed."

"Or Sam Buckley; would you box his ears, if he were to—you know?"

"Yes," she said. But there spread over her face a sudden crimson blush, like the rosy arch which heralds the tropical sun,[*] which made Jim laugh aloud.

"If you dared to say a word, Jim," she said, "I would never, never——"

Poor Cecil had taken his horse and had meant to ride home, but came back again at night, "just," he thought, "to have one more look at her; before he entered on some line of life which would take him far away from Garoopna and its temptations."

[*] A horrible plagiarism, Mr. Hamlyn—
"Your ripe lips moved not, but your cheek
Flushed like the coming of the day."—H. K.

The Doctor (who has been rather thrust aside lately in the midst of all this love-making and so on) saw that something had gone very wrong with Cecil, who was a great friend of his, and, as he could never bear to see a man in distress without helping him, he encouraged Cecil to stroll down the garden with him, and then kindly and gently asked him what was wrong.

Cecil told him all, from beginning to end, and added that life was over for him, as far as all pleasure and excitement went; and, in short, said what we have all said, or had said to us, in our time, after a great disappointment in love; which the Doctor took for exactly what it was worth, although poor little Cecil's distress was very keen; and, remembering some old bygone day when he had suffered so himself, he cast about to find some comfort for him.

" You will get over this, my boy," said he, " if you would only believe it."

" Never, never ! " said Cecil.

" Let me tell you a story as we walk up and down. If it does not comfort you, it will amuse you. How sweet the orange bloom smells ! Listen:—Had not the war broke out so suddenly, I should have been married, two months to a day, before the battle of Saarbruck. Catherine was a distant cousin, beautiful and talented, about ten years my junior. Before Heaven, sir, on the word of a gentleman, I never persecuted her with my addresses, and if either of them say I did, tell them from me, sir, that they lie, and I will prove it on their bodies. Bah ! I was forgetting. I, as head of the family, was her guardian, and, although my younger brother was nearer her age, I courted her, in all honour and humility proposed to her, and was accepted with even more willingness than most women condescend to show on such occasions, and received the hearty congratulations of my brother. Few women were ever loved better than I loved Catherine. Conceive, Cecil, that I loved her as well as you love Miss Brentwood, and listen to what follows.

" The war-cloud burst so suddenly that, leaving my bride that was to be, to the care of my brother, and putting him in charge over my property, I hurried off to join the Landsturm, two regiments of which I had put into a state of efficiency by my sole exertions.

" You know partly what followed,—in one day an army of 150,000 men destroyed, the King in flight to Königsberg, and Prussia a province of France.

" 1 fled, wounded badly, desperate and penniless, from that field. I learnt from the peasants, that what I had thought to be merely a serious defeat was an irretrievable disaster; and, in spite of wounds, hunger, and want of clothes, I held on my way towards home.

" The enemy were in possession of the country, so I had to travel by night alone, and beg from such poor cottages as I dared to approach. Sometimes I got a night's rest, but generally lay abroad in the fields. But at length, after every sort of danger and hardship, I stood above the broad, sweeping Maine, and saw the towers of my own beloved castle across the river, perched as of old above the vineyards, looking protectingly down upon the little town which was clustered on the river bank below, and which owned me for its master.

" I crossed at dusk. I had to act with great caution, for I did not know whether the French were there or no. I did not make myself known to the peasant who ferried me over, further than as one from the war, which my appearance was sufficient to prove. I landed just below a long high wall which separated the town from the river, and, ere I had time to decide what I should do first, a figure coming out of an archway caught me by the hand, and I recognised my own major-domo, my foster-brother.

" ' I knew you would come back to me,' he said, ' if it was only as a pale ghost: though I never believed you dead, and have watched here for you night and day to stop you.'

" ' Are the French in my castle, then ?'

" ' There are worse than the French there,' he said ; ' worse than the devil Bonaparte himself. Treason, treachery, adultery !'

" ' Who has proved false ?' I cried.

" ' Your brother ! False to his king, to his word, to yourself. He was in correspondence with the French for six months past, and, now that he believes you dead, he is living in sin with her who was to have been your wife.'

" I did not cry out or faint, or anything of that sort. I only said, ' I am going to the castle, Fritz,' and he came with me. My brother had turned him out of the house when he usurped my property, but by a still faithful domestic we were admitted, and I, knowing every secret passage in my house, came shoeless from behind some arras, and stood before them as they sat at supper. I was a ghastly sight. I had not shaved for a fortnight, and my uniform hung in tatters from my body ; round my head was the same bloody white handkerchief with which I had bound up my head at Jena. I was deadly pale from hunger, too ; and from my entering so silently they believed they had seen a ghost. My brother rose, and stood pale and horrified, and Catherine fell fainting on the floor. This was all my revenge, and ere my brother could speak, I was gone—away to England, where I had money in the funds, accompanied by my faithful Fritz, whom Mary Hawker's father buried in Drumston churchyard.

" So in one day I lost a brother, a mistress, a castle, a king, and a fatherland. I was a ruined, desperate man. And yet I lived to see old Blucher with his dirty boots on the silken sofas at the Tuileries, and to become as stout and merry a middle-aged man as any Prussian subject in her young Majesty's dominions."

CHAPTER XXXI.

HOW TOM TROUBRIDGE KEPT WATCH FOR THE FIRST TIME.

HUMAN affairs are subject to such an infinite variety of changes and complications, that any attempt to lay down particular rules for individual action, under peculiar circumstances, must prove a failure. Hence I consider proverbs, generally speaking, to be a failure, only used by weak-minded men, who have no opinion of their own. Thus, if you have a chance of selling your station at fifteen shillings, and buying in, close to a new gold-field on the same terms, where fat sheep are going to the butcher at from eighteen shillings to a pound, butter, eggs, and garden produce at famine prices, some dolt unsettles you, and renders you uncertain and miserable by saying that "rolling stone gathers no moss;" as if you wanted moss! Again, having worked harder than the Colonial Secretary all the week, and wishing to lie in bed till eleven o'clock on Sunday, a man comes into your room at half-past seven, on a hot morning, when your only chance is to sleep out an hour or so of the heat, and informs you that the "early bird gets the worms." I had a partner, who bought in after Jim Stockbridge was killed, who was always flying this early bird, when he couldn't sleep for musquitoes. I have got rid of him now; but for the two years he was with me, the dearest wish of my heart was that my tame magpie Joshua could have had a quiet two minutes with that early bird before any one was up to separate them. I rather fancy he would have been spoken of as "the late early bird" after that. In short, I consider proverbs as the refuge of weak minds.

The infinite sagacity of the above remarks cannot be questioned; their application may. I will proceed to give it. I have written down the above tirade, nearly, as far as I can guess, a printed pageful (may be a little more, looking at it again), in order to call down the wrath of all wise men, if any such have done me the honour of getting so far in these volumes, on the most trashy and false proverb of the whole: "Coming events cast their shadows before."

Now, they don't, you know. They never did, and never will. I myself used to be a strong believer in pre-(what's the word?— prevarications, predestinations)—no—presentiments; until I found by experience that, although I was always having presentiments, nothing ever came of them. Sometimes somebody would walk over my grave, and give me a creeping in the back, which, as far as I can find out, proceeded from not having my braces properly buttoned behind. Sometimes I have heard the death-watch, produced by a small spider (may the deuce confound him!), not to mention many other presentiments and depressions of spirit, which I am now firmly persuaded proceed from indigestion. I am far from denying the possibility of a coincidence in point of time between a fit of indigestion and a domestic misfortune. I am far from denying the possibility of more remarkable coincidences than that. I have read in books, novels by the very best French authors, how a man, not heard of for twenty years, having, in point of fact, been absent during that time in the interior of Africa, may appear at Paris at a given moment, only in time to save a young lady from dishonour, and rescue a property of ten million francs. But these great writers of fiction don't give us any warning whatever. The door is thrown heavily open, and he stalks up to the table where the will is lying, quite unexpectedly; stalks up always, or else strides. (How would it be, my dear Monsieur Dumas, if, in your next novel, he were to walk in, or run in, or hop in, or, say, come in on all-fours like a dog?—anything for a change, you know.) And these masters of fiction are right—"Coming events do not cast their shadows before."

If they did, how could it happen that Mary Hawker sat there in her verandah at Toonarbin singing so pleasantly over her work? And why did her handsome, kindly face light up with such a radiant smile when she saw her son Charles come riding along under the shadow of the great trees only two days after Cecil Mayford had proposed to Alice, and had been refused?

He came out of the forest shadow with the westering sunlight upon his face, riding slowly. She, as she looked, was proud to see what a fine seat he had on his horse, and how healthy and handsome he looked.

He rode round to the back of the house, and she went through to meet him. There was a square court behind, round which the house, huts, and store formed a quadrangle, neat and bright, with white quartz gravel. By the bye, there was a prospecting party who sank two or three shafts in the flat before the house last year; and I saw about eighteen pennyweights of gold which they took out. But it did not pay, and is abandoned. (This in passing, à propos of the quartz.)

"Is Tom Troubridge come home, mother?" said he, as he leaned out of the saddle to kiss her.

"Not yet, my boy," she said. "I am all alone. I should have had a dull week, but I knew you were enjoying yourself with your old friend at Garoopna. A great party there, I believe?"

"I am glad to get home, mother," he said. "We were jolly at first, but latterly Sam Buckley and Cecil Mayford have been looking at one another like cat and dog. Stay, though; let me be just, the fierce looks were all on Cecil Mayford's side."

" What was the matter ? "

" Alice Brentwood was the matter, I rather suspect," he said, getting off his horse. " Hold him for me, mother, while I take the saddle off."

She did as requested. " And so they two are at loggerheads, eh, about Miss Brentwood ? Of course. And what sort of a girl is she ? "

" Oh, very pretty ; deuced pretty, in fact. But there is one there takes my fancy better."

" Who is she ? "

" Ellen Mayford ; the sweetest little mouse——Dash it all ; look at this horse's back. That comes of that infernal flash military groom of Jim's putting on the saddle without rubbing his back down. Where is the bluestone ? "

She went in and got it for him as naturally as if it was her place to obey, and his to command. She always waited on him, as a matter of course, save when Tom Troubridge was with them, who was apt to rap out something awkward about Charles being a lazy young hound, and about his waiting on himself, whenever he saw Mary yielding to that sort of thing.

" I wonder when Tom will be back ? " resumed Charles.

" I have been expecting him this last week : he may come any night. I hope he will not meet any of those horrid bush-rangers."

" Hope not either," said Charles ; " they would have to go a hundred or two of miles out of their way to make it likely. Driving rams is slow work ; they may not be here for a week."

" A nice price he has paid ! "

" It will pay in the end, in the quality of the wool," said Charles.

They sat in silence. A little after, Charles had turned his horse out, when at once, without preparation, he said to her,—

" Mother, how long is it since my father died ? "

She was very much startled. He had scarcely ever alluded to his father before ; but she made shift to answer him quietly.

" How old are you ? "

" Eighteen ! " he said.

" Then he has been dead eighteen years. He died just as you were born. Never mention him, lad. He was a bad man, and by God's mercy you are delivered from him."

She rose and went into the house quite cheerfully. Why should she not ? Why should not a handsome, still young, wealthy widow be cheerful ? For she was a widow. For years after settling at Toonarbin, she had contrived, once in two or three years, to hear some news of her husband. After about ten years, she heard that he had been reconvicted, and sentenced to the chain-gang for life ; and lastly, that he was dead. About his being sentenced for life, there was no doubt, for she had a piece of newspaper which told of his crime,—and a frightful piece of villany it was,—and after that, the report of his death was so probable that no one for an instant doubted its truth. Men did not live long in the chain-gang, in Van Diemen's Land, in those days, brother. Men would knock out one another's brains in order to get hung, and escape it. Men would cry aloud to the judge to hang them out of the way! It was the most terrible punishment known, for it was hopeless. Penal servitude for life, as it is now, gives the very faintest idea of what it used to be in old times. With a little trouble I could tell you the weight of iron carried by each man. I cannot exactly remember, but it would strike you as being incredible. They were chained two and two together (a horrible association), to lessen the chances of escape; there was no chance of mitigation for good conduct; there was hard mechanical, uninteresting work, out of doors in an inclement climate, in all weathers: what wonder if men died off like rotten sheep? And what wonder, too, if sometimes the slightest accident, —such as a blow from an overseer, returned by a prisoner, produced a sudden rising, unpreconcerted, objectless, the result of which were half a dozen murdered men, as many lunatic women, and five or six stations lighting up the hill-side, night after night, while the whole available force of the colony was unable to stop the ruin for months?

But to the point. Mary was a widow. When she heard of her husband's death, she had said to herself, "Thank God!" But when she had gone to her room, and was sat a-thinking, she seemed to have had another husband before she was bound up with that desperate, coining, forging George Hawker—another husband bearing the same name; but surely that handsome curly-headed young fellow, who used to wait for her so patiently in the orchard at Drumston, was not the same George Hawker as this desperate convict? She was glad the convict was dead and out of the way; there was no doubt of that; but she could still find a corner in her heart to be sorry for her poor old lover,—her handsome old lover,— ah me!

But that even was passed now, and George Hawker was as one who had never lived. Now on this evening we speak of, his memory came back just an instant, as she heard the boy speak of the father, but it was gone again directly. She called her servants, and was telling them to bring supper, when Charles looked suddenly in, and said,—" Here they are!"

There they were, sure enough, putting the rams into the sheep-yard. Tom Troubridge, as upright, brave-looking a man as ever, and, thanks to bush-work, none the fatter. William Lee, one of our oldest acquaintances, was getting a little grizzled, but otherwise looked as broad and as strong as ever.

They rode in.o the yard, and Lee took the horses.

" Well, cousin," said Tom ; " I am glad to see you again."

" You are welcome home, Tom ; you have made good speed."

Tom and Charles went into the house, and Mary was about following them, when Lee said, in so low a tone, that it did not reach the others,—" Mrs. Hawker ! "

She turned round and looked at him ; she had welcomed him kindly when he came into the yard with Tom, and yet he stood still on horseback, holding Tom's horse by the bridle. A stern, square-looking figure he was ; and when she looked at his face, she was much troubled, at—she knew not what.

" Mrs. Hawker," he said, " can you give me the favour of ten minutes' conversation alone, this evening ? "

" Surely, William, now ! "

" Not now,—my story is pretty long, and, what is more, ma'am, somebody may be listening, and what I have got to tell you must be told in no ear but your own."

" You frighten me, Lee ! You frighten me to death."

" Don't get frightened, Mrs. Hawker. Remember if anything comes about, that you have good friends about you ; and, that I, William Lee, am not the worst of them."

Lee went off with the horses, and Mary returned to the house. What mystery had this man to tell her, " that no one might hear but she " ?—very strange and alarming ! Was he drunk ?—no, he was evidently quite sober ; as she looked out once more, she could see him at the stable, cool and self-possessed, ordering the lads about : something very strange and terrifying to one who had such a dark blot in her life.

But she went in, and as she came near the parlour, she heard Charles and Tom roaring with laughter. As she opened the door she heard Tom saying : " And, by Jove, I sat there like a great snipe, face to face with him, as cool and unconcerned as you like. I took him for a flash overseer, sporting his salary, and I was as thick as you like with him. And, ' Matey,' says I, (you see I was familiar, he seemed such a jolly sort of bird), ' Matey, what station are you on ? ' ' Maraganoa,' says he. ' So,' says I, ' you're rather young there, ain't you. I was by there a fortnight ago.' He saw he'd made a wrong move, and made it worse. ' I mean,' says he, ' Maraganoa on the Clarence side.' ' Ah ! ' says I, ' in the Cedar country ? ' ' Precisely,' says he. And there we sat drinking together, and I had no more notion of its being him than you would have had."

She sat still listening to him, eating nothing. Lee's words outside had, she knew not why, struck a chill into her heart, and as she listened to Tom's story, although she could make nothing of it, she felt as though getting colder and colder. She shivered, although the night was hot. Through the open window she could hear all those thousand commingled indistinguishable sounds that make the night-life of the bush, with painful distinctness. She arose and went to the window.

The night was dark and profoundly still. The stars were overhead, though faintly seen through a haze ; and beyond the narrow enclosures in front of the house, the great forest arose like a black wall. Tom and Charles went on talking inside, and yet, though their voices were loud, she was hardly conscious of hearing them, but found herself watching the high dark wood and listening to the sound of the frogs in the creek, and the rustle of a million crawling things, heard only in the deep stillness of night.

Deep in the forest somewhere, a bough cracked, and fell crashing, then all was silent again. Soon arose a wind, a partial wandering wind, which came slowly up, and, rousing the quivering leaves to life for a moment, passed away ; then again a silence, deeper than ever, so that she could hear the cattle and horses feeding in the lower paddock, a quarter of a mile off ; then a low wail in the wood, then two or three wild weird yells, as of a devil in torment, and a pretty white curlew skirled over the housetop to settle on the sheep-wash dam.

The stillness was awful ; it boded a storm, for behind the forest blazed up a sheet of lightning, showing the shape of each fantastic elevated bough. Then she turned round to the light, and said,—

" My dear partner, I had a headache, and went to the window. What was the story you were telling Charles just now ? Who was the man you met in the public-house, who seems to have frightened you so ? "

" No less a man than Captain Touan, my dear cousin ! " said Tom, leaning back with the air of a man who has made a point, and would be glad to hear " what you have to say to that, sir."

" Touan ? " repeated Mary. " Why, that's the great bushranger, that is out to the north ; is it not ? "

" The same man, cousin ! And there I sat hob and nob with him for half an hour in the ' Lake George ' public-house. If Desborough had come in, he'd have hung me for being found in bad company. Ha ! ha ! ha ! "

" My dear partner," she said, " what a terrible escape ! Suppose he had risen on you ? "

" Why I'd have broken his back, cousin," said Tom, " unless my right hand had forgot her cunning. He is a fine man of his weight : but, Lord, in a struggle for life and death, I could break his neck, and have one more claim on heaven for doing so ; for he is the most damnable villain that ever disgraced God's earth, and that is the truth. That man, cousin, in one of his devil's raids, tore a baby from its mother's breast by the leg, dashed its brains out against a tree, and then—I daren't tell a woman what happened."*

"Tom! Tom!" said Mary, "how can you talk of such things?"

"To show you what we have to expect if he comes this way, cousin; that is all."

"And is there any possibility of such a thing?" asked Mary.

"Why not? Why should he not pay us the compliment of looking round this way?"

"Why do they call him Touan, Tom?" asked Charles.

"Can't you see?" said Tom; "the Touan, the little grey flying squirrel, only begins to fly about at night, and slides down from his bough sudden and sharp. This fellow has made some of his most terrible raids at night, and so he got the name of Touan."

"God deliver us from such monsters!" said Mary, and left the room.

She went into the kitchen. Lee sat there smoking. When she came in he rose, and, knocking the ashes out of his pipe, touched his forehead and stood looking at her.

"Now then, old friend," she said, "come here."

He followed her out. She led the way swiftly, through the silent night, across the yard, over a small paddock, up to the sheep-yard beside the woolshed. There she turned shortly round, and, leaning on the fence, said abruptly—

"No one can hear us here, William Lee. Now, what have you to say?"

He seemed to hesitate a moment, and then began: "Mrs. Hawker, have I been a good servant to you?"

"Honest, faithful, kindly, active; who could have been a better servant than you, William Lee! A friend, and not a servant; God is my witness; now then?"

"I am glad to hear you say so," he answered. "I did you a terrible injury once; I have often been sorry for it since I knew you, but it cannot be mended now."

"Since you knew me?" she said. "Why, you have known me ever since I have been in the country, and you have never injured me since then, surely."

"Ay, but at home," he said. "In England. In Devonshire."

"My God!"

"I was your husband's companion in all his earlier villanies. I suggested them to him, and egged him on. And now, mind you, after twenty years, my punishment is coming."

* Tom was confusing Touan with Michael Howe. The latter actually did commit this frightful atrocity; but I never heard that the former actually combined the two crimes in this way. We must remember that barely four years from this present time (1858) a crime, exceeding this in atrocity, was committed in Van Diemen's Land, in open day. I refer to the murder of a lad returning from school.

She could only say still, " My God ! " while her throat was as dry as a kiln.

" Listen to what I have got to tell you now. Hear it all in order, and try to bear up, and use your common sense and courage. As I said before, you have good friends around you, and you at least are innocent."

" Guilty ! guilty ! " she cried. " Guilty of my father's death ! Read me this horrible riddle, Lee."

" Wait and listen," said Lee, unable to forego, even in her terror, the great pleasure that all his class have of spinning a yarn, and using as many words as possible. " See here. We came by Lake George, you know, and heard everywhere accounts of a great gang of bushrangers being out. So we didn't feel exactly comfortable, you see. We came by a bush public-house, and Mr. Troubridge stops, and says he, ' Well, lad, suppose we yard these rams an hour, and take drink in the parlour ? ' ' All right,' I says, with a wink, ' but the tap for me, if you please. That's my place, and I'd like to see if I can get any news of the whereabouts of the lads as are sticking up all round, because, if they're one way, I'd as lief be another.' ' All right,' says he. So in I goes, and sits down. There was nobody there but one man, drunk under the bench. And I has two noblers of brandy, and one of Old Tom ; no, two Old Toms it was, and a brandy ; when in comes an old chap as I knew for a lag in a minute. Well, he and I cottoned together, and found out that we had been prisoners together five-and-twenty years agone. And so I shouted for him, and he for me, and at last I says, ' Butty,' says I, ' who are these chaps round here on the lay' (meaning, Who are the bushrangers) ? And he says, ' Young 'uns—no one as we know.' And I says, ' Not likely, matey ; I've been on the square this twenty year.' ' Same here,' says the old chap ; ' give us your flipper. And now,' says he, ' what sort of a cove is your boss' (meaning Mr. Troubridge) ? ' One of the *real right sort*,' says I. ' Then see here,' says he, ' I'll tell you something : the head man of that there gang is at this minute a-sitting yarning with your boss in the parlour.' ' The devil ! ' says I. ' Is so,' says he, ' and no flies.' So I sings out, ' Mr. Troubridge, those sheep will be out ;' and out he came running, and I whispers to him, ' Mind the man you're sitting with, and leave me to pay the score.' So he goes back, and presently he sings out, ' Will, have you got any money ?' And I says, ' Yes, thirty shillings.' ' Then,' says he, ' pay for this, and come along.' And thinks I, I'll go in and have a look at this great new captain of bushrangers ; so I goes to the parlour door, and now who do you think I saw ? "

" I know," she said. " It was that horrible villain they call Touan."

" The same man," he answered. " Do you know who he is ? "

She found somehow breath to say, "How can I? How is it possible?"

"I will tell you," said Lee. "There, sitting in front of Mr. Troubridge, hardly altered in all these long years, sat George Hawker, formerly of Drumston,—your husband!"

She gave a low cry, and beat the hard rail with her head till it bled. Then, turning fiercely round, she said, in a voice hoarse and strangely altered,—

"Have you anything more to tell me, you croaking raven?"

He had something more to tell, but he dared not speak now. So he said, "Nothing at present, but if laying down my life——"

She did not wait to hear him, but, with her hands clasped above her head, she turned and walked swiftly towards the house. She could not cry, or sob, or rave; she could only say, "Let it fall on me, O God, on me!" over and over again.

Also, she was far too crushed and stunned to think precisely what it was she dreaded so. It seemed afterwards, as Frank Maberly told me, that she had an indefinable horror of Charles meeting his father, and of their coming to know one another. She half feared that her husband would appear and carry away her son with him, and even if he did not, the lad was reckless enough as it was, without being known and pointed at through the country as the son of Hawker the bushranger.

These were after-thoughts, however; at present she leaned giddily against the house-side, trying, in the wild hurrying night-rack of her thoughts, to distinguish some tiny star of hope, or even some glimmer of reason. Impossible! Nothing but swift, confused clouds everywhere, driving wildly on,—whither?

But a desire came upon her to see her boy again, and compare his face to his father's. So she slid quietly into the room where Tom and Charles were still talking together of Tom's adventure, and sat looking at the boy, pretending to work. As she came in, he was laughing loudly at something, and his face was alive and merry. "He is not like what his father was at his age," she said.

But they continued their conversation. "And now, what sort of man was he, Tom?" said Charles. "Was he like any one you ever saw?"

"Why, no. Stay, let's see. Do you know, he was something like you in the face."

"Thank you!" said Charles, laughing. "Wait till I get a chance of paying you a compliment, old fellow. A powerful fellow—eh?"

"Why, yes,—a tough-looking subject," said Tom.

"I shouldn't have much chance with him, I suppose?"

"No; he'd be too powerful for you, Charley."

A change came over his face, a dark, fierce look. Mary could see the likeness *now* plain enough, and even Tom looked at him for an instant with a puzzled look.

"Nevertheless," continued Charles, "I would have a turn with him if I met him. I'd try what six inches of cold steel between——"

"Forbear, boy! Would you have the roof fall in and crush you dead?" said Mary, in a voice that appalled both of them. "Stop such foolish talk, and pray that we may be delivered from the very sight of these men, and suffered to get away to our graves in peace, without any more of these horrors and surprises. I would sooner," she said, increasing in rapidity as she went on, "I would far sooner, live like some one I have heard of, with a sword above his head, than thus. If he comes and looks on me, I shall die."

She had risen and stood in the firelight, deadly pale. Somehow one of the bands of her long black hair had fallen down, and half covered her face. She looked so unearthly that, coupling her appearance with the wild, senseless words she had been uttering, Tom had a horrible suspicion that she was gone mad.

"Cousin," he said, "let me beseech you to go to bed. Charles, run for Mrs. Barker. Mary," he added, as soon as he was gone, "come away, or you'll be saying something before that boy you'll be sorry for. You're hysterical; that's what is the matter with you. I am afraid we have frightened you by our talk about bushrangers."

"Yes, that is it! that is it!" she said; and then, suddenly, "Oh! my dear old friend, you will not desert me?"

"Never, Mary; but why ask such a question now?"

"Ask Lee," she said, and the next moment Mrs. Barker, the housekeeper, came bustling in with smelling-salts, and so on, to minister to a mind diseased. And Mary was taken off to bed.

"What on earth can be the matter with her, cousin Tom?" said Charles, when she was gone.

"She is out of sorts, and got hysterical: that's what it is," said Tom.

"What odd things she said!"

"Women do when they are hysterical. It's nothing more than that."

But Mrs. Barker came in with a different opinion. She said that Mary was very hot and restless, and had very little doubt that a fever was coming on. "Terribly shaken she had been," said Mrs. Barker, "hoped nothing was wrong."

"There's something decidedly wrong, if your mistress is going to have a fever," said Tom. "Charley, do you think Doctor Mulhaus is at Baroona or Garoopna?"

"Up at the Major's," said Charles. "Shall I ride over for him? There will be a good moon in an hour."

"Yes," said Tom, "and fetch him over at once. Tell him we think it's a fever, and he will know what to bring. Ride like h—l, Charley."

As soon as he was alone, he began thinking. "What the *doose* is the matter?" was his first exclamation, and, after half-an-hour's cogitation, only had arrived at the same point, "What the *doose* is the matter?" Then it flashed across him, what did she mean by "ask Lee"? Had she any meaning in it, or was it nonsense? There was an easy solution for it; namely, *to* ask Lee. And so arising he went across the yard to the kitchen.

Lee was bending low over the fire, smoking. "William," said Tom, "I want to see you in the parlour."

"I was thinking of coming across myself," said Lee. "In fact I should have come when I had finished my pipe."

"Bring your pipe across, then," said Tom. "Girl, take in some hot water and tumblers."

"Now, Lee," said Tom, as soon as Lee had gone through the ceremony of "Well, here's my respex, sir," "Now Lee, you have heard how ill the mistress is."

"I have indeed, sir," said he; "and very sorry I am, as I am partly the cause of it."

"All that simplifies matters, Will, considerably," said Tom. "I must tell you that when I asked her what put her in that state, she said, 'Ask Lee.'"

"Shows her sense, sir. What she means is, that you ought to hear what she and I have heard; and I mean to tell you more than I have her. If she knew everything, I am afraid it would kill her."

"Ay! I know nothing as yet, you know."

Lee in the first place put him in possession of what we already know—the fact of Hawker's reappearance, and his identity with "The Touan;" then he paused.

"This is very astonishing, and very terrible, Lee," said he. "Is there anything further?"

"Yes, the worst. That man has followed us home!"

Tom had exhausted all his expressions of astonishment and dismay before this; so now he could only give a long whistle, and say, "Followed us home?"

"Followed us home!" said Lee. "As we were passing the black swamp, not two miles from here, this very morning, I saw that man riding parallel with us through the bush."

"Why did not you tell me before?"

"Because I had not made up my mind how to act. First I resolved to tell the mistress; that I did. Then after I had smoked a pipe, I resolved to tell you, and that I did, and now here we are, you see."

That was undeniable. There they were, with about as pretty a complication of mischief to unravel as two men could wish to have. Tom felt so foolish and nonplussed, that he felt inclined to laugh at Lee, when he said, "Here we are." It so exactly expressed the state of the case; as if he had said, "All so and so has happened, and a deuce of a job it is, and here sit you and I, to deliberate what's to be done with regard to so and so."

He did not laugh, however; he bit his lip, and stopped it. Then he rose, and, leaning his great shoulders against the mantelpiece, stood before the fireless grate, and looked at Lee. Lee also looked at him, and I think that each one thought what a splendid specimen of his style the other was. If they did not think so, "they ought to it," as the Londoners say. But neither spoke a few minutes; then Tom said,—

"Lee, Will Lee, though you came to me a free man, and have served me twenty years, or thereabouts, as free man, I don't conceal from myself the fact, that you have been convict. Pish, man! don't let us mince matters now,—a lag."

Lee looked him full in the face, without changing countenance, and nodded.

"Convicted more than once, too," continued Tom.

"Three times," said Lee.

"Ah!" said Tom. "And if a piece of work was set before me to do, which required pluck, honesty, courage, and cunning, and one were to say to me, 'Who will you have to help you?' I would answer out boldly, 'Give me Will Lee, the lag; my old friend, who has served me so true and hearty these twenty years.'"

"And you'd do right, sir," said Lee quietly. And rising up, he stood beside Tom, with one foot on the fender, bending down and looking into the empty grate.

"Now, Will," said Tom, turning round and laying his hand on his shoulder, "this fellow has followed us home, having found out who we were. Why has he done so?"

"Evident," said Lee, "to work on the fears of the mistress, and get some money from her."

"Good!" said Tom. "Well answered. We shall get to the bottom of our difficulty like this. Only answer the next question as well, and I will call you a Poly—, Poly—; d—n the Greek."

"Not such a bad name as that, I hope, sir," said Lee, smiling. "Who might she have been? A bad un, I expect. You don't happen to refer to Hobart-town Polly, did you, sir?"

"Hold your tongue, you villain," said Tom, "or you'll make me laugh; and these are not laughing times."

"Well, what is your question, sir?" asked Lee.

"Why, simply this: What are we to do?"

"I'll tell you," said Lee, speaking in an animated whisper. "Watch, watch, and watch again, till you catch him. Tie him tight, and hand him over to Captain Desborough. He may be about the place to-night: he will be sure to be. Let us watch to-night, you and I, and for many nights, till we catch him."

" But," whispered Tom, " he will be hung."

" He has earned it," said Lee.   " Let him be hung."

" But he is her husband," urged Tom, in a whisper.   " He is that boy's father.   I cannot do it.   Can't we buy him off ? "

" Yes," answered Lee in the same tone, " till his money is gone. Then you will have a chance of doing it again, and again, all your life."

" This is a terrible dilemma," said Tom ; and added in a perplexity almost comical, " Drat the girl !   Why didn't she marry poor old Jim Stockbridge, or sleepy Hamlyn, or even your humble servant ?   Though, in all honour I must confess that I never asked her, as those two others did.   No !   I'll tell you what, Lee : we will watch for him, and catch him if we can.   After that we will think what is to be done.   By the bye, I have been going to ask you :—do you think he recognised you at the public-house there ? "

" That puzzles me," said Lee.   " He looked me in the face, but I could not see that he did.   I wonder if he recognised you ? "

" I never saw him in my life before," said Tom.   " It is very likely that he knew me, though.   I was champion of Devon and Cornwall, you know, before little Abraham Cann kicked my legs from under me that unlucky Easter Monday.   (The deuce curl his hair for doing it !)   I never forgave him till I heard of that fine bit of play with Polkinghorn.   Yes ! he must have known me."

Lee lit the fire, while Tom, blowing out the candles, drew the curtains, so that any one outside could not see into the room. Nevertheless, he left the French window open, and then went outside, and secured all the dogs in the dog-house.

The night was wonderfully still and dark.   As he paused before entering the house, he could hear the bark falling from the trees a quarter of a mile off, and the opossums scratching and snapping little twigs as they passed from bough to bough.   Somewhere, apparently at an immense distance, a morepork was chanting his monotonous cry.   The frogs in the creek were silent even, so hot was the night.   "A good night for watching," said he to Lee when he came in.   " Lie you down ; I'll take the first watch."

They blew out the candle, and Lee was in the act of lying down, when he arrested himself, and held up his finger to Tom.

They both listened, motionless and in silence, until they could hear the spiders creeping on the ceiling.   There it was again ! a stealthy step on the gravel.

Troubridge and Lee crouched down breathless.   One minute, two, five, but it did not come again.   At length they both moved, as if by concert, and Lee said, " 'Possum."

" Not a bit," said Troubridge ; and then Lee lay down again, and slept in the light of the flickering fire.   One giant arm was thrown around his head, and the other hung down in careless grace;

the great chest was heaved up, and the head thrown back; the seamed and rugged features seemed more stern and marked than ever in the chiaroscuro; and the whole man was a picture of reckless strength such as one seldom sees. Tom had dozed and had awoke again, and now sat thinking, "What a terrible tough customer that fellow would be!" when suddenly he crouched on the floor, and, reaching out his hand, touched Lee, who woke, and silently rolled over with his face towards the window.

There was no mistake this time—that was no opossum. There came the stealthy step again; and now, as they lay silent, the glass-door was pushed gently open, showing the landscape beyond. The gibbous moon was just rising over the forest, all blurred with streaky clouds, and between them and her light they could see the figure of a man, standing inside the room.

Tom could wait no longer. He started up, and fell headlong with a crash over a little table that stood in his way. They both dashed into the garden, but only in time to hear flying footsteps, and immediately after the gallop of a horse, the echoes of which soon died away, and all was still.

"Missed him, by George!" said Lee. "It was a precious close thing, though. What could he mean by coming into the house, —eh?"

"Just as I expected; trying to get an interview with the mistress. He will be more cautious in future, I take it."

"I wonder if he will try again?"

"Don't know," said Troubridge; "he might: not to-night, however."

They went in and lay down again, and Troubridge was soon asleep; and very soon that sleep was disturbed by dreadful dreams. At one time he thought he was riding madly through the bush for his bare life; spurring on a tired horse, which was failing every moment more and more. But always through the tree-stems on his right he saw glancing, a ghost on a white horse, which kept pace with him, do what he would. Now he was among the pre-cipices on the ranges. On his left, a lofty inaccessible cliff; on the right, a frightful blue abyss; while the slaty soil kept sliding from beneath his horse's feet. Behind him, unseen, came a phantom, always gaining on him, and driving him along the giddiest wallaby tracks. If he could only turn and face it, he might conquer, but he dare not. At length the path grew narrower and narrower, and he turned in desperation and awoke—woke to see in the dim morning light a dark figure bending over him. He sprang up, and clutched it by the throat.

"A most excellent fellow this!" said the voice of Dr. Mulhaus. "He sends a frantic midnight message for his friend to come to him, regardless of personal convenience and horseflesh; and when this friend comes quietly in, and tries to wake him without disturbing the sick folks, he seizes him by the throat and nearly throttles him."

" I beg a thousand pardons, Doctor," said Tom; " I had been dreaming, and I took you for the devil. I am glad to find my mistake."

" You have good reason," said the Doctor; " but now, how is the patient?"

" Asleep at present, I believe; the housekeeper is with her."

" What is the matter with her?"

" She has had a great blow. It has shaken her intellect, I am afraid."

" What sort of a blow?" asked the Doctor.

Tom hesitated. He did not know whether to tell him or not.

" Nay," said the Doctor, " you had better let me know. I can help then, you know. Now, for instance, has she heard of her husband?"

" She has, Doctor. How on earth came you to guess that?"

" A mere guess, though I have always thought it quite possible, as the accounts of his death were very uncertain."

Tom then set to work, and told the Doctor all that we know. He looked very grave. " This is far worse than I had thought," he said, and remained thoughtful.

Mary awoke in a fever and delirious. They kept Charles as much from her as possible, lest she should let drop some hint of the matter to the boy; but even in her delirium she kept her secret well; and towards the evening the Doctor, finding her quieter, saddled his horse, and rode away ten miles to a township, where resided a drunken surgeon, one of the greatest blackguards in the country.

The surgeon was at home. He was drunk, of course; he always was, but hardly more so to-day than usual. So the Doctor hoped for success in his object, which was to procure a certain drug which was neither in the medicine-chest at the Buckleys' nor at Toonarbin; and putting on his sweetest smile when the surgeon came to the door, he made a remark about the beauty of the weather, to which the other very gruffly responded.

" I come to beg a favour," said Dr. Mulhaus. " Can you let me have a little—so and so?"

" See you d—d first," was the polite reply. " A man comes a matter of fourteen thousand miles, makes a pretty little practice, and then gets it cut into by a parcel of ignorant foreigners, whose own country is too hot to hold them. And not content with this, they have the brass to ask for the loan of a man's drugs. As I said before, I'll see you d—d first, AND THEN I WON'T." And so saying, he slammed the door.

Doctor Mulhaus was beside himself with rage. For the first and last time since I have known him he forgot his discretion, and instead of going away quietly, and treating the man with contempt, he began kicking at the door, calling the man a scoundrel, &c., and between the intervals of kicking, roaring through the keyhole, " Bring out your diploma; do you hear, you impostor ? " and then fell to work kicking again. " Bring out your forged diploma, will you, you villain ? "

This soon attracted the idlers from the public-house : a couple of sawyers, a shepherd or two, all tipsy of course, except one of the sawyers, who was drunk. The drunken sawyer at length made out to his own complete satisfaction that Doctor Mulhaus' wife was in labour, and that he was come for the surgeon, who was probably drunk and asleep inside. So, being able to sympathise, having had his wife in the straw every thirteen months regularly for the last fifteen years, he prepared to assist, and for this purpose took a stone about half a hundredweight, and coming behind the Doctor, when he was in full kick, he balanced himself with difficulty, and sent it at the lock with all the force of his arm, and of course broke the door in. In throwing the stone, he lost his balance, came full butt against Dr. Mulhaus, propelled him into the passage, into the arms of the surgeon, who was rushing out infuriated to defend his property, and down went the three in the passage together, the two doctors beneath, and the drunken sawyer on the top of them.

The drunken surgeon, if, to use parliamentary language, he will allow me to call him so, was of course underneath the others ; but, being a Londoner, and consequently knowing the use of his fists, ere he went down delivered a " one, two," straight from the shoulder in our poor dear Doctor's face, and gave him a most disreputable black eye, besides cutting his upper lip open. This our Doctor, being, you must remember, a foreigner, and not having the rules of the British Ring before his eyes, resented by getting on the top of him, taking him round the throat, and banging the back of his head against the brick floor of the passage, until he began to goggle his eyes and choke. Meanwhile the sawyer, exhilarated beyond measure in his drunken mind at having raised a real good promising row, having turned on his back, lay procumbent upon the twain, and kicking everything soft and human he came across with his heels, struck up " The Bay of Biscay, Oh," until he was dragged forth by two of his friends ; and being in a state of wild excitement, ready to fight the world, hit his own mate a violent blow in the eye, and was only quieted by receiving a sound thrashing, and being placed in a sitting posture in the verandah of the public house, from which he saw Doctor Mulhaus come forth from the surgeon's with rumpled feathers, but triumphant.

I am deeply grieved to have recorded the above scene, but I could not omit it. Having undertaken to place the character of that very noble gentleman, Doctor Mulhaus, before my readers, I was forced not to omit this.   As a general rule, he was as self-contained, as calm and as frigid as the best Englishman among us.   But under all this there was, to speak in carefully-selected scientific language, a substratum of pepper-box, which has been apparent to me on more than one occasion.   I have noticed the above occasion per force. Let the others rest in oblivion.   A man so true, so wise, so courteous, and so kindly, needs not my poor excuses for having once in a way made a fool of himself.   He will read this, and he will be angry with me for a time, but he knows well that I, like all who knew him, say heartily, God bless you, old Doctor !

But the consequences of the above were, I am sorry to say, eminently disastrous.   The surgeon got a warrant against Doctor Mulhaus for burglary with violence, and our Doctor got a warrant against him for assault with intent to rob.   So there was the deuce to pay.   The affair got out of the hands of the bench.   In fact they sent *both* parties for trial, (what do you think of that, my Lord Campbell ?) in order to get rid of the matter, and at sessions, the surgeon swore positively that Dr. Mulhaus had, assisted by a convict, battered his door down with stones in open day, and nearly murdered him.   Then in defence Doctor Mulhaus called the sawyer, who, as it happened, had just completed a contract for fencing for Mrs. May-ford, the proceeds of which bargain he was spending at the public-house when the thing happened, and had just undertaken another for one of the magistrates ; having also a large family dependent on him ; being, too, a man who prided himself in keeping an eye to windward, and being slightly confused by a trifling attack of delirium tremens (diddleums, he called it): he, I say, to our Doctor's con-fusion and horror, swore positively that he never took a stone in his hand on the day in question ; that he never saw a stone for a week before or after that date : that he did not deny having rushed into the passage to assist the complainant (drunken surgeon), seeing him being murdered by defendant ; and, lastly, that he was never near the place on the day specified.   So it would have gone hard with our Doctor, had not his Honour called the jury's attention to the discrepancies in this witness's evidence ; and when Dr. Mulhaus was acquitted, delivered a stinging reproof to the magistrates for wasting public time by sending such a trumpery case to a jury.   But, on the other hand, Dr. Mulhaus' charge of assault with intent, fell dead ; so that neither party had much to boast of.

The night or so after the trial was over, the Doctor came back to Toonarbin, in what he intended for a furious rage.   But, having told Tom Troubridge the whole affair, and having unluckily caught Tom's eye, they two went off into such hearty fits of laughter that poor Mary, now convalescent, but still in bed, knocked at the wall to know what the matter was.

CHAPTER XXXII.

WHICH IS THE LAST CHAPTER BUT ONE IN THE SECOND VOLUME.

THE state of terror and dismay into which poor Mary Hawker was thrown on finding that her husband, now for many years the *bête noire* of her existence, was not only alive, but promising fairly to cause her more trouble than ever he did before, superadded, let me say, for mere truth's sake, to a slight bilious attack, brought on by good living and want of exercise, threw her into a fever, from which, after several days' delirium, she rose much shattered, and looking suddenly older. All this time the Doctor, like a trusty dog, had kept his watch, and done more, and with a better will than any paid doctor would have been likely to do. He was called away a good deal by the prosecution arising out of that unhappy affair with the other doctor, and afterwards with a prosecution for perjury, which he brought against the sawyer; but he was generally back at night, and was so kind, so attentive, and so skilful that Mary took it into her head, and always affirmed afterwards, that she owed her life to him.

She was not one to receive any permanent impression from anything. So now, as day by day she grew stronger, she tried to undervalue the mischief which had at first so terrified her, and caused her illness;—tried, and with success, in broad daylight; but, in the silent dark nights, as she lay on her lonely bed, she would fully appreciate the terrible cloud that hung over her, and would weep and beat her pillow, and pray in her wild fantastic way to be delivered from this frightful monster, cut off from communion with all honest men by his unutterable crimes, but who, nevertheless, she was bound to love, honour, and obey, till death should part her from him.

Mrs. Buckley, on the first news of her illness, had come up and taken her quarters at Toonarbin, acting as gentle a nurse as man or woman could desire to have. She took possession of the house, and managed everything. Mrs. Barker, the housekeeper, the only one who did not submit at once to her kindly rule, protested, obstructed, protocolled, presented an ultimatum, and, at last, was so ill advised as to take up arms. There was a short campaign, lasting only one morning,—a decisive battle,—and Mrs. Barker was compelled to sue for peace. "Had Mr. Troubridge been true to himself," she said, "she would never have submitted;" but, having given Tom warning, and Tom, in a moment of irritation, having told her, without hesitation or disguise, to go to the devil (no less), she bowed to the circumstances, and yielded.

Agnes Buckley encouraged Dr. Mulhaus, too, in his legal affairs, and, I fear, was the first person who proposed the prosecution for perjury against the sawyer: a prosecution, however, which failed, in consequence of his mate and another friend, who was present at the affair, coming forward to the sawyer's rescue, and getting into such a labyrinth and mist of perjury, that the Bench (this happened just after quarter sessions) positively refused to hear anything more on either side. Altogether, Agnes Buckley made herself so agreeable, and kept them all so alive, that Tom wondered how he had got on so long without her.

At the end of three weeks Mary was convalescent; and one day, when she was moved into the verandah, Mrs. Buckley beside her, Tom and the Doctor sitting on the step smoking, and Charles sleepily reading aloud "Hamlet," with a degree of listlessness and want of appreciation unequalled, I should say, by any reader before; at such time, I say, there entered suddenly to them a little cattle-dealer, as brimful of news as an egg of meat. Little Burnside it was: a man about eight stone nothing, who always wore top-boots and other people's clothes. As he came in, Charles recognised on his legs a pair of cord breeches of his own, with a particular grease patch on the thigh: a pair of breeches he had lent Burnside, and which Burnside had immediately got altered to his own size. A good singer was Burnside. A man who could finish his bottle of brandy, and not go to bed in his boots. A man universally liked and trusted. An honest, hearty, little fellow, yet one who always lent or spent his money as fast as he got it, and was as poor as Job. The greatest vehicle of news in the district, too. "Snowy river Times," he used to be called.

After the usual greetings, Tom, seeing he was bursting with something, asked him, "What's the news?"

Burnside was in the habit of saying that he was like the Lord Mayor's fool—fond of everything that was good. But his greatest pleasure, the one to which he would sacrifice everything, was retailing a piece of news. This was so great an enjoyment with him that he gloried in dwelling on it, and making the most of it. He used to retail a piece of news, as a perfect novel, in three volumes. In his first he would take care to ascertain that you were acquainted with the parties under discussion; and, if you were not, make you so, throwing in a few anecdotes illustrative of their characters. In his second, he would grow discursive, giving an episode or two, and dealing in moral reflections and knowledge of human nature rather largely. And in his third he would come smash, crash down on you with the news itself, and leave you gasping.

He followed this plan on the present occasion. He answered Tom's question by asking,—

"Do you know Desborough?"

"Of course I do," said Tom; "and a noble good fellow he is."

"Exactly," said Burnside; "super of police; distinguished in

Indian wars; nephew of my Lord Covetown. An Irishman is Desborough, but far from objectionable."

This by way of first volume: now comes his second :—

"Now, sir, I, although a Scotchman born, and naturally proud of being so, consider that until these wretched national distinctions between the three great nations are obliterated we shall never get on, sir; never. That the Scotch, sir, are physically and intellectually superior——"

"Physically and intellectually the devil," burst in Tom. "Pick out any dozen Scotchmen, and I'll find you a dozen Londoners who will fight them, or deal with them till they'd be glad to get over the borders again. As for the Devon and Cornish lads, find me a Scotchman who will put me on my back, and I'll write you a cheque for a hundred pounds, my boy. We English opened the trade of the world to your little two millions and a half up in the north there; and you, being pretty well starved out at home, have had the shrewdness to take advantage of it; and now, by Jove, you try to speak small of the bridge that carried you over. What did you do towards licking the Spaniards, eh? And where would you be now, if they had not been licked in 1588, eh? Not in Australia, my boy! A Frenchman is conceited enough, but, by George, he can't hold a candle to a Scotchman."

Tom spoke in a regular passion; but there was some truth in what he said, I think. Burnside didn't like it, and merely saying, "You interrupt me, sir," went on to his third volume without a struggle.

"You are aware, ladies, that there has been a gang of bush-rangers out to the north, headed by a miscreant, whom his companions call Touan, but whose real name is a mystery."

Mrs. Buckley said, "Yes;" and Tom glanced at Mary. She had grown as pale as death, and Tom said, "Courage, cousin; don't be frightened at a name."

"Well, sir," continued Burnside, putting the forefinger and thumb of each hand together, as if he was making "windows" with soapsuds, "Captain Desborough has surprised that gang in a gully, sir, and," spreading his hands out right and left, "obliterated them."

"The devil!" said Tom, while the Doctor got up and stood beside Mary.

"Smashed them, sir," continued Burnside; "extinguished them utterly. He had six of his picked troopers with him, and they came on them suddenly and brought them to bay. You see, two troopers have been murdered lately, and so our men, when they got face to face with the cowardly hounds, broke discipline and wouldn't be held. They hardly fired a shot, but drew their sabres, and cut the dogs down almost to a man. Three only out of twelve have been captured alive, and one of them is dying of a wound in the neck." And, having finished, little Burnside folded his arms and stood in a military attitude, with the air of a man who had done the thing himself, and was prepared to receive his meed of praise with modesty.

" Courage, Mary," said Tom ; " don't be frightened at shadows." —He felt something sticking in his throat, but spoke out nevertheless.

" And their redoubted captain," he asked ; " what has become of him ? "

" What, Touan himself ? " said Burnside. " Well, I am sorry to say that that chivalrous and high-minded gentleman was found neither among the dead nor the living. Not to mince matters, sir, he has escaped."

The Doctor saw Mary's face quiver, but she bore up bravely, and listened.

" Escaped, has he ? " said Tom. " And do they know anything about him ? "

" Desborough, who told me this himself," said Burnside, " says no, that he is utterly puzzled. He had made sure of the arch-rascal himself ; but, with that remarkable faculty of saving his own skin which he has exhibited on more than one occasion, he has got off for the time, with one companion."

" A companion ; eh ? "

" Yes," said Burnside, " whereby hangs a bit of romance, if I may profane the word in speaking of such men. His companion is a young fellow, described as being more like a beautiful woman than a man, and bearing the most singular likeness in features to the great Captain Touan himself, who, as you have heard, is a handsome dog. In short, there is very little doubt that they are father and so."

Tom thought to himself, " Who on earth can this be ? What son can George Hawker have, and we not know of it ? " He turned to Burnside.

" What age is the young man you speak of ? " he asked.

" Twenty, or thereabouts, by all description," said the other.

Tom thought again : " This gets very strange. He could have no son of that age got in Van Diemen's Land : it was eight years before he was free. It must be some one we know of. He had some byeblows in Devon, by all accounts. If this is one of them, how the deuce did he get here ? "

But he could not think. We shall see presently who it was. Now we must leave these good folks for a time, and just step over to Garoopna, and see how affairs go there.

CHAPTER XXXIII.

THE morning after Cecil Mayford had made his unlucky offer to Alice, he appeared at Sam's bedside very early, as if he had come to draw Priam's curtains ; and told him shortly, that he had spoken, and had been received with contempt; that he was a miserable brute, and that he was going back home to attend to his business ; —under the circumstances, the best thing he could possibly do.

So the field was clear for Sam, but he let matters stay as they were, being far too pleasant to disturb lightly ; being also, to tell the truth, a little uncertain of his ground, after poor Cecil had suffered so severely in the encounter. The next day, too, his father and mother went home, and he thought it would be only proper for him to go with them, but, on proposing it, Jim quietly told him he must stay where he was and work hard for another week, and Halbert, although a guest of the Buckleys, was constrained to remain still at the Brentwoods', in company with Sam.

But at the end of a week they departed, and Jim went back with them, leaving poor Alice behind, alone with her father. Sam turned when they had gone a little way, and saw her white figure still in the porch, leaning in rather a melancholy attitude against the door-post. The audacious magpie had perched himself on the top of her head, from which proud elevation he hurled wrath, scorn, and mortal defiance against them as they rode away. Sam took off his hat, and as he went on kept wondering whether she was thinking of him at all, and hoping that she might be sorry that he was gone. " Probably, however," he thought, " she is only sorry for her brother."

They three stayed at Baroona a week or more, one of them riding up every day to ask after Mary Hawker. Otherwise they spent their time shooting and fishing, and speculating how soon the rains would come, for it was now March, and autumn was fairly due.

But at the end of this week, as the three were sitting together, one of those long-legged, slab-sided, lean, sunburnt, cabbage-tree-hatted lads, of whom Captain Brentwood kept always, say half-a-dozen, and the Major four or five (I should fancy, no relation to one another, and yet so exactly alike, that Captain Brentwood never called them by their right names by any chance) ; lads who were employed about the stable and the paddock, always in some way with the horses ; one of those representatives of the rising Australian generation, I say, looked in, and without announcing himself, or touching his hat (an Australian never touches his hat if he is a free man, because the prisoners are forced to), came up to Jim across the drawing-room, as quiet and self-possessed as if he was quite used to good society, and, putting a letter in his hand, said merely, ' Miss Alice," and relapsed into silence, amusing himself by looking round Mrs. Buckley's drawing-room, the like of which he had never seen before.

Sam envied Jim the receipt of that little three-cornered note. He wondered whether there was anything about him in it. Jim read it, and then folded it up again, and said " Hallo ! "

The lad,—I always call that sort of individual a lad ; there is no other word for them, though they are of all ages, from sixteen to twenty,—the lad, I say, was so taken up with the contemplation of a blown-glass pressepapier on the table, that Jim had to say, " Hallo there, John ! "

The lad turned round, and asked in a perfectly easy manner, " What the deuce is this thing for, now ? "

" That," said Jim, " is the button of a Chinese mandarin's hat, who was killed at the battle of Waterloo in the United States by Major Buckley."

" Is it now ? " said the lad, quite contented. " It's very pretty ; may I take it up ? "

" Of course you may," said Jim. " Now, what's the foal like ? "

" Rather leggy, *I* should say," he returned. " Is there any answer ? "

Jim wrote a few lines with a pencil on half his sister's note, and gave it him. He put it in the lining of his hat, and had got as far as the door, when he turned again. He looked wistfully towards the table where the pressepapier was lying. It was too much for him. He came back and took it up again. What he wanted with it, or what he would have done with it if he had got it, I cannot conceive, but it had taken his simple fancy more, probably, than an emerald of the same size would have done. At last he put it to his eye.

" Why, darn my cabbage-tree," he said, " if you can't see through it ! He wouldn't sell it, I suppose, now ? "

Jim pursed his lips and shook his head, as though to say that such an idea was not to be entertained, and the lad, with a sigh, laid it down and departed. Then Jim with a laugh threw his sister's note over to Sam. I discovered this very same note only last week, while searching the Buckley papers for information about the family at this period. I have reason to believe that it has never been printed before, and, as far as I know, there is no other copy extant, so I proceed to give it in full.

" What a dear, disagreeable old Jim you are," it begins, " to stay away there at Baroona, leaving me moping here with our daddy, wno is calculating the explosive power of shells under water at various temperatures. I have a good mind to learn the Differential Calculus myself, only on purpose to bore you with it when you come home."

" By the bye, Corrella has got a foal. Such a dear little duck of a thing, with a soft brown nose, and sweet long ears, like leaves! Do come back and see it; I am so very, very lonely!"

" I hope Mr. Halbert is pretty well, and that his wound is getting quite right again. Don't let him undertake cattle-drafting or anything violent. I wish you could bring him back with you, he is such a nice, agreeable creature."

" Your magpie * has attacked cocky, and pulled a yellow feather out of his crest, which he has planted in the flower-bed, either as a trophy, or to see if it will grow."

Now this letter is historically important, when taken in connexion with certain dates in my possession. It was written on a Monday, and Halbert, Jim, and Sam started back to Garoopna the next day, rather a memorable day for Sam, as you will see directly. Now I wish to call attention to the fact, that Sam, far from being invited, is never once mentioned in the whole letter. Therefore what does Miss Burke mean by her audacious calumnies? What does she mean by saying that Alice made love to Sam, and never gave the " poor boy " a chance of escape? Can she, Lesbia, put her hand on her heart and say that she wasn't dying to marry Sam herself, though she was (and is still, very likely) thirty years his senior? The fact is, Lesbia gave herself the airs, and received the privileges of being the handsomest woman in those parts, till Alice came, and put her nose out of joint, for which she never forgave her.

However, to return to this letter. I wonder now, as I am looking at the age-stained paper and faded writing, whether she who wrote it contemplated the possibility of its meeting Sam's eye. I rather imagine that she did, from her provoking silence about him. At any rate, Jim was quite justified in showing him the letter, " for you know," he said, " as there is nothing at all about you in it, there can be no breach of confidence."

" Well!" said Sam, when he had read it.

" Well!" said Jim. " Let us all three ride over and look at the foal."

So they went, and were strictly to be home at dinner-time; whereas not one of them came home for a week.

When they came to the door at Garoopna, there was Alice, most

---

* Magpie, a large, pied crow. Of all the birds I have ever seen, the cleverest, the most grotesque, and the most musical. The splendid melody of his morning and evening song is as unequalled as it is indescribable.

bewitchingly beautiful. Papa was away on the run, and Dr. Mulhaus with him; so the three came in. Alice was very glad to see Halbert—was glad also to see Sam; but not so glad, or, at all events, did not say so much about it.

" Alice, have you seen the newspaper?" said Jim.

" No; why?"

" There is a great steamer gone down at sea, and three hundred persons drowned." *

" What a horrible thing! I should never have courage to cross the sea."

" You would soon get accustomed to it, I think," said Halbert.

" I have never even seen it as yet," she said, " save at a distance."

" Strange, neither have I," said Sam. " I have dim recollections of our voyage here, but I never stood upon the shore in my life."

" I have beat you there," said Jim. " I have been down to Cape Chatham, and seen the great ocean itself: a very different thing from Sydney Harbour, I promise you. You see the great Cape running out a mile into the sea, and the southern rollers tumbling in over the reefs like cascades."

" Let us go and see it!—how far is it?" said Alice.

" About thirty miles. The Barkers' station is about half a mile from the Cape, and we could sleep there, you know."

" It strikes me as being a most brilliant idea," said Sam.

And so the arrangement was agreed to, and the afternoon went on pleasantly. Alice walked up and down with Sam among the flowers, while Jim and Halbert lay beneath a mulberry tree and smoked.

They talked on a subject which had engaged their attention a good deal lately. Jim's whim for going soldiering had grown and struck root, and become a determination. He would go back to India when Halbert did, supposing that his father could be tempted to buy him a commission. Surely he might manage to join some regiment in India, he thought. India was the only place worth living in just now.

" I hope, Halbert," he said, " that the Governor will consent. I wouldn't care when I went; the sooner the better. I am tired of being a cattle-dealer on a large scale; I want to get at some *man's* work. If one thing were settled I would go to-morrow."

" And what is that?" said Halbert.

Jim said nothing, but looked at the couple among the flower-beds.

" Is that all?" said Halbert. " What will you bet me that that affair is not concluded to-night?"

" I'll bet you five pounds to one it ain't," said Jim; " nor any

---

* Can this be the " President"?—H. K.

time this twelvemonth. They'll go on shilly-shallying half their lives, I believe."

"Nevertheless I'll bet with you. Five to one it comes off to-night! Now! There goes your sister into the house; just go in after her."

Jim sauntered off, and Sam came and laid his great length down by the side of Halbert.

They talked on indifferent matters for a few minutes, till the latter said,—

"You are a lucky fellow, Sam."

"With regard to what?" said Sam.

"With regard to Miss Brentwood, I mean."

"What makes you think so?"

"Are you blind, Sam? Can't you see that she loves you better than any man in the world?"

He answered nothing, but turning his eyes upon Halbert, gazed at him a moment to see whether he was jesting or no. No, he was in earnest. So he looked down on the grass again, and, tearing little tufts up, said,—

"What earthly reason have you for thinking that?"

"What reason!—fifty thousand reasons. Can you see nothing in her eyes when she speaks to you, which is not there at other times; hey, Bat?—I can, if you can't."

"If I could think so!" said Sam. "If I could find out?"

"When I want to find out anything, I generally ask," said Halbert.

Sam gave him the full particulars of Cecil's defeat.

"All the better for you," said Halbert; "depend upon it. I don't know much about women, it is true, but I know more than you do."

"I wish I knew as much as you do," said Sam.

"And I wish I knew as little as you do," said Halbert.

Dinner-time came, but the Captain and the Doctor were not to the fore. After some speculations as to what had become of them, and having waited an hour, Jim said, that, in the unexplained absence of the crowned head, he felt it his duty to the country, to assume the reins of government, and order dinner. Prime Minister Alice, having entered a protest, offered no further opposition, and dinner was brought in.

Young folks don't make so much of dinner as old ones at any time, and this dinner was an unusually dull one. Sam was silent and thoughtful, and talked little; Alice, too, was not quite herself. Jim, as usual, ate like a hero, but talked little; so the conversation was principally carried on by Halbert, in the narrative style, who really made himself very useful and agreeable, and I am afraid they would have been a very "slow" party without him.

Soon after the serious business of eating was over, Jim said,—

"Alice, I wonder what the Governor will say?"

"About what, brother?"

"About my going soldiering."

"Save us! What new crotchet is this?"

"Only that I'm going to bother the Governor till he gets me a commission in the army."

"Are you really serious, Jim?"

"I never was more so in my life."

"So, Mr. Halbert," said Alice, looking round at him, "you are only come to take my brother away from me!"

"I assure you, Miss Brentwood, that I have only aided and abetted: the idea was his own."

"Well, well, I see how it is;—we were too happy, I suppose."

"But, Alice," said Jim, "won't you be proud to see your brother a good soldier?"

"Proud! I was always proud of you. But I wish the idea had never come into your head. If it was in war time I would say nothing, but now it is very different. Well, gentlemen, I shall leave you to your wine. Mr. Halbert, I like you very much, but I wish you hadn't turned Jim's head."

She left them, and walked down the garden; through the twilight among the vines, which were dropping their yellow leaves lightly on the turf before the breath of the autumn evening. So Jim was going,—going to be killed probably, or only coming back after ten years' absence, "full of strange oaths and bearded like a pard!" She knew well how her father would jump at his first hint of being a soldier, and would move heaven and earth to get him a commission,—yes, he would go—her own darling, funny, handsome Jim, and she would be left all alone.

No, not quite! There is a step on the path behind her that she knows; there is an arm round her waist which was never there before, and yet she starts not as a low voice in her ear says,—

"Alice, my love, my darling, I have come after you to tell you that you are dearer to me than my life, and all the world besides. Can you love me half as well as I love you? Alice, will you be my wife?"

What answer? Her hands pressed to her face, with a flood of happy tears, she only says,—

"Oh! I'm so happy, Sam! So glad, so glad!"

Pipe up there, golden-voiced magpie; give us one song more before you go to roost. Laugh out, old jackass, till you fetch an echo back from the foggy hollow. Up on your bare boughs, it is dripping, dreary autumn: but down here in the vineyard are bursting the first green buds of an immortal spring.

There are some scenes which should only be undertaken by the hand of a master, and which, attempted by an apprentice like myself, would only end in disastrous failure, calling down the wrath of all honest men and true critics upon my devoted head,—not undeservedly. Three men in a century, or thereabouts, could write with sufficient delicacy and purity, to tell you what two such young lovers as Sam Buckley and Alice Brentwood said to one another in the garden that evening, walking up and down between the yellow vines. I am not one of those three. Where Charles Dickens has failed, I may be excused from being diffident. I am an old bachelor, too—a further excuse. But no one can prevent my guessing, and I guess accordingly,—that they talked in a very low tone, and when, after an hour, Alice said it was time to come in, that Sam was quite astonished to find how little had been said, and what very long pauses there had been.

They came in through the window into the sitting-room, and there was Doctor Mulhaus, Captain Brentwood, and also, of all people, Major Buckley, whom the other two had picked up in their ride and brought home. My information about this period of my history is very full and complete. It has come to my knowledge on the best authority, that when Sam came forward to the light, Halbert kicked Jim's shins under the table, and whispered, "You have lost your money, old fellow!" and that Jim answered, "I wish it was ten pounds instead of five."

But old folks are astonishingly obtuse. Neither of the three seniors saw what had happened; but entered *con amore* into the proposed expedition to Cape Chatham, and when bedtime came, Captain Brentwood, honest gentleman, went off to rest, and having said his prayers and wound up his watch, prepared for a comfortable night's rest, as if nothing was the matter.

He soon found his mistake. He had got his boots off, and was sitting pensively at his bedside, meditating further disrobements, when Jim entered mysteriously, and quietly announced that his whole life in future would be a weary burden if he didn't get a commission in the army, or at least a cadetship in the East India Company's service. Him the Captain settled by telling, that if he didn't change his mind in a month he'd see about it, and so packed him off to bed. Secondly, as he was taking off his coat, wondering exceedingly at Jim's communication, Sam appeared, and humbly and respectfully informed him that he had that day proposed to his daughter and been accepted,—provisionally; hoping that the Captain would not disapprove of him as a son-in-law. He was also rapidly packed off to bed, by the assurance that he (Brentwood) had never felt so happy in his life, and had been sincerely hoping that the young folks would fall in love with one another for a year past.

So, Sam dismissed, the Captain got into bed; but as soon as the light was blown out two native cats began grunting under the washing-stand, and he had to get out, and expel them in his shirt; and finally he lost his temper and began swearing. "Is a man never to get to sleep?" said he. "The devil must be abroad to-night, if ever he was in his life."

No sleep that night for Captain Brentwood. His son, asking for a commission in the army, and his daughter going to be married! Both desirable enough in their way, but not the sort of facts to go to sleep over, particularly when fired off in his ear just as he was lying down. So he lay tossing about, more or less uncomfortable all night, but dozed off just as the daylight began to show more decidedly in the window. He appeared to have slept from thirty to thirty-five seconds, when Jim woke him with,—

"It's time to get up, father, if you are going to Cape Chatham to-day."

"D—n Cape Chatham," was his irreverent reply when Jim was gone, which sentiment has been often re-echoed by various coasting skippers in later times. "Why, I haven't been to sleep ten minutes,—and a frosty morning, too. I wish it would rain. I am not vindictive, but I do indeed. Can't the young fools go alone, I wonder? No; hang it, I'll make myself agreeable to-day, at all events!"

CHAPTER XXXIV.

HOW THEY ALL WENT HUNTING FOR SEA ANEMONES AT CAPE CHATHAM— AND HOW THE DOCTOR GOT A TERRIBLE FRIGHT—AND HOW CAPTAIN BLOCKSTROP SHOWED THAT THERE WAS GOOD REASON FOR IT.

AND presently, the Captain, half dressed, working away at his hair with two very stiff brushes, betook himself to Major Buckley's room, whom he found shaving. "I'll wait till you're done," said he; "I don't want you to cut yourself."

And then he resumed: "Buckley, your son wants to marry my daughter."

"Shows his good taste," said the Major. "What do you think of it?"

"I am very much delighted," said the Captain.

"And what does she say to it?"

"She is very much delighted."

"And I am very much delighted, and I suppose Sam is too. So there we are, you see: all agreed."

And that was the way the marriage negotiations proceeded; indeed, it was nearly all that was ever said on the subject. But one day the Major brought two papers over to the Captain (who signed them), which were supposed to refer to settlements, and after that all the arrangements where left to Alice and Mrs. Buckley.

They started for Cape Chatham about nine o'clock in the day; Halbert and Jim first, then Sam and Alice, and lastly the three elders. This arrangement did not last long however; for very soon Sam and Alice called aloud to Halbert and Jim to come and ride with them, for that they were boring one another to death. This they did, and now the discreet and sober conversation of the oldsters was much disturbed by the loud laughter of the younger folks, in which, however, they could not help joining. It was a glorious crystal clear day in autumn; all nature, aroused from her summer's rest, had put off her suit of hodden grey, and was flaunting in gaudiest green. The atmosphere was so amazingly pure, that miles away across the plains the travellers could distinguish the herds of turkeys (bustards) stalking to and fro, while before them, that noble maritime mountain Cape Chatham towered up, sharply defined above the gleaming haze which marked the distant sea.

For a time their way lay straight across the broad well-grassed plains, marked with ripples as though the retiring sea had but just left it. Then a green swamp; through the tall reeds the native companion, king of cranes, waded majestic; the brilliant porphyry water hen, with scarlet bill and legs, flashed like a sapphire among the emerald green water-sedge. A shallow lake, dotted with wild ducks, here and there a group of wild swan, black with red bills, floating calmly on its bosom.—A long stretch of grass as smooth as a bowling-green.—A sudden rocky rise, clothed with native cypress (Exocarpus—Oh my botanical readers!), honeysuckle (Banksia), she-oak (Casuarina), and here and there a stunted gum. Cape Chatham began to show grander and nearer, topping all; and soon they saw the broad belt of brown sandy heath that lay along the shore.

"Here," said the Doctor, riding up, "we leave the last limit of the lava streams from Mirngish and the Organ-hill. Immediately you shall see how we pass from the richly-grassed volcanic plains, into the barren sandstone heaths; from a productive pasture land into a useless flower-garden. Nature here is economical, as she always is: she makes her choicest ornamental efforts on spots otherwise useless. You will see a greater variety of vegetation on one acre of your sandy heath than on two square miles of the thickly-grassed country we have been passing over."

It was as he said. They came soon on to the heath; a dark dreary expanse, dull to look upon after so long a journey upon the bright green grass. It stretched away right and left interminably, only broken here and there with islands of dull-coloured trees; as melancholy a piece of country as one could conceive: yet far more thickly peopled with animal, as well as vegetable life, than the rich pastoral downs further inland. Now they began to see the little red brush kangaroo, and the grey forester, skipping away in all directions; and had it been summer they would have been startled more than once by the brown snake, and the copper snake, deadliest of their tribe. The painted quail, and the brush quail (the largest of Australian game birds, I believe), whirred away from beneath their horses' feet; and the ground parrot, green, with mottlings of gold and black, rose like a partridge from the heather, and flew low. Here, too, the Doctor flushed a " White's thrush," close to an outlying belt of forest, and got into a great state of excitement about it. " The only known bird," he said, " which is found in Europe, America, and Australia alike." Then he pointed out the emu wren, a little tiny brown fellow, with long hairy tail-feathers, flitting from bush to bush; and then, leaving ornithology, he called their attention to the wonderful variety of low vegetation that they were riding through; Hakeas, Acacias, Grevilleas, and what not. In spring this brown heath would have been a brilliant mass of flowers; but now, nothing was to be seen save a few tall crimson spikes of Epacris, and here and there a bunch of lemon-coloured Correas. Altogether, he kept them so well amused, that they were astonished to come so quickly upon the station, placed in a snug cove of the forest, where it bordered on the heath beside a sluggish creek. Then, seeing the mountain towering up close to them, and hearing, as they stayed at the door, a low continuous thunder behind a high roll in the heath which lay before them, they knew that the old ocean was close at hand, and that their journey was done.

The people at the station were very glad to see them, of course. Barker, the paterfamilias, was an old friend of both the Major and the Captain, and they found so much to talk about, that after a heavy midday-meal, excellent in kind, though that kind was coarse, and certain libations of pale ale and cold claret and water, the older of the party, with the exception of Dr. Mulhaus, refused to go any farther; so the young people started forth to the Cape, under the guidance of George Barker, the fourth or fifth son, who happened to be at home.

" Doctor," said Alice, as they were starting, " do you remark what beautiful smooth grass covers the Cape itself, while here we have nothing but this scrubby heath? The mountain is, I suppose, some different formation?"

" Granite, my dear young lady," said the Doctor. " A cap of granite rising through and partly overlying this sandstone."

" You can always tell one exactly what one wants to know," said Alice; and, as they walked forwards, somehow got talking to Halbert, which I believe most firmly had been arranged beforehand with Sam. For he, falling back, ranged alongside of the Doctor, and, managing to draw him behind the others, turned to him and said suddenly,—

" My dear old friend! my good old tutor!"

The Doctor stopped short, pulled out a pair of spectacles, wiped them, put them on, and looked at Sam through them for nearly a minute, and then said:

" My dear boy, you don't mean to say——"

" I do, Doctor.—Last night.—And, oh! if you could only tell how happy I am at this moment! If you could but guess at it!——"

" Pooh, pooh!" said the Doctor; " I am not so old as that, my dear boy. Why, I am a marrying man myself. Sam, I am so very, very glad! you have won her, and now wear her, like a pearl beyond all price. I think that she is worthy of you: more than that she could not be."

They shook hands, and soon Sam was at her side again, toiling up the steep ascent. They soon distanced the others, and went forwards by themselves.

There was such a rise in the ground seawards, that the broad ocean was invisible till they were half way up the grassy down. Then right and left they began to see the nether firmament, stretching away infinitely. But the happy lovers paused not till they stood upon the loftiest breezy knoll, and seemed alone together between the blue cloudless heaven and another azure-sphere which lay beneath their feet.

A cloudless sky and a sailless sea. Far beneath them they heard but saw not the eternal surges gnawing at the mountain. A few white albatrosses skimmed and sailed below, and before, seaward, the sheets of turf, falling away, stretched into a shoreless headland, fringed with black rock and snow-white surf.

She stood there flushed and excited with the exercise, her bright hair dishevelled, waving in the free sea-breeze, the most beautiful object in that glorious landscape, her noble mate beside her. Awe, wonder, and admiration kept both of them silent for a few moments, and then she spoke.

" Do you know any of the choruses in the ' Messiah '?" asked she.

" No, I do not," said Sam.

" I am rather sorry for it," she said, " because this is so very like some of them."

" I can quite imagine that," said Sam. " I can quite imagine music which expresses what we see now. Something infinitely *broad* I should say. Is that nonsense now?"

" Not to me," said Alice.

" I imagined," said Sam, " that the sea would be much rougher than this. In spite of the ceaseless thunder below there, it is very calm."

" Calm, eh?" said the Doctor's voice behind them. " God help the ship that should touch that reef this day, though a nautilus might float in safety! See how the groundswell is tearing away at those rocks; you can just distinguish the long heave of the water, before it breaks. There is the most dangerous groundswell in the world off this coast. Should this country ever have a large coast-trade, they will find it out, in calm weather with no anchorage."

A great coasting trade has arisen; and the Doctor's remark has proved terribly true. Let the Monumental City and the Schomberg, the Duncan Dunbar and the Catherine Adamson bear witness to it. Let the drowning cries of hundreds of good sailors, who have been missed and never more heard of, bear witness that this is the most pitiless and unprotected, and, even in calm weather, the most danger-ous coast in the world.

But Jim came panting up, and throwing himself on the short turf, said—

"So this is the great Southern Ocean; eh! How far can one see, now, Halbert?"

"About thirty miles."

"And how far to India; eh?"

"About seven thousand."

"A long way," said Jim. "However, not so far as to England."

"Fancy," said Halbert, "one of those old Dutch voyagers driving on this unknown coast on a dark night. What a sudden end to their voyage! Yet that must have happened to many ships which have never come home. Perhaps when they come to explore this coast a little more they may find some old ship's ribs jammed on a reef; the ribs of some ship whose name and memory has perished."

"The very thing you mention is the case," said the Doctor. "Down the coast here, under a hopeless, black basaltic cliff, is to be seen the wreck of a very, very old ship, now covered with coral and seaweed. I waited down there for a spring tide, to examine her, but could determine nothing, save that she was very old; whether Dutch or Spanish I know not.* You English should never sneer at those two nations; they were before you everywhere."

"And the Chinese before any of us in Australia," replied Halbert.

"If you will just come here," said Alice, "where those black rocks are hid by the bend of the hill, you get only three colours in your landscape; blue sky, grey grass, and purple sea. But look, there is a man standing on the promontory. He makes quite an eyesore there. I wish he would go away."

"I suppose he has as good a right there as any of us," answered the Doctor. "But he certainly does not harmonise very well with the rest of the colouring. What a strange place he has chosen to stand in, looking out over the sea, as though he were a shipwrecked mariner—the last of the crew."

"A shipwrecked mariner would hardly wear breeches and boots, my dear Doctor," said Jim. "That man is a stockman."

* Such a ship may be seen in the eastern end of Portland Bay, near the modern town of Port Fairy.

"Not one of ours, however," said George Barker; "even at this distance I can see that. See, he's gone! Strange! I know of no way down the cliff thereabouts. Would you like to come down to the shore?"

So they began their descent to the shore by a winding path of turf, among tumbled heaps of granite; down towards the rock-walled cove; a horseshoe of smooth white sand lying between two long black reefs, among whose isolated pinnacles the groundswell leapt and spouted ceaselessly.

Halbert remarked, "This granite coast is hardly so remarkable as our Cornish one. There are none of those queer pinnacles and tors one sees there, just ready to topple down into the sea. This granite is not half so fantastic."

"Earthquakes, of which you have none in Cornwall," said the Doctor, "will just account for the difference. I have felt one near here quite as strong as your famous lieutenant, who capsized the Logan stone."

But now, getting on the level sands, they fell to gathering shells and sea-weeds like children. Jim, trying to see how near he could get to a wave without being caught, got washed up like jetsam. Alice took Sam's pocket-handkerchief, and filled it indiscriminately with flotsam, and everything she could lay her hand on, principally, however, lagend. Trochuses, as big as one's fist, and "Venus-ears," scarlet outside. And after an hour, wetfooted and happy, dragging a yard or so of sea-tang behind her, she looked round for the Doctor, and saw him far out on the reef, lying flat on his stomach, and closely examining a large still pool of salt water, contained in the crevices of the rocks.

He held up his hand and beckoned. Sam and Alice advanced towards him over the slippery beds of sea-weed, Sam bravely burying his feet in the wet clefts, and holding out his hand to help her along. Once there was a break in the reef, too broad to be jumped, and then for the first time he had her fairly in his arms and swung her across, which was undoubtedly very delightful, but unfortunately soon over. At length, however, they reached the Doctor, who was seated like a cormorant on a wet rock, lighting a pipe.

"What have you collected?" he asked. "Show me."

Alice proudly displayed the inestimable treasures contained in Sam's handkerchief.

"Rubbish! Rubbish!" said the Doctor, "Do you believe in mermaidens?"

"Of course I do, if you wish it," said Alice. "Have you seen one?"

"No, but here is one of their flower-gardens. Bend down and look into this pool."

She bent and looked. The first thing that she saw was her own exquisite face, and Sam's brown phiz peering over her shoulder A golden tress of hair, loosened by the sea breeze, fell down into the water, and had to be looped up again. Then gazing down once more, she saw beneath the crystal water a bed of flowers ; dahlias, ranunculuses, carnations, chrysanthemums, of every colour in the rainbow save blue. She gave a cry of pleasure : " What are they, Doctor ? What do you call them ? "

" Sea anemones, in English, I believe," said the Doctor, " actinias, serpulas, and sabellas. You may see something like that on the European coasts, on a small scale, but there is nothing I ever have seen like that great crimson fellow with cream-coloured tentacles. I do not know his name. I suspect he has never been described. The common European anemone they call ' crassicornis ' is something like him, but not half as fine."

" Is there any means of gathering and keeping them, Doctor ? " asked Sam. " We have no flowers in the garden like them."

" No possible means," said the Doctor. " They are but lumps of jelly. Let us come away and get round the headland before the tide comes in."

They wandered on from cove to cove, under the dark cliffs, till rounding a little headland the Doctor called out,—

" Here is something in your Cornish style, Halbert."

A thin wall of granite, like a vast buttress, ran into the sea, pierced by a great arch, some sixty feet high. Aloft all sharp grey stone : below, wherever the salt water had reached, a mass of dark clinging weed : while beyond, as though set in a dark frame, was a soft glimpse of a blue sky and snow-white seabirds.

" There is nothing so grand as that in Cornwall, Doctor," said Halbert.

" Can we pass under it, Mr. Barker ? " said Alice. " I should like to go through ; we have been into none of the caves yet."

" Oh, yes ! " said George Barker. " You may go through for the next two hours. The tide has not turned yet."

" I'll volunteer first," said the Doctor, " and if there's anything worth seeing beyond, I'll come for you."

It was, as I said, a thin wall of granite, which ran out from the rest of the hill, seaward, and was pierced by a tall arch ; the blocks which had formerly filled the void now lay, weed-grown, half buried in sand, forming a slippery threshold. Over these the Doctor climbed and looked beyond.

A little sandy cove, reef-bound, like those they had seen before, lay under the dark cliffs ; and on a water-washed rock, not a hundred yards from him, stood the man they had seen on the downs above, looking steadily seaward.

The Doctor slipped over the rocks like an otter, and approached the man across the smooth sand, unheard in the thunder of the surf. When he was close upon him, the stranger turned, and the Doctor uttered a low cry of wonder and alarm.

It was George Hawker! The Doctor knew him in a moment: but whether the recognition was mutual, he never found out, for Hawker, stepping rapidly from stone to stone, disappeared round the headland, and the thunderstruck Doctor retraced his steps to the arch.

There were all the young people gathered, wondering and delighted. But Alice came to meet him, and said,—

" Who was that with you just now?"

" A mermaid!" replied he.

" That, indeed!" said Alice. "And what did she say?"

" She said, ' Go home to your supper; you have seen quite enough; go home in good time.'"

" Doctor, there is something wrong!" said Alice. "I see it in your face. Can you trust me, and tell me what it is?"

" I can trust you so far as to tell you that you are right. I don't like the look of things at all. I fear there are evil times coming for some of our friends! Further than this I can say nothing. Say your prayers, and trust God! Don't tell Sam anything about this: to-morrow I shall speak to him. We won't spoil a pleasant holiday on mere suspicion."

They rejoined the others, and the Doctor said, "Come away home now; we have seen enough. Some future time we will come here again: you might see this fifty times, and never get tired of it."

After a good scramble they stood once more on the down above, and turned to take a last look at the broad blue sea before they descended inland; at the first glance seaward, Halbert exclaimed,—

" See there, Doctor! see there! A boat!"

" It's only a whale, I think," said George Barker.

There was a black speck far out at sea, but no whale; it was too steady for that. All day the air had been calm; if anything, the breeze was from the north, but now a strong wind was coming up from the south-east, freshening every moment, and bringing with it a pent bank of dark clouds; and, as they watched, the mysterious black speck was topped with white, and soon they saw that it was indeed a boat driving before the wind under a spritsail, which had just been set.

" That is very strange!" said George Barker. "Can it be a shipwrecked party?"

" More likely a mob of escaped convicts from Van Diemen's Land," said Jim. "If so, look out for squalls, you George, and keep your guns loaded."

" I don't think it can be that, Jim," said Sam. "What could bring them so far north? They would have landed, more likely, somewhere in the Straits, about the big lakes."

" They may have been driven off shore by these westerly winds which have been blowing the last few days," replied Jim, "and kept their boat's head northward, to get nearer the settlements. They will be terribly hungry when they do land, for certain. What's your opinion, Doctor?"

"I think that wise men should be always prepared. We should communicate with Captain Desborough, and set the police on the alert."

"I wonder," said Sam, "if that mysterious man we saw to-day, watching on the cliff, could have had any connexion with this equally mysterious boat. Not likely, though. However, if they are going to land to-night, they had better look sharp, for it is coming on to blow."

The great bank of cloud which they had been watching, away to the south-east, was growing and spreading rapidly, sending out little black avant-couriers of scud, which were hurrying fanlike across the heavens, telling the news of the coming storm. Land-ward, in the west, the sun was going down in purple and scarlet splendour, but seaward, all looked dark and ominous.

The young folks stood together in the verandah before they went in to dinner, listening to the wind which was beginning to scream angrily round the corners of the house. The rain had not yet gathered strength to fall steadily, but was whisked hither and thither by the blast, in a few uncertain drops. They saw that a great gale was coming up, and knew that, in a few hours, earth and sky would be mingled in furious war.

"How comfortable it is to think that all the animals are under shelter to-night!" said Sam. "Jim, my boy, I am glad you and I are not camped out with cattle this evening. We have been out on nights as bad as this though; eh? Oh, Lord! fancy sitting the saddle all to-night, under the breaking boughs, wet through!"

"No more of that for me, old Sam. No more jolly gallops after cattle or horses for me. But I was always a good hand at anything of that sort, and I mean to be a good soldier now. You'll see."

At dark, while they were sitting at dinner, the storm was raging round the house in full fury; but there, in the well-lighted room, before a good fire, they cared little for it. When dinner was over, the Doctor called the Captain and the Major aside, and told them in what manner he had seen and recognised George Hawker on the beach that day; and raised their fears still more by telling them of that mysterious boat which the Doctor thought Hawker had been watching for. None of them could understand it, but all agreed that these things boded no good; and so, having called their host into their confidence, with regard to the boat, they quietly loaded all the fire-arms in the place, and put them together in the hall. This done, they returned to the sitting-room, and, having taken their grog, retired to bed.

It must be remembered that hitherto Major Buckley knew nothing of George Hawker's previous appearance, but the Doctor now let him into the secret. The Major's astonishment and wrath may be conceived, at finding that his old *protégée* Mary, instead of being a comfortable widow, was the persecuted wife of one of the greatest bushrangers known. At first he was stunned and confused, but, ere he slept, his clear straightforward mind had come to a determination that the first evil was the worst, and that, God give him grace, he would hand the scoundrel over to justice on the first opportunity, sure that he was serving Mary best by doing so.

That night Jim and Sam lay together in a little room to the windward of the house. They were soon fast asleep, but, in the middle of the night, Jim was awoke by a shake on the shoulder, and, rousing himself, saw that Sam was sitting up in the bed.

" My God, Jim ! " said he,—" I have had such an awful dream ! I dreamed that those fellows in the boat were carrying off Alice, and I stood by and saw it, and could not move hand or foot. I am terribly frightened. That was something more than a dream, Jim."

" You ate too much of that pie at dinner," said Jim, " and you've had the nightmare,—that's what is the matter with you. Lord bless you, I often have the nightmare when I have eaten too much at supper, and lie on my back. Why, I dreamed the other night that the devil had got me under the wool-press, screwing me down as hard as he could, and singing the Hundredth Psalm all the time. That was a much worse dream than yours."

Sam was obliged to confess that it was. " But still," said he, " I think mine was something more than a dream. I'm frightened still."

" Oh, nonsense; lie down again. You are pulling all the clothes off me."

They lay down, and Jim was soon asleep, but not so Sam. His dream had taken such hold of his imagination, that he lay awake, listening to the storm howling around the house. Now and then he could hear the unearthly scream of some curlew piercing the din, and, above all, he could hear the continuous earth-shaking thunder of the surf upon the beach. Soon after daylight, getting Halbert to accompany him, he went out to have a look at the shore, and, forcing their way against the driving, cutting rain, they looked over the low cliff at the furious waste of waters beneath them, and saw mountain after mountain of water hurl itself, in a cloud of spray, upon the shore.

" What terrible waves, now ! " said Sam.

" Yes," replied Halbert; " there's no land to windward for six thousand miles or more. I never saw heavier seas than those. I enjoy this, Sam. It reminds me of a good roaring winter's day in old Cornwall."

" I like it, too," said Sam. " It freshens you up. How calm the water is to the leeward of the Cape ! "

" Yes ; a capital harbour of refuge that. Let us go home to breakfast."

He turned to go, but was recalled by a wild shout from Sam.

" A ship ! A ship ! "

He ran back and looked over into the seething hell of waters below. Was it only a thicker spot in the driving mist, or was it really a ship ? If so, God help her.

Small time to deliberate. Ere he could think twice about it, a full-rigged ship, about five hundred tons, with a close-reefed topsail, and a rag of a foresail upon her, came rushing, rolling, diving, and plunging on, apparently heading for the deadly white line of breakers which stretched into the sea at the end of the promontory.

" A Queen's ship, Sam ! a Queen's ship ! The Tartar, for a thousand pounds ! Oh, what a pity ; what a terrible pity ! "

" Only a merchant ship, surely," said Sam.

" Did you ever see a merchant ship with six such guns as those on her upper deck, and a hundred blue-jackets at quarters ? That is the Tartar, Sam, and in three minutes there will be no Tartar."

They had run in their excitement out to the very end of the Cape, and now the ship was almost under their feet, an awful sight to see. She was rolling fearfully, going dead before the wind. Now and then she would slop tons of water on her deck, and her mainyard would almost touch the water. But still the dark clusters of men along her bulwarks held steadfast, and the ship's head never veered half a point. Now it became apparent that she would clear the reef by a hundred yards or more, and Halbert, waving his hat, cried out,—

" Well done, Blockstrop ! Bravely done, indeed ! He is running under the lee of the Cape for shelter. Her Majesty has one more ship-of-war than I thought she would have had, five minutes ago."

As he spoke, she had passed the reef. The yards, as if by magic, swung round, and, for a moment, she was broadside on to the sea. One wave broke over her, and nought but her masts appeared above a sheet of white foam ; but, ere the water had well done pouring from her open deck ports, she was in smooth water, her anchor was down, and the topsail yard was black with men.

" Let us come down, Sam," said Halbert : " very likely they will send a boat ashore."

As they were scrambling down the leeward side of the cliff, they saw a boat put off from the ship, and gained the beach in time to meet a midshipman coming towards them. He, seeing two well-dressed gentlemen before him, bowed, and said,—

" Good morning ; very rough weather."

" Very, indeed," said Halbert. " Is that the Tartar, pray ? "

"That is the Tartar; yes. We were caught in the gale last night, and we lay-to. This morning, as soon as we recognised the Cape, we determined to run for this cove, where we have been before. We had an anxious night last night, I assure you. We have been terribly lucky. If the wind had veered a few more points to the east, we should have been done for. We never could have beaten off in such a sea as this."

"Are you going to Sydney?"

"No; we are in chase of a boat full of escaped convicts from Launceston. Cunning dogs; they would not land in the Straits. We missed them and got across to Port Phillip, and put Captain D—— and his black police on the alert; and the convicts have got a scent of it, and coasted up north. We have examined the coast all along, but I am afraid they have given us the slip; there is such a system of intelligence among them. However, if they had not landed before last night, they have saved us all trouble; and if they are ashore we wash our hands of them, and leave them to the police."

Halbert and Sam looked at one another. Then the former said,—

"Last night, about an hour before it came on to blow, we saw a boat making for this very headland, which puzzled us exceedingly; and, what was stranger still, we saw a man on the Cape, who seemed to be on the look-out."

"That is quite possible," replied the midshipman; "these fellows have a queer system of communication. The boat you saw must certainly have been them; and if they landed at all they must have landed here."

* * * * * *

I must change the scene here, if you please, my dear reader, and get you to come with me on board his (I beg pardon, her) Majesty's ship Tartar, for a few minutes, for on the quarter-deck of that noble sloop there are at this moment two men worth rescuing from oblivion.

The first is a stoutish, upright, middle-aged man, in a naval uniform, with a brickdust complexion, and very light scanty whiskers; the jolliest, cheeriest-looking fellow you are likely to meet in a year's journey. Such a bright merry blue eye as he has, too! This is Captain Blockstrop, now, I am happy to say, C.B.; a right valiant officer, as the despatches of Lyons and Peel will testify.

The other is a very different sort of man;—a long, wiry, brown-faced man, with a big forehead, and a comical expression about his eyes. This is no less a person than the Colonial Secretary of one of our three great colonies: of which I decline to mention. Those who know the Honourable Abiram Pollifex do not need to be told; and those who do not must find out for themselves. I may mention that he has been known to retain office seven years in succession, and yet he seldom threatens to resign his office and throw himself upon the country fewer than three times, and sometimes four, per annum. Latterly, I am sorry to say, a miserable faction, taking advantage of one of his numerous resignations, have assumed the reins of government, and, in spite of three votes of want of confidence, persist in retaining the seals of office. Let me add to this, that he is considered the best hand at quiet "chaff" in the House, and is allowed, both by his supporters and opponents, to be an honourable man, and a right good fellow.

Such were the two men who now stood side by side on the quarter-deck, looking eagerly at Sam and Halbert through a pair of telescopes.

"Pollifex," said the Captain, "what do you make of these?"

"Gentlemen," said the Secretary, curtly.

"So I make out," said the Captain: "and apparently in good condition, too. A very well fed man that biggest, I should say."

"Ye-es; well, ye-es," said the Secretary; "he does look well-fed enough. He must be a stranger to these parts; probably from the Maneroo* plains, or thereabout."

"What makes you think so?"

"Dear me," said the Secretary; "have you been stationed nearly three years on this coast, and ask how a man could possibly be in good condition living in those scrubby heaths?"

"Bad-looking country; eh?" said the Captain.

"Small cattle-stations, sir," said the Secretary, "I can see at a glance. Salt beef, very tough, and very little of it. I shall run a bill through the House for the abolition of small cattle-stations next session."

"Better get your estimates through first, old fellow. The bagpipes will play quite loud enough over them to last for some time."

"I know it, but tremble not," replied the undaunted Secretary; "I have got used to it. I fancy I hear Callaghan beginning now: 'The unbridled prodigality, sir, and the reckless profligacy, sir, of those individuals who have so long, under the name of government——'"

"That'll do, now," said the Captain; "you are worse than the reality. I shall go ashore, and take my chance of getting breakfast. Will you come?"

"Not if I know it, sir, with pork chops for breakfast in the cabin. Blockstrop, have you duly reflected what you are about to do? You are about to land alone, unarmed, unprovisioned, among the offscourings of white society, scarcely superior in their habits of life to the

---

* "Maneroo" is always pronounced "Maneera."

nomadic savages they have unjustly displaced. Pause and reflect, my dear fellow. What guarantee have you that they will not propose to feed you on damper, or some other nameless abomination of the same sort ? "

" It was only the other day in the House," said the Captain, " that you said the small squatters and freehold farmers represented the greater part of the intelligence and education of the colony, and now——"

" Sir! sir!" said the Secretary, " you don't know what you are talking about. Sir, we are not in the House now. Are you determined, then ? "

The Captain was quite determined, and they went down to the waist. They were raising a bag of potatoes from somewhere, and the Colonial Secretary, seizing two handfuls of them, presented them to the Captain.

" If you will go," he said, " take these with you, and teach the poor benighted white savages to plant them. So if you fall a victim to indigestion, we will vote a monument to you on the summit of the Cape, and write :—' He did not live in vain. He introduced the potato among the small cattle-stations around Cape Chatham.' "

He held out his potatoes towards the retiring Captain with the air of Burke producing the dagger. His humour, I perceive, reads poor enough when written down, but when assisted by his comical impassible face, and solemn drawling delivery, I never heard anything much better.

Good old Pollifex ! my heart warms towards him now. When I think what the men were whose clamour put him out of office in 184—, I have the conviction forced upon me, that the best among them was not worth his little finger. He left the colony in a most prosperous state, and, retiring honourably to one of his stations, set to work, as he said, to begin life again on a new principle. He is wealthy, honoured, and happy, as he deserves to be.

I cannot help, although somewhat in the wrong place, telling the reader under what circumstances I saw him last. Only two years ago, fifteen after he had left office, I happened to be standing with him, at the door of a certain club, in a certain capital, just after lunch time, when we saw the then Colonial Secretary, the man who had succeeded Pollifex, come scurrying round the corner of the street, fresh from his office. His face was flushed and perspiring, his hat was on wrong-side before, with his veil hanging down his back. In the one hand he held papers, in the other he supported over his fevered brow his white cotton umbrella ; altogether he looked harassed beyond the bounds of human endurance, but when he caught sight of the open club-doors, he freshened a bit, and mended his pace. His troubles were not over, for ere he reached his haven, two Irishmen, with two different requests, rose as if from the earth, and confronted him. We saw him make two promises, contradictory to each other, and impossible of fulfilment, and as he came up the steps, I looked into the face of Ex-Secretary Pollifex, and saw there an expression which is beyond description. Say that of the ghost of a man who has been hanged, attending an execution. Or say the expression of a Catholic, converted by torture, watching the action of the thumb-screws upon another heretic. The air, in short, of a man who had been through it all before. And as the then Secretary came madly rushing up the steps, Pollifex confronted him, and said,—

"Don't you wish you were me, T——?"

"Sir!" said the Secretary, "dipping" his umbrella and dropping his papers, for the purpose of rhetorically pointing with his left hand at nothing; "Sir! flesh and blood can't stand it. I resign to-morrow." And so he went in to his lunch, and is in office at this present moment.

I must apologise most heartily for this long digression. The Captain's gig, impelled by the "might of England's pride," was cleverly beached alongside of the other boat, and the Captain stepped out and confronted the midshipman.

"Got any news, Mr. Vang?"

"Yes, sir," said the midshipman. "These gentlemen saw the boat yesterday afternoon."

Sam and Halbert, who were standing behind him, came forward. The Captain bowed, and looked with admiration at the two highbred-looking men, that this unpromising desert had produced. They told him what they had told the midshipman, and the Captain said,— "It will be a very serious thing for this country side, if these dogs have succeeded in landing. Let us hope that the sea has done good service in swallowing fourteen of the vilest wretches that ever disgraced humanity. Pray, are either of you gentlemen magistrates?"

"My father, Major Buckley, is a magistrate," said Sam. "This gentleman is Lieutenant Halbert, of the Bengal Artillery."

The Captain bowed to Halbert, and turning to Sam, said,—"So you are the son of my old friend Major Buckley! I was midshipman in the 'Phlegethon' when she took him and part of his regiment to Portugal, in 1811. I met him at dinner in Sydney, the other day. Is he in the neighbourhood?"

"He is waiting breakfast for us not a quarter of a mile off," said Sam. "Will you join us?"

"I shall be delighted; but duty first. If these fellows have succeeded in landing, you will have to arm and prepare for the worst. Now, unless they were caught by the gale and drowned, which I believe to be the case, they must have come ashore in this very bay, about five o'clock last night. There is no other place where they could have beached their boat for many miles. Consequently, the thing lies in a nutshell : if we find the boat, prepare yourselves,—if not, make yourselves easy. Let us use our wits a little. They would round the headland as soon as possible, and probably run ashore in that furthest cove to our right, just inside the reef. I have examined the bay through a telescope, and could make out nothing of her. Let us come and examine carefully. Downhaul ! " (to his Coxswain). " Come with me."

They passed three or four indentations in the bay, examining as they went, finding nothing, but when they scrambled over the rocks which bounded the cove the Captain had indicated, he waved his hat, and laughing said,—

" Ha, ha ! just as I thought. There she is."

" Where, Captain Blockstrop ? " said Halbert. " I don't see her."

" Nor I either," said the Captain. " But I see the heap of seaweed that the cunning dogs have raked over her. Downhaul ; heave away at this weed, and show these gentlemen what is below it."

The Cockswain began throwing away a pile of sea-tang heaped against a rock. Bit by bit was disclosed the clear run of a beautiful white whale boat, which when turned over discovered her oars laid neatly side by side, with a small spritsail. The Captain stood by with the air of a man who had made a hit, while Sam and Halbert stared at one another with looks of blank discomfiture and alarm

CHAPTER XXXV.

A COUNCIL OF WAR.

" THIS is a very serious matter for us, Captain Blockstrop," said Sam, as they were walking back to the boats. " An exceedingly serious matter."

" I have only one advice to give you, Mr. Buckley," said the Captain ; " which is unnecessary, as it is just what your father will do. Fight, sir !—hunt 'em down. Shoot 'em ! they will give you no quarter : be sure you don't give them any."

A wild discordant bellow was here heard from the ship, on which the Captain slapped his leg and said,—

" Dash my buttons, if he hasn't got hold of my speaking-trumpet."

The midshipman came up with a solemn face, and, touching his cap, " reported,"—

" Colonial Secretary hailing, sir."

" Bless my soul, Mr. Vang, I can hear that," said the Captain. " I don't suppose any of my officers would dare to make such an inarticulate, no sailor-like bellow as that on her Majesty's quarter-deck. Can you make out what he says ? That would be more to the purpose."

Again the unearthly bellow came floating over the water, happily deadened by the wind, which was roaring a thousand feet over head.

" *Can* you make out anything, Mr. Vang ? " said the Captain.

" I make out ' pork chops ! ' sir," said the midshipman.

" Take one of the boats on board, Mr. Vang. My compliments, and will be much obliged if he will come ashore immediately ! on important business, say. Tell him the convicts have landed, will you ? Also, tell the lieutenant of the watch that I want either Mr. Tacks, or Mr. Sheets : either will do."

The boat was soon seen coming back with the Colonial Secretary in a statesmanlike attitude in the stern sheets, and beside him that important officer Mr. Tacks, a wee little dot of a naval cadet, apparently about ten years old.

" What were you bellowing about pork-chops, Pollifex ? " asked the Captain, the moment the boat touched the shore.

" A failure, sir," said the Colonial Secretary ; " burnt, sir ; disgracefully burnt up to a cinder, sir. I have been consulting the honourable member for the Cross-jack-yard (I allude to Mr. Tacks, N.C., my honourable friend, if he will allow me to call him so) as to the propriety of calling a court-martial on the cook's mate. He informs me that such a course is not usual in naval jurisprudence. I am, however, of opinion that in one of the civil courts of the colony an action for damages would lie. Surely I have the pleasure of seeing Mr. Buckley of Baroona ? "

Sam and he had met before, and the Secretary, finding himself on shore, and where he was known, dropped his King Cambyses' vein, and appeared in his real character of a shrewd, experienced man. They walked up together, and when they arrived at the summit of the ridge, and saw the magnificent plains stretching away inland, beyond the narrow belt of heath along the shore, the Secretary whispered to the Captain,—

" I have been deceived. We shall get some breakfast, after all. As fine a country as I ever saw in my life ! "

The party who were just sitting down to breakfast at the station were sufficiently astonished to see Captain Blockstrop come rolling up the garden walk, with that small ship-of-war Tacks sailing in his wake, convoying the three civilians ; but on going in and explaining matters, and room having been made for them at the table, Sam was also astonished on looking round to see that a new arrival had taken place since that morning.

It was that of a handsome singular-looking man. His hair was light, his whiskers a little darker, and his blonde moustache curled up towards his eyes like corkscrews or ram's horns (congratulate me on my simile). A very merry laughing eye he had, too, blue of course, with that coloured hair; altogether a very pleasant-looking man, and yet whose face gave one the idea that it was not at all times pleasant, but on occasions might look terribly tigerish and fierce. A man who won you at once, and yet one with whom one would hardly like to quarrel. Add to this, also, that when he opened his mouth to speak, he disclosed a splendid set of white teeth, and the moment he'd uttered a word, a stranger would remark to himself, " That is an Irishman."

Sam, who had ensconced himself beside Alice, looked up the long table towards him with astonishment. " Why, good gracious, Captain Desborough," he said, " can that be you ?"

" I have been waiting," said Desborough, " with the greatest patience, to see how long you would have the audacity to ignore my presence. How do you do, my small child ? Sam, my dear, if ever I get cashiered for being too handsome to remain in the Service, I'll carry you about and exhibit you, as the biggest and ugliest boy in the Australian colonies."

Captain Desborough has been mentioned before in these pages. He was an officer in the army, at the present time holding the situation of Inspector of Police in this district. He was a very famous hunter-down of bushrangers, and was heartily popular with every one he was thrown against, except the aforesaid bushrangers. Sam and he were very old friends, and were very fond of one another.

Desborough was sitting now at the upper end of the table, with the Colonial Secretary, Major Buckley, Captain Blockstrop, Captain Brentwood, and Doctor Mulhaus. They looked very serious indeed.

" It was a very lucky thing, Desborough," said the Major, " that you happened to meet Captain Blockstrop. He has now, you perceive, handed over the care of these rascals to you. It is rather strange that they should have landed here."

" I believe that they were expected," said the Doctor. " I believe that there is a desperate scheme of villany afloat, and that some of us are the objects of it."

" If you mean," said Desborough, " that that man you saw on the Cape last night was watching for the boat, I don't believe it possible. It was, possibly, some stockman or shepherd, having a look at the weather."

The Doctor had it on the tip of his tongue to speak, and astound them by disclosing that the lonely watcher was none other than the ruffian Touan, alias George Hawker ; but the Major pressed his foot beneath the table, and he was silent.

" Well," said Desborough, " and that's about all that's to be said at present, except that the settlers must arm and watch, and if necessary fight."

" If they will only do that," said the Colonial Secretary ; " if they will only act boldly in protecting their property and lives, the evil is reduced by one-half; but when Brallagan was out, nothing that I or the Governor could do would induce the majority of them to behave like men."

"Look here, now," said Barker, the host, "I was over the water when Brallagan was out, and when Howe was out too. And what could a lonely squatter do against half-a-dozen of 'em? Answer me that?"

"I don't mean that," said the Colonial Secretary; "what I refer to is the cowardly way in which the settlers allowed themselves to be prevented by threats from giving information. I speak the more boldly, Mr. Barker, because you were not one of those who did so."

Barker was appeased. "There's five long guns in my hall, and there's five long lads can use 'em," he said. "By-the-bye, Captain Desborough, let me congratulate you on the short work you made with that gang to the north, the other day. I am sorry to hear that the principal rascal of the lot, Captain Touan, gave you the slip."

The Doctor had been pondering, and had made up his mind to a certain course; he bent over the table, and said—

"I think, on the whole, that it is better to let you all know the worst. That man whom we saw on the cliff last night I met afterwards, alone, down on the shore, and that man is no other than the one you speak of, Captain Touan."

Any one watching Desborough's face as the Doctor spoke would have seen his eyebrows contract heavily, and a fierce scowl settle on his face. The name the Doctor mentioned was a very unwelcome one. He had been taunted and laughed at, at Government-house, for having allowed Hawker to outwit him. His hot Irish blood couldn't stand that, and he had vowed to have the fellow somehow. Here he had missed him, again, and by so little, too! He renewed his vow to himself, and in an instant the cloud was gone, and the merry Irishman was there again.

"My dear Doctor," he said, "I am aware that you never speak at random, or I should ask you, were you sure of the man? Are you not mistaken?"

"Mistaken in *him*,—eh?" said the Doctor. "No, I was not mistaken."

"You seem to know too much of a very suspicious character, Doctor!" said Desborough. "I shall have to keep my eye on you, I see!"

*   *   *   *   *   *

Meanwhile, at the other end of the table, more agreeable subjects were being talked of. There sat our young coterie, laughing loudly, grouping themselves round some exceedingly minute object, which apparently was between Sam and Alice, and which, on close examination, turned out to be little Tacks, who was evidently making himself agreeable in a way hardly to be expected in one of his tender years. And this is the way he got there :—

When Captain Blockstrop came in, Alice was duly impressed by the appearance of that warrior. But when she saw little Tacks slip in behind him, and sit meekly down by the door ; and when she saw how his character was appreciated by the cattle-dogs, one of whom had his head in the lad's lap, while the other was licking his face— when she saw, I say, the little blue and gold apparition, her heart grew pitiful, and, turning to Halbert, she said,—

" Why, good gracious me ! You don't mean to tell me that they take such a child as that to sea; do you ? "

" Oh dear, yes ! " said Halbert, " and younger, too. Don't you remember the story about Collingwood offering his cake to the first lieutenant ? He became, remember, a greater man than Nelson, in all except worldly honour."

" Would you ask him to come and sit by me, if you please ? " said Alice.

So Halbert went and fetched him in, and he sat and had his breakfast between Alice and Sam. They were all delighted with him ; such a child, and yet so bold and self-helpful, making himself quietly at home, and answering such questions as were put to him modestly and well. Would that all midshipmen were like him !

But it became time to go on board, and Captain Blockstrop, coming by where Alice sat, said, laughing,—

" I hope you are not giving my officer too much marmalade, Miss Brentwood ? He is over-young to be trusted with a jam-pot, —eh, Tacks ? "

" Too young to go to sea, I should say," said Alice.

" Not too young to be a brave-hearted boy, however ! " said the Captain. " The other day, in Sydney harbour, one of my marines who couldn't swim went overboard and this boy soused in after him, and carried the life-buoy to him, in spite of sharks. What do you think of that for a ten-year-old ? "

The boy's face flushed scarlet as the Captain passed on, and he held out his hand to Alice to say good-bye. She took it, looked at him, hesitated, and then bent down and kissed his cheek—a tender, sisterly kiss—something, as Jim said, to carry on board with him !

Poor little Tacks ! He was a great friend of mine ; so I have been tempted to dwell on him. He came to me with letters of introduction, and stayed at my place six weeks or more. He served brilliantly, and rose rapidly, and last year only I heard that Lieutenant Tacks had fallen in the dust, and never risen again, just at the moment that the gates of Delhi were burst down, and our fellows went swarming in to vengeance.

CHAPTER XXXVI.

AN EARTHQUAKE, A COLLIERY EXPLOSION, AND AN ADVENTURE.

So the Captain, the Colonial Secretary, and the small midshipman left the station and went on board again, disappearing from this history for evermore. The others all went home and grew warlike, arming themselves against the threatened danger; but still weeks, nay months, rolled on, and winter was turning into spring, and yet the country side remained so profoundly tranquil that every one began to believe that the convicts must after all have been drowned, and that the boat found by sagacious Blockstrop had been capsized and thrown bottom upwards on the beach. So that, before the brown flocks began to be spotted with white lambs, all alarm had gone by.

Only four persons, besides Mary Hawker herself, were conversant of the fact that the Bushranger and George Hawker were the same man. Of these only three, the Doctor, Major Buckley, and Captain Brentwood, knew of his more recent appearance on the shore, and they, after due consultation, took honest Tom Troubridge into their confidence.

But, as I said, all things went so quietly for two months, that at the end of that time no one thought any more of bushrangers than they would of tigers. And just about this time, I, Geoffry Hamlyn, having finished my last consignment of novels from England, and having nothing to do, determined to ride over, and spend a day or two with Major Buckley.

But when I rode up to the door at Baroona, having pulled my shirt collar up, and rapped at the door with my whip, out came the housekeeper to inform me there was not a soul at home. This was deeply provoking, for I had got on a new pair of riding trousers, which had cost money, and a new white hat with a blue net veil (rather a neat thing too), and I had ridden up to the house under the idea that fourteen or fifteen persons were looking at me out of window. I had also tickled my old horse, Chanticleer, to make him caper and show the excellency of my seat. But when I came to remember that the old horse had nearly bucked me over his head instead of capering, and to find that my hat was garnished with a large cobweb of what is called by courtesy native silk, with half-a-dozen dead leaves sticking in it, I felt consoled that no one had seen me approach, and asked the housekeeper with tolerable equanimity where they were all gone.

They were all gone, she said, over to Captain Brentwood's, and goodness gracious knew when they would be back again. Mrs.

Hawker and Mr. Charles were gone with them. For her part, she should not be sorry when Mr. Sam brought Miss Brentwood over for good and all. The house was terrible lonesome when they were all away.

I remarked, " Oho ! " and asked whether she knew if Mr. Troubridge was at Toonarbin.

No, she said ; he was away again at Port Phillip with store cattle ; making a deal of money, she understood, and laying out a deal for the Major in land. She wished he would marry Mrs. Hawker and settle down, for he was a pleasant gentleman, and fine company in a house. Wouldn't I get off and have a bit of cold wild duck and a glass of sherry ?

Certainly I would. So I gave my horse to the groom and went in. I had hardly cut the first rich red slice from the breast of a fat teal, when I heard a light step in the passage, and in walked my man Dick. You remember him, reader. The man we saw five and twenty years ago on Dartmoor, combining with William Lee to urge the unhappy George Hawker on to ruin and forgery, which circumstance, remember, I knew nothing of at this time. The same man I had picked up footsore and penniless in the bush sixteen years ago, and who had since lived with me, a most excellent and clever servant—the best I ever had. This man now came into Major Buckley's parlour, hat in hand, looking a little foolish, and when I saw him my knife and fork were paralysed with astonishment.

" Why, what the Dickens" (I used that strong expression) " brings you here, my lad ? "

" I went to Hipsley's about the colt," he said, " and when I got home I found you were gone off unexpectedly ; so I thought it better to come after you and tell you all about it. He won't take less than thirty-five."

" Man ! man ! " I said, " do you mean to say that you have ridden fifty miles to tell me the price of a leggy beast like that, after I had told you that twenty-four was my highest offer ? "

He looked very silly, and I saw very well he had some other reason for coming than that. But with a good servant I never ask too many questions, and when I went out a short time after, and found him leaning against a fence, and talking earnestly to our old acquaintance William Lee, I thought, " He wanted an excuse to come up and see his old friend Lee. That is quite just and proper, and fully accounts for it."

Lee always paid me the high compliment of touching his hat to me, for old Devon' sake I suppose. " How's all at Toonarbin, Lee ? " I asked.

" Well and hearty, sir. How is yourself, sir ? "

" Getting older, Lee. Nothing worse than that. Dick, I am

going on to Captain Brentwood's. If you like to go back to Toonarbin and stay a day or two with Lee, you can do so."

"I would rather come on with you, sir," he said eagerly.

"Are you sure?" I said.

"Quite sure, sir." And Lee said, "You go on with Mr. Hamlyn, Dick, and do your duty, mind."

I thought this odd; but knowing it useless to ask questions of an old hand, or try to get any information which was not volunteered, I held my tongue and departed, taking Dick with me.

I arrived at Captain Brentwood's about three o'clock in the afternoon. I flatter myself that I made a very successful approach, and created rather a sensation among the fourteen or fifteen people who were sitting in the verandah. They took me for a distinguished stranger. But when they saw who it was they all began calling out to me at once to know how I was, and to come in (as if I wasn't coming in), and when at last I got among them, I nearly had my hand shaken off; and the Doctor, putting on his spectacles and looking at me for a minute, asked what I had given for my hat?

Let me see, who was there that day? There was Mary Hawker, looking rather older, and a little worn; and there was her son Charles sitting beside pretty Ellen Mayford, and carrying on a terrible flirtation with that young lady, in spite of her fat jolly-looking mother, who sat with folded hands beside her. Next to her sat her handsome brother Cecil, looking, poor lad! as miserable as he well could look, although I did not know the cause. Then came Sam, beside his mother, whose noble happy face was still worth riding fifty miles to see; and then, standing beside her chair, was Alice Brentwood.

I had never seen this exquisite creature before, and I immediately fell desperately and hopelessly in love with her, and told her so that same evening, in the presence of Sam. Finding that my affection was not likely to be returned, I enrolled myself as one of her knights, and remain so to this present time.

The Major sat beside his wife, and the Doctor and Captain Brentwood walked up and down, talking politics. There were also present, certain Hawbucks, leggy youths with brown faces and limp hair, in appearance and dress not unlike English steeplechase-riders who had been treated, on the face and hands, with walnut-juice. They never spoke, and the number of them then present I am uncertain about, but one of them I recollect could spit a good deal farther than any of his brothers, and proved it beyond controversy about twice in every three minutes.

I missed my old friend Jim Brentwood, and was informed that he had gone to Sydney, "on the spree," as Sam expressed it, along with a certain Lieutenant Halbert, who was staying on a visit with Major Buckley.

First I sat down by Mary Hawker, and had a long talk with her about old times. She was in one of her gay moods, and laughed and joked continuously. Then I moved up by invitation, to a chair between the Major and his wife, and had a long private and confidential conversation with them.

" How," I began, " is Tom Troubridge ? "

" Tom is perfectly well," said the Major. " He still carries on his old chronic flirtation with Mary ; and she is as ready to be flirted with as ever."

" Why don't they marry ? " I asked, peevishly. " Why on earth don't they marry one another ? What is the good of carrying on that old folly so long ? They surely must have made up their minds by now. She knows she is a widow, and has known it for years."

" Good God ! Hamlyn, are you so ignorant ? " said the Major. And then he struck me dumb by telling me of all that had happened latterly : of George Hawker's reappearance, of his identity with the great bushranger, and, lastly, of his second appearance, not two months before.

" I tell you this in strict confidence, Hamlyn, as one of my oldest and best friends. I know how deeply your happiness is affected by all this."

I remained silent and thunderstruck for a time, and then I tried to turn the conversation :—

" Have you had any alarm from bushrangers lately ? I heard a report of some convicts having landed on the coast."

" All a false alarm ! " said the Major. " They were drowned, and the boat washed ashore, bottom upwards."

Here the Doctor broke in : " Hamlyn, is not this very queer weather ? "

When he called my attention to it, I remarked that the weather was really different from any I had seen before, and said so.

The sky was grey and dull, the distances were clear, and to the eye it appeared merely a soft grey autumnal day. But there was something very strange and odd in the deadly stillness of all nature. Not a leaf moved, not a bird sang, and the air seemed like lead. At once Mrs. Buckley remarked,—

" I can't work, and I can't talk. I am so wretchedly nervous that I don't know what to do with myself, and you know, my dear," she said, appealing to her husband, " that I am not given to that sort of thing."

Each man looked at his neighbour, for there was a sound in the air now—a weird and awful sound like nothing else in nature. To the south arose upon the ear a hollow quivering hum, which swelled rapidly into a roar beneath our feet ; then there was a sickening shake, a thump, a crash, and away went the Earthquake, groaning off to the northward.

The women behaved very well, though some of them began to cry; and hearing a fearful row in the kitchen I dashed off there, followed by the Doctor. The interior was a chaos of pots and kettles, in the centre of which sat the cook, Eleanor, holding on by the floor. Every now and then she would give a scream which took all the breath out of her; so she had to stop and fetch breath before she could give another. The Doctor stepped through the saucepans and camp-ovens, and trying to raise her, said—

" Come, get up, my good woman, and give over screaming. All danger is over, and you will frighten the ladies."

At this moment she got her " second wind," and as he tried to get her up she gave such a yell that he dropped her again, and bolted, stopping his ears; bolted over a teakettle which had been thrown down, and fell prostrate, resounding, like an Homeric hero, on to a heap of kitchen utensils, at the feet of Alice, who had come in to see what the noise was about.

" Good Lord! " said he, picking himself up, " what lungs she has got! I shall have a singing in my ears to my dying day. Yar! it went through my head like a knife."

Sam picked up the cook, and she, after a time, picked up her pots, giving, however, an occasional squall, and holding on by the dresser, under the impression that another earthquake was coming. We left her, however, getting dinner under way, and went back to the others, whom we soon set laughing by telling poor Eleanor's misadventures.

We were all in good spirits now. A brisk cool wind had come up from the south, following the earthquake, making a pleasant rustle as it swept across the plain or tossed the forest boughs. The sky had got clear, and the nimble air was so inviting that we rose as one body to stroll in groups about the garden and wander down to the river.

The brave old river was rushing hoarsely along, clear and full between his ruined temple-columns of basalt, as of old. " What a grand salmon-river this would be, Major! " said I; " what pools and stickles are here! Ah! if we only could get the salmon-spawn through the tropics without its germinating.—Can you tell me, Doctor, why these rocks should take the form of columns? Is there any particular reason for it that you know?"

" You have asked a very puzzling question," he replied, " and I hardly know how to answer it. Nine geologists out of ten will tell you that basalt is lava cooled under pressure. But I have seen it in places where that solution was quite inapplicable. However, I can tell you that the same cause which set these pillars here, to wall the river, piled up yon Organ-hill, produced the caves of Widderin, the great crater-hollow of Mirngish, and accommodated us with that brisk little earthquake which we felt just now. For you know that we mortals stand only on a thin crust of cooled matter, but beneath his feet is all molten metal."

"I wish you could give us a lecture on these things, Doctor," I said.

"To-morrow," said he, "let us ride forth to Mirngish and have a picnic. There I will give you a little sketch of the origin of that hill."

In front of the Brentwoods' house the plains stretched away for a dozen miles or so, a bare sheet of grass with no timber, grey in summer, green in winter. About five miles off it began to roll into great waves, and then heaved up into a high bald hill, a lofty down, capped with black rocks, bearing in its side a vast round hollow, at the bottom of which was a little swamp, perfectly circular, fringed with a ring of white gum-trees, standing in such an exact circle that it was hard to persuade oneself that they were not planted by the hand of man. This was the crater of the old volcano. Had you stood in it you would have remarked that one side was a shelving steep bank of short grass, while the other reared up some five hundred feet, a precipice of fire-eaten rock. At one end the lip had broken down, pouring a torrent of lava, now fertile grass-land, over the surrounding country, which little gap gave one a delicious bit of blue distance. All else, as I said, was a circular wall of grass, rock, and tumbled slag.

This was Mirngish. And the day after the earthquake there was a fresh eruption in the crater. An eruption of horsemen and horse-women. An eruption of talk, laughter, pink-bonnets, knives and forks, and champagne. Many a pleasant echo came ringing back from the old volcano-walls overhead, only used for so many ages to hear the wild rattle of the thunder and the scream of the hungry eagle.

Was ever a poor old worn-out grass-grown volcano used so badly? Here into the very pit of Tophet had the audacious Captain that very morning sent on a spring-cart of all eatables and drinkables, and then had followed himself with a dozen of his friends, to eat and drink, and talk and laugh, just in the very spot where of old roared and seethed the fire and brimstone of Erebus.

Yet the good old mountain was civil, for we were not blown into the air, to be a warning to all people picnicing in high places; but when we had eaten and drunk, and all the ladies had separately and collectively declared that they were *so* fond of the smell of tobacco in the open air, we followed the Doctor, who led the way to the summit of the hill.

I arrived last, having dragged dear fat old Mrs. Mayford up the slippery steep. The Doctor had perched himself on the highest flame-worn crag, and when we all had grouped ourselves below him, and while the wind swept pleasantly through the grass, and rushed humming through the ancient rocks, he in a clear melodious voice thus began:—

" Of old the great sea heaved and foamed above the ground on which we stand ; aye, above this, and above yon farthest snowy peak, which the westering sun begins to tinge with crimson.

" But in the lapse of ten thousand changing centuries, the lower deeps, acted on by some Plutonic agency, began to grow shallow ; and the imprisoned tides began to foam and roar as they struggled to follow the moon, their leader, angry to find that the stillness of their ancient domain was year by year invaded by the ever-rising land.

" At that time, had man been on the earth to see it, those towering Alps were a cluster of lofty islands, each mountain pass which divides them was a tide-swept fiord, in and out of which, twice in the day, age after age, rushed the sea, bringing down those vast piles of water-worn gravel which you see accumulated, and now covered with dense vegetation, at the mouth of each great valley.

" So twenty thousand years went on, and all this fair champagne country which we overlook became, first a sand-bank, then a dreary stretch of salt-saturated desert, and then, as the roar of the retiring ocean grew fainter and fainter, began to sustain such vegetation as the Lord thought fit.

" A thousand years are but as yesterday to Him, and I can give you no notion as to how many hundred thousand years it took to do all this ; or what productions covered the face of the country. It must have been a miserably poor region : nothing but the débris of granite, sandstone, and slate ; perhaps here and there partially fertilized by rotting sea-weed, dead fish and shells ; things which would, we may assume, have appeared and flourished as the water grew shallower.

" New elements were wanting to make the country available for man, so soon to appear in his majesty ; and new elements were forthcoming. The internal fires so long imprisoned beneath the weight of the incumbent earth, having done their duty in raising the continent, began to find vent in every weak spot caused by its elevation.

" Here, where we stand, in this great crack between the granite and the sandstone, they broke out with all their wildest fury ; hurling stones high in the air, making mid-day dark with clouds of ashes, and pouring streams of lava far and wide.

" So the country was desolated by volcanoes, but only desolated that it might grow greener and richer than ever, with a new and hitherto unknown fertility ; for, as the surface of the lava disintegrated, a new soil was found, containing all the elements of the old one, and many more. These are your black clay, and your red burnt soil, which, I take it, are some of the richest in the world.

" Then our old volcano, our familiar Mirngish, in whose crater we have been feasting, grew still for a time, for many ages probably;

but after that I see the traces of another eruption ; the worst, perhaps, that he ever accomplished.

"He had exhausted himself, and gradually subsided, leaving a perfect cup or crater, the accumulation of the ashes of a hundred eruptions ; nay, even this may have been filled with water, as is Mount Gambier, which you have not seen, forming a lake without a visible outlet ; the water draining off at that level where the looser scoriæ begin.

"But he burst out again, filling this great hollow with lava, till the accumulation of the molten matter broke through the weaker part of the wall, and rolled away there, out of that gap to the north-ward, and forming what you now call the 'stony rises,'—turning yon creek into steam, which by its explosive force formed that fan-tastic cap of rocks, and, swelling into great bubbles under the hot lava, made those long underground hollows which we now know as the caves of Bar-ca-nah.

"Is he asleep for ever ? I know not. He may arise again in his wrath and fill the land with desolation ; for that earthquake we felt yesterday was but a wild throe of the giant struggling to be free.

"Let us hope that he may not break his chains, for as I stand here gazing on those crimson Alps, the spirit of prophecy is upon me, and I can see far into the future, and all the desolate landscape becomes peopled with busy figures.

"I see the sunny slopes below me yellow with trellissed vines. They have gathered the vintage, and I hear them singing at the wine-press. They sing that the exhausted vineyards of the old world yield no wine so rare, so rich, as the fresh volcanic slopes of the southern continent, and that the princes of the earth send their wealth that their hearts may get glad from the juice of the Australian grapes.

"Beyond I see fat black ridges grow yellow with a thousand cornfields. I see a hundred happy homesteads, half-hidden by clus-tering wheatstacks. What do they want with all that corn ? say you ; where is their market !

"There is their market ! Away there on the barren forest ranges. See, the timber is gone, and a city stands there instead. What is that on the crest of the hill ? A steam-engine : nay, see, there are five of them, working night and day, fast and busy. Their cranks gleam and flash under the same moon that grew red and lurid when old Mirngish vomited fire and smoke twenty thousand years ago. As I listen I can hear the grinding of the busy quartz-mill. What are they doing ? you ask. They are gold-mining.

"They have found gold here, and gold in abundance, and hither have come, by ship and steamship, all the unfortunate of the earth. The English factory labourer and the farmer-ridden peasant ; the

Irish pauper; the starved Scotch Highlander. I hear a grand swelling chorus rising above the murmur of the evening breeze; that is sung by German peasants revelling in such plenty as they never knew before, yet still regretting fatherland, and then I hear a burst of Italian melody replying. Hungarians are not wanting, for all the oppressed of the earth have taken refuge here, glorying to live under the free government of Britain; for she, warned by American experience, has granted to all her colonies such rights as the British boast of possessing."

I did not understand him then. But, since I have seen the living wonder of Ballarat, I understand him well enough.

He ceased. But the Major cried out, "Go on, Doctor, go on. Look farther yet, and tell us what you see. Give us a bit more poetry while your hand is in."

He faced round, and I fancied I could detect a latent smile about his mouth.

"I see," said he, "a vision of a nation, the colony of the greatest race on the earth, who began their career with more advantages than ever fell to the lot of a young nation yet. War never looked on them. Not theirs was the lot to fight, like the Americans, through bankruptcy and inexperience towards freedom and honour. No. Freedom came to them, Heaven-sent, red-tape-bound, straight from Downing-street. Millions of fertile acres, gold in bushels were theirs, and yet——"

"Go on," said the Major.

"I see a vision of broken railway arches and ruined farms. I see a vision of a people surfeited with prosperity and freedom grown factious, so that now one party must command a strong majority ere they can pass a law the goodness of which no one denies. I see a bankrupt exchequer, a drunken Governor, an Irish ministry, a——"

"Come down out of that," roared the Major, "before I pull you down. You're a pretty fellow to come out for a day's pleasure! Jeremiah was a saint to him," he added, turning appealingly to the rest of us. "Hear my opinion, 'per contra,' Doctor. I'll be as near right as you."

"Go on, then," said the Doctor.

"I see," began the Major, "the Anglo-Saxon race——"

"Don't forget the Irish, Jews, Germans, Chinese, and other barbarians," interrupted the Doctor.

"Asserting," continued the Major, scornfully, "as they always do, their right to all the unoccupied territories of the earth——"

("Blackfellow's claims being ignored," interpolated the Doctor.)

"And filling all the harbours of this magnificent country——"

("Want to see them.")

"With their steamships and their sailing vessels. Say there be gold here, as I believe there is, the time must come when the mines will be exhausted. What then? With our coals we shall supply——"

(" Newcastle," said the Doctor, again.

" The British fleets in the East Indies——'

" And compete with Borneo," said the Doctor, quietly, " which contains more coal than ever India will burn, at one-tenth the distance from her that we are. If that is a specimen of your prophecies, Major, you are but a Micaiah after all."

" Well," said the Major, laughing, " I cannot reel it off quite so quick as you; but think we shall hardly have time for any more prophesying; the sun is getting very low."

We turned and looked to westward. The lofty rolling snow-downs had changed to dull lead-colour, as the sun went down in a red haze behind them; only here and there some little elevated pinnacle would catch the light. Below the mountain lay vast black sheets of woodland, and nearer still was the river, marked distinctly by a dense and rapidly-rising line of fog.

" We are going to have a fog and a frost," said the Major. " We had better hurry home."

Behind all the others rode Alice, Sam, and myself. I was fearful of being "de trop," but when I tried to get forward to the laughing, chattering, crowd in front, these two young lovers raised such an outcry that I was fain to stay with them, which I was well pleased to do.

Behind us, however, rode three mounted servants, two of Captain Brentwood's, and my man Dick.

We were almost in sight of the river, nearly home in fact, when there arose a loud lamentation from Alice.

" Oh, my bracelet! my dear bracelet! I have lost it."

" Have you any idea where you dropped it?" I inquired.

" Oh, yes," she said. " I am sure it must have been when I fell down, scrambling up the rocks, just before the Doctor began his lecture. Just as I reached the top, you know, I fell down, and I must have lost it there."

" I will ride back and find it, then, in no time," I said.

" No, indeed, Uncle Jeff," said Sam. " I will go back."

" I use an uncle's authority," I replied, " and I forbid you. That miserable old pony of yours, which you have chosen to bring out to-day, has had quite work enough, without ten miles extra. I condescend to no argument; here I go."

I turned, with a kind look from both of them, but ere I had gone ten yards, my servant Dick was alongside of me.

" Where are you going, sir?" said he.

" I am going back to Mirngish," I replied. " Miss Alice has dropped her bracelet, and I am going back for it."

" I will come with you, sir," he said.

"Indeed no, Dick; there is no need. Go back to your supper, lad, I shan't be long away."

"I am coming with you, sir," he replied. "Company is a good thing sometimes."

"Well, boy," I said, "if you will come, I shall be glad of your company; so come along."

I had noticed lately that Dick never let me go far alone, but would always be with me. It gave rise to no suspicion in my mind. He had been tried too often for that. But still, I thought it strange.

On this occasion, we had not ridden far before he asked me a question which rather surprised me. He said,—

"Mr. Hamlyn; do you carry pistols?"

"Why, Dick, boy?" I said, "why should I?"

"Look you here, Mr. Hamlyn," said he. "Have you tried me?"

"I have tried you for twenty years, Dick, and have not found you wanting."

"Ah!" said he, "that's good hearing. You're a magistrate, sir, though only just made. But you know that coves like me, that have been in trouble, get hold of information which you beaks can't. And I tell you, sir, there's bad times coming for this country side. You carry your pistols, sir, and, what's more, *you use 'em*. See here."

He opened his shirt, and showed me a long sharp knife inside.

"That's what I carries, sir, in these times, and you ought to carry ditto, and a brace of barkers besides. We shan't get back to the Captain's to-night."

We were rising on the first shoulder of Mirngish, and daylight was rapidly departing. I looked back. Nothing but a vast sea of fog, one snow peak rising from it like an iceberg from a frozen sea, piercing the clear frosty air like a crystal of lead and silver.

"We must hurry on," I said, "or we shall never have daylight to find the bracelet. We shall never find our way home through that fog, without a breath of wind to guide us. What shall we do?"

"I noticed to-day, sir," said Dick, "a track that crossed the hill to the east; if we can get on that, and keep on it, we are sure to get somewhere. It would be better to follow that than go blundering across the plain through such a mist as that."

As he was speaking, we had dismounted and commenced our search. In five minutes, so well did our recollection serve us, Dick had got the bracelet, and, having mounted our horses, we deliberated what was next to be done.

A thick fog covered the whole country, and was rapidly creeping up to the elevation on which we stood. To get home over the plains without a compass seemed a hopeless matter. So we determined to strike for the track which Dick had noticed in the morning, and get on it before it was dark.

We plunged down into the sea of fog, and, by carefully keeping the same direction, we found our road. The moon was nearly full, which enabled us to distinguish it, though we could never see above five yards in front of us.

We followed the road above an hour; then we began to see ghostly tree-stems through the mist. They grew thicker and more frequent. Then we saw a light, and at last rode up to a hut-door, cheered by the warm light, emanating from a roaring fire within, which poured through every crack in the house-side, and made the very fog look warm.

I held Dick's horse while he knocked. The door was opened by a wee feeble old man, about sixty, with a sharp clever face, and an iron-grey rough head of hair.

"Night, daddy," said Dick. "Can me and my master stay here to-night? We're all abroad in this fog. The governor will leave something handsome behind in the morning, old party, I know." (This latter was in a whisper.)

"Canst thou stay here, say'st thou?" replied the old fellow. "In course thou canst. But thy master's money may bide in a's pouch. Get thy saddles off, lad, and come in; 'tis a smittle night for rheumatics."

I helped Dick to take off the saddles, and, having hobbled our horses with stirrup-leathers, we went in.

Our little old friend was the hut-keeper, as I saw at a glance. The shepherd was sitting on a block before the fire, in his shirt, smoking his pipe and warming his legs preparatory to turning in.

I understood him in a moment, as I then thought (though I was much deceived). A short, wiry, black-headed man, with a cunning face—convict all over. He rose as we came in, and gave us good evening. I begged he would not disturb himself; so he moved his block into the corner, and smoked away with that lazy indifference that only a shepherd is master of.

But the old man began bustling about. He made us sit down before the fire, and make ourselves comfortable. He never ceased talking.

"I'll get ye lads some supper just now," said he. "There's na but twa bunks i' the hut; so master and man must lie o' the floor, 'less indeed the boss lies in my bed, which he's welcome to. We've a plenty blankets, though, and sheepskins. We'll mak ye comfortable, boys. There's a mickle back log o' the fire, and ye'll lie warm, I'se warrant ye. There's cowd beef, sir (to me), and good breed, no' to mind boggins o' tea. Ye'll be comfortable, will ye. What's yer name?"

"Hamlyn," I said.

" Oh, ay ! Ye're Hamlyn and Stockbridge ! I ken ye well ;
I kenned yer partner : a good man—a very good man, a man o' ten
thousand. He was put down up north. A bad job—a very bad
job ! Ye gat terrible vengeance, though. Ye hewed Agag in
pieces ! T' Governor up there to Sydney was wild angry at what ye
did, but he darena' say much. He knew that every free man's
heart went with ye. It were the sword of the Lord and of Gideon
that ye fought with ! Ye saved many good lives by that raid of
yours after Stockbridge was killed. The devils wanted a lesson, and
ye gar'd them read one wi' a vengeance ! "

During this speech, which was uttered in a series of interjections,
we had made our supper, and drawn back to the fire. The shepherd
had tumbled into his blankets, and was snoring. The old man,
having cleared away the things, came and sat down beside us. The
present of a fig of tobacco won his heart utterly, and he, having cut
up a pipeful, began talking again.

" Why," said he, " it's the real Barret's twist—the very real
article ! Eh, master, ye're book-learned : do you ken where this
grows ? It must be a fine country to bring up such backer as this ;
some o' they Palm Isles, I reckon."

" Virginia," I told him, " or Carolina, one of the finest countries
in the world, where they hold slaves."

" Ah," said he, " they couldn't get white men to mess with backer
and such in a hot country, and in course, every one knows that blacks
won't work till they're made. That's why they bothers themselves
with 'em, I reckon. But, Lord ! they are useless trash. White
convicts is useless enough ; think what black niggers must be ! "

How about the gentleman in bed ? I thought ; but he was snoring
comfortably.

" I am a free man, myself," continued the old man. " I never did
aught, ay, or thought o' doing aught, that an honest man should not
do. But I've lived among convicts twenty odd year, and do you know,
sir, sometimes I hardly know richt fra wrang. Sometimes I see things
that whiles I think I should inform of, and then the devil comes and
tells me it would be dishonourable. And then I believe him till the
time's gone by, and after that I am miserable in my conscience. So
I haven't an easy time of it, though I have good times, and money
to spare."

I was getting fond of the honest, talkative old fellow ; so when
Dick asked him if he wanted to turn in, and he answered no, I was
well pleased.

" Can't you pitch us a yarn, daddy ? " said Dick. " Tell us
something about the old country. I should like well to hear what
you were at home."

" I'll pitch ye a yarn, lad," he replied, " if the master don't want
to turn in. I'm fond of talking. All old men are, I think." he

said, appealing to me. "The time's coming, ye see, when the gift o' speech will be gone from me. It's a great gift. But happen we won't lose it after all."

I said, "No, that I thought not; that I thought on the other side of the grave we should both speak and hear of higher things than we did in the flesh."

"Happen so," said he; "I think so too, sometime. I'll give ye my yarn; I have told it often. Howsoever, neither o' ye have heard it, so ye're the luckier that I tell it better by frequent repetition. Here it is:—

"I was a collier lad, always lean, and not well favoured, though I was active and strong. I was small too, and that set my father's heart agin me somewhat, for he was a gran' man, and a mighty fighter.

"But my elder brother Jack, he was a mighty fellow, God bless him; and when he was eighteen he weighed twelve stone, and was earning man's wages, tho' that I was hurrying still. I saw that father loved him better than me, and whiles that vexed me, but most times it didn't, for I cared about the lad as well as father did, and he liked me the same. He never went far without me; and whether he fought, or whether he drunk, I must be wi' him and help.

"Well, so we went on till, as I said, I was seventeen, and he eighteen. We never had a word till then; we were as brothers should be. But at this time we had a quarrel, the first we ever had; ay, and the last, for we got something to mind this one by.

"We both worked in the same pit. It was the Southstone Pit; happen you've heard of it. No? Well, these things get soon forgot. Father had been an overman there, but was doing better now above ground. He and mother kept a bit shop, and made money.

"There was a fair in our village, a poor thing enough; but when we boys were children we used to look forward to it eleven months out o' twelve, and the day it came round we used to go to father, and get sixpence, or happen a shilling apiece to spend.

"Well, time went on till we came to earn money; but still we kept up the custom, and went to the old man reg'lar for our fairin', and he used to laugh and chaff us as he'd give us a fourpenny or such, and we liked the joke as well as he.

"Well this time—it was in '12, just after the comet, just the worst times of the war, the fair came round 24th of May, I well remember, and we went in to the old man to get summut to spend—just for a joke, like.

"He'd lost money, and been vexed; so when Jack asked him for his fairin' he gi'ed him five shillin', and said, 'I'll go to gaol but what my handsome boy shan't have summut to treat his friends to beer.' But when I axed him, he said, 'Earn man's wages, and thee'll get a man's fairin',' and heaved a penny at me.

"That made me wild mad, I tell you. I wasn't only angry wi' the old man, but I was mad wi' Jack, poor lad! The devil of jealousy had got into me, and, instead of kicking him out I nursed him. I ran out o' the house, and away into the fair, and drunk, and fought, and swore like a mad one.

"I was in one of the dancing booths, half drunk, and a young fellow came to me, and said, 'Where has thee been? Do thee know thy brother has foughten Jim Perry, and beaten him?'

"I felt like crying, to think my brother had fought, and I not there to set him up. But I swore, and said, 'I wish Jim Perry had killed un;' and then I sneaked off home to bed, and cried like a lass.

"And next morning I was up before him, and down the pit. He worked a good piece from me, so I did not see him, and it came on nigh nine o'clock before I began to wonder why the viewer had not been round, for I had heard say there was a foul place cut into by some of them, and at such times the viewer generally looks into every corner.

"Well, about nine, the viewer and underviewer came up with the overman, and stood talking alongside of me, when there came a something sudden and sharp, as tho' one had boxed your ears, and then a 'whiz, whiz,' and the viewer stumbled a one side, and cried out, 'God save us!'

"I hardly knew what had happened till I heard him singing out clear and firm, 'Come here to me, you lads; come here. Keep steady, and we'll be all right yet.' Then I knew it was a fire, and a sharp one, and began crying out for Jack.

"I heard him calling for me, and then he ran up and got hold of me; and so ended the only quarrel we ever had, and that was a one-sided one.

"'Are you all here?' said the viewer. 'Now follow me, and if we meet the afterdamp hold your breath and run. I am afraid it's a bad job, but we may get through yet.'

"We had not gone fifty yards before we came on the afterdamp, filling the headway like smoke. Jack and I took hold of each other's collars and ran, but before we were half way through, he fell. I kept good hold of his shirt, and dragged him on on the ground. I felt as strong as a horse; and in ten seconds, which seemed to me like ten hours, I dragged him out under the shaft into clear air. At first I thought he was dead, but he was still alive, and very little of that. His heart beat very slow, and I thought he'd die; but I knew if he got clear air that he might come round.

"When we had gotten to the shaft bottom we found it all full of smoke; the waft had gone straight up, and they on the top told us after that all the earth round was shook, and the black smoke and coal-dust flew up as though from a gun-barrel. Any way it was strong enough to carry away the machine, so we waited there ten minutes and wondered the basket did not come down; but they above, meanwhile, were rigging a rope to an old horse-whim, and as they could not get horses, the men run the poles round themselves.

" But we at the bottom knew nothing of all this. There were thirty or so in the shaft bottom, standing there, dripping wet wi' water, and shouting for the others, who never came; now the smoke began to show in the west drive, and we knew the mine was fired, and yet we heard nought from those above.

"But what I minded most of all was, that Jack was getting better. I knew we could not well be lost right under the shaft, so I did not swear and go on like some of them, because they did not mind us above. When the basket came down at last, I and Jack went up among the first, and there I saw such a sight, lad, as ye'll never see till ye see a colliery explosion. There were hundreds and hundreds there. Most had got friends or kin in the pit, and as each man came up, his wife or his mother would seize hold of him and carry on terrible.

" But the worst were they whose husbands and sons never came up again, and they were many; for out of one hundred and thirty-one men in the pit, only thirty-nine came up alive. Directly we came to bank, I saw father; he was first among them that were helping, working like a horse, and directing everything. When he saw us, he said, ' Thank the Lord, there's my two boys. I am not a loser to-day ! ' and came running to us, and helped me to carry Jack down the bank. He was very weak and sick, but the air freshened him up wonderful.

" I told father all about it, and he said, ' I've been wrong, and thou'st been wrong. Don't thou get angry for nothing; thou hast done a man's work to-day, at all events. Now come and bear a hand. T'owd 'ooman will mind the lad."

" We went back to the pit's mouth; the men were tearing round the whim faster than horses would a' done it. And first amongst 'em all was old Mrs. Cobley, wi' her long grey hair down her back, doing the work o' three men; for her two boys were down still, and I knew for one that they were not with us at the bottom; but when the basket came up with the last, and her two boys missing, she went across to the master, and asked him what he was going to do, as quiet as possible.

" He said he was going to ask some men to go down, and my father volunteered to go at once, and eight more went with him. They were soon up again, and reported that all the mine was full of smoke, and no one had dared leave the shaft bottom fifty yards.

" ' It's clear enough, the mine's fired, sir,' said my father to the owner. ' They that's down are dead. Better close it, sir.'

" ' What!' screamed old Mrs. Cobley, ' close the pit, ye dog, and my boys down there? Ye wouldn't do such a thing, master dear?' she continued; ' ye couldn't do it.' Many others were wild when they heard the thing proposed; but while they raved and argued, the pit began to send up a reek of smoke like the mouth of hell, and then the master gave orders to close the shaft, and a hundred women knew they were widows, and went weeping home.

" And Jack got well. And after the old man died, we came out here. Jack has gotten a public-house in Yass, and next year I shall go home and live with him.

" And that's the yarn about the fire at the Southstone Pit."

We applauded it highly, and after a time began to talk about lying down, when on a sudden we heard a noise of horses' feet outside; then the door was opened, and in came a stranger.

He was a stranger to me, but not to my servant, who I could see recognised him, though he gave no sign of it in words. I also stared at him, for he was the handsomest young man I had ever seen.

Handsome as an Apollo, beautiful as a leopard, but with such a peculiar style of beauty, that when you looked at him you instinctively felt at your side for a weapon of defence, for a more reckless, dangerous looking man I never yet set eyes on. And while I looked at him I recognised him. I had seen his face, or one like it, before, often, often. And it seemed as though I had known him just as he stood there, years and years ago, on the other side of the world. I was almost certain it was so, and yet he seemed barely twenty. It was an impossibility, and yet as I looked I grew every moment more certain.

He dashed in in an insolent way. " I am going to quarter here to-night and chance it," he said. " Hallo! Dick, my prince! You here? And what may your name be, old cock?" he added, turning to me, now seeing me indistinctly for the first time, for I was sitting back in the shadow.

" My name is Geoffry Hamlyn. I am a Justice of the Peace, and I am at your service," I said. " Now perhaps you will favour me with *your* name?"

The young gentleman did not seem to like coming so suddenly into close proximity with a " beak," and answered defiantly,—

" Charles Sutton is my name, and I don't know as there's anything against me at present."

" Sutton," I said; " Sutton? I don't know the name. No, I have nothing against you, except that you don't appear very civil."

Soon after I rolled myself in a blanket and lay down. Dick lay at right angles to me, his feet nearly touching mine. He began snoring heavily almost immediately, and just when I was going to give him a kick, and tell him not to make such a row, I felt him give me a good sharp shove with the heel of his boot, by which I understood that he was awake, and meant to keep awake, as he did not approve of the strangers.

I was anxious about our horses, yet in a short time I could keep awake no longer. I slept, and when I next woke, I heard voices whispering eagerly together. I silently turned, so that I could see whence the voices came, and perceived the hut-keeper sitting up in bed, in close confabulation with the stranger.

"Those two rascals are plotting some villany," I said to myself; "somebody will be minus a horse shortly, I expect." And then I fell asleep again; and when I awoke it was broad day.

I found the young man was gone, and, what pleased me better still, had not taken either of our horses with him. So, when we had taken some breakfast, we started, and I left the kind little old man something to remember me by.

We had not ridden a hundred yards, before I turned to Dick and said,—

"Now mind; I don't want you to tell me anything you don't like, but pray relieve my mind on one point. Who was that young man? Have I ever seen him before?"

"I think not, sir; but I can explain how you come to think you have. You remember, sir, that I knew all about Mrs. Hawker's history?"

"Yes! yes! Go on."

"That young fellow is George Hawker's son."

It came upon me like a thunderbolt. This, then, was the illegitimate son that he had by his cousin Ellen. Oh miserable child of sin and shame! to what end, I wondered, had he been saved till now?

We shall see soon. Meanwhile I turned to my companion and said, "Tell me how he came to be here."

"Why you see, sir, he went on in his father's ways, and got lagged. He found his father out as soon as he was free, which wasn't long first, for he is mortal cunning, and since then they two have stuck together. Most times they quarrel, and sometimes they fight, but they are never far apart. Hawker ain't far off now."

"Now, sir," he continued, "I am going to tell you something which, if it ever leaks out of your lips again, in such a way as to show where it came from, will end my life as sure as if I was hung. You remember three months ago that a boatful of men were supposed to have landed from Cockatoo?"

"Yes," I said, "I heard it from Major Buckley. But the police have been scouring in all directions, and can find nothing of them.

My opinion is that the boat was capsized, and they were all drowned, and that the surf piled the boat over with sea-weed. Depend on it they did not land."

"Depend on it they did, sir ; those men are safe and well, and ready for any mischief. Hawker was on the look-out for them, and they all stowed away till the police cleared off, which they did last week. There will be mischief soon. There ; I have told you enough to cut my throat, and I'll tell you more, and convince you that I am right. That shepherd at whose hut we stayed last night was one of them ; that fellow was the celebrated Captain Mike. What do you think of that ?"

I shuddered as I heard the name of that fell ruffian, and thought that I had slept in the hut with him. But when I remembered how he was whispering with the stranger in the middle of the night, I came to the conclusion that serious mischief was brewing, and pushed on through the fog, which still continued as dense as ever, and, guided by some directions from the old hut-keeper, I got to Captain Brentwood's about ten o'clock, and told him and the Major the night's adventures.

We three armed ourselves secretly and quietly, and went back to the hut with the determination of getting possession of the person of the shepherd Mike, who, were he the man Dick accused him of being, would have been a prize indeed, being one of the leading Van Diemen's Land rangers, and one of the men reported as missing by Captain Blockstrop.

"Suppose," said Captain Brentwood, "that we seize the fellow, and it isn't him after all ?"

"Then," said the Major, "an action for false imprisonment would lie, sir, decidedly. But we will chance it."

And when we got there we saw the old hut-keeper, he of the colliery explosion experiences, shepherding the sheep himself, and found that the man we were in search of had left the hut that morning, apparently to take the sheep out. But that going out about eleven the old man had found them still in the yard, whereby he concluded that the shepherd was gone, which proved to be the case. And making further inquiries we found that the shepherd had only been hired a month previously, and no man knew whence he came: all of which seemed to confirm Dick's story wonderfully, and made us excessively uneasy. And in the end the Major asked me to prolong my visit for a time and keep my servant with me, as every hand was of use ; and so it fell out that I happened to be present at, and chronicle all which follows.

CHAPTER XXXVII.

IN WHICH GEORGE HAWKER SETTLES AN OLD SCORE WITH WILLIAM LEE, MOST HANDSOMELY, LEAVING, IN FACT, A LARGE BALANCE IN HIS OWN FAVOUR.

I PAUSE here—I rather dread to go on. Although our course has been erratic and irregular; although we have had one character disappearing for a long time (like Tom Troubridge); and, although we have had another entirely new, coming bobbing up in the manner of Punch's victims, unexpected, and apparently unwanted; although, I say, the course of this story may have been ill-arranged in the highest degree, and you may have been continually coming across some one in Vol. II. who forced you to go back to Vol. I. to find out who he was; yet, on the whole, we have got on pleasantly enough as things go. Now, I am sorry to say I have to record two or three fearful catastrophes. The events of the next month are seldom alluded to by any of those persons mentioned in the preceding pages; they are too painful. I remark that the Lucknow and Cawnpore men don't much like talking about the affairs of that terrible six weeks; much for the same reason, I suspect, as we, going over our old recollections, always omit the occurrences of this lamentable spring.

The facts contained in the latter end of this chapter I got from the Gaol Chaplain at Sydney.

The Major, the Captain, and I, got home to dinner, confirmed in our suspicions that mischief was abroad, and very vexed at having missed the man we went in search of. Both Mrs. Buckley and Alice noticed that something was wrong, but neither spoke a word on the subject. Mrs. Buckley now and then looked anxiously at her husband, and Alice cast furtive glances at her father. The rest took no notice of our silence and uneasiness, little dreaming of the awful cloud that was hanging above our heads, to burst, alas! so soon.

I was sitting next to Mary Hawker that evening, talking over old Devon days and Devon people, when she said,—

" I think I am going to have some more quiet peaceful times. I am happier than I have been for many years. Do you know why? Look there."

I shuddered to hear her say so, knowing what I knew, but looked where she pointed. Her son sat opposite to us, next to the pretty Ellen Mayford. She had dropped the lids over her eyes and was smiling. He, with his face turned toward her, was whispering in his eager impulsive way, and tearing to pieces a slip of paper which he held in his hand. As the firelight fell on his face, I felt a chill come over me. The likeness was so fearful!—not to the father (that I had been long accustomed to), but to the son, to the half-brother—to the poor lost young soul I had seen last night, the companion of desperate men. As it struck me I could not avoid a start, and a moment after I would have given a hundred pounds not to have done so, for I felt Mary's hand on my arm, and heard her say, in a low voice,—

"Cruel! cruel! Will you never forget?"

I felt guilty and confused. As usual, on such occasions, Satan was at my elbow, ready with a lie, more or less clumsy, and I said, "You do me injustice, Mrs. Hawker, I was not thinking of old times. I was astonished at what I see there. Do you think there is anything in it?"

"I sincerely hope so," she said.

"Indeed, and so do I. It will be excellent on every account. Now," said I, "Mrs. Hawker, will you tell me what has become of your old servant, Lee? I have reasons for asking."

"He is in my service still," she said; "as useful and faithful as ever. At present he is away at a little hut in the ranges, looking after our ewes."

"Who is with him?" I asked.

"Well, he has got a new hand with him, a man who came about a month or so ago, and stayed about splitting wood. I fancy I heard Lee remark that he had known him before. However, when Lee had to go to the ranges, he wanted a hut-keeper; so this man went up with him."

"What sort of a looking man was he?"

"Oh, a rather large man, red-haired, much pitted with the small-pox."

All this made me uneasy. I had asked these questions by the advice of Dick, and, from Mrs. Hawker's description tallying so well with his, I had little doubt that another of the escaped gang was living actually in her service, alone, too, in the hut with Lee.

The day that we went to Mirngish, the circumstances I am about to relate took place in Lee's hut, a lonely spot, eight miles from the home station, towards the mountain, and situated in a dense dark stringy-bark forest—a wild desolate spot, even as it was that afternoon, with the parrots chattering and whistling around it, and the bright winter's sun lighting up the green tree-tops.

Lee was away, and the hut-keeper was the only living soul about the place. He had just made some bread, and, having carried out his camp-oven to cool, was sitting on the bench in the sun, lazily, thinking what he would do next.

He was a long, rather powerfully-built man, and seemed at first sight, merely a sleepy half-witted fellow, but at a second glance you might perceive that there was a good deal of cunning, and some ferocity in his face. He sat for some time, and beginning to think that he would like a smoke, he got out his knife preparatory to cutting tobacco.

The hut stood at the top of a lone gully, stretching away in a vista, nearly bare of trees for a width of about ten yards or so, all the way down, which gave it the appearance of a grass-ride, walled on each side by tall dark forest. Looking down this, our hut-keeper saw, about a quarter of a mile off, a horseman cross from one side to the other.

He only caught a momentary glimpse of him, but that was enough to show him that it was a stranger. He neither knew horse nor man, at least judging by his dress; and while he was still puzzling his brains as to what stranger would be coming to such an out-of-the-way place, he heard the "Chuck, kuk, kuk, kuk," of an opossum close behind the hut, and started to his feet.

It would of course have startled any bushman to hear an opossum cry in broad day, but he knew what this meant well. It was the arranged signal of his gang, and he ran to the place from whence the sound came.

George Hawker was there—well dressed, sitting on a noble chestnut horse. They greeted one another with a friendly curse.

As is my custom, when recording the conversations of this class of worthies, I suppress the expletives, thereby shortening them by nearly one half, and depriving the public of much valuable information.

"Well, old man," began Hawker, "is the coast clear?"

"No one here but myself," replied the other. "I'm hut-keeping here for one Bill Lee, but he is away. He was one of the right sort once himself, I have heard; but he's been on the square for twenty years, so I don't like to trust him."

"You are about right there, Moody, my lad," said Hawker. "I've just looked up to talk to you about him, and other matters,—I'll come in. When will he be back?"

"Not before night, I expect," said the other.

"Well," said Hawker, "we shall have the more time to talk; I've got a good deal to tell you. Our chaps are all safe and snug, and the traps are off. Only two, that's you and Mike, stayed this side of the hill; the rest crossed the ranges and stowed away in an old lair of mine in one of the upper Murray gullies. They've had pretty hard times, and if it hadn't been for the cash they brought away, they'd have had worse. Now the coast is clear, they're coming back by ones and twos, and next week we shall be ready for business. I'm going to be head man this bout, because I know the country better than any; and the most noble Michael has consented, for this time only, to act as lieutenant. We haven't decided on any plans yet, but some think of beginning from the coast, because that part will be clearest of traps, they having satisfied themselves that we ain't there. In fact, the wiseacres have fully determined that we are all drowned. There's one devil of a foreign doctor knows I'm round though: he saw me the night before you came ashore, and I am nigh sure he knew me. I have been watching him, and I could have knocked him over last week as clean as a whistle, only, thinks I, it'll make a stir before the time. Never mind, I'll have him yet. This Lee is a black sheep, lad. I'm glad you are here; you must watch him, and if you see him flinch, put a knife in him. He raised the country on me once before. I tell you, Jerry, that I'd be hung, and willing, to-morrow, to have that chap's life, and I'd have had it before now, only I had to keep still for the sake of the others. That man served me the meanest, dirtiest trick, twenty years ago, in the old country, that ever you or any other man heard of, and if he catches sight of me the game's up. Mind, if you see cause, you deal with him, or else,——" (with an awful oath) " you answer to the others."

" If he's got to go, he'll go," replied the other, doggedly. " Don't you fear me; Moody the cannibal ain't a man to flinch."

" What, is that tale true, then?" asked Hawker, looking at his companion with a new sort of interest.

" Why, in course it is," replied Moody; " I thought no one doubted that. That Van Diemen's Land bush would starve a bandicoot, and Shiner and I walked two days before we knocked the boy on the head; the lad was getting beat, and couldn't a' gone much further. After three days more we began to watch one another, and neither one durst walk first, or go to sleep. Well, Shiner gave in first; he couldn't keep his eyes open any longer. And then, you know, of course, my own life was dearer than his'n." *

" My God! That's worse than ever I did!" said Hawker.

" But not worse than you may do, if you persevere. You promise well," said Moody, with a grin.

Hawker bent and whispered in his ear; the other listened for a time, and then said,—

" Make it twenty."

Hawker after a little consideration nodded—then the other nodded—then they whispered together again. Something out of the common this must be, that they, not very particular in their confidences, should whisper about it.

---

* This story is true in every particular, and is, or was, notorious in Van Diemen's Land. Two convicts and a boy escaped, and, trying to cross the island, got short of provisions. They killed the boy, and lived on his flesh while it lasted. After that, one of the men murdered the other, whose flesh lasted long enough to take him back to the settlement, where he surrendered himself. I ought to apologize for telling such a terrible tale, but it is strictly true

They looked up suddenly, and Lee was standing in the doorway.

Hawker and he started when they saw one another, but Lee recovered himself first, and said,—

"George Hawker, it's many years since we met, and I'm not so young as I was. I should like to make peace before I go, as I well know that I'm the chief one to blame for you getting into trouble. I'm not humbugging you, when I say that I have been often sorry for it of late years. But sorrow won't do any good. If you'll forgive and forget, I'll do the same. You tried my life once, and that's worse than ever I did for you. And now I'll tell you, that if you want money to get out of the country and set up anywhere else, and leave your poor wife in peace, I'll find it for you out of my own pocket."

"I don't bear any malice," said Hawker; "but I don't want to leave the country just yet. I suppose you won't peach about having seen me here?"

"I shan't say a word, George, if you keep clear of the home station; but I won't have you come about there. So I warn you."

Lee held out his hand, and George took it. Then he asked him if he would stay there that night, and George consented.

Day was fast sinking behind the trees, and making golden boughs overhead. Lee stood at the hut door watching the sun set, and thinking, perhaps, of old Devon. He seemed sad, and let us hope he was regretting his old crimes while time was left him. Night was closing in on him, and having looked once more on the darkening sky, and the fog coldly creeping up the gully, he turned with a sigh and a shudder into the hut, and shut the door.

Near midnight, and all was still. Then arose a cry upon the night so hideous, so wild, and so terrible, that the roosting birds dashed off affrighted, and the dense mist, as though in sympathising fear, prolonged the echoes a hundredfold. One articulate cry, "Oh! you treacherous dog!" given with the fierce energy of a dying man, and then night returned to her stillness, and the listeners heard nothing but the weeping of the moisture from the wintry trees.

*   *   *   *   *   *

The two perpetrators of the atrocity stood silent a minute or more, recovering themselves. Then Hawker said in a fierce whisper,—

"You clumsy hound; why did you let him make that noise? I shall never get it out of my head again, if I live till a hundred. Let's get out of this place before I go mad; I could not stay in the house with it for salvation. Get his horse, and come along."

They got the two horses, and rode away into the night; but Hawker, in his nervous anxiety to get away, dropped a handsome cavalry pistol,—a circumstance which nearly cost Doctor Mulhaus his life,

They rode till after daylight, taking a course toward the sea, and had gone nearly twelve miles before George discovered his loss, and broke out into petulant imprecations.

" I wouldn't have lost that pistol for five pounds," he said ; " no nor more. I shall never have one like it again. I've put over a parrot at twenty yards with it."

" Go back and get it then," said Moody, " if it's so valuable. I'll camp and wait for you. We want all the arms we can get."

" Not I," said George ; " I would not go back into that cursed hut alone for all the sheep in the country."

" You coward," replied the other ; " afraid of a dead man ! Well, if you won't, I will : and, mind, I shall keep it for my own use."

" You're welcome to it, if you like to get it," said George. And so Moody rode back.

CHAPTER XXXVIII.

HOW DR. MULHAUS GOT BUSHED IN THE RANGES, AND WHAT BEFEL HIM THERE.

I MUST recur to the same eventful night again, and relate another circumstance that occurred on it. As events thicken, time gets more precious ; so that, whereas at first I thought nothing of giving you the events of twenty years or so in a chapter, we are now compelled to concentrate time so much that it takes three chapters to twenty-four hours. I read a long novel once, the incidents of which did not extend over thirty-six hours, and yet it was not so profoundly stupid as you would suppose.

All the party got safe home from the picnic, and were glad enough to get housed out of the frosty air. The Doctor, above all others, was rampant at the thoughts of dinner, and a good chat over a warm fire, and burst out, in a noble bass voice, with an old German student's song about wine and Gretchen, and what not.

His music was soon turned into mourning ; for, as they rode into the courtyard, a man came up to Captain Brentwood, and began talking eagerly to him.

It was one of his shepherds, who lived alone with his wife towards the mountain. The poor woman, his wife, he said, was taken in labour that morning, and was very bad. Hearing there was a doctor staying at the home station, he had come down to see if he could come to their assistance.

" I'll go, of course," said the Doctor ; " but let me get something to eat first. Is anybody with her ? "

"Yes, a woman was with her; had been staying with them some days."

"I hope you can find the way in the dark," said the Doctor, "for I can tell you I can't."

"No fear, sir," said the man; "there's a track all the way, and the moon's full. If it wasn't for the fog it would be as bright as day."

He took a hasty meal, and started. They went at a foot's pace, for the shepherd was on foot. The track was easily seen, and although it was exceedingly cold, the Doctor, being well wrapped up, contrived, with incessant smoking, to be moderately comfortable. All external objects being a blank, he soon turned to his companion to see what he could get out of him.

"What part of the country are you from, my friend?"

"Fra' the Isle of Skye," the man answered. "I'm one of the Macdonalds of Skye."

"That's a very ancient family, is it not?" said the Doctor at a venture, knowing he could not go wrong with a Highlander.

"Very ancient, and weel respeckit," the man answered.

"And who is your sheik, rajah, chieftain, or what you call him?"

"My lord Macdonald. I am cousin to my lord."

"Indeed! He owns the whole island, I suppose?"

"There's Mackinnons live there. But they are interlopers; they are worthless trash," and he spit in disgust.

"I suppose," said the Doctor, "a Mackinnon would return the compliment, if speaking of a Macdonald."

The man laughed, and said, he supposed "Yes," then added, "See! what's yon?"

"A white stump burnt black at one side,—what did you think it was?"

"I jaloused it might be a ghaist. There's a many ghaists and bogles about here."

"I should have thought the country was too young for those gentry," said the Doctor.

"It's a young country, but there's been muckle wickedness done in it. And what are those blacks do you think?—next thing to devils—at all events they're no' exactly human."

"Impish, decidedly," said the Doctor. "Have you ever seen any ghosts, friend?"

"Ay! many. A fortnight agone, come to-morrow, I saw the ghost of my wife's brother in broad day. It was the time of the high wind ye mind of; and the rain drove so thick I could no' see all my sheep at once. And a man on a white horse came fleeing before the wind close past me; I knew him in a minute; it was my wife's brother, as I tell ye, that was hung fifteen years agone for sheep-stealing, and he wasn't so much altered as ye'd think."

"Some one else like him!" suggested the Doctor.

"Deil a fear," replied the man, "for when I cried out and said, 'What, Col, lad! Gang hame, and lie in yer grave, and dinna trouble honest folk,' he turned and rode away through the rain, straight from me."

"Well!" said the Doctor, "I partly agree with you that the land's bewitched. I saw a man not two months ago who ought to have been dead five or six years at least. But are you quite sure the man you saw was hung?"

"Well nigh about," he replied. "When we sailed from Skye he was under sentence, and they weren't over much given to reprieve for sheep-stealing in those days. It was in consequence o' that that I came here."

"That's a very tolerable ghost story," said the Doctor. "Have you got another? If you have, I shouldn't mind hearing it, as it will beguile the way."

"Did ye ever hear how Faithful's lot were murdered by the blacks up on the Merrimerangbong?"

"No, but I should like to; is it a ghost story?"

"Deed ay, and is it. This is how it happened:—When Faithful came to take up his country across the mountains yonder, they were a strong party, enough to have been safe in any country, but whether it was food was scarce, or whether it was on account of getting water, I don't know, but they separated, and fifteen of them got into the Yackandandah country before the others.

"Well, you see, they were pretty confident, being still a strong mob, and didn't set any watch or take any care. There was one among them (Cranky Jim they used to call him—he has told me this yarn—he used to be about Reid's mill last year) who always was going on at them to take more care, but they never heeded him at all.

"They found a fine creek, with plenty of feed and water, and camped at it to wait till the others came up. They saw no blacks, nor heard of any, and three days were past, and they began to wonder why the others had not overtaken them.

"The third night they were all sitting round the fire, laughing and smoking, when they heard a loud co'ee on the opposite side of the scrub, and half-a-dozen of them started up and sang out, "There they are!"

"Well, they all began co'eeing again, and they heard the others in reply, apparently all about in the scrub. So off they starts, one by one, into the scrub, answering and hallooing, for it seemed to them that their mates were scattered about, and didn't know where they were. Well, as I said, fourteen of them started into the scrub, to collect the party and bring them up to the fire; only old Cranky Jim sat still in the camp. He believed, with the others, that it was the rest of their party coming up, but he soon began to wonder how it was that they were so scattered. Then he heard one of them scream, and then it struck him all at once that this was a dodge of the blacks to draw the men from the camp, and, when they were abroad, cut them off one by one, plunder the drays, and drive off the sheep.

"So he dropped, and crawled away in the dark. He heard the co'ees grow fewer and fewer as the men were speared one by one, and at last everything was quiet, and then he knew he was right, and he rose up and fled away.

"In two days he found the other party, and told them what had happened. They came up, and there was some sharp fighting, but they got a good many of their sheep back.

"They found the men lying about singly in the scrub, all speared. They buried them just where they found each one, for it was hot weather. They buried them four foot deep, but they wouldn't lie still.

"Every night, about nine o'clock, they get up again, and begin co'eeing for an hour or more. At first there's a regular coronach of them, then by degrees the shouts get fewer and fewer, and, just when you think it's all over, one will break out loud and clear close to you, and after that all's still again."

"You don't believe that story, I suppose?"

"If you press me very hard," said the Doctor, "I must confess, with all humility, that I don't!"

"No more did I," said Macdonald, "till I heard 'em!"

"Heard them!" said the Doctor.

"Ay, *and seen them!*" said the man, stopping and turning round.

"You most agreeable of men! pray, tell me how."

"Why, you see, last year I was coming down with some wooldrays from Parson Dorken's, and this Cranky Jim was with us, and told us the same yarn, and when he had finished, he said, ' You'll know whether I speak truth or not to-night, *for we're going to camp at the place where it happened.*'

"Well, and so we did, and as well as we could reckon, it was a little past nine when a curlew got up and began crying. That was the signal for the ghosts, and in a minute they were co'eeing like mad all round. As Jim had told us, one by one ceased until all was quiet, and I thought it was over, when I looked, and saw, about a hundred yards off, a tall man in grey crossing a belt of open ground. He put his hand to his mouth, gave a wild shout, and disappeared!"

"Thank you," said the Doctor. "I think you mentioned that your wife's confinement was somewhat sudden."

"Yes, rather," replied the man.

"Pray, had you been relating any of the charming little tales to her lately—just, we will suppose, to wile away the time of the evening?"

"Well, I may have done so," said Macdonald, "but I don't exactly mind."

"Ah, so I thought. The next time your good lady happens to be in a similar situation, I think I would refrain from ghost stories. I should not like to commit myself to a decided opinion, but I should be inclined to say that the tales you have been telling me were rather horrible. Is that the light of your hut?"

Two noble colley dogs bounded to welcome them, and a beautiful bare-legged girl, about sixteen, ran forth to tell her father, in Gaelic, that the trouble was over, and that a boy was born.

On going in, they found the mother asleep, while her gossip held the baby on her knee; so the Doctor saw that he was not needed, and sat down, to wait until the woman should wake, having first, however, produced from his saddle two bottles of port wine, a present from Alice.

The woman soon woke, and the Doctor, having felt her pulse, and left some medicine, started to ride home again, carrying with him an incense of good wishes from the warm-hearted Highlanders.

Instead of looking carefully for the road, the good Doctor was soon nine fathoms deep into the reasons why the mountaineers and coast folk of all northern countries should be more blindly superstitious than the dwellers in plains and in towns; and so it happened that, coming to a fork in the track, he disregarded the advice of his horse, and, instead of taking the right hand, as he should have done, he held straight on, and, about two o'clock in the morning, found that not only had he lost his road, but that the track had died out altogether, and that he was completely abroad in the bush.

He was in a very disagreeable predicament. The fog was thicker than ever, without a breath of air; and he knew that it was as likely as not that it might last for a day or two. He was in a very wild part of the mountain, quite on the borders of all the country used by white men.

After some reflection, he determined to follow the fall of the land, thinking that he was still on the water-shed of the Snowy-river, and hoping, by following down some creek, to find some place he knew.

Gradually day broke, cold and cheerless. He was wet and miserable, and could merely give a guess at the east, for the sun was quite invisible; but, about eight o'clock, he came on a track, running at right angles to the way he had been going, and marked with the hoofs of two horses, whose riders had apparently passed not many hours before.

Which way should he go? He could not determine. The horse-men, it seemed to him, as far as he could guess, had been going west, while his route lay east. And, after a time, having registered a vow never to stir out of sight of the station again without a compass, he determined to take a contrary direction from them, and to find out where they had come from.

The road crossed gully after gully, each one like the other. The timber was heavy stringy-bark, and, in the lower part of the shallow gullies, the tall white stems of the blue gums stood up in the mist like ghosts. All nature was dripping and dull, and he was chilled and wretched.

At length, at the bottom of a gully, rather more dreary looking, if possible, than all the others, he came on a black reedy waterhole, the first he had seen in his ride, and perceived that the track turned snort to the left. Casting his eye along it, he made out the dark indistinct outline of a hut, standing about forty yards off.

He rode up to it. All was as still as death. No man came out to welcome him, no dog jumped, barking forth, no smoke went up from the chimney; and, looking round, he saw that the track ended here, and that he had ridden all these miles only to find a deserted hut.

But was it deserted? Not very long so, for those two horsemen, whose tracks he had been on so long, had started from here. Here, on this bare spot in front of the door, they had mounted. One of their horses had been capering; nay, here were their footsteps on the threshold. And, while he looked, there was a light fall inside, and the chimney began smoking. " At all events," said the Doctor, " the fire's in, and here's the camp-oven, too. Somebody will be here soon. I will go in and light my pipe."

He lifted the latch, and went in. Nobody there. Stay—yes, there is a man asleep in the bed-place. " The watchman, probably," thought the Doctor, " he's been up all night with the sheep, and is taking his rest by day. Well, I won't wake him; I'll hang up my horse a bit, and take a pipe. Perhaps I may as well turn the horse out. Well, no. I shan't wait long; he may stand a little without hurting himself."

So soliloquised the Doctor, and lit his pipe. A quarter of an hour passed, and the man still lay there without moving. The Doctor rose and went close to him. He could not even hear him breathe.

His flesh began to creep, but his brows contracted, and his face grew firm. He went boldly up, and pulled down the blanket, and then, to his horror and amazement, recognised the distorted countenance of the unfortunate William Lee.

He covered the face over again, and stood thinking of his situation, and how this had come to pass. How came Lee here, and how had he met his death? At this moment something bright, half hidden by a blue shirt lying on the floor, caught his eye, and, going to pick it up, he found it was a beautiful pistol, mounted in silver, and richly chased.

He turned it over and over, till in a lozenge behind the

hammer, he found, apparently scratched with a knife, the name, " G. Hawker."

Here was light with a vengeance! But he had little time to think of his discovery, ere he was startled by the sound of horses' feet rapidly approaching the hut.

Instinctively he thrust the pistol into his pocket, and stooped down, pretending to light his pipe. He heard some one ride up to the door, dismount, and enter the hut. He at once turned round, pipe in mouth, and confronted him.

He was a tall, ill-looking, red-haired man, and to the Doctor's pleasant good morning, he replied by sulkily asking what he wanted.

" Only a light for my pipe, friend," said the Doctor; " having got one, I will bid you good morning. Our friend here sleeps well."

The new comer was between him and the door, but the Doctor advanced boldly. When the two men were opposite their eyes met, and they understood one another.

Moody (for it was he) threw himself upon the Doctor with an oath, trying to bear him down; but, although the taller man, he had met his match. He was held in a grasp of iron; the Doctor's hand was on his collar, and his elbow against his face, and thus his head was pressed slowly backwards till he fell to avoid a broken neck, and fell, too, with such force that he lay for an instant stunned and motionless, and before he came to himself the Doctor was on horseback, and some way along the track, glad to have made so good an escape from such an awkward customer.

" If he had been armed," said the Doctor, as he rode along, " I should have been killed : he evidently came back after that pistol. Now, I wonder where I am? I shall know soon at this pace. The little horse keeps up well, seeing he has been out all night."

In about two hours he heard a dog bark to the left of the track, and, turning off in that direction, he soon found himself in a court-yard, and before a door which he thought he recognised : the door opened at the sound of his horse, and out walked Tom Troubridge.

" Good Lord !" said the Doctor, " a friend's face at last; tell me where I am, for I can't see the end of the house."

" Why, at our place, Toonarbin, Doctor."

" Well, take me in, and give me some food; I have terrible tidings for you. When did you last see Lee ?"

" The day before yesterday; he is up at an outlying hut of ours in the ranges."

" He is lying murdered in his bed there, for I saw him so not three hours past."

He then told Troubridge all that had happened.

" What sort of a man was it that attacked you ?" said Troubridge. The Doctor described Moody.

" That's his hut-keeper that he took from here with him; a man he said he knew, and you say he was on horseback. What sort of a horse had he?"

"A good-looking roan, with a new bridle on him."

"Lee's horse," said Troubridge; "he must have murdered him for it. Poor William!"

But when Tom saw the pistol and read the name on it, he said,—

"Things are coming to a crisis, Doctor; the net seems closing round my unfortunate partner. God grant the storm may come and clear the air! Anything is better than these continual alarms."

"It will be very terrible when it does come, my dear friend," said the Doctor.

"It cannot be much more terrible than this," said Tom, "when our servants are assassinated in their beds, and travellers in lonely huts have to wrestle for their lives. Doctor, did you ever nourish a passion for revenge?"

"Yes, once," said the Doctor, "and had it gratified in fair and open duel; but when I saw him lying white on the grass before me, and thought that he was dead, I was like one demented, and prayed that my life might be taken instead of his. Be sure, Tom, that revenge is of the devil, and, like everything else you get from him, is not worth having."

"I do not in the least doubt it, Doctor," said Tom; "but oh, if I could only have five minutes with him on the turf yonder, with no one to interfere between us! I want no weapons; let us meet in our shirts and trowsers, like Devon lads."

"And what would you do to him?"

"If you weren't there to see, *he'd* never tell you."

"Why nourish this feeling, Tom, my old friend? you do not know what pain it gives me to see a noble open character like yours distorted like this. Leave him to Desborough,—why should you feel so deadly towards the man? He has injured others more than you."

"He stands between me and the hopes of a happy old age. He stands between me and the light, and he must stand on one side."

That night they brought poor Lee's body down in a dray, and buried him in the family burying-ground close beside old Miss Thornton. Then the next morning he rode back home to the Buckleys', where he found that family with myself, just arrived from the Brentwoods'. I of course was brimful of intelligence, but when the Doctor arrived I was thrown into the shade at once. However, no time was to be lost, and we despatched a messenger, post haste, to fetch back Captain Desborough and his troopers, who had now been moved off about a week, but had not been as yet very far withdrawn, and were examining into some "black" outrages to the northward.

Mary Hawker was warned, as delicately as possible, that her husband was in the neighbourhood. She remained buried in thought for a time, and then, rousing herself, said, suddenly,—

"There must be an end to all this. Get my horse, and let me go home."

In spite of all persuasions to the contrary, she still said the same.

"Mrs. Buckley, I will go home, and see if I can meet him alone. All I ask of you is to keep Charles with you. Don't let the father and son meet, in God's name."

"But what can you do?" urged Mrs. Buckley.

"Something, at all events. Find out what he wants. Buy him off, perhaps. Pray don't argue with me. I am quite determined."

Then it became necessary to tell her of Lee's death, though the fact of his having been murdered was concealed; but it deeply affected her to hear of the loss of her old faithful servant, faithful to her at all events, whatever his faults may have been. Nevertheless, she went off alone, and took up her abode with Troubridge, and there they two sat watching in the lonely station, for him who was to come.

Though they watched together, there was no sympathy or confidence between them. She never guessed what purpose was in Tom's heart; she never guessed what made him so pale and gloomy, or why he never stirred from the house, but slept half the day on the sofa. But ere she had been a week at home, she found out. Thus:—

They would sit, those two, silent and thoughtful, beside that unhappy hearth, watching the fire, and brooding over the past. Each had that in their hearts which made them silent to one another, and each felt the horror of some overflowing formless calamity, which any instant might take form, and overwhelm them. Mary would sit late, dreading the weary night, when her overstrained senses caught every sound in the distant forest; but, however late she sat, she always left Tom behind, over the fire, not taking his comfortable glass, but gloomily musing—as much changed from his old self as man could be.

She now lay always in her clothes, ready for any emergency; and one night, about a week after Lee's murder, she dreamt that her husband was in the hall, bidding her in a whisper which thrilled her heart, to come forth. The fancy was so strong upon her, that saying aloud to herself, "The end is come!" she arose in a state little short of delirium, and went into the hall. There was no one there, but she went to the front door, and, looking out into the profoundly black gloom of the night, said in a low voice,—

"George, George, come to me! Let me speak to you, George. It will be better for both of us to speak."

No answer: but she heard a slight noise in the sitting-room behind her, and, opening the door gently, saw a light there, and Tom sitting with parted lips watching the door, holding in his hand a cocked pistol.

She was not in the least astonished or alarmed. She was too much *tête montée* to be surprised at anything. She said only, with a laugh,—

" What! are you watching, too, old mastiff?—Would you grip the wolf, old dog, if he came ? "

" Was he there, Mary ? Did you speak to him ? "

" No! no! " she said. " A dream, a wandering dream. What would you do if he came,—eh, cousin ? "

" Nothing! nothing ! " said Tom. " Go to bed."

" Bed, eh ? " she answered. " Cousin; shooting is an easier death than hanging,—eh ? "

Tom felt a creeping at the roots of his hair, as he answered,— " Yes, I believe so."

" Can you shoot straight, old man? Could you shoot straight and true if he stood there before you? Ah, you think you could now, but your hand would shake when you saw him."

" Go to bed, Mary," said Tom. " Don't talk like that. Let the future lie, cousin."

She turned and went to her room again.

All this was told me long after by Tom himself. Tom believed, or said he believed, that she was only sounding him, to see what his intentions were in case of a meeting with George Hawker. I would not for the world have had him suppose I disagreed with him ; but I myself take another and darker interpretation of her strange words that night. I think, that she, never a very strong-minded person, and now grown quite desperate from terror, actually contemplated her husband's death with complacency, nay, hoped, in her secret heart, that one mad struggle between him and Tom might end the matter for ever, and leave her a free woman. I may do her injustice, but I think I do not. One never knows what a woman of this kind, with strong passions and a not over-strong intellect, may be driven to. I knew her for forty years, and loved her for twenty. I knew in spite of all her selfishness and violence that there were many good, nay, noble points in her character ; but I cannot disguise from myself that that night's conversation with Tom showed me a darker point in her character than I knew of before. Let us forget it. I would wish to have none but kindly recollections of the woman I loved so truly and so long.

For the secret must be told sooner or later,—I loved her before any of them. Before James Stockbridge, before George Hawker, before Thomas Troubridge, and I loved her more deeply and more truly than any of them. But the last remnant of that love departed from my heart twenty years ago, and that is why I can write of her so calmly now, and that is the reason, too, why I remain an old bachelor to this day.

CHAPTER XXXIX.

THE LAST GLEAM BEFORE THE STORM.

BUT with us, who were staying down at Major Buckley's, a fortnight passed on so pleasantly that the horror of poor Lee's murder had begun to wear off, and we were getting once more as merry and careless as though we were living in the old times of profound peace. Sometimes we would think of poor Mary Hawker, at her lonely watch up at the forest station; but that or any other unpleasant subject was soon driven out of our heads by Captain Desborough, who had come back with six troopers, declared the country in a state of siege, proclaimed martial law, and kept us all laughing and amused from daylight to dark.

Captain Brentwood and his daughter Alice (the transcendently beautiful!) had come up, and were staying there. Jim and his friend Halbert were still away, but were daily expected. I never passed a pleasanter time in my life than during that fortnight's lull between the storms.

"Begorra (that's a Scotch expression, Miss Brentwood, but very forcible)," said Captain Desborough. "I owe you more than I can ever repay for buying out the Donovans. That girl Lesbia Burke would have forcibly abducted me, and married me against my will, if she hadn't had to follow the rest of the family to Port Phillip."

"A fine woman, too," said Captain Brentwood.

"I'd have called her a little coarse, myself," said Desborough.

"One of the finest, strangest sights I ever saw in my life," resumed Captain Brentwood, "was on the morning I came to take possession. None of the family were left but Murtagh Donovan and Miss Burke. I rode over from Buckley's, and when I came to the door Donovan took me by the arm, and saying 'whist,' led me into the sitting-room. There, in front of the empty fireplace, crouched down on the floor, bareheaded, with her beautiful hair hanging about her shoulders, sat Miss Burke. Every now and then she would utter the strangest low wailing cry you ever heard: a cry, by Jove, sir, that went straight to your heart. I turned to Donovan, and whispered, 'Is she ill?' and he whispered again, 'Her heart's broke at leaving the old place where she's lived so long. *She's raising the keen over the cold hearthstone.* It's the way of the Burkes.' I don't know when I was so affected in my life. Somehow, that exquisite line came to my remembrance,—

'And the hare shall kindle on the cold hearthstone,'

and I went back quietly with Donovan; and, by Jove, sir, when we came out the great ass had the tears running down his cheeks. I have always felt kindly to that man since."

"Ah, Captain," said Desborough, "with all our vanity and absurdity, we Irish have good warm hearts under our waistcoats. We are the first nation in the world, sir, saving the Jews."

This was late in the afternoon of a temperate spring day. We were watching Desborough as he was giving the finishing touches to a beautiful water-colour drawing.

"Doctor," he said, "come and pass your opinion."

"I think you have done admirably, Captain," said the Doctor; "you have given one a splendid idea of distance in the way you have toned down the plain, from the grey appearance it has ten miles off to the rich, delicate green it shows close to us. And your mountain, too, is most aërial. You would make an artist."

"I am not altogether displeased with my work, Doctor, if you, who never flatter, can praise it with the original before you. How exceedingly beautiful the evening tones are becoming!"

We looked across the plain; the stretch of grass I have described was lying before one like a waveless sea, from the horizon of which rose the square abrupt-sided mass of basalt which years ago we had named the Organ-hill, from the regular fluted columns of which it was composed. On most occasions, as seen from Major Buckley's, it appeared a dim mass of pearly grey, but to-night, in the clear frosty air, it was of a rich purple, shining on the most prominent angles with a dull golden light.

"The more I look at that noble fire-temple, the more I admire it," said the Doctor. "It is one of the most majestic objects I ever beheld."

"It is not unlike Staffa," said Desborough. "There come two travellers."

Two dots appeared crawling over the plain, and making for the river. For a few minutes Alice could not be brought to see them, but when she did, she declared that it was Jim and Halbert.

"You have good eyes, my love," said her father, "to see what does not exist. Jim's horse is black, and Halbert's roan, and those two men are both on grey horses."

"The wish was parent to the thought, father," she replied, laughing. "I wonder what is keeping him away from us so long? If he is to go to India, I should like to see him as much as possible."

"My dear," said her father, "when he went off with Halbert to see the Markhams, I told him that if he liked to go on to Sydney, he could go if Halbert went with him, and draw on the agent for what money he wanted. By his being so long away, I conclude he has done so, and that he is probably at this moment getting a lesson at billiards from Halbert before going to dinner. I shall have a nice little account from the agent just now, of 'Cash advanced to J. Brentwood, Esq.'"

"I don't think Jim's extravagant, papa," said Alice.

"My dear," said Captain Brentwood, "you do him injustice. He hasn't had the chance. I must say, considering his limited opportunities, he has spent as much money on horses, saddlery, &c., as any young gentleman on this country side. Eh, Sam?"

"Well, sir," said Sam, "Jim spends his money, but he generally makes pretty good investments in the horse line."

"Such as that sweet-tempered useful animal Stampedo," replied the Captain, laughing, "who nearly killed a groom, and staked himself trying to leap out of the stockyard the second day he had him. Well, never mind; Jim's a good boy, and I am proud of him. I am in some hopes that this Sydney journey will satisfy his wandering propensities for the present, and that we may keep him at home. I wish he would fall in love with somebody, providing she wasn't old enough to be his grandmother.—Couldn't you send him a letter of introduction to some of your old schoolfellows, Miss Puss? There was one of them, I remember, I fell in love with myself one time when I came to see you; Miss Green, I think it was. She was very nearly being your mamma-in-law, my dear."

"Why, she is a year younger than me," said Alice, "and, oh goodness, such a temper! She threw the selections from Beethoven at Signor Smitherini, and had bread and water-melon for two days for it. Serve her right!"

"I have had a narrow escape, then," replied the father. "But we shall see who these two people are immediately, for they are crossing the river."

When the two travellers rose again in sight on the near bank of the river, one of them was seen galloping forward, waving his hat.

"I *knew* it was Jim," said Alice, "and on a new grey horse. I thought he would not go to Sydney." And in a minute more she had run to meet him, and Jim was off his horse, kissing his sister, laughing, shouting, and dancing around her.

"Well, father," he said, "here I am back again. Went to Sydney and stayed a week, when we met the two Marstons, and went right up to the Clarence with them. That was a pretty journey, eh? Sold the old horse, and bought this one. I've got heaps to tell you, sister, about what I've seen. I went home, and only stayed ten minutes; when I heard you were here, I came right on."

"I am glad to see you back, Mr. Halbert," said Major Buckley; "I hope you have had a pleasant journey. You have met Captain Desborough?"

"Captain Desborough, how are you?" says Jim. "I am very glad to see you. But, between you and I, you're always a bird of ill omen. Whose pig's dead now? What brings *you* back? I thought we should be rid of you by this time."

"But you are not rid of me, Jackanapes," said Desborough, laughing. "But I'll tell you what, Jim; there is really something wrong, my boy, and I'm glad to see you back." And he told him all the news.

Jim grew very serious. "Well," said he, "I'm glad to be home again; and I'm glad, too, to see you here. One feels safer when you're in the way. We must put a cheerful face on the matter, and not frighten the women. I have bought such a beautiful brace of pistols in Sydney. I hope I may never have the chance to use them in this country. Why, there's Cecil Mayford and Mrs. Buckley coming down the garden, and Charley Hawker, too. Why, Major, you've got all the world here to welcome us."

The young men were soon busy discussing the merits of Jim's new horse, and examining with great admiration his splendid new pistols. Charley Hawker, poor boy! made a mental resolution to go to Sydney, and also come back with a new grey horse, and a pair of pistols more resplendent than Jim's. And then they went in to get ready for dinner.

When Jim unpacked his valise, he produced a pretty bracelet for his sister, and a stockwhip for Sam. On the latter article he was very eloquent.

"Sam, my boy," said he, "there is not such another in the country. It was made by the celebrated Bill Mossman of the Upper Hunter, the greatest swearer at bullocks, and the most accomplished whipmaker on the Sydney side. He makes only one in six months, and he makes it a favour to let you have it for five pounds. You can take a piece of bark off a blue gum, big enough for a canoe, with one cut of it. There's a fine of two pounds for cracking one within a mile of Government House, they make such a row. A man the other day cracked one of them on the South Head, and broke the windows in Pitt Street."

"You're improving, master Jim," said Charles Hawker. "You'll soon be as good a hand at a yarn as Hamlyn's Dick." At the same time he wrote down a stockwhip, similar to this one, on the tablets of his memory, to be procured on his projected visit to Sydney.

That evening we all sat listening to Jim's adventures; and pleasantly enough he told them, with not a little humorous exaggeration. It is always pleasant to hear a young fellow telling his first impressions of new things and scenes, which have been so long familiar to ourselves; but Jim had really a very good power of narration, and he kept us laughing and amused till long after the usual hour for going to bed.

Next day we had a pleasant ride, all of us, down the banks of the river. The weather was slightly frosty, and the air clear and elastic

As we followed the windings of the noble rushing stream, at a height of seldom less than three hundred feet above his bed, the Doctor was busy pointing out the alternations of primitive sandstone and slate, and the great streams of volcanic bluestone which had poured from various points towards the deep glen in which the river flowed. Here, he would tell us, was formerly a lofty cascade, and a lake above it, but the river had worn through the sandstone bar, drained the lake, leaving nothing of the waterfall but two lofty cliffs, and a rapid. There again had come down a lava-stream from Mirngish, which, cooled by the waters of the river, had stopped, and, accumulating, formed the lofty overhanging cliff on which we stood. He showed us how the fern-trees grew only in the still sheltered elbows facing northward, where the sun raised a warm steam from the river, and the cold south wind could not penetrate. He gathered for Mrs. Buckley a bouquet of the tender sweetscented yellow oxalis, the winter flower of Australia, and showed us the copper-lizard basking on the red rocks, so like the stone on which he lay, that one could scarce see him till a metallic gleam betrayed him, as he slipped to his lair. And we, the elder of the party, who followed the Doctor's handsome little brown mare, kept our ears open, and spoke little,— but gave ourselves fully up to the enjoyment of his learning and eloquence.

But the Doctor did not absorb the whole party; far from it. He had a rival. All the young men, and Miss Alice besides, were grouped round Captain Desborough. Frequently we elders, deep in some Old World history of the Doctor's, would be disturbed by a ringing peal of laughter from the other party, and then the Doctor would laugh, and we would all join; not that we had heard the joke, but from sheer sympathy with the hilarity of the young folks. Desborough was making himself agreeable, and who could do it better? He was telling the most outrageous of Irish stories, and making, on purpose, the most outrageous of Irish bulls. After a shout of laughter louder than the rest, the Doctor remarked,—

"That's better for them than geology,—eh, Mrs. Buckley?"

"And so my grandmother," we heard Desborough say, "waxed mighty wrath, and she up with her gold-headed walking-stick in the middle of Sackville Street, and says she, ' Ye villain, do ye think I don't know my own Blenheim spaniel when I see him?' ' Indeed, my lady,' says Mike, ' 'twas himself tould me he belanged to Barney.' ' Who tould you?' says she. ' The dog himself tould me, my lady.' ' Ye thief of the world,' says my aunt, ' and ye'd believe a dog before a dowager countess? Give him up, ye villain, this minute, or I'll hit ye!'"

These were the sort of stories Desborough delighted in, making them up, he often confessed, as he went on. On this occasion, when he had done his story, they all rode up and joined us, and we stood admiring the river, stretching westward in pools of gold between black cliffs, toward the setting sun ; then we turned homeward.

That evening Alice said, " Now do tell me, Captain Desborough, was that a true story about Lady Covetown's dog ? "

" True ! " said he.   " What story worth hearing ever was true ? The old lady lost her dog certainly, and claimed him of a dog-stealer in Sackville Street; but all the rest, my dear young lady, is historic romance."

" Mr. Hamlyn knows a good story," said Charley Hawker, " about Bougong Jack.   Do tell it to us, Uncle Jeff."

" I don't think," I said, " that it has so much foundation in fact as Captain Desborough's.   But there must be some sort of truth in it, for it comes from the old hands, and shows a little more sign of imagination than you would expect from them.   It is a very stupid story too."

" Do tell it," they all said.   So I complied, much in the same language as I tell it now :—

You know that these great snow-ranges which tower up to the west of us are, farther south, of great breadth, and that none have yet forced their way from the country of the Ovens and the Mitta Mitta through here to Gipp's-land.

The settlers who have just taken up that country trying to penetrate to the eastward here towards us, find themselves stopped by a mighty granite wall.   Any adventurous men, who may top that barrier, see nothing before them but range beyond range of snow Alps, intersected by precipitous cliffs, and frightful chasms.

This westward range is called the Bougongs.   The blacks during summer are in the habit of coming thus far to collect and feed on the great grey moths (Bougongs) which are found on the rocks. They used to report that a fine available country lies to the east embosomed in mountains, rendered fertile by perpetual snow-fed streams.   This is the more credible, as it is evident that between the Bougong range on the west and the Warragong range on the extreme east, towards us, there is a breadth of at least eighty miles.

There lived a few years ago, not very far from the Ovens-river, a curious character, by name John Sampson.   He had been educated at one of the great English universities, and was a good scholar, though he had been forced to leave the university, and, as report went, England too, for some great irregularity.

He had money, and a share in his brother-in-law's station, although he never stayed there many months in the year.   He was always away at some mischief or another.   No horse-race or prize-fight could go on without him, and he himself never left one of these last-mentioned gatherings without finding some one to try conclusions with him. Beside this, he was a great writer and singer of comic songs, and a consummate horseman.

One fine day he came back to his brother's station in serious trouble. Whether he had mistaken another man's horse for his own or not, I cannot say; but, at all events, he announced that a warrant was out against him for horse-stealing, and that he must go into hiding. So he took up his quarters at a little hut of his brother-in-law's, on the ranges, inhabited only by a stock-keeper and a black boy, and kept a young lubra in pay to watch down the glen for the police.

One morning she came running into the hut, breathless, to say that a lieutenant and three troopers were riding towards the hut. Jack had just time to saddle and mount his horse before the police caught sight of him, and started after him at full speed.

They hunted him into a narrow glen; a single cattle-track, not a foot broad, led on between a swollen rocky creek, utterly impassable by horse or man, and a lofty precipice of loose broken slate, on which one would have thought a goat could not have found a footing. The young police lieutenant had done his work well, and sent a trooper round to head him, so that Jack found himself between the devil and the deep sea. A tall armed trooper stood in front of him, behind was the lieutenant, on the right the creek, and on the left the precipice.

They called out to him to surrender; but, giving one look before and behind, and seeing escape was hopeless, he hesitated not a moment, but put his horse at the cliff, and clambered up, rolling down tons of loose slate in his course. The lieutenant shut his eyes, expecting to see horse and man roll down into the creek, and only opened them in time to see Jack stand for a moment on the summit against the sky, and then disappear.

He disappeared over the top of the cliff, and so he was lost to the ken of white men for the space of four years. His sister and brother-in-law mourned for him as dead, and mourned sincerely, for they and all who knew him liked him well. But at the end of that time, on a wild winter's night, he came back to them, dressed in opossum skins, with scarce a vestige of European clothing about him. His beard had grown down over his chest, and he had nearly forgotten his mother tongue, but, when speech came to him again, he told them a strange story.

It was winter time when he rode away. All the table lands were deep with snow; and, when he had escaped the policemen, he had crossed the first of the great ridges on the same night. He camped in the valley he found on the other side; and, having his gun and some ammunition with him, he fared well.

He was beyond the country which had ever been trodden by white men, and now, for the mere sake of adventure, he determined to go further still, and see if he could cross the great White Mountains, which had hitherto been considered an insurmountable barrier.

For two days he rode over a high table-land, deep in snow. Here and there, in a shallow sheltered valley, he would find just grass enough to keep his horse alive, but nothing for himself. On the third night he saw before him another snow-ridge, too far off to reach without rest, and, tethering his horse in a little crevice, between the rocks, he prepared to walk to and fro all night, to keep off the deadly snow sleepiness that he felt coming over him. "Let me but see what is beyond that next ridge," he said, " and I will lie down and die."

And now, as the stillness of the night came on, and the Southern Cross began to twinkle brilliantly above the blinding snow, he was startled once more by a sound which had fallen on his ear several times during his toilsome afternoon journey : a sound as of a sudden explosion, mingled, strangely too, with the splintering of broken glass. At first he thought it was merely the booming in his ears, or the rupture of some vessel in his bursting head. Or was it fancy ? No ; there it was again, clearer than before. That was no noise in his head, for the patient horse turned and looked toward the place where the sound came from. Thunder ? The air was clear and frosty, and not a cloud stained the sky. There was some mystery beyond that snow-ridge worth living to see.

He lived to see it. For, an hour after daybreak next morning, he, leading his horse, stumbled over the snow-covered rocks that bounded his view, and, when he reached the top, there burst on his sight a scene that made him throw up his arms and shout aloud.

Before him, pinnacle after pinnacle, towered up a mighty Alp, blazing in the morning sun. Down through a black rift on its side, wound a gleaming glacier, which hurled its shattered ice crystals over a dark cliff, into the deep profound blue of a lake, which stretched north and south, studded with green woody islets, almost as far as the eye could see. Toward the mountain the lake looked deep and gloomy, but, on the other side, showed many a pleasant yellow shallow, and sandy bay, while between him and the lake lay a mile or so of park-like meadow-land, in the full verdure of winter. As he looked, a vast dislocated mass of ice fell crashing from the glacier into the lake, and solved at once the mystery of the noises he had heard the night before.

He descended into the happy valley, and found a small tribe of friendly blacks, who had never before seen the face of white man, and who supposed him to be one of their own tribe, dead long ago, who had come back to them, renovated and beautified, from the other world. With these he lived a pleasant slothful life, while four years went on, forgetting all the outside world, till his horse was dead, his gun rusted and thrown aside, and his European clothes long since replaced by the skin of the opossum and the koala. He had forgotten his own tongue, and had given up all thoughts of crossing again the desolate barriers of snow which divided him from civilization, when a slight incident brought back old associations to his mind, and roused him from sleep.

In some hunting excursion he got a slight scratch, and, searching for some linen to tie it up, found in his mi-mi an old waistcoat, which he had worn when he came into the valley. In the lining, while tearing it up, he found a crumpied paper, a note from his sister, written years before, full of sisterly kindness and tenderness. He read it again and again before he laid down, and the next morning, collecting such small stock of provisions as he could, he started on the homeward track, and after incredible hardships reached his station.

His brother-in-law tried in vain with a strong party to reach the lake, but never succeeded. What mountain it was he discovered, or what river is fed by the lake he lived on, no man knows to this day. Some say he went mad, and lived in the ranges all the time, and that this was all a mere madman's fancy. But, whether he was mad or not then, he is sane enough now, and has married a wife, and settled down to be one of the most thriving men in that part of the country.*

"Well," said the Doctor, thrusting his fists deep into his breeches pockets, "I don't believe that story."

"Nor I either, Doctor," I replied. "But it has amused you all for half an hour; so let it pass."

"Oh!" said the Doctor, rather peevishly, "if you put it on those grounds, I am bound, of course, to withhold a few little criticisms I was inclined to make on its probability. I hope you won't go and pass it off as authentic, you know, because if we once begin to entertain these sort of legends as meaning anything, the whole history of the country becomes one great fog-bank, through which the devil himself could not find his way."

"Now, for my part," said mischievous Alice, "I think it a very pretty story. And I have no doubt that it is every word of it true."

"Oh, dear me, then," said the Doctor, "let us vote it true. And, while we are about it, let us believe that the Sydney ghost actually did sit on a three-rail fence, smoking its pipe, and directing an anxious crowd of relatives where to find its body. By all means let us believe everything we hear."

The next morning our pleasant party suffered a loss. Captain Brentwood and Alice went off home. He was wanted there, and all things seemed so tranquil that he thought it was foolish to stay away any longer. Cecil Mayford, too, departed, carrying with him

* This legend is said to be among the "Archives" of one of our best North Border families. It is but little altered, since the author heard it narrated at a camp-fire, one night, in the western Port Phillip country.

the affectionate farewells of the whole party. His pleasant even temper, and his handsome face, had won every one who knew him, and, though he never talked much, yet, when he was gone, we all missed his merry laugh, after one of Desborough's good stories. Charley Hawker went off with him, too, and spent a few hours with Ellen Mayford, much to his satisfaction, but came in again at night, as his mother had prayed of him not to leave the Major's till he had seen her again.

That night, the Major proposed punch, and, after Mrs. Buckley had gone to bed, Sam sang a song, and Desborough told a story, about a gamekeeper of his uncle's, whom the old gentleman desired to start in an independent way of business. So he built him a new house, and gave him a keg of whiskey, to start in the spirit-selling line. " But the first night," said Desborough, " the villain finished the whiskey himself, broke the keg, and burnt the house down ; so my uncle had to take him back into service again after all." And after this came other stories, equally preposterous, and we went rather late to bed.

And the next morning, too, I am afraid, we were rather late for breakfast. Just as we were sitting down, in came Captain Brentwood.

" Hallo," said the Major; " what brings you back so soon, old friend. Nothing the matter, I hope ? "

" Nothing but business," he replied. " I am going on to Dickson's, and I shall be back home to-night, I hope. I am glad to find you so late, as I have had no breakfast, and have ridden ten miles."

He took breakfast with us and went on. The morning passed somewhat heavily, as a morning is apt to do, after sitting up late and drinking punch. Towards noon Desborough said,—

" Now, if anybody will confess that he drank just three drops too much punch last night, I will do the same. Mrs. Buckley, my dear lady, I hope you will order plenty of pale ale for lunch."

Lunch passed pleasantly enough, and afterwards the Major, telling Sam to move a table outside into the verandah, disappeared, and soon came back with a very " curious " bottle of Madeira. We sat then in the verandah smoking for about a quarter of an hour.

I remember every word that was spoken, and every trivial circumstance that happened during that quarter of an hour ; they are burnt into my memory as if by fire. The Doctor was raving about English poetry, as usual, saying, however, that the modern English poets, good as they were, had lost the power of melody a good deal. This the Major denied, quoting :—

" By torch and trumpet fast array'd."

" Fifty such lines, sir, are not worth one of Milton's," said the Doctor.

" 'The trumpet spake not to the armed throng.'

There's melody for you; there's a blare and a clang; there's a ——"

I heard no more. Mrs. Buckley's French clock, in the house behind, chimed three quarters past one, and I heard a sound of two persons coming quickly through the house.

Can you tell the step of him who brings evil tidings? I think I can. At all events, I felt my heart grow cold when I heard those footsteps. I heard them coming through the house, across the boarded floor. The one was a rapid, firm, military footstep, accompanied with the clicking of a spur, and the other was unmistakably the "pad, pad" of a black-fellow.

We all turned round and looked at the door. There stood the sergeant of Desborough's troopers, pale and silent, and close behind him, clinging to him as if for protection, was the lithe naked figure of a black lad, looking from behind the sergeant, with terrified visage, first at one and then at another of us.

I saw disaster in their faces, and would have held up my hand to warn him not to speak before Mrs. Buckley. But I was too late, for he had spoken. And then we sat for a minute, looking at one another, each man seeing the reflection of his own horror in his neighbour's eyes.

CHAPTER XL.

THE STORM BURSTS.

Poor little Cecil Mayford had left us about nine o'clock in the morning of the day before this, and, accompanied by Charles Hawker, reached his mother's station about eleven o'clock in the day.

All the way Charles had talked incessantly of Ellen, and Cecil joined in Charles's praises of his sister, and joked with him for being "awfully spooney" about her.

"You're worse about my sister, Charley," said he, "than old Sam is about Miss Brentwood. He takes things quiet enough, but if you go on in this style till you are old enough to marry, by Jove, there'll be nothing of you left!"

"I wonder if she would have me?" said Charles, not heeding him.

"The best thing you can do is to ask her," said Cecil. "I think I know what she would say, though."

They reached Mrs. Mayford's, and spent a few pleasant hours together. Charles started home again about three o'clock, and having gone a little way, turned to look back. The brother and sister stood at the house-door still. He waved his hand in farewell to them, and they replied. Then he rode on and saw them no more.

Cecil and Ellen went into the house to their mother. The women worked, and Cecil read aloud to them. The book was "Waverley;" I saw it afterwards, and when supper was over he took it up to begin reading again.

"Not that book to-night, my boy," said his mother. "Read us a chapter out of the Bible. I am very low in my mind, and at such times I like to hear the Word."

He read the good book to them till quite late. Both he and Ellen thought it strange that their mother should insist on that book on a week-night; they never usually read it, save on Sunday evenings.

The morning broke bright and frosty. Cecil was abroad betimes, and went down the paddock to fetch the horses. He put them in the stock-yard, and stood for a time close to the stable, talking to a tame black lad, that they employed about the place.

His attention was attracted by a noise of horses' feet. He looked up and saw about a dozen men riding swiftly and silently across the paddock towards the house.

For an instant he seems to have idly wondered who they were, and have had time to notice a thickset gaudily dressed man, who rode in front of the others, when the kitchen-door was thrown suddenly open, and the old hut-keeper, with his grey hair waving in the wind, run out, crying,—"Save yourself, in God's name, Master Cecil. The Bushrangers!"

Cecil raised his clenched hands in wild despair. They were caught like birds in a trap. No hope!—no escape! Nothing left for it now, but to die red-handed. He dashed into the house with the old hut-keeper and shut the door.

The black lad ran up to a little rocky knoll within two hundred yards of the house, and, hiding himself, watched what went on. He saw the bushrangers ride up to the door and dismount. Then they began to beat the door and demand admittance. Then the door was burst down, and one of them fell dead by a pistol-shot. Then they rushed in tumultuously, leaving one outside to mind the horses. Then the terrified boy heard the dull sound of shots fired rapidly inside the building (pray that you may never hear that noise, reader: it always means mischief), and then all was comparatively still for a time.

Then there began to arise a wild sound of brutal riot within, and after a time they poured out again, and mounting, rode away.

Then the black boy slipt down from his lair like a snake, and stole towards the house. All was still as death. The door was open, but, poor little savage as he was, he dared not enter. Once he thought he heard a movement within, and listened intently with all his faculties, as only a savage can listen, but all was still again. And then gathering courage, he went in.

In the entrance, stepping over the body of the dead bushranger, he found the poor old white-headed hut-keeper knocked down and killed in the first rush. He went on into the parlour; and there,— oh, lamentable sight!—was Cecil; clever, handsome little Cecil, our old favourite, lying across the sofa, shot through the heart, dead.

But not alone. No; prone along the floor, covering six feet or more of ground, lay the hideous corpse of Moody, the cannibal. The red-headed miscreant, who had murdered poor Lee, under George Hawker's directions.

I think the poor black boy would have felt in his dumb darkened heart some sorrow at seeing his kind old master so cruelly murdered. Perhaps he would have raised the death-cry of his tribe over him, and burnt himself with fire, as their custom is; but he was too terrified at seeing so many of the lordly white race prostrated by one another's hands. He stood and trembled, and then, almost in a whisper, began to call for Mrs. Mayford.

" Missis ;" he said, " Miss Ellen ! All pull away, bushranger chaps. Make a light, good Missis. Plenty frightened this fellow."

No answer. No sign of Mrs. Mayford or Ellen. They must have escaped then. We will try to hope so. The black boy peered into one chamber after another, but saw no signs of them, only the stillness of death over all.

Let us leave this accursed house, lest prying too closely, we may find crouching in some dark corner a Gorgon, who will freeze us into stone.

*   *   *   *   *   *

The black lad stripped himself naked as he was born, and running like a deer, sped to Major Buckley's before the south wind, across the plain. There he found the Sergeant, and told him his tale, and the Sergeant and he broke in on us with the terrible news as we were sitting merrily over our wine.

CHAPTER XLI.

WIDDERIN SHOWS CLEARLY THAT HE IS WORTH ALL THE MONEY SAM GAVE
FOR HIM.

THE Sergeant, as I said, broke in upon us with the fearful news as we sat at wine. For a minute no man spoke, but all sat silent and horror-struck. Only the Doctor rose quietly, and slipped out of the room unnoticed.

Desborough spoke first. He rose up with deadly wrath in his face, and swore a fearful oath, an oath so fearful, that he who endorsed every word of it then, will not write it down now. To the effect,

"That, he would take neither meat, nor drink, nor pleasure, nor rest, beyond what was necessary to keep body and soul together, before he had purged the land of these treacherous villains!"

Charles Hawker went up to the Sergeant, with a livid face and shaking hands; "Will you tell me again, Robinson, *are they all dead?*"

The Sergeant looked at him compassionately. "Well, sir," he said; "the boy seemed to think Mrs. and Miss Mayford had escaped. But you mustn't trust what he says, sir."

"You are deceiving me," said Charles. "There is something you are hiding from me. I shall go down there this minute, and see."

"You will do nothing of the kind, sir," said Mrs. Buckley, coming into the doorway and confronting him; "your place is with Captain Desborough. I am going down to look after Ellen."

During these few moments, Sam had stood stupified. He stepped up to the Sergeant, and said,—

"Would you tell me which way they went from the Mayfords'?"

"Down the river, sir."

"Ah!" said Sam; "towards Captain Brentwood's, and Alice at home, and alone!—There may be time yet."

He ran out of the room and I after him. "His first trouble," I thought,—"his first trial. How will our boy behave now?"

Let me mention again that the distance from the Mayfords' to Captain Brentwood's, following the windings of the river on its right bank, was nearly twenty miles. From Major Buckley's to the same point, across the plains, was barely ten; so that there was still a chance that a brave man on a good horse, might reach Captain Brentwood's before the bushrangers, in spite of the start they had got.

Sam's noble horse, Widderin, a horse with a pedigree a hundred years old, stood in the stable. The buying of that horse had been Sam's only extravagance, for which he had often reproached himself, and now this day, he would see whether he would get his money's worth out of that horse, or no.

I followed him up to the stable, and found him putting the bridle on Widderin's beautiful little head. Neither of us spoke, only when I handed him the saddle, and helped him with the girths, he said, "God bless you."

I ran out and got down the slip-rails for him. As he rode by he said, "Good-bye, Uncle Jeff, perhaps you won't see me again;" and I cried out, "Remember your God and your mother, Sam, and don't do anything foolish."

Then he was gone; and looking across the plains the way he should go, I saw another horseman toiling far away, and recognised Doctor Mulhaus. Good Doctor! he had seen the danger in a moment, and by his ready wit had got a start of every one else by ten minutes.

The Doctor, on his handsome long-bodied Arabian mare, was making good work of it across the plains, when he heard the rush of horse's feet behind him, and turning, he saw tall Widderin bestridden by Sam, springing over the turf, gaining on him stride after stride. In a few minutes they were alongside of one another.

"Good lad!" cried the Doctor; "On, forwards; catch her, and away to the woods with her. Bloodhound Desborough will be on their trail in half-an-hour. Save her, and we will have noble vengeance."

Sam only waved his hand in good-bye, and sped on across the plain like a solitary ship at sea. He steered for a single tree, now becoming dimly visible, at the foot of the Organ hill.

The good horse, with elastic and easy motion, fled on his course like a bird; lifting his feet clearly and rapidly through the grass. The brisk south wind filled his wide nostrils as he turned his graceful neck from side to side, till, finding that work was meant, and not play, he began to hold his head straight before him, and rush steadily forward.

And Sam, poor Sam! all his hopes for life are now brought down to this: to depend on the wind and pluck of an unconscious horse. One stumble now, and it were better to lie down on the plain and die. He was in the hands of God, and he felt it. He said one short prayer, but that towards the end was interrupted by the wild current of his thoughts.

Was there any hope? They, the devils, would have been drinking at the Mayfords', and perhaps would go slow; or would they ride fast and wild? After thinking a short time, he feared the latter. They had tasted blood, and knew that the country would be roused on them shortly. On, on, good horse!

The lonely shepherd on the plains, sleepily watching his feeding sheep, looked up as Sam went speeding by, and thought how fine a thing it would be to be dressed like that, and have nothing to do but to ride blood-horses to death. Mind your sheep, good shepherd; perhaps it were better for you to do that and nothing more all your life, than to carry in your breast for one short hour such a volcano of rage, indignation and terror, as he does who hurries unheeding through your scattered flock.

Here are a brace of good pistols, and they, with care, shall give account, if need be, of two men. After that, nothing. It were better, so much better, not to live if one were only ten minutes too late. The Doctor would be up soon; not much matter if he were, though, only another life gone.

The Organ hill, a cloud of misty blue when he started, now hung in aërial fluted cliffs above his head. As he raced across the long glacis which lay below the hill, he could see a solitary eagle wheeling round the topmost pinnacles, against the clear blue sky; then the hill was behind him, and before him another stretch of plain, bounded by timber, which marked the course of the river.

Brave Widderin had his ears back now, and was throwing his breath regularly through his nostrils in deep sighs. Good horse, only a little longer; bear thyself bravely this day, and then pleasant pastures for thee till thou shalt go the way of all horses. Many a time has she patted, with kind words, thy rainbow neck, my horse; help us to save her now.

Alas! good willing brute, he cannot understand; only he knows that his kind master is on his back, and so he will run till he drop. Good Widderin! think of the time when thy sire rushed triumphant through the shouting thousands at Epsom, and all England heard that Arcturus had won the Derby. Think of the time when thy grandam, carrying Sheik Abdullah, bore down in a whirlwind of sand on the toiling affrighted caravan. Ah! thou knowest not of these things, but yet thy speed flags not. We are not far off now, good horse, we shall know all soon.

Now he was in the forest again, and now, as he rode quickly down the steep sandy road among the bracken, he heard the hoarse rush of the river in his ears, and knew the end was well-nigh come.

No drink now, good Widderin! a bucket of champagne in an hour's time, if thou wilt only stay not now to bend thy neck down to the clear gleaming water; flounder through the ford, and just twenty yards up the bank by the cherry-tree, we shall catch sight of the house, and know our fate.

Now the house was in sight, and now he cried aloud some wild inarticulate sound of thankfulness and joy. All was as peaceful as ever, and Alice, unconscious, stood white-robed in the verandah, feeding her birds.

As he rode up he shouted out to her and beckoned. She came running through the house, and met him breathless at the doorway.

"The bushrangers! Alice, my love," he said. "We must fly this instant, they are close to us now."

She had been prepared for this. She knew her duty well, for her father had often told her what to do. No tears! no hysterics! She took Sam's hand without a word, and placing her fairy foot upon his boot, vaulted up into the saddle before him, crying,—"Eleanor, Eleanor!"

Eleanor, the cook, came running out. "Fly!" said Alice. "Get away into the bush. The gang are coming; close by." She, an old Vandemonian, needed no second warning, and as the two young people rode away, they saw her clearing the paddock rapidly, and making for a dense clump of wattles, which grew just beyond the fence.

"Whither now, Sam?" said Alice, the moment they were started. "I should feel safer across the river," he replied; "that little wooded knoll would be a fine hiding-place, and they will come down this side of the river from Mayford's."

" From Mayford's! why, have they been there?"

" They have, indeed. Alas! poor Cecil."

" What has happened to him? nothing serious?"

" Dead! my love, dead."

" Oh! poor little Cecil," she cried, " that we were all so fond of. And Mrs. Mayford and Ellen?"

" They have escaped!—they are not to be found—they have hidden away somewhere."

They crossed the river, and dismounting, they led the tired horse up the steep slope of turf that surrounded a little castellated tor of bluestone. Here they would hide till the storm was gone by, for from here they could see the windings of the river, and all the broad plain stretched out beneath their feet.

" I do not see them anywhere, Alice," said Sam presently. " I see no one coming across the plains. They must be either very near us in the hollow of the river-valley, or else a long way off. I have very little doubt they will come here, though, sooner or later."

" There they are!" said Alice. " Surely there are a large party of horsemen on the plain, but they are seven or eight miles off."

" Ay, ten," said Sam. " I am not sure they are horsemen." Then he said suddenly in a whisper, " Lie down, my love, in God's name! Here they are, close to us!"

There burst on his ear a confused sound of talking and laughing, and out of one of the rocky gullies leading towards the river, came the men they had been flying from, in number about fourteen. They had crossed the river, for some unknown reason, and to the fear-struck hiders it seemed as though they were making straight towards their lair.

He had got Widderin's head in his breast, blindfolding him with his coat, for should he neigh now, they were undone, indeed! As the bushrangers approached, the horse began to get uneasy, and paw the ground, putting Sam in such an agony of terror that the sweat rolled down his face. In the midst of this he felt a hand on his arm, and Alice's voice, which he scarcely recognised, said, in a fierce whisper,—

" Give me one of your pistols, sir!"

" Leave that to me!" he replied in the same tone.

" As you please," she said; " but I must not fall alive into their hands. Never look your mother in the face again if I do."

He gave one more glance round, and saw that the enemy would come within a hundred yards of their hiding-place. Then he held the horse faster than ever, and shut his eyes.

* * * * * *

Was it a minute only, or an hour till they heard the sound of the voices dying away in the roar of the river; and, opening their eyes once more, looked into one another's faces?

Faces, they thought, that they had never seen before,—so each told the other afterwards,—so wild, so haggard, and so strange! And now that they were safe and free again—free to arise and leave their dreadful rock prison, and wander away where they would, they could scarcely believe that the danger was past.

They came out silently from among the crags, and took up another station, where they could see all that went on. They saw the miscreants swarming about the house, and heard a pistol-shot—only one.

"Who can they be firing at?" said Alice, in a subdued tone. They were both so utterly appalled by their late danger, that they spoke in whispers, though the enemy were a quarter of a mile off.

"Mere mischief, I should fancy," said Sam; "there is no one there. Oh! Alice, my love, can you realize that we are safe?"

"Hardly yet, Sam! But who could those men be we saw at such a distance on the plain? Could they have been cattle? I am seldom deceived, you know; I can see an immense distance."

"Why," said Sam, "I had forgotten them! They must be our friends, on these fellows' tracks. Desborough would not be long starting, I know."

"I hope my father," said Alice, "will hear nothing till he sees me. Poor father! what a state he will be in. See, there is a horseman close to us. It is the Doctor!"

They saw Dr. Mulhaus ride up to one of the heights overlooking the river, and reconnoitre. Seeing the men in the house, he began riding down towards them.

"He will be lost!" said Alice. "He thinks we are there. Co'ee, Sam, at all risks."

Sam did so, and they saw the Doctor turn. Alice showed herself for a moment, and then he turned back, and rode the way he had come. In a few minutes he joined them from the rear, and, taking Alice in his arms, kissed her heartily.

"So our jewel is safe, then—praise be to God! Thanks due also to a brave man and a good horse. This is the last station those devils will ruin, for our friends are barely four miles off. I saw them just now."

"I wish, I only wish," said Sam, "that they may delay long enough to be caught. I would give a good deal for that."

There was but little chance of that though; their measures were too well taken. Almost as Sam spoke, the three listeners heard a shrill whistle, and immediately the enemy began mounting. Some of them were evidently drunk, and could hardly get on their horses, but were assisted by the others. But very shortly they were all clear off, heading to the north-west.

"Now we may go down, and see what destruction has been done," said Alice. "Who would have thought to see such times as these!"

"Stay a little," said the Doctor, "and let us watch these gentlemen's motions. Where can they be going nor'-west—straight on to the mountains?"

"I am of opinion," said Sam, "that they are going to lie up in one of the gullies this evening. They are full of drink and madness, and they don't know what they are about. If they get into the main system of gullies, we shall have them like rats in a trap, for they can never get out by the lower end. Do you see, Doctor, a little patch of white road among the trees over there? That leads to the Limestone Gates, as we call it. If they pass those walls upwards, they are confined as in a pound. Watch the white road, and we shall see."

The piece of road alluded to was about two miles off, and winding round a steep hill among trees. Only one turn in it was visible, and over this, as they watched, they saw a dark spot pass, followed by a crowd of others.

"There they go," said Sam. "The madmen are safe now. See, there comes Desborough, and all of them; let us go down."

They turned to go, and saw Jim coming towards them, by the route that Sam had come, all bespattered with clay, limping and leading his new grey horse, dead lame.

He threw up his hat when he saw them, and gave a feeble hurrah! but even then a twinge of pain shot across his face, and, when he was close, they saw he was badly hurt.

"God save you, my dear sister," he said; "I have been in such a state of mind; God forgive me, I have been cursing the day I was born. Sam, I started about three minutes after you, and had very nearly succeeded in overhauling the Doctor, about two miles from here, when this brute put his foot in a crab hole, and came down, rolling on my leg. I was so bruised I couldn't mount again, and so I have walked. I see you are all right though, and that is enough for me. Oh, my sister—my darling Alice! Think what we have escaped!"

So they went towards the house. And when Major Buckley caught sight of Alice, riding between Dr. Mulhaus and Sam, he gave such a stentorian cheer that the retreating bushrangers must have heard it.

"Well ridden, gentlemen," he said. "And who won the race? Was it Widderin, or the Arabian, or the nondescript Sydney importation?"

"The Sydney importation, sir, would have beaten the Arabian, barring accident," said Jim. "But, seriously speaking, I should have been far too late to be of any service."

"And I," said the Doctor, "also. Sam won the race, and has got the prize. Now, let us look forward, and not backward."

They communicated to Desborough all particulars, and told him of the way they had seen the bushrangers go. Every one was struck with the change in him. No merry stories now. The laughing Irishman was gone, and a stern gloomy man, more like an Englishman, stood in his place. I heard after, that he deeply blamed himself for what had occurred (though no one else thought of doing so), and thought he had not taken full precautions. On the present occasion he said,—

"Well, gentlemen, night is closing in. Major Buckley, I think you will agree with me that we should act more effectually if we waited till daylight, and refresh both horses and men. More particularly as the enemy in their drunken madness have hampered themselves in the mountains. Major, Doctor Mulhaus, and Mr. Halbert, you are military men—what do you say?"

They agreed that there was no doubt. It would be much the best plan.

"I would sooner he'd have gone to-night and got it over," said Charles Hawker, taking Sam's arm. "Oh! Sam, Sam! Think of poor Cecil! Think of poor Ellen, when she hears what has happened. She must know by now!"

"Poor Charley," said Sam, "I am so sorry for you! Lie down, and get to sleep; the sun is going down."

He lay down as he was bid, somewhere out of the way. He was crushed and stunned. He hardly seemed to know at present what he was doing. After a time, Sam went in and found him sleeping uneasily.

But Alice was in sad tribulation at the mischief done. All her pretty little womanly ornaments overturned and broken, her piano battered to pieces, and, worst of all, her poor kangaroo shot dead, lying in the verandah. "Oh!" said she to Major Buckley, "you must think me very wicked to think of such things at a time like this, but I cannot help it. There is something so shocking to me in such a sudden *bouleversement* of old order. Yet, if it shocks me to see my piano broken, how terrible must a visitation like the Mayfords' be! These are not the times for moralizing, however. I must see about entertaining the garrison."

Eleanor, the cook, had come back from her lair quite unconcerned. She informed the company, in a nonchalant sort of way, that this was the third adventure of the kind she had been engaged in, and, that although they seemed to make a great fuss about it, on the other side (Van Diemen's Land), it was considered a mere necessary nuisance; and so proceeded to prepare such supper as she could. In the same off-hand way she remarked to Sam, when he went into the kitchen to get a light for his pipe, that, if it was true that Mike Howe had crossed and was among them, they had better look out for squalls; for that he was a devil, and no mistake.

Desborough determined to set a watch out on the road towards the mouth of the gully, where they were supposed to be. "We shall have them in the morning," said he. "Let every one get to sleep who can sleep, for I expect every one to follow me to-morrow."

Charles Hawker had lain down in an inner room, and was sleeping uneasily, when he was awakened by some one, and, looking up, saw Major Buckley, with a light in his hand, bending over him. He started up.

"What is the matter, sir?" he asked. "Why do you look at me so strangely? Is there any new misfortune?"

"Charles," said the Major, "you have no older friend than me."

"I know it, sir. What do you want me to do?"

"I want you to stay at home to-morrow."

"Anything but that, sir. They will call me a coward."

"No one shall do so. I swear that he who calls you a coward shall feel the weight of my arm."

"Why am I not to go with them? Why am I to be separated from the others?"

"You must not ask," said the Major; "perhaps you will know some day, but not yet. All I say to you is, go home to your mother to-morrow, and stay there. Should you fire a shot, or strike a blow against those men we are going to hunt down, you may do a deed which would separate you from the rest of mankind, and leave you to drag on a miserable guilty life. Do you promise?"

"I will promise," said Charles; "but I wonder——"

"Never mind wondering. Good night."

The troopers lay in the hall, and in the middle of the night there was a sound of a horse outside, and he who was the nearest the door got up and went out.

"Who is there?" said the voice of Captain Brentwood.

"Jackson, sir."

"My house has been stuck up, has it not?"

"Yes, sir."

"And my daughter?"

"Safe, sir. Young Mr. Buckley rode over and caught her up out of it ten minutes before they got here."

"Long life to him, and glory to God. Who is here?"

The trooper enumerated them.

"And what has become of the gang?" asked the Captain.

"Gone into the limestone gully, sir. Safe for to-morrow."

"Ah, well, I shall come in and lie in the hall. Don't make a noise. What is that?"

They both started. Some one of the many sleepers, with that strange hoarse voice peculiar to those who talk in their dreams, said, with singular energy and distinctness,——

" I will go, sir; they will call me coward."

" That's young Mr. Hawker, sir," said the trooper. " His sweetheart's brother, Mr. Mayford, was killed by them yesterday. The head of this very gang, sir, that villain Touan—his name is Hawker. An odd coincidence, sir."

" Very odd," said the Captain. " At the same time, Jackson, if I were you, I wouldn't talk about it. There are many things one had best not talk about, Jackson. Pull out the corner of that blanket, will you? So we shall have some fun to-morrow, up in the pass, I'm thinking."

" They'll fight, sir," said the trooper. " If we can bail them up, they'll fight, believe me. Better so; I think we shall save the hangman some trouble. Good night, sir."

So Captain Brentwood lay down beside the trooper, and slept the sleep of the just among his broken chairs and tables. The others slept too, sound and quiet, as though there were no fight on the morrow.

But ere the moon grew pale they were woke by Desborough, tramping about with clicking spurs among the sleepers, and giving orders in a loud voice. At the first movement, while the rest were yawning and stretching themselves, and thinking that battle was not altogether so desirable a thing on a cold morning as it was overnight, Major Buckley was by Charles Hawker's bedside, and, reminding him of his promise, got him out unperceived, helped him to saddle his horse, and started him off to his mother with a note.

The lad, overawed by the Major's serious manner, went without debate, putting the note in his pocket. I have seen that note; Sam showed it to me the next day, and so I can give you the contents. It was from Major Buckley to Mary Hawker, and ran thus:—

" I have sent your boy to you, dear old friend, bearing this. You will have heard by now what has happened, and you will give me credit for preventing what might come to be a terrible catastrophe. The boy is utterly unconscious that his own father is the man whose life is sought this day above all others. He is at the head of this gang, Mary. My own son saw him yesterday. My hand shall not be raised against him; but further than that I will not interfere. Your troubles have come now to the final and most terrible pass; and all the advice I have to give you is to pray, and pray continually, till this awful storm is gone by. Remember, that come what may, you have two friends entirely devoted to you—my wife and myself."

Hurriedly written, scrawled rather as this note was, it showed me again plainer than ever what a noble clear-hearted man he was who had written it. But this is not to the purpose. Charles Hawker departed, carrying this, before the others were stirring, and held his way through the forest-road towards his mother's station.

This same two days' business was the best stroke of work that the Devil did in that part of the country for many years. With his usual sagacity he had busied himself in drawing the threads of mischief so parallel, that it seemed they must end in one and only one lamentable issue; namely, that Charles Hawker and his father should meet, pistol in hand, as deadly enemies. But at this last period of the game, our good honest Major completely check-mated him, by sending Charles Hawker home to his mother. In this terrible pass, after this unexpected move of the Major's, he (the Devil, no other) began casting about for a scoundrel, by whose assistance he might turn the Major's flank. But no great rogue being forthcoming he had to look round for the next best substitute, a great fool,—and one of these he found immediately, riding exactly the way he wished. Him he subpœnaed immediately, and found to do his work better even than a good rogue would have done. We shall see how poor Charles Hawker, pricking along through the forest, getting every moment further from danger and mischief, met a man charging along the road, full speed, who instantly pulled up and spoke to him.

This was the consummate fool, sent of the Devil, whom I have mentioned above. We have seen him before. He was the longest, brownest, stupidest of the Hawbuck family. The one who could spit further than any of his brothers.

" Well, Charley," he said, " is this all true about the bush-rangers ? "

Charles said it was. And they were bailed up in the limestone gully, and all the party were away after them.

" Where are you going then ?" asked the unfortunate young idiot.

" Home to my mother," blurted out poor Charles.

" Well ! " said the other, speaking unconsciously exactly the words which the enemy of mankind desired. " Well, I couldn't have believed that. If a chap had said that of you in my hearing, I'd have fought him if he'd been as big as a house. I never thought that of you, Charley."

Charles cursed aloud. " What have I done to be talked to like this ? Major Buckley has no right to send me away like this, to be branded as coward through the country side. Ten times over better to be shot than have such words as these said to me. I shall go back with you."

" That's the talk," said the poor fool. " I thought I wasn't wrong in you, Charley." And so Charles galloped back with him.

We, in the meantime, had started from the station, ere day was well broke. Foremost of the company rode Desborough, calm and serene, and on either side of him Captain Brentwood and Major Buckley. Then came the Doctor, Sam, Jim, Halbert, and myself; behind us again, five troopers and the Sergeant. Each man of us all was armed with a sword; and every man in that company, as it happened, knew the use of that weapon well. The troopers carried carbines, and all of us carried pistols.

The glare in the east changing from pearly green to golden yellow, gave notice of the coming sun. One snow peak, Tambo I think, began to catch the light, and blaze like another morning star. The day had begun in earnest, and, as we entered the mouth of the glen to which we were bound, slanting gleams of light were already piercing the misty gloom, and lighting up the loftier crags.

A deep, rock-walled glen it was, open and level; though, in the centre, ran a tangled waving line of evergreen shrubs, marking the course of a pretty bright creek, which, half-hidden by luxuriant vegetation, ran beside the faint track leading to one of Captain Brentwood's mountain huts. Along this track we could plainly see the hoof marks of the men we were after.

It was one of the most beautiful gullies I had ever seen, and I turned to say so to some one who rode beside me. Conceive my horror at finding it was Charles Hawker! I turned to him fiercely, and said,—

"Get back, Charles. Go home. You don't know what you are doing, lad."

He defied me. And I was speaking roughly to him again, when there came a puff of smoke from among the rocks overhead, and down I went, head over heels. A bullet had grazed my thigh, and killed my horse, who, throwing me on my head, rendered me *hors de combat*. So that during the fight which followed, I was sitting on a rock, very sick and very stupid, a mile from the scene of action.

My catastrophe caused only a temporary stoppage; and, during the confusion, Charles Hawker was unnoticed. The man who had fired at me (why at me I cannot divine), was evidently a solitary guard perched among the rocks. The others held on for about a quarter of an hour, till the valley narrowed up again, just leaving room for the track, between the brawling creek and the tall limestone cliff. But after this it opened out into a broader amphitheatre, walled on all sides by inaccessible rock, save in two places. Sam, from whom I get this account of affairs, had just time to notice this, when he saw Captain Brentwood draw a pistol and fire it, and, at the same instant, a man dashed out of some scrub on the other side of the creek, and galloped away up the valley.

"They have had the precaution to set two watches for us, which I hardly expected," said Captain Desborough. "They will fight us now, they can't help it, thank God. They have had a sharp turn and a merry one, but they are dead men, and they know it. The Devil is but a poor paymaster, Buckley. After all this hide and seek work, they have only got two days' liberty."

The troopers now went to the front with Halbert and the other military men, while Sam, Jim, and Charles, the last all unperceived by the Major in his excitement, rode in the rear.

"We are going to have a regular battle," said Jim. "They are bailed up, and must fight: some of us will go home feet foremost to-day."

So they rode on through the open forest, till they began to see one or two horsemen through the tree-stems, reconnoitring. The ground began to rise towards a lofty cliff that towered before them, and all could see that the end was coming. Then they caught sight of the whole gang, scattered about among the low shrubs, and a few shots were fired on both sides, before the enemy turned and retreated towards the wall of rock, now plainly visible through the timber. Our party continued to advance steadily in open order.

Then under the beetling crags, where the fern-trees began to feather up among the fallen boulders, the bushrangers turned like hunted wolves, and stood at bay.

CHAPTER XLII.

THE FIGHT AMONG THE FERN-TREES.

THEN Captain Desborough cried aloud to ride at them, and spare no man. And, as he spoke, every golden fern-bough, and every coigne of vantage among the rocks, began to blaze and crackle with gun and pistol shot. Jim's horse sprung aloft and fell, hurling him forcibly to the ground, and a tall young trooper, dropping his carbine, rolled heavily off his saddle, and lay on the grass face downward, quite still, as if asleep.

"There's the first man killed," said the Major, very quietly. "Sam, my boy, don't get excited, but close on the first fellow you see a chance at." And Sam, looking in his father's face as he spoke, saw a light in his eyes, that he had never seen there before— the light of battle. The Major caught a carbine from the hands of a trooper who rode beside him, and took a snap-shot, quick as lightning, at a man whom they saw running from one cover to another. The poor wretch staggered and put his hands to his head, then stumbled and fell heavily down.

Now the fight became general and confused. All about among the fern and the flowers, among the lemon-shrubs, and the tangled vines, men fought, and fired, and struck, and cursed; while the little brown bandicoots scudded swiftly away, and the deadly snake hid himself in his darkest lair, affrighted. Shots were cracking on all sides, two riderless horses, confused in the *mêlée*, were galloping about neighing, and a third lay squealing on the ground in the agonies of death.

Sam saw a man fire at his father, whose horse went down, while the Major arose unhurt. He rode at the ruffian, who was dismounted, and cut him so deep between the shoulder and the neck, that he fell and never spoke again. Then seeing Halbert and the Doctor on the right, fiercely engaged with four men who were fighting with clubbed muskets and knives, he turned to help them, but ere he reached them, a tall, handsome young fellow dashed out of the shrub, and pulling his horse short up, took deliberate aim at him, and fired.

Sam heard the bullet go hissing past his ear, and got mad. "That young dog shall go down," said he. "I know him. He is one of the two who rode first yesterday." And as this passed through his mind, he rode straight at him, with his sword hand upon his left shoulder. He came full against him in a moment, and as the man held up his gun to guard himself, his cut descended, so full and hard, that it shore through the gunbarrel as through a stick,* and ere he could bring his hand to his cheek, his opponent had grappled him, and the two rolled off their horses together, locked in a deadly embrace.

Then began an awful and deadly fight between these two young fellows. Sam's sword had gone from his hand in the fall, and he was defenceless, save by such splendid physical powers as he had by nature. But his adversary, though perhaps a little lighter, was a terrible enemy, and fought with the strength and litheness of a leopard. He had his hand at Sam's throat, and was trying to choke him. Sam saw that one great effort was necessary, and with a heave of his whole body, threw the other beneath him, and struck downwards, three quick blows, with the whole strength of his ponderous fist, on the face of the man, as he lay beneath him. The hold on his throat loosened, and seeing that they had rolled within reach of his sword, in a moment he had clutched it, and drawing back his elbow, prepared to plunge it into his adversary's chest.

But he hesitated. He could not do it. Maddened as he was with fighting, the sight of that bloody face, bruised beyond recognition by his terrible blows, and the wild fierce eyes, full of rage and terror, looking into his own, stayed his hand, and while he paused the man spoke, thick and indistinctly, for his jaw was broken.

"If you will spare me," he said, "I will be King's evidence."

* Lieutenant Anderson, unless I am mistaken, performed the same feat at the capture of a bushranger in '52.

"Then turn on your face," said Sam; "and I will tie you up."

And as he spoke a trooper ran up, and secured the prisoner, who appealed to Sam for his handkerchief. "I fought you fair," he said; "and you're a man worth fighting. But you have broken something in my face with your fist. Give me something to tie it up with."

"God save us all!" said Sam, giving him his handkerchief. "This is miserable work! I hope it is all over."

It seemed so. All he heard were the fearful screams of a wounded man lying somewhere among the fern.

"Where are they all, Jackson?" said he.

"All away to the right, sir," said the trooper. "One of my comrades is killed, your father has had his horse shot, the Doctor is hit in the arm, and Mr. James Brentwood has got his leg broke with the fall of his horse. They are minding him now. We've got all the gang, alive or dead, except two. Captain Desborough is up the valley now after the head man, and young Mr. Hawker is with him. D——n it all! hark to that."

Two shots were fired in quick succession in the direction indicated; and Sam, having caught his horse, galloped off to see what was going on.

*   *   *   *   *   *

Desborough fought neither against small nor great, but only against one man, and he was George Hawker. Him he had sworn he would bring home, dead or alive. When he and his party had first broken through the fern, he had caught sight of his quarry, and had instantly made towards him, as quick as the broken scrub-tangled ground would allow.

They knew one another; and, as soon as Hawker saw that he was recognised, he made to the left, away from the rest of his gang, trying to reach, as Desborough could plainly see, the only practicable way that led from the amphitheatre in which they were back into the mountains.

They fired at one another without effect at the first. Hawker was now pushing in full flight, though the scrub was so dense that neither made much way. Now the ground got more open and easier travelled, when Desborough was aware of one who came charging recklessly up alongside of him, and, looking round, he recognised Charles Hawker.

"Good lad," he said; "come on. I must have that fellow before us there. He is the arch-devil of the lot. If we follow him to h——ll, we must have him!"

"We'll have him safe enough!" said Charles. "Push to the left, Captain, and we shall get him against those fallen rocks."

Desborough saw the excellence of this advice. This was the last piece of broken ground there was. On the right the cliff rose precipitous, and from its side had tumbled a confused heap of broken rock, running out into the glen. Once past this, the man they were pursuing would have the advantage, for he was splendidly mounted, and beyond was clear galloping ground. As it was, he was in a recess, and Desborough and Charles pushing forward, succeeded in bringing him to bay. Alas, too well!

George Hawker reined up his horse when he saw escape was impossible, and awaited their coming with a double-barrelled pistol in his hand. As the other two came on, calling on him to surrender, Desborough's horse received a bullet in his chest, and down went horse and man together. But Charles pushed on till he was within ten yards of the bushranger, and levelled his pistol to fire.

So met father and son, the second time in their lives, all unconsciously. For an instant they glared on one another with wild threatening eyes, as the father made his aim more certain and deadly. Was there no lightning in heaven to strike him dead, and save him from this last horrid crime? Was there no warning voice to tell him that this was his son

None. The bullet sped, and the poor boy tumbled from his saddle, clutching wildly, with crooked, convulsive fingers, at the grass and flowers—shot through the chest!

Then, ere Desborough had disentangled himself from his fallen horse, George Hawker rode off laughing—out through the upper rock walls into the presence of the broad bald snow-line that rolled above his head in endless lofty tiers towards the sky.

Desborough arose, swearing and stamping; but, ere he could pick up his cap, Sam was alongside of him, breathless, and with him another common-looking man—my man, Dick, no other—and they both cried out together, "What has happened?"

"Look there!" said Desborough, pointing to something dark among the grass,—"that's what has happened. What lies there was Charles Hawker, and the villain is off."

"Who shot Charles Hawker?" said Dick.

"His namesake," said Desborough.

"His own father!" said Dick; "that's terrible."

"What do you mean?" they both asked aghast.

"Never mind now," he answered. "Captain Desborough, what are you going to do? Do you know where he's gone?"

"Up into the mountain, to lie by, I suppose," said Desborough.

"Not at all, sir! He is going to cross the snow, and get to the old hut, near the Murray Gate."

"What! Merryman's hut?" said the Captain. "Impossible! He could not get through that way."

"I tell you he can. That is where they came from at first; that is where they went to when they landed; and this is the gully they came through."

"Are you deceiving me?" said Desborough. "It will be worse for you if you are! I ain't in a humour for that sort of thing. Who are you?"

"I am Mr. Hamlyn's groom—Dick. Strike me dead if I ain't telling the truth!"

"Do you know this man, Buckley?" said Desborough, calling out to Sam, who was sitting beside poor Charles Hawker, holding his head up.

"Know him! of course I do," he replied; "ever since I was a child."

"Then, look here," said Desborough to Dick, "I shall trust you. Now, you say he will cross the snow. If I were to go round by the Parson's I shouldn't get much snow."

"That's just it, don't you see? You can be round at the huts before him. That's what I mean," said Dick. "Take Mr. Buckley's horse, and ride him till he drops, and you'll get another at the Parson's. If you have any snow, it will be on Broadsaddle; but it won't signify. You go round the low side of Tambo, and sight the .ake, and you'll be there before him."

"How far?"

"Sixty miles, or thereabouts, plain sailing. It ain't eleven o'clock yet."

"Good; I'll remember you for this. Buckley, I want your horse. Is the lad dead?"

"No; but he is very bad. I'll try to get him home. Take the horse; he is not so good a one as Widderin, but he'll carry you to the Parson's. God speed you."

They watched him ride away almost south, skirting the ridges of the mountain as long as he could; then they saw him scrambling up a lofty wooded ridge, and there he disappeared.

They raised poor Charles Hawker up, and Sam, mounting Dick's horse, took the wounded man up before him, and started to go slowly home. After a time, he said, "Do you feel worse, Charles?" and the other replied, "No; but I am very cold." After that, he stayed quite still, with his arm round Sam Buckley's neck, until they reached the Brentwoods' door.

Some came out to the door to meet them, and, among others, Alice. "Take him from me," said Sam to one of the men. "Be very gentle; he is asleep." And so they took the dead man's arm from off the living man's shoulder, and carried him in; for Charles Hawker was asleep indeed—in the sleep that knows no waking.

*　　*　　*　　*　　*　　*

That was one of the fiercest and firmest stands that was ever made by bushrangers against the authorities. Of the former five were shot down, three wounded, and the rest captured, save two. The gang was destroyed at once, and life and property once more secure, though at a sad sacrifice.

One trooper was shot dead at the first onset,—a fine young fellow, just picked from his regiment for good conduct to join the police. Another was desperately wounded, who died the next day. On the part of the independent men assisting, there were Charles Hawker killed, Doctor Mulhaus shot in the left arm, and Jim with his leg broke; so that, on that evening, Captain Brentwood's house was like a hospital.

Captain Brentwood set his son's leg, under Dr. Mulhaus' directions, the Doctor keeping mighty brave, though once or twice his face twisted with pain, and he was nearly fainting. Alice was everywhere, pale and calm, helping every one who needed it, and saying nothing. Eleanor, the cook, pervaded the house, doing the work of seven women, and having the sympathies of fourteen. She told them that this was as bad a job as she'd ever seen; worse, in fact. That the nearest thing she'd ever seen to it was when Mat Steeman's mob were broke up by the squatters; "But then," she added, "there were none but prisoners killed."

But when Alice had done all she could, and the house was quiet, she went up to her father, and said,—

"Now, father, comes the worst part of the matter for me. Who is to tell Mrs. Hawker?"

"Mrs. Buckley, my dear, would be the best person. But she is at the Mayfords', I am afraid."

"Mrs. Hawker must be told at once, father, by some of us. I do so dread her hearing of it by some accident, when none of her friends are with her. Oh, dear! oh, dear! I never thought to have had such times as these."

"Alice, my darling," said her father, "do you think that you have strength to carry the news to her? If Major Buckley went with you, he could tell her, you know; and it would be much better for her to have him, an old friend, beside her. It would be such a delay to go round and fetch his wife. Have you courage?"

"I will make courage," she said. "Speak to Major Buckley, father, and I will get ready."

She went to Sam. "I am going on a terrible errand," she said; "I am going to tell Mrs. Hawker about this dreadful, dreadful business. Now, what I want to say is, that you mustn't come; your father is going with me, and I'll get through it alone, Sam. Now please," she added, seeing Sam was going to speak, "don't argue about it; I am very much upset as it is, and I want you to stay here. You won't follow us, will you?"

"Whatever you order, Alice, is law," said Sam. "I won't come if you don't wish it; but I can't see——"

"There now. Will you get me my horse? And please stay by poor Jim, for my sake."

Sam complied; and Alice, getting on her riding-habit, came back trembling, and trying not to cry, to tell Major Buckley that she was ready.

He took her in his arms, and kissed her. "You are a brave, noble girl," he said; "I thank God for such a daughter-in-law. Now, my dear, let us hurry off, and not think of what is to come."

It was about five o'clock when they went off. Sam and Halbert, having let them out of the paddock, went in-doors to comfort poor Jim's heart, and to get something to eat, if it were procurable. Jim lay on his bed tossing about, and the Doctor sat beside him, talking to him, pale and grim, waiting for the doctor who had been sent for; no other than his drunken old enemy.

"This is about as nice a kettle of fish," said Jim, when they came and sat beside him, "as a man could possibly wish to eat. Poor Cecil and Charley; both gone, eh? Well, I know it ain't decent for a fellow with a broken leg to feel wicked; but I do, nevertheless. I wish now that I had had a chance at some of them before that stupid brute of a horse got shot."

"If you don't lie still, you Jim," said Sam, "your leg will never set; and then you must have it taken off, you know. How is your arm, Doctor?"

"Shooting a little," said the Doctor; "nothing to signify, I believe. At least, nothing in the midst of such a tragedy as this. Poor Mary Hawker; the pretty little village-maid we all loved so well. To come to such an end as this!"

"Is it true, then, Doctor, that Hawker, the bushranger, is her husband?"

"Quite true, alas! Every one must know it now. But I pray you, Sam, to keep the darkest part of it all from her; don't let her know that the boy fell by the hand of his father."

"I could almost swear," said Sam, "that one among the gang is his son too. When they rode past Alice and myself yesterday morning, one was beside him so wonderfully like him, that even at that time I set them down for father and son."

"If Hamlyn's strange tale be true, it is so," said the Doctor. "Is the young man you speak of among the prisoners, do you know?"

"Yes; I helped to capture him myself," said Sam. "What do you mean by Hamlyn's story?"

"Oh, a long one. He met him in a hut the night after we pic-nic'd at Mirngish, and found out who he was. The secret not being ours, your father and I never told any of you young people of the fact of this bushranger being poor Mrs. Hawker's husband. I wish we had; all this might have been avoided. But the poor soul always desired that the secret of his birth might be kept from Charles, and you see the consequence. I'll never keep a secret again. Come here with me; let us see both of them."

They followed him, and he turned into a little side room at the back of the house. It was a room used for chance visitors or strangers, containing two small beds, which now bore an unaccustomed burden, for beneath the snow-white coverlets lay two figures, indistinct indeed, but unmistakeable.

"Which is he?" whispered the Doctor.

Sam raised the counterpane from the nearest one, but it was not Charles. It was a young, handsome face that he saw, lying so quietly and peacefully on the white pillow, that he exclaimed—

"Surely this man is not dead!"

The Doctor shook his head. "I have often seen them like that," he said. "He is shot through the heart."

Then they went to the other bed, where poor Charles lay. Sam gently raised the black curls from his face, but none of them spoke a word for a few minutes, till the Doctor said, "Now let us come and see his brother."

They crossed the yard, to a slab outbuilding, before which one of the troopers was keeping guard, with a loaded carbine; and, the Sergeant coming across, admitted them.

Seven or eight fearfully ill-looking ruffians lay about on the floor, handcuffed. They were most of them of the usual convict stamp; dark, saturnine-looking fellows, though one offered a strange contrast by being an Albino, and another they could not see plainly, for he was huddled up in a dark corner, bending down over a basin of water, and dabbing his face. The greater part of them cursed and blasphemed desperately, as is the manner of such men when their blood is up, and they are reckless; while the wounded ones lay in a fierce sullen silence, more terrible almost than the foul language of the others.

"He is not here," said Sam. "Stay, that must be him wiping his face."

He went towards him, and saw he was right. The young man he had taken looked wildly up like a trapped animal into his face, and the Doctor could not suppress an exclamation when he saw the likeness to his father.

"Is your face very bad?" said Sam quietly.

The other turned away in silence.

"I'll tie it up for you, if you like," said Sam.

"It don't want no tying up."

He turned his face to the wall, and remained obstinately silent. They perceived that nothing more was to be got from him, and departed. But, turning at the door, they still saw him crouched in the corner like a wild beast, wiping his bruised face every now and then with Sam's handkerchief, apparently thinking of nothing, hoping for nothing. Such a pitiful sight—such an example of one who was gone beyond feeling hope, or sorrow, or aught else, save physical pain, that the Doctor's gorge rose, and he said, stamping on the gravel,—

"A man, who says that that is not the saddest, saddest sight he ever saw, is a disgrace to the mother that bore him. To see a young fellow like that with such a *physique*—and God only knows what undeveloped qualities in him—only ripe for the gallows at five-and-twenty, is enough to make the angels weep. He knows no evil but physical pain, and that he considers but a temporary one. He knows no good save, perhaps, to be faithful to his confederates. He has been brought up from his cradle to look on every man as his enemy. He never knew what it was to love a human being in his life. Why, what does such a man regard this world as? As the antechamber of hell, if he ever heard of such a place. I want to know what either of us three would have been if we had had his training. I want to know that now. We might have been as much worse than he is as a wolf is worse than an evil-tempered dog."

A beautiful colley came up to the Doctor and fawned on him, looking into his face with her deep, expressive, hazel eyes.

"We must do something for that fellow, Sam. If it's only for his name's sake," said the Doctor.

*　*　*　*　*　*

That poor boy, sitting crouched there in the corner, with a broken jaw, and just so much of human feeling as one may suppose a pole-cat to have, caught in a gin, is that same baby that we saw Ellen Lee nursing on the door-step in the rain, when our poor Mary came upon her on one wild night in Exeter.

Base-born, workhouse-bred! Tossed from workhouse to prison, from prison to hulk—every man's hand against him—an Arab of society. As hopeless a case, my lord judge, as you ever had to deal with; and yet I think, my lord, that your big heart grows a little pitiful, when you see that handsome face before you, blank and careless, and you try, fruitlessly, to raise some blush of shame, or even anger in it, by your eloquence.

Gone beyond that, my lord. Your thunderbolts fall harmless here, and the man you say is lost, and naturally. Yet, give that same man room to breathe and act; keep temptation from him, and let his good qualities, should he have any, have fair play, and, even yet, he may convert you to the belief that hardened criminals may be reformed, to the extent of one in a dozen; beyond that no reasonable man will go.

Let us see the end of this man. For now the end of my tale draws near, and I must begin gathering up the threads of the story, to tie them in a knot, and release my readers from duty. Here is all I can gather about him,—

Sam and the Doctor moved heaven, earth, and the Colonial Secretary, to get his sentence commuted, and with success. So when his companions were led out to execution, he was held back; reserved for penal servitude for life.

He proved himself quiet and docile; so much so that when our greatest, boldest explorer was starting for his last hopeless journey to the interior, this man was selected as one of the twelve convicts who were to accompany him. What follows is an extract which I have been favoured with from his private journal. You will not find it in the published history of the expedition;—

"Date — lat. — long. — Morning. It is getting hopeless now, and to-morrow I turn. Sand, and nothing but sand. The salsolaceous plants, so long the only vegetation we have seen, are gone; and the little sienite peak, the last symptom of a water-bearing country, has disappeared behind us. The sandhills still roll away towards the setting sun, but get less and less elevated. The wild fowl are still holding their mysterious flight to the north-west, but I have not wings to follow them. Oh, my God! if I only knew what those silly birds know. It is hopeless to go on, and, I begin to fear, hopeless to go back. Will it never rain again?

"Afternoon,—My servant Hawker, one of the convicts assigned to me by Government, died to-day at noon. I had got fond of this man, as the most patient and the bravest, where all have been so patient and so brave. He was a very silent and reserved man, and had never complained, so that I was deeply shocked, on his sending for me at dinner-time, to find that he was dying.

"He asked me not to deceive him, but to tell him if there was any truth in what the gaol-chaplain had said, about there being another life after death. I told him earnestly that I knew it as surely as I knew that the earth was under my feet; and went on comforting him as one comforts a dying man. But he never spoke again; and we buried him in the hot sand at sundown. The first wind will obliterate the little mound we raised over him, and none will ever cross this hideous desert again. So that he will have as quiet a grave as he could wish.

"Eleven o'clock at night.—God be praised. Heavy clouds and thunder to the north.—"

So this poor workhouse-bred lad lies out among the sands of the middle desert.

CHAPTER XLIII.

ACROSS THE SNOW.

HAWKER the elder, as I said, casting one glance at the body of his son, whom he knew not, and another at Captain Desborough, who was just rising from the ground after his fall, set spurs to his noble chestnut horse, and pushing through the contracted barriers of slate which closed up the southern end of the amphitheatre where they had been surprised, made for the broader and rapidly rising valley which stretched beyond.

He soon reached the rocky gate, where the vast ridge of limestone alternating with the schist, and running north and south in high serrated ridges, was cut through by a deep fissure, formed by the never idle waters of a little creek, that in the course of ages had mined away the softer portions of the rock, and made a practicable pass toward the mountains.

He picked his way with difficulty through the tumbled boulders that lay in the chasm; and then there was a cool brisk wind on his forehead, and a glare in his eyes. The chill breath of the west wind from the mountain—the glare of the snow that filled up the upper end of the valley, rising in level ridges towards the sky-line.

He had been this path before; and if he had gone it a hundred times again, he would only have cursed it for a rough desperate road, the only hope of a desperate man. Not for him to notice the thousand lessons that the Lord had spread before him in the wilderness! not for him to notice how the vegetation changed when the limestone was passed, and the white quartz reefs began to seam the slaty sides of the valley like rivers of silver! Not for him to see how, as he went up and on, the hardy Dicksonia still nestled in stunted tufts among the more sheltered side gullies, long after her tenderer sister, the queenly Alsophylla* had been left behind. He only knew that he was a hunted wild beast, and that his lair was beyond the snow.

The creek flashed pleasantly among the broken slate, full and turbid under the mid-day sun. After midnight, when its fountains are sealed again by the frosty breath of night, that creek would be reduced to a trickling rill. His horse's feet brushed through the delicate asplenium, the Venus'-hair of Australia; the sarsaparilla still hung in scant purple tufts on the golden wattle, and the scarlet correa lurked among the broken quartz.

---

* The two species of fern-tree.

Upwards and onwards. In front, endless cycles agone, a lava stream from some crater we know not of, had burst over the slate, with fearful clang and fierce explosion, forming a broad roadway of broken basalt up to a plateau twelve hundred feet or more above us, and not so steep but that a horse might be led up it. Let us go up with him, not cursing heaven and earth, as he did, but noticing how, as we ascend, the scarlet wreaths of the Kennedia and the crimson Grevillea give place to the golden Grevillea and the red Epacris; then comes the white Epacris, and then the grass trees, getting smaller and scantier as we go, till the little blue Gentian, blossoming boldly among the slippery crags, tells us that we have nearly reached the limits of vegetation.

He turned when he reached this spot, and looked around him. To the west a broad rolling down of snow, rising gradually; to the east, a noble prospect of forest and plain, hill and gully, with old Snowy winding on in broad bright curves to the sea. He looked over all the beauty and undeveloped wealth of Gipp's Land, which shall yet, please God, in fulness of time, be one of the brightest jewels in the King of England's crown, but with eyes that saw not. He turned towards the snow, and mounting his horse, which he had led up the cliff, held steadily westward.

His plans were well laid. Across the mountain, north of Lake Omeo, not far from the mighty cleft in which the infant Murray spends his youth, were two huts, erected years before by some settler, and abandoned. They had been used by a gang of bush-rangers, who had been attacked by the police, and dispersed. Nevertheless, they had been since inhabited by the men we know of, who landed in the boat from Van Diemen's Land, in consequence of Hawker himself having found a pass through the ranges, open for nine months in the year. So that, when the police were searching Gipp's Land for these men, they, with the exception of two or three, were snugly ensconced on the other water-shed, waiting till the storm should blow over. In these huts Hawker intended to lie by for a short time, living on such provisions as were left, until he could make his way northward on the outskirts of the settlements, and escape.

There was no pursuit, he thought: how could there be? Who knew of this route but himself and his mates? hardly likely any of them would betray him. No creature was moving in the valley he had just ascended, but the sun was beginning to slope towards the west, and he must onwards.

Onwards, across the slippery snow. At first a few tree-stems, blighted and withered, were visible right and left, proving that at some time during their existence, these bald downs had either a less eleva-tion or a warmer climate than now. Then these even disappeared, and all around was one white blinding glare. To the right, the snow-fields rolled up into the shapeless lofty mass called Mount Tambo, behind

c c

which the hill they now call Kosciusko,*—as some say, the highest
ground in the country,—began to take a crimson tint from the declining sun. Far to the south, black and gaunt among the whitened
hills, towered the rounded hump of Buffaloe, while the peaks of Buller
and Aberdeen showed like dim blue clouds on the furthest horizon.

Snow, and nothing but snow. Sometimes plunging shoulder deep
into some treacherous hollow, sometimes guiding the tired horse
across the surface frozen over unknown depths. He had been
drinking hard for some days, and, now the excitement of action had
gone off, was fearfully nervous. The snow-glint had dizzied his
head, too, and he began to see strange shapes forming themselves in
the shade of each hollow, and start at each stumble of his horse.

A swift-flying shadow upon the snow, and a rush of wings overhead. An eagle. The lordly scavenger is following him, impatient
for him to drop and become a prey. Soar up, old bird, and bide thy
time; on yonder precipice thou shalt have good chance of a meal.

Twilight, and then night, and yet the snow but half past. There
is a rock in a hollow, where grow a few scanty tufts of grass which
the poor horse may eat. Here he will camp, fireless, foodless, and
walk up and down the livelong night, for sleep might be death.
Though he is not in thoroughly Alpine regions, yet still, at this
time of the year, the snow is deep and the frost is keen. It were
as well to keep awake.

As he paced up and down beneath the sheltering rock, when night
had closed in, and the frosty stars were twinkling in the cold blue
firmament, strange ghosts and fancies came crowding on him thick
and fast. Down the long vista of a misspent, ruined life, he saw
people long since forgotten trooping up towards him. His father
tottered sternly on, as with a fixed purpose before him; his gipsy-
mother, Madge, strode forward pitiless; and poor ruined Ellen,
holding her child to her heart, joined the others and held up her
withered hand as if in mockery. But then there came a face
between him and all the other figures which his distempered brain had
summoned, and blotted them out; the face of a young man, bearing
a strange likeness to himself; the face of the last human creature he
had seen; the face of the boy that he had shot down among the fern.

Why should this face grow before him wherever he turned, so
that he could not look on rock or sky without seeing it? Why

---

* Mr. Macarthur, companion of Count Strzelecki, seems to believe that
Kosciusko is actually the highest point. But I believe Mr. Selwyn is of
opinion that there is a peak ("down" would be a more correct word) higher
yet. Mount Kosciusko is between 7,000 and 8,000 feet above the sea, from
which it is visible. It is hard to believe, however, that this is the highest
point in the Australian Alps. The nautical charts lay down here, "snowy
mountains, visible twenty-five leagues at sea." And considering that they
are at least fifteen leagues inland, I cannot help thinking, either that Kosciusko is not the highest point, or that its height is un lerrated.

should it glare at him through a blood-red haze when he shut his eyes to keep it out, not in sorrow, not in anger, but even as he had seen it last, expressing only terror and pain, as the lad rolled off his horse, and lay a black heap among the flowers? Up and away! anything is better than this. Let us stumble away across the snow, through the mirk night once more, rather than be driven mad by this pale boy's face.

Morning, and the pale ghosts have departed. Long shadows of horse and man are thrown before him now, as the slope dips away to the westward, and he knows that his journey is well-nigh over.

It was late in the afternoon before, having left the snow some hours, he began to lead his horse down a wooded precipice, through vegetation which grew more luxuriant every yard he descended. The glen, whose bottom he was trying to reach, was a black profound gulf, with perpendicular, or rather, over-hanging walls, on every side, save where he was scrambling down. Here indeed it was possible for a horse to keep his footing among the belts of trees, that, alternating with precipitous granite cliff, formed the upper end of one of the most tremendous glens in the world—the Gates of the Murray.

He was barely one-third of the way down this mountain wall, when the poor tired horse lost his footing and fell over the edge, touching neither tree nor stone for five hundred feet, while George Hawker was left terrified, hardly daring to peer into the dim abyss, where the poor beast was gone.

But it was little matter. The hut he was making for was barely four miles off now, and there was meat, drink, and safety. Perhaps there might be company, he hoped there might,—some of the gang might have escaped. A dog would be some sort of friend. Anything sooner than such another night as last night.

His pistols were gone with the saddle, and he was unarmed. He reached the base of the cliff in safety, and forced his way through the tangled scrub that fringed the infant river, towards the lower end of the pass. Here the granite walls, overhanging, bend forward above to meet one another, almost forming an arch, the height of which, from the river-bed, is computed to be nearly, if not quite, three thousand feet. Through this awful gate he forced his way, overawed and utterly dispirited, and reached the gully where his refuge lay, just as the sun was setting.

There was a slight track, partly formed by stray cattle, which led up it; and casting his eyes upon this, he saw the marks of a horse's feet. "Some one of the gang got home before me," he said. "I'm right glad of that, anything better than such another night."

He turned a sharp angle in the path, just where it ran round an abrupt cliff. He saw a horseman within ten yards of him with his face towards him. Captain Desborough, holding a pistol at his head.

"Surrender, George Hawker!" said Desborough. "Or, by the living Lord! you are a dead man."

Hungry, cold, desperate, unarmed; he saw that he was undone, and that hope was dead. The Captain had an easier prey than he had anticipated. Hawker threw up his arms, and ere he could fully appreciate his situation, he was chained fast to Desborough's saddle, only to be loosed, he knew, by the gallows.

Without a word on either side they began their terrible journey. Desborough riding, and Hawker manacled by his right wrist to the saddle. Fully a mile was passed before the latter asked sullenly,—

"Where are you going to take me to-night?"

"To Dickenson's," replied Desborough. "You must step out, you know. It will be for your own good, for I must get there to-night."

Two or three miles further were got over, when Hawker said abruptly,—

"Look here, Captain, I want to talk to you."

"You had better not," said Desborough. "I don't want to have any communication with you, and every word you say will go against you."

"Bah!" said Hawker. "I must swing. I know that. I shan't make any defence. Why, the devils out of hell would come into court against me if I did. But I want to ask you a question or two. You haven't got the character of being a brutal fellow, like O——. It can't hurt you to answer me one or two things, and ease my mind a bit."

"God help you, unhappy man;" said Desborough. "I will answer any questions you ask."

"Well, then, see here," said Hawker, hesitating. "I want to know—I want to know first, how you got round before me?"

"Is that all?" said Desborough. "Well, I came round over Broadsaddle, and got a fresh horse at the Parson's."

"Ah!" said Hawker. "That young fellow I shot down when you were after me, is he dead?"

"By this time," said Desborough. "He was just dying when I came away."

"Would you mind stopping for a moment, Captain? Now tell me, who was he?"

"Mr. Charles Hawker, son of Mrs. Hawker, of Toonarbin."

He gave such a yell that Desborough shrunk from him appalled, —a cry as of a wounded tiger, and struggled so wildly with his handcuff that the blood poured from his wrist. Let us close this scene. Desborough told me afterwards, that that wild, fierce, despairing cry, rang in his ears for many years afterwards, and would never be forgotten till those ears were closed with the dust of the grave.

CHAPTER XLIV.

HOW MARY HAWKER HEARD THE NEWS.

TROUBRIDGE'S Station, Toonarbin, lay so far back from the river, and so entirely on the road to nowhere, that Tom used to remark, that he would back it for being the worst station for news in the country. So it happened while these terrible scenes were enacting within ten miles of them, down, in fact, to about one o'clock in the day when the bushrangers were overtaken and punished, Mary and her cousin sat totally unconscious of what was going on.

But about eleven o'clock that day, Burnside, the cattle dealer, mentioned once before in these pages, arrived at Major Buckley's, from somewhere up country, and found the house apparently deserted.

But having coee'd for some time, a door opened in one of the huts, and a sleepy groom came forth, yawning.

" Where are they all? " asked Burnside.

" Mrs. Buckley and the women were down at Mrs. Mayford's, streaking the bodies out," he believed. " The rest were gone away after the gang."

This was the first that Burnside had heard about the matter. And now, bit by bit, he extracted everything from the sleepy groom.

I got him afterwards to confess to me, that when he heard of this terrible affair, his natural feeling of horror was considerably alloyed with pleasure. He saw here at one glance a fund of small talk for six months. He saw himself a welcome visitor at every station, even up to furthest lonely Condamine, retailing the news of these occurrences with all the authenticity of an eye witness, improving his narrative by each repetition. Here was the basis of a new tale, Ode, Epic, Saga, or what you may please to call it, which he Burnside, the bard, should sing at each fireside throughout the land.

" And how are Mrs. and Miss Mayford, poor souls? " he asked.

" They're as well," answered the groom, " as you'd expect folks to be after such a mishap. They ran out at the back way and down the garden towards the river before the chaps could burst the door down. I am sorry for that little chap Cecil, I am, by Jove! A straightforward, manly little chap as ever crossed a horse. Last week he says to me, says he, ' Benjy, my boy,' says he, ' come and be groom to me. I'll give you thirty pound a-year.' And I says, ' If Mr. Sam——' Hallo, there they are at it, hammer and tongs! Sharp work, that! "

They both listened intensely. They could hear, borne on the west wind, a distant dropping fire and a shouting. The groom's eye began to kindle a bit, but Burnside, sitting yet upon his horse, grasped the lad's shoulder and cried, "God save us, suppose our men should be beaten!"

"Suppose," said the groom, contemptuously shaking him off; "why then you and I should get our throats cut."

At this moment the noise of the distant fight breezed up louder than ever.

"They're beat back," said Burnside. "I shall be off to Toonarbin, and give them warning. I advise you to save yourself."

"I was set to mind these here things," said Benjy, "and I'm a-going to mind 'em. And they as meddles with 'em had better look out."

Burnside started off for Toonarbin, and when half-way there he paused and listened. The firing had ceased. When he came to reflect, now that his panic was over, he had very little doubt that Desborough's party had gained the day. It was impossible, he thought, that it could be otherwise.

Nevertheless, being half-way to Toonarbin, he determined to ride on, and, having called in a moment, to follow a road which took a way past Lee's old hut towards the scene of action. He very soon pulled up at the door, and Tom Troubridge came slowly out to meet him.

"Hallo, Burnside!" said Tom. "Get off, and come in."

"Not I, indeed. I am going off to see the fight."

"What fight?" said Mary Hawker, looking over Tom's shoulder.

"Do you mean to say you have not heard the news?"

"Not a word of any news for a fortnight."

For once in his life, Burnside was laconic, and told them all that had happened. Tom spoke not a word, but ran up to the stable and had a horse out, saddled in a minute, he was dashing into the house again for his hat and pistols when he came against Mary in the passage, leaning against the wall.

"Tom," she whispered hoarsely. "Bring that boy back to me safe, or never look me in the face again!"

He never answered her, he was thinking of some one beside the boy. He pushed past her, and the next moment she saw him gallop away with Burnside, followed by two men, and now she was left alone indeed, and helpless.

There was not a soul about the place but herself; not a soul within ten miles. She stood looking out of the door fixedly, at nothing, for a time; but then, as hour by hour went on, and the afternoon stillness fell upon the forest, and the shadows began to slant, a terror began to grow upon her which at length became unbearable, and well-nigh drove her mad.

At the first she understood that all these years of anxiety had come to a point at last, and a strange feeling of excitement, almost joy, came over her. She was one of those impetuous characters who stand suspense worse than anything, and now, although terror was in her, she felt as though relief was nigh. Then she began to think again of her son, but only for an instant. He was under Major Buckley's care, and must be safe; so that she dismissed that fear from her mind for a time, but only for a time. It came back to her again. Why did he not come to her? Why had not the Major sent him off to her at once? Could the Major have been killed? even if so, there was Doctor Mulhaus. Her terrors were absurd.

But not the less terrors, that grew in strength hour by hour, as she waited there, looking at the pleasant spring forest, and no one came. Terrors that grew at last so strong, that they took the place of certainties. Some hitch must have taken place, and her boy must be gone out with the rest.

Having got as far as this, to go further was no difficulty. He was killed, she felt sure of it, and none had courage to come and tell her of it. She suddenly determined to verify her thoughts at once, and went in doors to get her hat.

She had fully made up her mind that he must be killed at this time. The hope of his having escaped was gone. We, who know the real state of the case, should tremble for her reason, when she finds her fears so terribly true. We shall see.

She determined to start away to the Brentwoods', and end her present state of terror one way or another. Tom had taken the only horse in the stable, but her own brown pony was running in the paddock with some others; and she sallied forth, worn out, feverish, half-mad, to try to catch him.

The obstinate brute would not be caught. Then she spent a weary hour trying to drive them all into the stockyard, but in vain. Three times, she, with infinite labour, drove them up to the slip-rail, and each time the same mare and foal broke away, leading off the others. The third time, when she saw them all run whinnying down to the further end of the paddock, after half an hour or so of weary work driving them up, when she had run herself off her poor tottering legs, and saw that all her toil was in vain, then she sank down on the cold hard gravel in the yard, with her long black hair streaming loose along the ground, and prayed that she might die. Down at full length, in front of her own door, like a dead woman, moaning and crying, from time to time, " Oh, my boy, my boy."

How long she lay there she knew not. She heard a horse's feet, but only stopped her ears from the news she thought was coming. Then she heard a steady heavy footstep close to her, and some one touched her, and tried to raise her.

She sat up, shook the hair from her eyes, and looked at the man who stood beside her. At first she thought it was a phantom of her own brain, but then looking wildly at the calm, solemn features, and the kindly grey eyes which were gazing at her so inquiringly, she pronounced his name—" Frank Maberly."

" God save you, madam," he said. " What is the matter?"

" Misery, wrath, madness, despair!" she cried wildly, raising her hand. "The retribution of a lifetime fallen on my luckless head in one unhappy moment."

Frank Maberly looked at her in real pity, but a thought went through his head. " What a magnificent actress this woman would make." It merely past through his brain and was gone, and then he felt ashamed of himself for entertaining it a moment; and yet it was not altogether an unnatural one for him who knew her character so well. She was lying on the ground in an attitude which would have driven Siddons to despair; one white arm, down which her sleeve had fallen, pressed against her forehead, while the other clutched the ground; and her splendid black hair fallen down across her shoulders. Yet how could he say how much of all this wild despair was real, and how much hysterical?

" But what is the matter, Mary Hawker?" he asked. Tell me, or how can I help you?"

" Matter?" she said. " Listen. The bushrangers are come down from the mountains, spreading ruin, murder, and destruction far and wide. My husband is captain of the gang: and my son, my only son, whom I have loved better than my God, is gone with the rest to hunt them down—to seek, unknowing, his own father's life. There is mischief beyond your mending, priest!"

Beyond his mending, indeed. He saw it. " Rise up," he said, " and act. Tell me all the circumstances. Is it too late?"

She told him how it had come to pass, and then he showed her that all her terrors were but anticipations, and might be false. He got her pony for her, and, as night was falling, rode away with her along the mountain road that led to Captain Brentwood's.

The sun was down, and ere they had gone far, the moon was bright overhead. Frank, having fully persuaded himself that all her terrors were the effect of an overwrought imagination, grew cheerful, and tried to laugh her out of them. She, too, with the exercise of riding through the night-air, and the company of a handsome, agreeable, well-bred man, began to have a lurking idea that she had been making a fool of herself; when they came suddenly on a hut, dark, cheerless, deserted, standing above a black, stagnant, reed-grown waterhole.

The hut where Frank had gone to preach to the stockmen. The hut where Lee had been murdered—an ill-omened place; and as they came opposite to it, they saw two others approaching them in the moonlight—Major Buckley and Alice Brentwood.

Then Alice, pushing forward, bravely met her, and told her all—all, from beginning to end; and when she had finished, having

borne up nobly, fell to weeping as though her heart would break.
But Mary did not weep, or cry, or fall down. She only said, " Let
me see him," and went on with them, silent and steady.

They got to Garoopna late at night, none having spoken all the
way. Then they showed her into the room where poor Charles lay,
cold and stiff, and there she stayed hour after hour through the
weary night. Alice looked in once or twice, and saw her sitting on
the bed which bore the corpse of her son, with her face buried in her
hands ; and at last, summoning courage, took her by the arm and
led her gently to bed.

Then she went into the drawing-room, where, besides her father,
were Major Buckley, Doctor Mulhaus, Frank Maberly, and the
drunken doctor before spoken of, who had had the sublime pleasure
of cutting a bullet from his old adversary's arm, and was now in a
fair way to justify the *sobriquet* I have so often applied to him. I
myself also was sitting next the fire, alongside of Frank Maberly.

" My brave girl," said the Major, " how is she ?"

" I hardly can tell you, sir," said Alice : " she is so very quiet.
If she would cry now, I should be very glad. It would not frighten
me so much as seeing her like that. I fear she will die ! "

" If her reason holds," said the Doctor, " she will get over it.
She had, from all accounts, gone through every phase of passion
down to utter despair, before she knew the blow had fallen. Poor
Mary ! "

*   *   *   *   *   *

There, we have done. All this misery has come on her from one
act of folly and selfishness years ago. How many lives are ruined,
how many families broken up, by one false step ! If ever a poor
soul has expiated her own offence, she has. Let us hope that
brighter times are in store for her. Let us have done with moral
reflections ; I am no hand at that work. One more dark scene,
reader, and then.—

*   *   *   *   *   *

It was one wild dreary day in the spring ; a day of furious wind
and cutting rain ; a day when few passengers were abroad, and when
the boatmen were gathered in knots among the sheltered spots upon
the quays, waiting to hear of disasters at sea ; when the ships creaked
and groaned at the wharfs, and the harbour was a sheet of wind-
driven foam, and the domain was strewed with broken boughs. On
such a day as this, Major Buckley and myself, after a sharp walk,
found ourselves in front of the principal gaol in Sydney.

We were admitted, for we had orders ; and a small, wiry, clever-
looking man, about fifty, bowed to us as we entered the whitewashed
corridor, which led from the entrance hall. We had a few words
with him, and then followed him.

To the darkest passage in the darkest end of that dreary place; to the condemned cells. And my heart sunk as the heavy bolt shot back, and we went into the first one on the right.

Before us was a kind of bed-place. And on that bed-place lay the figure of a man. Though it is twenty years ago since I saw it, I can remember that scene as though it were yesterday.

He lay upon a heap of tumbled blankets, with his face buried in a pillow. One leg touched the ground, and round it was a ring, connecting the limb to a long iron bar, which ran along beneath the bed. One arm also hung listlessly on the cold stone, floor, and the other was thrown around his head. A head covered with short black curls, worthy of an Antinous, above a bare muscular neck, worthy of a Farnese Hercules. I advanced towards him.

The governor held me back. " My God, sir," he said, " take care. Don't, as you value your life, go within length of his chain." But at that moment the handsome head was raised from the pillow, and my eyes met George Hawker's. Oh, Lord ! such a piteous wild look. I could not see the fierce desperate villain who had kept our country-side in terror so long. No, thank God, I could only see the handsome curly-headed boy who used to play with James Stockbridge and myself among the gravestones in Drumston churchyard. I saw again the merry lad who used to bathe with us in Hatherleigh water, and whom, with all his faults, I had once loved well. And seeing him, and him only, before me, in spite of a terrified gesture from the governor, I walked up to the bed, and, sitting down beside him, put my arm round his neck.

" George ! George ! Dear old friend ! " I said. " O, George, my boy, has it come to this ? "

I don't want to be instructed in my duty. I know what my duty was on that occasion as well as any man. My duty as a citizen and a magistrate was to stand at the further end of the cell, and give this hardened criminal a moral lecture, showing how honesty and virtue, as in my case, had led to wealth and honour, and how yielding to one's passions had led to disgrace and infamy, as in his. That was my duty, I allow. But then, you see, I didn't do my duty. I had a certain tender feeling about my stomach which prevented me from doing it. So I only hung there, with my arm round his neck, and said, from time to time, " O George, George ! " like a fool.

He put his two hands upon my shoulders, so that his fetters hung across my breast, and he looked me in the face. Then he said, after a time, " What ! Hamlyn ? Old Jeff Hamlyn ! The only man I ever knew that I didn't quarrel with ! Come to see me now, eh ? Jeff, old boy, I'm to be hung to-morrow."

" I know it," I said. " And I came to ask you if I could do anything for you. For the sake of dear old Devon, George."

" Anything you like, old Jeff," he said, with a laugh, " so long as you don't get me reprieved. If I get loose again, lad, I'd do worse than I ever did yet, believe me. I've piled up a tolerable heap of wickedness as it is, though. I've murdered my own son, Jeff. Do you know that?"

I answered—" Yes; I know that, George; but that was an accident. You did not know who he was."

" He came at me to take my life," said Hawker. " And I tell you, as a man who goes out to be hung to-morrow, that, if I had guessed who he was, I'd have blown my own brains out to save him from the crime of killing me. Who is that man ?"

" Don't you remember him ?" I said. " Major Buckley."

The Major came forward, and held out his hand to George Hawker. " You are now," he said, " like a dead man to me. You die to-morrow; and you know it; and face it like a man. I come to ask you to forgive me anything you may have to forgive. I have been your enemy since I first saw you: but I have been an honest and open enemy ; and now I am your enemy no longer. I ask you to shake hands with me. I have been warned not to come within arm's length of you, chained as you are. But I am not afraid of you."

The Major came and sat on the bed-place beside him.

" As for that little animal," said George Hawker, pointing to the governor, as he stood at the further end of the cell, " if he comes within reach of me, I'll beat his useless little brains out against the wall, and he knows it. He was right to caution you not to come too near me. I nearly killed a man yesterday ; and to-morrow, when they come to lead me out——But, with regard to you, Major Buckley, the case is different. Do you know I should be rather sorry to tackle you; I'm afraid you would be too heavy for me. As to my having anything to forgive, Major, I don't know that there is anything. If there is, let me tell you that I feel more kind and hearty towards you and Hamlyn for coming to me like this to-day, than I've felt toward any man this twenty year. By-the-bye ; let no man go to the gallows without clearing himself as far as he may. Do you know that I set on that red-haired villain, Moody, to throttle Bill Lee, because I hadn't pluck to do it myself."

" Poor Lee," said the Major.

" Poor devil," said Hawker. " Why that man had gone through every sort of villany, from" (so and so up to so and so, he said ; I shall not particularise) " before my beard was grown. Why that man laid such plots and snares for me when I was a lad, that a bishop could not have escaped. He egged me on to forge my own father's name. He drove me on to ruin. And now, because it suited his purpose to turn honest, and act faithful domestic to my wife for twenty years, he is mourned for as an exemplary character, and I go to the gallows. He was a meaner villain than ever I was."

" George," I asked, " have you any message for your wife ?"

" Only this," he said ; " tell her I always liked her pretty face, and I'm sorry I brought disgrace upon her. Through all my rascalities, old Jeff, I swear to you that I respected and liked her to the last. I tried to see her last year, only to tell her that she needn't be afraid of me, and should treat me as a dead man; but she and her blessed pig-headed lover, Tom Troubridge, made such knife and pistol work of it, that I never got the chance of saying the word I wanted. She'd have saved herself much trouble if she hadn't acted so much like a frightened fool. I never meant her any harm. You may tell her all this if you judge right, but I leave it to you. Time's up, I see. I ain't so much of a coward, am I, Jeff? Good-bye, old lad, good-bye."

That was the last we saw of him; the next morning he was executed with four of his comrades. But now the Major and I, leaving him, went off again into the street, into the rain and the furious wind, to beat up against it for our hotel. Neither spoke a word till we came to a corner in George Street, nearest the wharf : and then the Major turned back upon me suddenly and I thought he had been unable to face the terrible gust which came sweeping up from the harbour : but it was not so. He had turned on purpose, and putting his hands upon my shoulders, he said,—

" Hamlyn, Hamlyn, you have taught me a lesson."

" I suppose so," I said. " I have shown you what a fool a tender-hearted soft-headed fellow may make of himself by yielding to his impulses. But I have a defence to offer, my dear sir, the best of excuses, the only real excuse existing in this world. I couldn't help it."

" I don't mean that, Hamlyn," he answered. " The lesson you have taught me is a very different one. You have taught me that there are bright points in the worst man's character, a train of good feeling which no tact can bring out, but yet which some human spark of feeling may light. Here is this man Hawker, of whom we heard that he was dangerous to approach, and whom the good Chaplain was forced to pray for and exhort from a safe distance. The man for whose death, till ten minutes ago, I was rejoicing. The man I thought lost, and beyond hope. Yet you, by one burst of unpremeditated folly, by one piece of silly sentimentality, by ignoring the man's later life, and carrying him back in imagination to his old schoolboy days, have done more than our good old friend the Chaplain could have done without your assistance. There is a spark of the Divine in the worst of men, if you can only find it."

In spite of the Major's parliamentary and didactic way of speaking, I saw there was truth at the bottom of what he said, and that he meant kindly to me, and to the poor fellow who was even now among the dead; so instead of arguing with him, I took his arm, and we fought homewards together through the driving rain.

Imagine three months to have passed. That stormy spring had changed into a placid, burning summer. The busy shearing-time was past; the noisy shearers were dispersed, heaven knows where (most of them probably suffering from a shortness of cash, complicated with delirium tremens). The grass in the plains had changed from green to dull grey; the river had changed his hoarse roar for a sleepy murmur, as though too lazy to quarrel with his boulders in such weather. A hot dull haze was over forest and mountain. The snow had perspired till it showed long black streaks on the highest eminences. In short, summer had come with a vengeance; every one felt hot, idle, and thirsty, and " there was nothing doing."

Now that broad cool verandah of Captain Brentwood's, with its deep recesses of shadow, was a place not to be lightly spoken of. Any man once getting footing there, and leaving it, except on compulsion, would show himself of weak mind. Any man once comfortably settled there in an easy chair, who fetched anything for himself when he could get any one else to fetch it for him, would show himself, in my opinion, a man of weak mind. One thing only was wanted to make it perfect, and that was niggers. To the winds with " Uncle Tom's Cabin," and " Dred " after it, in a hot wind! What can an active-minded, self-helpful lady like Mrs. Stowe, freezing up there in Connecticut, obliged to do something to keep herself warm,—what can she, I ask, know about the requirements of a southern gentleman when the thermometer stands at 125° in the shade? Pish! Does she know the exertion required for cutting up a pipe of tobacco in a hot north wind? No! Does she know the amount of perspiration and anger superinduced by knocking the head off a bottle of Bass in January? Does she know the physical prostration which is caused by breaking up two lumps of hard white sugar in a pawnee before a thunderstorm? No, she doesn't, or she would cry out for niggers with the best of us! When the thermometer gets over 100° in the shade, all men would have slaves if they were allowed. An Anglo-Saxon conscience will not, save in rare instances, bear a higher average heat than 95°.

But about this verandah. It was the model and type of all verandahs. It was made originally by the Irish family, the Donovans, before spoken of; and, like all Irish-made things, was nobly conceived, beautifully carried out, and then left to take care of itself, so that when Alice came into possession, she found it a neglected mine of rare creepers run wild. Here, for the first time, I saw the exquisite crimson passion-flower,* then a great rarity. Here, too,

---

* Passiflora Loudonia, I believe.

the native passion-flower, scarlet and orange, was tangled up with the common purple sarsaparilla and the English honeysuckle and jessamine.

In this verandah, one blazing morning, sat Mrs. Buckley and Alice making believe to work. Mrs. Buckley really was doing something. Alice sat with her hands fallen on her lap, so still and so beautiful, that she might then and there have been photographed off by some enterprising artist, and exhibited in the print shops as " Argia, Goddess of Laziness."

They were not alone, however. Across the very coolest, darkest corner was swung a hammock, looking at which you might perceive two hands elevating a green paper-covered pamphlet, as though the owner were reading—the aforesaid owner, however, being entirely invisible, only proving his existence by certain bulges and angles in the canvas of the hammock.

Now having made a nice little mystery as to who it was lying there, I will proceed to solve it. A burst of laughter came from the hidden man, so uproarious and violent, that the hammock-strings strained and shook, and the magpie, waking up from a sound sleep, cursed and swore in a manner fearful to hear.

" My dearest Jim ! " said Alice, rousing herself, " What is the matter with you ? "

Jim read aloud the immortal battle of the two editors, with the carpet bag and the fire shovel, in " Pickwick," and, ere he had half done, Alice and Mrs. Buckley had mingled their laughter with his, quite as heartily, if not so loudly.

" Hallo ! " said Jim ; " here's a nuisance ! There's no more of it. Alice, have you got any more ? "

" That is all, Jim. The other numbers will come by the next mail."

" How tiresome ! I suppose the governor is pretty sure to be home to-night. He can't be away much longer."

" Don't be impatient, my dear," said Alice. " How is your leg ? "

Please remember that Jim's leg was broken in the late wars, and, as yet, hardly well.

" Oh, it's a good deal better. Heigho ! This is very dull."

" Thank you, James ! " said Mrs. Buckley. " Dear me ! the heat gets greater every day. If they are on the road, I hope they won't hurry themselves."

Our old friends were just now disposed in the following manner :—

The Major was at home. Mary Hawker was staying with him. Doctor Mulhaus and Halbert staying at Major Buckley's, while Captain Brentwood was away with Sam and Tom Troubridge to Sydney ; and, having been absent some weeks, had been expected home now for a day or two. This was the day they came home, riding slowly up to the porch about five o'clock.

When all greetings were done, and they were sat down beside the others, Jim opened the ball by asking, "What news, father?"

"What a particularly foolish question!" said the Captain. "Why, you'll get it all in time—none the quicker for being impatient. May be, also, when you hear some of the news, you won't like it!"

"Oh, indeed!" said Jim.

"I have a letter for you here, from the Commander-in-Chief. You are appointed to the 3—th Regiment, at present quartered in India."

Alice looked at him quickly as she heard this, and, as a natural consequence, Sam looked too. They had expected that he would have hurra'd aloud, or thrown up his hat, or danced about when he heard of it. But no; he only sat bolt upright in his hammock, though his face flushed scarlet, and his eyes glistened strangely.

His father looked at him an instant, and then continued,—

"Six months' leave of absence procured at the same time, which will give you about three months more at home. So you see you now possess the inestimable privilege of wearing a red coat; and what is still better, of getting a hole made in it; for there is great trouble threatening with the Affghans and Beloochs, and the chances are that you will smell powder before you are up in your regimental duties. Under which circumstances I shall take the liberty of requesting that you inform yourself on these points under my direction, for I don't want you to join your regiment in the position of any other booby. Have the goodness to lie down again and not excite yourself. You have anticipated this some time. Surely it is not necessary for you to cry about it like a great girl."

But that night, after dark, when Sam and Alice were taking one of those agreeable nocturnal walks, which all young lovers are prone to, they came smoothly gliding over the lawn close up to the house, and then, unseen and unheard, they saw Captain Brentwood with his arm round Jim's neck, and heard him say,—

"O James! James! why did you want to leave me?"

And Jim answered, "Father, I didn't know. I didn't know my own mind. But I can't call back now."

Sam and Alice slipt back again, and continued their walk. Let us hear what conversation they had been holding together before this little interruption.

"Alice, my darling, my love, you are more beautiful than ever!"

"Thanks to your absence, my dear Sam. You see how well I thrive without you."

"Then when we are——"

"Well?" said Alice. For this was eight o'clock in the evening, you know, and the moon being four days past the full, it was pitch dark. "Well?" says she.

"When we are married," says Sam, audaciously, "I suppose you will pine away to nothing."

"Good gracious me!" she answered. "Married? Why surely we are well enough as we are."

"Most excellently well, my darling," said Sam. "I wish it could last for ever."

"Oh, indeed!" said Alice, almost inaudibly though.

"Alice, my love," said Sam, "have you thought of one thing? Have you thought that I must make a start in life for myself?"

No, she hadn't thought of that. Didn't see why Baroona wasn't good enough for him.

"My dear!" he said. "Baroona is a fine property, but it is not mine. I want money for a set purpose. For a glorious purpose, my love! I will not tell you yet, not for years perhaps, what that purpose is. But I want fifty thousand pounds of my own. And fifty thousand pounds I will have."

Good gracious! What an avaricious creature. Such a quantity of money. And so she wasn't to hear what he was going to do with it, for ever so many years. Wouldn't he tell her now? She would so like to know. Would nothing induce him?

Yes, there was something. Nay, what harm! Only an honest lover's kiss, among the ripening grapes. In the dark, you say. My dear madam, you would not have them kiss one another in broad day, with the cook watching them out of the kitchen window?

"Alice," he said, "I have had one object before me from my boyhood, and since you told me that I was to be your husband, that object has grown from a vague intention to a fixed purpose. Alice, I want to buy back the acres of my forefathers; I wish, I intend, that another Buckley shall be the master of Clere, and that you shall be his wife."

"Sam, my love!" she said, turning on him suddenly. "What a magnificent idea. Is it possible?"

"Easy," said Sam. "My father could do it, but will not. He and my mother have severed every tie with the old country, and it would be at their time of life only painful to go back to the old scenes and interests. But with me it is different. Think of you and I taking the place we are entitled to by birth and education, in the splendid society of that noble island. Don't let me hear all that balderdash about the founding of new empires. Empires take too long in growing for me. What honours, what society, has this little colony to give, compared to those open to a fourth-rate gentleman in England? I want to be a real Englishman, not half a one. I want to throw in my lot heart and hand with the greatest nation in the world. I don't want to be young Sam Buckley of Baroona. I want to be the Buckley of Clere. Is not that a noble ambition?"

"My whole soul goes with you, Sam," said Alice. "My whole heart and soul. Let us consult, and see how this is to be done."

"This is the way the thing stands," said Sam. "The house and park at Clere, were sold by my father for 12,000*l.* to a brewer. Since then, this brewer, a most excellent fellow by all accounts, has bought back, acre by acre, nearly half the old original property as it existed in my great grandfather's time, so that now Clere must be worth fifty thousand pounds at least. This man's children are all dead; and as far as Captain Brentwood has been able to find out for me, no one knows exactly how the property is going. The present owner is the same age as my father; and at his death, should an advantageous offer be made, there would be a good chance of getting the heirs to sell the property. We should have to pay very highly for it, but consider what a position we should buy with it. The county would receive us with open arms. That is all I know at present."

"A noble idea," said Alice, "and well considered. Now what are you going to do?"

"Have you heard tell yet," said Sam, "of the new country to the north, they call the Darling Downs?"

"I have heard of it from Burnside the cattle dealer. He describes it as a paradise of wealth."

"He is right. When you get through the Cypress, the plains are endless. It is undoubtedly the finest piece of country found yet. Now do you know Tom Troubridge?"

"Slightly enough," said Alice, laughing.

"Well," said Sam. "You know he went to Sydney with us, and before he had been three days there he came to me full of this Darling Down country. Quite mad about it in fact. And in the end he said: 'Sam, what money have you got?' I said that my father had promised me seven thousand pounds for a certain purpose, and that I had come to town partly to look for an investment. He said, 'Be my partner;' and I said, 'What for?' 'Darling Downs,' he said. And I said I was only too highly honoured by such a mark of confidence from such a man, and that I closed with his offer at once. To make a long matter short, he is off to the new country to take up ground under the name of Troubridge and Buckley. There!"

"But oughtn't you to have gone up with him, Sam?"

"I proposed to do so, as a matter of course," said Sam. "But what do you think he said?"

"I don't know."

"He gave me a great slap on the back," said Sam; "and, said he, 'Go home, my old lad, marry your wife, and fetch her up to keep nouse.' That's what he said. And now, my own love, my darling, will you tell me, am I to go up alone, and wait for you ; or will you come up, and make a happy home for me in that dreary desert? Will you leave your home, and come away with me into the grey hot plains of the west? "

"I have no home in future, Sam," she said, " but where you are, and I will gladly go with you to the world's end."

And so that matter was settled.

And now Sam disclosed to her that a visitor was expected at the station in about a fortnight or three weeks ; and he was no less a person than our old friend the dean, Frank Maberly. And then he went to ask, did she think that she could manage by that time to—, eh? Such an excellent opportunity, you know ; seemed almost as if his visit had been arranged ; which, between you and I, it had.

She thought it wildly possible, if there was any real necessity for it. And after this they went in ; and Alice went into her bed-room.

" And what have you been doing out there with Alice all this time, eh ? " asked the Captain.

" I've been asking a question, sir."

" You must have put it in a pretty long form. What sort of an answer did you get ? "

" I got ' yes ' for an answer, sir."

" Ah, well! Mrs. Buckley, can you lend Baroona to a new married couple for a few weeks, do you think ? There is plenty of room for you here."

And then into Mrs. Buckley's astonished ear all the new plans were poured. She heard that Sam and Alice were to be married in a fortnight, and that Sam had gone into partnership with Tom Troubridge.

" Stop there," she said ; " not too much at once. What becomes of Mary Hawker ? "

" She is left at Toonarbin, with an overseer, for the present."

" And when," she asked, " shall you leave us, Sam ? "

" Oh, in a couple of months, I suppose. I must give Tom time to get a house up before I go and join him. What a convenient thing a partner like that is, eh ? "

" Oh, by-the-bye, Mrs. Buckley," said Captain Brentwood, what do you make of this letter ? "

He produced a broad thick letter, directed in a bold running hand,

" Major Buckley,

" Baroona, Combermere County,

" Gipps-land.

" If absent, to be left with the nearest magistrate, and a receipt taken for it."

"How very strange," said Mrs. Buckley, turning it over. "Where did you get it?"

"Sergeant Jackson asked me, as nearest magistrate, to take charge of it; and so I did. It has been forwarded by orderly from Sydney."

"And the Governor's private seal, too," said Mrs. Buckley. "I don't know when my curiosity has been so painfully excited. Put it on the chimney-piece, Sam; let us gaze on the outside, even if we are denied to see the inside. I wonder if your father will come to-night?"

"No; getting too late," said Sam. "Evidently Halbert and the Doctor have found themselves there during their ride, and are keeping him and Mrs. Hawker company. They will all three be over to-morrow morning, depend on it."

"What a really good fellow that Halbert is," said Captain Brentwood. "One of the best companions I ever met. I wish his spirits would improve with his health. A sensitive fellow like him is apt not to recover from a blow like his."

"What blow?" said Mrs. Buckley.

"Did you never hear?" said the Captain. "The girl he was going to be married to, got drowned coming out to him in the Assam."

CHAPTER XLV.

IN WHICH THERE ARE SOME ASTONISHING REVELATIONS WITH REGARD TO DR. MULHAUS AND CAPTAIN DESBOROUGH.

At ten o'clock the next morning arrived the Major, the Doctor, and Halbert; and the first notice they had of it was the Doctor's voice in the passage, evidently in a great state of excitement.

"No more the common bower-bird than you, sir; a new species. His eyes are red instead of blue, and the whole plumage is lighter I will call it after you, my dear Major."

"You have got to shoot him first," said the Major.

"I'll soon do that," said the Doctor, bursting into the room-door. "How do you do, all of you? Sam, glad to see you back again. Brentwood, you are welcome to your own house. Get me your gun —where is it?"

"In my bedroom," said the Captain.

The Doctor went off after it. He reappeared again to complain that the caps would not fit; but, being satisfied on that score, he disappeared down the garden, on murderous thoughts intent.

Sam got his father away into the verandah, and told him all his plans. I need hardly say that they met with the Major's entire approval.

All his plans, I said; no, not all. Sam never hinted at the end and object of all his endeavours; he never said a word about his re-purchase of Clere. The Major had no more idea that Sam had ever thought of such a thing, or had been making inquiries, than had the owner of Clere himself.

"Sam, my dear boy," said he, "I am very sorry to lose you, and we shall have but a dull time of it henceforth; but I am sure it is good for a man to go out into the world by himself" (and all that sort of thing). "When you are gone, Brentwood and I mean to live together to console one another."

"My dear, are you coming in?" said Mrs. Buckley. "Here is a letter for you, which I ought to have given you before."

The Major went in and received the mysterious epistle which the Captain had brought the night before. When he saw it he whistled.

They sat waiting to know the contents. He was provokingly long in opening it, and when he did, he said nothing, but read it over twice, with a lengthening visage. Now also it became appa-rent that there was another letter inside, at the superscription of which the Major having looked, put it in his pocket, and turning round to the mantel-piece, with his back to the others, began drum-ming against the fender with his foot, musingly.

A more aggravating course of proceeding he could not have re-sorted to. Here they were all dying of curiosity, and not a word did he seem inclined to answer. At last, Mrs. Buckley, not able to hold out any longer, said,—

"From the Governor, was it not, my love?"

"Yes," he said, "from the Governor. And very important too," and then relapsed into silence.

Matters were worse than ever. But after a few minutes he turned round to them suddenly, and said,—

"You have heard of Baron Landstein?"

"What," said Sam, "the man that the Doctor's always abusing so? Yes, I know all about him, of course."

"The noble Landstein," said Alice. "In spite of the Doctor's abuse he is a great favourite of mine. How well he seems to have behaved at Jena with those two Landwehr regiments."

"Landsturm, my love," said the Major.

"Yes, Landsturm, I mean. I wonder if he is still alive, or whether he died of his wounds."

"The Doctor," said Sam, "always speaks of him as dead."

"He is not only alive," said the Major, "but he is coming here. He will be here to-day. He may come any minute."

"What! the great Landstein?" said Sam.

"The same man," said the Major.

"The Doctor will have a quarrel with him, father. He is always abusing him. He says he lost the battle of Jena, or something."

"Be quiet, Sam, and don't talk. Watch what follows."

The Doctor was seen hurrying up the garden-walk. He put down his gun outside, and bursting open the glass door, stepped into the room, holding aloft a black bird, freshly killed, and looking around him for applause.

"There!" he said; "I told you so."

The Major walked across the room, and put a letter in his hand, the one which was enclosed in the mysterious epistle before mentioned. "Baron," he said, "here is a letter for you."

The Doctor looked round as one would who had received a blow, and knew not who smote him. He took the letter, and went into the window to read it.

No one spoke a word. "This, then, my good old tutor," thought Sam, "turns out to be the great Landstein. Save us, what a piece of romance." But, though he thought this, he never said anything, and catching Alice's eye, followed it to the window. There, leaning against the glass, his face buried in his hands, and his broad back shaking with emotion, stood Doctor Mulhaus. Alas! no. Our kindly, good, hearty, learned, irritable, but dearly-beloved friend, is no more. There never was such a man in reality: but in his place stands Baron von Landstein of the Niederwald.

What the contents of the Doctor's (I must still call him so) letter, I cannot tell you. But I have seen the letter which Major Buckley received enclosing it, and I can give it you word for word. It is from the Governor himself, and runs thus:—

"MY DEAR MAJOR,

"I am informed that the famous Baron von Landstein has been living in your house for some years, under the name of Dr. Mulhaus. In fact, I believe he is a partner of yours. I therefore send the enclosed under cover to you, and when I tell you that it has been forwarded to me through the Foreign Office, and the Colonial Office, and is, in point of fact, an autograph letter from the King of P—— to the Baron, I am sure that you will ensure its safe delivery.

"The Secretary is completely 'fixed' with his estimates. The salaries for the Supreme Court Office are thrown out. He must resign. Do next election send us a couple of moderates.

"Yours, &c.   G. G."

This was the Major's letter. But the Doctor stood still there, moved more deeply than any had seen him before, while Alice and Sam looked at one another in blank astonishment.

At length he turned and spoke, but not to them, to the empty air. Spoke as one aroused from a trance. Things hard to understand, yet having some thread of sense in them too,

"So he has sent for me," he said, "when it seems that he may have some use for me. So the old man is likely to go at last, and we are to have the golden age again. If talking could do it, assuredly we should. He has noble instincts, this young fellow, and some sense. He has sent for me. If H——, and B——, and Von U——, and myself can but get his ear!

"Oh, Rhineland! my own beloved Rhineland, shall I see you again? Shall I sit once more in my own grey castle, among the vineyards, above the broad gleaming river, and hear the noises from the town come floating softly up the hillside! I wonder are there any left who will remember—"

He took two short turns through the room, and then he turned and spoke to them again, looking all the time at Sam.

"I am the Baron von Landstein. The very man we have so often talked of, and whose character we have so freely discussed. When the French attacked us, I threw myself into the foremost ranks of my countrymen, and followed the Queen with two regiments which I had raised almost entirely myself.

"I fled away from the blood-red sun of Jena, wounded and desperate. 'That sun,' I thought, 'has set on the ruins of Great Frederick's kingdom. Prussia is a province of France: what can happen worse than this? I will crawl home to my castle and die.'

"I had no castle to crawl to. My brother, he who hung upon the same breast with me, he who learnt his first prayer beside me, he whom I loved and trusted above all other men, had turned traitor, had sold himself to the French, had deceived my bride that was to be, and seized my castle.

"I fled to England, to Drumston, Major. I had some knowledge of physic, and called myself a doctor. I threw myself into the happy English domestic life which I found there, and soon got around me men and women whom I loved full well.

"Old John Thornton and his sister knew my secret, as did Lord Crediton; but they kept it well, and by degrees I began to hope that I would begin a new life as a useful village apothecary, and forget for ever the turmoils of politics.

"Then you know what happened. There was an Exodus. All those I had got to love, arose, in the manner of their nation, and went to the other end of the earth, so that one night I was left alone on the cliff at Plymouth, watching a ship which was bearing away all that was left me to love in the world.

"I went to Prussia. I found my brother had made good use of his prosperity, and slandered me to the King. His old treachery seemed forgotten, and he was high in power. The King, for whom I had suffered so much, received me coldly, and leaving the palace, I spoke to my brother, and said,—'Send me so much yearly, and keep the rest for a time.' And then I followed you, Major, out here.

" Shall I tell you any more, Sam ? "

" No !" said Sam, smiting his fist upon the table. " I can tell the rest, Baron, to those who want to know it. I can tell of ten years' patient kindness towards myself. I can tell—I can tell—"

Sam was the worst orator in the world. He broke down, sir. He knew what he meant very well; and so I hope do you, reader, but he couldn't say it. He had done what many of us do, tried to make a fine speech when his heart was full, and so he failed.

But Alice didn't fail,—not she, though she never spoke a word. She folded up her work ; and going up to the good old man, took both his hands in hers and kissed him on both his cheeks. A fine piece of rhetorical action, wasn't it? And then they all crowded round him, and shook hands with him, and kissed him, and God-blessed him, for their kind, true, old friend ; and prayed that every blessing might light upon his noble head, till he passed through them speechless and wandered away to his old friend, the river.

*　　*　　*　　*　　*　　*

About the middle of this week, there arrived two of our former friends,—Frank Maberly and Captain Desborough, riding side by side. The Elders, with the Doctor, were outside, and detained the Dean, talking to him and bidding him welcome. But Captain Desborough, passing in, came into the room where were assembled Alice, Sam, and Jim, who gave him a most vociferous greeting.

They saw in a moment that there was some fun in the wind. They knew, by experience, that when Desborough's eyes twinkled like that, some absurdity was preparing, though they were quite unprepared for the mixture of reality and nonsense which followed.

" Pace," said Desborough, in his affected Irish accent, " be on this house, and all in it. The top of the morning to ye all."

" Now," said Alice, " we are going to have some fun ; Captain Desborough has got his brogue on."

" Ye'll have some fun directly, Miss Brentwood," he said. " But there's some serious, sober earnest to come first. My cousin, Slieve-donad, is dead."

" Lord Slievedonad ? "

" The same. That small Viscount is at this moment in pur——. God forgive me, and him too."

" Poor fellow !"

" That's just half. My uncle Lord Covetown was taken with a fit when he heard of it, and is gone after him, and the Lord forgive him too. He turned me, his own brother's son, out into the world with half an education, to sink or swim ; and never a kind word did he or his son ever give me in their lives. It must have broken the old man's heart to think how the estate would go. But as I said before, God forgive him."

"You must feel his loss, Captain Desborough," said Alice. "I am very sorry for you."

"Ahem! my dear young lady, you don't seem to know how this ends."

"Why, no," said Alice, looking up wonderingly; "I do not."

"Why, it ends in this," said Desborough; "that I myself am Earl of Covetown, Viscount Slievedonad, and Baron Avoca, with twenty thousand a year, me darlin, the laste penny; see to there now!"

"Brogue again," said Alice. "Are you joking?"

"True enough," said Desborough. "I had a letter from my grandmother, the Dowager (she that lost the dog), only this very day. And there's a thousand pounds paid into the Bank of New South Wales to my account. Pretty good proof that last, eh?"

"My dear lord," said Alice, "I congratulate you most heartily. All the world are turning out to be noblemen. I should not be surprised to find that I am a duchess myself."

"It rests with you, Miss Brentwood," said Desborough, with a wicked glance at Sam, "to be a countess. I now formally make you an offer of me hand and heart. Oh! tell me, Miss Brentwood, will ye be Mrs. Mars—— I beg pardon, Countess of Covetown?"

"No, I thank you, my lord," said Alice, laughing and blushing. "I am afraid I must decline."

"I was afraid ye would," said Lord Covetown. "I had heard that a great six-foot villain had been trifling with your affections, so I came prepared for a refusal. Came prepared with this, Miss Brentwood, which I pray you to accept; shall I be too bold if I say, as a wedding present, from one of your most sincere admirers."

He produced a jewel case, and took from it a bracelet, at the sight of which Alice gave an honest womanly cry of delight. And well she might, for the bauble cost 150*l*. It was a bracelet of gold, representing a snake. Half-way up the reptile's back began a row of sapphires, getting larger towards the neck, each of which was surrounded by small emeralds. The back of the head contained a noble brilliant, and the eyes were two rubies. Altogether, a thorough specimen of Irish extravagance and good taste.

"Can you clasp it on for her, Sam?" said Lord Covetown.

"Oh, my lord, I ought not to accept such a princely present!" said Alice.

"Look here, Miss Brentwood," said Covetown, laying his hand on Sam's shoulder. "I find that the noblest and best fellow I know is going to marry the handsomest woman, saving your presence, that I ever saw. I myself have just come into an earldom, and twenty thousand a-year; and if, under these circumstances, I mayn't make that woman a handsome present, why then the deuce is in it, you know. Sam, my boy, your hand. Jim, your hand, my lad. May you be as good a soldier as your father."

"Ah!" said Jim. "So you're an earl, are you? What does it feel like, eh? Do you feel the blue blood of a hundred sires coursing in your veins? Do you feel the hereditary class prejudices of the Norman aristocracy cutting you off from the sympathies of the inferior classes, and raising you above the hopes and fears of the masses? How very comical it must be! So you are going to sit among the big-wigs in the House of Lords. I hope you won't forget yourself, and cry 'Faug a Ballagh,' when one of the bishops rises to speak. And whatever you do, don't sing, ' Gama crem'ah cruiskeen' in the lobby."

" My dear fellow," said he, " I am not in the House of Lords at all. Only an Irish peer. I intend to get into the Commons though, and produce a sensation by introducing the Australian ' Co'ee' into the seat of British Legislature."

How long these four would have gone on talking unutterable nonsense, no man can say. But Frank Maberly coming in, greeted them courteously, and changed the conversation.

Poor Frank! Hard and incessant work was beginning to tell on that noble frame, and the hard marked features were getting more hard and marked year by year. Yet, in spite of the deep lines that now furrowed that kindly face, those who knew it best, said that it grew more beautiful than it had ever been before. As that magnificent *physique* began to fail, the noble soul within began to show clearer through its earthly tenement. That noble soul was getting purified and ready for what happened but a few years after this in Patagonia. When we heard that that man had earned the crown of glory, and had been thought worthy to sit beside Stephen and Paul in the Kingdom; none of us wept for him, or mourned. It seemed such a fitting reward for such a pure and noble life. But even now, when I wake in the night, I see him before me as he was described in the last scene by the only survivor. Felled down upon the sand, with his arms before his eyes, crying out, as the spears struck him one after another, " Lord, forgive them, they know not what they do!"

CHAPTER XLVI.

IN WHICH SAM MEETS WITH A SERIOUS ACCIDENT, AND GETS CRIPPLED FOR LIFE.

WHAT morning is this, when Sam, waking from silver dreams to a golden reality, turns over in his bed and looks out of the open glass door; at dog Rover, propped up against the lintel, chopping at the early flies; at the flower-garden, dark and dewy; at the black wall of forest beyond, in which the magpies were beginning to pipe cheerily ; at the blessed dawn which was behind and above it, shooting long rays of primrose and crimson half-way up the zenith ; hearing the sleepy ceaseless crawling of the river over the shingle bars ; hearing the booming of the cattle-herds far over the plain ; hearing the chirrup of the grasshopper among the raspberries, the chirr of the cicada among the wattles—what happy morning is this ? Is it the Sabbath ?

Ah, no ! the Sabbath was yesterday. This is his wedding morn.

My dear brother bachelor, do you remember those old first-love sensations, or have you got too old, and too fat ? Do you remember the night when you parted from her on the bridge by the lock, the night before her father wrote to you and forbade you the house ? Have you got the rose she gave you there ? Is it in your Bible, brother ? Do you remember the months that followed—months of mad grief and wild yearning, till the yearning grew less—less wild —and the grief less desperate ; and then, worst of all, the degrading consciousness that you were, in spite of yourself, getting rid of your love, and that she was not to you as she had been ? Do you remember all this ? When you come across the rose in your Bible, do you feel that you would give all the honour and wealth of the world to feel again those happy, wretched old sensations ? Do you not say that this world has nothing to give in comparison to that ?

Not this world, I believe. You and I can never feel that again. So let us make up our minds to it—it is dead. In God's name don't let us try to galvanize an old corpse, which may rise upon us hideous, and scare us to the lower pit. Let us be content as we are. Let us read that Book we spoke of just now with the rose in it, and imitate the Perfect Man there spoken of, who was crucified 1800 years ago, believing, like Him, that all men are our brothers, and acting up to it. And then, Lord knows what may be in store for us.

Here's a digression. If I had had a good wife to keep me in order, I never should have gone so far out of the road. Here is Sam in bed, sitting up, with his happy head upon his hands, trying to believe that this dream of love is going to be realized—trying to believe that it is really his wedding morn.

It evidently is ; so he gets out of bed and says his prayers like an honest gentleman—he very often forgot to do this same, but he did it this morning carefully—much I am afraid as a kind of charm or incantation, till he came to the Lord's Prayer itself, and then his whole happy soul wedded itself to the eternal words, and he arose calm and happy, and went down to bathe.

Happy, I said. Was he really happy ? He ought to have been ; for every wish he had in this life was fulfilled. And yet, when Jim, and he, and Halbert, were walking, towel in hand, down the garden, they held this conversation :—

" Sam, my dear old brother, at last," said Jim, " are you happy ? "

" I ought to be, Jim," said Sam ; " but I'm in the most con-founded fright, sir."—They generally are in a fright, when they are going to be married,—those Benedicts. What the deuce are they afraid of ?

Our dear Jim was in anything but an enviable frame of mind. He had found out several things which did not at all conduce to his happiness ; he had found out that it was one thing to propose going to India, or No-man's-land, and cutting off every tie and association which he had in the world ; and that it was quite another thing to do that same. He had found out that it was one thing to leave his sister in the keeping of his friend Sam, and another to part from her probably for ever ; and, last of all, he had found out, ever since his father had put his arm round his neck and kissed him that night we know of, that he loved that father beyond all men in this world. It was a new discovery ; he had never known it till he found he had got to part with him. And now, when he woke in the night, our old merry-hearted Jim sat up in bed, and wept ; aye, and no shame to him for it, when he thought of that handsome, calm, bronzed face, tearless and quiet there, over the fortifications and the mathematics, when he was far away.

" He will never say a word, Sam," said Jim, as they were walking down to bathe this very morning of the wedding ; " but he'll think the more. Sam, I am afraid I have done a selfish thing in going ; but if I were to draw back now, I should never be the same to him again. He couldn't stand that. But I am sorry I ever thought of it."

" I don't know, Jim," said Halbert, pulling off his trowsers, " I really don't know of any act of parliament passed in favour of the Brentwood family, exempting them from the ordinary evils of humanity. Do you think now, that when John Nokes, aged nine-teen, goes into market at Cambridge, or elsewhere, and 'lists, and never goes home again ; do you think, I say, that that lad don't feel a very strange emptiness about the epigastric region when he thinks of the grey-headed old man that is sitting waiting for him at the cottage-door ? And," added Halbert, standing on the plungning-stage Adamically, without a rag upon him, pointing at Jim with his finger in an oratorical manner ; " do you think that the old man who sits there, year after year, waiting for him who never comes, and telling the neighbours that his lad who is gone for a sodger, was the finest lad in the village, do you think that old man feels nothing ? Give up fine feelings, Jim. You don't know what trouble is yet."

And so he went souse into the water.

And after the bathe all came up and dressed ;—white trowsers and brilliant ties being the order of the day. Then we all, from the bachelor side of the house, assembled in the verandah, for the ceremony was not to be performed till eight, and it was not more than half-past seven. There was the promise of a very awkward half hour, so I was glad of a diversion caused by my appearing in a blue coat with gilt buttons, and pockets in the tails,—a coat I had not brought out for twenty years, but as good as new, I give you my honour. Jim was very funny about that coat, and I encouraged him by defending it, and so we got through ten minutes, and kept Sam amused. Then one of the grooms, a lad I mentioned before as bringing a note to Baroona on one occasion, a long brown-faced lad, born of London parents in the colony, made a diversion by coming round to look at us. He admired us very much, but my gilt buttons took his attention principally. He guessed they must have cost a matter of twenty pound, but on my telling him that the whole affair was bought for three pounds, he asked, I remember :—

" What are they made on, then ? "

Brass I supposed, and gilt. So he left me in disgust, and took up with Jim's trowsers, wanting to know " if they was canvas."

" Satin velvet," Jim said ; and then the Major came out and beckoned us into the drawing-room.

And there she was, between Mrs. Buckley and Mary Hawker, dressed all in white, looking as beautiful as morning. Frank Maberly stood beside a little table, which the women had made into an altar, with the big Prayer-book in his hand. And we all stood around, and the servants thronged in, and Sam, taking Alice's hand, went up and stood before Frank Maberly.

Captain Brentwood, of the Artillery, would give this woman to be married to this man, with ten thousand blessings on her head ; and Samuel Buckley, of Baroona, would take this woman as his wedded wife, in sickness and health, for richer, for poorer, till death did them part. And, " Yes, by George, he will," says Jim to himself,—but I heard him, for we were reading out of the same Prayer-book.

And so it was all over. And the Doctor, who had all the morning been invisible, and had only slipt into the room just as the ceremony had begun, wearing on his coat a great star, a prodigy, which had drawn many eyes from their Prayer-books, the Doctor, I say, came up, star and all, and taking Alice's hand, kissed her forehead, and then clasped a splendid necklace round her throat.

Then followed all the usual kissings and congratulations, and then came the breakfast. I hope Alice and Sam were happy, as happy as young folks can be in such a state of flutter and excitement ; but all I know is, that the rest of the party were thoroughly and utterly miserable. The certainty that this was the break-up of our happy old society, that all that was young, and merry, and graceful, among us, was about to take wing and leave us old folks sitting there lonely and dull. The thought, that neither Baroona nor Garoopna could ever be again what they had once been, and that never again we should hear those merry voices, wakening us in the morning, or ringing pleasant by the river on the soft summer's evening; these thoughts, I say, made us but a dull party, although Covetown and the Doctor made talking enough for the rest of us.

There was something I could not understand about the Doctor. He talked loud and nervously all breakfast time, and afterwards, when Alice retired to change her dress, and we were all standing about talking, he came up to me in a quiet corner where I was, and took me by the hand. " My dear old frien¹," he said, " you will never forget me, will you ? "

" Forget you, Baron! never," I said. I ¹.ould have asked him more, but there was Alice in the room, in her pretty blue riding-habit and hat, ready for a start, and Sam beside her, whip in hand; so we all crowded out to say good-bye.

That was the worst time of all. Mrs. Buckley had said farewell and departed. Jim was walking about, tearless, but quite unable to answer me when I asked him a question. Those two grim old warriors, the Captain and the Major, were taking things very quietly, but did not seem inclined to talk much, while the Doctor was conducting himself like an amiable lunatic, getting in everybody's way as he followed Sam about.

" Sam," he said, " after Alice had been lifted on her horse, " my dear Sam, my good pupil, you will never forget your old tutor, will you ? "

" Never, never ! " said Sam; " not likely, if I lived to be a hundred. I shall see you to-morrow."

" Oh yes, surely," said the Baron; " we shall meet to-morrow for certain. But good-bye, my boy; good-bye."

And then the young couple rode away to Baroona, which was empty, swept, and garnished, ready for their reception. And the servants cheered them as they went away, and tall Eleanor sent one of her husband's boots after them for luck, with such force and dexterity that it fell close to the heels of Widderin, setting him capering;—then Sam turned round and waved his hat, and they were gone.

And we turned round to look at one another, and lo ! another horse, the Doctor's, was being led up and down by a groom, saddled; and, while we wondered, out came the Doctor himself and began strapping his valise on to the saddle.

" And where are you going to-day, Baron ? " asked the Major.

" I am going," said he, " to Sydney. I sail for Europe in a week."

Our astonishment was too great for ejaculations; we kept an awful silence; this was the first hint he had given us of his intention.

" Yes," said he, " I sail from Sydney this day week. I could not embitter my boy's wedding-day by letting him know that he was to lose me ; better that he should come back and find me gone. I must go, and I foresaw it when the letter came ; but I would not tell you, because I knew you would be so sorry to part. I have been inside and said farewell to Mrs. Buckley. And now, my friends, shorten this scene for me. Night and day, for a month, I have been dreading it, and now let us spare one another. Why should we tear our hearts asunder by a long leave-taking? Oh, Buckley, Buckley ! after so many years—"

Only a hurried shaking of hands, and he was gone. Down by the paddock to the river, and when he reached the height beyond, he turned and waved his hand. Then he went on his way across the old plains, and we saw him lessening in the distance until he disappeared altogether, and we saw him no more. No more !

In two months from that time Jim and Halbert were gone to India, Sam and Alice were away to the Darling Downs, Desborough and the Doctor had sailed for Europe, and we old folks, taking up our residence at Baroona, had agreed to make common house of it. Of course we were very dull at first, when we missed half of the faces which had been used to smile upon us ; but this soon wore off. During the succeeding winter I remember many pleasant evenings, when the Captain, the Major, Mrs. Buckley, and myself played whist, shilling points and the rigour of the game, and while Mary Hawker, in her widow's weeds, sat sewing by the fireside, contentedly enough.

CHAPTER XLVII.

HOW MARY HAWKER SAID " YES."

IT was one evening during the next spring, and the game of whist was over for the night. The servant had just brought in tumblers with a view to whiskey and water before bed. I was preparing to pay fourteen shillings to Mrs. Buckley, and was rather nervous about meeting my partner, the Major's eye, when he, tapping the table with his hand, spoke :—

" The most childish play, Hamlyn ; the most childish play."

" I don't defend the last game," I said. " I thought you were short of diamonds—at least I calculated on the chance of your being so, having seven myself. But please to remember, Major, that you yourself lost two tricks in hearts, in the first game of the second rubber."

" And why, sir ?" said the Major. " Tell me that, sir. Because you confused me by leading queen, when you had ace, king, queen. The most utterly schoolboy play. I wouldn't have done such a thing at Eton."

" I had a flush of them," I said eagerly. " And I meant to lead ace, and then get trumps out. But I put down queen by mistake."

" You can make what excuses you like, Hamlyn," said the Major. " But the fact remains the same. There is one great fault in your character, the greatest fault I know of, and which you ought to study to correct. I tell you of it boldly as an old friend. You are too confoundedly chary in leading out your trumps, and you can't deny it "

" Hallo !" said Captain Brentwood, " who comes so late ? "

Mary Hawker rose from her chair, and looked eagerly towards the door. " I know who it is," she said, blushing. " I heard him laugh."

In another moment the door was thrown open, and in stalked Tom Troubridge.

" By George !" he said. " Don't all speak to me at once. I feel the queerest wambling in my innards, as we used to say in Devon, at the sight of so many old faces. Somehow, a man can't make a new home in a hurry. It's the people make the home, not the house and furniture. My dear old cousin, and how are you ? "

" I am very quiet, Tom. I am much happier than I thought to have been. And I am deeply thankful to see you again."

" How is my boy, Tom ? " said the Major.

" And how is my girl, Tom ? " said the Captain.

" Sam," said Tom, " is a sight worth a guinea, and Mrs. Samuel looks charming, but— In point of fact, you know, I believe she expects— "

" No ! " said the Captain. " You don't say so."

" Fact, my dear sir."

" Dear me," said the Major, drumming on the table. " I hope it will be a b—. By the bye, how go the sheep ? "

" You never saw such a country, sir !" said Tom. " We have got nearly five thousand on each run, and there is no one crowding up yet. If we can hold that ground with our produce, and such store-sheep as we can pick up, we shall do wonders."

By this time Tom was at supper, and between the business of satisfying a hunger of fifteen hours, began asking after old friends.

" How are the Mayfords ? " he asked.

" Poor Mrs. Mayford is better," said Mrs. Buckley. " She and Ellen are just starting for Europe. They have sold their station, and we have bought it."

" What are they going to do in England ? " asked Tom.

" Going to live with their relations in Hampshire."

" Ellen will be a fine match for some young English squire," said Tom. " She will have twenty thousand pounds some day, I suppose."

And then we went on talking about other matters.

A little scene took place in the garden next morning, which may astonish some of my readers, but which did not surprise me in the least. I knew it would happen, sooner or later, and when I saw Tom's air, on his arrival the night before, I said to myself, "It is coming," and so sure enough it did. And I got all the circumstances out of Tom only a few days afterwards.

Mary Hawker was now a very handsome woman, about one and forty. There may have been a grey hair here and there among her long black tresses, but they were few and far between. I used to watch her sometimes of an evening, and wonder to myself how she had come through such troubles, and lived; and yet there she was on the night when Tom arrived, for instance, sitting quite calm and cheerful beside the fire in her half-mourning (she had soon dropped her weeds, perhaps, considering who her husband had been, a piece of good taste), with quite a placid, contented look on her fine black eyes. I think no one was capable of feeling deeper for a time, but her power of resilience was marvellous. I have noticed that before. It may, God forgive me, have given me some slight feeling of contempt for her, because, forsooth, she did not brood over and nurse an old grief as I did myself. I am not the man to judge her. When I look back on my own wasted life; when I see how for one boyish fancy I cut myself off from all the ties of domestic life, to hold my selfish way alone, I sometimes think that she has shown herself a better woman than I have a man. Ah! well, old sweetheart, not much to boast of either of us. Let us get on.

She was walking in the garden next morning, and Tom came and walked beside her; and after a little he said,—

"So you are pretty well contented, cousin?"

"I am as well content," she said, "as a poor, desolate, old childless widow could hope to be. There is no happiness left for me in this life!"

"Who told you that?" said Tom. "Who told you that the next twenty years of your life might not be happier than any that have gone before?"

"How could that be?" she asked. "What is left for me now, but to go quietly to my grave?"

"Grave!" said Tom. "Who talks of graves for twenty years to come! Mary, my darling, I have waited for you so long and faithfully, you will not disappoint me at last?"

"What do you mean? What can you mean?"

"Mean!" said he; "why, I mean this, cousin: I mean you to be my wife—to come and live with me as my honoured wife, for the next thirty years, please God!"

"You are mad!" she said. "Do you know what you say? Do you know who you are speaking to?"

"To my old sweetheart, Polly Thornton!" he said, with a laugh, —"to no one else in the world."

" You are wrong," she said ; " you may try to forget now, but you will remember afterwards. I am not Mary Thornton. I am an old broken woman, whose husband was transported for coining, and hung for murder, and worse ! "

" Peace be with him ! " said Tom. " I am not asking who your husband was ; I have had twenty years to think about that, and at the end of twenty years, I say, my dear old sweetheart, you are free at last : will you marry me ? "

" Impossible ! " said Mary. " All the country-side knows who I am. Think of the eternal disgrace that clings to me. Oh, never, never ! "

" Then you have no objection to me ? eh, cousin ? "

" To you, my kind, noble old partner ? Ah, I love and honour you above all men ! "

" Then," said Tom, putting his arm round her waist, " to the devil with all the nonsense you have just been talking, about eternal disgraces and so forth ! I am an honest man and you're an honest woman, and, therefore, what cause or impediment can there be ? Come, Mary, it's no use resisting ; my mind is made up, and you *must ! " *

" Oh, think ! " she said ; " oh, think only once, before it is too late for ever ! "

" I have thought," said Tom, " as I told you before, for twenty years ; and I ain't likely to alter my opinion in ten minutes. Come, Mary. Say, yes ! "

And so she said yes.

" Mrs. Buckley," said Tom, as they came up arm in arm to the house, " it will be a good thing if somebody was to go up to our place, and nurse Mrs. Sam in her confinement."

" I shall go up myself," said Mrs. Buckley, " though how I am to get there I hardly know. It must be nearly eight hundred miles, I am afraid."

" I don't think you need, my dear madam," said he. " My wife will make an excellent nurse ! "

" Your wife ! "

Tom looked at Mary, who blushed, and Mrs. Buckley came up and kissed her.

" I am so glad, so very glad, my love ! " she said. " The very happiest and wisest thing that could be ! I have been hoping for it, my love, and I felt sure it would be so, sooner or later. How glad your dear aunt would be if she were alive ! "

And, in short, he took her off with him, and they were married, and went up to join Sam and his wife in New England—reducing our party to four. Not very long after they were gone, we heard that there was a new Sam Buckley born, who promised, said the wise woman, to be as big a man as his father. Then, at an interval of very little more than two years, Mrs. Buckley got a long letter from Alice, announcing the birth of a little girl to the Troubridges. This letter is still extant, and in my possession, having been lent me, among other family papers, by Agnes Buckley, as soon as she heard that I was bent upon correcting these memoirs to fit them for the press. I will give you some extracts from it :—

. . . "Dear Mary Troubridge has got a little girl, a sweet, quiet, brighteyed little thing, taking, I imagine, after old Miss Thornton. They are going to call it Agnes Alice, after you and I, my dearest mother.

"You cannot imagine how different Mary is grown from what she used to be! Stout, merry, and matronly, quite! She keeps the house alive, and I think I never saw a couple more sincerely attached than are she and her husband. He is a most excellent companion for my Sam. Not to make matters too long, we are just about as happy as four people can be. Some day we may all come to live together again, and then our delight will be perfect.

"I got Jim's letter which you sent me. . . . Sam and his partner are embarking every sixpence they can spare in buying town and suburban lots at Melbourne. I know every street and alley in that wonderful city (containing near a hundred houses) on the map, but I am not very likely to go there ever. Let us hope that Sam's speculations will turn out profitable.

"Best love to Mr. Hamlyn." . . .

I must make a note to this letter. Alice refers to a letter received from Jim, which, as near as I can make the dates agree, must be the one I hold in my hand at this moment. I am not sure, but I think so. This one runs—

"Dear Dad, . . . I have been down among the dead men, and since then up into the seventh heaven, in consequence of being not only gazetted, but promoted. The beggars very nearly did for us. All our fortifications, the prettiest things ever done under the circumstances, executed under Bobby's own eye, were thrown down by— what do you think?—an earthquake! Perhaps we didn't swear— Lord forgive us! Akbar had a shy at us immediately, but got a most immortal licking!

"Is not this a most wonderful thing about Halbert? The girl that he was to be married to was supposed to be lost, coming out in the Assam. And now it appears that she wasn't lost at all (the girl I mean, not the ship), but that she was wrecked on the east coast of Madagascar, and saved, with five and twenty more. She came on to Calcutta, and they were married the week after he got his troop. She is uncommonly handsome and ladylike, but looks rather brown and lean from living on birds' nests and sea-weed for above six months of her life."

[Allow me to remark that this must be romance on Jim's part; birds' nests and trepang are not found in Madagascar.]

" My wound is nearly all right again. It was only a prick with a spear in my thigh—"

It is the very deuce editing these old letters without anything to guide me. As far as I can make out by myself (Jim being now down at Melton, hunting, and not having answered my letter of inquiries), this letter must have come accompanied by an Indian newspaper containing the account of some battle or campaign in which he was engaged. Putting this and that together, I am inclined to believe that it refers to the defence of Jellalabad by Sir Robert Sale, in which I know he was engaged. I form this opinion from the fact of his mentioning that the fortifications were destroyed by an earthquake. And I very much fear that the individual so disrespectfully mentioned above as " Bobby," was no other than the great Hero himself. In my second (or if that goes off too quick, in my third) edition, I will endeavour to clear this point up in a satisfactory manner.

After this time there was a long dull time with no news from him or from any one. Then Sam came down from New England, and paid us a visit, which freshened us up a little. But in spite of this and other episodes, there was little change or excitement for us four. We made common house of it, and never parted from one another more than a day. Always of an evening came the old friendly rubber, I playing with the Major, and Captain Brentwood with Mrs. Buckley. The most remarkable event I have to chronicle during the long period which followed, is, that one day a bushfire came right up to the garden rails, and was beaten out with difficulty; and that same evening I held nine trumps, Ace, Queen, Knave, Nine of hearts, and the rest small. I cannot for the life of me remember what year it was in, somewhere between forty-two and forty-five, I believe, because within a year or two of that time we heard that a large comet had appeared in England, and that Sir Robert Peel was distrusted on the subject of Protection. After all, it is no great consequence, though it is rather provoking, because I never before or since held more than eight trumps. Burnside, the cattle-dealer, claims to have had eleven, but I may state, once for all, that I doubt that man's statements on this and every other subject on which he speaks.—He knows where I am to be found.

My man Dick, too, somehow or another constituted himself my groom and valet. And the Major was well contented with the arrangement. So we four, Major and Mrs. Buckley, Captain Brentwood and I, sat there in the old station night after night, playing our whist, till even my head, the youngest of the four, began to be streaked with grey, and sixteen years were past.

CHAPTER XLVIII.

THE LATEST INTELLIGENCE.

IT is March, 1856. The short autumn day is rapidly giving place to night; and darkness, and the horror of a great tempest, is settling down upon the desolate grey sea, which heaves and seethes for ever around Cape Horn.

A great clipper ship, the noblest and swiftest of her class, is hurling along her vast length before the terrible west wind. Hour by hour through the short and gloomy day, sail after sail has gone fluttering in; till now, at night-fall, she reels and rolls before the storm under a single, close reefed, maintopsail.

There is a humming, and a roaring, and a rushing of great waters, so that they who are clinging to the bulwarks, and watching, awe-struck, this great work of the Lord's, cannot hear one another though they shout. Now there is a grey mountain which chases the ship, overtakes her, pours cataracts of water over her rounded stern, and goes hissing and booming past her. And now a roll more frantic than usual, nigh dips her mainyard, and sends the water spouting wildly over her bulwarks.

(" Oh, you very miserable ass," said Captain Brentwood; " to sit down and try to describe the indescribable. Do you think that because you can see all the scene before you now, because your flesh creeps, and your blood moves, as you call it to mind, do you think, I say, that you can describe it? Do you think that you can give a man, in black and white, with ink, and on paper, any real notion of that most tremendous spectacle, a sharp bowed ship running before a gale of wind through the ice in the great South Sea, where every wave rolls round the world? Go to—read Tom Cringle, who has given up his whole soul to descriptions, and see how many pictures dwell in your mind's eye, after reading his books. Two, or at most three, and they, probably, quite different from what he intended you to see, lovely as they are;—leave describing things, man, and give us some more facts."

Said Major Buckley, " Go on, Hamlyn, and do the best you can. Don't mind him." And so I go on accordingly.)

61° 30″ South. The Horn, storm-beaten, desolate, four hundred miles to the North, and barely forty miles to the South, that cruel, gleaming, ice barrier, which we saw to-day when the weather lifted at noon, and which we know is there yet, though we dare not think about it. There comes to us, though, in spite of ourselves, a vision of what may happen at any hour. A wild cry from the foretop. A mass, grey, indistinct, horrible, rising from the wild waters, scarce a hundred yards from her bowsprit. A mad hurrying to and fro. A crash. A great ruin of masts and spars, and then utter, hopeless destruction. That is the way the poor old Madagascar must have gone. The Lord send us safe through the ice.

Stunned, drenched to the skin, half-frightened, but wildly excited and determined to see out, what a landsman has but seldom a chance of seeing, a great gale of wind at sea, I clung tight to the starboard bulwarks of Mr. Richard Green's new clipper, Sultan, Captain Sneezer, about an hour after dark, as she was rounding the Horn, watching much such a scene as I have attempted to give you a notion of above. And as I held on there, wishing that the directors of my insurance office could see me at that moment, the first mate, coming from forward, warping himself from one belayingpin to another, roared in my ear, " that he thought it was going to blow."

" Man! man!" I said, " do you mean to tell me it is not blowing now?"

" A bit of a breeze," he roared; but his roar came to me like a whisper. However, I pretty soon found out that this was something quite out of the common; for, crawling up, along the gangway which runs between the poophouse and the bulwarks, I came with great difficulty to the stern; and there I saw the two best men in the larboard watch (let us immortalize them, they were Deaf Bob, and Harry the digger), lashed to the wheel, and the Skipper himself, steadfast and anxious, alongside of them, lashed to a cleat on the afterpart of the deck-house. So thinks I, if these men are made fast, this is no place for me to be loose in, and crawled down to my old place in the waist, at the after end of the spare topsail-yard, which was made fast to the starboard bulwarks, and which extended a little abaft of the main shrouds.

If any gentleman can detect a nautical error in that last sentence, I shall feel obliged by his mentioning it.

Somebody who came forth from the confusion, and was gone again, informed me that " He * was going to lay her to, and that I'd better hold on." I comforted myself with the reflection that I was doing exactly the right thing, holding on like grim death.

Then something happened, and I am sorry to say I don't exactly know what. I find in my notes, taken shortly afterwards, from the dictation of an intelligent midshipman, " that the fore-royal yard got jammed with the spanker-boom, and carried away the larboard quarterboat." Nautical friends have since pointed out to me that this involves an impossibility. I daresay it does. I know it involved an impossibility of turning in without subjecting yourself to a hydropathic remedy of violent nature, by going to bed in wet blankets, and of getting anything for breakfast besides wet biscuit and cold tea. Let it go; something went wrong, and the consequences were these.

* " He," on board ship, always means " the skipper."

A wall of water, looming high above her mainyard, came rushing and booming along, dark, terrible, opaque. For a moment I saw it curling overhead, and would have cried out, I believe, had there been time ; but a midshipman, a mere child, slipped up before me, and caught hold of my legs, while I tried to catch his collar. Then I heard the skipper roar out, in that hoarse throaty voice that seamen use when excited, " Hold on, the sea's aboard," and then a stunning, blinding rush of water buried us altogether. The Sultan was on her beam-ends, and what was more, seemed inclined to stay there, so that I, holding on by the bulwarks, saw the sea seething and boiling almost beneath my feet, which were swinging clear off the deck.

But the midshipman sung out that she was righting again, which she did rather quicker than was desirable, bringing every loose article on deck down to our side again with a rush. A useless, thundering, four-pounder gun, of which terrible implements of war we carried six, came plunging across from the other side of the deck, and went crashing through the bulwarks, out into the sea, within two feet of my legs.

" I think," I said, trying to persuade myself that I was not frightened, " I think I shall go into the cuddy."

That was not very easy to do. I reached the door, and got hold of the handle, and, watching my opportunity, slipped dexterously in, and making a plunge, came against the surgeon, who, seated on a camp-stool, was playing piquette, and overthrew him into a corner.

" Repique, by jingo," shouted Sam Buckley, who was the surgeon's opponent. " See what a capital thing it is to have an old friend like Hamlyn, to come in and knock your opponent down just at the right moment."

" And papa was losing, too, Uncle Jeff," added a handsome lad, about fifteen, who was leaning over Sam's shoulder.

" What are they doing to you, Doctor ? " said Alice Buckley, *née* Brentwood, coming out of a cabin, and supporting herself to a seat by her husband and son.

" Why," replied the surgeon, " Hamlyn knocked me down just in a moment of victory, but his nefarious project has failed, for I have kept possession of my cards. Play, Buckley."

Let us give a glance at the group which is assembled beneath the swing lamp in the reeling cabin. The wife and son are both leaning over the father's shoulder, and the three faces are together. Sam is about forty. There is not a wrinkle in that honest forehead, and the eyes beam upon you as kindly and pleasantly as ever they did ; and when, after playing to the surgeon, he looks up and laughs, one sees that he is just the same old Sam that used to lie, as a lad, dreaming in the verandah at Garoopna. No trouble has left its shadow there. Alice. whose face is pressed against his, is now a calm young matron of three or four-and-thirty, if it were possible, more beautiful than ever, only she has grown from a Hebe into a Juno. The boy, the son and heir, is much such a stripling as I can remember his father at the same age, but handsomer. And while we look, another face comes peering over his shoulder; the laughing face of a lovely girl, with bright sunny hair, and soft blue eyes; the face of Maud Buckley, Sam's daughter.

They are going home to England. Sam—what between his New England runs, where there are now, under Tom Troubridge's care, 118,000 sheep, and his land speculations at Melbourne, which have turned him out somewhere about 1,000 per cent. since the gold discovery—Sam, I say, is one of the richest of her Majesty's subjects in the Southern hemisphere. I would give 200,000*l.* for Sam, and make a large fortune in the surplus. "And so," I suppose you say, "he is going home to buy Clere." Not at all, my dear sir. Clere is bought, and Sam is going home to take possession. "Marry, how?" Thus,—

Does any one of my readers remember that our dear old friend Agnes Buckley's maiden name was Talbot, and that her father owned the property adjoining Clere? "We do not remember," you say; "or at least, if we do, we are not bound to; you have not mentioned the circumstance since the very beginning of this excessively wearisome book, forty years ago." Allow me to say, that I have purposely avoided mentioning them all along, in order that, at this very point, I might come down on you like a thunderbolt with this piece of information; namely:—That Talbot of Beaulieu Castle, the towers of which were visible from Clere Terrace, had died without male issue. That Marian and Gertrude Talbot, the two pretty girls, Agnes Buckley's eldest sisters, who used to come in and see old Marmaduke when James was campaigning, had never married. That Marian was dead. That Gertrude, a broken old maid, was sole owner of Beaulieu Castle, with eight thousand a-year; and that Agnes Buckley, her sister, and consequently, Sam as next in succession, was her heir.*

All the negotiations for the purchase of Clere had been carried on through Miss Gertrude and her steward. The brewer died, the property was sold, and Sam, by his agents, bought old Clere back, eight months before this, for 48,000*l.*

"Then, why on earth," says Mrs. Councillor Wattlegum (our colonial Mrs. Grundy), "didn't they go home overland? How

---

* If you will examine the most successful of our modern novels, you will find that the great object of the author is to keep the reader in a continual state of astonishment. Following this rule, I give myself great credit for this *coup de théâtre.* I am certain that the most experienced novel reader could not have foreseen it. I may safely say that none of my readers will be half so much astonished as I was myself.

could people with such wealth as you describe, demean themselves by going home round the Horn, like a parcel of diggers?"

"Because, my dear Madam, the young folks were very anxious to see an iceberg. Come, let us get on."

The gale has lasted three days, and in that time we have run before it on our course 970 miles. The fourth morning breaks gloriously bright, with the shadows of a few fleecy clouds flying across the bright blue heaving sea. The ship, with all canvas crowded on her, alow and aloft, is racing on, fifteen knots an hour, with a brisk cold wind full on her quarter, heeling over till the water comes rushing and spouting through her leeward ports, and no man can stand without holding on, but all are merry and happy to see the water fly past like blue champagne, and to watch the seething wake that the good ship leaves behind her. Ah! what is this, that all are crowding down to leeward to look at? Is this the Crystal Palace, of which we have read, come out to sea to meet us? No! the young folks are going to be gratified. It is a great iceberg, and we shall pass about a mile to windward.

Certainly worth seeing. Much more tremendous than I had expected, though my imagination had rather run riot in expectation. Just a great floating cluster of shining splintered crystals, about a mile long and 300 feet high, with the cold hungry sea leaping and gnawing at its base,—that is all. Send up those German musicians here, and let us hear the echo of one of Strauss' Waltzes come ringing back from the chill green caverns. Then away; her head is northward again now, we may sight the Falklands the day after to-morrow.

Hardly worth telling you much more about that happy voyage, I think, and really I remember but few things more of note. A great American ship in 45°, steaming in the teeth of the wind, heaving her long gleaming sides through the roll of the South Atlantic. The Royal Charter* passing us like a phantom ship through the hot haze, when we were becalmed on the line, waking the silence of the heaving glassy sea with her throbbing propeller. A valiant vain-glorious little gun-boat going out all the way to China by herself, giving herself the airs of a seventy-four, requiring boats to be sent on board her, as if we couldn't have stowed her, guns and all, on our poop, and never crowded ourselves! A noble transport, with 53 painted on her bows, swarming with soldiers for India, to whom we gave three times three. All these things have faded from my recollection in favour of a bright spring morning in April.

A morning which, beyond all others in my life, stands out clear and distinct, as the most memorable. Jim Buckley shoved aside my

* Alas! alas! how little did I think that in my second edition, I should have to remind my readers that this, the most beautiful of ships, had perished on the coast of Anglesey, with her 500 souls!

cabin door when I was dressing, and says he,—" Uncle Jeff, my Dad wants you immediately; he is standing by the davits of the larboard quarterboat."

And so I ran up to Sam, and he took my arm and pointed northward. Over the gleaming morning sea rose a purple mountain, shadowed here and there by travelling clouds; and a little red-sailed boat was diving and plunging towards us, with a red flag fluttering on her mast.

" What!" I said,—but I could say no more.

" The Lizard!"

But I could not see it now for a blinding haze, and I bent down my head upon the bulwarks — Bah! I am but a fool after all. What could there have been to cry at in a Cornish moor, and a Falmouth pilot boat? I am not quite so young as I was, and my nerves are probably failing. That must have been it. " When I saw the steeple," says M. Tapley, " I thought it would have choked me." Let me say the same of Eddystone Lighthouse, which we saw that afternoon; and have done with sentiment for good. If my memory serves me rightly, we have had a good deal of that sort of thing in the preceding pages.

I left the ship at Plymouth, and Sam went on in her to London. I satisfied my soul with amazement at the men of war, and the breakwater; and, having bought a horse, I struck boldly across the moor for Drumston, revisiting on my way many a well-known snipe-ground, and old trout-haunt; and so, on the third morning, I reached Drumston once more, and stabled my horse at a little public-house near the church.

It was about eight o'clock on a Tuesday morning; nevertheless, the church-bell was going, and the door was open as if for prayer. I was a little surprised at this, but having visited the grave where my father and mother lay, and then passed on to the simple headstone which marked the resting place of John Thornton and his wife, I brushed through the docks and nettles, towards the lychgate, in the shadow of which stood the clergyman, a gentlemanly looking young man, talking to a very aged woman in a red cloak.

He saluted me courteously, and passed on, talking earnestly and kindyl to his aged companion, and so the remarkable couple went into the church, and the bell stopped.

I looked around. Close to me, leaning against the gate, was a coarse looking woman about fifty, who had just set down a red earthen pitcher to rest herself, and seemed not disinclined for a gossip. And at the same moment I saw a fat man, about my own age, with breeches unbuttoned at the knee, grey worsted stockings and slippers, and looking altogether as if he was just out of bed, having had too much to drink the night before; such a man, I say, I saw coming across the road, towards us, with his hands in his pockets.

"Good morning," I said to the woman. "Pray what is the clergyman's name?"

"Mr. Montague," she answered, with a curtsey.

"Does he have prayers every morning?"

"Every marnin' of his life," she said. "He's a Papister."

"You'm a fool, Cis Jewel," said the man, who had by this time arrived. "You'm leading the gentleman wrong, he's a Pussyite."

"And there bain't much difference, I'm thinking, James Gosford," said Cis Jewell.

I started. James Gosford had been one of my favourite old comrades in times gone by, and here he was. Could it be he? Could this fat red-faced man of sixty-one, be the handsome hard-riding young dandy of forty years ago? It was he, doubtless, and in another moment I should have declared myself, but a new interruption occurred.

The bell began again, and service was over. The old woman came out of the porch and slowly down the path towards us.

"Is that all his congregation?" I asked.

"That's all, sir," said Gosford. "Sometimes some of they young villains of boys gets in, and our old clerk, Jerry, hunts 'em round and round all prayer time; but there's none goes regular except the old 'ooman."

"And she had need to pray a little more than other folks," said Cis Jewell, folding her arms, and balancing herself in a conversational attitude. "My poor old grandfather——"

Further conversation was stopped by the near approach of the old woman herself, and I looked up at her with some little curiosity. A very old woman she was surely; and while I seemed struggling with some sort of recollection, she fixed her eyes upon me, and we knew one another.

"Geoffry Hamlyn," she said, without a sign of surprise. "You are welcome back to your native village. When your old comrade did not know you, I, whose eyes are dim with the sorrow of eighty years, recognised you at once. They may well call me the wise woman."

"Good God!" was all I could say. "Can this be Madge?"

"This is Madge," she said, "who has lived long enough to see and to bless the man who saw and comforted her poor lost boy in prison, when all beside fell off from him. The Lord reward you for it."

"How did you know that, Madge?"

"Ask a witch where she gets her information!" laughed she. "God forgive me. I'll tell you how it was. One of the turnkeys in that very prison was a Cooper, a Hampshire gipsy, and he, knowing my boy to be half-blooded, passed all the facts on through the tribes to me, who am a mother among them! Did you see him die?" she added, eagerly putting her great bony hand upon my arm, and looking up in my face.

"No! no! mother," I answered: "I hadn't courage for that."

"I heard he died game," she continued, half to herself. "He should a done. There was a deal of wild blood in him from both sides. Are you going up to the woodlands, to see the old place? 'Tis all in ruins now; and the choughs and stares are building and brooding in the chimney nook where I nursed him. I shall not have much longer to wait; I only stayed for this. Good-bye."

And she was gone; and Gosford, relieved by her departure, was affectionately lugging me off to his house. Oh, the mixture of wealth and discomfort that house exhibited! Oh, the warm-hearted jollity of every one there! Oh, to see those three pretty, well-educated girls taking their father off by force, and making him clean himself in honour of my arrival! Oh, the merry evening we had! What, though the cyder disagreed with me? What, though I knew it would disagree with me at the time I drank it? That noisy, jolly night in the old Devonshire grange was one of the pleasantest of my life.

And, to my great surprise, the Vicar came in in the middle of it, and made himself very agreeable to me. He told me that old Madge, as far as he could see, was a thoroughly converted and orderly person, having thrown aside all pretence of witchcraft. That she lived on some trifle of hoarded money of her own, and a small parish allowance that she had; and that she had only come back to the parish some six years since, after wandering about as a gipsy in almost every part of England. He was so good as to undertake the delivery of a small sum to her weekly from me, quite sufficient to enable her to refuse the parish allowance, and live comfortably (he wrote to me a few months afterwards, and told me that it was required no longer, for that Madge was gone to rest at last); and a good deal more news he gave me, very little of which is interesting here.

He told me that Lord C——, John Thornton's friend, was dead; that he never thoroughly got over the great Reform debate, in which he over-exerted himself; and that, after the passing of that Bill, he had walked joyfully home and had a fit, which prevented his ever taking any part in politics afterwards, though he lived above ten years. That his son was not so popular as his father, in consequence of his politics, which were too conservative for the new class of tenants his father had brought in; and his religious opinions, which, said the clergyman, were those of a sound Churchman; by which he meant, I rather suspect, that he was a pretty smart Tractarian. I was getting won with this young gentleman, in spite of religious difference, when he chose to say that the parish had never been right since Maberly had it, and that the Dissenters always raved about him to this day; whereby, he concluded, that Frank Maberly was far from orthodox. I took occasion to say that Frank was the man of all others in this world whom I admired most, and that, considering he had sealed his faith with his life, I thought that he ought to be very reverently spoken of. After this there arose a little coolness, and he went home.

I went up to town by the Great Western, and, for the first time, knew what was meant by railway travelling. True, I had seen and travelled on that monument of human industry, the Hobson's Bay Railroad, but that stupendous work hardly prepared me for the Great Western. And on this journey I began to understand, for the first time in my life, what a marvellous country this England of ours was. I wondered at the wealth and traffic I saw, even in comparatively unimportant towns. I wondered at the beauty and solidity of the railway works; at the vast crowds of people which I saw at every station; at the manly, independent bearing of the men of the working classes, which combined so well with their civility and intelligence; and I thought, with a laugh, of the fate of any eighty thousand men who might shove their noses into this bee-hive, while there was such material to draw upon. Such were the thoughts of an Englishman landing in England, from whom the evils produced by dense population were as yet hidden.

But when I got into the whirl of London, I was completely overwhelmed and stupified. I did not enjoy anything. The eternal roar was so different to what I had been used to; and I had stayed there a couple of months before I had got a distinct impression of anything, save and except the Crystal Palace at Sydenham.

It was during this visit to London that I heard of the fall of Von Landstein's (Dr. Mulhaus') Ministry, which had happened a year or two before. And now, also, I read the speech he made on his resignation, which, for biting sarcasm and bitter truth rudely told, is unequalled by any speech I ever read. A more witty, more insolent, more audacious tirade, was never hurled at a successful opposition by a fallen minister. The K—— party sat furious, as one by one were seized on by our ruthless friend, held up to ridicule, and thrown aside. They, however, meditated vengeance.

Our friend, in the heat of debate, used the word, "Drummer-kopf," which answers, I believe, to our "wooden head." He applied it to no one in particular; but a certain young nobleman (Bow-wow Von Azelsberg was his name) found the epithet so applicable to his own case, that he took umbrage at it; and, being egged on by his comrades, challenged Von Landstein to mortal combat. Von Landstein received his fire without suffering, adjusted his spectacles, and shot the young gentleman in the knee, stopping *his* waltzing for ever and a day. He then departed for his castle, where he is at this present speaking (having just gone there after a visit to Clere) busy at his great book, " The History of Fanatics and Fanaticism, from Mahomet to Joe Smith." Beloved by all who come in contact with him; happy, honoured, and prosperous, as he so well deserves to be.

But I used to go and see everything that was to be seen, though, having no companion (for Sam was down at Clere, putting his house in order), it was very wretched work. I *did*, in fact, all the public amusements in London, and, as a matter of course, found myself one night, about eleven o'clock, at Evans's in Covent Garden.

The place was crowded to suffocation, but I got a place at a table about half-way up, opposite an old gentleman who had been drinking a good deal of brandy and water, and was wanting some more. Next me was an honest-looking young fellow enough, and opposite him his friend. These two looked like shop-lads, out for a " spree."

A tall old gentleman made me buy some cigars, with such an air of condescending goodwill, that I was encouraged to stop a waiter and humbly ask for a glass of whiskey and water. He was kind enough to bring it for me; so I felt more at ease, and prepared to enjoy myself.

A very gentlemanly-looking man sang us a song, so unutterably funny that we were dissolved in inextinguishable laughter; and then, from behind a curtain, began to come boys in black, one after another, as the imps in a pantomime come from a place I dare not mention, to chase the clown to his destruction. I counted twelve of them and grew dizzy. They ranged themselves in a row, with their hands behind them, and began screeching Tennyson's " Miller's Daughter " with such a maximum of shrillness, and such a minimum of expression, that I began to think that tailing wild cattle on the mountains, at midnight, in a thunderstorm, with my boots full of water, was a far preferable situation to my present one.

They finished. Thank goodness. Ah! delusive hope. The drunken old miscreant opposite me got up an encore with the bottom of his tumbler, and we had it all over again. Who can tell my delight when he broke his glass applauding, and the waiter came down on him sharp, and made him pay for it. I gave that waiter sixpence on the spot.

Then came some capital singing, which I really enjoyed; and then came a remarkable adventure; " an adventure! " you say; " and at Evans's! " My dear sir, do you suppose that, at a moment like this, when I am pressed for space, and just coming to the end of my story;—do you suppose that, at a moment like this, I would waste your time at a singing-house for nothing?

A tall, upright looking man passed up the lane between the tables, and almost touched me as he passed. I did not catch his face, but there was something so *distingué* about him that I watched him. He had his hat off, and was smoothing down his close-cropped hair, and appeared to be looking for a seat. As he was just opposite to us, one of the young clerks leant over to the other, and said,—

" That is———." I did not catch what he said.

" By George," said the other lad. " Is it now ? "

" That's *him*, sir," said the first one, with a slight disregard of grammar.

The new comer was walking slowly up the room, and there began to arise a little breeze of applause, and then some one called out, " Three cheers for the Inkerman pet," and then there was a stamping of feet, and a little laughter and cheering, in various parts of the room ; but the new comer made one bow and walked on.

" Pray, sir," said I, bending over to one of those who had spoken before, " who is that gentleman ? "

He had no need to tell me. The man we spoke of reached the orchestra and turned round. It was Jim Brentwood !

There was a great white seam down his face, and he wore a pair of light curling moustachios, but I knew him in a moment ; and, when he faced round to the company, I noticed that his person seemed known to the public, for there was not a little applause with the bottoms of tumblers, not unlike what one remembers at certain banquets I have been at, with certain brethren, Sons of Apollo.

In one moment we were standing face to face, shaking one another by both hands ; in another, we were arm in arm, walking through the quiet streets towards Jim's lodgings. He had been in Ireland with his regiment, as I knew, which accounted for my not having seen him. And that night, Major Brentwood recounted to me all his part in the last great campaign, from the first fierce rush up the hill at the Alma, down to the time when our Lady pinned a certain bit of gun metal on to his coat in St. James's Park.

A few days after this, Jim and I were standing together on the platform of the Wildmoor station, on the South-Western Railway, and a couple of porters were carrying our portmanteaus towards a pair-horse phaeton, in which stood Sam Buckley, shouting to us to come on, for the horses wouldn't stand. So, in a moment, I was alongside of Sam in the front seat, with Jim standing up behind, between the grooms, and leaning over between us, to see after Sam's driving ; and away we went along a splendid road, across a heath, at what seemed to me a rather dangerous pace.

" Let them go, my child," said Jim to Sam, " you've got a fair mile before you. You sit at your work in capital style. Give me time and I'll teach you to drive, Sam. How do you like this, Uncle Jeff ? "

I said, " That's more than I can tell you, Master Jim. I know so little of your wheeled vehicles that I am rather alarmed."

" Ah ! " said Jim, " you should have been in Calcutta when the O'Rourke and little Charley Badminton tried to drive a pair of fresh imported Australians tandem through the town. Red Maclean and I looked out of the billiard-room, and we saw the two horses go by with a bit of a shaft banging about the wheeler's hocks. So we ran and found Charley, with his head broke, standing in the middle of the street, mopping the blood off his forehead. ' Charley,' says I, ' how the deuce did this happen ? ' ' We met an elephant,' says he, in a faint voice."

" Have you heard anything of the Mayfords lately ? " said Jim.

" You know Ellen is married ? " said Sam.

" No ! Is she ? " I said. " And pray to whom ? "

" The Squire of Monkspool," he answered. " A very fine young fellow, and clever withal."

" Did old Mrs. Mayford," asked Jim, " ever recover her reason before she died ? "

" Never, poor soul," said Sam. " To the last she refused to see my mother, believing that the rivalry between Cecil and myself in some way led to his death. She was never sane after that dreadful morning."

And so with much pleasant talk we beguiled the way, till I saw, across a deep valley on our right, a line of noble heights, well timbered, but broken into open grassy glades, and smooth sheets of bright green lawn. Between us and these hills flowed a gleaming river, from which a broad avenue led up to the eye of the picture, a noble grey stone mansion, a mass of turrets, gables, and chimneys, which the afternoon sun was lighting up right pleasantly.

" That is the finest seat I have seen yet, Sam," I said. " Whose is that ? "

" That," said Sam, " is Clere. My house and your home, old friend."

Swiftly up under the shadow of the elm avenue, past the herds of dappled deer, up to the broad gravelled terrace which ran along in front of the brave old house. And there beneath the dark wild porch, above the group of servants that stood upon the steps to receive their master, was Alice, with her son and daughter beside her, waiting to welcome us, with the happy sunlight on her face.

*　　*　　*　　*　　*　　*

I bought a sweet cottage, barely a mile from Clere, with forty acres of grass-land round it, and every convenience suited for an old bachelor of my moderate though comfortable means.

I took to fishing, and to the breeding of horses on a small scale, and finding that I could make myself enormously busy with these occupations, and as much hunting as I wanted, I became very comfortable, and considered myself settled.

I had plenty of society, the best in the land. Above all men I was the honoured guest at Clere, and as the county had rallied round Sam with acclamation, I saw and enjoyed to the fullest extent that charming English country-life, the like of which, I take it, no other country can show.

I was a great favourite, too, with old Miss Gertrude Talbot at the castle. Her admiration and love for Sam and his wife was almost equal to mine. So we never bored one another, and so, by degrees, gaining the old lady's entire confidence, I got entrusted with a special mission of a somewhat peculiar character.

The leading desire of this good old woman's life was, that her sister Agnes should come back with her husband, the Major, and take possession of the castle. Again, Alice could not be content, unless her father could be induced to come back and take up his residence at Clere. And letters having failed to produce the desired effect in both instances, the Major saying that he was quite comfortable where he was, and the Captain urging that the English winters would be too rigorous for his constitution ; under these circumstances, I say, I, the *confidant* of the family, within fifteen months of landing at Plymouth, found myself in a hot omnibus with a Mahomedan driver, jolting and bumping over the desert of Suez on my way back to Australia, charged to bring the old folks home, or never show my face again.

And it was after this journey that the scene described in the first chapter of this book took place ; when I read aloud to them from the roll of manuscript mentioned there, my recollections of all that had happened to us during so many years. But since I have come back to England, these "Recollections" have been very much enlarged and improved by the assistance of Major Buckley, Agnes, and Captain Brentwood.

For I succeeded in my object, and brought them back in triumph through the Red Sea, across the Isthmus of Suez, and so by way of the Mediterranean, the Bay of Biscay, the English Channel, Southampton Water, the South-Western railway, and Alice's new dark-blue barouche, safe and sound to Clere and the castle, where they all are at present speaking, unless some of them are gone out a-walking.

As for Tom Troubridge and Mary, they are so exceedingly happy and prosperous, that they are not worth talking about. They will come either by the Swiftsure or the Norfolk, and we have got their rooms ready for them. They say that their second child, the boy, is one of the finest riders in the colony.

"You have forgotten some one after all," says the reader after due examination. "A man we took some little interest in. It is not much matter though, we shall be glad when you have done."

Is this the man you mean ?

I am sitting in Sam's "den" at Clere. He is engaged in receiving the "afterdavy" of a man who got his head broke by a tinker at the cricket-match in the park (for Sam is in the commission, and sits on the bench once a month "a perfect Midas," as Mrs. Wattlegum would say). I am busy rigging up one of these wonderful new Yankee spoons with a view to killing a villanous pike, who has got into the troutwater. I have just tied on the thirty-ninth hook, and have got the fortieth ready in my fingers, when a footman opens the door, and says to me,—

" If you please, sir, your stud-groom would be glad to see you."

I keep two horses of all work and a grey pony, so that the word " stud " before the word " groom " in the last sentence must be taken to refer to my little farm, on which I rear a few colts annually.

" May he come in, Sam ? " I ask.

" Of course ! uncle Jeff," says he.

And so there comes a little old man, dressed in the extreme of that peculiar dandyism which is affected by retired jockeys and trainers, and which I have seen since attempted, with indifferent success, by a few young gentlemen at our great universities. He stands in the door and says,—

' Mr. Plowden has offered forty pound for the dark chestnut colt, sir."

" Dick," I say (mark that if you please), " Dick, I think he may have the brute."

And so, my dear reader, I must at last bid you heartily farewell. I am not entirely without hope that we may meet again.

THE END.

PRINTED BY W. H. SMITH AND SON, 186, STRAND, LONDON.

19—4—79   D—56

PART 2

Excerpts from Novels

The Two Cadets*

CHAPTER I

... In Australia, year glides into year, and one almost un-distinguishable season fades into another, and time, divided and unmarked by events, goes on with equal pace. The years are not *marked* as with us, by the snows and frosts of Christmas, or by leafless trees. In winter there the grass is greener than the trees; in summer the trees, though remaining the same colour, are greener than the grey dried grass. That is all the change, except some little in temperature.

Ten years had gone over Lionel's head, and he was a steady, rich, sedate magistrate of three-and-thirty before he could believe such a thing possible.

He was wealthy even for the wealthy community in which he lived. Besides his vast flocks of sheep, he had made some singularly bold and lucky investments in town lands. He had no genius for commerce, but he was a steady, contemplative, quiet man, who did not care about making money, and still his money grew. He had no partner, but lived alone, about 250 miles from town.

A very pleasant place was this solitary station of his, ten miles from the next neighbours. A creek, overarched by vast white-

*Reprinted from *Old Margaret and Other Stories* (London: Ward Lock, n.d.). Originally in *Hetty and Other Stories* (London: Bradbury Evans, 1871), with publication prior to that in *Once a Week* XVI (23 February 1867): 214–20; (2 March 1867): 246–53.

stemmed trees, running in a deep glen cut out of the table-land, wandered on between the forest and the plain, and in one of the pleasantest of its bends his house was placed overlooking it. The house stood quite by itself, in the midst of a beautiful garden, which grew everything, from gooseberries to peaches. The great outbuildings, which were necessary for his wool and his men, were a quarter of a mile off. He had a quiet place.

The time did not go unpleasantly to him. He had his books, carefully added to year after year; and what is more, he read them. He had his newspapers and magazines in those days three months after date. He had expeditions to Sydney, at that time even growing to be a beautiful place; and long rides over plain and through forest, after his business. Last, and not least, he had his sporting.

He got to be the greatest sportsman of those parts. His "run", as they call the ground occupied under lease from Government by a squatter, was a vast stretch of country, twenty-five miles by twenty; nearly all bare, rich, level plain, at a considerable elevation above the sea, almost entirely without wood, and only marked here and there by two or three grass-grown extinct volcanoes, which rose perhaps three or four hundred feet above the level of the table-land. It was one of the richest "runs" in those parts, keeping a sheep to every three acres, but it was a very bad sporting run. There were many lakes upon it, swarming with waterfowl, from the gigantic pelican and black swan, down to the tiny grey grebe; but it was a bad country for sport. He hardly ever fired a gun on his own run, save at the ducks, and more particularly at one other species of game, which I shall notice directly.

But his house stood at the very edge of his run, close to the "plough line" which separated him from his neighbours. And behind his house began the great forests of which his neighbours' run consisted. These forests, at first open, that is to say, formed by large trees without underwood, rolled up into a densely-thicketed (scrubby) region of greater elevation—a wilderness of flowers, a paradise of game; at that time, merely a wild labyrinth of rocky gullies, or little glens, where the virgin gold lay about on the surface, shining, after each shower, out of the red clay which formed the soil, like the window of a jeweller's shop. Afterwards this very hunting-ground of Lionel's held a population of thirty thousand souls; now, like the "Fiery Creek", for instance, it has nearly returned to its original solitude. Nobody was more amused than himself when he heard of the vast treasures which his old hunting-ground had yielded, from the surface and from a few feet deep.

To show that one does not exaggerate, I myself knew well a tract of low-lying forest ranges, at the foot of Mount Cole, in Victoria, utterly desolate and uninhabited, a place to which our lost sheep wandered and died of foot-rot. I saw that same tract of country *after* it had supported a population of fifty thousand souls, and was still supporting about ten thousand. With gold, however, we have nothing to do, and only with hunting for a specific purpose.

For these upland gullies—all a-blossom in spring with *Grevilleas*, *Epacris*, and innumerable other beautiful flowers (the exquisite series of Australian orchids trampled under one's horse's feet unnoticed)—these sparsely timbered flower-gardens became his hunting-ground. They lay higher than the great forest, but not high enough to get the fresh breeze from the mountain, which still towered above and beyond them: and in spring and early summer they were hot, bright, happy sorts of places, smelling not unlike an old-fashioned walled garden in England. Nobody ever went there; there was nothing to attract the cattle or the sheep, for the soil was bare of grass, showing the red clay everywhere through the flowers, and the gold too, had any one had eyes to see it: and "shikarees" (like the late Mr Wheelwright, the "old bushman" of the Field), did not exist in Australia in those days. It was an utterly desolate region, and Lionel himself only rode into it accidentally on one occasion, when he was steering for his head-station by compass.

He often came again. Your horse could not go fast in consequence of the abruptness of the gullies and the denseness of the flowering shrubs, and you seldom rode far in a contemplative mood, without becoming dimly aware of a presence, and an eye; and, on looking more carefully, finding that you were within a few yards of a great grey (or sometimes red) kangaroo, sitting up like a small donkey on its hind-legs, and going away, click, click, fifteen miles an hour as soon as you noticed it. Then, again, coming round the corner of a belt of shrubbery, you would come on a knot of birds, standing from six to eight feet high, which, after examining you, would get a panic, and race away twenty miles an hour—Emus to wit. Parrots—why thicker than sparrows and linnets in England; cockatoos, lorekeets; *Scansores* innumerable, sulphur-crested, rose-crested, black and red, black and yellow, beyond telling; eagles, larger than any European species, would come from the great blue overhead and almost brush your ear with their wings; and alighting on a bare bough close by, would sit and watch you. Snakes? why, unfortunately, yes; some almost steel-coloured, gliding softly among the flowers; others more deadly and more horrible, lying with their soft bodies fitting to the ground as if they had grown there, and only raising their flat unutterably wicked heads as you passed. Monster lizards, five, ay, and seven feet long; other lizards of all colours; one a mass of evil horns and wings (the "Moloch"). For the rest—scorpions, centipedes, ridiculously fantastic beetles; *Mantidae*, like straws and sticks and leaves, which crawled on your blankets if you camped there; and stinging ants, with a grievance against the rest of animated nature, always promptly revenged. A "paradise", as I said, in the sense in which old Xenophon* uses the word. In another sense of the word, it was a "paradise" to Lionel. One of the *spécialités* of his order for all time has been that of the destruction of wild animals. From the hero of the *Ter centum millia perdicum* in "Sartor Resartus", up to——K.G., statesman and sportsman, it has always been the same. Lionel did not belong to the school who are shocked at the killing of poor innocent dumb animals; in fact, the school scarcely existed then, certainly not in that part of the world; for I greatly fear that some animals by no means dumb had been shot down in those parts; and though Lionel's hands were clean, he was an exception. Sport of some kind was one of the traditions of the order, and he found sport in these secondary gullies which lay under the great dominating mountains, and followed it.

In his own way. At first he took the usual course which is followed in the colonies, and had dogs, half-bred greyhounds, for the kangaroos, but he lost half of them; then he tried on many occasions to ride down emus on his best horses, but he lamed his horses, lost his emus, and once had a serious accident against a tree himself. He put his wits to work. Stalking was quite impossible on account of the snakes, but in those early times any kind of game would allow the close approach of a horse; while, in consequence of their being used to an attack by natives, no kind of game in any way worth having would allow the approach of a man on foot. He got himself a carbine, and looked about for a horse who would stand the firing of this same carbine from his back.

His stock horses, the horses employed in driving in his cattle, being used to the stock-whip, which makes a report like a pistol, could be got to stand it after a time. But stock horses do not do for sporting purposes. One leg among four of them is a good average. He took his youngest and best horse, and carefully trained him to standing fire. He got some terrible falls, but the British aristocracy,

---

* παραδεισος.

though, as some say, wanting in all the cardinal virtues, have never been accused of having less pluck than other folks, and he persevered. He got a high-bred young horse to stand fire, after which he had splendid sport. He would ride up to a kangaroo, and shoot it dead with a single bullet from his carbine; he would ride into a flock of turkeys (bustards) on his own plains, and with the reins on his spirited young horse's neck, would pick off three or four before the foolish creatures thought it time to move.

So far. He vegetated on here with his accumulating wealth, with his books, his business, and his sport, and there was but little to disturb him. Old memories were getting very dim; and the most painful parts of them, with the dark exception of his most unhappy duel, were getting so mellowed by time as to be almost pleasant. So when he, after five years' vegetation, got the intelligence that his cousin, the Honourable Edward Hornby, had come into the colony, and had been made inspector of police for the southern district (Victoria was a mere district then, though central now), he did not care very much. It was all over and done with so many years ago, and the sun had gone to sleep with her last light upon the peaceful eastern hills so often. In that land of untellable melancholy peace called Australia, the setting of the sun—a peaceful event everywhere—is more peaceful, more calm, possibly more beautiful, than in any other country in the world. Once see for yourself those dim, lonely, long-drawn plains of grey grass, and see the sunlight die on the solitary wooded peak which stands out from them twenty miles away, and then you will know what I mean. Lionel had seen this awful sunset spectacle every day for five years, and he said, "Who am I, that the sun should go down on my wrath?"

He had met Edward Hornby at sessions, with an open brow and an open hand, two years after he had heard of his being in the colony as police inspector, which was seven years after his own arrival, when he was getting to be a wealthy and well-to-do man. The meeting on his part was cordial, and on that of his cousin's apparently so. But he was very much struck by his cousin's appearance.

He did not look dissipated: all his nerve and vitality were left, but there was a wild, fierce, bandit-look about the man for which he could not in any way account. He asked the head stipendiary magistrate about him in confidence. This officer was a very dear friend of his, and they had a mutual respect for one another.

"It is an awful shame," said the stipendiary magistrate to Lionel;

"the Home Government serves us shamefully.* This is a home appointment. This man, this cousin of yours, my dear Lionel, is a desperate man: he has been kicked out of every billiard-room from Brussels to Naples. But his cousin and your cousin, Lady Alice ——, married Lord Granton; and so, when Europe is too hot to hold him, he is foisted on us as police inspector. It is too monstrous. We are not strong enough to cast the old country off, but the time will come when we shall be. You are making your fortune, you have your position, you will go home and go into Parliament. Do for heaven's sake tell the assembled British nation that we are sick already of having ill-reputed cadets thrust upon us in responsible positions. Do for heaven's sake, man, tell them that we are forced to stand it now, but that the time will come when we will stand it no longer."

Lionel saw but little of his cousin after this. When Edward, as inspector of police, came his way, he was always absent from the bench. The last time—save two—he ever saw him was at a fancy ball at Government House. Edward was dressed as a bandit, and Lionel was obliged to agree that he looked the part to perfection.

Now one has to explain again, for we fear that few of our readers know the meaning of the word "bushranger".

The first bushrangers were escaped convicts from Sydney. Bushranging began almost as soon as the Blue Mountains were crossed and the great interior opened; making the strict police, possible while the colony was confined to the eastward of that mountain chain, now impossible. After this, bushranging spread far and wide: more to the north, towards the Hunter and Clarence at first; but afterwards, as the flocks went south, into the most outlying districts in that direction. The object of these bushrangers was to avenge themselves on the society which they had once defied, by new crimes; and if you will take the newest digest of the criminal laws, and run your eye down the list of crimes, you will find not one which they did not commit. Such were the first generation of bushrangers. The second were hardly so brutal; but, strange to say, young men whose fathers had been convicts, but who were reformed and were doing well—getting rich indeed—joined this second generation of bushrangers from mere love of adventure and of old association. I date the second generation of bushrangers at 1830; what shall we say of 1865—of the *third* generation—when no road in New South Wales was safe, and when the *grandsons* of the original

---

*"We have changed all that". I am speaking of old times—"Killing extinct Satans".

convicts join the bushrangers and defy the police? On one occasion, in 1865, they actually held a town for two days and gave a ball, at which the policemen were obliged to dance. If it is so in 1865, what must it have been in 1830? Is it at all surprising that the feeling of the respectable colonists like Lionel Horton, with the dread of horrors to which those of the sack of St Sebastian are child's play, hanging over them, should be one of intense wrath, bordering on ferocity.

In his quiet southern home, with his flocks grazing far across the plains, and the *stolos* of old, quiet, good-humoured, contented London pickpockets and forgers around him, he had troubled himself but little about these bushrangers. His people were all rogues and convicts. He knew that very well; but they were not men who had been convicted of violent crimes, with the exception of one, who had fired a loaded pistol at his colonel at Gibraltar, because the colonel had refused to let him marry.* This would-be murderer was a great friend of Lionel's. On the whole, he felt perfectly safe about his people.

"I debauched my moral sense among these people, you know," he said once to Lady Granton, whilom his cousin Alice. "They didn't care anything for me, though I was a magistrate. I assure you these people are much nicer than your people. Take yourself, for instance: you are supposed to know everybody; but you don't know anybody who has robbed a goldsmith, and is perfectly ready to tell you all about it. And you are supposed to know the world. Oh! my poor cousin".

It was about the eighth year of his calm sojourn in these quiet solitudes, that there came a noise or report from the north, dim and vague at first, and clouded with a mist of incidents and anecdotes which the younger folks took to be original, but which the older hands recognized as mere replicas of old stories. But, in spite of the surrounding mist of old stories reproduced, the noise or report began to shape itself into form, and at last crystallized itself into certainy. There was a great gang of bushrangers abroad; by rumour more numerous, more bold, more cunning, and more cruel than any which had appeared on the continent. One had to go to the legends of the neighbouring island of Van Diemen's Land to match them for strength and for ferocity.

* A fact. A *difficult* man, but not what I should call an *awkward* man. You had to smooth him the right way. If he threw down his pack or his tools, you must leave him alone. If you had gone about further with him, I should suspect that he would become dangerous. I never tried the experiment, and so the reader has the present story.

There was little doubt about their leader: he had been seen many times, and could be sworn to by a hundred mouths—no less a person than Mike Howe, the baby-killer of Van Diemen's Land. This was not true: Howe never went into the bush on the mainland, as far as I can gather. But that awful name was sufficient to cause a panic among the outlying settlers, and many of the outlying squatters (country gentlemen) removed their books and their wives, and went to Sydney, leaving ex-convict overseers to make the best bargain they could with the terrible bandit.

A fearful bandit he was. The foulest, fellest, and fiercest with which the land had ever been plagued. The three types of bushrangers which came most naturally to one's memory are those represented by Mike Howe, Rocky Whelan, and Melville. Michael Howe was a handsome devil—a man beside whom Nana Sahib appears only as an enraged patriot with a personal grievance. He took the child from the mother's breast, and beat its brains out against a tree. Rocky Whelan was a feller devil even than this—a murderer from sheer love of seeing his victim die. Melville was different to either of them, and by far the most remarkable. A smallish man, the son of a Scotch clergyman, of the most intense vitality, with a courage of the most transcendent order. A man utterly without fear; not, as far as I know, either cruel or unclean, but a man whose whole soul was, for no reason whatever, in utter rebellion against order, law, society; nay, I fear against God Himself. The man could never have shed blood, or he would have been hanged without mercy. He was never hanged, for there never was anything against him worse than highway robbery. He was under sentence for something like thirty years, when, in one of his mad attempts to escape from the hulk, he got drowned.

This last man is a puzzle to me still. I would give much to have a talk to him. I had a chance once; I might have got near the man. But who can undertake to talk with a man mad in two-thirds of his soul, in flat rebellion against society and her ministers, tearing furiously at his iron bars like a hungry disappointed tiger . . .

The Boy in Grey*

CHAPTER XII

Gil Macdonald and Prince Philarete went safely round Cape Horn in about fifteen hours, and this was, for one reason at least, the most remarkable part of their voyage.

Not because it was done in a birch-bark canoe, against the great booming west wind which plagued Magellan and nearly ruined Anson. Pigafetta felt it, and Byron will tell you of that wind. The reason why this part of their journey was the most remarkable was this. When they came through Canada they saw plenty of things; round the Horn they saw *nothing at all*.

You say that there is nothing remarkable about that. I beg your pardon. Did *you* ever see nothing at all? *I* never did, and should very much like to make the acquaintance of a man who had.

Because, don't you see, you *cannot* see nothing at all. And yet that was all they saw, and therefore they must have seen that.

Let us be cool and logical. Let us not heat ourselves unnecessarily over this question. Let us get at the crux of it. There is no greater

*Reprinted from *The Boy in Grey and Other Short Stories and Sketches* (London: Ward Lock, n.d.). *The Boy in Grey* was printed first as a serial in *Good Words for the Young*, March–September 1869; June–July 1870; and published as a book by Strahan & Co., London, in 1871. Ward, Lock and Bowden published Kingsley's collected works in 1895.

mistake in this world than unnecessary heat over deep matters of thought like this. It involves the great question of Iamity.

They did not see anything at all, and therefore they saw nothing. But you cannot see nothing. But they did. Therefore they couldn't have.

Nonsense? Yes. But you will have worse and more pernicious nonsense than this to sort out for yourself before you have worn out three pair of trousers—that is, if you mean to be a man.

Well, they saw something when they approached the Australian shore. All the male adult colonists were down on the shore; and every man had brought his grandmother, and every man had brought an egg, and was showing his grandmother how to suck it.

"Come here," they cried, as Gil and the Prince coasted along; "come here, you two, and learn to suck eggs. We will teach you to suck all kinds of eggs, not merely those of the emu and talegalla, but those of the blue-throated warbler. And we will teach you to suck eggs which we have never seen. Come ashore, come ashore."

But they never came ashore for all that, but coasted on till the high wooded capes, no longer jutting into the sea, trended inland, and at last were lost to the eye. Then began a long continuous beach of sand, backed with low rolling sandhills. Then even these were gone, and the coast got so low that it was only distinguished from the grey wild sea by the line of mad bursting surf which broke up. The sea which the Greeks called barren was swarming with life, beauty, and vitality; the land was barren, hideous, and seemed accursed.

A long black cloud lay along their southern horizon towards the Pole, and from it came a blast from the Antarctic ice, cold as the hand of death upon the heart, yet as mad in its rage as the Mistral. A pelting, pitiless shower deluged them, and hid sea and sky and land as Gil hurried their frail bark towards the leaping breakers, and whispered—

"Ye must land here. Good-bye."

That was all. How it happened he does not know; how long it took he does not know. There was wild confusion for a little time, and then he found himself standing high and dry on the awful desolate shore alone—with God.

The blinding shower had cleared away, but the deadly cold wind remained. He looked towards the sea—a mad wild stretch of tumbled waters gnawing at the land. No signs of Gil or the canoe. Gil had disappeared by glamour of his nation; his mother had been a noted spaewife, so that was not surprising. He turned towards the land; it was nothing but a level sea of sand and salt, stretching away indefinitely northward, hideous, barren, but only marked by the track of two resolute naked little feet, not yet obliterated by the driving dust.

He was on the track now, and the ruby blazed and flamed out finely, warming his heart. And he broke into song, even in that hideous place, which God seemed to have forgotten.

> All alone, thou and I in the desert,
>   In the land all forgotten of God,
> In the land the last raised from the ocean,
>   In the land which no footsteps have trod,
> In the land where the lost pioneer
>   Falls stricken in heart as in head,
> In the land where his bones lie sand-buried,
>   In the land of the dead.
>
> Hear me, darling, the hope of the nation,
>   Stay thy feet as thou crossest the sand:
> Thou art far on before me to landward;
>   I look seaward—no help is at hand.
> Stay thy feet in thy swiftness, I pray thee,
>   Through this region of drouth and of light:
> Boy in Grey, I beseech thee to stay thee;
>   Let me meet thee at night.
>
> One said, who was never in error,
>   That the poor we had with us alway,
> And in all times of sadness and terror,
>   When night is more bright than the day,
> We can then lay our heads on thy bosom,
>   And, forgetful of false friends and old,
> Find there all we wanted in this world,
>   Warm when others were cold.

CHAPTER XIII

He was so very much pleased with his little song that he thought the best thing he could do would be to sing it over again. A theatrical friend of mine tells me that encores are very seldom successful: this one was a failure.

He began—

> All alone, thou and I in the desert,
>   In the land all forgotten of God—

and there he broke down. *Was* it forgotten of God?

It seemed like it. A plain of level baking sand and salt as far as the eye could reach, with a sky of brass overhead: not one blade of grass or one drop of fresh water. Surely forgotten of God if ever land was. He tried the song once more, but the words stuck in his throat.

"Peem! Peem!" Who is this alone with us in this hideous blazing desert? A little golden fly; in some ways more beautifully organized than ourselves: a beautiful little golden fly, in comparison to whose flight that of the eagle is a clumsy flapping, and that of the woodcock a clumsy dash. That little fly makes nine thousand strokes a minute with his pretty little wings. What does he say as he hovers before Philarete, passes him, goes behind him, round his head, and at last lights on his shoulder? He is a very little fly, like a small stingless wasp, and he says this—

"We are rather out of bounds, you and I. This is the desert, where God is at work to found in future ages a new place for the Boy in Grey's plough. This weary land is, chemically speaking, already richer than the Polders which the Dutch reclaimed. It is being gradually upheaved so that it can carry watercourses in hollow places where there is but little evaporation. And the armies of God are advancing on it, to shield it from the sun. A few hundred miles northward you will meet their advance guard: first skirmishers of bent grass, the little whorls of Banksia; then a forest of full-grown trees; then Casuarinae, at which point man can live. Walk swiftly, and you will be among the towering box forests of the gold land before you know where you are."

And so the fly flew away, and the Prince sped on several hundred miles, until out of the salt desert he saw a small shattered mountain, and under that mountain was a pool of fresh water, with an old gum tree by the side of it. And the pool of fresh water said to him—

"I am Jackson's Creek, and I am the finish and end of it. I can't get any further at present, but I will be down to the sea some day."

And the old blue gum said, "You and I have been a long time about it."

"I am not going to be much longer," said the water-hole: "there has been a great storm up northward."

And as he spoke the Prince saw a hill of water coming down the gully, carrying with it broken boughs, and sticks, and straw, and dead kangaroos. And it burst into the pool and went seaward, making a largeish lake in the desert, but scooping out a fresh-water hole below the other.

"He is off," said the old gum-tree; "we will soon have the place in order at this rate.—Hi! here! don't go yet."

This last exclamation was not addressed to Prince Philarete, but to a small tortoise, who had emerged from the old water-hole, and was steadily bent down the side of the new stream to the desert.

"I'm off too," said the tortoise. "I'm sick of seeing your old boughs blown about. And you have been struck with lightning three times—a thing you can't deny. I'm off to see the fun." And away he pegged, twenty yards an hour.

"They are all leaving me," said the gum tree, weeping resinous tears like the Prince's ruby. "The opossums will come soon and live in my inside, and keep me awake all night; the centipedes will come and give me the tic-douloureux; and the cockatoos will come and pull and peck. And then the blackfellows will come and make shields out of my bark, and will cut steps in me to get at the opossums, and very likely set me on fire to burn them out. I wish I was dead! There is no place left in the world for a gentleman of fixed opinions."

"You take this matter too much to heart, sir," said the Prince.

"Heart!" said the gum tree. "If you could only see my inside, you would see that it has been gone for years. I shall flare up like a foul chimney when they do set me on fire."

So he did; but the oddest thing is that, although set on fire three times, he is as well as ever. I have a personal acquaintance with him, and on one occasion took the liberty of lighting a fire in front of him, and sleeping inside him.

About a hundred miles on, the Prince came into a very pretty country of acacias, with grass and everlasting flowers, where he met a running brook, and he asked the brook where it was going; for, do you see, he had come that way himself, and wondered.

And the brook said, "As far as I can at present. Not farther than the larger Banksias. This evaporation is telling on my constitution already."

"You will not get to the sea, then?"

"Not for a thousand years. In about that time I shall get there."

"Hawk! crawk! chawk! Wee! wah! chawk!" said somebody, to whom the Prince turned and wished "Good morning."

"Say that again."

"Good morning, sir."

"Ho! I am the Black Cockatoo with the yellow tail. I am the worst tempered among the Scansores. I am the biggest blackguard under the sun: that is about what I am." And he hung upside down, and pecked, and bit, and clawed, using *the most awful language* all the time, until the Prince walked away and left him, never stopping until he was brought up by a pair of eyes in the grass.

"How do you do?" said the Prince. But the eyes were there still, though the mouth belonging to them said not one word.

This was not very comfortable. So the Prince advanced towards the eyes, and found that they belonged to an insignificant looking grey lizard, not nine inches long.

"Get up," he said.

Whereupon the lizard said, "Piperry wip!" emphatically, and bolted out of the grass down the sandy path, full gallop, as if he was going in for the Derby: he made such caracoles and demivoltes as you never saw in your life; and when he had gone down the path for about fifty yards, he dashed into the heather again, and was gone, leaving a cloud of dust behind him. I do not know this gentleman's name. Philarete calls him the galloping lizard.

Now in this sandy path there was a strange thing. The naked footsteps of the Boy in Grey were plain enough, but in the sandy path Philarete began to be aware that they were accompanied by a fresh trail, and wherever he saw the Boy's footsteps in the sand after this, even to nearly the last (as you will hear), he saw this strange trail beside the Boy in Grey's naked footprints.

It puzzled him. The trail was so singular that I, who have seen it often, can scarcely describe it. It was as though you put your hand into the surface of the sand, and at intervals pushed it from right to left; that was all. What could it be?

In a turn of the road, in a pleasant, happy, quiet little gully, such as are to be seen in Australia and nowhere else—in a gully of shadow, and trickling waters, and flowers, and the murmur of birds, in the earthly Paradise of the Australian spring—Philarete met a quaint pretty little fellow, something like a small raccoon, with white bands all over him, and a brush like a fox; and, seeing something intelligent in his eye, determined to converse with him on the subject of this strange trail, now parallel to that of the Boy in Grey.

"What is your name, if you please?" asked Philarete.

"They call me Myrmecobius now," he said; "but I have not got any real name. I was born before man and before speech, and I have thirty-three molars. I am the oldest beast alive, and the she-oak is the oldest tree. The she-oak has no real name either, it is only a consolidated Equisetum."

"That is a very fine name, though," said Philarete. "But look here, I want you to tell me something. What is the name of that—

person—who seems to be leaving his trail beside my friend the Boy in Grey?"

"Why," said the Myrmecobius, "the settlers call him the Carpet Snake."

"Is that his real name?"

"Well, it is hard to say what his real name is," said the Myrmecobius.

"Is he, like you, too old to *have* a name?"

"Oh no, he comes into historical times. You can read of him in the third chapter of Genesis. He has kept his name, too, very well. Cuvier gives him exactly the same name as the old Greeks did."

"And what is that?"

"Python."

"The snake of Apollo?"

"The very same. Some call him 'Science' now; and he still lives in the tree of knowledge of good and evil, which, as you are doubtless aware, grows between the devil and the deep sea."

The frightened Prince said, "Why does he go with the Boy in Grey?"

"To catch you and speak to you."

"Will he follow the Boy in Grey to the end?"

"No; your turn first, his afterwards. The time for the meeting of the Python and the Boy in Grey alone is not yet. If the two meet without you, there will be evil such as no man has seen. Is Athanasio with you?"

"No."

"I wish he was. There is a great deal more to be got out of *him* yet; however, if you must get on without him, get on. Don't hurry, and don't dawdle. There is plenty of time, but remember that the night cometh in which no man can work." After saying which the Myrmecobius quietly skulked away into the heather.

The next person he met was an American professor of natural history, in green spectacles, who was, as he said, "Kinder looking round and sorting things." He never said one single word, but he took off the Prince's cap and felt his head, after which he went straight off, and wrote his great paper on the solitary occurrence of a Doleco-cephalous Pithecoid in the interior of Australia. Such is democratic respect for princes!

The moment he was out of sight there was such a noise as you never heard. If all the beasts in the Regent's Park were to have nothing to eat for a fortnight, there would be a fine noise, I doubt not; but it would be nothing to the noise which arose the instant the naturalist's back was turned. The Prince stopped his ears, but all the beasts and the birds in the bush resolved themselves into an indignation meeting, and carried him into the chair by acclamation.

White's thrush (who had been in America) always declared to the day of his death that all the pow-wows he'd ever seen were fizzle to this.

Philarete, finding himself actually in the chair, bethought himself of his *princely duties*, and called for "Order!" to which the spur-winged plover began yelling "Hear! hear!" and found himself unable to leave off for above a quarter of an hour, notwithstanding that all the other birds kept yelling and howling "Silence!" at him.

At last there was a dead silence, which was broken by the kangaroo, who moved the first resolution by saying "Poof".

"I deny it," said the scorpion, running round and round in the sand; "I deny it."

Whereupon the laughing jackass came down off his tree, ate up the scorpion, and flew up into his tree again; whereupon the duck-billed porcupine, bristling up his quills, moved that the "laughing jackass was out of order".

The laughing jackass replied only "Ho! ho! ho! Hah! hah! he!"

The porcupine was not going to be laughed out of his motion to order. He called for a seconder.

The brush-turkey said "that two courses only were open to the meeting, either to condemn the laughing jackass for his proceedings with regard to the scorpion, or not to do so. For his part he recommended the meeting to do neither."

The crow said that that was a recurrent negation.

The brush-turkey said he had left his dictionary on the piano, and so he could not reply to his honourable friend's long words.

Meanwhile there had come about a free fight between the opossum and the native cat, who had got their teeth into one another, and were making the dust fly, I can tell you. The meeting were highly delighted and excited; making a disorderly ring round the combatants.

"Go it!" yelled the eagle; "three to two on the native cat! Go it, Dasyurus! get your teeth in his nose and hold on. Go it!" And the old rascal, who had no more fight in him than your grandmother, went on bobbing up and down in the most ridiculous manner, drooping his wings and yelling, until the Prince caught him a good box on the ears, and sent him sprawling.

"What are they fighting about?" asked the Prince of the kangaroo, who seemed the most sensible person present.

"Nothing at all," said the kangaroo; "that is the point of the joke. It's a prize fight."

"It is one of our national sports," said the porcupine.

"Oh! it is one of your national sports, is it? And what is the object of this meeting?"

"To protest against the naturalist, who has been killing us for specimens," said the kangaroo. "We have not been able to call our souls our own. He says he wants to observe our habits, and immediately kills us indiscriminately. I don't call that natural history. Blow that. Poof."

"He wants to examine your internal construction," said the Prince, who, like all true princes, was a patron of science.

"Internal construction!" said the porcupine, with all his quills up. "What odds is my inside to *him?* I don't want to bother with *his* inside. If I had the examination of his internal construction, I'd do it in a way *he* wouldn't like: yes, indeed."

The Prince argued that some of our highest poets and novel-writers were in the habit of turning themselves inside out for the inspection of the public, and that when the public got tired of that, they generally took an historical or other character and tried to turn *him* inside out; but the porcupine could not be brought to see matters in this light.

"Let him leave my inside alone, and I'll go bail I leave *his* alone," was all that he would say, and that very sulkily.

The Prince finding that the rest of the meeting were all mad over the prize fight between the opossum and the native cat, and that to argue about the first principles of art with an ignorance as crass as that of the porcupine, was useless, quietly vacated the chair and slipped away into the wood.

CHAPTER XIV

Now he came into the solemn towering box forest. All around him were great trees, as large as his father's largest oaks, beneath which the level turf stretched away for miles in long flats, with brave flowers, orchises and everlasting flowers; and sometimes these forest flats would be broken by little abrupt rocky ridges, with red clay and white quartz showing amidst the scant grass and thick flowers; and here the gold lay about so thick that you could see it as you walked;

and on one hillside there were sapphires like blue stars, and they told him of the Boy in Grey, and how he had gone by with a sapphire on his bosom bigger than any of them.* Here also were snakes in plenty, harmless and venomous; but they never troubled him, poor things, any more than they will trouble you, if you leave them alone. These rocky rises, with glimpses of the distant blue mountains between the tree-stems, were the most peaceful and beautiful places which he had seen; and here he met the king of the kangaroos. And the king of the kangaroos asked him what o'clock it was.

"Greenwich time?" asked Philarete.

"Did you say Greenwich fair?" said the kangaroo, who stood seven feet high and looked rather stupid.

"No, Greenwich time. Eight hours difference, you know."

"Ho!" said the kangaroo; "just scratch my head, will you have the goodness?"

And the Prince did so.

"I have got a message for you," said the kangaroo.

"From the Boy in Grey?"

"Yes."

"And what is it?"

"I have forgotten all about it. Or at least I have forgotten whether I remember it or not; or, to be more correct, I can't remember whether I have forgotten it."

"Can't you think of it?" said Philarete.

"Oh, yes, I can think of it, but I can't remember one word of it."

"What was it about?"

"It was about as long as my tail," said the kangaroo.

"How did it begin?"

"At the beginning," returned the kangaroo, promptly. "At least, I am not sure that it did not begin in the middle."

"Do you think it began at the end?"

"Very likely, for aught I know," said the kangaroo.

It was no use talking to the silly thing, and so he walked on. But he had not gone a hundred yards before the kangaroo called out, "Hi! hullo! come back!" And the Prince went.

"Just scratch my head, will you?" said the kangaroo. And Philarete walked away quite angry.

There were parrots enough here of all colours to have stocked Jamrach's for a twelvemonth, whistling and jabbering and

---

*Black Hill, Buninyong. The writer there found a greater number of sapphires, but, not thinking what they were, ultimately lost them all.

contradicting. A solemn emu whom he met, and of whom he asked the way, told him that this place was called Jaw Fair, corresponding to Bunyan's Prating Row, and that this was the great day of the year with the Parrots' Benefit Societies, on which they spent annually twenty-five per cent of their savings. Pretty as the parrots were, Philarete was glad enough to get out of the noise, and thankfully accepted a seat on the emu's back: who nevertheless stood still after the Prince was comfortably between his shoulders, and bent his beautiful neck and head in all directions.

"I am waiting for the white cockatoo," he explained. "He has to come with us. He is attending Jaw Fair."

"Does *he* spend his money?" asked Philarete.

The emu made a noise in his stomach like the rattling of pebbles. It was his way of laughing.

"Not *he*," he said. "He is too wide-awake for that. But he likes society, and has great powers of conversation; so he goes. There is the eagle ready for us there on that bough. Oh, here is the cockatoo. So off we go."

He bent his breast nearly to the ground, and away they went twenty miles an hour. The eagle dipped off his bough, rushed upwards like a rocket into the sky until he seemed a speck, wheeled round, and came rushing close past the Prince's ear like a whirlwind; after which he took up the position which he held all through their wonderful journey, just a hundred yards in front of the emu, ten feet from the ground.

The swift elastic motion of the emu at first engaged Philarete's attention, and then he began looking at the eagle as they sped headlong forward. With wings fifteen feet across, this bird held his magnificent course before them. Through the deep forest, where the green and yellow lights fell flickering on his chocolate and orange back, he held on like a meteor before them, until the forest grew thinner and thinner, and they came on the wild wide open plain, with a dim blue mountain here and there upon the wide sea-like horizon—still before them always the steadfast eagle, with his flying shadow upon the golden grass.

Northward ever, beyond the bounds of human knowledge, past solitary lakes covered with black swans, ducks, and pelicans; now racing across the lower spurs of some lonely extinct volcano, now crossing some deep ravine scooped out of the table-land by some fretting creek, growing silent before the coming summer. But as day waned, the day of all days in the Prince's life, they came to a pleasant peaceful granite country, where there were trees and ferns, as if in a European park, and a silent creek, with lilies, and reeds, and rushes, which whispered and rustled in the melancholy evening wind.

The eagle sat upon a tree, and the emu drank at the creek, holding up his head after each draught, like the Interpreter's fowl, to give thanks to Heaven. Now for the first time the Prince saw that the cockatoo was with them, and thought that he would like a little conversation; but the cockatoo only said in a whisper, "We cannot talk here."

"What place is this," said Philarete, "so solemn, so sad, and yet so beautiful?"

"This is the Creek Mestibethiwong, the Creek of the Lost Footsteps: follow me."

So he flew a little way and lighted on a tree, under which there lay a human figure on its side, withered long since by rain and sun, with the cheek pressed in the sand. So lies Leichhardt, so lay Wills.

While Philarete was looking on him, not with terror but with deep pity, the cockatoo lit upon his shoulder, and said—

"He set his feet before the feet of his fellows, and here his feet failed him, and he lay down and died."

"All alone?" said Philarete. "Alas! to die so, away from all! All alone?"

"Not alone," whispered the pretty bird. "See there, go and look. You are not afraid."

Philarete went up undismayed to look. By the dead man's hand was a Bible, and Philarete read—

"When thou passest through the waters, I will be with thee; and through the rivers, they shall not overflow thee."

"Not alone," said Philarete; "I see."

At this moment there burst on his astonished ear such a ravishing flood of melody that his breath came thick and short with pleasure. Beginning with a few short sharp notes of perfect quality, it rolled up into a trumpet-like peal, and then died off in a few bars like the booming of minster-bells on a still evening in a deep wooded valley, in the land which had become a dim memory.

"In all my father's land are no such bells as those. Who is it that rings them over the dead man?"

"That is the Australian magpie," said his companion. "Now lie down a little."

The setting sun was smiting the highest boughs as he laid his head on the sand. For a little time he looked across to where the dead man lay, and in a little time he slept. When he awoke it was dark night, and his clothes were wet with dew. The emu, the eagle, and the cockatoo were gone, and he was alone by the silent creek with the dead man.

Philarete rose, and in the daze which followed his sleep called to the dead pioneer to arise also. But the dead pioneer was past calling by all princes: he lay quite quiet by the side of the Creek of the Lost Footsteps. Philarete was now absolutely alone, with a horror upon him. Now he knew that the dead man was dead; now he knew that he was fourteen thousand miles from home, alone and without help, in the company of a dead man who had lain down and died here. Who could help him in this terrible strait and in this black midnight, under the strange Southern Cross, and Magellan's clouds?

There was but One who could help the poor child, God Himself; and the poor little man knelt down in the sand and prayed that God would tell him how to follow the Boy in Grey, as Christ did, and that he would be good to Arturio, Polemos, and Athanasio. The boy was very humble. He was alone with death, and he did not wish to die until he had seen the Boy in Grey. Sometimes he wished he was back with his toys, sometimes he wished he was with rioting Polemos, sometimes he wished that he was with Arturio, in spite of Arturio's priggishness; but when he said his poor little prayer he thought more of Athanasio than any one; for Athanasio had loved the Boy in Grey, and his family had quarrelled with the family of Athanasio on the subject. But the poor little Prince said his prayer, as he looked on the dead man by the silent creek, and his prayer was answered in a most singular and remarkable way. From this moment he had no fear whatever. He knew now that he could dree out his weird to the end, without any fear of failure. He had been doing his very best, and his work had been accepted; the Great Cause was sending to him inferior beasts to teach him the great lesson, that the higher animals are far before us men in what is now called virtue. The poor little man had been taught to pray, and he prayed; and his poor little prayer, arriving from his heart, was answered.

There was a tiny wind on his cheek, and a tiny voice in his ear: a little bird lit on his shoulder, I doubt a democratic bird, and said, "Don't be afraid of it now, Prince; go through with it. He is not far"; and then the Prince saw that the emu wren had lit on his left shoulder; then he remembered what the elephant had told him in India. He had no fear now, for the Elephant's words were coming true, word for word. No fear or halting now: the emu wren was on his shoulder, and the Boy in Grey was not far.

"Will you come on to my finger?" said the Prince.

The emu wren did so. When he saw it the Prince gave a great sigh. It was only a little bird, one of the smallest birds in existence; it was only a little grey bird, without any "tropical" colour at all; but yet the most astoundingly beautiful bird in creation. Conceive a little tiny wren, which has a grey tail more delicate than that of the Bird of Paradise. How did it get that tail? I, believing in a good God, cannot tell you. Competition and selection I do believe in, but I have seen things which tell me that there is a great *Will*, and the emu wren is one.

Such a very little bird, with such a very long tail. It lit on the Prince's forefinger in the dark, and it said, "Look at my tail."

"I can't see," said the Prince; "and he is dead."

"I am sorry you can't see my tail," said the emu wren, "because I am a very humble little bird, and I like to be admired sometimes. However, I had to come to you in the dark, and I have come. Do you think that my tail came by competition or selection?"

"I don't suppose it matters much," said the Prince.

"He don't think it matters much," said the emu wren. "Pipe up."

"Who are you talking to?" said the Prince, with that disregard for grammar which is not confined to princes, but which has actually been attributed to deans.

(If you want a piece of fun, young man, just examine the "grammar" of the last sentence—"a disregard of grammar which is not confined to princes". It means absolutely nothing at all, but you never would have seen it if I hadn't told you).

"Who are you talking to?" he repeated.

"It's White's thrush," said the emu wren; and White's thrush flew up on a tree, and said, "Toroo! toroo! the night is dark, but he must meet him before the morning, or the world will lapse back into its old folly. Hurry him on. I live in all lands, and I tell you he must go."

"Take me on your shoulder," said the emu wren.

"Bonny sweet, of course I will," said the Prince. "But why?"

"Because of the carpet snake."

"Must I meet him?" said Philarete.

"Yes, he is slower than the Boy in Grey: You must be quiet, and let him have his will of you. You must be very quiet and submissive, or you will never see the Boy in Grey, and then the whole world will be ruined."

They sped on, these three, through the night, leaving the dead man, the lost pioneer, lying where he was by the creek; it seemed nearly morning, when White's thrush said, "Toroo! here he is."

"The Boy in Grey?" whispered Philarete.

"No, the python," said White's thrush.

They were rising on to the mountains now, and Philarete put his friend the emu wren off his shoulder on to a bush, for the python, or carpet snake, had ceased following the Boy in Grey, and was lying a dark mass on the sandy path before him. You see that the emu wren had a suspicion or fancy, and the Prince, being a real prince, was afraid that the snake of Apollo would charm her, and then gobble her up and swallow her. The Prince, being *au fait* with affairs, knew that the thing had happened several times before, and his *statesmanlike intellect* told him that it was very likely to happen again (as it has). So he put the emu wren on a bush before he had his interview with the python, or carpet snake.

Yet the ruby on his breast was blazing out now with a vengence. The Boy in Grey is not far off when the python is near. The carpet snake raised his head from the ground, and lashing its tail round the Prince's heel, passed his head between his legs, and raised his head so that it nearly touched the Prince's face. Its eyes were for one instant like beryl, and the Prince said, "I understand, and I will go first": then the python, or carpet snake, uncoiled himself from the boy's body and let him go. The Prince was alone with the emu wren and White's thrush, and it was very dark, but he knew that if he could dree out the weird a light would break on the world such as the world had never seen yet. He looked into the python's eyes, and he had learnt something, for you learn quick in that school. He had learned something from the King and Queen, his father and mother; now the only thing was to catch the Boy in Grey before it was too late.

Some people older than children will read this story; to them we should say, "Help to catch the Boy in Grey. Whether you are Dissenters, Romanists, Tractarians—whatsoever you are, catch the Boy in Grey, even if you walk as far as Philarete after him." Speaking now to my equals or superiors, I do appeal in favour of the Boy in Grey. It would seem that they are going to keep the very Bible from him. "*Aux armes, Citoyens!*"

The Python dropped from Philarete's body into the sand, and he was free to go on through the darkness of the Australian night, through the rustling Australian forest. The Prince went very quickly; the emu wren and White's thrush said each of them that they had something to say to him, but the Prince only said, "I have seen the python". The boy said that it was merely a matter of time; the python had not spoken to him, but he had seen two things in the eyes of the python—Love and Hate. Young man, you had better listen to this: Love, played with and abused, is very apt to become furious Hate. I heard of a country called Ireland once; but that is no matter. Prince Philarete saw that he must hurry after the Boy in Grey.

Whither? There were no footsteps in the sand now. White's thrush had left him, and would guide him no more; only the little emu wren was on his finger, and he asked her, "How shall we find the Boy in Grey?" and she said, "I don't exactly know."

"I would give you anything," said Philarete, "if you could guide me to him."

"My dear," said the emu wren, "we have neither of us got anything, that would come to the same thing in the end, and it is not the least use asking the black cockatoo, he is so terribly *emporté*."

"Hah! hah! you two," said a voice over their heads. "Wee, wah! you're a pretty couple of fools. I saw Eyre through the great Australian bight. I *am* the black cockatoo, and I have heard every word you have said. I was Eyre's pilot. Do you think I could not manage two such twopenny fools as you? The Boy in Grey is just over the mountain. Look sharp!"

"I am afraid you are a very sad blackguard, sir," said the Prince.

"Well, if ye have not found out *that* before you *must* be a fool," said the black cockatoo. "You keep my counsel, and hang Henderson, that's all we convicts want of you. We black cockatoos don't like Henderson—he knows too much. We don't mind Bruce so much, but we don't like Henderson.

But we are leaving our Prince alone, utterly alone in the desert. The black cockatoo flew away *before* the Prince in the direction of the Boy in Grey, and the emu wren stepped away and saw she could go no farther.

The night was very dark and the wood was very wild, the hill was very steep, too, now, and he was utterly and entirely alone. There was a great thicket of *Eucalyptus Dumosa* in her way, but the naked feet of the Boy in Grey had crushed it down right and left so that the Prince could follow.

But as he rose into the dim breezy solitude of the upper and more open forest, he saw that he was getting into such a presence as he had never seen before. The night was very dark and dim, and night winds were making lonely whispers like the voices of dead men among the boughs of the mountain forest trees. Yet there was a light growing in his eye, and before he could tell what light that was, he was out of the dark wood on to a breezy down, where the night wind sighed old memories in the grass. Before him was a profound valley, dark as the pit, and beyond that a vast alp leaping up into the black sky with sheets of snow. That was the light.

It was such a wild, bare, bald down, and it was so far from home, and such a hopeless place, that the Prince would have been frightened had not Cowardice and he parted company. So unutterably solitary so terribly magnificent. Around him, hundreds of miles in every direction, was an ocean of rolling woodlands, untrodden by human foot. The solitude of the plains is terrible, but the solitude of the mountain forest is overwhelming.

The wind whistled through the grass and moved it. There seemed to be nothing here save himself, and the stars, and the alp; but there was something else too. There was the Boy in Grey. A cry rose in that solitary desert which seemed to bring fresh flashes from the Southern Cross, for the Boy in Grey, with naked feet, was lying in the grass before him, and the Prince cried out, "My darling, I have got you at last! let us lie warm together, for I am so very very cold."

So prince and peasant lay together in the long grass on the windy solitary down. And as the Prince kissed the Boy in Grey, with one kiss for Henri, one for Louis, and one for Philarete, morning came down on the summit of the alp and made it blaze again.

Reginald Hetherege*

CHAPTER XXXVI

SYDNEY

It is not to be supposed that the arrival of a man-of-war at the great port of Sydney creates half so much sensation in these days, when Sydney is one-fourth larger, and when the colonists have ships of their own, as it did in 1847. The arrival of such a fine ship was a great sensation; salutes were exchanged with the two other ships there, and the names of all the officers were published in the papers next morning.

Visits were at once interchanged with the other ships: and then the most hospitable of cities in the Pacific surpassed herself; balls and picnics took place nearly every day, and both soldiers and civilians vied with one another in giving the blue jackets a most hearty welcome.

Crowds of new faces passed so very quickly over the eye that many were forgotten almost as soon as seen, and the whirl of new scenes and new amusements was so great that George was quite confused, and more than once made the mistake of calling people by their wrong names, which was amusing to the people, but a source of

*Reprinted from *Reginald Hetherege* (London: Ward Lock, n.d.), prior to 1888. The novel was first published in three volumes by Richard Bentley, London, in 1874.

overwhelming confusion to the young gentleman himself, he being of an extremely modest and retiring disposition. But a week had not passed when he began to think that he saw one face oftener and in a greater variety of places than any other. At first he thought that it was fancy, but at last he was perfectly sure of it. An amiable-looking old man, with a very full complexion and rather stout, certainly met him in a great many strange places, though he never addressed him. The old man was dressed in well-made clothes, such as a gentleman would wear, white trousers and waistcoat, and a maize-coloured coat, with an expensive Panama hat. Somehow, in spite of his good clothes and his heavy watch-chain, George came to the conclusion that he was not a gentleman.

Yet he attracted his curiosity. He was in the theatre, in the bar-room, in the billiard-room, in the church, in Pitt Street, on the Quay, in the Domain, but never at any private house, or at any entertainment where the officers of George's ship were invited. He asked a few of his Sydney acquaintances who the old gentleman was, but none of them had noticed him or knew anything about him.

One morning, riding ten miles from the town, he met him on a very beautiful horse, which he seemed unable to manage. He seemed so extremely disturbed and nervous that George, who was of an obliging disposition, and very much attached to the society of old people, proffered his assistance, which was at once thankfully accepted, and words for the first time passed between them . . .

[*George and the old gentleman exchanged horses and proceeded to the latter's home.*]

It of course never entered his head that the old gentleman had expressly got up the whole scene for the purpose of making acquaintance with him, and had at last succeeded in doing what was very difficult for a man like himself, not known in Sydney society, to do—had got on speaking terms with an officer in the Royal Navy.

The road wound very pleasantly under over-arching trees, the sandy track being bounded on each side by fern and heath. Sometimes there was a pretty clearing, fenced with post and rails, which were concealed by towering hedges of scarlet geranium, a wonder to George. Each wooden farmhouse stood in a wilderness of flowers, while the orchards consisted, not of apple and pear trees, but of peach and orange. The summer air was faint with scents of all kinds, partly European, certainly, but overwhelmed by the rich aromatic smell of the bush, which in addition to scent, emitted sound in the shape of large insects and the pleasant whistling of parrots, or rather parakeets. They came to a small town, with a little church and court-house, where the young men were playing at cricket; then they came down to a pleasant river, bubbling over stones now, in the summer, but spanned with a noble wooden bridge thirty feet above its level, which was so built, George's companion told him, to provide against the winter floods. The old gentleman's conversation was very interesting and agreeable, and George liked him more and more. He knew more of the interior of the country and of the strange life and ways there than any of his aristocratic acquaintances in the town, some few of whom, at all events, had, George thought, the fault of being "genteel", a very sad fault, never committed by a gentleman. They rode on until at a smaller river they saw a charming little stone house in a nook among gently sloping heights, which came down to the stream. The wooden verandah surrounding it was nearly as large as the house itself, and had one *spécialité*, which took George's sailor-boy fancy immensely. On the roof of the verandah had been planted water-melons, which had rambled clean over the highest ridge of the house, covering it and hiding it from sight with a mass of broad leaves, yellow flowers, and enormous green fruit. He had never seen such a garden on the house-top before, and seldom such a garden as there was on the ground, covering the earth with gaudy masses of colour; and climbing up the pillars of the verandah, there were creepers of all kinds to mix with the water-melons on the roof . . .

Had he told any of his new Sydney friends how he had passed the afternoon, they would have done nothing more than tell him that fellows older than himself were very careful not to get too thick with Miss Ada Honey, for her father notoriously wanted to marry the poor girl above her station, and would most certainly bring any man to book who gave him the chance. There was not one breath against the girl's character in any way; she was a very good girl, but would most certainly marry the first gentleman who would ask her; and she would have a very nice penny of money.

We are obliged to explain this, though George knew nothing of it, and after he had found this fairy bower hardly talked about the matter at all, thinking that he would keep a good thing to himself. He was only a boy of little more than seventeen, and was of a privileged age, when a lad may play fast and loose with any woman. Had he mentioned the matter at all, men a little older would have said that they would be glad to be in his place, but they dare not be . . .

The afternoon passed most agreeably, and he was pleased in every way. What with the agreeable company of the young lady and her saint-like mamma, the day slipped on so that he had to ride like mad into Sydney, to get on board his ship in proper time. He tumbled into the last of his ship's boats in a great hurry, and next morning asked for five days' leave.

"I expect that we shall sail as soon as the *Torch* comes in," said Captain Hickson. "Where do you want to go?"

"A gentleman I have met in the bush, sir, tells me that he can show me some fine kangaroo hunting only forty miles south."

"Well, I have no objection," said Hickson. "Yes; you and your messmate may go if you like. I suppose you want leave for a messmate as well—put a name to him."

"The invitation only extends to myself, sir.". . .

CHAPTER XXXVII

THE SHADOW OF DEATH

George was back at Mr Clumber's house soon after ten. He had left the ship by the first boat, with a hurried farewell to Captain Hickson, and a promise to be punctually back from his leave. He had some wild idea that he might want money, and so he put a bill for fifty pounds in his pocket; he was in such a hurry to see the house of the flowers and the agreeable young lady again that he cared for no breakfast, but trusted to getting it on shore. As the boat pushed off, he gave a look at the dear old ship, in which he had learnt so much, and suffered not a little.

"The tall masts quivered as they lay afloat."

He felt that he loved the old ship dearly, but more dearly than her the man who stood upon her quarter-deck,—the man who had done him the compliment of trying him so hardly, and who had done him the high honour of telling him that he had been more than worthy of his trial. The boy left the ship with his heart beating wild with new hopes, new thoughts and ambitions, all to be told to the beautiful girl who was his friend, before the sun was high. He was not a handsome fellow, but the bare-necked, bare-breasted sailors at the oars could not help but notice that the most popular youngster in the ship looked more gay and pleasant than ever.

The bank was open early in that weather, and he got his bill cashed. Then he got his breakfast at the hotel, and ordered the horse which he had hired during the stay of the ship: for he was always in funds—the richest of his messmates. Then he dressed himself carefully in the best costume of the country, and rode away through the suburbs to his pleasant new acquaintances who lived among the flowers in the aromatic forest.

According to the rules of a certain kind of high art, he ought to have ridden over a black snake in the grass, as a warning not to go on. Aunt Hester, in her style of art, would most certainly have done so, and would either have made him turn back and be saved, or proceed to his destruction. We no more pretend to emulate Aunt Hester's genius than we do to emulate her virtues. We can only say that he saw no snake in the grass, and that if he had he would certainly not have turned back for it.

When he arrived at Mr Clumber's his young lady was on the lawn in a riding-habit. Her eyes were not so bright as they were the day before, and George, with the pleasant boldness of a sailor, asked her if she had been crying for his absence. She said no, but she seemed very much inclined to cry then; for she had heard enough of the conversation between her mother and stepfather on the afternoon before to make her very anxious, little as it was. And she had reason to cry, for, honest and good girl as she was, she knew more of the ways of this wicked world than George did: and George—God help her!—was the first gentleman she had ever met in her life, and she loved him.

Her stepfather came out, and George heard him say, "Go and tell your mother he is come, and bid her see to breakfast." But Mrs Clumber was ill, and did not appear. They had breakfast, and then they rode southward, followed by two grooms and one dog, a colly.

Ada was not herself by any means; beautiful she was, with that blazing Australian beauty which fades so soon, but her vivacity was gone this morning. The conversation was principally between Mr Clumber and George for many miles.

The Blue Mountains on their right, they rode pleasantly on through forest and over plain, through a beautiful English-like country all the morning, and stayed at a settler's house at mid-day. It was as good a house as many which he had passed or had entered, but there was a *je ne sais quoi* about the people in it which puzzled him extremely. They were utterly different to the squatters he had met in Sydney; they were not ladies and gentlemen, and were extremely constrained in their manners before him. They were dressed much the same as other people, but there were a hundred points of want of refinement which he noticed, and, as a general rule, they seemed very much surprised at his capture by Clumber, and rather afraid of him. The children, however, particularly the boys, came out in their true colours as the unmitigated little savages they were. George devoutly hoped that there would be no children at the next house they stayed at.

There were not, and the people were a slight improvement on the last, but by no means up to the Sydney mark. They slept here, and were to hunt the next day.

In the morning they started out into the delicious air, full of scent of flowers and song of birds, before the sun was up, and when the east was in colour a primrose green. The dogs barked joyfully, and the horses neighed their pleasure; it was impossible to resist the air and the beauty of all things around, and George gave loose to his spirits and became confidential to the strangers who surrounded him, numbering about seven or eight, and forgot the fact that they were a sad contrast to the real bush gentlemen he had met. If he had only known the fact, he was among one of the rowdiest set of blackguards in the colony. They talked with their grooms like equals on all kinds of subjects, and were by no means improving society.

Neither Mr Clumber nor Ada went with them, the former pleading age and fatigue, and the latter, of course, her sex and weakness. The ground over which they began to ride was almost mountainous, deeply timbered, with open valleys of exquisite beauty between the ridges. They had ridden scarcely a quarter of a mile when George saw something large in front of them moving slowly up and down: it was a large brown kangaroo. The next instant the dogs had seen him; the beast was off at full speed, and the sticks were flying about like mad. George forgot everything at once in the wild gallop which followed. The great creature, with infinite dexterity and speed, was going in a manner which would be thought impossible by those who have only seen them in a menagerie. Up hill and down hill were alike to them all now; a mile or two passed, some heavy in and out leaps were taken by George among the branches of giant trees fallen in the forest, but still the pretty animal steered ahead among the bushes and obstacles nearly in a straight line, as fast as ever; and still close to George rode one of Clumber's grooms, whom he afterwards found out to be his head stockman, encouraging him and guiding him.

At the foot of a very steep hill, in a very secluded valley, the kangaroo went to soil in a water hole and was killed. The whole party were up at the death, and they at once, as the horses were fresh, agreed to hunt another; "And," said one of the young men, "let us turn him homeward, and we shall come in for lunch." Everyone agreed to that as a "very good idea". George took occasion quietly to thank the stockman for his advice and assistance, and, considering himself the guest of the party, thought it only proper to slip two sovereigns into the stockman's hand. In doing so he looked at him. He was a rough-looking fellow about thirty, but in spite of the strange, defiant, sulky look, which all of the present company had, he did not seem to be entirely a bad fellow. He looked at the money and hesitated, then he looked rather earnestly into George's face, and seemed to deliberate, as if he was thinking of a very important matter. At last he seemed resolved, and put George's money in his pocket with an oath, and no other kind of recognition or thanks whatever.

George thought these strange manners, but he reflected that he was at the Antipodes, where everything is exactly the reverse of everything in Europe, consequently that it might possibly be the correct thing for a man to swear at you for giving him a couple of sovereigns. A diversion to his thoughts soon occurred, which made him think again that he was at the Antipodes: the determination of the whole party was to hunt the next kangaroo towards home: the instant the animal was seen, however, the host's son most dexterously turned it in exactly the opposite direction to that of the way home. It was certainly the longest, for the kangaroo would have had to go round the world in the present cruise to take them one foot nearer the station. One or two of the party swore and turned back, but the others swore and went on; as they none of them seemed to do anything without swearing, this did not surprise George. He went off at a good pace after the dogs, with his friend, the stockman, keeping close to him. This was a harder run than the other, for the dogs were a little tired, and the horses were getting so. One by one the party tailed off, only George and the stockman following the chase, which seemed very long; at last, as they got into a thick scrub, the kangaroo seemed likely to have by far the best of it, and the stockman drew his bridle, causing George to do the same.

"It is bellows to mend, young master," he said; "we had better follow in the trail of the dogs, for there is one I should not like to lose. Will you come on with me?"

George at once consented, and followed his companion through scrub denser than he had ever seen before, for several miles.

"I am glad you are with me," said George, with no notion of danger; "for I should never be able to find my way back!"

"No, master," said the stockman. "There's me and about five others could get out of this here scrub alive. If I was to have your life and blood at this here minute, and pitch you in there, all the traps in Sydney side would never find your bones. You can't see the sun, that's what beats you, and you goes rambling round and round till your tongue gets dry and swoll, and then you goes mad and busts up; and then the eagle hawk has your flesh and the warragals picks your bones, that's nigh about the size of it. But I'll fetch you to a place of safety, and you shan't be harmed, because of them sovereigns what you gave me."

George rather wished that he would have shown an inclination to assist him without the sovereigns, but as that seemed to please him he said that he should be most happy to give him a couple more when they got home.

"No, no," said the man; "them first was given willing; I'll do all I can for you."

George began to get uneasy, he knew not why. The stockman was talking very strangely to him, and he could not make it out. He was utterly unarmed, and no match for the man either in strength or courage. He had heard strange tales of bushrangers from his friends in Sydney, and some were out now. What if this man were one?

He might have made his mind perfectly easy on that score. The man, undiscovered, unconvicted, was one of the great go-betweens or "fences" among all the bushrangers in New South Wales, and probably might now and then do a little amateur business himself.

"Had we not better turn back?" said George.

"Burn me if I don't think we had," said the other, and he reversed his horse's head, passed George, and began apparently riding in the opposite direction. He was doing nothing of the kind, and had made a perfect semicircle in half a mile, carrying George further and further away from the staion, with a view, it is very possible, to "plant" him, or hide him away for his own purpose; but nothing was ever proved against the man, for accident upset all calculations, and no one ever knew the truth for some time after, except those principally concerned.

They passed through the scrub, and came into an open cheerful valley, down which ran a small creek, murmuring over iron-stone boulders, with here and there some lightwood on its banks, and here and there blue gum. They rode down to cross it, George taking his line under an aged gum. Suddenly the stockman cried out "Mind!"

and before George had time to attend, his horse gathered himself together and was clambering up the boulders on the other side, while George's chest was brought sharply against an overhanging bough which would not give way. George checked him suddenly, and he and the horse came clattering down together on the cruel stones. The horse rolled partly over him and injured him, then got up and trotted away. George lay perfectly helpless, in agony of mind and body inconceivable, unable to move.

The stockman dismounted, and said, "Now you *have* done it, young master; who would have thought of this?" . . .

The Mystery of the Island*

CHAPTER X

PRITCHARD'S ESCAPE

James Pritchard's attempt was one of the most remarkable ever made. It was *one* of the most remarkable, we most advisedly say, because it was not so splendid as Governor Eyre's solitary march of seven hundred miles round the Great Bight.

The furthest point of civilization to the north, at that time, was at the mouth of the Murchison river; there was only a hut there inhabited by a stockman and a hutkeeper, the latter of whom had rather a weary life of it, and was glad to see any new face—a gratification which he seldom enjoyed.

One day, when looking out at the driving rain, a young man, a sailor, with a gun in his hand, stood before him, and he said, "Where the dickens have you dropped from? Come in, mate; these rains are enough to float Noah's ark." And James Pritchard came in, and, opening his peacoat, showed his sailor's shirt, with his ship's name upon it.

"I have been out at sea for two days," he said.

"Are you wet, man?" said the hut-keeper.

"Ask a fellow that, with these rains?" said James Pritchard.

"Well," said the hutkeeper, bestirring himself, to make the fire

*Reprinted from *The Mystery of the Island* (London: Gibbings, 1896). First published by William Mullan, London, 1877.

burn, "I needn't have asked that. Is there a ship cast away, or have you run?"

"Run."

A sacred person now was James Pritchard. The poor ex-convict hutkeeper had the same instinct about hunted people which was shared by my Lord Marcus D'Este and his grandmother, Lady Dunorrin. One touch of nature makes the whole world kin. I do not say that this instinct of shielding hunted things is peculiarly moral; but people do it. The late Dr Johnson was a moral man, and enthusiastically admired the conduct of Mrs Flora Macdonald in shielding the Pretender. I will say no more.

"Now, where are you going, mate?" said the hut-keeper; "we can keep you here, or if the troopers come round we can put you in the bush. Besides, none of them would bother you if they did come. We are thorough good friends with the troopers."

"I will rest and dry myself before I answer you," said James Pritchard. "Who is your stockman?"

"Well," said the hut-keeper, "as we are all in the same boat, I may tell you that I am sevenpence and he is one shilling and twopence."*

"Fourteenpence," said James Pritchard, "that is a long chalk up."

"It is," said the hut-keeper.

James Pritchard looked at him for the first time very closely. He was a good-looking young man, but appeared to want vitality; James Pritchard seemed to feel that he could trust him in spite of the "sevenpence", but he thought it far wiser not to say that he had got sevenpenny-worth himself.

"I want to confide in you," said James Pritchard. "I am not a blameless person myself. I want to ask you this—is your stockman likely to round?"

"The last man to do it. See here he comes; as perfect a gentleman as you ever saw."

They saw him take the rails down, turn his horse loose in the paddock, then they saw him coming towards the hut after putting the rails up. James Pritchard went to meet him, and held out his hand.

"I am afraid that I ought not to take the hand of a sailor," said the stockman, "because I am only a convict."

James Pritchard said, after one glance at him, "I am a convict also, and I want your advice."

*A convict's way of expressing seven and fourteen years' transportation.

"You a convict!" said the stockman; "you have not the look of it."

"Neither have you," said James Pritchard.

Certainly not; he was a large, tall, melancholy man, with a carefully-tended moustache, but no beard or whiskers. A very brown man in complexion, and extremely comely in figure. The sort of man who could be backed to get the Victoria Cross every time he got the chance. He was a very gentle man. He put his hand on James—

"I think that we understand one another," was all that he said, before he passed into the hut with his saddle and bridle on his arm.

"I do not quite understand you," said James Pritchard.

"I only mean that we are both innocent," said the stockman.

"I am not perfectly innocent," said James Pritchard; "I have been fearfully careless, and I am suffering for it."

"I," said the stockman, "have not been careless. I intended doing a certain thing for certain purposes, and *another* man did what I intended at one time to do. The other man was my brother, but I pleaded guilty to save him."

"But why did not your brother come forward?" said James Pritchard; "He must have been a mean creature."

"He had got my mother and five sisters to keep, so what could he do?" said the stockman; "you don't understand Ireland at all. Well, come in, I will help you as far as I can."

They went in together, but as they went in the stockman whispered to him:—"Don't make the hut-keeper jealous."

So they sat together and talked. The hut-keeper listened all the time, and they therefore spoke on general subjects, such as horses, sheep, and other things which would only be partially understood by the English reader.

After a time the hut-keeper put the supper on the table, and, when they had eaten and drank, and were smoking, he said—

"This man has run his ship. I doubt that he will get three months if he goes back to Perth. We had better get the boss (master) to take him on for six months. He and you are much of a size; you can give him a suit of clothes."

"Well said, James Norton," said the stockman. "We will put him in some of my clothes, and ride over and see the governor to-morrow. You can ride, mate, I suppose—all sailors can ride a little."

"I have ridden very much in South America, when I was in the Royal Mail service."

"Then you can ride anywhere," said the stockman. "Now we can go to bed."

CHAPTER XI

PRITCHARD DISAPPEARS

The next morning beheld a strange transformation in James Pritchard; he was dressed exactly like the stockman. The hut-keeper asked him how he had slept, and he answered remarkably well. He then asked the hut-keeper how he had slept, and the hut-keeper replied that he had never waked once in the night, a fact of which James and the stockman were perfectly aware, as they had been walking up and down in front of the hut talking, from the time when he first went to sleep until a very late hour.

"You will give me no other name but George," said James Pritchard.

"No," said the stockman; "my father's name is disgraced through me, though not by my means, and I will not reveal it."

"Are you going to make any effort to get out of this place?"

"I am hemmed in on all sides," said the man whom we shall for the present call "George".

"What do you know about the Murchison river?" said James Pritchard.

"More than you do," said George; "know it for two hundred miles."

"Is there any chance that way?" asked James Pritchard.

"I should say every chance in the world," said George; "but what do you know about the Murchison?"

"I guessed that there was a chance there, that is all," said James Pritchard. "I only know about it from Gregory's map."

"But if we do sight the telegraph wires," said George, "we have no money. I'll be hanged if I don't think that we had better stay where we are, all said and done."

They sat down together under a banksia tree, and James Pritchard told George a certain secret.

"It is obvious," said George, "that we could never escape through the colony. I suppose we had better try the Murchison. Is it not an awful pity that you took that nobleman's gold?"

"He made a good bargain," said James, laughing, and thinking of the match-box.

James and George, the stockman, rode away the next morning for the purpose of getting James employment at the station. They were never heard of any more. The hut-keeper thought that they were going to Mr Stanford's, and said so. Mr Stanford said that they had never come near him. They got lost in the bush, and died. Of that there was no doubt whatever.

Whenever you read about a matter being perfectly certain, you may, nine times out of ten, decide that it is totally untrue. If you notice, certain great papers seldom use that formula. Some of the Australian papers said that it was perfectly certain that the men were lost; a few others said that there was no proof whatever of the fact. It is certain that they never reappeared; but it is equally certain that they were never, except for a short time, lost.

A very said thing occurred up the Murchison that year. At the very furthest station on that river, a very poor old cockney was hut-keeper to a Scotch shepherd. The Londoner, not a physically good specimen of his class, probably the most plucky in the world, has got the Scotch shepherd's tea ready, and his Bible on the table, when the shepherd came in. The shepherd did not eat his tea or read his Bible. He talked to the Londoner about many things, but he was most certainly ill; he had caught a cold in the drenching rains, and he took to his bed with ague.

The Londoner nursed him tenderly. When two men are alone together, far from help or hope, it is a fearful thing for one to fall sick. No one knows what it is save those who have experienced it. The Londoner read his Bible to him as long as he could hear it; and when the cold stark look of death came into his face, he went for help. But he was frightened, and lost his way: he wandered through glens and gullies, through scrub and forest, until he found himself surrounded by a tribe of black fellows.

They treated him in the kindest manner, and communicated with other tribes, who were in communication with the authorities. A sergeant, a cadet, and three troopers were sent; they brought the man back, and the magistrate at Perth said that he had lost his senses in the bush. He was found 126 miles beyond the country previously known by Europeans, and yet he declared that when he was lying in the bush at that point, he saw two gentlemen ride past him on roan horses, and tried to make them hear. He was examined, not of course officially, by a judge, and the judge, in an able paper, quotes this delusion as the best instance of bush-madness he had ever observed.

Judge Merton, however, being on circuit, met the tribe who had found the hut-keeper, and asked them collectively if they had ever seen the two gentlemen on horseback. "Oh, dear, no," the chief answered. "Hut-keeper fellow plenty frighten. Rain tumble down;

thunder tumble down; hut-keeper fellow tumble down. Baaly mine make a light of two gentlemen in the bush."

It was no business of Judge Merton's, but he reserved his opinion.

We now bid farewell to James Pritchard and George the stockman, at least for the present.

PART 3

Short Prose

*Travelling in Victoria**

I have not had the honour of seeing the State of New York; but I am told by those who have seen both, that its feverish energy is only surpassed in one place—Melbourne. The utter ignorance of home-dwellers about this place is extraordinary; they think it is a howling wilderness. I have seen people landing in 1857 with bowie-knives in their belts, and much astonished, instead of meeting bushrangers, at being put into a comfortably padded railway carriage, and whisked up, if it so pleased them, to a first-rate hotel. I have dined at the Wellington in Piccadilly, and I have dined at the Union in Bourke Street; and I prefer the latter. A man asked me the other day whether there were any theatres in Melbourne. I referred him to Miss Swanborough and Mr G.V. Brooke. There is no account extant of the Melbourne of to-day; even Mr Westgarth's admirable book is out of date. Let us have a glance at the every-day life of this *terra incognita.*

Day after day I and a friend of mine stayed in town, comforting one another with false excuses. Our business was well concluded, but still we lingered on, in spite of visions which occasionally arose before us of a face we knew, waiting for us, two hundred and fifty miles away on old Wimmera, and which face would probably exclaim with a look of triumph when it caught sight of us, "I knew you would stop for the race!"

For, the next day, Victoria and New South Wales were to meet in deadly conflict. Veno, the long-legged chestnut from Sydney, was to

* Reprinted from *Macmillan's Magazine* III (January 1861): 140–50.

run the great inter-colonial match with Alice Hawthorne, our plucky little grey. Both Houses were adjourned *nem. con.*, so that the collective legislative wisdom of the colony might have an opportunity of drinking its cobblers, and making its bets on the grand stand; and you may depend upon it, that, when your honourables adjourn, there is something worth seeing; and that was why we stayed in town.

And so there was something worth seeing. His Excellency himself was worth all the money, with his blue coat and white waistcoat, and his brown, shrewd, handsome face. It was worth while to see our bishop and the Roman Catholic prelate bowing and kootooing together, and pleasanter yet to hear the Wesleyan's wife tell Father G——, the jolly Irish priest, that she and her husband had come to see the "trial of speed," and "that it was quite like a race, really," and Father G—— offering her absolution. Pleasant to look at were the crowded steamers, and the swarming heights around the course, and pleasantest of all was it to see the scarlet jacket (New South Wales) and the dark blue jacket (Victoria) lying side by side, all through the deadly three-mile struggle, till the poor little grey was just beat at the finish, and then to see every man who had won five shillings batter a guinea hat to pieces in the exuberance of his joy.

Now the reason I mentioned this was, firstly, to make some sort of excuse to my reader for what may otherwise appear to have been inexcusable dawdling; and, secondly, because in consequence of this delay we were forced to do in two days what we should otherwise have taken four at.

Our horses were at a station not far from the great new digging of Mount Ararat, in the Portland Bay district. Mount Ararat was two hundred miles off; for the last sixty miles there was no road; and yet we coolly said to one another at breakfast-time next morning, "We shall get in to-morrow night."

I lingered over my breakfast as one lingers on the bank of the stream, on a cold day, before plunging in. I knew that in ten minutes more I should be no longer a man with a free will, but a bale of goods ticketed and numbered, temporarily the property of the Telegraph Company, tossed from boat to rail, from rail to coach, like a portmanteau, with this difference, that if a portmanteau is injured, you can make the company pay, but if a man is damaged, they consider themselves utterly irresponsible, and, in fact, the ill-used party.

We can see from our window right down the wharf; and our little steamer is getting up her steam under the tall dark warehouses. We must be off. Good bye! "Good bye," says Jack, who ain't going, puffing at his last new Vienna meerschaum; "good bye, boys, and a happy journey."

So we raced along past the Great Princes bridge (copied in dimensions from the middle arch of London bridge), and the Hobson's Bay railway station, along the broad wharfs, with all the Flinder Street warehouses towering on our right, and the clear river on our left. Now we were among the shipping; barques, schooners, and brigs of light draught which work up the river from the bay. Here comes our little steamer, the *Comet,* ready to start, with the captain on the bridge—"Only just in time. Good morning, captain. Portmanteau's aboard. All right, captain. Cut away."

Ha! A little rest after that run is rather pleasant. Let us look about us; plenty to be seen here. The river is about the size of the Thames at Oxford, but deep enough to allow ships of two hundred tons and upwards to lie along the wharfs. So here we see the coasting traders in plenty, regular Australians bred and born, in all their glory. That schooner yonder is unloading cedar from the dark jungles of the Clerance far away there in the north, while her next-door neighbour is busy disgorging nuts and apples from Launston in Van Diemen's Land (I humbly ask pardon—Tasmania); and the clipper barque, whose elegant bows tower over our heads, is a timber ship from New Zealand loaded with Kauri pine, and what not. There goes the seven o'clock train across the wooden viaduct! They say that Hobson's Bay railway is paying its eighteen per cent. Ha, here we are off at last!

Here we are off at last, panting down the river. "Where to?" say you. Well, I'll tell you. We are going down the Yarra to catch the first train from Williamstown to Geelong; from Geelong we go to Ballarat by coach, where we sleep; and to-morrow morning we mean to coach it on to Ararat, and then, picking up our horses, to get to our home on the Wimmera.

If our reader has never been in Australia, he will hardly understand what are the sensations of a man, long banished, when he first realizes to himself the fact, "I am going home". Home! No one ever says, "I am going to Europe, sir", or "I am going to England, sir". Men say, "I am thinking of taking a run home, Jim" (or Tom, as the case may be). Then you know Jim (or Tom) considers you as a sacrosanct person, and tires not in doing errands for you—will wade the mud of little La Trobe Street for you, and tells you all the time that, when so-and-so happens (when the kye come home, in fact), he means to run home too, and see the old folk.

We are steaming at half speed past the sweet-smelling slaughter-houses, with the captain on the bridge swearing at a lumbering Norwegian bark who has got across the river, and whose skipper replies to our captain's Queen's English in an unknown and barbarous tongue. The custom-house officer on board is known to us; so the captain makes a particular exception of his eyes, beyond that of the Norwegian skipper and his crew, gives them a thump with his larboard paddlebox which cants the bark's head up stream again, and on we go.

Plenty to see here, for those who do not choose to shut their eyes, as we steam down the narrow deep river between walls of tea scrub (a shrub somewhat resembling the tamarisk). Here are some fellows fishing and catching great bream; and now, above the high green wall, we begin to see the inland landscape of broad yellow plains intersected with belts of darksome forest, while beyond, distant but forty miles, is the great dividing range, which here approaches nearer to the sea and gets lower than in any other part of its two-thousand-mile course. Mount Macedon (three thousand feet), Mount Blackwood with its rich goldmines, and Pretty Sally's Hill (Apollo, what a name!), are the three principal eminences in sight of Melbourne. It is hard to believe that that wooded roll in the land is one hundred and fifty feet higher than majestic Cader Idris, but so it is.

Now the river grows apace into a broad estuary, and now suddenly rounding an angle we see busy Williamstown before us on the right bank—a group of zinc-roofed houses, a battery, two long dark stone jetties, and a tall white lighthouse. Now we open on the bay too; there are the convict hulks under the battery, with the two ships of war lying close beyond, and away to the left the crowded shipping.

There begins a buzz of conversation now; men ask which is the *Swiftsure* (a new clipper of Green's, just arrived in sixty-seven days). That's her next the *Red Jacket*. A black ship with a white beading. The Queen's ship, the *Electra*, is to sail this morning for England; there she goes—that gun is to weigh anchor, and lo! in an instant her yards are blackened by two hundred men, and, rapidly as a trick in a pantomime, her masts become clothed with a cloud of canvas, and, as we touch the railway pier, the good old ship is full sail for England.

As I find that we are only a quarter of an hour behind the time of the train's starting, and as I see a guard violently gesticulating at us to run or we shall be too late, I, who have before travelled by this line, become aware that we have a good half hour to spare; and so we turn into the refreshment room to discuss a bottle of pale ale, and look through the morning's *Argus*. This being leisurely accomplished, we are sulkily taken into custody by the guard and locked up in a comfortable first-class carriage.

There is a gentleman at the farther end with his arm full of papers. This turns out to be his Honour Justice Blank, going on the Dash circuit—a very great person; and, after a few frigid commonplaces, we turn round and look out on to the platform.

There is a group of respectably-dressed men, neat, clean, and shaved, standing together; they are diggers, who have been to town for a day or two, and are now going back to resume work. Near them are two men, who are intending to be diggers, and who have evidently not been many weeks in the country. They are dressed in the traditional old style of the digger in the pictures, the like of which was never seen, and I hope never will be, except among exceeding green new chums. They have got on new red shirts, and new wide-awakes, new moleskins, and new thigh-boots, and huge beards. One of them, too, carries a bowie-knife in a leather belt—a piece of snobbishness he will soon get laughed out of at the mines. Ah, well, we won't laugh at these two poor bears, with their sorrows before; they will be mightily changed in a year's time, or I am mistaken!.
Ah, well, we won't laugh at these two poor bears, with their sorrows before; they will be mightily changed in a year's time, or I am mistaken!

There is a group much more pleasant to contemplate. Two lanky, brown-faced, good-looking, and evidently brothers—are standing side by side, alike in face, figure, and dress; one is an inch longer than the other, but it is impossible to tell them apart. They are not bad specimens of Australian youth before the flood (of gold); and, as being characteristic, I will take notice of them in lieu of giving you statistics about the returns per share of the railway; about which the less that is said the better. They are dressed in breeches and boots, in brilliant-patterned flannel shirts of the same pattern, in white coats of expensive material, with loosely-tied blue handkerchiefs round their necks, and cabbage-tree hats on their heads. Each one has in his hand a stock-whip, some fourteen feet long, and there lies at the feet of each saddle and bridle. They stand side by side silent. They have that patient, stolid look, which arises from an utter absence of care, and from, let us say, not too much education. Look at the contrast they make to that lawyer, fuming up and down the platform, audibly cross-examining imaginary witnesses as to when the dawdling, jolter-headed idiots, are going to start this lumbering train of theirs. Would all the gold in Ballarat induce him to stand as quiet and unheeding as those two lads have done for half an hour? He could not do it. But our two brothers, *they* are in no hurry, bless you. They ain't hungry or thirsty, or too hot or too cold, or tired with standing; they have plenty of money, and an easy round of duties, easily performed. They would as soon be there as elsewhere. They have never—oh, my pale friends, who are going into the schools next term to try for a first—they have never tasted of the tree of knowledge. Think and say, would you change with them?

These two brown-faced lads are known to us; so we beckon them to come into our carriage. After a quick flash of recognition from the four blue eyes, guard is beckoned up to open the door. The saddles are taken up, and the two brothers prepare to enter. Guard objects that the saddles must go in the luggage-van. Guard's suggestion is received with lofty-scorn. Elder brother demands of guard whether he (guard) thinks him such a fool as to shy a thirteen-guinea saddle into the luggage-van, and have everybody else's luggage piled atop of it. Younger brother suggests that they shall go in the luggage-van themselves, and take care of their saddlery. Guard submits that the saddles will annoy the other passengers. His honour, the judge, without raising his eye from the foolscap sheet he is reading at the other end of the carriage, says, in a throaty voice, as if he was summing up, that if the young gentlemen don't bring their saddles in he shall leave the carriage. So the valuable property is stowed away somehow, and we are once more locked up.

All this waiting about is altered now. Then there was but one line of rails, and an accident every day; now the trains run, I understand, with wonderful punctuality. At this time we waited nearly an hour altogether; but, being men of contented disposition, did not get very much bored. The lawyer aforementioned was enough to amuse one for a time. This leading counsel and MLC grew more impatient as the time went on, and at last, having drawn the station-master out of his private office as a terrier draws a badger, he so bullied and aggravated that peaceable man that he retired into his house in high wrath, sending this Parthian arrow at the lawyer: "If I thought there were half-a-dozen such aggravating chaps as you in the train, I'd start her immediately, and have you all smashed to punk ashes against the goods before you'd gone ten miles."

A train comes sliding in alongside of us, and then off we go. Past the battery and the lighthouse, away on to the breezy plains, with the sea on our left.

> "The plain is grassy, wild and bare,
>   Wide and wild, and open to the air."

On every side a wide stretch of grey grass, with here and there a belt of dark timber, seen miles off, making capes and islands in the sea of herbage. A piece of country quite unlike anything one can see in England. Here and there is a lonely station, apparently built for the accommodation of the one public-house which stands about one hundred yards off, the only house in sight. Here two farmers get out (one of whom has lost his luggage), and two get in (one of whom is drunk, through having waited too long at the public-house for the train). Here also the station-master holds a conversation with the guard on the most personal and private matters, every word of which is perfectly audible to the whole train, and highly interesting. And then on we go again.

A pretty blue peaked mountain right before us; the mountain grows bigger and bigger, and at length, racing along under its hanging woods and granite crags, we find that the long-drawn bay on our left is narrowing up, and that the end of our journey is near. Then we see a great town (thirty thousand inhabitants) built of wood, painted white, of red brick and grey stone, with one or two spires, and a great iron clock-tower. Then the train stops; we have come thirty miles, and we are in Geelong.

There was no time then to notice what we had been enabled to notice on former occasions—that the Geelong terminus was a handsome and commodious building, in a suburb of the second city in Victoria, in the port of Great Ballarat; no time for that now. There stands before the gateway of the station a coach like a cricket-drag, with an awning of black leather, and curtains of the same. It holds about ten people, is drawn by four splendid horses, and is driven by a very large, very fresh-coloured, and very handsome Yankee, who is now standing up on his box, and roaring in a voice half sulky, half frantic, "Now then here, now then, all aboard for Ballarat. All aboard for Ballarat". We tumble on board as fast as we can, and find that our driver is inclined to attribute the lateness of the train to a morbid wish on the part of his passengers to make themselves disagreeable to their driver. This very much embittered the relations between the ten passengers on the one hand, and the driver on the other. The latter, indeed, was the most conceited and sulky I ever met among his very sulky and conceited class.

At length all was ready, the horses were standing immoveable, the driver settled himself firmly, and said—"Ho!"

With one mad bound the four horses sprang forward together,

one of the leaders fairly standing on his hind legs. Three more fierce plunges, and the coach was fairly under weigh, and the four bays were cantering through the shabby suburbs of the town.

One remarks principally that the houses are of one storey, of wood and iron, and that the population don't comb their hair, and keep many goats, who have no visible means of subsistence. Now the streets get handsomer, and the shops exhibit more plate glass; now passing through a handsome street, with some fine stone houses, and seeing glimpses of the bright blue sea down lanes, we pull up suddenly in a handsome enough market square, with a singularly pretty clock-tower in the centre. There is a pause for a moment at the post-office; and then, before we have time to think of where we are, we are up the street, up the hill, on to the breezy down, with a long black road stretching indefinitely before us.

There is a noble view beneath us now. As we look back, a circular bay, intensely blue, with a shore of white sand; a white town, pretty enough at this distance; two piers with shipping, and a peaked mountain rising from the sea on the left—as like, I suspect, to Naples and Vesuvius as two peas. The myrtle-like shrubs which fringe the shore, and the trim white villas peeping out from among them, carry out the idea amazingly, until the eye catches a tall red chimney-stack or two, and watches a little cloud of steam flying above the line miles away, and then we know that we are not, indeed, looking at a scene of Italian laziness, but on a good, honest, thriving, busy English town.

Now the whole scene has dipped down below the hill, and we are looking inland over some wooded hills, with a noble, vast stretch of corn-land, dairyfarm, and vineyards on the left. The road goes straight as a line, apparently without a break; and we think it looks level enough until we come to a grand precipitous ravine, about five hundred feet deep, and at the bottom a little river, fringed with green trees, and a pretty village, with a public-house or two, and a blacksmith's shop.

We travelled fast, and were soon up the hill, through the wood, and away over the plains again—long weary yellow stretches of grass, bounded by dull she-oak woods, with one shabby inn by the roadside, visible for miles—the external prospect being so dull that we turned to look at our fellow passengers. There were six in our compartment; let us see what they were like. A tolerably cosmopolitan collection, upon my word. My *vis-a-vis* was a Chinaman, with a round, smooth, beardless face, displaying no trace of human emotion or intelligence—not unlike a cocoa-nut from which the hair has been removed. He was dressed in the height of European dandyism, save that he wore over all a tunic of sky-blue watered silk. He goggled his eyes, and looked at nothing. He did not look out of the window, or at me, or at the bottom of the carriage — he looked nowhere. He had just come back from some villainous expedition in town, and I have no doubt had a cool hundred or two stowed about him for travelling expenses. Next to him sat a big-chested, black-haired, handsome man, whom we knew. He was a French baker on a large scale; and his mission seemed to be to make himself agreeable—which he did, setting us all talking to one another, save the surly driver and the Chinaman. He tried his hand on coachman too; but, only getting an oath for his pains, he desisted, with a shrug; after which, he and his neighbour the Irishman kept us alive for a mile or two by various antics, while a Scotchman looked on approvingly, and took snuff, and a German smoked and dozed.

Such were our companions. As for the scenery we were passing through, or the road we were travelling on, the less that is said of either the better. It is hard for an Englishman to imagine a forest which is in every respect dreary and hideous; yet such is the case with the stunted belt of honeysuckle forest which generally makes its appearance between the sea and the mountains, which must be crossed before one gets into the beautiful glades and valleys among the quartz ranges. Travellers are very apt to condemn Australian woods wholesale, by their first impressions of them from the dreary she-oaks and honeysuckles near the coast—forgetting that after-wards, they saw a little farther in the interior forests more majestic, ay, and more beautiful in their way, though thin in foliage, than it will be easy to find in more than a few places in England. But whoever says that a honeysuckle forest is beautiful deserves to live in one for the rest of his life. It consists of mile beyond mile of miserable clay-land, far too rotten and uneven to walk over with comfort. Its only herbage is sparse worthless tussock-grass; its only timber very like unhappy old apple-trees after a gale of wind.

And the road through this aforesaid honeysuckle forest? Well, it is a remarkable provision of nature that the road (unless macadamized) is so unutterably bad that it quite takes off your attention from the scenery around you—one continual bump, thump, crash; crash, thump, bump. Every instant you are lifted off the seat four inches, and let down again (no cushions, mind you), as if you were playing at see-saw, and the other boy had slid off just when you were at your highest. Your head is shaken till you fear fracture of the base of the skull. The creak, jump, jolt of the vehicle begins to form itself into a tune from its monotony (say the Bay of Biscay or Old Robin Grey), until some more agonizing crash than usual makes you wickedly hope for an upset, that you may get a quiet walk in peace for a mile or two.

No such luck; the driver goes headlong forward, with whip, and voice—a man of one idea—to do it as quickly as possible. "Jerry, Jerry, jo; snap (from the whip). Jerry, hi. Snap, snap. Blank, blank, your blank, blank". This last to his horses. I cannot render it here. Then snap, snap again. A dead fix, and we dream foolishly of getting out and walking. Ν ηπίοι He is only gathering his horses together for a rush. Then the original Ho! and we are all right again, going along at full gallop.

The horrible discomfort of our present mode of transit would render it totally impossible for any one who had not been this road before to make any observations, whether general or particular, on the immense amount and variety of traffic which we are meeting and overtaking. We, however, who have in times heretofore, jogged leisurely along the road on horseback—we, I say, can give some sort of idea of what this hideous phantasmagoria of men, horses, drays, women, and children, which to us, in our headlong course, appear to be tumbling head over heels and making faces at us, would appear to some happier traveller who has not bartered comfort, safety, and money for mere speed.

In one place a string of empty drays passes us going towards the town, each drawn by two horses, very similar in breed and make to inferior English hunters (for your heavy dray-horse, your Barclay and Perkins, would soon bog himself in these heavy roads). Then, again, we overtake a long caravan of loaded horse-drays toiling wearily up country with loads of all conceivable sorts of merchandise; and immediately afterwards, a caravan of bullock-drays, each drawn by eight oxen apiece, going the same way with ourselves, yet empty. How is this? say you, why thus. These bullock-drays belong to the settlers, and have been carrying down wool for shipment, and are returning. As I speak, we meet a wool-dray, piled to a dangerous height with the wool-bales, and threatening each instant to topple over, which threat it religiously fulfils about every fifty miles.

Now we overtake a long file of Chinamen, just landed, all in their native dress, dusky-looking blue smocks, loose drawers of the same, and hats like Indian pagodas. They are carrying their worldly goods over their shoulders, on bamboos, as in the willow-pattern plate; and as they pass, to my astonishment, my goggle-eyed Chinese *vis-a-vis* wakes up, puts his head out of where the window should be, and makes a noise like a door with rusty hinges, but ten times as loud. He is replied to by the head man of the travelling Chinamen in a sound as though one were playing a hurdy-gurdy under the bed-clothes. Our Chinaman draws his head back, and looks round upon his fellow-travellers with the air of one who has said something rather clever, he believes; and before I have time to ask him, angrily, what the deuce he means by making that noise before a gentleman, I see something which puts Chinamen out of my head altogether.

A dray is upset by the roadside, evidently the dray of a newly-arrived emigrant, and all the poor little household gods are scattered about in the dirt. Poor old granny is sitting by the roadside, looking scared and wringing her hands, while the young mother is engaged half in watching her husband among the struggling horses, and half in trying to soothe the baby by her breast. She has had a sad cut, poor soul, I can see by her crumpled bonnet; and she looks pale and wild, but brave withal. A girl about fourteen is nursing and quieting a child of six, while a boy of ten helps his father. There is the bonnet-box, crushed flat by the hair trunk. Alas! for the poor Sunday bonnet inside, brought with such proud care so many miles, the last memento of happy summer church-goings in England. Poor bonnet! becoming poetical only in thy destruction! There, too, the box with the few poor books has burst open, and "The Farmer of Englewood Forest" and "Fatherless Fanny" are in the mud with their old friend and companion, the fiddle. God speed you, my poor friends; be brave and careful, and the worst will soon be over. A twelve-month hence you shall be sitting by the fireside laughing at all these mishaps and annoyances, bitter as they are now.

If this purgatory of jolting continues much longer, a crisis must supervene—death, probably, or insanity. Two or three thousand years ago, as near as I can compute, there was a short cessation of it—a dream, as of being taken into an inn and having a dinner, and seeing the Chinaman eat with his knife and his fingers, dismissing his fork from office without pension; but since then things have been worse than ever; and now a change is coming over me. I must be going mad. That Chinaman's head is no more fixed on his shoulders than King Charles the First's. He has got a joint in his neck like those nodding *papier mâché* mandarins we used to have at home. How I should like to knock his head off, only I am so sleepy. Ah! that is it; before I have time to think about it, I am asleep.

I woke whenever we changed horses at a country township, and saw the same sight everywhere,—two or three large wooden hotels, with a few travellers loitering about in the verandahs, unwilling to shoulder their heavy bundles and proceed. A drunken man dragged out and lying prone by the door, with his patient dog waiting till he should arouse himself and come home. The blacksmith's shop, with its lot of gossiping idlers. The store, or village shop, with the proprietor at his door, with his hands in his pockets; half-a-dozen houses around, little wooden farmhouses like toys, standing just inside the three-railed fence, which inclosed the 80, 160, or 640 acre lots belonging to them; and around and beyond all the forest, now composed of Eucalypti (box and stringy bark here), and infinitely more beautiful than the miserable Banksia forest on which we poured the vials of our wrath.

But at a place called Burat-bridge, I woke up for good; for in that place the plank road begins, and from that place the troubles of the traveller into Ballarat end. The road is of wooden planks, laid crosswise, and the coach runs as on a railway. This is an American invention. Let me do the Americans full justice. In spite of the bad and "wooden nutmeg" quality of nine-tenths of their importations, they have taught the Victorians one invaluable lesson—how to travel with speed over rough bush roads. Their double-ended Collins' picks, too, are more useful and handy than any imported from home.

We dash on through the darkening glades of a beautiful forest, the topmost boughs overhead growing more and more golden under the slanting rays of the sinking sun. As the tallest feathery bough begins to lose the light, and the magpie most glorious of song-birds, croons out his vespers, I lean out of the coach to feast my eyes on a sight which, though so often seen, has never palled upon me—one of the most beautiful mountains in the world, Mount Buninyong. It is the extreme southern lip of a great volcanic crater, which runs up suddenly near a thousand feet above the road, covered from the dark base to where the top-most trees stand, feathering up against the crimson west, with some of the largest timber in the world. Northwards, and towards Ballarat, the lava has burst down the rim of the cup on all sides, pouring in bands from forty to sixty feet thick over the gold-beds, to the everlasting confusion of miners; but at the south end it stands up still as abrupt and lofty as it did when all the fertile country was a fiery desert—when the internal fires were vitrifying every seam in the slate-rock, and sublimating its vapour into gold.

Buninyong. Three large hotels, and a blacksmith's shop. A stoppage. A drunken man, who is anxious to fight any man in the coach for half-a-crown. The return gold escort from Geelong; ten troopers, in scarlet shirts, white breeches, and helmets; two carts, driven tandem, and an officer in a blue cloak, all of her majesty's 12th regiment; fifty or sixty dogs, who sit perfectly quiet till we start, and then come at us pell-mell, and gnaw our wheels in their wrath; then darkness again, and the forest.

Forest, and a smooth turnpike road. Sleep and dreams. Dreams of the forest getting scanter as we go; of long-drawn gullies running up into the hills, with all the bottom of them turned up in heaps of yellow clay, as though one were laying on the gas in the New Forest. Of tents; sometimes one alone, sometimes twenty together, with men and women standing outside, looking at the coach. Of a stoppage at a store, supposed to be the post-office, where was a drunken man who disparaged us, and, like Shimei, went on his way, cursing. Of another bit of forest. Of more tents, and then of waking up and looking over a magnificent amphitheatre among the hills, with ten thousand lights on hill and bottom, and a hundred busy steam-engines fuming and grinding away in the darkness. Of a long street of canvas stores and tents; of a better street of stone and wood; of handsome shops, and then of pulling up opposite a handsome hotel. Ballarat.

We had an excellent supper in a handsome room, and, smoking our pipes after it, were joined by a gentleman in yellow clay-stained moleskin trousers, a blue shirt, and a white cap. This gentleman had not been invited to join our little party, but he did so with the greatest condescension. We soon found that he was a gentleman with a grievance, and that his grievance was Bath's hole.

I give you my word of honour, that, although he bored us with Bath's hole, and his relations therewith, for an hour and a half, I have not the slightest idea what his grievance was. His strong point was this, that although Bath (the excellent landlord of the hotel in which we were staying) had hit gold, it wasn't the gravel-pits. We, knowing something about the matter, were unfortunately of opinion that it was the gravel-pits, and no other lead; so the discussion was indefinitely prolonged, until we went out to look at the hole itself, just in front of the hotel—an erection like a bankrupt windmill, with a steam-engine inside, standing over a shaft of three hundred feet deep; and then we went to bed.

But not to sleep—oh dear, no! I was in bed at a quarter before eleven. At eleven, two dogs had a difference of opinion under my window; they walked up and down, growling, till, as near as I can guess, a quarter past eleven; when they departed without fighting, at which I was sorry. At half-past eleven (I merely give you approximation as to time; I did not look at my watch), a drunken man fell into the gutter, and, on being helped out by another man, pitched into him savagely. They fought three rounds, and *exeunt*. At twelve, the bar was cleared, and a gentleman, of the name of Bob, was found to be unequal to the occasion, and lay down in the mud, pulling a wheelbarrow over him, under the impression that it was the bed-clothes. Bob's mates fell out as to a score at the blacksmith's for sharpening gads. Fight, and grand *tableau—exeunt*. At half-past twelve, a drunken Irishwoman was conducted home by two policemen; on reaching my window, she declined to proceed on any terms whatever, and committed a series of savage assaults on the constabulary. At one, a gentleman from over the way came out of his house, and, without notice or apparent reason, discharged a six-barrelled revolver; which reminded another neighbour that he might as well let off a two-barrelled fowling-piece; which caused a third neighbour to come out and swear at the other two like a trooper.

And so the night wore on. We got to sleep somewhere in the small hours, and then were awakened by the "night-shift" from that abominable "Bath's hole" afore-mentioned, who arrived at the surface of the earth at four A.M. in a preternatural state of liveliness, and murdered sleep. A difference of opinion seemed to exist as to whether a gentleman of the name of Arry was, or was not, an etcetera fool. It was decided against Arry, by acclamation, and they went to bed.

In the grey light of the morning a vindictive waiter brought me my boots, and announced, in a tone of savage, implacable ferocity, that the coach would be ready in half an hour. So I again found myself opposite my old friend the Chinaman, plunging headlong through one of the worst roads in the world, north-west for Mount Ararat.

Mount Ararat, I must tell you here, at the risk of boring you, was the place at which all men in that year (1857) who cared to win gold were congregated. Eight "leads" of gold were being worked, and the population was close on sixty thousand.

There was breakfast in an hotel beside a broad desolate-looking lake, with a lofty volcanic down—a "bald hill", as they call them here—rolling up on the right; then "Fiery Creek", an immense deserted diggings among romantic gullies at the foot of a mountain; then we began to pass some very beautiful scenery indeed—flat plains, interspersed with belts of timber, and two fine isolated mountains, four thousand feet or so in height, rising abruptly on the left, the nearest of which rejoiced in the hideous name of "Tuckerimbid" (Mount Cole), and the farthest one in the exceedingly pretty one of Laningeryn. This latter mountain had two sharp peaks like Snowdon; but, like all other high mountains in Australia (except the Alps), was wooded with dense timber from base to summit—a circumstance which considerably mars the beauty of mountain scenery in those parts.

What I am going to tell you now is nothing more than the truth, whatever you may be inclined to think. We were going down a steep hill towards a creek, when the Chinaman, who sat opposite, suddenly, without notice or provocation, levelled his head, and brought it full against what Mr Sayers would call my bread-basket with astonishing force that I had no breath left to cry for assistance. I made a wild clutch at his pigtail, with the intention of holding on by that while I punched his head. That intention was never fulfilled; for, ere my hand reached his head, the whole *orbis terrarum*, the entire cosmos, utterly disappeared, and was replaced by a summer sky with floating clouds. The end of all things had come, and I was floating through space alone with a lunatic Chinaman.

But we did not float long. We came back to earth again with a crash enough to break every bone in our bodies, one would think; and I am happy to say that the Chinaman fell under me. Up rising, we saw that the coach had been upset, and rolled completely over. Our friend the French baker was wiping the blood from a terrible cut in the fore-head; the Yankee driver lay on his back, as I thought dead; and two of the party were cautiously approaching the four mad struggling horses.

In time the traces were cut; in time the driver came to himself, and swore profane oaths; in time the Frenchman got his head plastered, and was merry over our mishap, and, in time, we got to Ararat.

A great dusty main street of canvas stores, hotels, bagatelle-rooms, and bowling-alleys, outside of which on each side were vast mounds of snow-white pipe-clay, each one of which was surmounted by a windlass attended by two men. Due west, well in sight, rose Mount William, the highest mountain in Portland bay, rising 4,500 feet above the table-land, 6,000 feet above the sea. The main street in which we stop was primeval forest two months ago; and we may remark that the country round lies between the bald volcanic plains and the great ranges, consisting of a poor scrubby heath (more brilliant with flowers in spring than a duke's garden), over which was a sparse forest of stunted gum-trees.

Our coach journey is over, and we are put down at our hotel. Then we wander forth among the "holes" and converse with the miners, while supper is getting ready. A hole is pointed out to us as being remarkable. The men who are working it expect to raise about sixty load, and are certain of washing out eleven ounces to the load, which will give them somewhere about £600 a man for three weeks' work. We go and look at the hole. It is a pyramid of white pipeclay, about twenty feet high, with a windlass atop, and two handsome young Norfolk men working at it. We hear that their shaft is ninety feet deep, and several other particulars. But what takes our attention more than anything is this. At the foot of the great mound of pipeclay, in the very centre of this roaring mass of advancing civilization, there sit three native black fellows. Naked save for a dirty Government blanket, pinned over their shoulders with a wooden skewer, there they sit, stupid and stunned. On the very place where a short year ago they had been hunting their wallaby and brush kangaroo, the billiard balls are clicking and the fiddles are playing. A rush of sixty thousand Europeans has come into their quiet forest, after that curious yellow metal, of whose existence they had never known; and they sit there stunned and puzzled. The eldest among them can remember the happy old times, when kangaroos were plenty and white men had not been heard of; the youngest can remember the quiet rule of the squatters, when all their work consisted in supplying the settler's table with game. And now! Their time is come, and they know it; there is no place left for them in the land. These white men have brought drink with them, and that will make them forget their troubles for a time. Let them cringe and whine, and prostitute their wives for it, and then die for it; that is all left for them. Alas! poor black fellows, I have left a little bit of my heart among you, and that is the truth.

Five hundred black fellows in full corroborry would have had a sedative tendency compared to what I had to suffer in the way of aggravating noises after I got to bed that night. Our hotel was built of calico; so, as you may suppose, one gathered a tolerable idea of what was going on around one. I got into bed with great confidence at eleven, and then discovered that I was within three statute feet of a bowling-alley. I listened for one hour to the "trundle, trundle, clink, clink", of that exciting game; and then the proprietor of the place put the candle out, and cleared the alley, and I composed myself to sleep.

Then I became painfully conscious that there was a bagatelle-board in my immediate neighbourhood, and that two men were playing on it, and, what was worse, that a dozen or so of other men were looking on, and discussing every stroke. A gentleman of the name of "Nipper", obviously disguised in liquor, was betting on one of the players, called "Sam". I was rather glad when Nipper and Sam fell out, and Sam hit Nipper over the head with the cue; but I was not glad when they came out with the intention of fighting, and wrangled for near upon three-quarters of an hour against my bed.

Then a drunken man came, and fell down on the other side of the calico, within two feet of me, and, being under the impression that he was lost in the bush, began singing out, "Coo'ee", as loud as he could. I suggested to him that he shouldn't make such a noise against a man's tent, whereat he cursed me, demanding what I meant by putting my tent in his way, and, receiving no answer, said that I was always at it.

And on the morrow we were on horseback once more, and, leaving all the dust and turmoil behind, were holding our way across the breezy plains towards the peaceful sunny stations of the west.

My Landladies*
Chapters of a Digger's Life

I

MRS MACKINNON

I have had so many landladies, and I have suffered first and last so very heavily from them, that I think (and Mr Bentley also thinks) I have a perfect right to be revenged on them. The most abominable part of the matter is, that I never had a landlady yet who was not transcendently virtuous and religious. I suppose that landladies are infinitely the most virtuous ladies in the whole world. I never met a landlady who was not; and yet—— Well. Let us take them in detail. Let us begin with Mrs Mackinnon.

The only fault I have to find with Mrs Mackinnon is that she was always drunk when she had the money; and that I, then a young man of twenty-five, used to attract too much attention from her. I happened to be enamoured of her eldest daughter, who never cared twopence for me. This gave rise to complications, and ultimately to a fight.

I must premise, however, that I am speaking of Australia, and that Mrs Mackinnon was an old convict, otherwise I shall never be understood. At the same time Bob Hart was a fool about the whole

*Reprinted from *Temple Bar*, XXXVI (October 1872): 371–90. This was the only one published—Kingsley apparently discontinued the series after this appeared.

matter. And I will swear there was not a man in the colony I was so loth to thrash.

It fell out just like this. (I beg you to understand that I never said one word to the young woman, beyond taking her to church. I hope it will be understood that *I never said anything to the young woman*.) The old woman said a good deal to me, however, a great amount of which might have been unsaid.

It all came out of the breaking up of the old Red Hill gang. We stayed on at the Red Hill long after every one else was gone. We were comfortable enough together, and on the whole did not do badly for a time.

There were about twenty-five of us altogether, men I mean, and we generally lived in pairs, in small tents. I lived in the same tent with an old bricklayer named Harris, a Londoner, and he worked with me, and on Saturday night used to come home extremely drunk, and have to be put to bed. Now getting drunk every Saturday night is a matter between a man and his conscience; but it is most emphatically a matter between a man and his mate. One Saturday night I kicked him out of the tent, and made him lie in the rain till he had cooled himself. I most emphatically was not going to have him raising Cain on me in the middle of the night, as drunk as an owl. I beg it to be understood that I speak of *him*, not of myself. Being unused to literary composition I must guard myself from misrepresentation. The only stimulant I ever indulged in at that time was cold tea.

After I pitched old Harris out of the tent he served me a completely new trick. Instead of coming home drunk, like a decent man, on Saturday night, he got afraid of me, and he used to sleep out all Sunday and come back in a crapulous state about twelve o'clock on Monday. So that I actually had to be let down the shaft (forty feet) by a neighbour before I could get to work. One Monday he never came at all, and I had to leave all the wash dirt in the drive. This does not seem much to you, I dare say, but at the same time you must remember that it was pretty near death for a drunken man to walk about on that lead among the deserted shafts. A man was safer in the light cavalry charge at Balaklava, which occurred just at that time.

This dreadful old man of the sea who had fastened himself on my back had an equally dreadful dog. I cannot describe all this dog's specialities, further than that he used diligently to howl all night. Also, when he came home drunk with his master, my dog Rover used to get him down and make night hideous. The number of times the silent Australian forest has seen me out in my shirt, bare-legged, separating those two dogs, with barefooted kicks, for which Rover cared not one penny, and which the other dog resented by biting my tendon Achilles—the number of times, I say, when I have exhibited my legs to the blacks who slept outside our tent I am unable to remember.

I am leading up to Mrs Mackinnon. I could not live with the old fellow Harris any longer. I only lived with him so long because he had a nose for gold like a hound. I believe every man has some speciality, and old Harris's speciality was gold. However, it could not continue. The end came in this way.

There were a great many Scotch on the Red Hill; and being a very thrifty people, they helped to build a church before the Anglicans, who came soon after. The church was of course Presbyterian, and I went the first Sunday; and Rover, my dog, followed: a fact I did not notice till I came to the church door. I saw many others with their dogs, for some of the Scotch shepherds had heard of the church being opened. One grey-headed old Scotchman who spoke to me told me that he had started at two o'clock in the morning and had walked eighteen miles to worship in the church of his fathers once more before he died. I told the glorious old fellow that I was an Episcopalian, but he liked me the better for that; the Scottish gentry mostly were, he said. Then I told him that I was an Englishman, and he said, "There'll be no Scotch and English in heaven". I went in with him and our dogs came also. I do not profess to be an extremely religious person, but the sensation of worshipping among one's fellow-men after an interval of three years would make any man sensitive and sentimental.

I am afraid that old memories of my father's church were crowding on me so strongly that my cheeks were wet when the first hymn was sung. The whole thing was destroyed by that tipsy old vagabond Harris. I could have killed him.

He not only came to church extremely drunk, but he brought his dog. Rover, who was as good as gold with the dear old Scotch shepherd's dogs, saw old Harris's dog and fell on him tooth and nail. The whole service was stopped, and I had to get Rover away, with angry glances from the congregation. I waited outside for Mackinnon; told him that I could live with old Harris no longer, and asked him if he could take me in to board.

Mackinnon asked me if I would step round and see his good wife. I stepped round. The first thing I did was to fall violently in love with Elsie Mackinnon as she opened the door, after which I asked her if her mother was at home.

She said that her mother was at home, but was lying down. I remarked that I had been sent by her father, and that I proposed to board and lodge with the family. She went away to her mother, and then I remarked that there were five young persons beside Elsie, who was about sixteen. I object to children as a rule, considering them to be a mistake; but had there been fifty it would have been the same to me. Elsie was there, and I knew nothing whatever about Bob Hart. If mother Mackinnon had known the state of my feelings she might have doubled her charges. She did not.

It is to be remembered that nothing whatever had passed between Elsie and I further than her opening the door, and the dialogue which is written above.

I discoursed with the eldest boy Alick, a boy of thirteen, who, as I afterwards found, kept the whole family in bread, besides supplying his mother in liquor, by what is called "fossicking" in the creek for wasted gold. I liked the boy very much, but I liked his sister better.

In a few minutes Mrs Mackinnon came in. I discovered afterwards that Alick had got a twenty pennyweight piece on the creek, and that his mother had been having a big drink on it. That, as I see matters now, accounts for the huskiness of her voice, and also for the fact that her petticoat came down during our interview, and that she removed it without the smallest symptoms of discomposure. Young as I was amongst landladies, it seemed to me that this accident was of frequent occurrence; and looking round on the faces of the assembled family, I saw no expressions of surprise or dismay whatsoever. They were used to it.

"Well, young man," she said, "what's up."

"Your good gentleman, madam," I replied, "thought that you could take me in to board and lodge. May I venture to ask your terms?"

"Three pound a week," she said; which was a pound over the ordinary price. But I loved Elsie and I liked the poor boy, and so I said "Yes."

Mrs Mackinnon instantaneously borrowed four pounds sterling. With the one-pound notes in one hand, and her petticoat in the other, she went back to bed; and immediately afterwards I saw the youngest—but one was sent across to the public-house for a bottle of brandy.

I went and fetched away my kit from the old tent in a dray. I sold the dear old hole I had worked so long for five ounces. When I went the old Red Hill gang was broken up entirely. I was the first deserter, and all the others came away. I wonder where they are now.

The day I took possession of my new home I noticed a great many things. I saw that Mrs Mackinnon was given to drinking, and I also saw that the children were perfectly aware of the fact, but that they looked on it as a disease, which they had not caught, and that they were quite respectful to their mother in spite of it.

The place where they lived was a very large tent, almost a house, down by the river Avoca. The good children had nearly filled it with birds. Mary, the second girl, took me into her confidence about some of the birds. The magpie (who was allowed to go loose) was most emphatically determined to kill the budgery ghahs, who were in a cage. The lady budgery ghah had been setting hard on a lump of white sugar for three weeks, under the impression that it would develop into a parrakeet. At this point the opossum nimbly ran up my back ankd sat on my head, while the magpie began digging into my heels. Mrs Mackinnon, hearing me yell, dashed out and kissed me; then the opossum bit her in the nose, while the magpie pegged away at *her* legs as hard as he could go.

I don't want to praise that bird, because he will probably read this, and he might get too conceited. But that was the cleverest bird to dig into your heels when you thought that he was miles away which I ever saw. As for the bird's language I simply cannot write it down. I have offered specimens of it to Mr Bentley, and he says that it will *not* do.

The cockatoo also was an extremely clever bird. He was not noticeable when I arrived. I put my things right, and then I sat down to afternoon tea. I must call your attention to the fact that this was the day *after* I had settled the bargain, and that Mrs Mackinnon was comparatively sober.

I came in and saw my bed, then I had my tea. Then I sat down on a stool, and Mrs Mackinnon asked me my name, I said "Dick". She at once burst into tears, said that she had lost a son of that name fifteen years before; and concluded by requesting me to step across to the public-house and get her a pint of gin. I did so, and she kissed me. Soon afterwards she went and laid down.

The pretty boy came to me and seemed to take to me very much. Elsie brought her work and chatted. She said that she thought she should like me. I most emphatically thought that I should like her. The boy Alick admired a nugget ring I had; I gave it to him at once, and he wondered. How would poor Alick have wondered had he known that I would have given the price of it ten times over for the right to give it to his sister?

I was sitting smoking my pipe and talking to Elsie when I felt something crawling up my back. Elsie said, "Be quiet, it is only the native bear", and for one word of her delicate voice I was perfectly silent. The gridiron of St Quentin would have silenced me if she had said the word. The bear got on my head, and I tried to think that I liked it (for her sake, you will understand), when the opossum ran up my back and gave the bear a savage bite behind, and then ran down, knocked up the tom cat, and had really, as Elsie said, a splendid turn-up with him. The bear remained sitting on the top of my head. He had made a perfectly stupid effort to fight the opossum, and Elsie told him that he was very good. I wish that he had been good anywhere else; but Elsie said he was good, and so I thought he was.

Suddenly the cockatoo saw the bear on my head, and down she came like an eagle. She fixed her claws in the bear's head, and the bear held on to my hair. Elsie laughed. Alick tried to mend matters, but only succeeded in getting bitten by the bear and the cockatoo at one and the same time. The magpie and the opossum had a beautiful turn-up, (the bombardment of Montmedy was an inferior business), but that was only witnessed by Tommy, who said that the magpie had the best of the opossum.

All these small matters were brought to an end by Mrs Mackinnon rushing into the tent, hitting me violently over the head with a broom (composed of *epacris kennedya* on a stick of *eucalyptus dumosa*, and that is no joke, I can tell you, leaving alone the botanical names). She hit me vertically on the head with a broom, which, if properly named, would have made a new quarrel between Ayrton and Hooker. She accused me of making love to her daughter, which was perfectly false, because I happened to be opening ground by making love to her daughter's brother, a very common procedure; in my opinion the best way to go to work. We will let that pass. I must go on to tell about my first night with the Mackinnons, of the fight with Bob Hart, and of the end of the whole business.

When Mrs Mackinnon had hit me over the head with the *eucalyptus epacris* broom, she seized me by the throat and offered to shove me into the middle of next week. I offering no objection at all, she cuffed me a little about the head and burst into tears. She then asked for my arm to take her to bed. I gave her my arm to bed. I beg to state that there was no impropriety of any sort or kind in this. Mrs Mackinnon's way of going to bed was not exactly primitive, because she never took a rag off her body. The most proper man of these times might have seen her to bed. I, quite as proper a man as any other, have seen her to bed a dozen times. She used to put the brandy bottle under the pillow (*on her own side*) hoist herself on the bed, and immediately, with a rapidity which would surprise you, sleep the sleep of the just.

This was all very pleasant for herself. For her really good husband it was not so very pleasant.

I and the boy Alick sat up very late. I tell the fair truth when I say that I loved Alick. I think that if Alick's mother had been more sober Alick might be taking his place in London to-day. Meanwhile I was making love to him to get at his sister. I am, however, only at my first night.

Mackinnon came home, and he sent the boy to bed. "Will you mind sleeping with Alick for a night or so?" he said, wearily. As I most decidedly intended to marry Alick's sister, I did not object to sleeping with her brother. So I consented, and asked him if he would sit with me a little, and have a pipe and a glass of grog. It so happened that I had a very little rum in a case bottle. I had also any amount of tobacco. Mackinnon said to me that he would have some, and I fetched it out.

Mackinnon was one of the most astounding fellows I ever met. I want to say this of him. He would help any man he had ever seen. He would put up with conduct from his wife which no other man would suffer. And yet that man was the most transcendent and outrageous liar with whom I ever met.

I am only telling the plain truth about the man. He romanced like a novelist. No one ever believed him. I had been warned about this, and I honestly believe that one of the few times he talked the truth was when he spoke to me that night. Everything he said was confirmed afterwards. Alick said to me, "You must not believe father except when mother is in question"; and the boy was right.

"Dick," said Mackinnon, "I'm off."

"Where are you going?"

"Fiery Creek. I can't stand this. The old girl is drunk every night."

"*Every* night!" I said.

"You judge for yourself."

I began to think that I had made a mistake in moving from old Harris, who, at all events, was available from Tuesday until Saturday.

"I'm off, Dick," said Mackinnon; "keep a hand on the house for me. I want to get to the bush, and there she will be away from the liquor. Dick, my boy, I should hang myself if it was not for the children. You have had a fine education, take care of the children.

Take care of Elsie."

Then I made my grandest *bêtise*. "Mackinnon," I said, "I will do everything you ask me if you will make me your father-in-law."

He was utterly puzzled.

"In twenty-four hours," I said, "I have fallen in love with your daughter."

"Which one?"

"Elsie."

"The devil. Can't you fall in love with Mary?"

"No."

"Bob Hart is engaged to Elsie," said he. Then he put his pack on his shoulder and departed. For me, I stayed on, and I forgot Bob Hart. I licked Bob Hart, but Elsie loved him all the better afterwards. And the worst of it was, I loved her more than ever.

One of the most astonishing things was that Alick was my second in this fight. We, however, had uglier work to the fore. Our bitter trouble was approaching.

I had money. Bob Hart had no money at all. We fought about Elsie, and I saw that the girl loved him, and so I moved no more in the matter. I told him that I would not, and I never did. We were perfectly good friends; in fact, fast friends. I did not know in any way that he had won Elsie's heart, or I would never have thought of her. I was, however, left practically in charge of the family.

Bob Hart was one of the old Red Hill men. And one Sunday he and I and Alick went shooting to the mountain. We shot everything we could see, and then we lay down in the grass.

The boy Alick said: "When you marry Mary, Dick, we will have a farm here, and will all be happy."

"Who told you that I was going to marry Mary, young one?"

"You are a fool if you don't," said Alick.

Bob Hart said, "I am sorry we had that quarrel about Elsie, old boy; but for some reason she likes me better than she does you. I can't think why."

"Let bygones be bygones," I said. "I am quite well now."

"Quite well?"

"Quite well."

"Dick," said Hart, "I wish I could get some money to keep her. Your rent and Alick's fossicking is not enough to keep the old woman and the children. I wish I could get on some lay."

"Ah, that would be a grand thing," said Alick. And the boy laid his head on my breast; and I thought, what would I have given to have his sister's head here three weeks agone. I would not have given twopence for it now, except, of course, as a delicate attention on the part of the young lady, which I should probably have resented, and which Bob Hart most certainly would at the risk of another thrashing.

For I had by this time written a most beautiful ballad on the subject of Elsie's infidelity (she had never been unfaithful, but that is nothing in poetry); and when a man comes to that there is not much the matter with him. I had got over the business; and although as a general rule I think that boys are the greatest nuisances under the sun, yet I liked Alick better than either of his sisters. When you find a real good boy, with the pluck and sagacity of a man, he makes a fine friend. To say one word of anything wrong to such a boy is to call our Lord's curse on you: "It were better that a millstone were hanged round your neck, and you were cast into the sea."

If it mattered, Alick was violently in love himself. He told me of it as we lay awake one night. He was going to marry Jenny Bart, or perish. He did so marry that young lady, at that time eleven years of age; when they married he was seventeen and she fifteen.

Well, I am to a certain extent travelling out of the record. On that summer day's shooting we came to a resolution which altered all our lives.

The day was nearly done, and the sun was blazing on the highest summit of the Australian Pyrenees, when I began speaking.

"Alick," I said, "you were down Dickson's Hole when they got that twenty-pennyweight piece, and lost the lead?"

"Yes, Dick."

"Dry?"

"Yes, Dick."

"Which way did the brown sand go?"

"The brown sand came to an end, Dick; we came to pink dirt, which led up."

"Did they keep to the bottom?"

"No, Dick; they lost the colour* and held upwards."

"Did they move any boulders?" I asked.

"No; they funked. Their last tub was three pennyweights, and they would not go on. Then came the Canadian rush, and nobody bottomed."

"Alick and Hart," I said, "I am of opinion that we could drop down on it. What was the depth, Alick? I was not in it."

*These details, though intelligible by an old Australian gold miner, are barely in place here. The "colour" means only the glimmer of the gold.

"It was between ninety-seven and a hundred feet," said Alick.

"There was no water?" I asked once more.

"Not a drain," said Alick.

"Let us have a turn at it, my boys," I said.

"That is all very well," said Hart; "I like the idea immensely; but who is to find the money? I have none."

"I have got money," I said; "the difficulty is about men. My proposal is to go a hundred-and-twenty yeards in front of the lost lead, and get a prospecting claim.* What men are there at the Red Hill?"

"Devil a one except the mad old Frenchman; they are all off to Fiery Creek," said Hart.

"We shall want a fourth man," I said. "We must be quick; we must see the colour before we get the double claim. I must get a fourth man (I count you as one, Alick), and a man we can trust. You are not strong enough for the windlass with two heavy men like Hart and I. I wish your father was here."

"Try my mother," said Alick, suddenly.

I replied, "A heavy man does not care to come up on the rope with a woman at the windlass."

"My father and mother hit the fifteen-foot lead at Daisy Hill," said Alick; "and if you keep her from the drink she is as good as any man."

"That is so," said Hart.

And I had an interview with her. She was to share for her husband; Alick was to have a fourth share, just like a man. (The boy's powers of sinking were splendid.) Mrs Mackinnon was not to touch liquor; or in case she did, was to forfeit her share. The two men and the boy were to run the shaft down, and I was to find the money.

I went out on the Monday morning and pegged out the claim. Mrs Mackinnon had been drinking on the Saturday, and was a little crapulous now. I brought her a bottle of beer, and made her drink half of it. She thanked me very heartily, and then she went and moved my pegs.

"My dear madam!" I said.

"I am absolutely certain," she said. "Pray do not interfere. If people would only notice things for themselves, they would see that when a lead passes into a deep lead it follows water. The larger box trees only grow with water at their roots."

---

*These details about the old gold-digging laws may be uninteresting to the English reader, but to the Australian they show that this story is true.

I submitted. The woman had found one lead; she might find another.

We did not trouble her much that day; she helped us to get the windlass on, and then went home. If one could have kept the drink from that woman, there were few women like her.

We three—the two men and the boy—were down fifteen feet that day. Elsie used to bring us our dinner for the next eight days. Mrs Mackinnon worked like a horse, but she had no word from her husband.

We were extremely anxious to keep the shaft very straight and square; this was necessary in case we should hit the water. Therefore I never cut any foot-holes, and we always came up by the windlass. We were forty feet down, and Mrs Mackinnon was at the windlass. It was dinner-time, and she sang out to me to come up.

I said, "Tell Hart to tackle-to, and I will come."

She said, "Hart is gone home, and Alick also. Put your foot in, and I will have you up."

I submitted. It was a rather nervous thing to be drawn up by a lady forty feet; but I hitched the hook round the rope, put my left foot in, and Mrs Mackinnon fetched me up as well as a Life Guardsman could.

"Well done, old girl!" I said.

She immediately kissed me. I was rather afraid that she had been at the brandy bottle, but I did her an injustice. She began crying as we went home, and I asked the reason.

She immediately sat down among a bed of orchises and grevilleas, and cried louder.

"I have drove my old man out of the house with the drink and my going on, and I can't get no word from him any how; I am a disgrace to my daughters and to him. I wish I was dead."

"My good soul," I said, "you are an honour to your family now. How many women have your pluck and resolution! Give up that terrible drink and we will all be happy."

"I've give up the drink," she said, rising; "but it is too late now. I have been a bad wife to him."

Ninety feet and no water at all; one hundred and four feet, and no water, and yet Mrs Mackinnon had an idea that the sign of gold would be water. She was utterly wrong in her calculations, the whole thing was a piece of transcendent luck.

One hundred and ten feet, and a boulder as large as a decanter, packed in soft greasy clay and gravel. More boulders, ever growing larger, and at last one as big as a bucket. Dinner-time was come, and

Mrs Mackinnon and I were alone: she at the windlass, I at the pick one hundred feet below her. I called up the shaft to her:

"Old woman, I believe I am bottoming. Mind this boulder, for it will hardly go into the bucket."

I was very anxious, for it would hardly go into the bucket, and if it slipped out I was in all likelihood a dead man. I saw her haul it out dexterously into the bright sunshine, and then I looked down at the place it had come from.

Its removal had discovered a layer of gravel the colour of pink blotting-paper, I could see that, although it was very dark at that depth, and you never or seldom use a candle in sinking at these small depths. I called up the shaft:

"Old woman, have you got a bit of candle"?

"No, I'll cut and fetch a bit from the Chinese store."

"Do."

How my heart beat while she was gone! She was not very long, however, and I amused myself in my deadly anxiety by gently turning up the pink gravel with my pick. The old woman dexterously lowered me a lighted candle-end, and when it came down I looked at my work. If any man at that moment had offered me £4000 for the hole I should have refused it; it was worth much more as it turned out afterwards.

I put some of the stuff (not much, for I was a heavy load myself for the old woman) into the bucket, and then taking it in my hand I told my landlady to pull me up. She accomplished it splendidly, and when she had me safe "to bank", as the colliers say, she asked:

"Are we bottomed?"

I pointed to the gravel at the bottom of the bucket. It was simply blazing with gold, and my hands were trembling violently as I turned it over silently (for I was unable to speak) and showed it to her.

She uttered a cry like a hyena. She threw herself on the ground, and clutched at the grass with her fingers. "Oh, my old man! Oh, my old man! The best old man that ever lived. Now that I have driven you to death by my wicked ways this wealth has come on us."

The wild fit went off very soon, and a silent one came on. She seemed to me dazed and stunned, as I was myself to a certain degree; but she was thinking. She took the bucket and walked home with me; and half-way home she turned to me and said:

"Dick."

"Yes, Mrs Mackinnon."

Dare I tell the story? Well, I think I dare.

"Dick," said Mrs Mackinnon, "he was very good to me." No, I cannot go on. Aposiopesis is the only thing for it.

"After it all," continued Mrs Mackinnon, having told one of the saddest stories I ever heard, "when he was so good and kind (remember I told him every thing before we were married), then I behaved so that it was hard for him to keep a house over his head. Dick, I want you to do something."

"Well?"

"Trust Bob Hart and I and Alick with the hole, and go and bring my old man back to me. You are so clever, and you have been in the police; do go, Dick, and trust us."

I should have not trusted Mrs Mackinnon a month before; but I trusted her now. I went to the camp and announced the discovery, getting a double claim. I then made Alick and Hart move up a small tent to the hole and sleep there, then I went to the farm where my horse was and got him, and assuming bush dress, so different from diggers' dress, I put on breeches and boots, and went after Mackinnon. I thought I should be about three days; I was much longer. So long, indeed, that I had another landlady or two before I came back.

Mac was not at the Fiery Creek, I found that out in a day amidst a population of eighty thousand; he had gone on, it was said, to Ararat, then a place of no significance. I was puzzled at this; but I was forced to stay a night at the Fiery Creek, and as I knew that Mrs Primrose was there, and that I should probably get a severe thrashing from her if I went to any other house than her own (that was the way in which she showed her affection to Primrose, and her affection for me was most notorious), I went there.

Mrs Primrose was an extremely short and ferocious ex-convict woman, with a face like a prize-fighter's, and a voice like a costermonger's. She could thrash her husband; her husband could thrash Jack Simmonds; and he could give me quite as good as I brought him. Neither of us ever knew which was best man. If you will reckon up this, you will see that I had the strongest reasons for entertaining the very highest esteem and respect for Mrs Primrose.

When I had put up my horse and arrived at the bar, I arrived at a somewhat unfortunate moment.

Mr Dennis Moriarty, not having the fear of the priest before his eyes, had got himself disguised in liquor, and finding it pleasant had determined in his own mind to stay so. Mr Primrose declined that arrangement, on the ground that he was a married man with a wife and five children; that Mrs Moriarty had always been a good wife to him, and that his duty as a man was to take his earnings home to his wife, and not make a beast of himself with them. This advice coming from an ex-convict publican, backed up by his ex-convict wife, struck me as extremely good, but Mr Moriarty did not see his way to it all. His thesis was, that a publican was bound to serve out "licker" as long as it was paid for.

Mrs Primrose traversed all his arguments by saying that she would see—never mind what Mrs Primrose was prepared to see— before she would draw another drop for him. She reiterated the fact that Biddy Moriarty was a good woman for a Tipperary woman (I must mention that the Connaught Irish are as unpopular as the northern and midland Irish are popular in those parts), and that she would be no party to his getting drunk at her house. Mr Moriarty was ill-advised enough to call her an "Ould Sydney hand".

That means death or near it. If you ever wander to Australia, my dear sir, pray never, in general company, speak of Sydney or Hobart Town. It is not polite. It is a *casus belli*. Mr Moriarty, a most excellent gentleman, was ill-advised. The moment he said this Mrs Primrose told her husband to turn him out. To hear was to obey with Mr Primrose; he dashed out of the house and had Mr Moriarty down in an instant. But Mr Moriarty was a most excellent fighting man, and the Sydney man was no match for him at all. Mr Moriarty gave a most admirable and excellent account of Mr Primrose. I never saw a better account given of any man in my life. At the last rally I was laughing, with my saddle and bridle over my left arm, and the defeat of Mr Primrose was so very emphatic that I was knocked over in his fall, and found myself sitting, in tight cord breeches, on a heap of broken lemonade bottles in a corner.

"Primrose, with eye like a violet,
  Arose from the earth with his red rose wet."

(Shade of Shelley, forgive me!) Mr Moriarty was in a triumphant state and wanted to fight *me* (I had been doing nothing except laughing) when Mrs Primrose said to her husband, "You old fool, there was a time when you could fight as well as any man. Here, catch hold of the child and let me go in at him."

Mr Primrose took the child, and Mrs Primrose went in at Mr Moriarty. He was out of that house in less than two minutes.

When she had put Mr Moriarty out, she took the baby from her husband, and gave him a kiss. (I am writing down things exactly as I saw them). Then she turned to me, and said:

"My dear Mr Blank, I am so sorry that you should have come at such a time; but I believe I would have given it you as bad as I did him if you had *dared* to go anywhere else. Come in, my dear, and be comfortable; it is so pleasant to have a gentleman in the place. You must not fight, my boy. Why on earth did you turn up with Bill Simmonds, he as near as twopence got the best of you.''

"Oh, it was only a boxing-match," I said. "There was no quarrel.''

You finish your catechism," she said. "You fought Bob Hart.''

"We are mates now," I said.

"Hah! you will get overhauled some day. You are too quarrelsome. You will have a turn-up with me. What right has a gentleman to go fighting?''

"We fight at our public schools."

"Yes, but not when you are grown up men. Come in. Geordie'' (to the barman), "what beds have we?''

"None, Mrs Primrose.''

"Then turn Dick Allen out, and say that he can't sleep here any longer. I want the bed for Mr Blank.''

"My dear madam," I said, "this is rather sharp practice.''

"If you would like to manage the establishment yourself," she said; "my old man will sell it for four thousand pounds. If you are not prepared to take it, do not interfere.''

The splendid and terrible old savage cooked my supper for me with her own hands. It was a very good supper, and I told her so.

"I learnt cooking," she said, "when I was serving my time. Have you seen Mrs Mackinnon lately?''

"I have just left her.''

"Is the report true that you and her boy have hit it.''

"It is perfectly true.''

"Why are you away from the hole, then?'' she asked, sharply.

"Because Mrs Mac has asked me to find her husband, who has bolted.''

"I thought it would be so," she said. "Primrose, come here.''

Primrose came and sat down. "Prim," she said, "What would you do if I was to take to drinking?''

"Cut my throat," was the prompt answer.

"Now, Prim, old boy, you don't fight as well as you did.''

"I'm fifty-three," said Mr Primrose, apologetically.

"Yes, old man. Never mind that; I'll fight for you. But now I want to talk to you about the Mackinnons. Mrs Mac has taken to the drink, and Mac has bolted.''

"Mac was a good man," said Primrose; "I have heard tell he was religious, as the Scotch mainly are at times. What more?''

I have omitted some conversation which I had with Mrs Primrose; a conversation which put her in possession of the facts, and the unnecessary recapitulation of which would be wearisome.

Mrs Primrose said, "This young gentleman, who for some reason has come to Australia, and for other reasons has chosen to leave the bush, has been living with the Mackinnons. Old man," she added, putting her hand round his neck, "they have hit the lead on the Avoca, down in the four-mile flat."

"I ought to be off in an hour," said Mr Primrose.

"So you shall; but hear me say something else. This young gentleman has left the hole in trust with Bob Hart, the old woman and Alick, and has come away to find Mac. Why has he done so?"

"Because he is a young gentleman, I suppose," said the convict Primrose.

"Spoke like my own husband," said the convict woman. "Give us a kiss, old boy. We must find Mac."

"I can't," said Mr Primrose. "I saw him a day or two ago, and he said everywhere that he was going to Ararat. But I know that he never went there."

"Which way did he go?" I asked.

"He went towards Mitchell's," said Mr Primrose. "Kelly the trooper, you mind him, you were a comrade of his at Richmond; he told me that he see him going through the bush towards Mitchell's. And says he to Kelly, I am going to Mitchell's, he says, for a job of shearing. And Kelly laughed, and he says, 'You've been on the burst my lad, shearing is over this three months.' And Mac says 'Life has been over this three years.' And in my opinion, Mr Blank, if you want your man you had better ride to Mitchell's at once. I shall go to the Avoca in an hour. Have you got any dirt, sir?"

I had and showed him some.

"And you have left that hole with old mother Mac, Bob Hart, and the boy!" He said, "Why, it is three ounces to the tub!"

Still I rode across to Mitchell's to try and find my man. I was deeply anxious about it. As it happened, I had made my fortune during my absence twice over. That I will tell about afterwards.

Mitchell was out, at which I was disappointed, because he as a magistrate might have helped me. His housekeeper, Mrs Bryon, was in, however, and my horse was lame, and the grooms were both out, and when they came home were totally unable to get a fresh horse for me. And so Mrs Bryon possessed herself of my person, put me in my dear old bedroom, and fed me on the fat of the land. The grooms were her sons, and all in the conspiracy. There were above fifty horses on the run, but I was not allowed one of them. I had submitted to Mrs Bryon before, but had fought her on the subject of my kangaroo. She was then my servant. Now she was my landlady I submitted to her entirely.

I was nearly three days there, and on the third I was so worried and anxious that I told Mrs Bryon that I should like to lay down my head and die there in my happy old home. She asked me "Why did I ever leave it?" and I said "I am sure I don't know."

But there was no news about Mac—none whatever. I was always considered to be in possession there whenever I went, because the chief overseer, while possessed of every Christian virtue, was not a gentleman, and yet was so far a gentleman that he would not show. My time was getting short. I must go. When my landlady, Mrs Bryon, came flying in and cried, "Oh, Mr Blank, the judge is coming!"

Bryon, came flying in and cried, "Oh, Mr Blank, the judge is coming!"

I thought she meant the day of judgment, and ran into the verandah to look eastward. It was only Judge Hundford coming on circuit with a couple of troopers behind him. Instead of being frightened, however, I told her to get lunch. Which she did.

I was cool with the judge, as I did not like him; and finding that both his troopers were cadets, I made them come in and sit with us. He was very cross at first, and Mrs Bryon was scared. But as I pointed out to the judge privately that in all probability the two young gentlemen would be lieutenants in two months, he quite saw his way to this arrangement.

The judge was new to the colony, and was nervous about my opening the French window and admitting my old emeu, who, I regret to say, pecked him on the top of his head, and proposed to line a nest with his hair. He did not like me at all, because he did not understand my position, and the reason why I treated him *de haut en bas*. I was perfectly civil to him on the whole, however, because I wanted to get something out of him. I thought of champagne, and made my present landlady, Mrs Bryon, get a bottle of it, and the judge drank it all up while the cadets went out to their horses.

"Can you tell me, your honour," I asked, "anything about a man called Mackinnon?"

"Yes," said the judge. "He has headed this new gang of bushrangers!"

In vino veritas!

"What Christian name?" I asked.

He pulled out his papers. "Christian name, Colin. Age 48. Wife took to drinking. Previous character good. Left the Avoca three months ago. Is that your man?"

"I fear it is, your honour."

"Do you know his wife?"

"Yes, your honour."

"She should keep from drink, my dear sir. A man who drinks is one thing, but when a woman takes to it her virtue is not safe. We look at these things in a practical manner, you see."

I made my *congé* to him and asked for my horse. George Bryon was there on another.

"Where are you going, George?"

"He is going with you," said his mother. "You are not fit to take care of yourself."

"I'll give him good work," I said, and we rode away.

The last of the dear old place. The very last, except in dreams. The old court-yard, and the judge, bare-headed, beside Mrs Bryon. Behind them the emeu, pawking and gandering about. Behind the emeu the troopers, tall, blue, and majestic, waving their hands to me; behind them a wilderness of petunias and geraniums; beyond this, the forest. Oh, the Australian life! how can one exist in Europe after it?

I rode back to the Avoca very fast, but my news was before me. George Bryon pointed it out to me first, in a large placard on a large tree.

"£100 Reward.

V.R.

"Whereas Colin Mackinnon and others are now ranging the bush in the Wunmera district; and whereas the said Colin Mackinnon has killed no less than two policemen, and Lieutenant Moore has been wounded by him; a reward of one hundred pounds is offered for his body alive or dead. Any trooper capturing him will be at once promoted to sergeant. Any cadet to lieutenant."

I hardly dared go home. When I got there I found only Alick, Elsie, and the children.

"Where is mother?" I whispered to Alick.

"Gone after him."

"Alone?"

"Ah. She said she would put a knife in me if I came. We have taken the bottom off the hole, and it came to nearly a thousand pounds. I have got your share. We must have another partner now. Mother is gone to fetch father out of it. Will they hang him?"

"I can't tell; it is a horrible business."

"Can you do nothing?"

"Nothing except work the hole. Your father will be brought to trial, and we shall want every penny we can scrape together."

George Bryon came into the concern with the greatest pleasure, and we set to work with this horrible cloud over us.

It was like quarrying gold more than anything else. We netted an amazing sum of money; the boy Alick, who was allowed full shares, got £2500 when we washed up. Elsie, who was our mistress now, said that she would go down into the drive, and take all she could see. We said yes, and lowered her with a knife in her hand. I can see her pretty head swinging round and round as she turned into the darkness of the shaft. When we pulled her up again she had gold, which she sold to the bank of Sydney for £56. We were terribly prosperous.

The lead was narrow, and by some wondrous stroke of good luck Mr Primrose had hit on the lead in front of us. So he never troubled us by driving into our ground. Meanwhile Bob Hart and I had made a fortune in another way.

Part of the land close to the lead was for sale, months and months before. We had bought it, he only buying 7 acres, I 640 acres. A whole township was erected on our land, and one Saturday night we quietly served notices, through a policeman, that every store and grog shop was to be removed. They paid us £7000 for leave to stay, and Mrs Primrose said that if she had not been my old landlady she would have broken my head. She put the baby down, and gave Bob Hart a black eye, but she never touched me; and, as a fact, I sent their money back, for they were good people, say what you will.

Still there was no word whatever from the Mackinnons. Months went on, and the weather got wild. The Avoca had not run from one water-hole to another for two years, but now it began to run, and more than run, to flood. The lead was being nearly worked out, and the cold bitter June of the southern hemisphere was settling down upon us. We had worked out our gold, and sold it. We were rich, and George Bryon was blessing his stars for the day when he came away with me.

We were all round the fire. The wind was whistling through the hut overhead, and the rain was pouring steadily; it was fearfully dull, and we had not heart for a song, or for anything cheerful.

The door was opened, and Mrs Mackinnon stepped in, wet, draggled, and worn, more like a ghost than a human being.

So changed, as I noticed in a moment. Alick and Elsie were at her feet in one instant, but she looked at George Bryon.

"Who is that young man?" she said hoarsely.

"A friend of mine, landlady," I said.

"To be trusted?"

"George! George!" I said, "you would never betray us!"

"I am not a dog, Mr Blank," said George, with a smile.

"I will trust you all," said Mrs Mackinnon. "Black death light on you if you betray me. I have promised him that I will never touch liquor again. And I have got him away from that gang; and the *Benjamin Elkin* sails from Port Fairy next week, and we could have gone right there, only the poor old boy wanted to see his children again before he went to South America. He wanted to see Elsie, and give her his blessing before she was married. Give me some bread."

Elsie, shaking her brave bosom with emotion, got her some. My landlady ate it like a wolf.

"Ah! I have been a bad mother to you, girl; but Bob Hart will be a good husband. Well, my old man wants to see his children again, but there are police here, and he did not venture across the creek until I had seen things square. So I came across the old boy, and what you have got to do some of you, my dears, is to go out and put the police off the lay till after daybreak."

Alick looked at me quietly, and left the room. What is human morality? Why did I, a man who would risk my life in defending a policeman, actually kiss that boy the next evening when I found that there was not a policeman to be found for the whole day within several miles of the Avoca? What masterly fiction did he invent! One thing is certain, however, he got rid of the police. One trooper was subsequently found a week afterwards wandering about on the Murray at a distance of two hundred miles from his head-quarters, and had an acrimonious and personal squabble with the Right Honourable Mr Childers because Mr Childers declined to give him promotion for distinguished services. The Right Hon. Hugh Eardley Childers did not see his way to it.

But my poor landlady, she was very wet, and she saw that the Avoca was flooding. She must get to her old man in the morning, and they would go away together. "I have ruined him, Dick," she said to me; "but we have made it up now. I'll be faithful and true to him. I want to know what money we have to take for our share."

"I suppose about three thousand pounds," I said.

"Can you give me two hundred?"

"I will not give you a farthing until you have changed your clothes," I said.

"I'll do it," she said; "the old man has money, but it is not good money—not well come by. Elsie, take me in and change my clothes. And, Dick, you must write *your* name on the back of every note you give me."

I gave her two hundred pounds in notes with my name on the back, and leaving her with Elsie I went to sleep.

But not for long. I was used to the whispering of the summer wind in the acacias, and its pleasant passage over the grass. I was used to the strident chirp of the cicada, and to the illimitable clanjamfray of ten opossums backed up by twenty native cats (*en passant*, as it has nothing whatever to do with the matter, I may remark that you can actually get used to barrel organs by a certain mental process). I was used to every sort of bush sound, but this night I heard a new one: the death-note of my poor old landlady.

A low continuous hiss, which sometimes swelled into a roar. I got out of bed and looked forth. The black fellows had told me that this happened sometimes, but I never believed them. The gentle Avoca was in furious flood. There was a quarter of a mile of raging water before me. As day dawned I saw that the river had risen thirty feet.

Hush! let us be short over such things. It is as plain to me now as the ghastly rattle of Sedan. I went out and looked at the awful rolling waters. On the other wise I saw a solitary horseman splashing across the meadows. I waved him back, but he took no notice and came on. I felt a hand on my shoulder—it was that of my landlady, Mrs Mackinnon.

"It's my old man coming to meet me," she said; "better to meet like this. Come, darling, come to me."

One great log, about one hundred feet long, was still unmoved by the flood. My landlady ran out to the end of it and held up her arms like a cross.

I knew what would happen; any bushman would know. Mackinnon rode straight on towards her, and got into the stream. In a moment the horse was off its legs, and in the terrible current was upset, carrying Mackinnon under it. I saw the four feet of the horse in the air for a moment, and then I saw Mackinnon trying to swim towards his wife. Then she jumped off the log and tried to clutch him, and then they were both in one another's arms, and then two more ruined souls, loving each other almost to madness, went down the wild stream to death.

PART 4

Australian Reviews and Articles on Exploration

A Successful Exploration through the Interior of Australia*

A Successful Exploration through the Interior of Australia. From the Journals of W.J. Wills. Edited by his Father. 8vo. London. Bentley. 1863.

In September, 1845, Charles Sturt, up to that time the most successful of Australian explorers, reached a point in the interior of Australia, which can only be represented to the reader by the formula, long. 138 15 ′31 ″E.; lat. 24 40 ′00 ″; or, in other words, as far as we can make out, with considerable care, a point, roughly speaking, thirty miles north-east of the furthest known bend of Eyre's Creek; and some thirty miles south-west by west of the place known in the book under review as "Boochas Rest".

"Grass and water," he says, "had both failed, nor could I see the remotest chance of any change in the character of the country. It was clear, indeed, that until rain should fall, it was perfectly impracticable. I felt it would be endangering the lives of those who were with me." And Sturt looked to the north-west at sundown, and went home, and went blind. He had failed for the first time. But his reputation was so great, his previous discoveries had been so vast and so astonishing (surpassing anything done in this century, Livingstone's discoveries, perhaps, excepted) that people said to one another, "Where Sturt has failed it is no use to try". And so for fifteen years the map of Australia presented an enormous blank of

*Reprinted from *The Reader* I (21 February 1863): 183–84.

nearly eighteen hundred miles square, with one little thin line running about one-third of the way across, the end of which was marked "Sturt's Furthest, 1845".

And so matters stood for fifteen years. Sturt's furthest was Sturt's furthest, and that was the end of it. But in 1860 the map of Australia was strangely altered. A fresh comet had come blazing through space, leaving his orbit clearly marked. Stuart had got on horseback with four comrades, had passed 300 miles to the west of Sturt's furthest, and had stopped and turned when he was 750 miles to the north-west of it. And old Australians met one another at the street corners in London, and said "Do you believe it? Did you ever? Who could have thought it?"

Almost simultaneously with Stuart's expedition, an expedition was started from Melbourne, with the intention of penetrating due north from the city to the Gulf of Carpentaria. The *spécialités* of this expedition were, that camels were to be used, and that the whole business was, by previous arrangement, to be the most shamefully blundering piece of mismanagement since the Walcheren expedition. The history of this glorious and successful expedition,— successful in spite of the utter incapacity of nearly all those employed in it, and the hesitation and carelessness of a sort of Aulic council of a committee in Melbourne,—is contained in the volume under review.

The command of the expedition was given to a brave and enterprising, but hot-tempered and injudicious, inspector of police, by name O'Hara Burke. The second place was given to Mr Landells, who had succeeded in persuading the committee that the camels would die without him (he had brought them from India), who quarrelled with Mr Burke, and left the expedition before it was out of the settled districts; and the third to William John Wills, the subject of this book, decidedly the best man in the expedition, a young surveyor from Totnes, in Devonshire.

The doctors selected were, a Dr Beckler, evidently a German, of whom we know nothing, save that he is described as utterly unfit for his post, and that he resigned with Mr Landells; and poor old Ludwig Becker, who actually lay down and died before they were beyond the settlement. It was cruelty to ask him to go. Were there no gallant young surgeons, fresh from the hall and college, in the billiard-room at the Union? Melbourne must be strangely changed if there were not. Young fellows with courage, strength, and good-humour enough to take them anywhere. Young fellows who would have commanded that particular form of familiar reverence and

obedience, which is never accorded to the captain or the parson,—
only to the doctor.

Such as it was, without any doctor at all, the expedition reached
Cooper's Creek (latitude, say, 27½; longitude, say, 141). And on the
16th of December 1860, a party of four men, consisting of Mr Burke,
Mr Wills, King and Gray; with six camels, one horse, and three
months' provisions, started for the north, leaving behind a party
under Mr Brahe, at Cooper's Creek, to keep up their line of
communication with their base of operations on the Darling. The
gallant little band of four, leaving Sturt's Furthest to the west,
penetrated seven hundred miles to the north; and striking a water
which they called the Cloncurry (which we believe to be the main
headwater of Leichhardt's "Flinders"), they left Gray and King
behind; Mr Burke and Mr Wills pushing on alone on foot, until,
after about a day and a half walking, they came to a place where the
tide rose and fell two feet, and they listened to Carpentaria snarling
upon his coral reefs. Here they turned—the first men who had ever
crossed the continent from north to south.

In drawing this wonderful new line across the map of Australia,
they crossed very little bad country, none unfit to support human
life, for natives were in sight the whole way. Sturt's good fortune had
deserted him in that expedition to the interior, to put it one way; to
put it another, it pleased Almighty Providence that the natives
should enjoy that country for fifteen years more. Their time is come
now. They are cumbering land which will, some of it, carry a sheep
to four acres. They will have to be protected. Only fair play, this
time, gentlemen; and let us have no arsenic dampers.

So Burke and Wills, the proudest and happiest men on earth that
day, turned to go home. Although only thrown together for the first
time by the exigencies of the expedition, it is evident that a deep
friendship had by this time sprung up between these noble fellows.
They pushed rapidly southward again, towards their comrades at
Cooper's Creek, talking pleasantly about what this one would say,
and how proud another one would be. They were getting a little
shaky in the legs, all the four of them;—one, poor Gray, more so
than the other three. Gray stole some flour and ate it; Mr Wills told
Mr Burke of it, and Mr Burke gave Gray what he called "a good
thrashing". "Two or three good slaps of the head," says King. Mr
Burke struck him because he thought he was shamming ill, but he
was not, or else shammed very well, for he died and was buried, and
stole no more flour.

The three others pushed on to Cooper's Creek as fast as possible, for they were getting ill with scurvy, but were in high spirits. On April the 21st, they came in sight of the camp after a severe push of thirty miles. Burke called out, "There they are, I see them"; but it was not so. The camp was deserted, they had been left to perish.

Burke threw himself on the ground, and from that moment, as we believe, gave up all for lost. Brahe's party had despaired of them and gone. But the most terrible part of the business is this, that Brahe's party had not started much more than six hours, that they were probably not more than twelve miles' distance, or less, and we believe that by burying and firing their powder horns they might have made them hear.

Wills behaved nobly. Burke madly determined to strike to the southwest, *because some one had told him in Melbourne that there was a cattle station within one hundred miles of Cooper's Creek*. Here, on the first great trial, his head gave way; and we must blame Mr Wills also, for not urging his opinion more strongly. However, it was determined, instead of striking for the Darling, to strike southwest, towards the South Australian cattle stations; and from this time the man King, about whom we know nothing, save that he was "a common soldier", begins to develop into a true hero.

Mr Wilkie Collins, with all his wonderful ingenuity of plot, never *dared* to twist affairs into such cross purposes as those which follow. Burke, Wills, and King left Cooper's Creek on April 23rd, having buried their journal, but *by some fatal oversight, leaving no sign of their having been there*. A fortnight afterwards, Mr Wright came up from the Darling, looked round the camp, saw no sign of their having been there, and so turned and went home again,—while their journals were under his feet, and they themselves not more than twenty miles down the creek. Mr Wright, also, left no mark of his having been there; so that a fortnight after, when Mr Wills returned to the camp to deposit some fresh journals, he writes, "No trace of any one having been here, except blacks". And so Wright gave up Burke and Wills as lost, and they gave themselves up as deserted.

Those who care to trace two such noble specimens of humanity through misery to death, must read the book. The end came in this way: They wandered up and down, and lived on a seed called "Nardoo", (about which we know nothing; having never met with anything corresponding to it), and on what they could beg from the blacks, who treated them very kindly. The nights got deadly cold; Mr Wills got weaker and weaker, as did also Mr Burke; King held out best of all. The blacks went away. It was voted necessary, as a last chance, that Mr Burke and King should follow them; and so

Wills wrote a letter to his father, and gave Burke his watch; and they left him alone with his God knowing that they should see his face no more.

The last act of the tragedy approaches. The noble King and poor Burke went out into the bush together, and Burke broke down. "I hope," he said to King, "that you will stay by me till I am quite dead; it is a comfort to know that some one is by. But when I am dying, it is my desire that you should place my pistol in my right hand, and leave me unburied as I lie."

King now "felt very lonely", but managed to wander back to Wills,—who was of course dead some days now,—and scraped some sand over him. After this he went and lived with the blacks, who were very kind to him, particularly an old woman called Carrawaw. And this was the end of the whole business. King was rescued by Mr Howitt, who rewarded the faithful blacks.

But the results of the three last explorations are most important. Australia has been proved capable of supporting a population of at least thirty million; and all the old bugbear about a central desert has been dissipated for ever.

Reminiscences of a Thirty Years' Residence in New South Wales and Victoria*

Reminiscences of a Thirty Years' Residence in New South Wales and Victoria. By R. Therry, Esq., late one of the Judges of the Supreme Court of New South Wales. One Vol., 8vo. Sampson Low, Son, & Co.

To those acquainted with Australian affairs, it would be quite unnecessary to mention one word about Mr Therry's antecedents; but for the benefit of the majority who are not, it may be as well to mention that he was trusted by Mr Canning to edit his speeches; that he wrote a memoir of Mr Canning, which both Lady Canning and Mr Stapleton mention with praise; and that for thirty years he held high legal offices in New South Wales and Victoria—latterly the office of Judge in the Supreme Court, the appeal from which is to the House of Lords.

Residing, as he did, in that colony from 1829 till 1859, in high official positions, with means of information utterly beyond such colonial historians as Sidney and Westgarth, he gains our ear at once, and makes us listen to him with respect. We opened the book with intense interest, and we confess that we have not been disappointed. The book gives us the history of the wealthiest possession of the British Crown (for the history of New South Wales, up to 1850, includes that of Victoria) for the thirty most important years of its existence. To use Edie Ochiltree's words, Mr Therry "kenned the bigging o' it".

*Reprinted from *The Reader* I (14 March 1863): 256–57.

Mr Therry is a Roman Catholic. This no one would have guessed, had he not plainly told us so, for anything more liberal and generous than his treatment of other creeds cannot be conceived; but Mr Therry is also an Irishman, and with all respect we venture to think that his Irishism is too strong. A man who does not love his own country better than any other must be a poor fellow; but when an unbiassed reader, in the first twenty pages of a book, "breaks his shins" over a flowery comparison between Sydney harbour and the lakes of Killarney, we put it to Mr Therry whether or no that reader is not inclined afterwards to conclude that the book is written from an exclusively Irish point of view? There are mountains at Killarney, there are none at Sydney. The south side of Sydney harbour is occupied by a city of eighty thousand inhabitants; we have heard of no such city at Killarney. "There is a river in Macedon, and there is a river at Monmouth—and there is salmon in both." That is about the value of Mr Therry's comparison. It is through such outbreaks of Irishism as this, that he forces us to tell our readers that his statements are perfectly impartial.

To give here the *résumé* of a book which includes the political gossip of a large community for thirty years, would be quite impossible. It only remains to point out such portions of it as are interesting to the general reader.

When Mr Therry arrived in the colony in 1829, the population of England was twelve million,—of the colony, fifty thousand. In England there were executed that year fifty-three persons,—in the colony, fifty. But in the year 1860, when Mr Therry left, the population of England was nineteen million; that of the colony, three hundred and fifty thousand. That year there were twelve people executed in England, while in New South Wales, in the year 1856, *there was not one*—a rather startling fact concerning a penal colony.

But here we must again find fault with Mr Therry. He is, at time, inaccurate in his figures. His comparison, above referred to, is based on the number of the population of *England and Wales*, which he puts at twenty-nine million in 1861, and which we have taken the liberty of correcting for him. He goes on, also, page after page, talking of the *Paris* Exhibition of 1851. These things are trifles; but when people see such obvious carelessness in small matters, which they do know all about, they are apt to get distrustful of the accuracy of his figures in larger matters, which would be doing him a very great injustice. Moreover, when "a compendious little essay" on female emigration "read before the Social Congress of Dublin" makes the utterly incredible statement that "a short time since 810 women applied for one situation of £15 per annum", we must say that the author of that "little essay" had better give us a few names and dates, or we shall remember that Mr Peel, in 1828, wrote to Lord Anglesey, "I have learnt by long experience the necessity of distrusting Irish information". We cannot contradict this statement. It may be true. The colony may have changed for the worse since we knew it. Only when we have thundered into one ear the demand for female emigration, and into the other the statement that nearly one thousand women are racing after a situation of £15 per annum, we do not know what to believe.

While reviewing recently in these pages a book on Australian exploration, and referring to the fact that enormous new tracts were about to be taken up in Australia for pastoral purposes, we spoke about "arsenic dampers", an expression which puzzled some of our friends. What we alluded to was the practice prevalent in many districts (the Glenelg had a bad name) of poisoning the unfortunate aborigines like vermin. Mr Therry (Judge of the Supreme Court at Sydney, be it remembered) alludes to this practice, and confirms it. But he tells us a tale about a "black" massacre, which sounds only the more wild and terrible, from being given in the clumsy and confused language of the witness-box. And it is right that we who have so often raised the voice of indignation against the Americans for the treatment of their negroes, should know what was going on in one of our own colonies in the year of grace 1838. And let the reader remember that the unproved crime of which these blacks were accused, was that of having *speared some cattle sixty miles away*, near which place they had not been for three months.

Mr Hobbs, an overseer, who seems to have been a just and humane man, stayed for a fortnight at his hut, and while there noticed that some fifty blacks were living round the hut inoffensively and quietly; half the number were women and children. He left home for ten days, and on his return found them gone. He soon got a hint that something was wrong, and noticing some eagles hovering in the air, he directed his steps to a place some half-mile from the hut, where he found twenty-eight bodies, with the heads cut off, partly consumed by fire.

Then the whole ghastly story came out. Mr Therry gives it to us from the notes of Mr Justice Dowling and Sir W. Burton, taken on the trial. The principal witness was George Anderson, hutkeeper to Mr Hobbs, and from his witness-box English we gather the following. On one winter's night in the middle of June, everything was still round the hut, except, perhaps, the sounds which always proceed from a black encampment; at one time the bab-bab-ah of an infant feeling for its mother in the dark; at another, the low petulant whimper of some old woman shoved by the younger women out into the cold, and complaining under her voice lest she should awaken the lord and master, and get beaten for disturbing him. But about ten o'clock there was a new sound altogether: the noise of ten men, who rode armed up to the hut, and began to talk angrily together. And when the poor blacks heard these men, they all, men, women, and children, to the number of nearly fifty, crowded into the hut, calling on Anderson to protect them. Anderson was at this time outside the hut, while the poor blacks were inside. The murderers went into the hut, leaving him alone; and then "I heard the crying of the blacks for relief or assistance to me and Kilmeister. They were moaning the same as a mother and children would cry." Soon after they were brought out of the hut, tied to a tether rope (about twenty-five yards long), and led away over the hill, to their death. Two old men were not tied up with the rest. "Old Daddy", a giant, and another old man followed, whimpering and unwilling, knowing what was to come. Some of the children were tied, others were not, but followed their mothers. The stockmen led them over the hill, and murdered them in cold blood, and afterwards attempted to burn the bodies. As they were starting from the hut, the witness, George Anderson, managed to save one boy by shutting him up in the hut, for which deed, done, as it was, at the risk of his life, he will, we hope, have his reward. But perhaps the strangest part of the story remains to be told. As these devils were driving off these poor blacks over the hill, one of them relented; he took up a black boy, who had been a favourite of his, and put him behind a tree, telling him to wait till he returned. The boy would not, but followed his mammy over the hill, and was slaughtered with the rest. And it is with a feeling passing awe, that we read in this hard lawyer's evidence, that the identification of the body of this boy was the one fact which led to the conviction and execution of the murderers.

The colony rose in furious indignation; not, however, against the murderers, but against the Attorney-General, Mr Plunkett, who had the audacity to get these murderers executed. There can be no doubt that there are many cases (the case of the murder of the Wills family in Queensland, for instance), where reprisals are necessary to keep the blacks in order. But the case quoted above is one of those which are utterly intolerable and abominable, and which must never be heard of again. While contemplating such an excessively black pot as this, one must really pronounce the South Carolina kettle to be white by comparison, although that is dirty enough.

New Australian Exploration*

Tracks of McKinlay and Party across Australia. By John Davis, one of
the Expedition. Edited from Mr Davis's Manuscript Journal.

The work of Australian exploration goes bravely on. The present
volume is the chronicle of a journey from Adelaide to the Gulf of
Carpentaria, and from thence to Port Denison in Queensland—a
distance of twenty-five hundred miles, mostly over new ground,
during the greater part of which grass, water and natives were met
with in considerable quantities.

A few months ago we reviewed the account of Burke's expedition,
which, though eminently successful, terminated so disastrously. We
may remind our readers that he, starting from Melbourne,
proceeded, roughly speaking, due north, until he struck the Gulf of
Carpentaria at the mouth of the Flinders, having crossed the
continent for the first time. McKinlay, who was sent in search of
him, has now crosed the continent a second time, having started
from Adelaide, crossed Burke's route in lat. 27°, kept to the east of it
until lat. 19°, crossed it again, and struck the Gulf near the mouth of
the Leichhardt, some sixty miles to the east of where Burke and Wills
met the sea.

Thus, although McKinlay has gone over new ground, yet still he
is, so to speak, in old country. Landsborough and the settlements are
to the east of him, Burke to the west, and Stuart to the far, far west.
Stuart remains still the pioneer who has been furthest into the

* Reprinted from *The Reader* I (27 June 1863): 618–19.

unknown West, having passed five degrees west of Sturt's furthest, in long 138° lat. 25°, which was for fifteen years the Ultima Thule of Australian explorers.

About one-half the island remains untraversed; and this, in many respects, is the most promising half. Eyre, during his unparalleled solitary journey round the bight, was always getting track of a better country being near him on the north. We confess we should like to see another attempt or two made from the west coast—from the Abrolhos up the Murchison for instance—with larger means than have been used hitherto.

The task of reviewing this book is rendered all the more simple by a masterly *précis* of its contents, given, in the introduction, from the familiar pen of Mr Westgarth. The main part of the book consists of the Journal of Mr Davis, one of the expedition under Mr McKinlay. It is very amusingly written. One would think, from the style in which Mr Davis writes, that the expedition was the great joke of his existence—a kind of enormous "lark". His shrewdness, his patience, and his never-failing good-humour must have been a perfect God-send to this or any other expedition. Any bushman knows by experience the depressing, dulling influence which one croaker can produce on a party, and, on the other hand, knows the blessing of having one face which is always good-humoured and smiling, and whose smiles are always reflected on the faces of his companions. Such a face Mr Davis's seems to have been.

Starting from Adeliade, McKinlay proceeded due north, and after four hundred miles came to Lake Torrens. This great inland sea, four hundred miles long and twenty broad, so familiar to every one who has ever looked at a map of Australia—the sea which had the honour of stopping such men as Sturt and Eyre—was now perfectly dry. They crossed the bed of it, and saw no water on either horizon. It was gone; but it will probably be there again next year. It is merely a great accumulation from the floods of the enormous river-system of the Barcoo and the Cooper—rivers which, though of immense length, are in most years merely a chain of water-holes. Crossing then the dry Lake Torrens, they came to the Desert of Sturt—which also appears to be flooded in very wet seasons, for the expedition were nearly swept away by a flood; and, passing from this region, where excessive inundation alternates with excessive drought, in 25° south, they came to a region of flowery swamps, containing plenty of water, and crossed the dividing range in 22°— a little north of where Stuart passed it on his track to the east. It would therefore appear, from what we can gather, that the strike of the dividing range is here, about northeast by east—not nearly north, as in the auriferous ranges of Victoria. But this is mere conjecture of our own; and our duty is to review, not to theorize.

Entering the tropics, they were struck by the fact that the vegetation underwent little or no change, and that the features of the country (fauna, flora, and all) were very like what they would have found eighteen hundred miles south—park-like glades of grass, fringed with gum-trees. The soil improves as one goes north, the heat is greater, and the mosquitoes more troublesome; but it is Australia still; and those who have once seen any part of the most beautiful melancholy sea-coast of that wonderful country are not likely to forget it, or to compare it with the coast of any other country. By all accounts the mouth of the Leichhardt in the Indian Ocean is exactly like the mouth of the Garra, two thousand miles south of it; only, instead of mangrove on the Leichhardt, you have tea-scrub on the Garra. When almost within hail of the Indian Archipelago, you still find yourself among the old familiar fauna. The platypus, the emu, and the kangaroo are found equally plentiful, and equally at home, at points varying from one another in position and in climate as much as do Edinburgh and Constantinople.

After having struck the Indian Ocean, McKinlay turned southeast, and soon found himself in the great wave of advancing colonization which was creeping on from the east. The old work was going on—driving sheep to new pastures, building outlying huts, butchering blacks, and all the rest of it. And, as in old times, no one to blame, my dear sir, except the blacks themselves! This, however, is an ugly subject. If people choose to reckon on the blindness of God, it is no business of a mere reviewer. The mere reviewer has only to remark, in conclusion, that the names of McKinlay and Davis are added to the list of English worthies; and that the result of their expedition is to confirm fully our most sanguine hopes about the interior of Australia.

Charles Sturt
A Chapter from the History of Australian Exploration*

Just now, when so much attention is being called to Australian exploration, and while the work is going on so very satisfactorily, it may not be amiss if we while away half-an-hour in recalling the deeds of an earlier adventurer in the same field, at a time when the nature of the country towards the interior was utterly unknown, when nearly every plant was new, and when no navigable river had been discovered to the eastward of the Blue Mountains. Let us follow the footsteps of the first successful explorer of the interior of the great continent—of the man who penetrated almost to the centre of it, and who left his name like a monument on the great bare map of Australia for twenty years, hundreds and hundreds of miles beyond the boldest of his contemporaries. Let us follow the track of Charles Sturt, the father of Australian exploration. . .

[*To the early settlement at Port Jackson, the Blue Mountains in the west "hung like a dark curtain, and shut out the knowledge of all beyond". Following a drought in 1813, Blaxland, Wentworth and Lawson, "fought their way to the summit, and looked over into the glorious western land". Discovery of the Macquarie, Lachlan, and Castlereagh rivers followed but whither they flowed seemed unanswerable.*]

* Reprinted (with some omissions, as marked) from *Macmillan's Magazine* XI (Jan. 1865): 204–17. It was reprinted in *Hornby Mills and Other Stories* (London: Tinsley, 1872) as "The March of Charles Sturt", under which title it also appears, with other stories and sketches, in *The Boy in Grey* (London: Ward, Lock, and Bowden, 1895).

So stood the question until 1828. In 1826 another fearful drought set in, and lasted for two years. After that time, the western rivers were reported to be lower than they had ever been seen; and it became evident that now or never was the time to penetrate the vast reedy marshes which had stopped Oxley, and, by crossing them, to see what lay beyond. An expedition was formed, and the command of it was given to Captain Charles Sturt, of the 39th Regiment. He started from Paramatta on the 9th of November, 1828; and on the 26th of December, having proceeded about a hundred miles down the Macquarie, and having passed for some days through a level, dreary flat, with belts of reeds, he came to a wall of reeds, which prevented his further progress by land, and necessitated the launching of his boat.

At first the course of the river was narrow and tortuous; but at length, in a very few miles, it grew broader. This, so far from being a good sign, was a bad one. The river was spreading out into the marsh; for the flood-marks, which formerly were many feet above the water, were now barely a foot. It was evident that the river was losing power; the current grew almost imperceptible, and at this point, also, the trees disappeared. Three miles further the river, thirty yards broad as it was, came to an end; the boat grounded, and Captain Sturt got out; and, for his own satisfaction, walked right round the end of it, and got in again. There was an end of the Macquarie.

Unsupplied by any tributaries, and receiving its waters entirely from mountains two hundred miles away, the time had come for the river when its mountain supply was counterbalanced in the very dry season by evaporation. In very wet seasons the surplus water is carried westward by fifty tiny channels. Carried westward, but whither. Into an inland sea, or into a great watercourse running northwest? That was the problem before Captain Sturt—the problem he solved at last.

Having rowed back to his camp, Captain Sturt made an expedition, a circuit of some two hundred miles to the northwest, which resulted in nothing. From this time till the 18th of January the whole party persevered in their efforts to get round the north of the miserable country which surrounded the marshes. Every attempt to the westward was foiled. The ascent of a small mountain rising out of the waste revealed nothing whatever except the horrible level expanse, stretching westward like a sea. They were, in fact, standing on the St Kilda of the dividing range, and looking over the Atlantic of low land so recently raised from the sea.

So they struggled, westward and northward, without hope, down a dry creek, with sometimes, but very seldom, a pool of water in it. And suddenly, without expectation or preparation of any kind, they came to the edge of a cliff some fifty or sixty feet high, at the base of which flowed a magnificent river, stretching away from northeast to southwest in vast reaches, eighty yards broad, and evidently of great depth. Splendid trees grew on its banks; its waters were covered with countless legions of pelicans, swans, and ducks; the native paths on each side of it were as broad as roads. It was a magnificent discovery. In one instant it dispelled the notion—which had arisen one hardly knows how—that the trend of land was towards the northwest. It proved at a glance that this was a great trench, carrying off all the innumerable eastern rivers southward, and showed that the Southern Ocean, and not Torres Straits, received their waters. That its sources and its *embouchure* were both far distant from the place where Sturt stood, in silent gratitude, was evident from its great size and depth; and from this moment the Darling took its place for ever among the great rivers of the world, and Charles Sturt's name was written down among the foremost of the great band of successful explorers.

Though a great geographical blunder, involving an error of nearly two thousand miles, had been cleared up, it fared but poorly with the expedition. In five minutes, or less, congratulations and hand-shakings were exchanged for looks of incredulous horror. They forced their way to the banks of the stream, and found it was salt, too salt to be drunk.

But little more remains to be said of this great river in this place. They followed it down for many miles, subsisting precariously on the puddles of fresh water which lay about the bank. The river at night was covered with leaping fish; innumerable wild fowl still floated on its bosom; the banks were fertile and beautiful; but the water was salt. The bullocks stood in it, with only their noses above water, and refused to drink it; the men who attempted to do so were made fearfully ill. At one time they found a current in it, which they discovered was fed by great brine springs; at another it ceased altogether, and a bar of dry sand, over which you might ride, crossed it. A strange, weird, anomalous river, on whose banks they were nigh dying of thirst!

It was necessary to turn. It was resolved on. Captain Sturt was merely to go a few miles down the river, on a forlorn hope, leaving the party behind in camp. The day was intensely clear and cloudless, burning hot, without a breath of air. Captain Sturt and

Mr Hume were sitting on the ground together, making their chart, when they heard the boom of a great cannon, fired apparently about five miles to the northwest. The whole expedition heard it; there was no doubt about it. A man was sent up a tree, and reported nothing but perfectly level wooded country in every direction. What that sound was we shall never know. Neither the captain in the army, nor the brave gentleman-pioneer and bushman, nor the convicts, could make head or tail of it. No doubt, coming at such a time, "it made a strong impression on us for the rest of the day."

Captain Sturt, with Mr Hume, went forty miles down the river, and found it stretching away southwest, in reaches grander and more majestic than before, covered with wildfowl, swarming with fish, but as salt as ever. There he left it, to meet it twice again—once higher up, as we shall see immediately; and once again hundreds of miles away, in the most awful moment of his adventurous life.

We need say but little more. After terrible hardships the expedition succeeded in striking the Darling ninety miles higher up than the first point of discovery, and recognized it in an instant. The same long canal-like reaches; the same clouds of waterfowl and shoals of fish; the water still intensely salt! They had now seen it through 150 miles of its course, and found no change. It was time to abandon the expedition. They got back in safety, having by tact and courage avoided any collision with the natives. The results were important. The trend of the interior basin was southward, not northward! From the water-marks by the shore of this great canal-like river, it was evident that in nine summers out of ten, in any season almost but this, the driest hitherto known in the history of the colony, the rainfall would be sufficiently great to overpower the brine springs in its bed, and make it run fresh. And, lastly, from the size of the channel, it was inferred that the sources of the river were many hundred miles to the north, probably within the tropic.*

And now we come to the second and greater expedition. The question remained, "What becomes of the Darling towards the southwest?"

It seemed an utterly hopeless task to carry boats back to the point at which Captain Sturt had touched it, to launch them on its waters, and to run down. The plan evidently was to try and cut it at a point lower down; but how? The Macquarie had been tried, as we see.

*This branch of the Darling, which may be called the true Darling, loses its name higher up, but may be roughly said to rise in the latitude of Moreton Bay (27°). The lower part, however, receives waters from far inside the tropic.

The Lachlan was known to be a miserable poor thing of a river, worse than the Macquarie. What remained? What river was there flowing west with vitality sufficient to reach the Darling before it perished?

The Morumbidgee? Well, that did seem something of the kind—rising here behind Mount Dromedary, fed by a thousand streaming creeks, from a thousand peaceful gullies, till it grew to manhood, to strength, to passion, and hurled itself madly from right to left, against buttress after buttress of its mountain-walled prison, until it was free; and then sweeping on, sleeping here, snarling there, under lofty-hanging woodlands, through broad rich river flat, through a country fit for granary of an empire, sometimes in reaches still as glass, sometimes in long foaming shallows of frosted silver. A river among rivers, growing in majesty and beauty, as a hundred tributaries added to its volume, until at last, where the boldest stockman had left it and turned, it went still westward, a chain of crimson reaches, towards the setting sun! Could this river die, save in the great eternal ocean? Was there a curse on the land, that such a thing should happen?

This is very unbusiness-like language. But I think it must have been something of this kind which Charles Sturt meant, when he said that the attention of the Colonial government was, under these circumstances, drawn to the fact that the volume of water in the Morumbidgee was more considerable than that in either of the rivers before mentioned, and did not seem to decrease, but rather the contrary, in a westerly direction. So they deputed Captain Sturt to follow down the Morumbidgee, and find out whether he could carry it on until it cut the Darling. Saul went after his father's asses, and found a kingdom. Captain Sturt went to look after that miserable old Darling, and found a kingdom also, and a very fine one too.

But there was another reason which gave people great hopes that the Morumbidgee went somewhere, and not nowhere, like other Australian rivers. In 1825 Mr Hume (before-mentioned) and Mr Hovell, had gone a strange journey to the south-west, keeping great mountains on their left, to the south and east, nearly all the way, through an utterly unknown, but fine and well-watered, country, until, when five hundred miles from Sydney, they came on a great arm of the sea, and came back again, disputing whether or no they had reached the Port Phillip of Collins, or the western port of Bass. It was, in fact, the former, though they could not decide it. This journey of theirs, down to the desolate shores of a lonely sea, was made only thirty-eight years ago; yet the best way to describe it now is to say that they passed through the towns of Yass, Goulbourn, Albury (with the wonderful bridge), Wangaratta, Benalla, Seymour, and Kilmore, until they came to the city of Melbourne, which is now slightly larger than Bristol, and exports eleven millions a year. "Darn'em," said an old Yankee to me once, *apropos* of the new South Australian discoveries, "they're at it again you see."

On their route they crossed three large streams, going north and west from the mountains which were between them and the sea, which they named the Hume, the Ovens, and the Goulbourn. Now, if either of these streams joined the Morumbidgee, there were great hopes that their united tides would be strong enough to bear one on to the junction with the Darling. These were the prospects of the expedition. We will now resume our narrative.

A whale-boat was constructed, fitted loosely, and taken to pieces again and packed in the drays, ready for construction in the interior. A still was also provided, lest the waters of the Darling should be found salt where they struck it. The expedition started from Sydney on the 3rd of November, 1829, exactly a year after the starting of the previous one, whose course we have so shortly followed. Mr Hume was unable to accompany Captain Sturt on this journey. His principal companions were, Mr George Macleay; Harris, his soldier servant; Hopkinson, soldier friend of Harris; Frazer, an eccentric Scot, declining to forego his uniform; dogs; a tame black boy on horseback; Clayton, a stolid carpenter; the rest convicts.

On the 21st of the month, they were getting among the furthest stations. "From east-south-east to west-north-west, the face of the country was hilly, broken and irregular, forming deep ravines and precipitous glens, amid which I was well aware the Morumbidgee was still struggling for freedom; while mountains succeeded mountains in the background, and were themselves overtopped by lofty and distant peaks." So says Captain Sturt, in his vigorous, well-chosen language.

At last they reached the river of their hopes, rushing, crystal clear, over a bed of mountain *debris,* in great curves and reaches, across and across the broad meadows, which lay in the lap of the beautiful wooded mountains which towered up on all sides, and which, in places, abutted so closely on the great stream that they had to cross and recross it many times, with great difficulty. Immediately they were beyond the limits of all geographical knowledge; the last human habitation was left behind at the junction of the Tumut, a river as big as the Morumbidgee, about ten miles above the present town of Gundaqui, which has since acquired a disastrous notoriety for its fatal floods. The river was stronger and broader than ever, leading them on towards the great unknown southwest.

The reaches grew broader, and the pasture on the flats more luxuriant; yet still hope grew stronger. The natives, such as they saw, were friendly; they caught fish, one of which weighed 40 pounds, (a small thing that, though; they run up to 120 pounds). The ranges still continued on either hand. Hope grew higher and higher—it was to be a mere holiday expedition! At length they left the ranges, and came out on to the great basin of the interior once more; and a dull unexpressed anxiety began to grow on them hour after hour. The country was getting so horribly like the miserable desert which had balked them before, on the Macquarie.* Still the river held on bravely, and any unexperienced man would have scouted the idea of its losing itself among reed marshes. But ugly symptoms began to show themselves. The soil grew sandy, and was covered with the claws of dead crayfish. The hated cypress began to show too. Two blacks, who had been induced to accompany them, turned back, evidently never expecting to see them again. Things began to look bad.

And worse as they went on. They began to get among the reeds again. The plains stretched away treeless and bare to the north-east as far as they could see, and the river, their last hope, began to grow smaller. They got entangled among sheets of polygonum (a gloomy and leafless bramble); the crested pigeon and the black quail appeared—all strong symptoms of the interior desert.

Toiling over a dreary sand plain, in which the dray horses sunk fetlock-deep, they came to a broad, dry creek, which seemed to be the junction or one of the junctions of the Lachlan. They headed back to the river again; but one of the men, sent on on horseback, rode back to say that the noble river was gone—that there was nothing to be seen but reeds, reeds, reeds in all directions. They had been deceived by another Macquarie!

Fortunately not. After a terrible day on horseback, Sturt forced his way to the river once more, and lay down, half dead with fatigue, in utter despair on its banks. He could not sleep, but, as he lay awake under the winking stars, his purpose grew. At daybreak he was up

---

*How greatly would their anxiety have been increased had they been aware, as we are now, that the river had actually bifurcated already immediately below the beautiful Hamilton Plains, and, that after a ramble of 150 miles, with more or less prosperity, the smaller arm reached the Murray 11 miles above the junction of the main channel!

and on horseback with Macleay. They rode till noon through belts of reeds, the river still holding its own to the south-west. At noon Sturt reined up, and the deed was done. He asked no advice, he allowed no discussion. He told Mr Macleay that to push round the reeds toward the northwest in search of the Darling was to endanger the expedition—that the river was still alive; that at any moment it might join a stream from the southeast (he meant one of the three streams discovered by Hovell and Hume, before mentioned); that his fixed and unalterale purpose was to send the drays and horses back, to put together the whale boat, and to row down the river into such country and towards such fate as Providence should will.

One can fancy the smile that came over Macleay's face as his tall, gaunt chief sat upright in his saddle and announced his determination to take this bold and desperate step, for such it was. All the expedition, convicts and all, understood the situation perfectly, and worked accordingly. *In seven days not only had the whale boat been put together, but a tree had been felled from the forest, sawn up, and another boat built and painted; and at the end of the seventh day both were in the water ready for loading.*

Of the convicts he took the carpenter, Clayton, who had superintended and mainly done this wonderful week's work (what *could* such a fine fellow have been doing to get transported?), Mulholland, and Macnamee; of free men, Harris, the captain's servant, Hopkinson, and Frazer (all these three, I believe, soldiers). The others were sent home, under charge of *Robert* Harris, with despatches . . .

[*Eight days later, after difficult navigation, the party was still hoping to encounter the stream they believed lay ahead.*]

At one o'clock they stopped for a short time, and then proceeded, the banks becoming more narrow and gloomy, the turns in the river more abrupt, and the stream very swift. At three o'clock Hopkinson, who was in the bows, called out that they were approaching a junction; in less than one single minute afterwards, they were shot, like an arrow from a bow, through a narrow channel into a magnificent river. The Morumbidgee was no more; and they, dazed and astonished, were floating on the bosom of the majestic Murray, henceforth one of the great rivers of the world.

What a moment in the man's life! It was not merely that a desperate adventure had terminated—as it would seem at the moment—favourably. There was more to congratulate himself on than the mere lucky issue of an adventure. A very carefully

considered geographical problem, originated by his sagacity, had
been solved by his perseverance. He had argued that the Hume,
Ovens, and Goulbourn, seen by Hume and Hovell flowing north,
would "form a junction", or, as vulgarians would say, "join", and
that the Morumbidgee would retain sufficient strength to carry its
waters to them. The one difficulty had been the Morumbidgee, and
that river had not deceived him, though he had so cruelly suspected
it. Sturt must have felt on that afternoon, as Adams did, when,
having finished his vast calculations, he sat looking through his
telescope, and saw the long-expected Neptune roll into the field, or
as Herschel and his sister felt, after their three months' labour to
correct one unfortunate mistake, when they saw a dim needle of
light in the west, which was not a star.

If one had to find fault with Captain Sturt's proceedings, one
would be forced to say that it would have been better, on the
discovery of this great river, to have gone back at once, to have
brought on his depot, to have communicated with his base of
operations at Sydney, and to have done the whole thing with a
Fluellen-like attention to the rules of war. I am happy to say such a
thing never entered into his head. Sir Galahad saw his horse,
armour, and sword, and recognized it as the means of reaching the
Sangreal. Sturt saw his boat full of convicts, and recognized it as the
means of solving the great problem of the outfall of the western
waters. I say I am glad that Sturt committed himself to this strange,
wild adventure without one moment's hesitation, like a knight-
errant; if for no other reason, because one is glad to see the spirit of
the sixteenth century so remarkably revived in the nineteenth.
Charles Sturt, the Dorsetshire squire's son, turned his boat's head
westward, down the swift current of the great new river, knowing
well that each stroke of the oar carried him further from help and
hope, but knowing also that a great problem was before him, and
begrudging any other man the honour of solving it. It is not well for
us to sneer at motives such as these. We must recognize personal
ambition as a good and necessary thing, or half our great works
would be left undone. He disconnected himself from his base, and
began to move his little flying column. Whither?

It seems, from a later passage in his journal, that he had some
notion of reaching the Southern Ocean, and coasting back in his
whaleboat. I cannot but think that he (who afterwards shewed
himself so patient and so sagacious in his unparalleled journey to the
centre of the continent) had, on this occasion, calculated, to some
extent, the chances against him; yet by his journal one finds no trace

of any calculation whatever. Here was the great river, flowing swiftly westward, and he turned his boat's head down it, "*vogue la galère*".

The Murray, where he joined it, was 120 yards broad; say, roughly, one third broader than Henley reach. The Murray, however, above its junction with the Morumbidgee, is both swifter and deeper, as well as broader, than the Thames at Henley. Captain Sturt speaks of it as being perfectly clear. It doubtless was so in January; but later on in the summer I think he would have found it assume a brown, peaty colour. At least, such is my impression. I used to notice this fact about nearly all the rivers I knew in Australia Felix. While the vegetable matter was thoroughly washed out of them and diluted by the winter floods, they were—instance the Yarra, Goulbourn, and Ovens—very clear. But later on in the summer, towards February, they began, as the water got lower, to get stained and brown, although not foul; and the little cor- reginus(?) of the Yarra, the only one of the salmonidae which, as far as I am aware, exists to any extent in Australia, seems only to rise to the fly while the waters are clear and green, but to go to the bottom during the summer.

On the lower part of the Morumbidgee they had seen no natives; but on the very first day on the Murray, as we now call this great river, natives reappeared. In the evening a large band of them, painted and prepared for war, advanced on Sturt and his few companions, through the forest. The sight was really magnificent. They halted and broke out into their war-cry. They threatened and gesticulated; but at last, when they had lost their breath, they grew calm, nay, began to get rather alarmed, for no one took the slightest notice of them—which was very alarming indeed. Sturt got them to come down to him, and gave them presents; then put them in a row, and fired his gun in the air. The result was an instant and frantic "stampede". However, after a time, they were induced to return, and sixteen of them, finding no one was the worse for the gun, stayed with them all night. Next day they followed them, and entreated them to stay with them. Their astonishment at the gun shows that Sturt and his party were the first white men they had seen.

It was, in all human probability, *these very blacks*, at least the children and young men among them, who gave some curious trouble to the police at Swanhill, as late as 1854. I say, in all human probability, for Sturt was at this time barely sixty miles from the town we now call Swanhill, though then close upon four hundred miles from human habitation . . .

[Here, Kingsley digresses to tell of the capture and subsequent release of a Chinese emigrant from Amoy. The secrecy of his capture was breached by a jealous visitor of another tribe and a policeman later effected his return to Swanhill.]

Such were these poor children of the wilderness in 1854, who were frightened by Sturt's gun in 1829. Poor wretches! It unluckily happened, by mismanagement on both sides, that it came to be a struggle for bare existence between them and the first squatters. Horrible atrocities were committed on both sides; Glenelg poisonings and severe stockmen massacres on the part of the whites, and innumerable butcheries of lonely shepherds on the part of the blacks. Having heard the case argued so very often as I have, I cannot pronounce any sweeping condemnation on either blacks or whites. If you deny the squatters the right to defend their lives and property, you come inexorably to the conclusion that we have no business in Australia at all. Have we, or have we not, a right to waste lands occupied by savage tribes? If we have not, the occupation of Australia is an act of piracy. If we have, then the confiscation of the Waikato lands ought to have been done thirty years ago, before we supplied the Maories with guns. This is the sort of result you come to, if you apply any general rule to our colonial policy. The law of purchase, which makes us legal owners in New Zealand, proves us to be pirates in Australia.

Meanwhile Sturt sleeps his first night on the Murray. It is time that he, Macleay, and his boatful of soldiers and convicts should awaken and go on . . .

[Nine days later, after a near capsize and help by Aborigines, the party was still making progress.]

The river still perversely held to the north of west, but the friendly natives, in describing its course, always pointed a *little* to the south of west. But, besides this, they made a curious diagram by placing sticks across one another, which no one could understand. Frazer, the Scot, played with them; he sat up with them all night, to his and their infinite contentment; but in the morning they were gone.

The reason was soon apparent,—they were approaching another tribe. The next morning, the river being so much wider, they hoisted a sail, and sailed pleasantly on. They saw vast flocks of wildfowl overhead; and, after nine miles, looking forward, saw that they were approaching a band of magnificent trees, of dense, dark foliage; and beneath them was a vast band of natives, in full war-paint, chanting their war-songs, and standing line behind line, quivering their spears. The passage of the river was about to be disputed at last.

At first Sturt thought nothing of it. The river was so broad that he could easily pass them. But the blacks knew what they were about. The river suddenly shoaled; the current was swift; and Sturt saw that a great sandbank stretched suddenly one-third across the river below. This the natives took possession of, and this Sturt had to pass.

It seemed a perfectly hopeless business. The expedition was within five minutes of its conclusion. The people at home in Dorsetshire yonder, praying for those travelling by land or by water that Sunday, would have prayed a little more eagerly, I take it, if they had known to what pass tall young Squire Charley had brought himself at eleven o'clock that morning. Macleay and two of the men were to defend the boat with the bayonet; Captain Sturt, Hopkinson, and Harris were to keep up the fire. There would not have been much firing or bayoneting either, after the first flight of a couple of hundred spears or so, each one thrown by a man who could probably hit a magpie at ten yards.

The boat drifted on, the men again behaving nobly. Sturt fixed on a savage, and said he must die; his gun was at his shoulder, but it was never fired. Before he pulled the trigger, Macleay called his attention to the left bank. A native, running at the top of his speed, dashed into the water, swam and splashed across, seized the native at whom Sturt was aiming by the throat, and forced him back; and then, driving in the natives who were wading towards the boat, back on to the sand-bank by the mere strength of his fury, the noble fellow stood alone before the whole tribe of maddened savages, before three hundred quivering spears, stamping, gesticulating, threatening, almost inarticulate in his rage.

They were saved. They were just drifting past their preserver when the boat touched on a sand-bank; in an instant they had her off. For a minute or two they floated like men in a dream, incredulous of their safety; and, while they were preparing to go back to the assistance of the gallant savage, they looked to their right, and saw the Darling—saw it come rolling its vast volume of water in from the northward. The Darling—the river they had tried to follow the year before, five hundred miles to the north, in the miserable desert—found once more, at this terrible time, when each man sat on his thwart, paralyzed with the fear of the terrible danger just overpast!

They saw about seventy natives on the bank of the new river, and landed among them. Seeing this, the others, on the tongue of land between the two rivers, began to swim across, unarmed, in curiosity. Now, they saw the extent of their danger. Captain Sturt, a soldier, used to calculate numbers of men, puts the number of hostile natives at no less than six hundred. They soon became quiet. Sturt rewarded his friend with every expression of good will, but refused to give anything to the hostile chiefs. After rowing a few miles up the Darling, which he found a more beautiful stream than the Murray, and perfectly fresh, he turned his boat's head and renewed his voyage, running up the Union Jack and giving three cheers. They hoisted their sail, and went onwards with their strange adventure.

The channel grew to be much obstructed with large fallen logs of timber, and sand-banks began to appear. Sturt considers that, just after the junction of the Darling, they were not more than fifty feet above the level of the sea. Enormous flocks of wild-fowl flew high over head. The blacks were friendly enough and curious enough. They broke up the skiff they had towed so far, and found the river, since the junction, holding, as the black fellows had shown them, slightly south of west on the whole. They had now been rowing rapidly down stream for eighteen days.

Day succeeded day, and they still rowed on. After they had passed the junction of the Darling, no further hostility was exhibited by the natives. Their valiant friend, who had risked his life to save theirs, had done his work well. They now found themselves passed on, from tribe to tribe, by ambassadors, and treated in the most friendly way. Seldom do we get an instance of the action of one powerful mind producing such remarkable results. The poor savage was a typical person. In reading the history of the encroachments of the white race on the coloured race, one always finds a Montezuma, a man in advance of the thoughts of his countrymen—a man who believes in us and our professions, and thinks that the great hereafter will be a millennium of tomahawks, looking-glasses, and Jews'-harps. This poor fellow could hardly have succeeded in keeping the blacks quiet without some degree of eloquence. That, when he, single-handed, drove two or three hundred of them on the sand-bank, he merely frightened them by his fury into believing that the whites were a sacred and terrible race, I can quite believe. But after this he must have gone into particulars, and, shewing the tomahawks Sturt had given them, have begun to lie horribly. There is no other way of accounting for the singular change in the behaviour of the natives. Captain Sturt's great gun-trick fell perfectly dead on the audience at this part of the river. They had heard of it, and never so much as winked an eye at the explosion, but sat defiantly still. The temper of the natives must have been at this time neutral. They were determined to give these men—these white men—these men who came from the land of looking-glasses—these distributors of tenpenny nails—these fathers of Jews'-harps—a fair trial, on condition of their acting up to the character given of them by those natives who already had received tomahawks—on condition, in short, of being each one furnished with a looking-glass, a string of beads, and a tomahawk. This being impossible, Sturt was treated very much like an impostor on his way back, being made answerable for the wild representation of his friends. If the blacks had any cause for their behaviour, it must have been this.

They let them pass on from tribe to tribe, undergoing the most loathsome examination from the poor diseased savages. And now a new feature showed itself upon the river. The left banks became lofty, above one hundred feet high, of fantastically water-worn clay, apparently like the domes of the Mississippi, or the cliffs near Bournemouth. The natives as yet gave no information about the sea . . .

[*After further hardships Sturt arrived within one hundred miles of the rivermouth.*]

When this weary hundred miles was nearly passed they found that there was a tide in the river of nearly eight inches; and next day Sturt got out of the boat and climbed a hill, and saw that the end of it all was come. *Thalatta! Thalatta!* There it was at last, in the distance, with one great solitary headland, wrapped in a mist of driving sea-spray.

Between where he stood and the sea, the river expanded into a large lake, and this he determined to cross for the purpose of seeing whether there was a practicable channel into the sea. The spot on which he stood is nearly identical with the Ferry, at Wellington, a township on the Adelaide road. The nearest human habitation to him at that time, 1829, must have been nearly seven hundred miles away as the crow flies. Now, if he stood there, he would be able to take a coach to the city of Adelaide, fifty miles distant, containing twenty-five thousand inhabitants, and would pass through a beautiful settled country all the way. Or he could get on board one of the fleet of steamers which now ply on this river, and might go up in her above a thousand miles into the network of rivers which spread out of the Murray and the Darling.

Lake Alexandrina was the name he gave to this beautiful lake, fifty miles in length, across which they sailed in one day, and at sunset heard the surf bursting in on the sand. The next day they went down to the shore, and bathed in the great Southern Ocean.

There was no available passage into the sea. Had there been, Sturt thinks he would have made for Van Dieman's Land. As it was, he was eight hundred miles from help, with failing provisions and sickening men, a strong current, a danger of natives, who had by this time repented allowing them to pass, and violent physical pain of his own to contend with. Was ever man in such a case?

The men could not have rowed all the way, as became evident afterwards. God, it seemed, would not have the expedition perish, and most unexpectedly He sent a strong south wind, which lashed the broad lake and the long reaches of the Murray into waves, and before which they hoisted their sail and sped away homewards, across the solitary lake, among the swift sea-fowl, as though their whaleboat was seized with a panic as soon as they turned, and was flying for life . . .

[*The return journey was equally fraught with danger from both river and Aborigines.*]

We return to him entering the Morumbidgee, since leaving which they had rowed fifteen hundred miles, through an unknown desert country. Pause and think of this an instant; it is really worth while to do so. On the fifty-fifth day from their leaving it, they re-entered the narrow, gloomy channel of the tributary: the navigation was much obstructed, in consequence of the river having fallen. On the seventy-seventh day, having reached the place where the whaleboat had been launched, after a voyage of two thousand miles, they met with their greatest disappointment. Their companions were not there. The drays had failed to meet them, and the depot was deserted.

The men lost heart now for the first time. The river suddenly rose, and for seventeen terrible days longer they rowed without energy—almost without hope—against a swift current. They became terribly haggard, and at last the first man went mad, and showed the others the terrible fate in store for them, and forced them, in addition to their own gloomy thoughts, to listen to the raving of a lunatic. The mind of the chief himself became a little off its balance. With his noble simplicity he says:—"I became captious, and found fault when there was no occasion, and lost the equilibrium of my temper in contemplating the condition of my companions. . . . No murmur, however, escaped them. Macleay preserved his good humour to the last."

At Hamilton Plains, being still ninety miles from assistance by land, they abandoned the boat and took to the bush. It became necessary to send the two strongest men for assistance. Hopkinson and Mulholland were honoured by the selection, and the others remained camped. On the eighth day Sturt served out the last ounce of flour, and prepared to move his foodless and exhausted men on the way towards assistance. Suddenly there was a shout, and they knew that aid was come one way or another. Hopkinson and Mulholland had found the drays; and then these noble fellows, disregarding their fearful condition, had hastened back with a few necessaries to their chief, to fall utterly exhausted on the ground before him, but to tell him with smiling faces that he was saved.

The two great successful river-adventures of this century are undoubtedly Sturt's discovery of the Murray and Speke's discovery of the source of the Nile. But Sturt's discovery has of course led to commercial results far greater than any which can come from that of Speke. The Murray, draining a basin nearly equal to that of the true Mississippi (omitting the Missouri and Arkansas basins) is now covered with steam-boats, and flows through three splendid republics, whose presidents are nominated by the British Crown. No city stands on the Murray, in consequence of the unfortunate bar at the mouth, and so the dockyards required by the fleet of steamers are on Lake Victoria. But the beautiful city of Adelaide is but seventy miles off, and now, unless I am mistaken, connected with it by the Goolwa railway. And Charles Sturt has earned for himself the title of the father of Australian exploration.

Eyre, the South Australian Explorer*

The colony of South Australia, now the largest of the five colonies, was, about the year 1841, practically the smallest. The area available, either for cultivation or pasturage, seemed at that time to be extremely limited. Northward of the colony lay, or seemed to lie, the hideous, hopeless basin of Lake Torrens—a land of salt mud and shifting sand, from the description of Sturt and Eyre, in which human life was impossible, and the external aspects of which were so horrible that the eye wearied with looking on them, and the sickened soul soon brooded itself into madness. North-westward nothing had as yet been discovered but grassless deserts, while westward no human foot had penetrated beyond Eyre's peninsula. But the coast line to the west, between Port Lincoln, in South Australia, and King George's Sound, in West Australia, a distance of thirteen hundred miles, had been surveyed by Flinders from the sea, and pronounced by him to be what it is.

That main part of the South Australian coast called the Australian Bight is a hideous anomaly, a blot on the face of nature, the sort of place one gets into in bad dreams. For seven hundred miles there is no harbour fit to shelter a mere boat from the furious south wind, which rushes up from the Antarctic ice to supply the vacuum caused by the burning, heated, waterless continent. But

*Reprinted (with omissions as marked) from *Macmillan's Magazine* XII (October 1865): 501–10 and XII (November 1865): 55–63. It was republished as "Eyre's March" with "The March of Charles Sturt" in 1872 and 1895 (see note p.532).

there is worse than this. For *eleven hundred* miles no rill of water, no, not the thickness of a baby's little finger, trickles over the cruel cliffs into the sailless, deserted sea. I cast my eye over the map of the world, and see that it is without parallel anywhere. A land which seems to have been formed not by the 'prentice hand of nature, but by nature in her dotage. A work badly conceived at first, and left crude and unfinished by the death of the artist. Old thoughts, old conceptions which produced good work, and made the earth glad cycles agone, attempted again with a failing hand. Conceive digging through a three-foot crust of pleiocene formation, filled with crude, almost imbecile, forms of the lowest animal life, millions of ages later than Eozoon Canadense, yet hardly higher; and then finding shifting sea-sand below! Horrible, most horrible!

This, the most awful part of the earth's crust, a thousand miles in length, has been crossed once and once only. Not by a well-appointed expedition with camels, with horse-drays, preserved meats, and a fiddler; but by a solitary man on foot. A man irritated by disappointment; nigh worn-out by six months' dread battle with nature in her cruelest form: a man who, having been commissioned to do something in the way of exploration, would not return home without results: a man in whose path lurked murder, foul, treacherous, unexpected—the murder of a well-tried friend. To such a man has hitherto been reserved the task of walking a thousand miles round the Australian Bight. Was there ever such a walk yet? I have never heard of such another.

Of this Mr Eyre, who made this unparalleled journey, I know but little, save this:—He knew more about the aboriginal tribes, their habits, language, and so on, than any man before or since. He was appointed Black Protector for the Lower Murray, and did his work well. He seems to have been (*teste* Charles Sturt, from whom there is no appeal) a man eminently kind, generous, and just. No man concealed less than Eyre the vices of the natives, but no man stood more stedfastly in the breach between them and the squatters (the great pastoral aristocracy) at a time when to do so was social ostracism. The almost unexampled valour which led him safely through the hideous desert into which we have to follow him, served him well in a fight more wearing and more dangerous to his rules of right and wrong. He pleaded for the black, and tried to stop the war of extermination which was, is, and I suppose will be, carried on by the colonists against the natives in the unsettled districts beyond reach of the public eye. His task was hopeless. It was easier for him to

550 REVIEWS AND ARTICLES

find water in the desert than to find mercy for the savages. Honour to him for attempting it, however.

It is interesting to remember also, that this band of country of which we have been speaking practically divides the penal settlement of Western Australia from the civilized republics of the eastern coast, and must be crossed by any convict who should make his escape. The terror of the colonists which showed itself in such extreme irritation the other day, when it was proposed to send more criminals to Perth, was not without foundation, however. There is very little doubt that a practicable route exists from the east to the west, in the centre of the continent, about a thousand miles to the north of the southern coast—probably, I have thought for a long time, by the Valley of the Murchison.

It was originally proposed to send out an expedition under the command of Mr Eyre, to cross the bight to the westward; but his opinion was that although a light party might force their way, yet their success would be in the main useless, as it would be impossible ever to follow with stock in consequence of the badness of the country, and thus the main object of the expedition would be missed, and the expense incurred without adequate commercial results. The committee, therefore, yielding to his representations, commissioned him to go north, and attempt to explore the interior.

In this he was unsuccessful. Four hundred miles to the north of Adelaide he got into the miserable country, known then as the basin of Lake Torrens—now known as Lakes Gregory, Torrens, and Blanche—a flat depressed region of the interior, not far from equal to the basin of Lake Superior, of alternate mud, brackish water, and sand; after very wet seasons probably quite covered with water, but in more moderate ones intersected with bands of dry land varying in size. It is certain that in 1841 Eyre found a ring of water round him five hundred miles in extent, and that in 1860 MacKinlay crossed it, finding nothing but a desert fifty miles broad, without water visible on either hand,—came immediately into good country abounding with water, and crossed the continent from south to north.

Such an achievement was not for Eyre. To MacKinlay and others was left the task of showing the capabilities of Australia: to Eyre that of showing her deficiencies. Beaten back from the north at all points, he determined to follow out the first plan of the expedition, and try the coast-line westward. He forced his way out of this horrid barren region, bounded (if the reader will kindly look at his Keith Johnston, plate 19, enlarged plate of Australia in the corner, or at any available map of Australia) by Lakes Torrens, Gregory, and

Blanche—crossing the quasi-embouchure of Lake Torrens into the sea, and crossing that great peninsula which now bears his name, "Eyria"; and, after various difficulties and aggravations, he formed a depot of his party at Streaky Bay, just a thousand miles on the eastern or wrong side of King George's Sound, the object of his journey.

Here weary months were past, in desperate fruitless efforts to find a better country to the westward or northward. No water was to be had except by digging, and that was generally brackish, sometimes salt. The country was treeless and desolate, of limestone and sand, the great oolite cliffs, which wall the ocean for so many hundred miles, just beginning to rise towards the surface. The heat was so fearful that, on one of the expeditions which Mr Eyre made westward, a strong courageous man lay down, as uneducated men will do when things get to a certain stage of desperation. But Eyre got him up again, and got him down to the shore, where they found the shadow of a great rock in that weary land, and saved themselves by bathing the whole afternoon. This was the sort of country they had to contend with.

Eyre succeeded in rounding the head of the bight by taking a dray full of water with him, making a distance of 138 miles. The country, however, did not improve, and after seven months, he was back at his depot at Fowler's Bay (lat. 32° S. long. 132° E.) with no better results than these.

The expedition had hitherto consisted of Mr Eyre, Mr Scott, Mr Eyre's overseer, two Englishmen, a corporal of engineers, and two natives. Moreover, a small ship had been at its command, and had more than once communicated with Adelaide. It had been Mr Eyre's later plan to take part of his party overland, and keep this vessel to co-operate with him; but the answer from Adelaide was inexorable, though polite: the vessel must not leave the limits of the colony—must not, that is to say, go further west than long. 130° E.; no further, indeed, than Eyre had been himself. This was a great disappointment and perplexity. What to do?—But home save by one route—never! After very little cogitation he came to the following desperate resolution,—to dismiss the whole of the expedition except one man and with three natives to face the thing out himself.

Taking his young companion, Mr Scott, to walk with him upon the shore, he unfolded his plan to him, and gently but firmly dismissed him. Scott pleaded hard to share the danger, but Eyre was immoveable. He had selected another, a trusty, tried servant and comrade for years past, the man hitherto mentioned as his overseer.

This man Mr Eyre took on one side, and spoke to most earnestly. He pointed the almost hopelessness of their task—the horror of the country before them, the perils of thirst, the perils of savages, the awful distance, nine hundred miles. Then he told him that he was free to return to Adelaide and civilization, and leave him alone; and then he asked him, Would he go now? And the answer was, "Yes, by heaven, to the very end!"

His name is worth recording—John Baxter. A good sound, solid English name. The man himself, too, seems to have been nobly worthy of his name, and to have possessed no small portion of the patient and steadfast temper of his great Shropshire namesake . . .

[*They remained in camp for six weeks preparing for the expedition. The party now comprised Eyre, Baxter, and three Aborigines.*]

The six weeks passed; the horses and men got into good condition, as well fit for their hopeless journey as horses and men were ever likely to be. It became time to start, and they prepared to start; and here occurs one of those curious coincidences of time which do not startle us in a novel like "Aurora Floyd", because we know that the author has command of time and space, and uses them with ability for our amusement, but which do startle us, and become highly dramatic, when we find them in a commonplace journal, like that of Eyre. Eyre and Baxter were engaged in burying such stores as they could not take with them, when they heard a shot from the bay. Thinking some whalers had come in, they hurriedly concealed their work, and went towards the shore. It was no whaler. It was their own cutter, the *Hero*, which had been to Adelaide, and had returned. The two men they met on the shore were the captain of the *Hero* and young Scott, who brought a message, and innumerable letters . . .

[*Despite the many requests contained in the letters, Eyre refused to abandon the expedition and return home without result.*]

One of these savages requires notice from us; his name was Wylie. A frizzly-haired, slab-sided, grinning, good-natured young rascal; with infinite powers of giggling on a full belly, and plaintively weeping on an empty one—at least so I should guess. But withal some feeling of a faithful doglike devotion in the darkened soul of him, as events proved—something more in the inside of the man than any marmoset or other monkey ever had got, or ever would get after any number of cycles, one cannot help thinking. This fellow

Wylie was a *man* after all; as were, indeed, the other two natives, though bad enough specimens of the genus.

Having now brought my reader on to the real starting point of the great adventure, we may as well sum up the forces, by which this campaign against nature, in her very worst mood, was to be accomplished. The party which accompanied Mr Eyre when he took a final farewell of Mr Scott, on the morning of the 25th of February, 1841, consisted of—John Baxter, the useful hero; the black boy, Wylie, before spoken of; two other black boys; nine horses; a Timor pony (a small kind of fiend or devil, who has been allowed, for purposes, to assume the form of a diminutive horse, and in comparison with which Cruiser, or Mr Gurney's grey colt, would show like Cotswold lambs who have joined the Band of Hope); a foal (the best part of one of your high-bred weedy Australian colts is a certain cut out of the flank; if you are lucky enough to happen upon a Clydesdale foal, try a steak out of the shoulder (but this is mere cannibalism); and six sheep—merinos (ten pounds to the quarter, at the outside). Along the shore Eyre had, in a previous expedition, buried flour enough to last the party, at the rate of six pounds a week, for nine weeks. With this army, and with these resources, Eyre formed a flying column, cut himself off from his base of operations, and entered on a march of eight hundred and fifty miles through a hopelessly hostile country. Hostile, not so much because the natives he might meet on his march outnumbered him as fifty to one, but because Nature herself was in her cruel thirsty sleep of summer, and was saying to him, in every high floating yellow cloud which passed over his head southward, "Fool, desist; I am not to be troubled yet". Murder too was looking at him out of two pairs of shifting eyes; but he did not see her, and went on.

On the 26th of February, 1841, they made a place called by the few scattered natives Yeercumban Kowee, the furthest point they had hitherto reached in any of their excursions from the camp. It is so much less abominable than the country around that the natives have thought it worthy of a name. It is in fact a few hills of driving sand, where, by digging, one may obtain water; but, for all that, the best place in seven hundred miles of coast. It is the sort of place in which an untravelled reader would suppose a man would lie down and die in despair, merely from finding himself there: would suppose so until he found out how very little man can live with, and how very, very dear life gets in great solitude. Or, to correct myself once more, how very, very strong in such situations becomes the desire of seeing a loved face again; or, failing that, of seeing a face which will connect one, however distantly, with the civilization which is so far off, with the face of a man who will at all events tell those for whose applause we strive how we strove and how we died.

Here the terrible part of his adventure begins. From this he was 128 miles without water, toiling over the summit of those great unbroken cliffs which form the southern buttress of Australia . . .

[*Water was to prove a problem and, with all the hardships involved, Eyre traversed 135 miles before discovering some abandoned native water holes. Proceeding from that point the party was to travel a further 160 miles before obtaining relief, being, at one stage, reduced to collecting dew.*]

The miserable details are wearisome to write down. At the 160th mile from the last water, after seven days' drought for the horses and their one sheep, and two for themselves, Eyre and the overseer having gone on in desperation alone, digging in the first likely spot they had seen, found the sand moist and fresh, and soon came on an abundance of excellent water.

Among these sand-hills they stayed for twenty-eight days, Eyre going back alone with a boy to recover the baggage. On the occasion of this expedition they speared a sting ray, and ate him. This proved a somewhat valuable discovery, as it eked out their fast failing provisions. The weather became cold, but no rain fell, though there were occasionally heavy thunderstorms. The cliffs again approached the shore about fourteen miles to the westward; and Baxter went forward to examine them. His report was exceedingly unfavourable. Of course it was impossible for them to go any way but along the top of them, and the downs appeared to be grassless and waterless. Baxter was anxious to go back, but Eyre quietly determined to go on.

They killed one of their horses, and the natives feasted on it all day long, while they made some unsuccessful efforts to jerk it. The effect of this great feed of meat was exactly such as Mr Bumble would have expected. The natives grew rebellious, announced their intention of shifting for themselves, and marched off. Even the gentle Wylie, the King George's Sound native, shared in the revolt. The younger of the two Port Lincoln Blacks, however, was sufficiently under command to obey the eye and voice of Mr Eyre, and to remain behind.

Still they lingered here, unwilling to face the next 150 miles of cliff, where they knew there could be no water without rain. But the rain did not come; and, having kills their last sheep, they prepared to set forward. The night before they started, however, the two native deserters, beaten back by hunger and thirst, returned. Wylie was frankly penitent, and acknowledged that he had made a fool of himself; but the Port Lincoln blacks sat sulking by the fire, refusing to speak.

They now went on their weary way and ascended the cliffs. The downs were, as Baxter had reported, waterless and stony, with a dwarf tea-scrub (much like our chalk-down juniper). The first night, for the first time on the journey, the blacks were set to watch the horses.

Eyre had intended to travel the main part of the next night; but when it came on, Baxter urged him so strongly to remain that he yielded, the more easily as Baxter's reasons appeared good. Rain was threatening, and they were now in a place where water might be collected from the rock-pools, whereas, were they to advance, and the country to get sandy, the rain would be of no use to them. So they stayed where they were, and it was Baxter and Eyre's turn to watch the horses. Eyre, not being sleepy, took the first watch, and Baxter and the natives lay down to sleep.

The night was cold and wild, with scud driving across the moon, and a rushing wind which tossed the shrubs and sang loudly among the rocks. The place was very solitary—a high treeless down four hundred feet above the vast Southern Ocean: a place not unlike the great down above Freshwater. The horses were very restless, keeping Eyre moving up and down, till at half-past ten he had lost sight of the camp fires. While he was looking round to catch a sight of them he saw a gun fired about a quarter of a mile off. Calling out, and receiving no answer, he ran towards the spot, and was met by Wylie, crying, "Come here! Come here!" He ran in terror on to the camp fire, and there he found poor Baxter weltering in his blood inarticulate. How many minutes it was before he died, Eyre cannot say; but he did not speak or recognize him. The poor tortured body sank into quiescence, without one word having passed the lips; and the soul, still in its agony of torture, of indignation, of horror, with a burthen of explanations and messages to loved ones at home still struggling and struggling in vain to get sent by its usual channel, went wandering away over the desolate down-lands to ——

And poor Eyre was left alone in the waterless desert, five hundred miles from help, with terror, unutterable grief, and despair for his companions. No others, unless it were the crawling sea, the thirsty down, and a crouching whining savage, who wrung his hands and whimpered! None other, indeed, except the God in whom he trusted, and who delivered him even out of this!

PART II

Five hundred miles from any hope of help, in the very centre of the most horrible waterless desert on the face of the earth, poor Eyre stood that night, on the desolate down above the desolate sea, all alone save for one crouching, guilty-looking savage, and the corpse of his dearly loved companion lying stark and bloody in the flying gleams of the moon.

First terror, then indignation, then grief, then the dull horror of utter loneliness and despair, and the indescribable ghastly oppression of great and hopeless distance, which clawed at his heart like a nightmare; these were his other companions. Sometimes he prayed, sometimes he wept, sometimes he walked up and down, in short, tiger-like snatches, in his furious indignation meditating revenge before death. But all the time the cold chill wind rushed over the down, drove the sparks of the fire landward, and moved the dead man's hair. Whose imagination is powerful enough to conceive the unutterable horrors of such a night, in such a place?

The man was a high-strung and very sensitive man. This mad journey of his would prove it to a thoughtful reader, even if he would not take my word for it. But, high-strung and sensitive as he was, he was as *indestructible* a man as Big Boone himself. Nay, if Big Boone had, with his vast frame, found himself in this match against Nature, I think, if I may be allowed a sporting phrase, that I should have backed Nature.

But there was such an irrepressible vitality about this man, such a dexterous manipulation of the very worst materials, that he could not be beaten. In the midst of his very despair he had taken measures for continuing the struggle, and had completed them long before the morning dawned. The first discovery he made in the dark was the very unpleasant one that he was left without the means of self-defence, or, what was dearer just now, Revenge; that the two blacks had got the available firearms, and were lurking round among the scrub with them; and that his life was not worth five minutes' purchase of any one's money. He had pistols, but no cartridges. His only other hope was in a rifle, which they had not taken. But this rifle was unserviceable. The murdered man had, a few days before, done the only undexterous thing recorded of him—tried to wash out the rifle while it was loaded. By the time he had found out it *was* loaded, he had wetted and partly washed out the powder, so that it was impossible to get it out; they had no screw to draw the bullet, and the rifle had been thrown aside as utterly useless. (Rifles are the most utterly useless trash in Australia, even for kangaroo-shooting. Eley's green cartridge in a double barrel is the only arm which a reasonable man uses for the larger game.) This disabled rifle was his only hope, and his only chance of getting it to work was to melt out the bullet. He put the barrel in the fire; but there was powder enough left to explode, and the bullet whizzed close by his ear. After such an accident at such a time he may be considered safe.

When the rifle was loaded he felt more secure. The next thing which engaged the attention of our πολυμητις was the horses, on whom everything depended. He went into the scrub after them at the risk of being shot, and got them. After this he waited for morning.

The raving wind went down towards morning, and by degrees the grey dawn crept over the desolate down, and bit by bit showed him all the circumstances and all the extent of the horrible midnight disaster. Baxter lay in his shirt about five yards from his bed, shot through the breast, soaking in blood; his eyes, Eyre tells us, were still open, but glazed in death; and the same expression of stern resolution which he had worn in life was still on the face of the corpse. The camp was plundered, and everything was broken by the murderers. After examination he found that all they left was forty pounds of flour and four gallons of water.

Before he started westward, one duty remained to him, that of paying the last tribute of decency and friendship to his dead friend. The soil was bare limestone rock for miles around, and time was life. All that he could do for the poor senseless corpse was to wrap its head decently in a blanket, and leave it to wither in the woods. There it lies still, and there most likely it will lie for ever. Old Earth is such a bitter cruel stepmother in that accursed country, that she even refuses to take her dead children back to her bosom . . .

[*Eyre believed Wylie capable of being a plunderer but not a murderer. On the other hand the other two Aborigines, he considered, menaced his life.*]

Wylie was a very good, a somewhat exceptional, specimen of his people, as Eyre, a lover and protector of the blacks, allows. Now, you know these people must *go*. God never made the Portland Bay district for *them*. All one asks is, that the thing should be done with decency, and with every sort of indulgence; whereas it is not, but in a scandalous and disgraceful manner. Of course these Australians must be improved, but let the improvement be done with some show of decency. But we may preach and preach, and the same old story will go on, now there is no Governor Gipps; and so we will leave preaching, and mind our business, for public opinion, unbacked by a Governor Gipps, is but a poor thing for the blacks.

The above paragraph was written yesterday, and, under ordinary circumstances, I should have altered it, and polished it down. But this morning I got my *Times*, and read about the massacre of the Indians on the Colorado; and that seemed to illustrate what I have said above in such a singular manner that I determined to let the paragraph stand, just as I had jotted it down, as a matter of curiosity. The leading article in the *Times* this morning was remarkably sensible. When the colonists are left to administer justice in their own way, they do invariably say, "We must fight as they fight", and they not only say so, but do so. For very decency's sake, this improving business should be done by paid third parties, if it were only to avoid scandal. *So* we are going to withdraw the imperial troops from New Zealand, and do the business in a shorter and cheaper manner.

Eyre, however, as he started at eight o'clock on the morning after the murder, with his forty pounds of flour and his four gallons of water, was not, probably, in the humour to think deeply over this question. His life's work had been, and was to be, the protection of these savages against the whites. But on this particular morning things had gone so very cross with him, that he found the leading resolution in his very resolute mind was to cut off the first one caught sight of, like a rabbit. "How circumstances do change people." His horses had now been three days without water, and where the next was to be got he had no idea. However, he started over the downs, on his five hundred miles tramp, in an exceedingly defiant mood. "Not an ounce of die in him", as I heard a cockney blacksmith say about a sick friend.

He had one interview, and one only, with these murderous young vagabonds. At four o'clock in the afternoon, he saw them approaching cautiously. One cannot help wishing that he had had an Enfield rifle, instead of one of those miserable things we called rifles in those days; but he had not. A rifle of those times was not sighted above a hundred yards, and they would not give him a shot. He walked towards them, but they kept beyond distance; and at last, in despair, he threw down his own rifle, and advanced unarmed, hoping to get near enough to run in on one of them, wrest his loaded gun from him, and &c. If I am not mistaken, the Victoria Cross has been given for less than this. But they would not come near him, but kept away, crying out for Wylie. Master Wylie, to whom every cry of theirs was a fresh piece of evidence as to his complicity in the murder, did not know them, had never seen these low coloured persons before, wondered what they could possibly mean by hollering after him, and so on, with all the transparent childish cunning of a savage; leading his horses on, and leaving the question in the hands of Providence, and those of an extremely infuriated English gentleman called Eyre; and walked calmly on in saint-like innocence.

Eyre could do nothing with them; they only went on running away, and implicating Wylie's character to an extent which must have exasperated that young gentleman to a pitch many degrees beyond murder. After a time Eyre came back, picked up his rifle, and saw them no more.

What they did, or what became of them, we shall never know exactly. If they did not die of famine, they were most certainly murdered by the first natives they came across. One can guess at their motives in plundering the camp and murdering Baxter. They possibly (I will go no further than possibly) wanted a good feed, and hated Baxter. But this is an exceptional case. In general, you can form no guess whatever of an Australian black's motives. If you notice, you will find yourself very much puzzled by the motives of your own children. But their motives for action are the hardest common sense, if you compare them with those of an Australian black. The only crime which I have heard of on this side of the water, and which I can compare to the aimless murders so common among these queer Australians, is the murder committed by Constance Kent on her little brother. It was Australian "all over". I knew the old hand at once.

Allow me to tell an anecdote in illustration. I was staying in an Australian country house once, in the far west,—a real Australian country house, where the kangaroos came skipping and staring, and gandering past the dining-room windows; where the opossums held high jinks and murdered sleep in the shrubberies every night; where the native cats stowed themselves under your bed until you had gone to sleep, and then proclaimed their case against an ungrateful world in a noise which might be achieved in an inferior degree by a wicked old tom cat, carefully trained by a howling ape and a hyena;—a house with a flower-garden, at the bottom of which was a lake on which no one was allowed to fire a shot, and which swarmed all through the burning summer's day with teal, widgeon, great cranes, pelicans, black swans, and purple water-hens;—a house in which the scorpions came tittle, tittle, tittle, along the passage, looked in at the library door to see how you were getting on, and then packed themselves away under the doormat; where enormous centipedes came from under the fender at a terrific pace, eight inches long, twenty legs a side, struck with a sudden uncontrollable impulse to walk up the leg of your trousers, and see what *that* was like;—a house where some one was always going to bed after breakfast, and "coming down" as fresh as paint, just out of his bath, to an eight o'clock dinner; where you slept all day, and went out a-fishing as soon as the night was dark enough; where your papers were the *Spectator* and the *Illustrated London News*, and one's drink weak claret and water;—a real old hundred thousand acre, two thousand a year, Australian country house, in short.

In such a house as this, it once befell that I had to stay for an indefinite time. On the first morning, when I came down (there was only one storey, but I will continue the fiction) to breakfast, I found a very smart-looking native girl, dressed much as your own housemaid is dressed, dusting the room. She looked so much smarter and brighter than any native woman I had ever seen before, that I asked Mrs L—— (may her days be long in the land), the Scotch housekeeper, about her antecedents.*

There was a queer story about her. Her brother, a native, was one groom, and another young native was another groom; and one day, not two months before, these two young rascals had agreed to murder her. There was no more cause for it than there is for your murdering me, but they thought they would like to do it; they had not tasted blood lately, and, although they were very well off, had plenty to eat, worked no more than they chose, and so on, yet things were rather slow in these parts; so they thought they would murder this young woman. They proceeded to do so; they had got her down, her brother was throttling her—hope was lost—it was a matter of moments—when—

Here comes your sensation—Mrs L——, a very strong and opinionated Scotchwoman came in and caught them at it. Not only caught them at it, but caught the principal offender across the back of the head with a carpet-broom, stopped the whole business, and routed the enemy single-handed. It is time we walked on with Eyre, and so we must have done with Mrs L——; I have no more to tell you of her than this: When the station was attacked by the blacks, she and the two gentlemen of the house were alone. The two hundred savages were so near accomplishing their object that they

---

*Editor's note: Mrs Laidlaw of Rolf Boldrewood's station, Squattleseamere.

actually were upon the roof, and were casting their spears in upon the three. The roof would not fire, in consequence of a heavy rain, and my two hosts picked off every man who appeared in the gap of the roof which they had made. Mrs L—— all the time stood between them, loading their guns and handing them to them alternately, until assistance came from Port Fairy. Another fact about her is this: I never could convince her that the great wedge-tailed eagle of Australia was to be compared to our own twopenny-halfpenny golden eagle. The colonists have, for their own reasons, christened these birds "eagle hawks". "Ye have no been to Scotland?" she would say; "I tell ye, sir, they are naething to the Scottish eagle." Common specimens measured fifteen feet across the wings!

What with Mrs L—— and the eagles, we have left poor Eyre on his waterless down, five hundred miles from help, somewhat too long. We shall have one more terrible push with him, and then the story will become more pleasant, or rather less horrible, to read . . .

[*After encountering the murderers, Eyre and Wylie pushed on rapidly. As they progressed westwards the horse was killed for food and more favourable country was encountered.*]

It got bitter cold, so that a new fear took possession of him—whether or no he should be able to face the next three hundred miles with cold and starvation as his companions. Scurvy, according to all precedent, would soon set in; and already he had to use force to get Wylie to move after sitting down. Really it seemed a hopeless business even now. He little knew what a glorious piece of good fortune God's providence had in store for him. One cannot help seeing that, but for one singular accident, the chances were still a hundred to one against him.

The French whaler, *Mississippi,* commanded by one Rossiter, an Englishman, had found herself in these Australian seas just as the Pritchard-Tahitian dispute had breezed up to that extent that war between France and England seemed almost a matter of certainty. Rossiter became very much alarmed. To go home and lose his voyage was ruin; to be captured by a British cruiser was ruin and imprisonment besides; yet there was no coast but that of the enemy for some thousands of miles. Under these circumstances he betook himself to the most desolate and out-of-the-way place he could think of, and anchored in a bay in lat. 34° long. 122°, behind an island. It was a fine enough anchorage, but in those times it had no name. It was so desolate and so utterly out of the way of all human knowledge, that in the year of grace 1841 it had actually had no name, for the simple reason that no one had ever been there before.

"A waste land where no one comes,
  Or hath come since the making of the world."

They knew this coast—that it was waterless and uninhabited for a thousand miles. It did not matter to them: they had their ship, and cared little for the shore. They used to see it there every day, yellow and bare and treeless, with a few mountains on the left in the dim hot distance; so it had been for ever, and would be for evermore. But one day it had a strange new interest for them: they, as they were idly busying themselves with cleaning their cables, which were foul, saw a man moving on the shore. It seemed incredible, but their glasses confirmed it. It was a white man, who knelt on a point and was making a fire to signal them. Half a dozen of them tumbled into a whale boat; and, as the beautiful craft came leaping and springing towards the shore, their wonder grew into amazement. It was a white man indeed, but such a man as they had never seen before. He was wan and thin, his clothes were ragged; he seemed wild, and looked like one who had risen from the dead: a man who had evidently such a story to tell that you trembled while you waited for him to begin. Such a man stood on the very verge of a wave-worn rock among the climbing surge, with strained eyes and parted lips, eagerly holding out his wasted hands towards them.

To say that they had him into the plunging boat off the slippery sea-weed in a minute; to say that they embraced him, patted him on the back, and looked fondly at him, that they in one breath demanded his story of him, and in the next forbade him to open his mouth until he had refreshed himself—is only to say that they were sailors, and, what is more, Frenchmen. Here was something which suited their great sailor hearts entirely. Here was unprecedented headlong courage: here was endurance equally unprecedented: here was a man who had been where no one had been before, and had seen what no one could ever see again. To be blown a thousand miles out of your course was one thing, but to have *walked* a thousand miles was quite another. If Eyre had done the distance in a fast spring cart (that mode of locomotion which a sailor specially affects), it would have been a noble action. But to have walked (a sailor never walks), seemed, I suspect, to put a halo of romance about the affair which it would not have had otherwise. At all events, their hearts were in the right place; and Eyre, from a lonely, hopeless wanderer, found himself suddenly transformed into a hero.

One must be allowed to be mildly jocular for a moment, for the story has been so miserably tragical hitherto. We would try to avoid the sin of jocularity as much as possible; there is very little temptation to it here; and yet I should be disposed to guess that Eyre was inclined to laugh boisterously at the smallest joke.

That night he slept on board the *Mississippi*. As the night darkened, the wind rose and moaned till the moan grew into a shriek, and then raved on till it became a gale. But the good ship *Mississippi*, in the lee of the island, cared little for this, and Eyre less. Lying warm and snug in his bunk, between the blankets, he only heard the slopping tread of the officer of the watch over head, and so knew it was raining: only heard the wild wind aloft among the rigging, and so knew that it was blowing. He thought how that rain was beating and that wind was tearing among the desolate sand-hills, where he would have lain this night had it not been for the providence of a merciful God, who, it seemed to him, was resolved to see him through it all, and not let his adventure end in utter useless disaster. So, every time he was awakened by the officer of the watch or the wind in the rigging, he said a short fervent prayer of deep thankfulness to Almighty God for His mercy, and then turned himself to happy sleep once more, only to hear the wild rain and the wilder wind singing a pleasant bass through his hopeful dreams.

For, if he *could* get through with this business, he had done what no man had ever done before, or would ever do again. The thing could never be repeated; there was not, and there is not, room on the earth for the repetition of such an adventure by a sane man. If he did it—if the cup was not dashed from his lips now—he would be immortal. It is perfectly certain that his adventure was, in its way, the greatest ever carried through; but, as for the immortality of it, I cannot find any one in London who ever heard of it or of him. A few of the oldsters in Melbourne, and a few more in Sydney, remember the thing being done; but the expedition led to nothing positive—only proved in the most offensively practical way that you *could not*, whereas Eyre's duty as a man and explorer had been supposed to be to prove that you *could*.

He stayed a fortnight with Captain Rossiter, who treated him with the extremest kindness, though he himself was in deep anxiety about the war and the fate of his ship. He fitted out Eyre with every necessary and luxury, and started him again on his journey with every good wish. Eyre gave him bills on his agent at Albany for the things he had, but they were never presented. He never again saw or heard of the man to whom he was so deeply indebted.

He had now been a year exactly on his expedition. The splendid staff of companions with which he had started was dwindled down to one solitary savage, and there were yet two hundred and fifty miles of distance; but still hope grew stronger each mile they made forward through the driving bitter weather. The country got more interesting as his journal becomes less so.

One morning when he rose he told Wylie that they would see the mountains beyond the Sound before night. Wylie was very sceptical about it—in fact, never really believed that they would reach the Sound at all. But in the afternoon the grand rugged outline of his native hills broke upon his view, and he gave way to the wildest transport of joy. He knew every valley in them, and every tree which feathered their sides. There his own brothers and relations were waiting for him now.

The fourth day from this they left their horses and pushed on rapidly. It was a fearfully wet day, and, though they were close to the town, they had not met a living creature facing the furious weather. The first creature they met was a native, who knew Wylie, and from him they learnt that they had been given up two months before. Shortly after Wylie was in the bosom of his enraptured tribe, and Eyre was shaking hands with Lady Spencer.

Wylie was pensioned by Government, and retired to his tribe, where, I have no doubt, he took heartily to lying about his journey, and in due time got to believe his own lies. He may be alive now, and may have seen Redpath. Peace be with him!

Mr Eyre had now finished his journey. From the time he had dismissed the rest of his staff, and had come on with the overseer alone, he had been four months and ten days, and had travelled in actual distance about a thousand miles. Since Baxter was murdered, and he was entirely alone with Wylie, he had been two months and five days, and had come between five and six hundred miles. The distance passed over, without finding one drop of surface water, was seven hundred miles, the distance from London to Vienna. He returned to Adelaide, and met with the welcome he deserved, and so the great adventure came to an end. That dreadful band of country has never been invaded since, and Baxter's bones still lie out on the desolate down, bleaching in the winds.

The Last Two Abyssinian Books*

. . . It is most likely that our hotter spirits will find themselves utterly disappointed of any sort or kind of fighting whatever. It happened once that I formed part of an expedition, nearly, if not quite, fifty thousand strong, during which every man did what seemed right in his own eyes, and the very policemen sent for our protection were hunted away, into a country which, from all I can hear, was worse than the most part of Abyssinia. Our real basis of operations was two hundred miles away. If it be said that we were not advancing into an enemy's country, and that we had no lines of communication to preserve, I answer that the ruffians—convicts and bushrangers— who hung on our flank and rear, did far more to interrupt our communications than the Shoho tribe is ever likely to do. And yet this expedition, fifty thousand strong, in which every man shifted for himself, was thoroughly successful. I do not think that there were any deaths from such causes as we anticipate in the Abyssinian expedition. Men were certainly killed by careless mining, and a policeman was shot dead in trying to arrest a bushranger; but these were the only serious casualties I can call to mind. No one ever wanted anything to eat that I heard of, if he had money to pay for it: if he had not, somebody was sure to give it to him. As for enough to drink, there was a great deal too much champagne in certain quarters. The quieter souls amongst us wished that there had been

*Reprinted from *The Fortnightly Review* VIII (November 1867): 547–58, and refers to Sir Samuel White Baker's *The Nile Tributaries of Abyssinia*, and *Narrative of a Journey through Abyssinia in 1862–3* by Henry Dufton.

less. Water, however, was not very abundant. All that was procurable was contained in a river which pleases to call itself the Hopkins. I am at a loss to find a river sufficiently familiar with my readers, and sufficiently small to illustrate the Hopkins. "I forget at this moment," says Mr Dickens somewhere, in speaking of a very small steamer in which he travelled, "how short this boat was, or how narrow." In the same way I am puzzled to find a river in England, with a name, sufficiently small to bring the Hopkins before my reader's eye. Most people have passed Twyford on the Great Western Railway, where the Loddon divides into *three* (not as old Camden says, into *two*) streams. The smallest of these streams, which united have scarcely strength to reach the Thames, is, for all practical purposes, a perfect Mississippi to the Hopkins. And, in addition to this, the Loddon is, in its smallest branch, perennial and well aërated. Now, the Hopkins was not perennial; it was merely a chain of water holes; and yet this creek, for river it was not, was perfectly sufficient to supply fifty thousand souls with water, not only for drinking purposes, but for the purpose of washing thousands of tons of auriferous dirt.

Therefore, with the personal experience of the great Ararat rush before me, I honestly confess that I have no fear of our soldiers wanting water. We neither wanted water nor anything else. An objector may say—"You, however, had no commissariat officers", to which I am dumb.

In this place, if I may be allowed a few lines' space to say what is perhaps irrelevant, I should like to note that it was the *Chinese* who crept up and found the spot; and moreover, that the people who undertook to keep up our communications with our basis of operations by coaches, were all Americans; Yankees almost universally from the Northern States. It is like Hebrew to speak to an English reader about "Cobb's line", but I cannot help whimsically wondering whether, if our military authorities had contracted with "Cobb's line" for the transport of the Abyssinian expedition, these wonderful Americans, who drive their coaches across America among hostile Indians, would not have done it for them, at least quite as well as they will do it for themselves.

We have this fact, then, fifty thousand people poured themselves into a very poorly-watered, porous sandstone country, with a mere supply and demand commissariat, and did well. So far all seems to be promising well. But there is another instance of swarming, in which a very few people got into one of the finest regions in the whole world—a very land of streams; but being too far from their base of operations, perished miserably. The Ararat rush, or swarm, of which I have given a description, was successful. The great Omco rush was one of the most unfortunate things—one of the very saddest and most miserable things which ever happened. How many perished we shall never know; those who got safely across the mountains to Beechworth saved themselves; and I myself sat in Beechworth, and heard from a man who had followed us, a man who looked more dead than alive, the story of the awful disaster which had happened in our rear.

Nature in these uncertain latitudes must not be trifled with. You may play with her in the Arctic regions with greater safety than you can play with her when her number gets about thirty-five, or below. If you do, she has a fearful habit of destroying you in a fit of passion and fury, in comparison with which her Arctic anger is as cold as the cold ice by which she works it out . . .

PART 5

Extracts from The Daily Review *(Edinburgh)*

1871

The Daily Review *Editorial of 1 October 1869**

. . . The staff of the paper will remain unaltered, and we shall, one and all, be bent on increasing, instead of merely maintaining, its efficiency. Our political and religious views remain entirely unchanged: present and approaching affairs will be treated with liberality and without prejudice, as heretofore: our object being to assure ourselves of what is right by consideration, and then pursue it unflinchingly. New features will be introduced and old ideas developed.

Literature will take a still more prominent place with us than heretofore. As far as space will in any way permit, all books of sufficient merit will be from time to time reviewed; not with reckless, hurried sciolism, but with due care and diligence. Books of high scientific or historic interest will be carefully read, and their chief points of interest shown, with a view of informing those whose engagements do not permit them the time for reading such works. Books of slighter interest, again, will be freely commented on; always in a kindly spirit, yet without any lack of bold speaking, wherever bold speaking seems to be necessary.

Great diligence will be used in pointint out to the readers of the *Daily Review* such articles in the quarterly and monthly periodical literature as may seem to be of higher interest, with more or less comment upon them. This is a task by no means useless or

*Kinglsey's editorial appeared on his assumption of the editorship. His engagement lasted for eighteen months.

unnecessary; the mass of periodical writing is far too great for any ordinary reader to wade through, and amidst much that is indifferent, or difficult to read, there will be found by those who seek some jewels of literature—frequently by young and unknown hands—which left unnoticed might attract but little attention.

Another feature will also be introduced, that of frequent extracts and translations from foreign papers, showing the state of public opinion abroad. Every week, also, we shall prepare a column of causeries, both serious and amusing, from various sources.

With a programme like this, capable of great expansion, we hope to retain the confidence of old readers and to attract new. To sum up, all our object will be to keep our readers, with as little trouble to themselves as possible, completely *au fait* with the latest facts and the newest ideas.

*Victoria as a Field for Emigration**

Sixteen years ago all the British and Irish world were mad on one point—emigration, and emigration to one single country, Australia, and to one single province, Victoria. There was actually a partial exodus from the United States to that wonderful province; and indeed there was quite sufficient reason for it. California had been a great thing, but it had never been anything to Victoria: California had done its eight millions of exports, Victoria was threatening to get on to twelve. The Minas-Geraes in the last century had nearly equalled California, nothing had ever come near Victoria. The world, or at least representatives of it, from noblemen to sweeps, went. The noblemen came away having satisfied their curiosity: there were many who could not get away at all, and have stood there ever since.

A very large number of people went there who were utterly unfitted for the place: not in the way of training very often, for young gentlemen, highly educated, turned often into very good workmen: but utterly unfitted through want of experience, of experience which was seldom gained before the emigrant found his capital, whatever it might have been, gone, and his hands utterly tied by poverty. Great numbers, misled by high prices, took out their little all in the shape of goods, to find the market glutted, and to sell their goods at such miserable prices that the Jews made fortunes by reimporting them to England. The town was not built either,

*Reprinted from *The Daily Review*, 16 October 1869, p.2, col. 2-3.

although the population of it quadrupled in no time. Tradesmen took leases at gold prices, and found the leases left on their hands to their great distress when rents had fallen. The land was practically in the hands of the squatters (great sheep-owners), and what between one thing and another, there arose a cry which seemed very reasonable, that the labour market was overstocked, and although a good steady emigration has been going on, yet Victoria and her six hundred thousand inhabitants have rather dropped out of popularity as a field of emigration among the thirty million of the British Islands.

The fact of the matter is that, now the gold fever is gone, and gold mining is only a steady trade like any other mining, the United States offer a field so very desirable to the emigrant that a great many will not take the trouble to examine any other. Now, it so happens that there are some people so naturally perverse and wicked that they dislike American institutions, American manners and have the strangest and most rooted objection to the general run of American people. When they get to the United States, if they do well they generally get to be rather caricatured Yankees, if they do ill they steadily abuse it: but a vast number of people would far sooner try any other country in the world than the United States. To people who like to find an England in a new land, to people who want to change as little as possible, certainly many places are preferable to the United States, and Victoria is one of them.

No book save the most recent can be trusted to give any reliable information about this colonial republic, for matters change so very swiftly there. For a long time the principal power of the legislative body was in the hands of the squatters—a kind of territorial aristocracy of vast wealth, who held all the lands on leases from Government at peppercorn rents, and were taxed according to the number of their sheep or cattle. For a long time they practically had the making of the laws, and it as with great difficulty that the cry of "unlock the land" was listened to: land was extremely difficult to get, and the sentimental grievance was very great indeed. Small people whose hope—nay, whose passion—it was to get a freehold of their own were half ruined by rent in bad lodgings; but one change after another, each more and more liberal as the new constitution came into full action, came on, and at last, in the year 1865, the system of free selection before surveying came into full operation, and the people came into their magnificent inheritance. Among six hundred thousand of them there was open for their selection this splendid kingdom.

Of rich loams and alluvial flats, twenty-three millions of acres; of the unequalled black and chocolate soil, which is in places six feet thick, and will grow fifty bushels of the very finest wheat ever seen in Mark Lane, eight millions of acres; of lighter and more sandy granite soils, five millions of acres. Here is a country for half the poor in England (we do not mean the *paupers*, but the poor who will work); let us see on what terms these thirty-six millions of acres of land are to be had: they are to be had practically for nothing.

The provisions of the new Act are these. Any person may select land not alienated from the Crown, in any part of the colony, in a quantity not exceeding a square mile, or six hundred and forty acres. A yearly licence will be issued for this land, the fee being two shillings per annum per acre, payable in advance half-yearly. The holding must be fenced in within eighteen months, and one acre out of every ten selected must be brought under cultivation; and moreover the licensee must reside on his farm for six months. In three years the settler must have made improvements on his land to the extent of £1 per acre, and at the end of that time he can exchange his licence for a lease extending over ten years at the original price of two shillings per acre; and at the payment of the last year's rent, his farm will be conveyed to him, happy man, free of charge, from the Crown, to be his own property and that of his descendants. The leaseholder may at any time pay off the whole of the rental, and so receive his lands in fee simple at once, and should the rental be paid at the end of three years' licence, his land will not cost him more than sixteen shillings an acre.

Such are the opportunities open to an emigrant for making a new home in a country, for all practical purposes, as highly civilized as this in which we live. The country is intersected by railways, and netted with telegraph wires. Churches of all denominations abound. The schools are equal to our own. For higher education there is the Melbourne University, officered by picked men from the English universities—men selected for their acquirements regardless of expense. The country is very beautiful, and the climate like that of the south of France—that is to say, not so good as our own with regard to extreme heat, and subject to more rapid changes; yet far superior to it in the matter of heat. A common custom for English doctors now is to send their patients to Australia. The city of Melbourne is rather bigger than Bristol, full of beautiful buildings, and surrounded by fine gardens and parks; life and property are more secure than in London, and in every respect the country is rapidly advancing. Fever and ague, the curses of newly settled lands, are unknown; and, in short, Victoria is one of the finest heritages into which the English race have come. It offers freedom, cultivation, education, and moderate wealth to every well-conducted citizen, without any reference to birth, religion, or nation. What could any land offer more? We propose, in our next article, to discuss one of the Western States of North America, and see what advantage our American cousins have to offer to the shifting population of the old country in comparison to this beautiful possession of our own.

Queensland*

Any one intending to emigrate, and seeking such information as he may require, must be exceedingly cautious before he commit his whole future prosperity to one cast of the die. Now, in seeking information, two classes of people must be to some extent looked on with distrust—the one interested, the other entirely disinterested and enthusiastic. In any of our colonies it is extremely rare to find any man, or still less any woman, who has been sober, diligent, and respectable, and yet who in the long run has gone wrong. Yet all should remember that these colonies are in a state of transition— that what is true of them to-day is not true to-morrow—that what is true of them this year may not be true of them next, but will be pretty sure to be true the year after. In the Australian colonies particularly, there are great temporary changes in prosperity. A great drought, like that of last year; a sudden find of gold, not sustained, bringing in a flux of immigration and a sudden glut of prosperity, frequently ending in a financial crisis, may convert for a little time one of those splendid colonies into a place by no means desirable for a penniless man. In a less degree also, two classes of people, the one, as we said, interested, that is the shipowners, and the other utterly disinterested, the philanthropists, are very apt to bring about a glut in the labour market, and earn the hearty malediction of the emigrant. These things should be guarded against.

*Reprinted from *The Daily Review*, 26 October 1869, p.2, col.2–3.

If an emigrant gets a fancy for any new country, he buys the last book or pamphlet on the subject, and in that book or pamphlet he is pretty sure to find the place described as a terrestrial paradise. We have more than once seen the Moreton Bay district, now called Queensland, described as such, whereas it is nothing of the kind, but only a very excellent place in its way, with a good many drawbacks which an emigrant should know about before he goes. The only use of such articles as those which we are now writing is to let people know, as far as we can, the real state of the case. Queensland is an excellent country, but it would be a bad thing to do anything to produce a glut on the labour or capital market there now.

Queensland is a vast territory, almost entirely tropical, and an anomaly in that land of anomalies, Australia: for it produces at once high-class wool, with cotton, coffee, and sugar—a fact which points it out at once as the land rather of the British capitalist than of the British labourer. Still there is a very good opening for the skilled British labourer here, and some slight opening for the unskilled one. In this colony the European labourer must expect to find himself more, year after year, in face with coolie labour—with the labour of men more fit than himself to stand tropical heat. A European labourer cannot stand cotton or coffee work as a rule, and last year Queensland had exported no less than £68,000 worth of cotton; and the sugar plantations are going ahead hand over hand. Still there is a demand, and what is more a *safe* but very *steady* one, for skilled European labour, with which the Polynesian coolies cannot compete, and there is also a demand for a certain amount of unskilled labour, but the unskilled labourer must be more careful here than elsewhere. That the demand for European labour exists is proved very plainly by the colony offering advantageous terms for it; for free passages are offered to married farm labourers having not more than one child. The future of such a man would be this. He would receive six shillings a day, keeping himself, with bread at nine-pence the four pound loaf: or he would have from £25 to £35 a year, with lodging and as much to eat as he could manage: in fact, with similar rations we have known thrifty married couples sell a good bit of flour in the year. When he has saved enough to capitalize, he can get good land in the suburbs at £1 an acre (upset price, subject to be run up at auction as we understand); in the country at fifteen, ten and five shillings per acre on the same terms. This is not a bad prospect even after such a long voyage, and the chances of a little ague, but not more of that than he would have in nearly all the Western States with the exception of Iowa.

Skilled labour is valuable here as elsewhere, blacksmiths getting eight shillings a day, but a blacksmith who works long for wages in Australia must be a poor creature, not very likely to do well any where. In a pastoral country like Queensland, the blacksmith, the wheelwright, and, we are sorry to say, the publican, are people of very considerable importance, forming with the storekeeper a small middle class between the aristocrat of the leased Government lands and the "hand" or labourer, and very frequently getting possession of great capital themselves and make vast fortunes. The richest man in Australia was, we believe, a butcher.

To rise a little further on the "capital" scale: the Queensland Government holds out singular baits to a very small kind of capitalist. It offers to every man who pays his own passage £30 worth of land perfectly free, open to his own selection, in the settled parts of the colony; this is a very great temptation to a man with about £300 and a sharp head on his shoulders; but now we must speak a little more at large about larger figures.

We dismiss the gold. There is gold there, but let no emigrant be tempted to look at it. Where an emigrant will make his account of the gold is by feeding and supplying the miners: he will be rich faster than they will: we say dismiss the gold and come to the wool.

Setting aside the fact that in Queensland there are no convicts, that country may be roughly described as being in the state in which New South Wales was for about twenty years before the gold discovery; it is the country to make a small capital into a large one without any great risk, and at the sacrifice of fifteen or twenty years in a very pleasant country, where after a few years you will find yourself in possession of most European luxuries. At the present time the pastoral or squatting interest is much depreciated; and had a man with capital enough to wait a few years without realizing been on the spot last year, he might have made a great deal of money in a short time. But by this time matters have probably recovered themselves. It is pretty certain, however, that if a shrewd young fellow with from £2000 to £6000 were to set aside £400 for voyage there (and back if necessary), and half-a-year's travelling in the colony, he would meet with an investment which would make his fortune. The longer he waited before investing the more certain he might be to succeed. In the old times we have known perfectly ignorant gentlemen received on first-class stations like gentlemen, and taught their trade, merely because they could be trusted as men of higher education and responsibility. We have known young Scotch farmers taken on to their relative stations, put into places of trust, and started on the road to fortune, on a system of shares in two years. But a man as a rule should have capital, and should put it into the bank (getting safe interest) for at least a year. Then he may do well. A man of ordinary intelligence should know enough about the matter to invest, at least a part, in twelve months.

The climate is very charming for all the year except two months, when it is hot, with furious thunderstorms and a very great rainfall. Of course it differs from the rest of Australia in its productions, as all tropical fruits flourish there. As in the other parts of the island, a man either drinks or does not; if he drinks beyond a certain quantity he dies, and the temptation is very great in a country where the lassitude produced by the climate makes men fancy that they require stimulants. But, summing up all, it is a very fine possession, and will no doubt surely, if slowly, rise into the first rank of the young British States. To invest labour, prospects, or capital in it requires such diligence, thrift, and caution as is required in all undertakings.

*Advice to Emigrants**

A few months ago we published a series of articles on Emigration, in which we tried seriously to discuss, and put fairly before our readers the various fields which were open to the emigrant, without fear or favour. In one of our *causeries* we also warned the emigrant against the folly of believing all that was said by private emigration agents about the climate and prospects of the new countries which are being overrun by our countrymen. We went to the extreme length of offering a penny copy of the *Weekly Review* to any emigration agent who had *not* said that the climate of his particular colony was the finest in the world. No answer came, either the bait was not sufficiently large, or the emigration agents felt guilty. It is possible that the former supposition is true, and that they would not commit themselves for a penny, but we rather think that there are very few of them who could come to us with clean hands, and undergo cross-examination.

The responsibility of writing articles recommending emigration to particular places is, as regards this paper, very heavy. Since writing these articles on emigration, we have had letters from people who have taken our advice and gone to the new settlements of which we spoke favourably. We have sent more than one to Ontario, and more than one to Iowa. We believe in these countries, and the emigrants have believed in us. The responsibility is fearful. We got the best information we could, and those articles were written;

*Reprinted from *The Daily Review*, 21 May 1870, p.2, col.2–3.

whether we have made lives or marred lives we cannot tell. The man might have done better here for all we know; we only did our best, and tried to direct the outpouring stream of emigration to the best point. But people believe in newspapers, and will believe in newspapers until the coming of the Cocigrues. We have fairly done our duty. We wish that the emigration agents would do theirs. We selected Victoria, Iowa, and Ontario. We think now as we thought then, that if a man cannot get on in those countries, he may as well turn detective. One of those districts is known by us most familiarly; with regard to the other two, we have only taken our information from the very best sources. But we do earnestly hope that none of our readers will take private statements about other colonies or other fields for labour from private agents. We have a conscience, private agents have none. With regard to emigration generally, we emphatically affirm from our own experience that there is no country like the British Islands. We have seen some thousands of emigrants from these islands, and we never heard but one key-note among them, and that was "Home".

It is a bitter thing to say, but at times it is necessary to say bitter things. Nine times out of ten a man does not improve himself by emigration, and the proof of the pudding is in the eating; *all men come back who can*. Every one of our colonies has run away into a petty bastard imitation of the British Constitution and of the Constitution of Washington, and is making by no means fine weather of it. With New York we have no business. With Victoria we have. One of the most prominent members of the Melbourne Parliament was a very small linen draper at Chelsea. What New York is the *New York Tribune* takes care to tell us: what Victorian politics are we may read from the *Argus*: we could only ask what the number of men is who can dare to call themselves gentlemen, either in the one Legislature or the other. The Anglo-Teutonic race has desired to be ruled by the most worthless of its members, and seems to have had its will. An educated emigrant, if honest and decent, must give up all hopes of political life until he comes back repentant to the old country.

So far that is to be marked: but other things are to be marked also. We believe that a man may feed, like a hog in his stye, in Iowa, Ontario, or Victoria: but that is not life. A man had better do that than starve here; but a man had far better fight his way out here to the bitter end, than rot in idle gross luxury, in climates which are not suited to his constitution. There is no *life* for an educated man in America or Australia: he has only his choice between rowdyism and Lotos eating. Robert Lowe and Childers? Well, *they* came home again, and neither of them is more remarkable for temper than the Premier himself.

Emigration is no remedy, no specific, it is merely an operation: and very seldom a successful one. Now the great United States are a case of emigration, and we very much doubt whether they are the great success which they say they are. "The Brahmin of New England" still exists—in this last generation: but does not seem to be reproducing himself. The Americans have spent more money in four years than any other nation ever spent in fifteen. Their credit is so awfully bad after Fiske's Erie business that no sane man would lend them a bad farthing; they are in debt head over ears, and one of the few gentlemen in the land who has gone into politics is working most nobly against repudiation. The future of Australia may be a grand one, if she keeps the scum of her large towns in order, as we do here: we can only hope that it may be something better than that of the great United States, because the position of a nation which cannot externally borrow a solitary brass farthing from any one out of Bedlam or Morningside may be grand, but is not exactly respectable. The question is beginning to arise in some minds whether or no the United States of North America are not the most pretentious "fizzle" on the face of the earth. *We* hope not.

More people than many would believe go to the United States under the impression that in those States there is an immunity from war. Many who went there under this impression before the rebellion are undeceived now, but in the next world, not in this. Emigrants should remember that America submitted to a thing which we never submitted to, to the conscription. That war is over certainly, but no one knows when the next will begin: the United States are essentially a weak power; two twopenny steamers, which were let to depart from our ports through the sheer imbecility of Lord Russell destroyed their commerce, and they are grumbling about it now. They cannot smite, save in Canada, and only there at the price of their remaining commerce: and again only at the price of an alliance with Russia. Were Russia a free State this alliance would be dangerous to us, but Russia has about forty millions of slaves in her rear, wherever she goes, and those slaves seem to be exhibiting just now a tendency to *jacquerie*, far uglier than anything heard of in the French Revolution. We think that if we can keep France with us we can hold our own; but at the same time an emigrant must remember that the danger of joining the United States consists not so much in the external dangers of that very shaky dominion, but in its interior dangers. What has happened once may happen again. Iowa is a happy and prosperous State, one of the few Western States which are tolerably free from fever and ague; yet New York is between Iowa and the sea, and how long such States as Iowa are going to tolerate the ghastly and iniquitous Sodom, which men call New York, is only a question of time. Still a man who emigrated to Iowa might get the chance, were there ever a quarrel, of giving the devil a rap over his ears, which is something.

There is no possible fear of war either in Australia or New Zealand. In Ontario there will be war sooner or later, but it is difficult for a coward to hide his head in these days. All men, we think, had better try to fight out their lives in the dear old islands, but certainly a man who is afraid of war had better not emigrate, save to safe places. In the meantime, we beg to give a very important warning to people who are intending to emigrate. We speak very cautiously when we say that there are wolves in sheep's clothing who for their own interest seduce emigrants to parts of the world unfit for human habitation, and leave them to starve. We are quite unable to particularize, because we are responsible for what we say: but in heaven's name let no fellow-citizen of ours go to any colony save these—Ontario, Iowa, Victoria, New Zealand, New South Wales, and Queensland—without carefully possessing himself of facts. And even going to any of these great new States the danger is not inconsiderable. *Go nowhere without getting a letter from a person whom you can trust from the colony.* But lastly, for any sake beware of South America: we dare say no more.

PART 6

Selected Criticism

A Word of Remonstrance with Some Novelists*

BY A NOVELIST

Shades of Shakespeare and Sir Walter, what would you think of our new heroines, our charming criminals, our fascinating plots of mystery and wickedness? You dealt with wickedness, but you had a simple habit of calling things by their right names, and awarding vice its true desert. Suppose your tragedies and novels were re-written in the present day, how all would be changed. Lady Macbeth would wash her little hands quite clean; then having disposed of Macbeth by a lucky accident at Dunsinane, would marry Malcolm Canmore, or become a second wife to Macduff.

Othello, after his murder of Desdemona, would think better of it and only slay Iago, not himself. He would then begin life anew with Emilia, who would lay aside her guile and hardness for the occasion, and start afresh sincere and transparent as the day,—filching no more handkerchiefs, putting them to no more treacherous uses. You can easily fancy her hanging over the cradle of her first-born little Moor. Would she ever hear "Willow, Willow", I wonder? Othello and she would rather sing, "Happy, tawny Moor" together, and be content.

*Reprinted from *Good Words* IV (1863): 524–26.

Cordelia would have no interest for us as the sweet low-voiced daughter of Lear. Pooh! Cordelia, where would be the excitement in so tame, commonplace, milk-and-water, bread-and-butter character and feelings as hers! All our sympathies would fly to Regan and Gonerel, "sublime in passion", spurning weakness, loving "not wisely but too well", wild in love and hate. What a pity that one or other was not rewarded by being suddenly transformed into a dying saint, if not into a bountiful, blessed wife and mother!

We would have no time to waste over Portia's pleading, unless there was an ugly suspicion that she had in her early youth, when she bought her necklaces, entered into a private marriage with Shylock, who had so far forgot his ducats as to become enamoured of the high-spirited Christian maiden.

In the modern version Rebecca would elope with Bois Gilbert, and, returning penitent, wed poor Ivanhoe.

And with regard to Jeanie and Effie Deans, what a tremendous mistake we and the author together have made in being (like Reuben Butler and Dumbiedikes) devoted lovers of homely, noble Jeanie, and travelling every step with her in that long journey to England, when we had the sinners Effie and George Robertson to engross our thoughts and facies. What a poor figure Jeanie makes without stage accessories, what a small sensation now-a-days standing up in the court and crying out "Alack, alack, she never breathed a word to me about it", rather than tell one little lie to save her sister—what a poor figure beside our modern heroines, with their all-excusing taint of insanity, or their glow of impulse, yet who are not so impulsive but that they keep hideous secrets "gnawing at their hearts" for weeks, months, and years,—whose whole life is a cheat and a lie?

Yet we were wont to set store on immortal Will and Sir Walter, and call their art true art, and boast how they had enlightened and bettered the world. How much health and happiness will redound to society through this modern treatment of sin is a very dubious question.

For a time our rage after criminal heroines owned certain bounds. It began with a frenzy for supercilious or violent damsels, rampagious young women whose waywardness and perversity, that is their selfishness, folly, and slightly-veiled coarseness, came to be harped upon as their chief attractions. We have long passed these respectable bounds. Falseness, dishonesty, murder even, are rapidly claiming our most intense sympathies. It is the old Jack Sheppard mania, with female Jack Sheppards. We began our infatuation by executing the sentence of reprobation on our favourites. We hanged them like Captain Rock—we banished them—at least, we exiled them and condemned them to die, however becomingly and edifyingly, of remorse and misery. But now, even this small concession is cast aside, and after a little temporary anguish we bring back our criminals to sit at our tables, and "take sweet counsel with us", as if Jezebel, after having painted her face and tired her head, in place of being thrown to the dogs, was rescued and restored to a dignified palace and an undisturbed reign.

Decidedly the latest, most enticing, engrossing, breathlessly delightful heroine, is she who is in some form connected with the crime of bigamy. I beg to propose, if this style of novel continue in fashion, that the scene be removed to the more appropriate locality of the Mormons' city. By this means a great deal of invention, some improbability, and a few moral and religious scruples may be saved, although there will no doubt be a falling off in the element of danger. Or if this is not granted, then I would suggest the introduction of the slight variety of one man with two wives, and so shift the responsibility in fairness to the opposite side of the house.

I once knew a case of bigamy, and its facts were these. A working man married unhappily, and within a week of his marriage quarrelled with and separated from his wife by mutual consent, neither party seeing nor seeking to see the other's face again. The man removed to a different locality, lived alone for seven years, and then, actuated by an erroneous idea, not rare among the lower class, that seven years' separation breaks the marriage vow, set about courting another wife. He was not guilty of concealment; he told the circumstances of his former life to his intended wife. She was a bold lass, unreflecting, and no＇ ＇scrupulous. She consented to marry him; still there was no doubt ʼing, both man and woman were aware of the facts. They even took some steps to consult higher authorities; but unfortunately gave up the process as a tedious and contradictory one.

They found a clergyman, who was also made aware, I think, of the old transaction that barred the new, but who, I suspect, shared the ignorance and delusion of those who fancied it of no matter—a thing ended and gone. At all events he married the couple openly, in the circle of their friends. Within a few weeks a charge of bigamy was brought against the man, not at the instance of his first wife, who desired to have nothing more to do with him, and was on the point of a second marriage herself, but upon the information of an old acquaintance. Without any ceremony the man was thrown into gaol. He and the second wife—who, not very consistently or justly, resented her downfall—did not meet after their honeymoon was thus rudely broken up, until both parties were on their way to the circuit court, the man in his fustian, to be tried as a criminal, the woman in some of her dearly bought marriage finery, to be examined as a witness. Then the man seized an opportunity to speak reproachfully to her with a certain rough pathos, because she deserted him in the day of his calamity.

The court condemned the man, but in consideration of his self-deception and openness, awarded no severer sentence than a few months' imprisonment, while it censured the woman for her heartlessness and rashness.

The poor woman returned to her father's house, and remained there till her baby was born. Then, broken in character, and ruined in prospect, she was persuaded into the sin of returning to the man, and living with him in an illegal connection. The gaol brand had burnt into him, and the degradation of her position taunted her, so the couple fell fast into vice and poverty. The man lost his industrious habits and took to drinking. At last the woman wandered back to her first home, a baby in her arms, a baby on her back, a baby at her knee, with white lips and shrunk arms and defiant eyes, to beg bread for her starving children.

A haggard tale enough, but still with no spurious sentiment in it, craving no morbid attraction towards its weak and wretched victims. Yet for this couple in their ignorance and rudeness, I say it advisedly, there are excuses and palliatives a thousand-fold stronger than can be urged for our favourite heroines. This poor man and woman were straight as cedars, and pure as snow, beside them.

I do not protest against the introduction of wickedness into art, living as we do in a wicked world. I believe "terror and pity purge the human heart", but let wickedness be painted as William Hogarth painted it, in its loathsome, ghastly, downward career, ending in the gallows, the kennel, the mad-house. Do not let us have liars and cheats, and false wives, transformed by a touch into dying saints and honourable matrons. Do not let crime or its penalty be the crucible which converts our dross into gold.

"The greatest sinner may repent." Thank God, she may; so, also, "while there is life there is hope". But do not our hearts quake when this is all the assurance that the pitying doctor dare afford us in our friend's peril?

Is it honest or benevolent to take the exceptional cases, flaunt them, distort them, exaggerate them, so that sinners may indulge in excess, clinging to the faith that if they do not become reformed and prosperous men and women, they are at least likely to wipe out the past, by quitting this world as martyrs and saints? It is unutterably mean to lead a life of imposture, under whatever motives of revenge and retribution the life be undertaken, and no mortal can deliberately and persistently follow it who is not a debased being in the beginning and in the end. One true act can no more make a true woman, than one swallow can make a summer.

In the name of a holy and merciful religion let us profoundly pity and tenderly succour the miserable, but do not let us commit the grave error of preferring degradation to renown, and the infinitely more heinous error of preferring guilt to innocence. When the prodigal's father received the lost son with the kisses of love and the music of joy, he did not fail to answer the protest of the elder brother, "Son, thou art ever with me, and *all* that I have is thine". Is it possible we are more merciful than He who was the type of Divine mercy?

In Solomon's day it was held that jealousy was the rage of a man, and that there was one disgrace which could not be wiped away till the black curtain of death descended and hid it from the appalled, horror-stricken sight. Why do we depart from the wisdom of the wise king, and believe that it is not a virtuous woman, but a deceiver or a betrayer, whose price is above rubies, and that it is she alone who should usurp our regard, and awe our admiration?

I humbly pray our good writers, moralists, satirists, humourists, by precept and example, by tongue and pen, to exorcise this evil possession of our literature; that we may not have the sorrow and shame of knowing that the reign of good Queen Victoria, our true woman and wife, will be identified in after generations with the reign of female criminals in English literature.

WALTER SCOTT*

The good Sir Walter was far too good at a plot to allow a trifle of history to stand in his way. Charlotte de la Tremouille, the Lady of Latham, is represented in "Peveril of the Peak" as a Roman Catholic, and some of the finest and most subtle parts of the story rest on that circumstance. But she was in fact a French Protestant: just take "Peveril of the Peak" and read it, making Lady Derby a Protestant, you would spoil a good half of it. That is why Scott, who knew what he was about, (for he coolly tells you so), just let history take care of itself. In "Kenilworth", however, he is still more audacious, really laughably so: he must have smiled himself when he wrote some parts of "Kenilworth". His object was to exhibit Queen Elizabeth in a fury of jealous rage with Leicester, and so he used his wife for the purpose at the revels of "Kenilworth". Now Amy Robsart, Lady Dudley, had had a somewhat famous coroner's inquest on her unfortunate body twelve years before at Cumnor Hall. Her husband was away at Windsor, and the occasion was Abingdon Fair. She sent all her servants there, and was in the house alone, when a lady, a neighbour of hers, came in and urged her to go. She refused, on the ground that the first day was not the fit day for a lady to go. The neighbour left her, and when the servants came

*Reprinted from *The Daily Review*, 16 October 1869, p.2, col. 5.

home she was found lying dead at the bottom of the stairs. The man Foster also, who is represented by Scott as a villain, was, it appears, a very good fellow. There is a tomb to him in Abingdon Church. But perhaps the most singular violation of possibility for effect is to be found in this novel, where Shakespeare is represented as a young poet at Leicester's levee. Shakespeare at that time was twelve years of age. Scott's object was to write a splendid story, and in that object he has succeeded like no other man.

WORD PAINTING†

Novelists of the present age have a great tendency to what is called "word painting"; in fact, among our numerous sins we have tried the thing ourselves. But let us all listen humbly to the voice of our master, Walter Scott. Ruskin has some very grand passages in which he tries to bring nature before us in printer's ink, but he has, we think, no passage so splendid as the following, which we quote from "The Heart of Midlothian", chapter 50. Swinburne or Shelley have scarcely matched it anywhere, which is saying a great deal. The passage we allude to is this:—"*She could see the crest of the torrent fling loose down the rock, like the mane of a wild horse.*" We cannot write like that now.

CHARACTER NAMING*

There is a point in novel writing to which very few novelists ever attend, and that point is the invention of names. Dickens, Balzac, and George Eliot have taken their own line in this matter. Dickens has resorted to fantacism as in "Martin Chuzzlewit", "Nicholas Nickleby", and so on: that king and lord of humour has seldom hit off a humourous name. "Pecksniff" is poor, probably the most subtly humorous of his names is "Gamp". There is a delicious subtlety about that great name which can no more be analyzed than the perfume of the rose. Balzac, it is said, got his names from shop doors, attending merely to the element of *bissarrerie*. George Eliot's

†Reprinted from *The Daily Review*, 19 March 1870, p.2, col. 4.
*Reprinted from *The Daily Review*, 29 January 1870, p.2, col. 4.

names are excessively poor and unworthy of her, mere reflexes of what we would call the Midland school of thought, *i.e.*, that the central counties of England contained a race of people which could not be equalled elsewhere. Such names as "Adam Bede" and "Silas Marner" show only a reflection of the perversity of thought of which the late Mrs Gaskell was chief prophetess. It is strange to find such amazing and unexampled genius as that of George Eliot, without one touch of true humour from first to last. Half a dozen sentences in "King Lear" or "Twelfth Night" would exhaust all the humour in George Eliot's novels, or any novels by any hand save those of Dickens, Thackeray, or Scott.

We would engage to prove our thesis had we space. All novelists, ourselves included, are tolerably tolerable to us until they become funny. Then we must part company with all novelists with the exception of Scott, Dickens, and Thackeray for English writers, and Hawthorne and Holmes for American; as a French humourist we might put in a claim for the Comtesse de Segur, but out present *tenu* is that of the invention of names. And really the necessity of our theme forces us to give another word to the Comtesse de Segur. Her "enragée" woman is Madame "Bonbeck". Her Pole is "Coserzinki" which is given up as a bad job, and shortened into "Cos". She shows an amazing genius for inventing names, far greater than that of George Sand for example.

But the two men who have invented names, who have cast their whole soul into the invention of names, are most undoubtedly Scott and Thackeray. Let us being in Scotland take Scott first, though we would gladly put him in the place of honour, last: he nearly equalled Thackeray at his own game. An English lad of five and twenty years ago *lived* on Scott. Scott *made* him. Scott was the only man previous to Dickens who showed that true pure humour did not consist in the stupid brutalities of Smollett. It is hard if Scotchmen will not listen to the praise of nearly the greatest man they even sent out, in a mere detail of wit.

Look at Scott's names. "Peter Peebles". See how wonderfully that name gives one the idea of loose, inconsecutive, voluble imbecility. Then, again, "Drumthwackit", you would bet your life that you would get a hot screed of doctrine in *that* parish. We have no space to analyze Scott's wondrous wit in these names, for the analysis of his wit would fill a volume. We must leave such immortal names as that of "Jedediah Cleishbotham", the typical Scotch schoolmaster, who, if you won't have your learning at one end is prepared to put it into you at the other (we beg pardon, it is Sir

Walter, not us), we must pass from comedy, and come to deep wild tragedy.

There he stares us in the face with his magnificent genius. In "Old Mortality" we know partly what is coming. He knows entirely, for the necessity of the situation is forced on him. We see that a supreme time is coming, and we know that Sir Walter has a man to meet him. He tells us his tale and leaves us breathless when he names his man of the time. Habakuk Mucklewrath. Shakespeare has never shown such a dexterity in names as is shown in that one. No one else ever has, as far as we know. The tale is told by that one name. The transcendently beautiful passage about Habakuk's experiences among the sea fowl at the Bass Rock is unnecessary to thoughtful people. After giving him such a name Sir Walter might have left him dumb.

But he would not. Scott's genius was too great to let him do that. He made him speak; and speak in words which will never be forgotten, we should hope. The speech of Habakuk Mucklewrath, not only approaches some of the finest passages in Shakespeare, but has also a very singular political significance at the present moment. We however are dealing with names.

It would be an endless business to summarize that wonderful beauty of Thackeray's names. We believe, and always shall, that the most splendid of them is that of the great German Princess Potztausend Donnerwelter.

Nathaniel Hawthorne in England

Passages from the English Note-Books of Nathaniel Hawthorne. 2 Vols.
Strahan and Co., 56 Ludgate Hill, London. 1870.*

Every one who loves and appreciates literature as a fine art will turn
with eagerness to these handsome volumes, containing as they do
the unfinished sketches, the rough materials of one of the most
consummate literary artists the world has ever seen. Every one that
knows anything of Hawthorne's work—and who is there that does
not?—knows that, apart from his merits as a subtle analyst of
character and motive, as a powerful delineator of the most moving
and tragic passions, as a weird explorer into the dark recesses of the
human soul, as a painter of all the dark shadows of life, of the night
side of nature, he has a claim to immortality in the simple fact of his
being one of the greatest—with the exception of Thackeray and
Goldsmith—perhaps the greatest master of style English literature
can boast of. It is a style that has a distinct individuality about it, of
course, otherwise it would be no style at all worth speaking about.
But when we try to describe it we break down. Our bravest attempts
are baffled, and we confess to ourselves the utter impossibilty of
giving our readers any idea of the exquisite, impalpable charm that
it conveys—a charm which is, notwithstanding its airiness and
exquisiteness, a distinct reality, but which one can no more describe

*Reprinted from *The Daily Review*, 31 October 1870, p.5, col.2–5.

in words than one can describe or paint the fragrance brought us on the wings of the south wind as it passes over a bed of violets. Longfellow said of Hawthorne's style that it was as clear as running waters, and that it seemed as though his words were merely used as stepping-stones upon which, with a free and youthful bound, his spirit crossed and recrossed the bright and rushing stream of thought. No one can read a few even of his most hasty sketches without noticing how beautifully the sentences are constructed. Not a single false metaphor—not one single ugly unappropriate word—not a single halt or stumble—to jar upon the ear and mar that sad, sweet music which in Hawthorne's sentences is never absent, and which imparts to them not a little of their nameless but exquisite charm. No man when he had a thing to say ever said it in a more graceful or beautiful manner than Nathaniel Hawthorne. "Thought, if left to itself," said a very beautiful prose writer by whose untimely death literature suffered a very serious loss, "will dissipate and die—it is style alone that preserves it as balsams preserve the Pharaoh." We don't mean to say this is absolutely true; but if it were, then assuredly Hawthorne's most trivial thoughts, his very lightest fancies, are destined to be imperishable and immortal. His sentences are worth very careful study and very careful dissection. The exquisite fitness of his epithets—the cunning turns of expression—the neatness and fine taste with which he lays in a bit of bright colour in the way of imagery where the sentence was becoming flat, and freshens and touches it up with a little epigrammatic glitter where it was beginning to get dead and lose the fulness of vitality which characterizes all his works, and imparts to them so much of their peculiar fascination. Like all truly great authors, Hawthorne has with all those who love his style and read him, for the sake of that alone, the reputation of being a subtle thinker and speculator, and yet it would be impossible to point out any positive proofs of his claims to such a title. The fact is, there is such an amount of communicativeness about his style that we always fancy we hear him musing at our elbow, and shyly whispering to us his quaint speculations and his wild weird fancies. Hawthorne's books are always thoughtful books, and if the writer of a thoughtful book is a thinker, then Hawthorne *was* one almost without peer or rival. But a book which impresses us as a thoughtful book, and as the work of a great thinker, is not so much a book that is teeming with mighty thoughts and fine subtle fancies as one that puts thoughts and fancies of that sort into the heads of those that read it. We do not care twopence for a book that does no more than tell us what the author thinks upon this or that subject. What we revel in is a book that besides and beyond all that makes *us* think and speculate for ourselves, not only on the themes of which the author treats, but on other ones which they summon up to our minds. Anybody can write an *instructive* book—but one author in a thousand only can write a *suggestive* book, and that one is *par excellence* a great thinker. In this sense Hawthorne was a thinker, and a profound one; and in this sense his books are simply invaluable . . .

He was so shy that you had to woo his shrinking soul from its hiding-place with as much tact and delicacy as though it had been a schoolgirl's. Yet to this feminine delicacy and quickness of perception and feelings he added a most wonderful masculine breadth and sweep of creative genius. This it was that enabled him to give to the world that sublime tragedy "The Scarlet Letter". For the power it has of haunting the imagination for ever and for ever it is only surpassed by Dickens's "Tale of Two Cities". The painful intensity of the interest of this terrible story may be a little morbid, and it may be that it is "not the glow of life but the hectic fire of disease that burns on the cheeks of the actors", yet the darkest passions, the most subtle forms of sin and suffering are delineated with terrible impressiveness and truth, and there pervades it a spirit of the most delicate purity, which Hawthorne's femininely-sensitive taste inspired, a lofty sympathy which his femininely tender heart enabled him to feel; severe portioning out of justice and retribution, which his masculine sense of right enabled him to express . . .

His office was one that brought him in contact with all sorts of queer characters—with outlaws, and imposters, and beggars, and destitute men of all sorts who came to claim the charity of the representative of the Great Republic. With the touch of a master we have them photographed for us in these notes. Not a striking face but he noticed, not a single bit of tragedy or comedy in real life escaped him. He seemed fond of mixing up the grave and gay, and jotting down these little stories of people he came in contact with in a half-laughing, half-sighing sort of way . . .

We don't think any one but Hawthorne, with his quaint, keen insight into life and character, and with his curious propensity for working out the "night side" of nature, would have caught the true import—the mixture of humour, of fun, and of sadness—in a drive with an undertaker in a sable-plumed coach, talking about graves.

The keen eye he had for available material was most wonderful. He never missed a dramatic situation in the street, and the most common sights seem to have been constantly suggesting to his fertile imagination all sorts of quaint and curious fancies—which, as a perusal of these note-books shows, he always jotted down as "things to be done" . . .

A facsimile reproduction of page 520, *The Hillyars and the Burtons*. This is one of thirty-nine sheets of manuscript known to be extant. Of interest is the deleted sentence referring to Langi Willi. The reproduction is by permission of the Librarian, University of California, Los Angeles.

Select Bibliography

WORKS OF HENRY KINGSLEY

Books

The Recollections of Geoffry Hamlyn. 3 vols. Cambridge: Macmillan, 1859.

Ravenshoe. 3 vols. Cambridge: Macmillan, 1862. *Macmillan's Magazine*. January 1861 – July 1862.

Austin Elliott. 2 vols. London: Macmillan, 1863.

The Hillyars and the Burtons: A Story of Two Families. 3 vols. London: Macmillan, 1865. *Macmillan's Magazine*. November 1863 – April 1865.

Leighton Court: A Country House Story. 2 vols. London: Macmillan, 1866.

Silcote of Silcotes. 3 vols. London: Macmillan, 1867. *Macmillan's Magazine*. July 1866 – September 1867.

Mademoiselle Mathilde. 3 vols. London: Bradbury, Evans, 1868. *The Gentleman's Magazine*, April 1867 – May 1868.

Robinson Crusoe. Edited after the original editions with biographical introduction, London: Macmillan, 1868.

Tales of Old Travel: Re-Narrated. London: Macmillan, 1869.

Stretton. 3 vols. London: Tinsley Brothers, 1869. *The Broadway Annual*, September 1868 – August 1869.

The Boy in Grey. London: Strahan, 1871. *Good Words for the Young*, March – September 1869; June – July 1870.

The Lost Child. London: Macmillan, 1871.

Hetty. London: Bradbury, Evans, 1871. *Once a Week*, February – May 1869.

Hetty and Other Stories. London: Bradbury, Evans, 1871.

Old Margaret. 2 vols. London: Tinsley Brothers, 1871.

Hornby Mills and Other Stories. 2 vols. London: Tinsley Brothers, 1872.

Valentin: A French Boy's Story of Sedan. 2 vols. London: Tinsley Brothers, 1872. *Routledge's Every Boy's Annual for 1873*, ed. Edmund Routledge, London.

The Harveys. 2 vols. London: Tinsley Brothers, 1872.

Oakshott Castle: Being the Memoirs of an Eccentric Nobleman. 3 vols. London: Macmillan, 1873.

Reginald Hetherege. 3 vols. London: Richard Bentley, 1874.

Number Seventeen. 2 vols. London: Chatto and Windus, 1875.

The Grange Garden: A Romance. 3 vols. London: Chatto and Windus, 1876. *St. James Magazine*, April 1875 – August 1876.

Fireside Studies. 2 vols. London: Chatto and Windus, 1876.

The Mystery of the Island. London: William Mullan, 1877.

Selected Short Stories, Reviews and Articles

"Wild Sports of the Far South". *Fraser's Magazine* LIX (May 1859) pp. 587–97.

"Travelling in Victoria". *Macmillan's Magazine* III (January 1861) pp. 140–50.

Review of *A Successful Exploration through the Interior of Australia,* from the Journals of W.J. Wills, edited by his Father. *The Reader* I (21 February 1863) pp. 183–84.

Review of *Reminiscences of a Thirty Years' Residence in New South Wales and Victoria* by R. Therry. *The Reader* I (14 March 1863) pp. 256–57.

"New Australian Exploration". Review of *Tracks of McKinlay and Party across Australia*, by John Davis. *The Reader* I (27 June 1863) pp. 618–19.

"Charles Sturt: A Chapter from the History of Australian Exploration". *Macmillan's Magazine* XI (January 1865) pp. 204–17.

"Eyre, The South Australian Explorer". *Macmillan's Magazine* XII (October 1865) pp. 501–10; XII (November 1865) pp. 55–63.

"The Last Two Abyssinian Books". *The Fortnightly Review* V (August 1866) pp. 654–69.

"The Two Cadets". *Once a Week* XVI (23 February 1867) pp. 214–20; (2 March 1867) pp. 246–53.

"The New Church at the Mistibithiwong". *Good Words* IX (1868) pp. 322–28.

"My Landladies—Chapters of a Digger's Life". *Temple Bar* XXXVI (October 1872) pp. 371–90.

WORKS ABOUT HENRY KINGSLEY

Argyle, Barry. *An Introduction to the Australian Novel, 1830–1930*. Oxford: Clarendon Press, 1972.

Barnes, John. *Henry Kingsley and Colonial Fiction*. Australian Writers and Their Work series, Melbourne: Oxford University Press, 1971.

Baxter, Rosilyn. "Henry Kingsley and the Australian Landscape". *Australian Literary Studies* 4, no. 4 (October 1970) pp. 395–98.

Boldrewood, Rolf. *Babes in the Bush*. London: Macmillan, 1900.

Byrne, Desmond. *Australian Writers*. London: Richard Bentley, 1896.

Croft, Julian. "*Is Geoffry Hamlyn* a creole novel?", *Australian Literary Studies* 6, no. 3 (May 1974) pp. 269–76.

Dixon, Robert. "Kingsley's *Geoffry Hamlyn* and the Art of Landscape", *Southerly*, no. 3 (September 1977) pp. 274–99.

Elliott, Brian. "The Composition of *Geoffry Hamlyn:* The Legend and the Facts", *Australian Literary Studies* 3, no. 4 (October 1968) pp. 271–89.

Ellis, S.M. *Henry Kingsley 1830–1876: Towards a Vindication*. London: Grant Richards Pronto, 1931.

Green, H.M. *A History of Australian Literature*. Sydney: Angus & Robertson, 1961.

Hamer, Clive. "Henry Kingsley's Australian Novels", *Southerly*, no. 26 (1966) pp. 40–57.

Hancock, W.K. *Discovering Monaro: A Study of Man's Impact on his Environment*. Cambridge University Press, 1972.

Hergenhan, L.T. "*Geoffrey Hamlyn* through Contemporary Eyes", *Australian Literary Studies* 2, no. 4 (December 1966) pp. 289–95.

Horner, J.C. "*Geoffry Hamlyn* and its Australian Setting", *Australian Literary Studies* 1, no. 1 (June 1963) pp. 3–15.

Kingsley, Maurice. "Personal Traits of Henry Kingsley", *The Book Buyer*, XI, no. 12 (January 1895) pp. 727–31.

Kramer, Leonie J. *Henry Kingsley: Some Novels of Australian Life*, The Commonwealth Literary Fund Lectures, 1954.

——. Introduction to *The Hillyars and the Burtons: A Story of Two Families* by Henry Kingsley, facsimile of 1865 edition, Sydney University Press, 1973.

Lansbury, Coral. *Arcady in Australia: The Evocation of Australia in Nineteenth-Century English Literature*. Melbourne University Press, 1970.

McLaren, John. "*Geoffry Hamlyn* and the Australian Myth", *Segment* 2 (1973) pp. 6–12.

Mares, F.H. "Henry Kingsley, Marcus Clarke and Rolf Boldrewood", in *The Literature of Australia*, edited by Geoffrey Dutton, Melbourne: Penguin, 1964.

Mellick, J.S.D. "Henry Kingsley in Australia", *Australian Literary Studies* 6, no. 1 (May 1973), pp. 91–94.

——. "Henry Kingsley—Mounted Policeman?" *Australian Literary Studies* 7, no. 4 (October 1976) pp. 416–20.

Ryan, J.S. "The Prose Style of Henry Kingsley", *Armidale and District Historical Society Journal and Proceedings* no. 19 (April 1976) pp 63–72.

Sadleir, Michael. *Things Past*. London: Constable, 1944.

Scheuerle, William H. *The Neglected Brother: A Study of Henry Kingsley*. Tallahassee: Florida State University Press, 1971.

——. Introduction to *Ravenshoe* by Henry Kingsley, reprint of 1862 edition, Lincoln: Nebraska University Press, 1967.

——. "*Romantic Attitudes in Geoffry Hamlyn*", *Australian Literary Studies* 2, no. 2 (December 1965).

Shorter, Clement. "A Note on Henry Kingsley", in *The Recollections of Geoffry Hamlyn*. London: Ward, Lock & Bowden, 1895.

Sutherland, Bruce. "Henry Kingsley and Australia", *The Australian Quarterly*, XVII, no. 2 (June 1945) pp. 98–105.

Wellings, N.G. "Henry Kingsley: *Ravenshoe*", *Australian Literary Studies*, 4, no. 2 (October 1969) pp. 115–29.

Wilkes, G.A. "Kingsley's *Geoffry Hamlyn*: A Study in Literary Survival", *Southerly* 32, no. 4 (1972) pp. 243–54.

Wolff, Robt. L. "Henry Kingsley", *Harvard Library Bulletin* XIII, no. 2 (Spring 1959) pp. 195–226.

04